CARRICKMINES CASTLE
RISE AND FALL

Carrickmines Castle:
rise and fall

Mark Clinton

Wordwell

In Memoriam:
Stephen Devaney, Barrister
Dominic Dunne, Environmentalist
Barry Raftery, Academic
who were not found wanting when Carrickmines Castle
was in its final hour of need.

First published in 2019
Wordwell Ltd
Unit 9, 78 Furze Road, Sandyford Industrial Estate, Dublin 18
www.wordwellbooks.com

Front cover image—Standing remnant of Carrickmines Castle. (Photo: Mark Clinton)

ISBN 978-1-9164922-7-1

British Library Cataloguing-in-Publication Data.
A catalogue record for this book is available from the British Library.

Typeset in Ireland by Wordwell Ltd
Copy-editor: Emer Condit
Index: Geraldine Begley
Cover design and artwork: Wordwell Ltd
Printed by Gráficas Castuera, Pamplona

o'connell & clarke solicitors

The author and publisher would like to acknowledge the generous financial contribution made by O'Connell & Clarke Solicitors to the preparation and publication of this book.

Contents

FOREWORD AND ACKNOWLEDGEMENTS vii

INTRODUCTION: THE EARLY HISTORICAL BACKGROUND 1

Viking/Scandinavian settlement — The Angevin intervention

PART 1: CARRICKMINES: EARLY TENURES AND TENANTS 15

The Butlers of south Dublin and north Wicklow — Edward Bruce — Aunger Lissebon — Church property — Roger FitzDavid — Maurice Howel — Trade and productivity in south Dublin — The Black Death — The Rokeby line — Janico Dartasso — The Walshes of Carrickmines — Henry Walsh of Carrickmines — The second Henry Walsh

PART 2: THE SHIFTING SANDS OF THE SIXTEENTH CENTURY 55

The Great Earl — The Pale — Garret Óg Fitzgerald — The insurrection of 1534 — Realignments — The Walshes of Three Castles — A new order — The Walshes of Shanganagh — The Walshes of Balally — Munster — Leinster — The Second Desmond Rebellion — The Walshes of Kilgobbin — The North — The Walshes of Killincarrig — Feagh Mac Hugh O'Byrne — The aftermath

PART 3: THEOBALD WALSH: A TIME OF PEACE, POLITICS AND FOREIGN ADVENTURES 107

After-effects of the Treaty of Mellifont — The parliament of 1613 — Crisis of consciences — Richard Walsh, soldier of fortune — The Battle of Lützen — Theobald Walsh — Confessional contradictions — The great assembly — The Walsh cadet houses — Thomas Wentworth, earl of Strafford — Lord deputy of Ireland — The parliament of 1634 — Church reform — The threat of confiscation — Life at Carrickmines — The parliament of 1640 — Two parliaments in England — The drift towards conflict — The conflict and Carrickmines — The level of participation by Theobald Walsh — The Walshes of Wicklow — The local theatre — Carrickmines Castle

PART 4: SIR SIMON HARCOURT AND THE FALL OF CARRICKMINES CASTLE 177

Family background — The Palatinate — The Low Countries — The Spanish Siege of Breda — The Siege of Oldenzaal — The Siege of Groll (Groenlo) — The Siege of 's-Hertogenbosch (Bois-le-Duc) — The capture of Venlo, Strale and Roermond — The Siege of Maastricht — Limbourg, Orsoy and Rheinberg — The Siege of Tienen (Tirlemont) — Schenkenschans — The Dutch Siege of Breda — The Battle of Kallo — Scotland — The campaign — Interlude — The second campaign — Final campaigns in the Netherlands — Chester — Ireland — Swords — Wicklow — Clontarf — Santry and Finglas — Munster — South County Dublin and County Kildare — Rathcoole, Saggart and Artane — The Battle of Dean's Grange — The Battle of Kilsallaghan Castle — The relief of Drogheda and its aftermath — County Kildare — Carrickmines Castle

THE EPILOGUE 273

A LOYAL LOVE-LETTER (From a Maid ...) 283
—A seventeenth-century ballad

GENEALOGICAL TABLES 285

BIBLIOGRAPHY 289

INDEX 315

FOREWORD AND ACKNOWLEDGEMENTS

It has taken a while to research and write this book—five years in physical terms, and a lot longer to reach the point of equanimity. To quote Charles Dickens, 'It was the best of times, it was the worst of times': an enthralling site, a highly committed crew and an emerging hideous mess leading to an An Bord Pleanála review, an EU-commissioned report, three High Court cases and three Supreme Court cases. I had arrived at Carrickmines as a trusting archaeologist and historian but I departed as an entrenched preservationist and active environmentalist. Above all other concerns and agendas, however, Carrickmines Castle has a truly fascinating story. It deserves to be told.

I would like to express my sincere thanks to the staff of the various institutions in which I assembled the history of Carrickmines Castle and its long-term owners, the Walshes, and especially to Siobhán O'Rafferty and Pat Kelly of the Royal Irish Academy, Gerry Kavanagh and Lidia Laube of the National Library of Ireland, Eva Oledzka and Gillian Humphreys of the Bodleian Library in Oxford, Aisling Lockhart of Manuscripts and Archives, Special Collections, Trinity College Dublin, and Paul Ferguson of the Map Library, TCD. My thanks to Ken Nicholls for additional information on the genealogy of the Walshes of Carrickmines. Once again my thanks to my long-time (40 years!) 'pardner' Dr Matthew Stout for preparing the maps and the genealogical tables for publication; to Nick Maxwell for tracking down my wish-list of visual representations; to Sara Nylund and Rob Goodbody for photography; to my old mate Laurie Lewis in London for successfully leading the relentless hunt for a genuine image of Sir Simon Harcourt, followed by that of the good Lady Anne; to Erika Ingham of the National Portrait Gallery in London for greatly assisting us in this epic quest; to the Courtauld Institute; to Turtle Bunbury for interceding, and to Arabella Bishop of Sotheby's for permission to use the photograph of the portrait of Lady Harcourt.

Over the course of its long history Carrickmines evolved from an open settlement to a defended farmstead, then to a strong military outpost and finally to a

Pl. 1—Carrickmines at the beginning of the 1960s. The landscape was to remain unchanged for almost the next 40 years. Note the earthworks in the lower right-hand corner of the photograph (the western defences of the northern enclosure).

wealthy manorial centre. The Walsh family were established at Carrickmines by 1400. Over the following two and a half centuries they would expand their holdings in south County Dublin and north County Wicklow. They would in time occupy other castles and fortified dwellings, at Shanganagh, Kilgobbin, Balally, Old Court, Cork, Old Connaught and Killincarrig. They would also hold additional estates—Clonmannan, Phrompstown and Jamestown, amongst others.

The Walshes, dwelling in their castles, did not exist in serene and glorious isolation. Trouble would come to them all. From the beginning of the 1400s to the disastrous events of March 1642 not only Ireland but also the wider world was invariably in turmoil. The Walshes found themselves in the thick of it both at home and abroad. Neither did the arrival of the Reformation herald Continental brotherhood. Warfare became even more rife. The religious conflicts of the seventeenth century proved to be particularly vicious.

The final act in the saga was played out in March 1642. The events of one weekend were to have calamitous consequences in the lives of two men and their spouses. Theobald and Maria Walsh were the owners of Carrickmines Castle; Sir Simon Harcourt was the besieger beyond its walls. His wife and confidante, Anne, awaited his return in Oxfordshire. Both men were experienced soldiers. Theobald had served alongside his father Richard in the imperial forces of the Habsburg Empire.

Pl. 2—Aerial view of the Carrickmines Castle complex under excavation, 2000–2. (Photo: Mark Clinton)

Simon had soldiered in Germany, the Netherlands and Scotland. Neither man would die peacefully in his bed.

In August 2000 I completed work on a destroyed section of the Pale Ditch at Balally in south County Dublin. With the remnants of my small crew (Damian Shiels, Åsa Carlsson, Aoife Coghlan, Peter King, Cathy Ambrey and Brian Armstrong) I departed for Carrickmines. There our ranks were expanded to 22—a large team, we thought. We found ourselves encamped in a sleepy, leafy valley. On the first morning we assisted the farmer, Patsy Mooney, to move the bull and cattle to a field across the Glenamuck Road. The No. 63 single-decker bus passed by the site a couple of times a day on its meandering journey to the pleasant rural village of Kiltiernan. How convenient! We expected to be there, at the longest, for a matter of months. I wondered where my next commission would be, but that was not the way things worked out ('Events, dear boy, events').

I will be forever thankful to the excavation crew at Carrickmines Castle, not least to all of those who worked long hours of unpaid overtime for the integrity of the site. Many of the friendships forged there under fire have endured—and even some of the romances! Over the course of the two years in the trenches, from 2000 to 2002, several hundred workers from at least eleven countries passed through the ranks. These served under the very able leadership of Charlie Arthur (the 525th), Åsa Carlsson (the 837th), Dr Sharon Greene and Brian Ó Donnchadha (the 370th), Malcolm Hope and Ros Ó

Maoldúin (the 612th), Noelle Mitchell (the 445th), Paul O'Keeffe (the 863rd), Damian Shiels (the 598th), Jim Wheeler (the 804th) and Marianne Nolan and Ken Curran (the FRG).

From the very beginning Brian Ó Donnchadha worked hard to instil an *esprit de corps* in the camp. Morale was maintained by Stephen 'Legend' Devlin with his 'Castle Days' and sundry other distractions. Meanwhile, Jim Wheeler amazed us all by persuading Dublin Bus to put on our own double-decker, the No. 46C, at knocking-off time (Monday to Friday)—surely a first for an archaeological excavation! The comradeship forged with Paul, Albert and Ron, the drivers on our faithful morning No. 63 bus, undoubtedly helped the union to agree to the special service. Literally nothing stopped our devoted Finds Officer, Clare Nolan, from processing the constant avalanche of finds with the help of various ailing 'out-of-front-line-service' assistants; Alva McGowan and Sara Nylund set about drawing these finds with skill; Cara O'Doherty shepherded the pots; and Dr Linda Fibiger treated the human remains with professionalism and dignity. Paul O'Keeffe in his role as CQ kept the crew fully booted and H&S suited; Tom Moran became 'Mr Fixit' on site; Frank Spain made sure that the post got through despite hail, rain, heatwaves, snowdrifts and the inevitable mud; and solidarity came from our beleaguered neighbour, Gerald Sands, holding out for as long as he could in his beloved but condemned 1700s-built home, 'Hinchoge House'.

As our outpost came under increasing pressure, Åsa, Sharon and Noelle became the Castellans of Carrickmines: nobody thereafter got in unchallenged! Quietly Damian took on *Abwehr* duties, while Fin Dwyer (unbeknownst to us!) did likewise with *la Résistance*. We would not go quietly into the night.

We were not alone. There were friendly voices out there. My sincere thanks to P. David Sweetman (Chief Archaeologist), Chris Corlett, Con Manning and Tom Condit of the National Monuments Service; Dr Patrick Wallace (Director), Eamonn P. Kelly (Keeper of Antiquities, who vigorously and ruthlessly took to the field of battle), Nessa O'Connor, Mary Cahill and Dr Andrew Halpin of the National Museum of Ireland; the academics Dr David Edwards, Professor Seán Duffy, Professor Rolf Loeber, Dr Emmett O'Byrne and Dr Niall Brady; and my old C.-in-C. and comrade, the late Professor Barry Raftery.

Meanwhile, the heritage advocates and environmentalists were taking no prisoners. The remains of the castle complex and the medieval/post-medieval landscape—the manorial centre, the associated village, the fair green, the ancient roadway and river-crossing—were all about to be destroyed to facilitate the construction of a major junction. This was one of a chain of five junctions occurring within a ten-minute drive on a motorway originally designed to move national traffic, unimpeded by local traffic, around the city of Dublin—a motorway whose original course had been altered, thus bringing it into contact with the castle site, without explanation, and a major junction not connecting with any national primary route or road of significance! What could the explanation possibly be? The activists had a fair idea. We could only stand back and admire them. There was Peter Sweetman (the Alchemist), Ruadhán Mac Eoin (the Indomitable Spirit), Shirley O'Brien (the

Archivist), Michael Smith (Chair of An Taisce, who forged an alliance of the willing), Ian Lumley (Heritage Officer, An Taisce), Tony Lowes (Friends of the Irish Environment), Dominic Dunne, Michael Mulcreevy, Gordon Lucas, Anthony Murphy, David Healy, Cian O'Callaghan, and many others; the legal eagles, Frank Callanan, Colm Mac Eochaidh, Barra Ó Cuiv, Gerard Hogan, Jim Bridgeman and especially Stephen Devaney and Colman Fitzgerald; the politicians, with Senator Victor Boyhan, Proinsias de Rossa MEP, Ciarán Cuffe TD and Patricia McKenna MEP to the fore.

Finally, I would like to express my thanks to VJK for the invitation and opportunity to direct excavations at Carrickmines Castle. A special thanks to Cormac Bruton (Surveyor) and all the staff at HQ in Kilkenny; to Matt Seaver and Cóilín Ó Drisceoil, my fellow site-directors in the South-Eastern Theatre, for many informative discussions; and especially to Clare McCutcheon and Adrian Kennedy, specialists, for keeping us in the loop.

Last, but never least, my gratitude to my long-enduring family: my wife Alison Kelly for tracking down ever-more-obscure books in libraries at home and abroad and for epic photocopying, my daughters Ruth and Emily Clinton for accepting my many mental absences, and Mr P for his constant companionship deep into the many long, candle-burning nights.

INTRODUCTION

The early historical background

The early medieval kingdom of Leinster was centred on the valleys of the rivers *Liphe* or *Ruirthech* (Liffey), *Berba* (Barrow) and *Sláine* (Slaney). Its borders were topographically protected by the bogs of the midlands, the forests to the north of the Liffey and the coastline stretching along the eastern and south-eastern flanks (Byrne 1973, 130, 150). Giraldus Cambrensis in the late twelfth century described the Laigen/Osraige (Leinster/Ossory) border as being impassable in many places owing to the presence of woods and bogs (Scott and Martin 1978, 36–7).

The kingship of Leinster in the seventh century was held by representatives of the Uí Máil, the Uí Dúnlainge and the Uí Cheinnselaig (Bhreathnach 2000, 304–5; Byrne 1973, 288–90; Smyth 1994, 91). By the mid-eighth century three ruling dynastic segments in the Uí Dúnlainge had emerged and would rotate the overkingship of Leinster over the ensuing three centuries. This rotation, however, was not 'as orderly and resolute' (see MacNeill 1981, 126; Byrne 1973, 150) as often believed (Bhreathnach 2000, 305). In south Leinster the Uí Cheinnselaig were the corresponding dominant power. The biaxial division into a northern and a southern sphere inspired the occasionally used title *rí Diabul-Laigen* ('king of the double Laigin') (Byrne 1973, 131).

The territories of the three Uí Dúnlainge dynastic groups—the Uí Muiredaig, the Uí Fáeláin and the Uí Dúnchada—stretched from south Kildare through the Liffey valley to the southern limits of Dublin. There is evidence to suggest that the Uí Dúnchada had a royal seat in the district of *Liamain* (Bhreathnach 2000, 310), which has been identified as Lyons in south County Dublin (Price 1940, 127). The three kingdoms were ruled by the descendants of three brothers, Muiredach, Fáelán and Dúnchad, whose deaths occurred towards the middle of the eighth century. Their collective ancestor, Dúnlaing (whose sons died in 527 and 548), had a brother called Brión Lethderg from whom descended the Uí Briúin Chualann (Byrne 1973, 288–9; Smyth 1994, 61, 81).

The place-name 'Cualu' was manifest in one of the symbols of royal power in

Leinster—the *Coirm Cualann*, the '(ale-drinking) horn of Cualu' (Byrne 1973, 153; Bhreathnach 2014, 31). The genealogical and annalistic evidence establishes that Cualu was divided into two kingdoms: Uí Chellaig Chualann and Uí Briúin Chualann (Bhreathnach 2014, 242). In the seventh century the Uí Máil had occupied the western and north-western foothills of the Wicklow Mountains (Smyth 1994, 92). The last ruler of Uí Máil to hold the overkingship of Leinster was Cellach Cualann, who died in 715 (Byrne 1973, 288; Smyth 1994, 97). His descendants, the Uí Chellaig Chualann, survived. Dubhaltach Mac Firbhisigh, the seventeenth-century genealogist, recorded the names of twelve generations of the dynasty (O'Donovan 1854, II, 313, fn. h). They dwelt in northern Cualu, south of Tallaght, along the foothills of the Dublin Mountains and along the north-western reaches of the Wicklow–Kildare border (Smyth 1994, 97). By the mid-eleventh century the Uí Muiredaig were increasing pressure on the Uí Chellaig Chualann in the uplands of south County Dublin (Duffy 2000, 352).

In 819 the Annals of Ulster had described the 'land of Cualu' as extending as far south as *Glenn da Locha* (Glendalough) (Mac Airt and Mac Niocaill 1983, 274–5). Eastern Cualu was occupied by the territory known as Uí Briúin Chualann, the name reflecting its possession by the Uí Briúin sept. The territory extended from south County Dublin into coastal Wicklow as far south as Newcastle (Etchingham 1994, 121). Price (1954, 72) identified several locations within Uí Briúin Chualann: *Deilginis* (Dalkey), *Senchill* (Shankill), *Tulach na n-Epscop* (Tully), *Glenn Munire* (Ballyman, a.k.a. Glenmunder, to the immediate west of Old Connaught), *Dun Bréa* (probably Bray), *Teach Conaill* (near Powerscourt) and *Dergne Mogoroc* (Delgany).

VIKING/SCANDINAVIAN SETTLEMENT

The first documented appearance of the Vikings in east Leinster occurred in 827, when 'an encampment of the Laigin' was 'overwhelmed by the heathens'. Amongst the fallen was Conall, son of Cú Chongalt, 'king of the Fortuatha' (Mac Airt and Mac Niocaill 1983, 284/5). The *Fortuatha Laigen*, the 'alien tribes of Leinster', i.e. those not regarded as ethnically Laigin, occupied the eastern face of the Wicklow Mountains (Byrne 1973, 130). In 836 Kildare was 'plundered by heathens from *Inber Dea* (Mac Airt and Mac Niocaill 1983, 294–5). The general consensus of opinion is that *Inber Dea* represents Arklow (Etchingham 1994, 114), the Gaelic place-name *An tInbhear Mór* ('the big estuary') being superseded by the contracted Nordic personal name Arnketil + *ló* ('low-lying land at the water's edge') (Fellows-Jensen 2015, 279).

The foundation of a permanent base, the *longphort*, at Dublin in 841 would inevitably have centralised Viking activities in the region. The resulting settlement would steadily evolve and grow, with documented interruptions, over the ensuing centuries.

The hinterland of Dublin was referred to in the late Icelandic sagas as *Dyflinnarskíri* (the shire of Dublin) (Halliday 1884, 138). The northern part of the region was termed *Fingal/Fine Gail* ('the land of the foreigners') by the Irish (Fellows-Jensen 2015, 280).

The evidence establishes that the extent of *Dyflinnarskíri* expanded and contracted over the years (Bradley 2009, 47). In 902 the Vikings were physically driven out of Dublin, and presumably its hinterland, by the combined forces of the kingdoms of Laigen and Brega (Mac Airt and Mac Niocaill 1983, 352–3). They were back in occupation of the city by 917. The battle of *Temair* (Tara) in 980 resulted in the crushing defeat of the Vikings of Dublin and their allies from the Isles by the high-king Máel Sechnaill son of Domnall (*ibid.*, 414–15). The Christian king of Dublin, Amlaib Cúarán (Óláfr kváran), abdicated in the wake of the defeat and went on pilgrimage to Iona, where he died. A poem dedicated to Amlaib in the Metrical Dindshenchas was composed by Cináed ua hArtacáin, who upon his death in 957 was described in the Annals of Ulster as the 'chief poet of Ireland'. An accompanying gloss described him as being *do sil cornaigh sotail* (*ibid.*, 412–13); Cernach Sotal (d. 668) was the ancestor of the kings of Lagore/South Brega (Byrne 1973, 281). The poem described Amlaib as *Amlaib Átha Cliath cétaig, rogab rígi i mBeind Étair; tallus lúag mo dúane de, ech d'echaib ána Aichle* (Gwynn 1991, 52). The translation reads: 'Amlaib of Áth Cliath the hundred-strong, who gained the kingship in Bend Etair; I bore off from him as price of my song a horse of the horses of Achall' (*ibid.*, 53). Achall is the name of the Hill of Skreen, across the valley from Tara. Doherty (1998, 298) has observed that 'Bend Étair' was used as a synonym for the kingship of Brega. He further noted that, as the gifted horse came from the horses of Achall, it was perfectly plausible that Amlaib was in fact ruling South Brega prior to his defeat. The Dublin Hiberno-Norse were still attempting to control the region in the twelfth century. Control, however, is not synonymous with settlement. Significantly, the Annals of Clonmacnoise reported that it was into *Fingale* that the victorious forces of Máel Sechnaill proceeded in the wake of the battle, with the objective of wreaking vengeance on 'the Danes'. There they 'remained three nights and three days' with the knowledge that it was 'the place of greatest strength with the Danes'. Great numbers of people living in 'servitude and bondage' there were set free (Murphy 1896, 159).

Evidence for dwellings outside Dublin may be found in an entry in the Annals of the Four Masters, *s.a.* 1014 (*recte* 1015): 'An army was led by Maelseachlainn [...] to Ath-cliath; and they burned the fortress, and all the houses outside the fortress [...]' (O'Donovan 1854, II, 782–3).

A reference in the Annals of the Four Masters, *s.a.* 1052, to *Fine Ghall* illustrates that prior to the mid-eleventh century the term was being applied to a territory and not, as in the ninth century, to a people (*ibid.*, 860). In that year the territory was raided by Diarmait mac Máil na mBó, king of Leinster, in his ongoing quest for the high-kingship. Diarmait successfully installed his son Murchad as king of Dublin (Byrne 1973, 272). The annalist described the burning of the territory as extending from *Áth-Cliath* to *Albene*, i.e. from Dublin to the River *Ailbine* (the modern Delvin). Reeves (1857, 110 fn. i) described this area as 'afterwards known as Fingall'. In *Cogadh Gaedhel re Gallaibh* it is related how the *Gaill* (foreigners) 'saw the conflagration' '*i Fini*' and the district of '*Edar* (Howth)' and raised their standards on *Magh nElda*. Todd (1867, 154–5, clxxi fn. 6) described the latter area as the great plain lying between the Hill of Howth and the Hill of *Tamhlacht* (Tallaght). In his work on the Annals of Clonmacnoise, Murphy (1896, 13 fn. 1) also identified 'the playnes of *Moynealta*' as extending 'from Howth to Tallaght'. The twelfth-century notes to the Martyrology of Oengus refer to '*Magh n-elta*' in '*Gaill*'. Other locations in Fingal were identified in this work: Lusk; *Duilech* (i.e. *Clochar Dúilig*, St Doulough's Church), which is described as being located south of *Faeldrum* (Feltrim); *Cenn Sáli* (Kinsealy); and *Inis mac Nessáin* (Ireland's Eye) (Stokes 1905, 243, 203, 169, 99). Glasnevin (*Glais nóiden*) was placed *hi nGallaib* (*ibid.*, 222).

Lambay, which lies off the coast of north County Dublin, takes its name from the Nordic *Lamba-ey*, i.e. 'lamb's island' (Fellows-Jensen 2015, 275). To the west of the city lay *Lax-hleypa*, i.e. 'salmon's-leap' (Leixlip) (*ibid.*, 280). There was also a documented outpost at Clondalkin (Doherty 2000, 184). In 867 Amlaib's fort at *Cluain Dolcáin* was burned and 'a hundred of the leaders of the foreigners' slaughtered (Mac Airt and Mac Niocaill 1983, 322–3). The Annals of the Four Masters (AFM), *s.a.* 915, reported that 'Sitric, the grandson of Imhar, with his fleet, took up at *Ceann-fuait*, in the east of Leinster' (O'Donovan 1854, II, 588–9). *Ceann-fuait* was identified as Confey, near Leixlip (*ibid.*, 589). The 'plundering of *Cill-dara* by the Foreigners of *Ceann-Fuaid*' was also recorded (*ibid.*, 590–1). The western boundary of 'all that was under the dominion of the foreigners' (AFM, *s.a.* 936) was marked by the ford near Mullaghmast on the River Greese in south County Kildare named *Áth-Truisten* (*ibid.*, 635 fn. p).

The place-name evidence to the south of the River Liffey includes Dalkey. Its original name was *Deilginis Cualann*, 'the thorn (or cloak-pin) island of Cuala'. This may well have influenced the Nordic appellation of *Dalkeye*, i.e. *dalk* (cloak-pin or dagger) + *ey* (island) (Fellows-Jensen 2015, 276). There are also examples of Nordic personal names in hybrid language place-names: *Baile Thurmot* (Ballyfermot), *Baile mhic Thorcaill* (Curtlestown) and *Baile Amhlaibh* (Balally) (*ibid.*, 281).

A group of grave-slabs in the Rathdown area feature a distinctive series of motifs whose origin is diverse, with many apparently having roots in Northumbria and Pictland. The evidence indicates a Viking origin for the Rathdown slabs. Indeed, many of the motifs may be found on objects discovered during excavations conducted in Viking Dublin (Healy 2009, 70–1). While Healy (*loc. cit.*) gave a dating range from the mid-ninth to the mid-twelfth century, Corlett (2015, 444, 448) has advanced a late eleventh- to mid-twelfth-century floruit.

Additional archaeological evidence for Scandinavian settlement in the hinterland of Dublin is exiguous. A nineteenth-century excavation at Donnybrook recorded the presence of a Viking burial (Frazer 1879–88, 29, 116). A male skeleton was accompanied by a sword of early ninth-century date (Walsh 1998, 226), in addition to a spearhead and (probably) three arrowheads. The burial was located within an indigenous cemetery of the late first millennium AD (O'Brien 1992, 170).

Despite the unprecedented level of development in the hinterland of Dublin over the past 25 years, with a high level of archaeological monitoring and/or investigation, the sparseness of hitherto-unknown Viking or Scandinavian-related sites is striking. There have, however, been two notable recent discoveries.

In 1999 a longhouse and two later buildings, one an aisled house, were excavated at Cherrywood, 16km south-east of Dublin. The longhouse compares to examples found in Sweden and on the Shetland Islands (Ó Néill 2013, 72). A ringed-pin and fragments of a bone comb were found in association with the aisled house. A decorated whalebone plaque was found in a large rectangular pit along with a ringed-pin, a three-pronged socketed iron object and some fragmentary bronze objects (*ibid.*, 69). The whalebone plaque is of later ninth-century date and of classic Norwegian style. These plaques are typically found in association with the remains of wealthy Norse women (Ó Néill 2000). Unfortunately, the relationship between the longhouse, which was of tenth-century date, and the pit could not be determined (Bradley 2009, 48–9).

In 2004 the burial place of a woman was discovered in Finglas, 6.5km north-west of Dublin. The presence of two oval brooches, the better-preserved one gilded in gold and silver, in the grave established its late ninth-century Viking credentials. The burial was located within the area of an early monastic enclosure (Kavanagh 2007). The oval brooches are paralleled at Hedeby in Denmark (Bradley 2009, 59).

Large monastic settlements were the natural focal points of industrial pursuits and trade by the latter centuries of the first millennium AD. The present writer has previously suggested that, given their trading *métier*, the Vikings would naturally have been drawn to these centres. In the early phase their primary mission would have been to loot and pillage. The monastery of *Glass Mór* near Swords was so badly damaged by Vikings, apparently based on the estuary of Malahide (*Inber Domnann*), that it ceased to exist (Bradley 2009, 61). As is evident from the annals, however, after the establishment of the permanent *longphort* at Dublin in 841 all Viking raiding in the area ceased (*ibid.*, 53). Major monastic foundations, for example Tallaght, thrived into the twelfth century. There is every possibility that large numbers of the Scandinavian settlers were residing in these commercial centres as opposed to isolated farmsteads (Clinton 2000, 293). Ultimately, the loss of control of the eighteen monastic sites located in the south County Dublin area can only have had a detrimental effect on the economic stability of the Uí Dúnchada polity. The last overking of Leinster drawn from the kingdom was deposed in 1003 (Ó Corráin 1972, 127; Byrne 1973, 289).

THE ANGEVIN INTERVENTION

Martin (2011, 104) has described the Angevin arrival in Ireland as 'a casual, almost an accidental affair'. What had started out as a bitter personal struggle between Diarmait MacMurrough, king of Leinster, and Tiernán O'Rourke of Breifne was to lead to what was probably the most dramatic sea change in Irish history.

Diarmait slipped away quietly in August 1166. The burning of his *caput* at Ferns had signalled that the end was nigh. Abandoned by his allies and hounded by his enemies, he had no choice. With few friends and little succour available at home, he was left with only the hope that he could attract support abroad. He reportedly sailed with his wife, Mór, and a daughter, possibly Aífe (Scott and Martin 1978, 288 fn. 11), accompanied by at least three score followers, from *Korkeran* (Orpen 1892, 18). The Corock River flows into the north-eastern extremity of Bannow Bay, and there is a small port along the western shore of the bay named after St Kieran. It has been suggested that a variant of 'Corock-Kieran' is the origin of *Korkeran* (Roche 1970, 115; Scott and Martin 1978, 287–8 fn. 11). Their first port of call was Bristol (Orpen 1892, 18–19). Diarmait had to journey to the Continent to find Henry II, and he finally caught up with the king at Saumur (Swift 2015, 102). The men were not strangers. In 1165 Henry had hired the Dublin fleet from Diarmait to participate in his abortive campaign in north Wales (Byrne 1973, 272). Whilst he already had the king's goodwill and now received his permission to recruit from amongst his subjects, there was no guarantee given regarding any direct royal intervention. After a slow and disappointing start, Diarmait eventually found the men he was seeking on the Welsh frontier. He struck a bargain with Richard FitzGilbert de Clare, the earl of Strigoil. In return for marriage to Diarmait's daughter Aífe and the right to succeed to the kingdom of Leinster, de Clare, known as Strongbow, would arrange an interventionist force. Other knights signed on, including Maurice FitzGerald and Robert FitzStephen. In Pembrokeshire Diarmait recruited members of the imposed Flemish community, for example the Prendergasts, Roches, Flemings and Synotts. Inevitably, many indigenous Welshmen were also enlisted. Indeed, many of the knights had Welsh blood in their veins. The remarkable Welsh princess Nest (or Nesta) was the common thread between several of the leading players. She was the daughter of Rhys ap Tewdwr, king of the south-western kingdom of Deheubarth. She was first documented in 1108 as the wife of Gerald of Windsor, castellan of Pembroke. Their sons included William FitzGerald, lord of Carew, the father of Raymond le Gros; Maurice FitzGerald, whose daughter Nesta married Hervey de Montmorency, Strongbow's uncle; and David, bishop of St David's. A daughter, Angharad, married William de Barry; they were the parents of Robert de Barry and the historian Giraldus Cambrensis. Nest was also the mother of Robert FitzStephen, by Stephen the castellan of Cardigan, and of William FitzHay, by an unknown lover. In 1144 Henry I was engaged in waging war against the kingdom of Powys. Owain ap Cadwgan of Powys had abducted Nest, his cousin, leading to a violent backlash. Owain subsequently fled to Ireland. As David Crouch put it, either the English king seduced Nest or she seduced him. The resulting child was Henry FitzHenry. He was the father of Meiler and Robert FitzHenry (*ODNB*, XL, 441–2).

Diarmait returned to Ireland, and early in May 1169 Robert FitzStephen landed at Bannow Bay in County Wexford. According to the *chanson de geste* now known as 'The Song of Dermot and the Earl', he was accompanied by approximately 300 men, including Hervey de Montmorency, Meiler FitzHenry and Miles, son of Bishop David (Orpen 1892, 34–5). Giraldus put the number at 390 (30 knights, 60 men wearing mail and *c.* 300 archers/foot-soldiers) (Scott and Martin 1978, 30–1). The later editions of Giraldus's late twelfth-century text *Expugnatio Hibernica* recorded the arrival of Maurice de Prendergast on the following day with an additional ten knights and 'a large body of archers' (*ibid.*, 293 fn. 28). He was accompanied by Robert de Barry. These men were probably Flemings. The next to arrive was Maurice FitzGerald, with ten knights, 30 mounted archers and *c.* 100 archers/foot-soldiers (Orpen 1892, 92–3; Scott and Martin 1978, 50–1). About 1 May 1170 Raymond le Gros arrived on the orders of Strongbow. He brought between 80 and 100 men with him, including around ten knights (Orpen 1892, 104–7; Scott and Martin 1978, 56–7). Finally, on 23 August 1170, Strongbow arrived. Giraldus Cambrensis put the numbers of his contingent at 'two hundred knights and about a thousand others' (Scott and Martin 1978, 64–5). The 'Song' put the number at 1,500 (Orpen 1892, 112–13). Frame (1981, 16) has observed that the strength of Strongbow's forces may have been somewhat exaggerated.

Wexford had already been taken and Waterford now followed. It was there that Aífe, the daughter of Diarmait MacMurrough and Mór Uí Tuathail, married Strongbow.

Diarmait and Strongbow decided to march on Dublin. Ahead of them the high-king, Ruaidrí O'Connor, supported by O'Rourke, lay in wait at Clondalkin. Besides blocking the main highway from the south, the high-king's forces also sealed the coastal routes. Diarmait, however, simply outmanoeuvred them by leading the Leinster and Angevin forces along pathways through the dense forests covering the Wicklow and Dublin mountains. They suddenly appeared before the walls of the town.

The Norse king of Dublin, Askulv Mac Turcaill, began negotiations through the archbishop of Dublin, St Laurence O'Toole, Diarmait's brother-in-law. Milo de Cogan and Raymond le Gros lost patience, however, and broke into the town. According to the Annals of the Four Masters, the attacking force 'made a slaughter' of many in the town (O'Donovan 1854, II, 1176–7). Askulv and his surviving fellow citizens fled; they sailed to the Hebrides. As of 21 September 1170, Dublin became an Angevin stronghold.

When Diarmait MacMurrough suddenly took ill, Strongbow journeyed south to see him. The king died about 1 May 1171. In Strongbow's absence the Scandinavians led by Askulv arrived in a 60-ship fleet drawn from the Hebrides, the Isle of Man and Norway. The Northmen advanced towards the east gate of the town. These warriors wore long breastplates or shirts of mail; their shields were round, bound with iron and coloured red. According to Giraldus Cambrensis, although Milo's forces made little headway in the fighting, his brother Richard carried the day. Slipping out by the southern (or western, according to 'The Song') gate, his cavalry fell on the Ostmen's rear. Fierce fighting ensued. An Ostman leader named John the Wode was slain in personal combat by Walter de Ridelesford. The Ostmen lines broke (Scott and Martin 1978, 76–7). The attack on the town faltered and failed: 'many were slaughtered on both sides' (O'Donovan 1854, II, 1184–5). Askulv was captured and beheaded before his people (Orpen 1892, 180–1).

Strongbow returned in time to meet a new threat with the arrival of O'Connor and O'Rourke. The resulting two-month siege led to near-starvation in the town. At that point, however, the high-king decided to move against the Leinstermen while deploying the cavalry drawn from Breifne and Airgialla to 'burn the corn of the Saxons'. Thereupon detachments from the besieged town, led by Miles de Cogan, Strongbow and Raymond le Gros, swept into Ruaidrí's camp. The remnants of his army fled, leaving many dead, with their full provisions and weaponry left intact behind (O'Donovan 1854, II, 1184–5; Scott and Martin 1978, 82–3, 307 fn. 123; Orpen 1892, 138–9). The surviving Hiberno-Scandinavian population of the town were forcibly resettled across the River Liffey in what became known as *Villa Ostmannorum*, Ostman's town, Oxmanstown (Purcell 2003, 193). Dublin remained in Angevin hands.

The family of the executed Ostman king of Dublin were dispossessed of their lands to the north and south of the town. The Meic Turcaills had been the leading Ostman family in Uí Briúin Chualann and had ruled the town of Dublin for most of the twelfth century (O'Byrne 2003b, 230). Their origins are unclear. Etchingham (1994, 129) has suggested that perhaps the Turcaill, son of Eóla, whose death was recorded in the early eleventh century was the eponymous ancestor. The Annals of Inisfallen, *s.a.* 1093, refer to the slaying of this Turcaill alongside Rhys ap Tewdwr, king of Deheubarth in south-west Wales, by the 'French' (Mac Airt 1951, 244–5).

There is no available documentation recording the full extent of the holdings of the Meic Turcaill extended family. Three 'sons of Thorkil'—Sitriuc, Pole and Brodar—donated land to the Priory of the Holy Trinity. Sitriuc was the donor of *Achatillagh na escop* (modern Tully) to the church (Mills 1894, 164; Brooks 1951, 120). This grant would probably have included Carrickmines. Pole and Brodar gifted *Balyucharan* and *Tirodran* respectively to the priory (McNeill 1950, 28). Curtlestown, *Baile mhic Thorcaill*, which is located to the west of Powerscourt in north County Wicklow, preserves the family name (Price 1954, 74). Mills (1894, 164) proposed the parish of Tully as representing the northern limits of the Meic Turcaill lands, and suggested that their holdings extended as far south as Bray.

Ironically, the eclipse of the Meic Turcaills facilitated the rise to prominence of kindred lineages, amongst them the Harolds (O'Byrne 2004, 115). The Harolds were of Scandinavian origin, as were possibly the Archbolds (Curtis 1923, 196 fn.; Nicholls 1998a, 17). The Harolds became well established in the lands of Rathfarnham (Ball 1902–17, II, 116) and in the parish of Whitechurch, where the townland of Haroldsgrange still preserves their name (*ibid.*, III, 57–8). In an early seventeenth-century grant the parish of Cruagh was referred to as 'Harold's Country' (D'Alton 1838, 796). They gained possession of Kilgobbin from the Hackets in the early thirteenth century.

By 1141 Uí Briúin Chualann had been annexed by the Uí Dúnchada. Under that year the Annals of the Four Masters recorded that Muirchertach Mac Gilla Mo-Cholmóc, 'lord of *Feara-Cualann*', was blinded by Diarmait MacMurrough, king of Leinster (O'Donovan 1854, II, 1064/5). Mac Gilla Mo-Cholmóc was the surname adopted by the kings of Uí Dúnchada (Byrne 1973, 151).

The Annals of Tigernach recorded that Domnall Mac Gilla Mo-Cholmóc, king of Uí Dúnchada, was slain in 1166 by 'the sons of Mac Braenáin' at 'the instigation of

Mac Murchada' (Stokes 1897, 270). He was succeeded by his namesake Domnall Mac Gilla Mo-Cholmóc (Flanagan 2005, 275). The latter Domnall's marriage to Derbforgaill, a daughter of MacMurrough, establishes that a *rapprochement* was subsequently achieved. The marriage probably took place following Diarmait's return from exile in the autumn of 1167.

O'Byrne (2003a, 21) has observed that Domnall's integration into Angevin society would not have entailed any dramatic changes in lifestyle. He already owned a property in the town and would have been well accustomed to the multinational culture of the community. Its clothes, coinage, wines and trappings would all have been familiar to him. His guile is very plain to see. Being a son-in-law of MacMurrough and a brother-in-law of Strongbow certainly eased his path into the new order, yet during the pitched battle between the expelled King Askulv and the de Cogans in May 1171 he remained neutral, awaiting the outcome. In a rather cynical manner, he perched himself and his captains on the summit of the Thingmote outside the town to watch the encounter unfold. As the 'Song of Dermot' recalled the event: 'On the summit of the Howe (*de sur la hogges*) over the Stein, in a plain outside the city, to watch the contest, they there assembled' (Orpen 1892, 168–71).

Domnall and Derbforgaill had two sons, Diarmait and Donnchad (Flanagan 2005, 275). On 12 November 1207 King John granted to 'Dermot Mac Gilmeholmoc all the land held by Gilleholmoc, his father, namely *Lymerhim* with fifteen carucates of land in the vale of Dublin and his burgage in Dublin' (Sweetman 1875–81, I, 53).

The success of the Mac Gilla Mo-Cholmócs in retaining their lands was matched by the archbishop of Dublin and the Priory of the Holy Trinity. This meant that of the four major landholders in Uí Briúin Chulann only the Meic Turcaills were dispossessed by the new Angevin rulers. In turn, this resulted in a large degree of continuity in settlement.

Henry II arrived in Ireland in the autumn of 1171. As Frame (1981, 18) succinctly phrased it, his arrival was 'prompted by a desire to assert control over a process of conquest that was taking place almost despite him'.

Henry's arrival signalled a spate of formal submissions from most of the Irish kings. Amongst the notable exceptions were most of the dynasties of Ulster, who were too far removed geographically to take any interest in the proceedings. According to 'The Song of Dermot and the Earl', Henry arrived at the head of an army 4,000 strong, including 'four hundred armed knights' (Orpen 1892, 188–9). The Annals of the Four Masters put the number of ships transporting the army at 240 (O'Donovan 1854, II, 1186–7). Giraldus Cambrensis credited Henry's army with 'about 500 knights and many mounted and foot archers' (Scott and Martin 1978, 92–3). Henry's apparent intention to curb the aggrandisement of his nobles would have encouraged the submissions of the Irish rulers. By the time of his departure in April 1172 the towns of Dublin, Wexford and Waterford, with their environs, had been taken into royal ownership. Leinster had been formally granted to Strongbow.

The Tuscan-born Pope Alexander III was pleased to hear of Henry's intervention in Ireland. In a letter to the king dated 20 September 1172, he expressed his 'delight' at the news of Henry's 'triumph over the Irish people'. His enthusiasm was fired by the expectation that Henry would bring to an immediate end the 'abominable practices' prevalent in the Irish church. These 'illicit practices' had been brought to his attention by the Irish hierarchy. In a contemporary letter addressed to the 'Kings and Princes of Ireland', the pope wrote that he 'has learnt with joy that they have taken Henry King of England for their King, and sworn fealty to him' (Sweetman 1875–81, I, 7).

In October 1175 the Treaty of Windsor was concluded between Henry and representatives of Ruaidrí O'Connor. The former, and his nobles, would retain possession of the (aforementioned) east coast towns, Leinster, Meath and part of Munster, while Ruaidrí would hold suzerainty over the rest of the island. Crucially, Ruaidrí would recognise Henry as his overlord. Whether Ruaidrí could hold ground against all his rival domestic contenders, not to mention the external mavericks, would be his problem.

When Henry granted Leinster to Strongbow, the two cantreds nearest to Dublin were exempted. This tranche of land extended as far south as Newcastle McKynegan in County Wicklow (Price 1954, 76).

Walter de Ridelesford was the chief recipient of lands in the area. He was granted '*Brien* and the land of the sons of Mac Turcaill' (Mills 1894, 163). His grant of ten ploughlands (*c.* 1,200 acres of arable land) was for the fee of one knight (Otway-Ruthven 1959, 10). Price (1954, 72) emphasised that *Brien*, while identifiable as Uí Briúin Chualann, did not equate with the territory in its entirety, nor did 'the land of the sons of Turchil' embrace all the former holdings of the Meic Turcaill family. The Priory of the Holy Trinity and the Abbey of St Peter of Glendalough, for example, held a considerable portfolio of properties in the territory and had no intention of surrendering any of it. Until the sees of Dublin and Glendalough were united in 1216 the abbey of Glendalough had many holdings in both the Wicklow Mountains and the adjoining lowlands. The '*Concessio*', a charter of confirmation of its lands to the abbey issued by Strongbow in 1173, indicates the extent of these holdings (Manning 1893, 351). Within the *terra de Magillamocholmog* (the lands of the Mac Gilla Mo-Cholmóc dynasts) alone it held nine churches and their appurtenances. Amongst the locations identified were *Techdologa* (Templeogue), *Cell adgair* (Killegar), *Deirgni* (Delgany) and *Cell mo mothenoe* (Kilmacanogue) (*ibid.*, 366). In 1192 Prince John, as lord of Ireland, confirmed the holdings of the abbey. In 'the land of Macgilleholmoche' again we find *Thegdeloge*, *Keladger*, *Dergni* and *Kelmahenoc* (McNeill 1950, 21). Price, who compiled the index for McNeill's work, identified *Kelmacaburun* as Kilmacberne in north-east County Wicklow. He also placed *Glenmuneri* 'at Ballyman' in south County Dublin. Kilmacberne was later attached to the archbishop's manor of Shankill (*DKR 36* (1904), 36). In the case of the Meic Turcaills, as noted above, the family had already donated some of their land to the church. Furthermore, their extensive holdings at Portrane, Kilbarrack, Portmarnock and Malahide to the north-east of Dublin (O'Byrne 2004, 115), which were all confiscated, were not subsequently granted to de Ridelesford.

The de Ridelesfords appear to have been a Yorkshire family (Brooks 1951, 115; Frame 1981, 92). Walter was a senior member of Strongbow's forces. 'The Song of Dermot and the Earl' described him as 'a brave and noble warrior' (Orpen 1892, 132–3) and recorded that he was granted 'twenty fiefs in *Omurethy*' by 'the noble earl' (*ibid.*, 224–7). These twenty knights' fees in the territory of the Uí Muiredaig were in the Castledermot area of south Kildare (Brooks 1951, 117). De Ridelesford was also granted ten carucates close to the southern limits of Dublin city, including Donnybrook (*Duvenalbroc*). Walter was married to Amabilis FitzHenry, presumably the sister of Meiler FitzHenry (Scott and Martin 1978, 305 fn. 113). They had five known children: two sons, Walter and Haket, and three daughters, Basilia (married to Richard de Cogan), Sonand (married to Eustacius de Rupe) and Elena (married to Hugh de Aston) (Brooks 1951, 130). Walter would appear to have died about the year 1200 (*ibid.*, 117).

On 12 November 1207 King John granted and confirmed the lands donated by Walter de Ridelesford to the convent and nuns of St Mary of *Grane*, namely twenty carucates (Sweetman 1875–81, I, 53). Graney is located two and a half miles to the north-east of Castledermot in County Kildare (Orpen 1892, 305; Fitzgerald 1912–14, 373).

The extensive holdings acquired by Walter de Ridelesford were inherited by his son and heir Walter II and his wife Amicia. They had two daughters. Emeline was first married to Hugh de Lacy, the earl of Ulster (Sweetman 1875–81, I, 397), and secondly to Stephen de Longespée, who subsequently became justiciar of Ireland (Brooks 1951, 137). Their second daughter, Margaret, married Robert de Marisco. Walter's last appearance in the records was in October 1237 (Orpen 1892, 285; Brooks 1951, 137). On 12 December 1280 Margaret's daughter, the Lady Christiana de Marisco, reached an agreement with King Edward I and his consort, Queen Eleanor. In return for 'lands in England to the same value', she would surrender 'all her castles, fortresses, lands, with advowsons of churches, knight's fees, homages and services, villeins and their offspring' in Ireland to the king (*Cal. close rolls, Edward I*, 111–12). The properties acquired in England included *Langeleye* (Langley) and *Wyrardesbury* (Wraysbury) in Buckinghamshire (*ibid.*, 312). The lands in Ireland included properties in Connacht, Kildare, south Dublin and north-east Wicklow. The manors in County Kildare were *Kilkea*, *Garnenagh* and *Tristeldermot* (modern Castledermot) (Sweetman 1875–81, II, 377). The estates in south Dublin/north-east Wicklow were listed as *Bere*, *Balimachinan*, *Cnoctalafintyn*, *Caocro*, *Done*, *Nachbrok*, *Kylleymen*, *Kilmatheh*, *Baliculan*, *Little Tattom*, *Brun* and *Balimolys* (*ibid.*). There is an error in the transcript. '*Done*' and '*Nachbrok*' should be read as '*Donenachbrok*', i.e. Donnybrook. Brooks (1952, 49) offered identifications for nearly all these locations. His identifications would suggest that most of the holdings were in two clusters. One group was in the general area of Knocklyon: *Cnoctalafintyn* (Knocklyons), *Baliculan* (Ballycullen, adjoining to the south), *Kilininny* (Killininny, to the west/south-west) and *Balimoly* (Ballymaice, to the south-west). The second group lay in north-east Wicklow and south-east Dublin: *Brun*, i.e. *Obrun*, Uí Briúin, the territory of Uí Briúin Chulann, and *Bere* (the manor of Bray). Brooks did

(a)

not offer an identification for *Balimachinan*. It is possible that it could have been the pre-castle name for Newcastle McKynegan (i.e. *Baile Machinan*) to the south of Kilcoole. A legal suit in 1204 involving the bishop of Glendalough concerned four properties including a Balimaclinan (Sweetman 1875–81, I, 38). Hogan (1910, 82) suggested a location in the diocese of Glendalough for the said place, rendering it *Baile mac linan*. The parish of Newcastle is in that diocese. Brooks proposed Kilmashoge for *Kilmatheh*. An alternative suggestion could be Kilmartin, which lies to the immediate south of Newcastle McKynegan. Brooks provided 'Cnocro' for *Caocro*. Knockroe lies to the north of Kilcoole. He offered 'Tagony' for *Little Tattom*. The conjoined townlands of Tigroney (East and West) are located between Rathdrum and Arklow. Christiana was also credited with six carucates of arable, meadow and pasture in the manor of *Curtun* in *Kinelahun* in the county of Wexford (Sweetman 1875–81, II, 378). This manor could possibly be identified as Courtown in the parish of Kintennel. Interestingly, the manor was described as lying in 'waste and uninhabited' owing to warfare.

The O'Tooles (Ua Tuathail) and the O'Byrnes (Ua Broin) took their family names from Tuathal Mac Augaire of the Uí Muiredaig and Bran Mac Maelmórda of the Uí Fáeláin respectively. Both men held the kingship of Leinster. Tuathal died in 958 and Bran was blinded and deposed in 1018 (Byrne 1973, 151, 289). The O'Tooles and the O'Byrnes were displaced from their lands in south and north Kildare in the wake of the late twelfth-century Angevin conquest of the Liffey and Barrow river basins

Pl. 3—The watermill at Carrickmines; the dendrochronological dates and the associated pottery indicate that it was active in the twelfth century. (a) (left) The wheel-pit with wooden base-plates of the mill building. The millstones would have been located on an upper floor (connected by a vertical shaft to the horizontal millwheel sited below in the lower wheelhouse). (b) (above) Millstone. (Photos: Mark Clinton)

(Smyth 1994, 41). Like many Leinster dynasties before them, they took refuge in the mountainous terrain of Wicklow. The O'Byrnes occupied *Críoch Branach* ('the Byrnes Country') and *Raghnallach*, the O'Tooles *Imaal* and *Fercullen* (Nicholls 1998a, 7–8; Smyth 1994, 41). Basically, the O'Byrnes were pre-eminent in the east and the O'Tooles in the west (Lydon 1994, 153).

Archaeological evidence has established that there was a marked increase in arable farming in Ireland during the ninth century. Of the 35 relevant mills dated, two-thirds were built between 790 and 870 (Stout 2017, 134). The horizontal watermill (Pl. 3) uncovered during excavations at Carrickmines was dated, on dendrochronological evidence, to the early/mid-twelfth century (Clinton 2003, 228). There are a limited number of known horizontal watermills of late contemporaneous date (Stout 2017, 135). The indigenous nature of this structure would suggest that the inhabitants of this early settlement were of native stock. They may have represented an 'underclass' that had managed to survive the imposition of a Scandinavian landowning élite. In other words, Sitriuc may have owned Carrickmines prior to donating it to Holy Trinity but the tenants in occupation would appear to have been Irish.

PART I

Carrickmines: early tenures and tenants

The earliest apparent reference to Carrickmines is to be found in a document dating from 28 May 1231. The king, at the request of Richard de Burgh, the justiciar of Ireland, granted the custody of land in Dublin and in *Karmein* to Ralph Brund (or Brunt). The latter was a servant of de Burgh (Sweetman 1875–81, I, 281) who had been tasked in September 1230, along with George Defuble, with delivering 1,000 marks from Ireland into the custody of William de Putot, the sheriff of Gloucester. The sheriff had conveyed the money to the king's coffers by late October/early November (*ibid.*, 275, 276, 277). The 1231 document contains further information. The owner of the land was named as a Roger Fitz Brito le Butiller. This man had apparently died, leaving his heirs in their minority. The king retained the 'custody and marriage' rights of the children (*ibid.*, 281). *Karmein* is very compatible phonetically with *Carmayn* (see below).

THE BUTLERS OF SOUTH DUBLIN AND NORTH WICKLOW

The Butler profile in the south County Dublin/north Wicklow area held throughout the medieval period. By 1290 Theobald (V) le Botiller was in possession of the manor of *Bree* (Bray), which he held of the Crown *in capite*. The service due was the provision of 'an armoured horse at the gate of the Castle of Dublin' when required (Sweetman 1875–81, III, 315). D'Alton (1838, 909) wrote that Theobald purchased the manor of Bray 'with all the lands of the O'Byrnes' in 1297, in the wake of his service in Scotland with King Edward I. Lodge and Archdall (1789, IV, 6) had Theobald purchasing the manor in 1297 from a Philip de Rupella. 'The land of the O'Byrnes' would be a reference to Uí Briúin Chualann.

On 1 March 1326 James, the son of Edmund Butler, the earl of Carrick, and brother to the heirless Theobald (V), 'had a grant and confirmation of the prize-wines'. The prisage of wines represented the right to two tuns (large casks), each containing

252 gallons, from every ship importing twenty tuns or more. James was created the first earl of Ormond on 2 November 1328 (*ibid.*, 7). Lodge and Archdall (*ibid.*, 3) state that King Henry II had granted the prisage of wines in Ireland to Theobald (I) Butler during his 1172 visit to Ireland. Cokayne (1910–59, II, 447) credited the grant to Lord (later King) John in the 1180s.

In 1345 Elias 'de Asshebourne' (i.e. Archbold) accounted for the 'lands and tenements' that he held from the king in *Balyhauly* (Balally), *Balytir* (Ballinteer) and *Balyhamond*. It was observed that these holdings had belonged to Geoffrey le Botiller. The lands and tenements and the marriage rights of the heir were now in the possession of the king. Elias was granted the custody of the holdings for one year (*DKR 54* (1927), 22, 60).

In 1395 Richard Butler was pardoned on the grounds of self-defence for the killing of one William Horsley. He was resident in Ballyfermot (Ball 1902–17, IV, 102).

Thomas le Botiller held the priorship of the Hospital of St John of Jerusalem at Kilmainham in 1401, and again from 1410 to 1413. He was an illegitimate son of James, the fourth earl of Ormond (D'Alton 1838, 617), and was popularly known amongst the Irish as Tomás Bacach ('Thomas the Lame') (O'Donovan 1854, IV, 841 fn. y). He apparently also served as deputy to Thomas of Lancaster, the lord lieutenant of Ireland from 1401 to 1403 and from 1408 to 1409. In 1409 he presided over a meeting of parliament that passed a statute forbidding any mariners from conveying labourers out of the country without licence (Berry 1907, 517, 520). Thomas le Botiller led a force of 1,600 men to France in support of King Henry V. They took part in the siege of Rouen, which lasted from the end of July 1418 until 19 January 1419 (Burton 1843, 91, 212). According to the Annals of the Four Masters, Thomas and most of the men in his service died during the campaign (O'Donovan 1854, IV, 841).

Theobald (I) le Botiller (d. 1205/6) had four brothers. Hubert held the offices of chancellor, chief justice and treasurer of England and also served as archbishop of Canterbury. He died in July 1205. The other three brothers, Walter, Roger and Hamon, are not so well documented, and their progeny even less so (Carte 1736, I, 4; Lodge and Archdall 1789, IV, 3). The shadowy Roger Fitz Brito le Botiller may have been amongst their number.

EDWARD BRUCE

Robert the Bruce, king of Scotland, was descended from a knight who in 1066 had accompanied William the Conqueror to England. On 27 March 1306 he was crowned king of Scotland at Scone Abbey in Perthshire. The early days of his reign were a disaster and he was obliged to take refuge on Rathlin Island, off the coast of County Antrim. His comeback culminated in a great victory over the sizeable forces of King Edward II at Bannockburn on 24 June 1314.

Robert's attention then turned to Ireland. He was already married to Elizabeth, daughter of Richard de Burgh, earl of Ulster. He could expect support there from Domnall O'Neill of Tír Eógain, who in return would expect greater liberty in Ulster (Frame 1981, 132).

In May 1315 Edward, Robert's brother and lieutenant, landed in Ireland at the head of an army. He was joined by many of the leading Ulstermen. Dundalk was quickly taken and burned on 29 June. Soon afterwards Edward was crowned king of Ireland. There followed a victory over the forces of the earl of Ulster. Edward advanced southwards through the counties of Louth and Meath, leaving a trail of destruction in his wake. The Gaelic forces of the Wicklow Mountains and east Leinster began raiding south County Dublin and the Barrow Valley. The settlement at Carrickmines would have been fortunate to escape the turmoil. An engagement fought near Athy, Co. Kildare, between the English settlers and the Scots was followed by the latter's withdrawal to the north. The arrival of King Robert in early 1317 renewed hostilities. The Bruces advanced as far as Dublin but the city refused to surrender. The Scottish army proceeded south but, running desperately short of supplies, withdrew once again into Ulster. Stalemate ensued. In October 1318 Edward Bruce once again advanced southwards. At Faughart in north County Louth he was confronted and defeated by a force raised from the gentry of the county led by John de Bermingham and Milo de Verdon (Frame 1981, 133–4; Smith 1999, 105–6).

The defeat and death of Bruce certainly did not upset the annalist compiling the Annals of Loch Cé: 'Edward Bruce, the destroyer of all Erinn in general, both Foreigners and Gaeidhel, was slain by the Foreigners of Erinn, through the power of battle and bravery, at Dún Dealgan … and no better deed for the men of all Erinn was performed since the beginning of the world' (Hennessy 1871, I, 595). This sentiment was echoed in both the Annals of Ulster (Hennessy and MacCarthy 1887–1901, II, 433) and the Annals of the Four Masters (O'Donovan 1854, III, 521). All three entries observed that the 'universal famine' that resulted from the three and a half years of conflict had driven many people to 'devour the other'. The devastation wrought by the burning and looting of the marauding Scottish forces was seriously exacerbated by the simultaneous failed harvests (owing to 'intolerable, destructive bad weather') and the resulting famines of 1315–17 (Lydon 1973, x).

AUNGER LISSEBON

An Irish exchequer memorandum from the reign of King Edward I contains a reference to *Carecmayn*. The original draft of the document appears to date from between 1272 and 1305 (Bateson 1903, 503). The full entry read: '*De Aungero de Lyssebon i servientem pedes de Carecmayn*', i.e. Aunger de Lissebon owed the military service of one foot- (*pedes*) serjeant (*servientem*, from the Medieval Latin *servientum*) to the king for *Carecmayn*. The corresponding entry in the Book of Howth reads: '*De Aungero de Lysseton 1 servicium et carucat*' (Brewer and Bullen 1867–73, V, 231). The reference to the carucate (*carucata*), i.e. as much land as can be ploughed by one team

Pl. 4—Silver penny of Edward I, struck in Dublin, 1280.
Obverse: inverted triangle containing facing crowned bust, trefoil of pellets on breast. Inscription: EDW. R. ANGL. D NS. hYB ('Edward King of England, Lord of Ireland').
Reverse: long cross, three pellets in each angle. Inscription: CIVITAS DUBLINIE ('City of Dublin'). (Photo: Sara Nylund)

Pl. 5—Silver penny of Alexander III, 1280–6.
Obverse: crowned bust facing right with sceptre. Inscription: ALEXANDER DEI GRA ('Alexander by the Grace of God').
Reverse: long cross with a voided mullet of six points in each angle. Inscription: REX SCOTORUM ('King of Scots'). (Photo: Sara Nylund)

of eight oxen in a year, is of particular interest. An Edward I penny, minted in Dublin in 1281–2, was discovered within the footprint of a medieval house at Carrickmines (Clinton 2002, 263–4), and a contemporary penny of Alexander III of Scotland was found approximately 6m away in the environs of a hearth (*ibid.*, 283) (Pls 4–6).

Aunger Lissebon's name appears in the chartularies of St Mary's Abbey. He was one of three recorded sons of Lissebon. The father witnessed a number of documents. One was a grant of '*unam carucatum terre que dicitur Baliofelennan*' (Gilbert 1884, I, 32–3) made by Derbforgaill, the daughter of Diarmait MacMurrough, king of Leinster,

Pl. 6—Hearth associated with open settlement at Carrickmines. It was composed of four main stones, including a rotary quern-stone, and also incorporated two fragments of millstone. (Photo: Mark Clinton)

and the wife of Domhnall Mac Gilla Mo-Cholmóc, lord of Uí Briúin Chualann (O'Byrne 2003a, 20–1). Flanagan (2005, 275) has dated the charter in question to between 1186 and 1195. Another charter witnessed by Lissebon concerned *Tylechstelan* and *Glinculin*. This grant to St Mary's was made by William de Karru (Gilbert 1884, I, 110). Mills (1894, 166) equated *Tulacstelen* with Kiltiernan. *Glinculin*, of course, is Glencullen. These lands had been held by William de Karru from Mac Gilla Mo-Cholmóc at a very early date (*ibid.*, 169). A *c.* 1200 charter of Walter the Goldsmith granting 'certain lands' (*quadam terra*) to the Hospital of St John the Baptist without the New Gate, Dublin, was also witnessed by Lissebon (Brooks 1936, 114).

Lissebon made a grant of his own land in Dublin to the abbey. This land was described as being held by Roger the Carpenter and as lying between the lands held by Ade Faber and Roger the Chaplain. The charter was witnessed by, amongst others, his sons John, William and Aunger (Gilbert 1884, I, 457). John Lissebon in turn issued two related charters concerning the rents of adjacent holdings. Aunger and William witnessed the documents. The location of the land was described as '*in suburbia Dublin*'. John also expressed his wish to be interred in St Mary's (*ibid.*, 457, 458). These grants were later ratified by a William Tallen (*ibid.*, 459).

Aunger, in his own right, witnessed the confirmation of a grant by a Philip of Flanders (*ibid.*, 204) and a grant of the lands and church of *Douenachmor* (i.e. *Domhnach Mór*) by Milo le Bret (*ibid.*, 127). He was joined by his brother William in witnessing a chirograph (a personally written and subsequently formally split legal parchment) relating to the boundaries of Glencullen (*ibid.*, 117). In 1230 Aunger witnessed the charter by which Luke, the archbishop of Dublin, granted the land of Grenoc and land adjacent to Newcastle to Henry de Tauelaght (McNeill 1950, 65).

A survey of the lands in the valley of Dublin formerly held by Walter de Ridelesford was conducted in or about October–November 1248 by a panel including William and Aunger Lissebon, Nicholas de Feld, Richard de Stanconi, Ralph Clement, Robert Thursken and others (Sweetman 1875–81, I, 443).

At some date between 1257 and 1263 John Lissebon served as a juror at an inquisition held to hear law cases concerning the *Senkelle* (Shankill), *Raith Mikills* (Rathmichael) and Dalkey areas (McNeill 1950, 112).

William Lissebon witnessed a grant to the Priory of All Saints, Dublin, of a carucate of arable land in *Balyofryn* made by Claricia, daughter of Gilbert, son of Griffin. The holding was described as adjacent to the land of John Harold of *Kylgabanyn*, i.e. Kilgobbin. *Balyofryn* may therefore be suggested as representing Ballyogan. The grant was made before 1276 (Butler 1845, lxix, 70–1). The Priory of All Saints, or All Hallows, stood where Trinity College Dublin now stands. The FitzGriffins and the de Karrus were descended from William de Karru (de Carew), son of Gerald of Windsor (Ó Conbhuí 1962, 60). Claricia would have been a first cousin once removed of the William de Karru who made grants to St Mary's Abbey, Dublin.

William was the son and heir of John Lissebon. It is apparent that he either inherited or accumulated a sizeable estate. In a transaction pre-dating 1260, William granted 'all his land of *Clonmour*, *Fermoffyn*, *Maghreulyn*, and *Tirmagarran*', in addition to 'the vill of *Carriklydan*' and four carucates 'beside the Archbishop's land of *Shenkyll* which is called *le Dalgin*', to the master and brethren of the Knights Templar. William's *caput* was identified as *Clonmour* (McNeill 1950, 91). In a charter dating from *c.* 1217 Milo le Bret had granted 20s. (*xx solidis*) of the rent from the land *qui dicitur Karrecclidan* that Aunger Lissebon held of him to the Hospital of St John the Baptist without the New Gate, Dublin (Brooks 1936, 228–9). It would thus appear that Aunger had no direct heir and that his holding at *Carriklydan/Karrecclidan* had therefore passed to his nephew, William Lissebon.

By *c.* 1260 the holding at '*Carrikdolgyn* by *Shenkill*' was in the possession of Fromund le Brun senior. He confirmed a grant, 'in free alms 4 marks', from the rent of the holding to the Templars. The holding was identified as the land 'which William, son and heir of John de Lysbon', had previously granted to the Templars (McNeill 1950, 91). Carrickgollogan is the name of a hill that lies in the south-western area of the townland of Shankill.

In 1284 an investigation was made into the full extent of the lands held in Ireland by Christiana de Marisco. Christiana, the granddaughter of Walter de Ridelesford, was in the process of swapping her estates in Ireland for land in England. Amongst the holdings was 'a tenement held by John Lissebon' in Bray (Brooks 1952, 51). Lissebon's occupancy can hardly have been contemporaneous with the investigation, given that the date is rather late.

Pl. 7—The north-western corner of the northern enclosure. These earthworks were identified by Paddy Healy in 1983 (see Map 2). The northern enclosure was the first fortification constructed at Carrickmines, probably in the thirteenth century, and appears to have constituted an irregular-shaped moated site or ringwork castle.

The north-western corner, as illustrated, was destroyed in 1996 by the construction of a major drainage pipeline. A strip of land, 145m long and 25m wide, was cut through the archaeological site from the Glenamuck Road to the Ballyogan Road. (Photo: courtesy of Rob Goodbody.)

Aunger Lissebon was found liable for 5s. for the service of a foot-sergeant representing Carrickmines in July 1324–5 (*DKR 42* (1911), 53). This liability was in relation to the 'Army of *Tylagh*' (Tullow) proclaimed during John Darcy's time as justiciar of Ireland. The Gaelic kingdoms and lordships were resurgent in the 1320s. In the midlands the English settlers were coming under increasing pressure from, amongst others, the O'Carrolls, the MacGillapatricks and the O'Briens. Donnchadh Fionn O'Carroll, the king of Ely (*Éile*, in modern north Tipperary), was a ruthlessly ambitious man. In 1325 alone he was credited with 'scarcely' leaving an English 'house, castle, or town' (*domum, castrum, aut villam*) in Ely unburnt (Butler 1849, 17). Brian Bán O'Brien, a dissident nobleman from Thomond, also took the field and ravaged Ossory. Significantly, he was aided by some of the English settlers of Ely (*ibid.*). John de Bermingham, earl of Louth and justiciar, raised an army and moved against O'Carroll, accompanied by Thomas le Botiller, first baron of Dunboyne (*ibid.*). The same year also witnessed two government expeditions against Uí Cheinnselaig (O'Byrne 2003a, 89). And yet the Gaelic revival continued. In 1327 the Leinstermen endorsed their first king since Diarmait MacMurrough. His first act was to 'place his standard within two miles of Dublin' (Butler 1842, 106 fn. c; Curtis 1923, 205).

On 23 November 1323 King Edward II instructed the treasurer, barons and chamberlains of the exchequer in Dublin to immediately pay a quarter of his salary to John Darcy, the newly appointed justiciar of Ireland (*Cal. close rolls, Edward II*, 43). Letters to, amongst others, Richard de Burgh, earl of Ulster, Thomas (son of John), earl of Kildare, John de Bermingham, earl of Louth, and Thomas le Botiller followed, ordering them to provide 'aid and counsel' to Darcy (*ibid.*, 145). Darcy's first term of office ran until 12 March 1327 (*ODNB*, XV, 127). Further terms were served from *c.* May 1329 to 12 February 1331, from 13 February 1333 to 13 August 1333, from 19 January 1334 to 19 April 1335 and from 8 April 1340 to 9 February 1344 (Sayles 1961, 227). He had been knighted upon his arrival in Dublin.

John was the son of Sir Roger Darcy and his wife Isabel D'Alton (Cokayne 1910–59, IV, 54). He served as the sheriff of Nottinghamshire and Derbyshire between 1319 and 1323, of Lancashire from February 1322/3 to July 1323 and of Yorkshire (1327/8). He was on the king's service against the Scots from 25 February 1322/3 until 4 April 1323 (*ibid.*, 55). He married Joan of Maynooth on 3 July 1329. She was the daughter of Richard de Burgh, the second earl of Ulster, and the widow of the earl of Kildare (*ibid.*, 58). Darcy led an army from Ireland to Scotland in 1335 and laid waste to Arran and Bute. He served as steward of the king's household from March 1336/7 to December 1340 (*ibid.*, 56). It proved necessary to create the post of deputy justiciar of Ireland on 16 March 1340/1, given King Edward III's constant calls on Darcy's time (*ibid.*, 57). John Darcy died on 30 May 1347 (*ibid.*, 58).

In July 1344 King Edward III appointed Ralph D'Ufford as justiciar of Ireland. Ralph was following in the footsteps of his grandfather, Robert, who had served from 1268 to 1270 and from 1276 to 1281 (Frame 1981, 78). Ralph was brother to Robert, the first earl of Suffolk. They were the sons of Robert D'Ufford, the first baron of Ufford in Suffolk. Ralph was married to Maud Plantagenet, the daughter of Henry, third earl of Lancaster, and widow of William de Burgh, the murdered third earl of Ulster (Gilbert 1865, 197).

With great pomp and ceremony, the justiciar and his wife entered Dublin at the head of a large troop of soldiers under the banners of England. They took up residency in the affluent surroundings of the Knights Hospitaller's priory of Kilmainham. It was said that the countess 'lived royally, with her friends about her, like a queen in the island of Ireland' (*ibid.*, 198).

D'Ufford summoned a parliament in Dublin in June 1345. The earl of Desmond not only failed to attend but also instead invited the nobility to a summit meeting in Callan, Co. Kilkenny.

Ralph D'Ufford took up the gauntlet. Having dissuaded the nobles from attending the meeting in Callan, he quickly raised an army drawn from the men of Leinster, Munster and Connacht. Sums due for services in respect of 'the army of *Moydesshell*' included '5s. for the service of a foot serjeant' from Aunger Lissebon (*DKR 54* (1927), 23).

Maurice FitzThomas had been elevated to the earldom of Desmond in 1329. It was an unwarranted honour. From the time of the Bruce invasion he had aspired to the kingship of Ireland. He was aware that to achieve his burning ambition he would have to garner support from both English and Irish quarters. His ambitions were advanced by events in England. The dysfunctional reign of King Edward II culminated in the challenge mounted in September 1326 by his own wife, Queen Isabella, and her lover, Roger Mortimer. Ireland, inevitably, had to be left to its own devices (Sayles 1961, 206). Desmond's attempts to forge an alliance in Ireland stalled. One of his prospective allies, the earl of Kildare, accepted the justiciarship on 12 March 1327, while another, the earl of Louth, was slain on 10 June 1329 by the gentry of the county (Smith 1999, 115), possibly at the instigation of Roger Mortimer (*ibid.*, 117).

Desmond's main Irish ally, Brian Bán O'Brien, waged a vicious campaign. On the last day of April 1330 he slew James de Beaufo, the sheriff of Limerick, and 200 others while ravaging the countryside. On 17 July 1330 the deputy justiciar, Roger Outlaw, launched an offensive against O'Brien. The new sheriff of Limerick, Thomas de Lees, was ordered to seize all of O'Brien's livestock and cattle but was intimidated by Desmond into returning it all (Sayles 1961, 210). The deputy justiciar's arrival led to the imprisonment of Desmond. O'Brien soldiered on and destroyed Bunratty Castle in July 1332. In early June 1333 Desmond was released from Dublin Castle but by the turn of the decade was the cause of renewed conflict (*ibid.*, 215–16).

Laoiseach O'More had become the most powerful of the petty kings in the midlands (O'Byrne 2003a, 88). In 1336 there was war between O'More and Fulco de la Frene, who was in command of *Anglicorum Ossorie* (Butler 1849, 27). Sums due for service 'in respect of the army of *Kylkenny*' included 5s. for the service of one foot-serjeant from Aunger Lissebon (*DKR 45* (1913), 25–6). The date given was 1337–8, in 'the time of John Darcy, Justiciar of Ireland'.

In the wake of the aborted summit at Callan, 'the army of *Moydesshell*' swept south-westward. Desmond's castle at Iniskisty was taken, followed by Askeaton Castle on 30 September 1345. Finally, Desmond's impregnable fortress at Castle Island, near Tralee, was besieged. The commanders, Eustace le Poer, the baron of Kenlis in Ossory, and William le Grant, refused to surrender to D'Ufford despite his unfurling of the standard of England. Two weeks later, on 21 October, the fortress finally fell. Both le Poer and le Grant were hanged, as was Desmond's seneschal John Coterel, who also had his intestines burned, his head severed and his limbs distributed for public display throughout the province (Gilbert 1865, 200; Sayles 1961, 222).

Desmond's luck turned, however. Ralph D'Ufford, the justiciar, took ill and died at Kilmainham on Palm Sunday, 9 April 1346 (Gilbert 1865, 201). His successor, Roger Darcy, was not as indomitable. Incredibly given his history, after a period of supplication in England the earl of Desmond was allowed to return to Ireland in 1350, and on 8 July 1355 was appointed to represent the king in Ireland. He served as justiciar from 17 August 1355 until his death on 25 January 1356 (Sayles 1961, 225, 227).

Aunger Lissebon: chronology

Clearly there are problems regarding the dating span of the documentary references to Aunger Lissebon. How could the same man be witnessing a charter in 1230 and still be liable for the cost of a military service in 1345? There would be the possibility, as in the case of the references relating to Walter de Ridelesford, that there was an eponymous father and son in the equation. There is, however, no supportive evidence for the existence of a son of any name. There is also the fact that Carrickmines would appear to have been in different hands by 1295 and again in 1326 (see below). The logical explanation, therefore, is that the latter-day references to Aunger's service obligations at Carrickmines are in fact 'formulae in aspic'. In other words, on the later occasions that 'Aunger Lissebon' is found to be liable for the cost of the service of a foot-serjeant on behalf of Carrickmines, what was actually meant in the documents dating from 1324–5, 1337–8 and 1345 was that the 'current occupant' of Carrickmines was liable for the contribution formerly paid by Aunger Lissebon.

CHURCH PROPERTY

The Church was the major landholder in County Dublin, holding close to half of all the land. Of the 222,710 acres in the county, at least 104,710 were in the possession of the Church (Otway-Ruthven 1959, 3; 1961, 56). The lands of the archbishop, amounting to 53,200 acres, constituted half the total (Otway-Ruthven 1961, 54, 56). South of the River Liffey the archiepiscopal lands included the parish of Dalkey (467 acres) and the parishes of Rathmichael and Shankill (1,592 acres) (*ibid.*, 58). The manor of Clonkeen, in the parishes of Tully and Kill, constituted 2,578 acres of the total of 10,538 acres held by Christchurch (Holy Trinity Priory) (*ibid.*, 59). Carrickmines lies within the parish of Tully. St Mary's Abbey was the largest landowner among the monastic houses, holding a total of 17,125 acres, including the parish of Kiltiernan (3,166 acres) and the parish of Monkstown (2,052 acres) (*ibid.*, 62). The lands held by St Mary's Abbey in the barony of Rathdown were clustered into three groups, one group of lands spilling into the neighbouring barony of Uppercross (Ó Conbhuí 1962, 54). The Knights Hospitaller held approximately 6,316 acres, north and south of the River Liffey. In the parishes of Rathmichael and Old Connaught they held 1,141 acres (Otway-Ruthven 1961, 65–6). This land passed from the Templars to the Hospitallers in the wake of the 1308 confiscation of Templar lands. It was, as previously noted, William, the son of John Lissebon, who had granted four ploughlands of the land to the Templars (*ibid.*, 66).

The prior of Holy Trinity throughout the 1280s was Adam de la More (Archdall 1873, 5). In 1282, according to the *Liber Niger*, he purchased the advowson of *Acherlar* with 120 acres, seven acres in *Balliardur* and seven acres *incremanta de Kartmayn* (Lawlor 1908–9, 66). Lawlor identified *Archerlar* as Killahurler in the parish of Arklow, Co. Wicklow (*ibid.*, 70). Ball (1902–17, III, 57) placed *Balliardur* (Ballyardor) in modern Kilmashogue (to the west of Stepaside, to the south-east of Ballinteer). If *Kartmayn* is accepted as a variation of *Karmein*, it can be identified as *Carrickmayn*. The transaction of 1282 would therefore represent the date when the holdings of the Priory of the Holy Trinity 'expanded' or 'increased' (*incrementa*) to incorporate the heartland of Carrickmines.

Pl. 8—The bivallate defences along the western flank of the northern enclosure at Carrickmines. (Photo: Mark Clinton)

ROGER FITZDAVID

In the late twelfth century, the earl of Strigoil had granted Walter de Ridelesford lands around Castledermot (Mills 1894, 164). The roll of service of *Tristledermot* (Castledermot) for Michaelmas term 1295 listed Roger FitzDavid as being liable for 5s. for *Karrkmayn*, alongside William Haket, who was liable for one mark for *Staglorgan* (Sweetman 1875–81, IV, 100). *Stachlorcan* was the old form of Stillorgan (Price 1940, 131). Roger son of David had served as a juror at an inquisition held in Dublin on 1 July 1295. Upon their oath the jury found that 'John Walhope, deceased, held of the king *in capite* at his death, five carucates of land in *Balyhawyl* (Balally), *Balytire* (Ballinteer), *Balyhamond*, and half a carucate in *Garvath*' (Sweetman 1875–81, IV, 100). The receipt of service of the term of St Hilary 1297–8 recorded *Roger David de Carmayn* as having been liable for 5s. (*ibid.*, 222). At an inquisition taken before the treasurer and barons of the Dublin exchequer on 6 May 1298 the jury included a Roger David (*ibid.*, 202).

Pl. 9—The moat along the north-eastern flank of the northern enclosure at Carrickmines. Later features, such as stone-lined wells and the basal courses of a high-status building, may also be seen. (Photo: Mark Clinton)

The pipe roll dated xxx Edward I (i.e. 1301–2) recorded that 'Roger Dauy' was liable for '5s. for the service of one foot serjeant from *Carrickmayn*'. Significantly, he owed the payment 'for Aunger de Lisbon' (*DKR 38* (1906), 61). This could imply that Roger son of David was renting Carrickmines from Aunger Lissebon or it might be an elaboration on the formula that would subsequently appear in the previously mentioned military service-related documents of 1324–5, 1337–8 and 1345 (see above)—in other words, that Roger son of David was holding Carrickmines either directly from the king or from an unknown intermediary by 1295 and that Aunger Lissebon was in fact no longer involved with the property. The most persuasive evidence comes from the accounts of Walter de Istelep, the escheator. It is made clear that in 1312 the holding was in the hands of the king's representatives. Furthermore, it is stated that the 40 acres, six 'cottars' and pasturage rights which he had rented out formerly 'belonged to Roger son of David', who had recently died. After two months the land was delivered to Roger's son, John (*DKR 39* (1907), 61). Interestingly, the estate apparently held additional 'demesnes' that lay 'between the Mountains and the Irish'. These lands then lay waste 'for want of tenants' (*ibid.*, 62). Unfortunately, the place-names of the additional demesnes were not recorded.

MAURICE HOWEL

In *c.* 1326 Maurice Howel held 40 acres in *Carricmayn* for 40s. a year from the Priory of the Holy Trinity, along with '2 crofts, *penes* (with) *Villam Corner*', for which he paid 20d. a year. In addition, he held *Balybrenan* (Brenanstown) for 50s. a year (Mills 1891, 195; McEnery and Refaussé 2001, 144–5). *Villam Corner*, Cornerstown, Cornelscourt, is adjacent to Cabinteely (Mills 1891, 194 fn. 2). Maurice Howel was a leading citizen in south County Dublin. In November 1337 the priory's account roll noted the purchase of wine for the refreshment of Maurice, a John Aket (Hacket?) and others (*ibid.*, 1). In the early part of the fourteenth century Howel accounted to the Crown for the rents of Much Bray (Ball 1902–17, III, 102).

On 21 June 1312 a Maurice Howel failed to appear to serve in Kildare as a juror in a trial for theft and the contracting of a killing (Wood *et al.* 1957, 243). A marginal note recorded that he was later excused (*ibid.*, 243 fn. 1). He did serve in Kildare as a juror on 21 April 1314 in a trial for theft (*ibid.*, 318).

Ball (1902–17, I, 105) described Maurice as 'a leader of the militia and [a] large farmer'. In fact, Howel was of sufficient importance to the government that, in return 'for the good service often done to the King' 'in fighting the Irish felons of the mountains of Leinster' and in Offaly, he was pardoned on 25 February 1314 for 'all trespasses and felonies' committed to date. The record covering the pardon is of further significance in that it names many of Maurice's relatives, i.e. Archebaud, Alexander, Walter, John, Richard, William and Philip Howel, and some of his associates, e.g. Richard le Waleys, Richard Roth le Waleys, Robert le Waleys and William Crok. The blanket pardon was extended to them all (Wood *et al.* 1957, 315). Interestingly, there is no mention of Peter Howel, who contemporaneously held *Balymorthan*, also known as *Ballymolghan*, an area now represented by Murphystown and Blackthorn (Mills 1891, 194 fn. 3; McEnery and Refaussé 2001, 144–5). This holding would have lain to the immediate north-west of Carrickmines.

About 1316 'a confederacy of O'Tooles, O'Byrnes, and the hibernicised Ostmen—the Harolds and Archbolds, attacked the marches from Arklow to Bray' (Curtis 1923, 234). In November 1316 the privy council assigned Maurice Howel to the defence of Newcastle McKynegan. The castle was deemed to be under threat of attack or siege. He accordingly led a force of 29 hobelars (lightly armed horsemen) and 60 foot-soldiers to its defence, and they remained there until the end of January 1317 (Connolly 1998, I, 239–40). He led his force through the marches again in 1324–5, keeping watch on the mountain passes used by the Irish raiding parties (*ibid.*, 303). The damage wrought by the raiders is apparent in Archbishop Alen's Register, where under 14 March 1326 it was recorded that 'there were no buildings' left standing in *Senekyll* (Shankill). They had all been 'burned and thrown down by Irish felons'. 'Nine score and five acres', hitherto under the plough, lay 'waste and untilled for want of *tenants*'. Similarly, at Rathmichael there were no tenants left (McNeill 1950, 194).

Howel served as 'a Captain' in the July 1330 campaign against the previously mentioned Brian O'Brien in Munster. He was entitled to 29 days' pay according to the army's clerk, Thomas de Warylowe. Alexander, the archbishop of Dublin, duly paid his wages (*DKR 43* (1912), 43). Soon afterwards he was in action in Wicklow. He was paid £10 for the subsequent delivery of prisoners into the custody of the agents of the king. The prisoners were named as William son of 'Donwyth' O'Toole, and Richard and William the sons of Simon O'Toole (Connolly 1998, II, 371). Elsewhere Howel is described as a 'king's yeoman' (*vallettus*) (*ibid.*, 616).

A John Howel was referred to in a 1309 document pertaining to the Hospital of St John the Baptist without the New Gate, Dublin. He witnessed a charter regarding the granting of a property in *Clocher* to the hospital *c.* 1315 (Brooks 1936, 334, 340). Henry Howel served as a juror in Kildare in a trial for theft on 25 November 1311 (Wood *et al.* 1957, 226).

TRADE AND PRODUCTIVITY IN SOUTH DUBLIN

Despite the ongoing hostilities, there was trade between the Gaelic lordships and the colonial community. Wool and timber were readily available in the mountainous region. Wine, weapons and livestock were high on the reciprocal list of goods (O'Byrne 2004, 144).

The demesne lands of the manor of Clonkeen, a property of the Priory of the Holy Trinity, lay around Kill-of-the-Grange. The tenants owing service to the manor lived in an area stretching from *Ballymolghan* (*Balymorthan*), i.e. modern Murphystown and Blackthorn, to Killiney (Mills 1891, 174).

An account roll for 1344–5 kept by John Chamburleyn, the bailiff at Clonkeen, contains invaluable information regarding daily life at a manorial centre in south County Dublin. The economic profile of Carrickmines would have mirrored its neighbouring manor at Clonkeen but on a much-reduced scale. The discovery of a keyhole-shaped corn-drying kiln during excavations at Carrickmines indicated the ongoing importance of grain at the castle site in the late thirteenth/fourteenth century (Clinton 2003, 359) (Pl. 10).

The harvest of 1344 at Clonkeen lasted from Thursday 5 August until Saturday 4 September. The work, however, was confined to eighteen days. Different numbers of workers were deployed on the various occasions, for example 88 men on the first day (*ibid.*, 64, 67). The cereal crops harvested were wheat, oats and barley (*ibid.*, 85, 86, 87). Legumes (both peas and beans) were grown (*ibid.*, 83). The employment of 64 hoers may have been related to the tending of the latter two crops (*ibid.*, 79). Frame (1981, 95) has drawn attention to the fact that landholders were heavily dependent on the casual paid labour that they would hire at, for example, harvest time. He noted the sporadic nature of the work, i.e. the 'occasional ploughing, hoeing, reaping, and carting services', that was necessary to a functioning manorial estate.

The barley grown would have constituted the bulk of the raw material used for the ale malted at the manor. Practically all the wheat grown would have been used to bake bread. Oats, when baked as flat cakes or used in stews, were a source of 'cheap

Pl. 10—Corn-drying kiln. Keyhole-shaped kilns date from the late medieval and post-medieval periods. Two grain-drying kilns were excavated at Carrickmines. (Photo: Mark Clinton)

and plentiful' food (Murphy and Potterton 2010, 313). The scale of grain production is illustrated by the purchase of timber 'for the making of 12 new ploughs' (Mills 1891, 57). 'Bullocks' were purchased to pull ploughs, horses to pull carts (*ibid.*, 62, 82).

A 'haggard' was an enclosed area adjacent to a farmstead and was used to store hay and grain. It was also where threshing took place. In the autumn of 1344 Walter Harold was engaged in 'stacking' in the haggard at Clonkeen (*ibid.*, 67). Two other men were 'forking' corn there, while one woman was binding sheaves (*ibid.*, 68).

Besides paying their workers 1d. a day, the manor also had to feed them. Bread, beef, mutton, chicken, goose, herring, ale and wine all made appearances on the menu (*ibid.*, 67, 72–3). The wine, of course, would have been imported.

Pigs were kept on the manor. The fact that a man was employed to make sure that they did not cause 'injury' to the neighbours (*ibid.*, 79) suggests that they roamed free. It is not impossible that they foraged in the 'Wood of *Clonken*' (*ibid.*, 64). There was also a 'keeper of cows and lambs' (*ibid.*, 85). Indeed, the farmyard contained a cowhouse as well as at least one barn (*ibid.*, 79, 86).

Rabbits, which had been brought to Ireland by the Angevin settlers, were a source of meat and fur. Rabbit warrens are a known feature of some manorial centres (O'Conor 1998, 34).

The manor traded in turf and clay. The clay was of the type used for the making of earthen jars (*de argilla pro ollis luteis*) (Mills 1891, 55). The sale of wool suggests the keeping of sheep (*ibid.*, 56).

The manor of Clonkeen also played a security role in the locality. An entry in the account roll records the payment of 4d. to two men for spending two nights on 'the tops of the mountains' keeping watch, 'from fear of the *Hibernicorum*' (*ibid.*, 64).

THE BLACK DEATH

John Clyn recorded the 'Black Death' as having first arrived in 1348 through the ports of Howth and Drogheda, and reported the widespread fear of the 'pestilencie' and its devastating effect on the citizens of Drogheda and Dublin (Butler 1849, 35). The Annals of Ross also recorded the arrival of the plague under the year 1348 and the resulting *mortalitas magna* (*ibid.*, 23).

The Black Death naturally took a greater toll in the confined spaces of urban settlement. It is estimated, for example, that between 30% and 50% of the population of Dublin city perished within six to nine months (Dwyer 2016, 63). The plague thus had a disproportionately greater impact on the urban-based English settlers than on the rural Irish (*ibid.*, 69, 88). As the numbers of the colonist community drastically declined, the frontier areas increasingly came under threat and inevitably began to contract.

THE ROKEBY LINE

In December 1349 Sir Thomas de Rokeby took up the office of justiciar of Ireland. He was referred to as *L'Uncle* to differentiate him from his nephew of the same name (Gilbert 1865, 205). De Rokeby was coming to a kingdom laid waste by plague and famine and now suffering from an extreme dearth of labour, especially of skilled workers. As a veteran soldier, he immediately took the field in both Leinster and Munster (Lydon 1973, 80). His salary of £500 was for his own benefit and for the maintenance of twenty men-at-arms and twenty mounted archers. He was authorised to supplement this detachment with an additional twenty men-at-arms and 40 mounted archers from England. These military provisions were undoubtedly underscored by a contemporary official appraisal of the state of Ireland, which found that the country was 'neither in a good plight nor at peace' (Gilbert 1865, 205). De Rokeby was loyal to his troops; he was reported to have stated in public that he would happily use wooden dishes, platters and cups 'rather than not pay in gold and silver the wages of his men' (*ibid.*, 206). Neither did he tolerate corruption, and thus the treasurer, Robert Embleton, was amongst the government officials prosecuted and convicted (*ibid.*, 205).

A successful campaign was conducted in 1353 in Munster, but Leinster soon became troublesome again. Expeditions, deploying around 1,000 men, were launched against the rebellious factions in late 1353, in the autumn of 1354 and in the spring of 1355 (Lydon 1973, 82). In October 1354 John mac Taidhg O'Byrne defeated de Rokeby and besieged him in Wicklow Castle (O'Byrne 2003a, 100). There was no escaping the fact that the government was lamentably lacking in proper resources. The official responses of occasional scaled-down expeditionary forays would never succeed in achieving a comprehensive victory.

Besides his military operations, de Rokeby set about pragmatically placating the Gaelic lords and marcher families. He signed accords with the O'Byrnes, Archbolds and Harolds. The border areas close to Tallaght he secured by monetary means. Aodh O'Toole was to provide a force of twenty hobelars, who would each be paid 4d. per day, and a troop of 40 foot-soldiers, who would each be paid 2d. per day. Aodh himself would be paid ten marks, his brother Shane (of Imail) 40s. and his marshall 20s. His chaplain would receive 6s. 8d. to gather intelligence on the movements of elements hostile to the Crown (Gilbert 1865, 206). De Rokeby also devised a policy of supporting dissidents and dynastic rivals throughout the various lordships and petty kingdoms. The assassination of hostile nobles was encouraged with offers of reward. Their heads would be displayed on the battlements of Dublin Castle (*ibid.*). Self-serving alliances were not uncommon in what O'Byrne (2005, 18) has described as 'the merry-go-round' of marchland politics in the fourteenth century. King Edward III issued a proclamation in 1353: no settlers would be granted permission to depart from the kingdom (Gilbert 1865, 207).

By the 1350s de Rokeby had initiated a policy of constructing a chain of castles to protect the city of Dublin and those parts of east Leinster vulnerable to the predations of the O'Byrnes, the O'Tooles, the MacMurroughs and O'Nolans. The settlers there had become prey to constant occurrences of 'homicides, depredations, burnings and other crimes' (Connolly 1998, II, 472). In 1352 the king was anxious to ascertain whether or not the constables of his castles and fortalices had them in proper order and well defended (Barry 1995, 224). It is important to note that he made a distinction between the two types of fortification. Barry (*loc. cit.*) has noted that there is evidence to establish that fortalices were being built in south County Dublin in the mid-1350s. He also raised the possibility that some of these fortalices were constructed of timber or other non-permanent materials (*ibid.*). When John de Troye was appointed baron of the exchequer *c.* 1355–6 he embarked on a programme of strengthening and supervising these wards/fortalices, including the one at *Carrigmayn* (Maps 1 and 2). The line of castles around the Wicklow Mountains and foothills stretched from Kilmartin, Newcastle McKynegan and Bray on the County Wicklow coast, to Carrickmines and Dundrum, to Tallaght and Saggart, to Rathmore and Ballymore in County Kildare and to Graney, close to the border with County Carlow (Frame 1981, 140) (Map 6). The Lawlesses held the fortresses at Kilmartin, Newcastle McKynegan and Killoughter. The family were embroiled in a 'fight to the death' with the O'Byrnes (O'Byrne 2004, 140). Newcastle McKynegan is referred to in the documentation as *Novum Castrum McKynegan* to distinguish it from *Novum Castrum de Leuan*, i.e. Newcastle (Lyons) in County Dublin (Orpen 1908, 126).

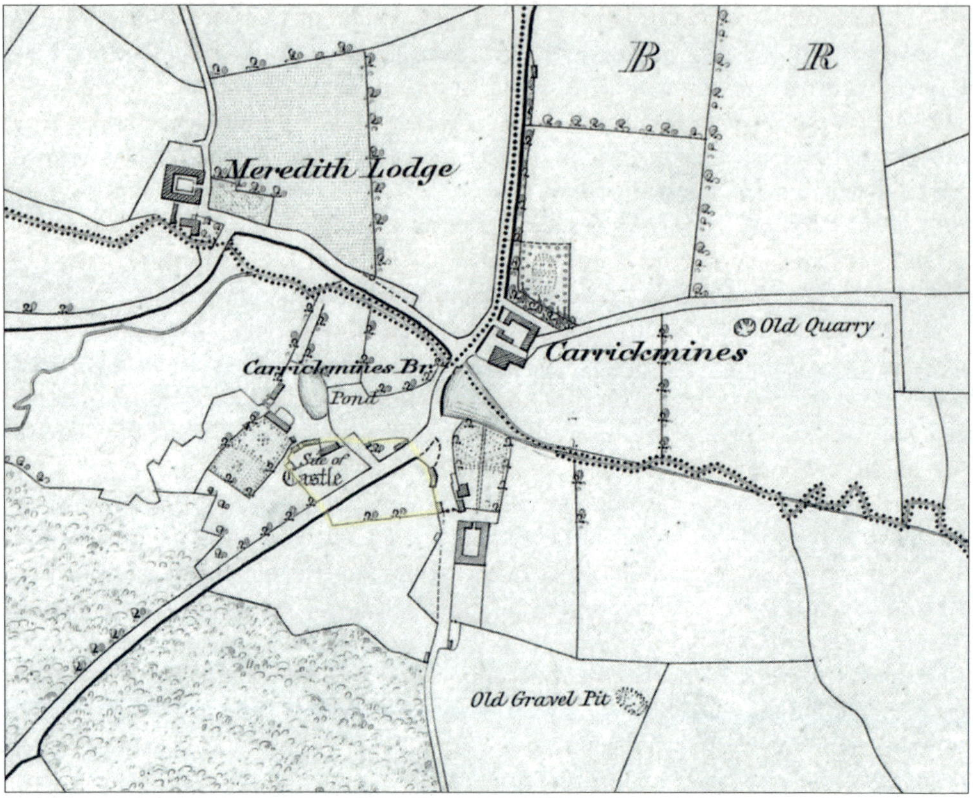

Map 1—The south-eastern enclosure of Carrickmines Castle as indicated on the 1843 Ordnance Survey map.

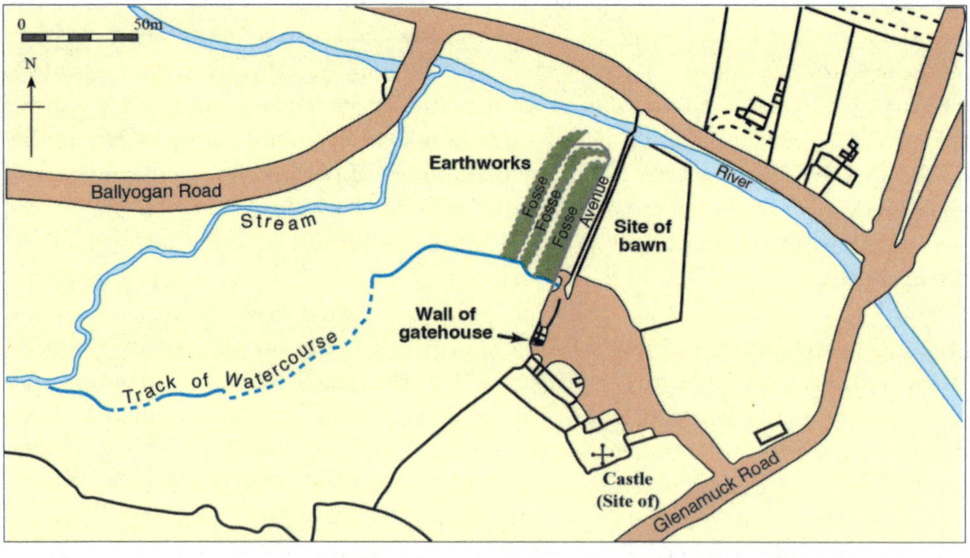

Map 2—The northern enclosure of Carrickmines Castle as identified by Paddy Healy in 1983.

John de Troye apparently spent 'no small time' touring the wards 'with many armed men and archers'. Improvements were made, 'not without heavy labours and expenses'. There was also a detailed examination of the reliability and suitability of those appointed to administer the wards. Failure to furnish sufficient 'horses and arms' to the wards by these administrators would result in penalties (Connolly 1998, II, 472).

The need for the line of defensive wards to the south of Dublin city was obvious. Only seven of the years between 1320 and 1344 had been free of strife in Leinster (Frame 1982, 310). Further to the south, the Barrow valley, the main route to Munster, was coming under increasing threat (*ibid.*, 313). The death of de Rokeby in April 1357 was followed by the short-lived tenure of Amaury de St Amand. In early 1359 Maurice FitzMaurice Butler, the second earl of Ormond, was appointed as justiciar of Ireland (*ibid.*, 299). His first major concern was the revival of the MacMurroughs under the leadership of Murchertach MacMurrough, the self-styled 'King or Prince of Leinster' (*ibid.*, 312). Murchertach had the support of the Gaelic families in the Wicklow Mountains. In the summer of 1359 Ormond gave battle to the O'Tooles at Carrickmines (*ibid.*, 314). In the 33rd year of the reign of King Edward III (i.e. 1359–60), an armed force led by John de Bermingham was engaged in resisting the O'Byrnes and the O'Tooles *in partibus de Carrigmayn* ('in parts of Carrickmines') (Tresham 1828, 79).

The penny finally dropped in London and King Edward III agreed to dispatch an army to Ireland under the command of his son, Lionel, earl of Ulster (Frame 1982, 296).

In September 1361 Lionel landed at the head of an army 800–900 strong. Importantly for the colony, the expense was to be borne by the English exchequer (Frame 1982, 333; 1981, 147; Lydon 1973, 89). Lionel had more than a passing interest in Ireland. Indeed, he and his wife, Elizabeth de Burgh, on paper owned 'close on half the territorial area' of the island (Frame 1982, 334). The details of Lionel's campaigns in Ireland are sketchy. A campaign was conducted in Wicklow in the early days of his tenure (Lydon 1973, 91). About 100 soldiers were lost in an attack conducted by Sir John O'Byrne and Lionel was forced to withdraw into Wicklow town (O'Byrne 2004, 141). His forces were in action there again in 1364 (*ibid.*, 92). Lionel was to serve as his father's lieutenant in Ireland until November 1366. Except for a gap of eight months in 1364 he remained permanently on the island (Frame 1981, 149). Despite the great expectations of the king and the colonists, Lionel did not achieve any major victories. The fundamental problem was that there was no primary foe to challenge and defeat—just an array of petty kings and chieftains scattered the length and breadth of the island.

Lionel's most enduring legacy was enacted at a parliament summoned in February 1366. The Statute of Kilkenny was designed to rein in those English settlers—or, to be more precise, their descendants—who were increasingly adopting Gaelic laws, language and attire. Intermarriage and alliances were also widespread but not universal. The legislation now enacted made it unlawful to enter into a marriage, form an alliance, foster children, engage in concubinage or conduct business with Gaelic society. All colonists must henceforth use the English language, be called by English names, follow English customs, and dress and ride horses in the correct mode.

Recourse to brehon law was forbidden, as was the retaining of Gaelic musicians, storytellers or rhymers (on the suspicion that these individuals could be acting as spies) (Gilbert 1865, 224–5). In fact, very little of the legislation was technically new (Lydon 1973, 95). Frame (1981, 151) has observed, however, that it was 'much more clearly directed'. He also drew attention to the fact that the legislation insisted that the early colonists were entitled to be treated as well as the recent arrivals (*ibid.*, 150).

The war of attrition continued unabated. Both the Annals of the Four Masters and the Annals of Ulster, *s.a.* 1369, credit a mysterious figure, 'the Black Knight' (*An Ridire Dubh*), with the slaying of Gerald Kavanagh, 'heir to the King of Leinster' (O'Donovan 1854, III, 647; Hennessy and MacCarthy 1887–1901, II, 537). The latter annals recorded that it was also *An Ridire Dubh* who captured ('in treachery') Diarmait Laimhdearg MacMurrough. The entry concluded by reporting that Diarmait Laimhdearg, the king of Leinster, was later 'drawn asunder' in Dublin.

The pressure on Carrickmines increased dramatically in 1374–5. The treasurer of Ireland, John Colton, was obliged to serve two tours of duty at the *vill* of *Carrykmayn*. The first lasted for eight days, the second a month. He was accompanied by 'a large company of men' (*magna comitiva homines*), greater than his regular escort (Tresham 1828, 87). John Colton was born in Norfolk. In 1373 he was appointed lord treasurer of Ireland and in 1374 dean of St Patrick's. Later, on 9 March 1382, he would become primate of Ireland (Reeves 1850, i–ii). Newcastle McKynegan and Wicklow castles were captured briefly by the O'Byrnes in 1374 and again in 1376 (Nicholls 1998a, 17) and both were broken down in the wake of their 1374 capture (*ibid.*, 19). John Colton promptly counter-attacked and the two castles were rebuilt. Newcastle McKynegan was destroyed again in the wake of the 1376 attack and its garrison all killed (*ibid.*, 20). It was around this period that the Lawlesses finally threw in the towel and abandoned their east Wicklow estates, withdrawing to their lands in Old Connaught and Shanganagh to the north of Bray (O'Byrne 2004, 143). Carrickmines was now decidedly in the front line (Map 3) (Pls 11–13).

Richard of Bordeaux, the ten-year-old grandson of Edward III, succeeded him as king in June 1377. His father, Edward the Black Prince (his sobriquet came from the colour of his armour), a knight of some renown, had died the previous year. In the absence of a formally appointed regent, the boy's uncle, John of Gaunt, duke of Lancaster, was the power behind the throne.

On 26 October 1386 the notification of a levy on the landholders of Fingal was recorded. They would pay 2s. per carucate and the money was to be used to sustain '40 *hobellar & sagittar*' at *Carrykmayne* for fifteen days to resist the O'Byrnes and the O'Tooles (Tresham 1828, 136). Hobelars were spearmen who rode small horses known as hobins. Archers (*sagittarii*) started to appear in the literature after 1337. Never that common in Ireland, they used the English longbow (Frame 1989, 114, 115).

Peace with France, after prolonged warfare, and a truce with Scotland finally allowed London to address Irish affairs decisively. In the autumn of 1394 Richard II arrived at the head of a sizeable army, the first English monarch to set foot in Ireland since 1210 (Lydon 2011, 134).

Pl. 11—The revetted inner rock-cut fosse of the trivallate south-eastern enclosure at Carrickmines. The middle fosse was also rock-cut, while the outer fosse was earth-cut. There would have been intervening earthen banks. The revetment, which was 217m in length, survived to a height of 2m in a remnant buried in an early nineteenth-century roadside ditch. Its supporting bank was probably originally topped by a wooden palisade. The south-eastern enclosure was probably created, or at least significantly strengthened, in the mid-fourteenth century. It was damaged in 1996 by a drainage pipeline scheme and again in 1998 by the laying of a major gas pipeline. (Photos: Mark Clinton)

Pl. 12 (above)—Causeway connection between the south-eastern and south-western enclosures. (Photo: Mark Clinton)

Pl. 13 (left)—The sloping ramp entrance to the Carrickmines Castle complex. The north-eastern terminal section of the revetted fosse of the south-eastern enclosure may be observed along its 'right-hand' flank. There was evidence for the former presence of a tower at the entrance to the complex. (Photo: Mark Clinton)

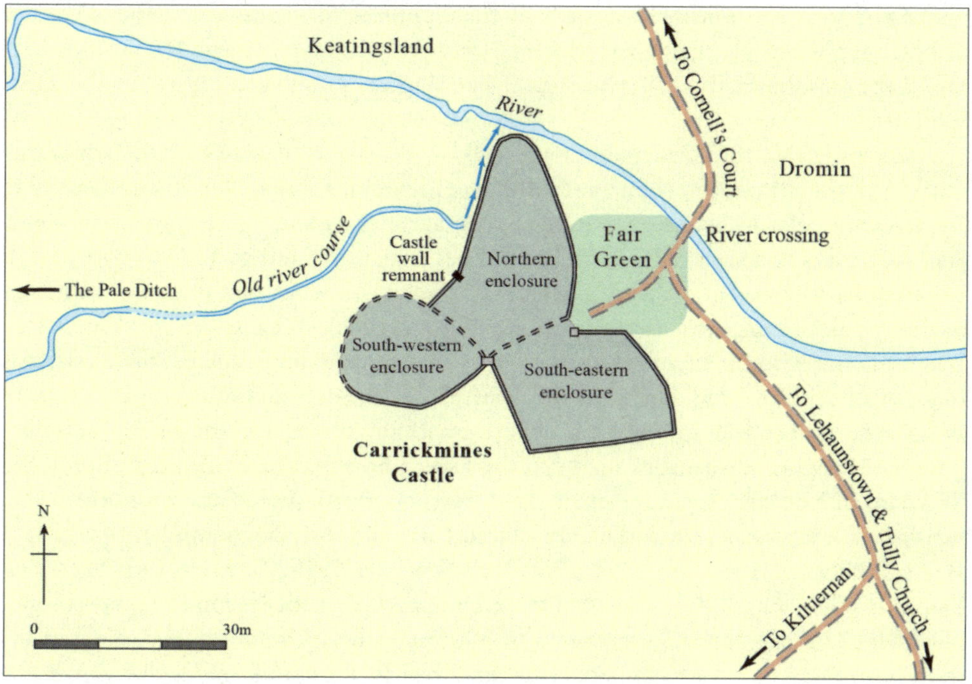

Map 3—The Carrickmines Castle complex and landscape in medieval times.

Art Mór MacMurrough, self-declared king of Leinster since April 1378 (Frame 1995, 168), was the son of Art MacMurrough (d. 1362) and a daughter of Philip O'Byrne (O'Byrne 2003a, 104). He had skilfully exploited the vacuum created by the withdrawal of the justiciar, William of Windsor, in 1376 to consolidate his position. Throughout the 1380s he collected a steady and very tidy income from the Dublin government to 'maintain the peace' in Leinster (Frame 1995, 169). It is credible that he collected 'several hundred pounds' a year for his 'loyalty' (*ibid.*). Art had the enduring support of his O'Byrne cousins. The intermarrying of his children with the O'Byrnes was pronounced (O'Byrne 2003a, 104).

It was inevitable that Richard II and Art MacMurrough, given the geographical position of Leinster in relation to Dublin, would come to blows sooner rather than later. It was ironic that the successors of King Henry II and King Diarmait MacMurrough should now confront each other 'in the woods and glens of Leinster' (Frame 1995, 156).

JANICO DARTASSO

Janico Dartasso (Dartas), according to the *DIB*, was a native of Navarre in the western Pyrenees. The town of Artaxo, to the south-east of Pamplona, has been identified as his probable place of birth (*DIB*, III, 61; Walker 1999, 33). Writers have for long focused on the fact that he was termed *Janico de Arthois Gaiscoyn* (Curtis 1924–7, 297).

Gascony lay to the immediate north of the Pyrenees in south-west France. Walker (1999, 33, 50) accepts the theory that Dartasso was a Basque. Curtis (1933, 183) had raised the possibility that Dartasso was a Fleming or 'some such native' of the Low Countries.

Curtis (1933, 182) described Dartasso as 'a gallant personage who rides across the stage in all the valour, gaiety and colour of late medieval Europe'. A contemporary, the French chronicler Jean Creton, noted his reputation as a good fighter ('*Jenico, qui tenoit pour bon routier*') (Webb 1823, 322). He first set foot in Ireland in 1394 as part of the expeditionary force led by King Richard II. This was not his first military excursion by any means. From 1367 onwards he served a succession of causes, from Charles 'the Bad' of Navarre to Sir Henry 'Hotspur' Percy's naval expedition against the Scots, the duke of Bourbon's siege of the Tunisian port of al-Mahdiya and the campaign waged in Prussia against the Lithuanians by Henry Bolingbroke, earl of Derby, and the Teutonic Knights. His patrons included the earl of Northumberland and Bishop John Waltham of Salisbury, treasurer of England. He undertook diplomatic missions to the north Italian city-states (including Venice), to Paris and to Cologne on behalf of King Richard between 1392 and 1397 (*DIB*, III, 61; Walker 1999, 37–8). In October 1393 Dartasso was granted 40 marks for life, serving as one of the 'esquires of the [king's] chamber'. The payment had increased to 100 marks by November 1395. He had by then been retained 'to stay for life with the King' (*Cal. pat. rolls, Richard II (1391–6)*, 320, 671).

In the campaign of 1394 Dartasso held an independent command (Curtis 1933, 186; *DIB*, III, 61). After an intensive assault on the Irish of Leinster, culminating in the torching of the royal abode of Art MacMurrough, the latter, along with his captains Gerald O'Byrne, Felim O'Toole and Donal O'Nolan, submitted in person to King Richard (Curtis 1924–7, 281).

The key to King Richard's vision of a fully 'Anglo' Leinster was the voluntary transportation of Art, his captains' and allies' fighting men and their followers to unspecified pastures new (Curtis 1936, 126; Lydon 1973, 115). Art led his delegation to meetings in Tullow on 7 January 1395 and Balygory on 16 February. With the fruition of his plan in sight, the king began to grant sizeable portions of the 'soon to be vacated' lands to the likes of Sir John de Beaumont, the duke of Gloucester and William le Scrope (Curtis 1924–7, 281–2).

Janico Dartasso was not forgotten. As a reward for 'his excellent service against the Irish of Leinster and for his constant loyalty', he was granted a clutch of manors to the south of Dublin city (Curtis 1933, 187; Lydon 1973, 117). The manors were named as *Kenlyestoun* (Kindlestown), *Suttonestoun* (Killincarrig), *Kilfernok*, *Carrykmayne*, *Whitestoun*, *Termok*, *Killaghtre* (Killoughter), *Kilmartoun* (Kilmartin), *Ballyronan* and *Kilmol*. He was also granted land formerly in the possession of John, the son of James Archbold, and Sir Hugh Lawless (Tresham 1828, 154). Kilmartin and Killoughter, two fortalices, lay to the south of Newcastle in County Wicklow. Ballyronan (to the west of Kilcoole), Kindlestown (to the west of Greystones) and Killincarrig (to the immediate south of Greystones) were also located in the shadow of O'Byrne power.

The identity and location of the other manors is unclear. There is a Whitestown to the west of the O'Toole stronghold of the Glen of Imaal. *Kilmol* might possibly be interpreted as Killmalum, a place that lies to the south-west of Blessington.

King Richard's grand design came to naught. The MacMurroughs, O'Tooles, O'Byrnes and O'Nolans were going nowhere. Janico's new fiefdom was worth next to nothing. He did see the irony in his predicament. It is extremely fortunate that the content of a letter written by Janico has survived (the only such artefact from an occupier of Carrickmines in its entire history to do so). In an oft-quoted section, he wrote (to his old patron the bishop of Salisbury):

> '[...] and please you to know, my reverend lord, that our lord the King has granted me a parcel of land in the country of the Irish rebels, which if it were in the parts of London would be worth by the year fifty thousand marks, but, by my faith, I have so much trouble holding on to it that I would not like to lead such a life for long for even a quarter of the land' (Curtis 1924–7, 296).

Curtis (*op. cit.*, 296 fn. 30) calculated that, given the overall size of the combined holdings, Dartasso was probably jesting about their potential value. He also speculated that by 'a quarter of the land' Dartasso was implying 'a quarter of the Earth!' (*ibid.*, fn. 31).

Dartasso was not impressed by the Irish he had encountered: 'the people are so false that no man can believe them' (*ibid.*, 296). It does sound like Janico may have made some effort to secure at least part of his land bank, for he stated that 'I have so much trouble holding on to it'. Given its location and proven defensive qualities, it is not impossible that he based himself at Carrickmines. If he did, however, he was not there for long. King Richard returned to England on 1 May 1395 and Dartasso travelled with him (*DIB*, III, 62).

As far as the king was concerned, all was now orderly in his lordship in Ireland. Indeed, he had received the formal submissions of most of the principal Gaelic rulers, representing, for example, the O'Neills, the O'Briens, the MacCarthys and the MacMurroughs (Curtis 1933, 188). Three years later the illusion was shattered. Roger Mortimer, the fourth earl of March, was the serving governor of Ireland. He was Richard's cousin and, in the absence of any children, his designated heir. After his appointment as governor, he resolved to enforce compliance on the Leinster leadership regarding their previous commitments and agreements (*ibid.*, 189). On 20 July 1398, at the petty battle of Kellistown in County Carlow, he was slain whilst engaged in combat with the O'Byrnes and the O'Tooles (Nicholls 1998a, 20; O'Donovan 1854, IV, 761). An outraged Richard dispatched his nephew Thomas Holland, duke of Surrey. Janico Dartasso accompanied him and again held his own command. His detachment was credited with the slaying of 200 foes in County Kildare (Webb 1823, 93; Curtis 1924–7, 297). On 1 June 1399 Richard himself landed in Waterford with vengeance on his mind. Art MacMurrough, however, had learnt his lessons well, and during Richard's second expedition he successfully ducked and dodged through the wild Wicklow and Wexford terrain of mountains, deep woods, bogs and hidden valleys. By rigidly employing this strategy he successfully managed to avoid full contact with the royal forces throughout the campaign (Frame 1995, 172). It was time for the king to rethink his own strategic approach, but he did not get the opportunity.

John of Gaunt, duke of Lancaster, the fourth son of Edward III, had died in February. His son Henry Bolingbroke, after a quarrel with Thomas Mowbray, the first duke of Norfolk, had been banished from the kingdom in 1398 by his cousin, King Richard. Upon the death of John of Gaunt, Richard had seized the family's vast estates and assets, an opportunistic act that could only be regarded as a dangerous precedent by the leading nobility of England. Richard's subsequent departure to Ireland was premature, if not ill judged.

Henry Bolingbroke, duke of Hereford, left France and landed in Yorkshire at the end of June. The earl of Northumberland was the first of many to rally to his standard. Curtis (1933, 190) observed that had Richard sailed immediately from Dublin he would have been in a good position to oppose Henry. Instead he decided to march to Waterford, thus losing eighteen crucial days (Webb 1823, 75).

By the time that Richard, disguised as a Franciscan, arrived at Conway Castle in north Wales in early August his cause was lost (Walker 1999, 31; Webb 1823, 77 fn. w). His return to England had been chaotic. His fleet had scattered to ports as far apart as Bristol and Plymouth and Dartmouth on the south Devonshire coast. Some of the ports of arrival had already been taken by Henry's forces. Furthermore, a significant quantity of arms, munitions and equipment still lay stranded in Dublin (McGettigan 2016, 185). To the surprise of all, not least of Jean Creton, the French chronicler, the king slipped away from Milford (Haven) with a mere handful of attendants (Webb 1823, 76–7). He surrendered to Henry on 19 August at Flint. His abdication of the throne was read to parliament and on 30 September the reign of King Henry IV began. It is possible that Richard's detention at Pontefract Castle in Yorkshire might have been prolonged but a failed conspiracy to restore him sealed his fate. By 14 February 1400 he had died in mysterious circumstances.

Janico Dartasso, the holder of Carrickmines, had remained by Richard's side when most of his other attendants and followers had faded away. Creton recorded that he had absolutely refused to remove Richard's White Hart emblem from his person upon his capture (Webb 1823, 93, 152). He was imprisoned in Chester Castle with little apparent prospect of a guaranteed release or future.

THE WALSHES OF CARRICKMINES

Previous writers have confirmed the existence of a Welsh presence in the Dublin area prior to the Angevin intervention in 1169. Cynan, the son of Iago, the Welsh dynast, was married to Ragnhildr, the daughter of Amlaib (Olaf) of Dublin, and apparently spent many years in exile there (Duffy 1995, 381, 386). According to the twelfth-century text *Historia Gruffud vab Kenan*, Cynan's son Gruffudd would appear to have been born in

Dublin and reared in Swords, to the north of the town (*ibid.*, 394). The invasion force that he raised to retake the kingdom of Gwynedd (north Wales) *c.* 1081 was comprised of men of Ostman, Irish and Welsh blood (*ibid.*, 395). Gruffudd ruled until his death in 1137. His son, Owain Gwynedd, had an Irish wife and at least four of their sons seem to be associated with estates in north County Dublin and in Dublin town. He ruled until his death in 1170 (Duffy 2015, 104). Many Welsh refugees would inevitably have taken up permanent residence. O'Byrne (2003b, 231) noted that the origins of the Fitzrery family of Cloghran in north County Dublin were rooted in the kingdom of Gwynedd. The Walshes in the northern part of the county were to be found at Courtlough and Grallagh, lying to the south and south-west of Balbriggan. Walshestown (*Baile na mBretnach*) lies to the west of Courtlough, separated by just one small townland.

The obvious place-name evidence in the original name of Kilgobbin, i.e. *Tech na mBretnach*, 'the house of the Welshmen' (McNeill 1950, 3 fn. 2), and of Brenanstown (a.k.a. *Ballybrenan*), *Baile na mBretnach*, 'the town of the Welshmen', indicates their presence in south County Dublin. The Howels, a family whose patronymic surname was rooted in the forename Hywel, were clearly of Welsh descent (Curtis 1910, 119). Maginn (2004, 120) has described them as a 'relatively small lineage'. They would certainly appear to have become extinct by the latter part of the fourteenth century (*ibid.*, 127). O'Byrne (2003b, 240) has suggested that Howel heiresses 'probably' married leading members of the Walsh family, drawing attention to the subsequent use of 'Howel' and 'Maurice' as forenames by the Walshes. It should be observed, however, that in a family of Welsh origin these forenames would have been likely to appear regardless. There is certainly a notable commonality in the lands held by the Howels and later by the Walshes. In 1331–2 Maurice Howel held lands from the king at Bray, and in Balally, Edmondstown and Ballinteer (Mills 1891, 143–4). He also held lands in Carrickmines and Brenanstown from Holy Trinity (*ibid.*, 144).

It is possible that the Walshes of Carrickmines emerged from the indigenous pre-Angevin settler population of south County Dublin, but this is not certain.

The family had achieved status by the mid-fourteenth century, and not always in a good light. In March 1326, according to a sixteenth-century gloss, the Walshes, in league with the Harolds, the Archbolds, the O'Byrnes and the O'Tooles, laid waste the lands to the south of the walls of Dublin city (McNeill 1950, 172, fn. 16; Maginn 2004, 127). The tenants of these lands were unable to work them and were afraid to remain on their holdings in the marches after dark (McNeill 1950, 170). In 1350 Walter Harold was chosen as the head of the Harold family at a convention overseen by the justiciar, Sir Thomas de Rokeby. Representatives of the leading lineages of south County Dublin, including the Lawlesses, the Howels, the Archbolds and the Walshes, underwrote the agreement. Elias, son of Robert, was the nominated Walsh. Curtis (1910, 119) observed that the Walshes were 'considerable landowners in the country west of Dalkey'. He identified an Elias le Waleys as being amongst their number in the late thirteenth century. Le Waleys, however, was associated with such properties as *Vill Walensis* and *Balymolyn* (Sweetman 1875–81, II, 232). There are no Walshestowns in south County Dublin, and *Balymolyn* was part of the 'tenement' of Newcastle Lyons in south-west County Dublin (*DKR 41* (1909), 25). The same convention also witnessed the election of the 'captains' of the Archbold and O'Byrne lineages, Matthew and John respectively. The supervised election of heads of lineages was a first for a justiciar of Ireland. De Rokeby was in effect developing existing arrangements to the advantage of the government (Maginn 2004, 122–5).

There are two other possibilities regarding the genesis of the Walshes of Carrickmines that should also be considered. In County Kilkenny the Walshes were settled within the orbit of the Butlers. As late as the early seventeenth century they were described as an important element in the military composition of the Butler forces of the earldom of Ormond (Brewer and Bullen 1867–73, IV, 448). Given the proven Butler presence in the south County Dublin area (see above), it is not unlikely that they brought members of the Walsh family with them from Ormond. Indeed, Hussey Walsh (1900–1, 217) has advanced the suggestion that there was a direct close familial connection between the Walshes of Carrickmines and Kilkenny.

Another possibility that should be explored is that the founding members of the Carrickmines lineage at the beginning of the fifteenth century were more recent arrivals. The presence of Welshmen in State service in Ireland is attested by the payment of £59 25s. 4d. in 'stipends' covering their costs incurred from 1278 to April 1285 (Sweetman 1875–81, III, 22). In 1289 King Edward I ordered the treasurer of Ireland to dispatch a trusted aide to Wales in order to recruit an unspecified number of Welshmen to serve in Ireland. Their passage and expenses were to be paid for with the authority of the justiciar (*ibid.*, 245). Again, in 1296 money was required to cover the payment of 'Welshmen abiding in divers places of defence in Ireland'. These men were engaged in the 'fortification of castles and lands' (Sweetman 1875–81, IV, 164). The ongoing influx from Wales is exemplified in an entry in the Annals of Ross. In 1337 the justiciar, John Darcy, arrived in Ireland accompanied by 200 Welshmen (*cum 200 Walensibus*) (Butler 1849, 23). These men were clearly being brought in by the justiciar to serve the Dublin administration. Unfortunately, in what capacity they were to serve was not specified.

There is no available evidence to suggest that the Walshes were significant landholders in south County Dublin before the early fifteenth century (Maginn 2004, 127). They do sporadically appear as witnesses to documents and as inquisitors. A Thomas le Waleys served at inquisitions held in Dublin in February 1326 and November 1338 (McEnery and Refaussé 2001, 75, 77). On 12 December 1336 William Walsh, along with two bailiffs and some other men, witnessed a grant of land in High Street to Holy Trinity Priory (*ibid.*, 76–7). Roger Walsh witnessed a land grant in *Menesrath* (Rathmines) in April 1399 (McNeill 1950, 234). On 27 February 1421 Thomas Walsh, a lawyer, was a witness to a deed issued by the archbishop of Dublin regarding Holy Trinity (McEnery and Refaussé 2001, 87).

The first documented Walsh occupant of land in the area appeared in May 1372. Sir Thomas Walsh, a chaplain of Tully church (Ball 1902–17, I, 105), was leased 'the town of *Balybrenan*' by the Priory of the Holy Trinity. The lease was for twenty years, the rent four marks per annum. He was bound to 'do suit of court' at Clonkeen twice yearly. He was also obliged to construct and maintain a stone house within four years (McEnery and Refaussé 2001, 168). This townland, represented by modern Brenanstown, lies to the immediate north of Carrickmines. There are no indications as to Sir Thomas's family connections or place of origin. A chaplain of Tully church could have come from anywhere.

HENRY WALSH OF CARRICKMINES

Henry IV had taken the crown by force. His grip on power was by no means iron-tight. Revenue could not be raised at will, as the nobility might at best refuse to comply or at worst rebel. In fact, the new monarch had to crush a rebellion led by the earls of Kent, Huntington and Salisbury within months of taking the throne.

Wales rebelled shortly afterwards (Lydon 1973, 141). Although the revolt was eventually quelled, its leader, Prince Owain Glyndwr, continued to elude capture and carried on the fight for several years. At one stage he unsuccessfully tried to lure Gaelic Ireland and Scotland into the fray (*ibid.*). King Henry's eldest son, Henry, only sixteen years of age, fought alongside his father.

The king's second son, Thomas of Lancaster, despite being only fourteen years of age, was appointed lord lieutenant of Ireland. In April 1401 he departed for Dublin. Clearly it was inevitable that he would need the advice and protection of dependable companions. His father's choices were Sir Stephen Scrope, Sir Edward Perrers and Janico Dartasso (Curtis 1933, 192).

Dartasso had fared much better than many others in the wake of the fall of Richard and the rise of Henry. Friends with influence had quickly come to his rescue on hearing of his imprisonment in Chester Castle. Within days Sir Thomas Walker and Sir John Stanley went guarantor for him. He was released on the condition that he remained within the walls of the city (Walker 1999, 41). The Percys of Northumberland also facilitated his rehabilitation. Whether because of their shared service with the Teutonic Knights or simply out of appreciation for an intensely loyal soldier, it was not long before King Henry recruited Janico for the royal household (*ibid.*).

Curtis (1924–7, 297) indicated that there was no evidence to suggest that Dartasso retained an interest in any of the estates granted to him by King Richard, including Carrickmines. A grant, however, was made on 19 November 1399, i.e. after his engagement by Henry IV, authorising him to 'occupy' all his 'lands, rents and possessions' in Ireland with 'attorneys, bailiffs and servants'. They in turn would be empowered to 'levy the issues thereof' and forward the income to him in England for the next eight years (*Cal. pat. rolls, Henry IV (1399–1401)*, 131). There is no further mention of these assets. Instead, there is a stream of new sources of income flowing into the coffers of Janico Dartasso: 100 marks a year from 'the issues' of the town of Drogheda 'because the King has retained him for life' (*ibid.*, 74), and 40*l.* a year for life from 'the issues' of the city of Dublin in 'recompense' for the loss of the barony of Norragh (*ibid.*, 154). The following year (1400) he was granted custody of the wealthy lordship of Trim during the minority of the Mortimer heir (Walker 1999, 41). A prison break from Trim Castle in May 1400 resulted in the escape of approximately 30 inmates, including both offenders and hostages. Amongst the escapees were O'Hanlons, McCartans, a Peter Hacket and, interestingly, an Adam Walsh. This event occurred during Dartasso's stewardship, and forfeits due to the king were accordingly awarded to him (*Cal. pat. rolls, Henry IV (1399–1401)*, 289). In 1401 Janico was awarded the constableship of Dublin Castle and was also appointed as deputy, with responsibility for Ireland, to Thomas Rempston, the admiral of the southern fleet (*ibid.*, 448, 446). In 1399 he had married Joan Taafe, a wealthy widow of the colony (Curtis 1933, 194; Walker 1999, 40). Between the income from her estates in Meath and Ulster and his own recent acquisitions, Janico Dartasso was apparently now a man no longer concerned with the fraught lifestyle and insecurities of a marcher lord.

On 20 December in the seventh year of the reign of King Henry IV, i.e. 1405, John and David Walsh transferred their properties at *Carrickemayne*, *Ballyroe* and *Annodan* in the county of Dublin to Henry, the son of Adam Walsh. Henry was to hold the properties for life. The 'remainder' was to go to William Walsh 'and his heirs male'; the 'remainder' to Maurice Walsh 'and his heirs male'; 'with divers other remainders' (Morrin 1861–2, I, 95). William was the name of Henry's son and heir; Maurice may have been another son. Henry was already settled at *Cairykmayn* by 11 March 1400. In that month the 'receivers or farmers' of the manor of Thorncastle in County Dublin were ordered to pay him 100s. per year 'for good service' to the king (Stamp 1927, 69). A patent roll bearing the same date also documented the award. In addition, it recorded the granting by the Crown of the 'lands and tenements' in *Balyhauley*, *Balyhamond*, *Balytire* and *Balymargy* in the county of Dublin, to the value of 10*l.* yearly, to 'Henry Adamesone of *Cairykmayn*' (*Cal. pat. rolls, Henry IV (1399–1401)*, 237). As John and David Walsh were transferring their property in Carrickmines to Henry Walsh of Carrickmines, the logical explanation is that there was more than one property trading under the name in the 'townland'. The 1405 land transaction by John and David can be explained as an expansion and consolidation of the part already held by Henry Walsh.

The relationships between John, David and Henry were not explained. As we know, Henry's father was called Adam. Were John and David his uncles? Or did all three simply share a surname or place of origin? Henry may have been a government employee. He was certainly in favour, given his appearance as an inquisitor in August 1382. The inquisition in question was held in Dublin and was chaired by William Fitzwilliam, the escheator of Ireland. Also serving was a John Walsh of *Thorgeteston* and a William Hacket (McEnery and Refaussé 2001, 84). An equally important question is how John and David Walsh and Henry Walsh came into possession of Carrickmines and ancillary properties. Could any or all of them have been amongst the 'attorneys' and 'bailiffs' appointed by Janico Dartasso? Unfortunately, we do not know. It has been suggested by O'Byrne (2003b, 241) that they acquired the land from Janico Dartasso. It is equally feasible that the Crown granted them the properties. Alternatively, could they have been government-installed employees? As already discussed, Carrickmines had on occasion found itself in the care of officials. Flanagan (2005, 86, 109 fn. 9) observed that, in breach of the more customary practice, the lay witnesses, including Lissebon (father of Aunger, a holder of Carrickmines), preceded the clerical witnesses in a specific charter. As Lissebon was not a significant landowner, his prestige can only have come from his occupation, more than likely as an employee of the State. Indeed, his son Aunger's tenure at Carrickmines was most likely facilitated by Lissebon's political connections.

It was not long before Henry Walsh experienced the periodically occurring threat of the O'Byrnes. The decision by Domhnall, the head of the O'Byrnes (Nicholls 1998a, 20), to settle mercenaries in the vicinity of Bray forced the administration in Dublin to take action. The lord mayor, John Drake, led the forces of the city and the southern marches against the mercenaries. Amongst their ranks was Henry Walsh, 'Captain of the Walsh men' (Ball 1901, 197). The Battle of the Bloody Bank was fought on 11 July (Lydon 1994, 179) or in August 1402 (O'Byrne 2003b, 241; D'Alton 1838, 909). The site of the battle was in Little Bray (Simpson 2003, 293). The Annals of Connacht recorded the victory of 'the Galls of Dublin' and the deaths of 'many of the hired Munster troops', including their leader Tadc O'Mechair (Freeman 1944, 381). The very precise figure of 'foure hundred ninety three, being all men of warre', appeared in another account (Ware 1809, (b), 18; Lydon 1994, 179). Domhnall O'Byrne quickly made his peace on 8 November with Sir Stephen Scrope, deputy to the new lord lieutenant (Nicholls 1998a, 20). He vowed to 'conduct himself' and to 'make amends for all injuries and damages which have been done by him'. He also handed back possession of Newcastle McKynegan (Brewer and Bullen 1867–73, V, 480–1). The Annals of Connacht recorded that the castle was 'demolished' in 1405 by the O'Byrnes (Freeman 1944, 393).

There is no recorded date for the death of Henry Walsh. In late October 1407 ('before the Feast of St Martin') we find his son and heir William taking possession of his father's manors of *Ballyhawly*, *Ballyhammond* and *Ballytir* (Hunter 1834, 45). Earlier that year, an inquisition held on 6 March established that William was then residing in *Symondeston*, where he held tenure for life (*ad terminum vite sue*). The holding was to revert to St Mary's Abbey upon his demise (Gilbert 1884, I, 280). Ball (1902–17, I, 99) described *Symondstown* as 'part' of the lands of Carrickmines. In the October document William was described as *Willelmus Walsh de Carrykmayn*. Does this reassignment suggest that Henry had died in the interim? One condition imposed on William was that he should build a fortalice within three years on the lands of *Ballyhawly*. A patent roll dated 27 September 1430 recorded that William had died within the designated period of three years without work on the fortalice being completed (Tresham 1828, 249). This document establishes that William died between 1407 and 1410. Ball (1901, 197) had placed William's death in 1420. The 1430 patent also revealed that William had a brother named Howell.

After the hands-on policies and strategies of Richard II, his successors to the throne kept their distance. The approach of his immediate successor, Henry IV, for example, was weak and ineffectual in relation to Ireland—not that he had many options.

Thomas of Lancaster may have been the son of the king but financial support was simply not forthcoming. In 1402, for example, the chancellor of Ireland and the archbishop of Dublin wrote to London to complain that there was no money left with which to govern the lordship. Similarly, the prince, assisted by Dartasso, wrote a letter pleading for funding (Curtis 1933, 192). It is evident that Janico Dartasso would not have had the opportunity, even if he had the inclination, to personally defend or invest in his mostly untenable grants from Richard II. Prince Thomas returned to England and was replaced with deputies—Stephen Lescop, followed by Gerald, the fifth earl of Kildare.

Henry V was crowned in Westminster Abbey on 9 April 1413 in succession to his father, whose declining health had resulted in an inglorious culmination to his reign. The new king had been a renowned warrior since his youth. In fact, as the mumblings of discontent grew during his father's decline there was talk of him seizing the throne. Once installed as king, he turned his attention towards France, launching an invasion on 11 August 1415. Sailing with the king was Janico Dartasso (Walker 1999, 45). The Battle of Agincourt, fought on 25 October, resulted in a crushing French defeat. Prior to the battle Henry had taken the town of Harfleur. Dartasso was certainly serving with the garrison there in 1416 (*ibid.*) and thus may not have fought at Agincourt.

Despite the English victories the war dragged on. Normandy was taken in 1419. Prince Thomas was killed at the Battle of Baugé in 1421, and Henry himself died from a fatal illness in August 1422 at the age of 34. He had never shown any particular interest in his lordship of Ireland.

THE SECOND HENRY WALSH

In 1420 Henry Walsh, William's son, was still a minor. In that year parts of his pending inheritance, at *Ballycarryk* and *Adovan*, were placed in the hands of a cleric (*clericus*) by the name of Richard Northorp. He was not obliged to render any account of his tenure during Henry's minority (Hunter 1834, 67; Ball 1902–17, I, 99).

John Talbot, later first earl of Shrewsbury, had been appointed lieutenant of Ireland in 1414. After five years in office he departed to fight in France. He briefly returned to serve in Ireland in 1425 and again in 1446–7. He was to fall in battle in France in 1453.

Talbot concluded agreements in 1425 with An Calbhach O'Connor, king of Offaly, and Donnchadh O'Byrne, 'Chief of his Nation of the O'Byrnes' (Gilbert 1865, 320–1). O'Connor was obliged to release prisoners, including Henry Mac Adam, seneschal of the 'Viceroy's manor of *Loghsueedy*, in West-Meath' (i.e. the medieval manor of Ballymore Lough Sewdy); to desist from collecting 'Black Rent'; to make many promises of good behaviour; etc. O'Byrne vowed to protect the tenants of Talbot's holdings in Wexford. He also agreed to allow the archbishop of Dublin (Talbot's brother) to collect his legally due rents from his territories (*ibid.*).

Talbot's younger brother, Richard, was installed as archbishop of Dublin in 1417. In 1423 he began his long tenure as chancellor of Ireland. He also served as his brother's deputy and as justiciar. His epic feuds with John Swayne, the archbishop of Armagh, and James Butler, the fourth earl of Ormond, had a seriously debilitating effect on the position of the English colony in Ireland. Lydon (1973, 137) has described the vendetta between Talbot and Butler as 'the greatest feud, which dominated Ireland for thirty years'. When James Butler, commonly called 'the White Earl', succeeded to his lands and inheritance in 1412, he would have had every expectation, despite his youthful age, of taking the premier role in the administration of the colony. The appointment of Talbot, therefore, could only be regarded as an affront.

The overall condition of the colony was seriously debased. Archbishop Swayne of Armagh wrote an official report on the state of the country in 1427, painting a dismal picture of shrinking territory, the flight of droves of 'husband people', internal strife and bad government (*ibid.*, 139). By 1430 the counties of Dublin, Meath, Kildare and Louth were being described as 'for the most part destroyed and wasted by the Irish enemies (and English) rebels' (Berry 1910, 33). The necessary remedies from Westminster were not, however, forthcoming.

Henry VI had been a mere nine months old when his father died in 1422. Thanks to his father's campaigns and political machinations, he not only succeeded to the throne of England but was also crowned king of France. The southern French provinces, however, declared for the son of their late king. The power in England and France respectively was vested largely in the hands of Humphrey, duke of Gloucester, and (until his death in 1435) John, duke of Bedford, the king's uncles. Henry, Cardinal Beaufort, his great-uncle, contested their power. Owing to his lineage the young Richard, duke of York, had a legitimate claim to the throne. There certainly was a lot at stake, as King Henry, a pious and studious man, had little interest in governing his kingdoms or lordships. Meanwhile, the Hundred Years' War dragged on. It would end in defeat in 1453, causing the king to suffer a catatonic breakdown or, possibly, a bout of mental illness. This necessitated the appointment of a lord protector to administer the realm.

By 1441 neither the lords nor the commons of the Irish parliament were satisfied with the performance as lord deputy of James Butler, fourth earl of Ormond ('the White Earl'). In a petition to King Henry VI they described him as 'aged, unwiledie, and unlustie' and as totally failing to curtail the activities of the enemies of the throne (Berry 1910, 50).

Henry Walsh of *Carrikmayne* was awarded ten marks by the exchequer in 1442 'for his great expense (incurred) on the frontier of the March of Dublin resisting the King's enemies' (Tresham 1828, 263; Connolly 1998, II, 578). The jury of an inquisition held in the time of Abbot White (i.e. 1438–63) to determine the extent of the lands of St Mary's Abbey included 'Harry Walshe Captayne of the Walsche men'. The jury on which he served was tasked with 'tryyng the meyres of *Kilternane*' (Nolan 1939, 38).

The common apparel worn by both the Gaelic Irish and the marchers was also of concern to the authorities, who complained that it caused confusion as to the identity of those travelling on the 'high roads'. The resulting infiltration had led to widespread robbery, pillage, the murder of 'husbandmen in the nights' and the billeting of raiders on the 'common people'. As a reaction, in 1447 it was ruled that all those who were to be accounted Englishmen were henceforth to shave regularly above the lip in order to distinguish themselves from the Irish. An ordinance passed by the Dublin authorities in 1457–8, referring to the 'bardys above the mouth' of the Irishmen, barred them—and specifically those with horses—from the city (Gilbert 1889–1944, I, 298).

Richard Plantagenet, duke of York, was dispatched to Ireland as lieutenant in 1447. There is good reason to believe that he was given the role to get him out of England. Edward Beaufort, second duke of Somerset, and William de la Pole, earl of Suffolk, were anxious to see the back of him. In the wake of the suspicious death of his patron, Humphrey, duke of Gloucester, Richard became the inevitable cynosure for the disillusioned and discontented (Curtis 1923, 308). Lydon (1973, 145) has observed that there was 'a real need in Ireland for someone like York'. Richard arrived in Howth in July 1449 accompanied by his wife, the renowned beauty Cicely Neville (Cosgrove 2011, 138–9). He was always going to take an interest in Ireland, given that he was heir to the property empire of the Mortimers. A great-grandson of King Edward III, he was born in 1411, the son of Richard, earl of Cambridge, and Anne, the daughter of Roger Mortimer, the fourth earl of March. The Annals of the Four Masters record that the duke received a warm reception from both the colonists and the Irish dwelling adjacent to Meath (O'Donovan 1854, IV, 965). When Cicely gave birth to their son George (later duke of Clarence), the baby's baptismal sponsors were the earls of Ormond and Desmond (Cosgrove 2011, 140).

Richard received many submissions from the nobility of Leinster, Ulster and the midlands. Lydon (1973, 146) has drawn attention to the fact that the submissions were made to York personally as opposed to the king. Clearly the duke was building support for future endeavours. The earl of Ormond, for one, entered into sworn allegiance.

With the death of Edmund in 1446 the leadership of the O'Byrnes had passed to his second cousin, Dúnlang ('Dowling'). Within three years he was dead and was succeeded by Edmund's nephew, Bran ('Bernard') (Nicholls 1998a, 22). It was Bran who was forced to submit to York in late 1449 in the wake of the wasting of the O'Byrne territories. He swore to become the 'Kyngs trewe servant' and would, as would his children, 'weer English array and lern English' (Curtis 1932, 166; Lydon 1994, 179–80).

As Cosgrove (2011, 143–4) succinctly put it, the reconquest of Ireland would have required a level of expenditure 'far beyond what any English king was prepared to spend'. The only viable alternative, therefore, allowing for the inherent dangers, was to place the government of the island in the hands of powerful colonist magnates. These men would have the advantage of already being well placed, connected and largely self-resourced.

In October 1427 Thomas Fitzgerald had become the seventh earl of Kildare on the death of his father, John. The duke of York first appointed Thomas as lord deputy in 1454 and he was to administer the lordship until 1459 (Gilbert 1865, 367). Several parliaments were held under his auspices in Dublin and Naas. In 1456 one of these parliaments (O'Byrne 2002, 15) issued an edict demanding that a named list of people surrender to the constable of Dublin Castle and remain there for eight days or face the confiscation of their goods. These men were indicted on various charges of extortion, oppression, robbery, felony and trespass. Amongst their ranks were Henry Walsh of *Carrikmayn* and his son William. Also listed were a Maurice Walsh and a Thomas Maurice Adamson (Berry 1910, 441–5). Henry subsequently remained at large but apparently redeemed himself. This redemption, however, was not without blemish, as there was a further public disturbance. In 1458 a gentleman called John Ley complained to parliament that 'on the 18th day of October last', whilst in the company of the mayor of Dublin and the city's bailiffs, he was set upon by William Walsh, the son of Henry Walsh, 'with force and arms'. The assault occurred on 'the King's highway' leading to 'the place of the said Henry', 'one league beyond the water of the Dodder'. It was there that William killed the horse John Ley was riding 'with the cast of a lance'. The horse was valued at five marks. In his testimony Ley observed that Henry and William Walsh had failed to surrender themselves to the constable of Dublin City; neither were they 'amenable to the laws of the King' (Berry 1910, 565–7). The Walshes were only held liable for the price of the dead horse (Maginn 2004, 128 fn. 115). The parliament, held at Naas by the earl of Kildare, repealed the enactment that had convicted Henry Walsh, his son William, Thomas Maurice Adamson and Maurice Walsh, amongst others, of various misdemeanours. This was done after consideration of the 'laudable services' performed by the said gentlemen and their cohorts. They had resisted, 'at their own expense, the malice of the Irish enemies' of the king (Berry 1910, 557–61).

The state of the countryside around Dublin in the mid-fifteenth century is made clear in representations made to Rome by Archbishop Michael Tregury, who reported that the castles, possessions and lands belonging to the archbishopric were 'utterly destroyed' for a radius of twelve miles around the city. He was accordingly granted financial assistance in December 1451 (Berry 1898, xx). The unprotected nature of the road from Bray towards Dublin (the '*Boher* of Bray') posed a threat, and the Commons finally addressed the problem in 1459. It was observed that this was the main route employed by the O'Byrnes to raid the marchlands, and an offer of £10 was made to whoever would construct a castle or fortalice, '40 of Paul's feet' (i.e. the modern length) in height and '16 feet broad', adjacent to the aforementioned road in the lands of Cork. This area lies to the north of Bray. The apparent danger carried by this road would have been of great import to the Walshes. Shanganagh lay alongside the road a little further to the north, and Carrickmines was located within striking distance of the road. The Walshes of Shanganagh later held a castle and lands in Cork.

Henry did not behave himself for long. In 1460 the Commons proclaimed that Henry Walsh of *Carrykmain* 'oppresses and destroys the liege people of the King'. Recently he had seized the cattle of the collector of the barony of Rathdown and 'still detains them unlawfully'. He was ordered to appear before the lord lieutenant to answer the charges (Berry 1910, 767–9).

In typical fashion, Henry balanced his 'bad' deeds with his 'good' services. An edict from the parliament in 1460 authorised, amongst others, Michael Tregury and Henry Walsh to summon one man from every house in the baronies of Newcastle Lyons and Rathdown. The workforce thus raised was to be used for the 'throwing up of dykes and cutting of ditches' for the protection of the marches. They were to report for duty equipped with 'a spade, a barrow or a pickaxe' on a yearly basis (Berry 1910, 757). The defences were clearly intended to prevent the endless cattle-rustling incursions from the mountains. To control 'the enemy within' the defences, a by-law had been passed in 1454 banning all Irishmen and women (by blood) from the city unless they had been resident for the past twelve years. The list of 'undesirables' included *nonnys* (nuns), *clerkys* (clerics), journeymen, *prentesys* (apprentices) and beggars (Gilbert 1889–1944, I, 280). Two of the city constables who naturally would be tasked with implementing the ordinance were Christopher Walsh and Peter Walsh (*ibid.*, 282, 299). This by-law was reminiscent of a statute passed in England in the second year of the reign of King Henry IV (i.e. 1400–1), which ordained that no Welshman, either by birth or parentage, would be allowed to purchase lands or tenements in Chester—or, indeed, in any other merchant town adjoining the marches (Luders *et al.* 1810–28, II, 124).

The duke of York became increasingly embroiled in events that would ultimately lead to the War of the Roses in England. In the wake of the king's mental collapse in 1453, Richard was appointed lord protector and administered the realm during the king's illness. The birth of an heir on 10 October 1453, however, crushed his hopes of a peaceful succession (Curtis 1932, 177). Civil war was now inevitable. It would ultimately lead to the end of the era of the House of Lancaster and the crowning of Richard Plantagenet's son Edward in 1461.

Upon the death of Richard himself at the Battle of Wakefield in December 1460, the council in Dublin elected Thomas Fitzgerald as justiciar. During the reign of King Edward IV he was reappointed to this position and in January 1464 was appointed lord chancellor of Ireland for life (Fitzgerald 1858, 38; Crooks 2017, 250).

Michael Tregury, the archbishop of Dublin, had ambitions to expand the portfolio of his assets and holdings. In 1460 he made the plea to parliament that 'from ancient time' his predecessors held 'great property upon the borders of the marches of the County of Dublin'. This 'great property' extended from Dalkey to Ballymore. His justification for the restoration of such a great estate is that it would be suitably endowed to provide the protection and maintenance currently explicitly absent from the marches. The archbishop had already appointed a Thomas Walsh as the constable of the manor and castle of Tallaght (Berry 1910, 771, 773). Tregury was seized and abducted in November 1462. In a subsequent letter to Pope Pius II he named his captors as Geoffrey Harold and his sons Thomas and Edmund, in league with Patrick O'Byrne and many others. The pope ordered their public excommunication. Archbishop Alen's gloss identified Geoffrey Harold as the 'Captain of his perverse nation'. Two other 'perverse' nations identified were the Walshes and the *Tolys* (i.e. the

O'Tooles) (McNeill 1950, 242 fn. 1). In August 1463 a band of men 'in warlike manner' descended on *Ballawly* (Ballaly), Dundrum, Mulchanstown and *Balloure* (Leopardstown). There they 'feloniously killed' eight men and pillaged the named 'villages'. They also made off with 200 cows, 40 *afers* (affers, i.e. plough horses) and 100 sheep. The leader of the raiding party was William Harold (Berry 1914, 67). The same year Richard Harold, 'a common notorious robber', described as the illegitimate son of Robert Harold, raided the holding of Christopher Shirborne, a Dublin merchant, at Newtown near Rathcoole. His raiding party consisted of 'Irish enemies' and 'English rebels' (*ibid.*, 215). The Harolds were increasingly perceived as *personae non gratae*. An ordinance passed in 1461 had prohibited any dialogue between the citizens of Dublin and the Harolds, 'duryng thar being under wode' (i.e. whilst they lived in the woods, that is to say while they remained outside the law). That same year witnessed the prohibition of the sale of corn to the *Irys men* (Gilbert 1889–1944, I, 309).

An unnamed leader of the O'Byrnes was slain in 1463 whilst engaged in action against the colonists, specifically the Walshes of south County Dublin (Freeman 1944, 513; Nicholls 1998a, 22). The colonists, however, were defeated in the engagement, and some of the sons of Henry Walsh were taken prisoner (O'Byrne 2002, 15; 2003b, 245).

The Irish captured the castle at *Bree* (Bray). The lord deputy, Thomas, seventh earl of Desmond, retook and regarrisoned it in August 1464 (Gilbert 1889–1944, I, 143).

Thomas ('the Great Earl of Desmond') had been appointed deputy to the lord lieutenant, George, duke of Clarence, lord of Richmond, on 1 April 1463 (*Cal. pat. rolls, Edward IV (1461–7)*, 270). Desmond had defeated the forces of Sir John Butler, brother of the late earl of Ormond, and over the course of seventeen days had 'burned, wasted, and destroyed' the Ormond territories. The pro-Yorkist colonists referred to his adversary as 'the great rebel, John of Ormonde' (Gilbert 1865, 380). Desmond's rewards kept on coming. In August 1462 he had been granted the office of steward of Connacht and 100 marks yearly from the liberty of Meath (*Cal. pat. rolls, Edward IV (1461–7)*, 196). This grant was followed by the constableship of the king's castle of Limerick. Both grants were for life (*ibid.*). In 1464 he was granted the manors of *Trym* (Trim), *Kildalke* (Kildalkey) and *Rathtouth* (Ratoath) in County Meath; *Rathwere* (Rathwire) and *Foure* (Fore) in County Westmeath; and *Belgard* in south County Dublin, again for life (*ibid.*, 340). His son and heir, James, was later to be granted the office of constable of Limerick Castle and 10*l.* yearly from the 'fee farm of the city of Limerick' in June 1476 (*Cal. pat. rolls, Edward IV, Henry VI (1467–77)*, 595).

Thomas's fall from favour was swift and dramatic. Over the course of ten days in February 1468 he was 'arrested, attainted and executed' (Crooks 2017, 223). As Crooks (2017, 252) summarised the events, Desmond had fallen foul of 'the topsy-turvy world of courtly intrigue, dynastic paranoia and summary blood justice that characterised the early reign of Edward IV'. The violent reaction of the Geraldines and their allies to the execution forced the king to call on the earl of Kildare to restore order throughout the lordship of Ireland. Thus the breaking of Desmond was, ironically, to be the making of his fellow Geraldines in the House of Kildare.

Parliament granted Henry Walsh of *Carykmayne* a pardon in 1465. Also pardoned were his brother Esmond (Edmund of Shanganagh?), his son John and his kinsman Thomas Walsh of Kilgobbin. Accused of 'divers offensives, trespasses, and injuries', they had thrown themselves on the mercy of the lord deputy (Desmond) and were duly forgiven (Berry 1914, 399–401). Maginn (2004, 131) refers to this episode as an indication of the 'indispensable' role of the Walshes in the defence of the march as far as the authorities were concerned.

The commons in the parliament of 1467 listed the many 'extortions, oppressions, larcenies' and 'robberies' inflicted on the 'faithful liege people' by many named individuals. Amongst the perpetrators were Henry Walsh, his sons William, John and Tibbot (Theobald); Esmund Walsh of Shankill and his sons; and Thomas Walsh of Kilgobbin and his sons. Also named were Maurice Walsh, 'servant to the Earl of Kildare', and two 'idlemen' (i.e. men of substance), Shane Walsh and Walter Walsh. The parliament enacted the necessary legislation to force the said parties to surrender themselves to the relevant authority, the constable of Dublin Castle, by the following 4 March 1468 (Berry 1914, 443–7).

The lordship of Dalkey came within the remit of the archbishopric of Dublin. Alexander Trewoff was the selected candidate of Michael Tregury, the archbishop of Dublin, for the post of water bailiff in Dalkey. The archbishop complained to parliament in 1467–8 that Trewoff, his cousin, had neglected to take up his post and now found himself dispossessed by 'one Henry Walsh'. He objected to the fact that Henry not only applied 'Irish rule' (i.e. law) but had also adopted Irish 'habit' (i.e. dress). More importantly, the archbishop was perturbed that Henry's administration of the office was ruining its business: 'merchants and mariners' were now reportedly afraid to use Dalkey. He further accused Henry of having pocketed all the income from the port. Parliament ruled that should Henry persist in occupying the office a 100*l.* levy would be exacted from his 'lands, rents, goods and chattels' (*ibid.*, 461–3). The outcome is unknown but the Walshes did continue to be major stakeholders in Dalkey, holding leases from the archbishopric over the next two centuries (Smith 1996, 52–3).

The increasingly volatile nature of the south Dublin marches is illustrated in a number of late fifteenth-century accounts. In 1470 the tenants of the town of Saggart had entered a truce and placed themselves under the protection of the O'Tooles. Needless to say, this protection came at a financial cost. The authorities in Dublin were less than impressed. The town used to be 'guarded with lookers-out and watchers'. These men had served not only the town but also the surrounding marchland. The tenants were duly ordered to terminate the deal with the O'Tooles forthwith (Berry 1914, 665). The consequences were not long in coming. An attack by the O'Byrnes, including the O'Byrnes of Ranelagh (*Raghnallach*), and the O'Tooles in 1471–2 resulted in the burning of part of the town. Several of the inhabitants fled and others were planning to leave. The defences were deemed to be deficient and badly in need of work. To remedy this deficiency, a workforce of 'four score able labourers' was to be raised in both the barony of Balrothery and the barony of Coolock in north County Dublin. The barony of Castleknock, to the west, was to contribute another 80 men. The work would take three days and the workers were obliged to bring their own supplies. The objective was to enclose the town with substantial fosses. A simultaneous operation was to be undertaken by four score labourers from the barony of Newcastle on the town of the same name, the work lasting for a period of six days (*ibid.*, 809). By 1471 the 'Harold's country', which was located in the barony of Newcastle, 'under the mountains', had become a no-go area for residents of the colony. It was noted as being 'in rebellion', with an active fear of loss of life or capture for sale to 'the Irishmen' (*ibid.*, 667). The increasing threat to the colony about 1472–3 prompted the lord deputy to establish a standing guard, to consist of '8 score archers and 63 spears'. The force was to operate in counties Dublin, Meath, Kildare and Uriel (Louth). The captain in command was to be Gerald fitz Maurice, son and heir of the lord deputy, Thomas, the seventh earl of Kildare (Morrissey 1939, 131).

When Maurice Óg Fitzgerald and many other Geraldines were charged with treason *c.* 1473, amongst his followers was John Walsh, the son of Henry Walsh (*ibid.*, 125).

Henry Walsh clearly employed Irish legal stratagems and adopted Irish dress when it suited his purposes. O'Byrne (2004, 144; 2005, 19) maintains that Henry could speak Irish, which of course is very likely, given his interaction with the Gaelic families of the mountains. It is equally true that he at times abided by the English legal code and on other occasions blatantly defied or abused it. Ultimately, however, when it came to the crux the Walshes would inevitably have to side with the Dublin authorities. They were literally wedged between the O'Byrnes and O'Tooles, hungry for good land, on their southern flank and the forces of the Dublin city enclave to the north. Indeed, as Maginn (2004, 129) has observed, the increasing strength of the Walshes was 'the closest thing resembling an English counter-offensive' to the Irish advance. The O'Byrnes and the O'Tooles could not threaten the survival of the Dublin city enclave as long as the Walshes were entrenched in their path. Again, as Maginn (2004, 125) has put it, the adoption by the Walshes and other marcher families of aspects of Gaelic culture did not 'amount to a political defection'. Expediency was the prime motivator in their battle for survival.

PART 2

The shifting sands of the sixteenth century

THE GREAT EARL

Garret (Gerald) Mór Fitzgerald, eighth earl of Kildare, popularly known as 'the Great Earl', succeeded his father in 1478. He was not long in consolidating the power and wealth of the family. As lord deputy he could frame favourable legislation with which to exploit the considerable personal wealth at his disposal. This *modus operandi* is succinctly exemplified in the concession whereby he obtained the right to retain all Crown land recovered from rebellious factions (Ellis 2017, 327, 338), providing a strong incentive to remain militarily active in the field (Lydon 1973, 155).

Kildare's proactive endeavours could only be good for stability in the Pale. As long as the Gaelic lords were on the defensive the Pale could develop its agrarian and commercial pursuits. The perpetual infiltration of cattle-rustlers and pillagers had clearly had a detrimental effect on the economy of the colony. There is a memorandum in the official records of Dublin stating that 'no business of the city was transacted on the fourth Friday after Easter [1480], because the Mayor, Bailiffs, and commons were, at that time, with Garret, Earl of Kildare, deputy in Ireland for Edward IV, engaged in devastating O'Byrnes' country' (Gilbert 1889–1944, I, 357). In the late 1490s the earl expelled the O'Tooles from their estates in Fercullen. Ellis (2017, 336) has linked these developments with the increased agricultural productivity in the barony of Rathdown, where the subsidy assessment rose from the twelve ploughlands recorded in 1479 to the twenty ploughlands recorded by the beginning of the 1500s. The Walshes would undoubtedly have benefited from this increased prosperity. The primary form of direct personal taxation in late medieval Ireland was calculated on the quantity of cultivated arable land held, measured in 'ploughlands'. Overall the number of documented ploughlands rose between 1479 and 1500 from 793 to 831. By the 1530s tillage had risen by 20% (Ellis 2011, 17). Wheat remained the primary grain crop in the area (Murphy and Potterton 2010, 305–6). By the late fifteenth century the horse was replacing the ox for ploughing (*ibid.*, 348). This growth in agricultural productivity was a pure reflection of the increasingly stable conditions in and about the Pale (Ellis 2011, 17).

It was in this quiet twilight of his days that Henry Walsh of Carrickmines passed the reins to his son John. Judging by the primacy given to him in earlier documents, it would appear probable that William was Henry's eldest son. His subsequent disappearance from the records indicates that he had *decessit vita patris*. Hence it was the second son, John, who inherited from his father. The conveyance document, dated 16 October 1481, lists his holdings as 'all the ... lands and tenements in *Carrickmayne*, *Balliroe*, *Anodan*, *Ballyhanley*, *Balhamond*, and *Ballityre*' (Morrin 1861–2, I, 96). In a deed (no. 332), dated 27 March 1482, John Walsh, 'late of *Stalorgane*' (Stillorgan), was bound to Holy Trinity to 'keep the peace'. A threat of a fine of 100 marks hung over his head (McEnery and Refaussé 2001, 96). The threat was extended to his brothers Theobald (of '*Balybother*', Booterstown) and Nicholas (of '*Dondrom*', Dundrum) should he fail to 'abide by his agreement' (deed no. 333) (*ibid.*, 96–7). The brothers were further bound by bonds of £20 each, as were their kinsmen Charles Walsh of Shanganagh and Maurice Walsh of Kilgobbin (*ibid.*, 212). It is not certain that this John was the John of Carrickmines. It would be questionable that he should be described as 'late of Stillorgan' rather than 'of Carrickmines', unless of course that had been his abode prior to inheriting the family estate. The properties in Booterstown and Dundrum held by the brothers of 'John of Stillorgan' must have been leased from non-family individuals, as they are not listed amongst the family's core holdings. Should this John be accepted as the man who inherited Carrickmines in 1481, it would be established that he had an otherwise undocumented brother named Nicholas. A statute roll entry dating from 1467/8 identified three of the sons of Henry Walsh, i.e. William, John and Tibbot (Theobald) (Berry 1914, 444–5). Significantly, two other Walshes named in this indictment were Esmund of Shankill (this would be Esmund of Shanganagh, the father of Charles—see above) and Thomas, the son of Maurice Walsh of Kilgobbin.

Henry Walsh had one documented daughter, Katherin. She was married to Thomas Harold of *Kilmahioke* (Genealogical Office MS 48, 18). Kilmashogue lies to the south-west of Ballinteer and to the west of Stepaside. This Thomas may be the son of Geoffrey Harold of Kilmashogue. Geoffrey had at least two sons, Thomas and Edmund (Ball 1902–17, III, 58).

John Walsh, the son of Henry Walsh, along with Nicholas Harold and many others, was summoned to answer for treason committed under the leadership of Maurice Óg Fitzgerald in 1473–4 (Morrissey 1939, 125).

The supporters of two Yorkist pretenders, Lambert Simnel in 1487 and Perkin Warbeck in 1491, used Ireland as a springboard for their aspirations to seize the throne of England. Henry VII could not allow this to happen again. The experienced soldier Sir Edward Poynings was accordingly appointed lord deputy of Ireland in 1494 (MacCurtain 1972, 7; Cosgrove 2011, 145). Kildare was not in the least impressed with this show of royal authority. He was, however, expected to support the initiative. Poynings moved against the north but got no further than southern Ulster, where Kildare took exception to Butler's ravaging of the O'Hanlon lands. Poynings was having none of it and the expedition petered out in animosity (Lydon 1973, 194).

In late 1494 Poynings summoned a parliament to be held in Drogheda. It was to sit from 1 December until the following February (O'Byrne 2003a, 147) and its most enduring legacy was the passing of an act that forbade the convening of any Irish parliament without the king's permission. Henry VII was determined to prevent any future pretenders to the English throne from using the Irish parliament as a springboard, as had been done in the case of Lambert Simnel in 1487.

In February 1495 Kildare was arrested on a charge of treason and transported to London (O'Donovan 1854, IV, 1210–11). He was accused of having held secret communications with the Ulster Gaelic lords (Ellis 2017, 330), and specifically of collusion with the O'Hanlons (O'Byrne 1998a, 71; 2003a, 147). His brother, Sir James Fitzgerald, rose in rebellion and seized Carlow Castle. Despite having enjoyed the fruits of the Geraldine 'peace', the Walshes and the Harolds of south Dublin nevertheless chose to stand against them. Theobald Walsh, who had inherited Carrickmines from his brother John, and Edmund Harold organised local forces in the marches on behalf of the government (Ellis 1995, 73). Their stance resulted from the direct contacts made by Poynings. In March 1496 Theobald Walsh arrived in Dublin, along with a captain of the O'Byrnes, to pledge their allegiance to the government. Theobald was then in command of twenty horse and twenty foot (Maginn 2004, 134).

Poynings returned to England and by August 1496 Kildare had been reinstated as deputy in Ireland. He finally found his niche. The king realised that it was better to have the earl in his service than brooding and scheming in opposition. The charges of treason were quietly dropped. A marriage (his second) to Elizabeth St John, the king's cousin, sealed the new working relationship (Ellis 2017, 331, 337). His return to power curtailed the activities of the temporarily unfettered O'Byrnes and O'Tooles; this in turn brought renewed security, peace and prosperity to the Pale (Maginn 2005, 18).

Secure in his consolidated lordship and with the trust of the king, the earl embarked on a programme of military expeditions and visitations of far-flung towns and territories. In 1498 he took the castle of *Dun-Genainn* (Dungannon in modern County Tyrone) at the instigation of Toirdhealbach, son of Conn Ó Néill (Hennessy and MacCarthy 1887–1901, III, 437, 439). The following year he led 'a great hosting' into Connacht and took four castles (Athleague, Roscommon, Tulsk and Castlerea) (*ibid.*, 443).

The growing trust and favour of the king were in evidence in 1503. Having been summoned to London, Kildare returned to Ireland 'at the end of a week of Harvest' with his son Garret (Gerald), who had been held as a hostage for the preceding eight years. That same year he visited Carrickfergus and demolished the castle at Belfast (Hennessy and MacCarthy 1887–1901, III, 465; O'Donovan 1854, V, 1270–1). In 1504 a hosting led by the earl into Connacht incorporated, according to the Annals of Ulster, 'a very great part of the *Gaidhil*'. They were opposed by Ulick Burke of Clanrickard with the support of Toirdhealbach O'Brien, king of Thomond. The two armies fought a pitched battle at *Cnoc-tuagh* (Knockdoe) in modern County Galway. The ferocity and scale of the battle were remarked upon by the annalists. The Annals of Ulster noted that its like 'was not found … in the latter time' (Hennessy and MacCarthy 1887–1901, III, 469), while the Annals of Connacht observed that 'so great a battle had not been fought among Galls and Gaels in latter times' (Freeman 1944, 609).

January 1510 saw the earl leading his forces, including the Leinster Irish, into Munster. He was supported by his ally Aodh O'Donnell. They captured the castles of *Cenn-tuirc* (Kanturk) and *Pailis* (near Beaufort in modern County Kerry), and were joined by the forces of the earl of Desmond under the command of his son James. The army of Toirdhealbach O'Brien met and opposed them at the site of a bridge over the River Shannon. The only result was a slight skirmish that favoured the Thomond forces, although O'Donnell distinguished himself in a rear-guard action (Hennessy and MacCarthy 1887–1901, III, 491; O'Donovan 1854, V, 1306–7; Freeman 1944, 615).

The castle of Belfast was taken by the earl in 1512 in a campaign that also saw the demolition of a castle belonging to the Mac Eoins and the plundering of the Glens (of Antrim). In the same year he plundered Connacht, took Roscommon Castle and garrisoned it (Freeman 1944, 617, 621).

The death of King Henry VII did not impinge on Kildare's power. Indeed, he took advantage of the situation to have himself appointed justiciar of Ireland by the council. Henry VIII ascended the throne on 22 April 1509.

It was fitting that the Great Earl of Kildare should die under arms. The Annals of the Four Masters record an attack on the castle at *Leim Ui Bhanain* (Leap) (O'Donovan 1854, V, 1326–7). During a lull in the assault, the earl was watering his horse at the Greese River near Kilkea in modern County Kildare when he was shot by one of the O'Mores. A few days later, on 3 September 1513, he died from his wounds (O'Byrne 2003a, 150; Ellis 2017, 325). The Annals of Ulster described Kildare as 'the unique Foreigner who was the best and was of most power and fame and estimation'. He was credited with seizing more castles from the Gaelic lords and building more castles for the colonial community than any of his predecessors (Hennessy and MacCarthy 1887–1901, III, 507). The Annals of Connacht hailed him as the 'best and foremost of all the Galls that had ever arisen for power, renown and dignity'. Again, he was credited with conquering more territory from the Irish and 'demolishing the greatest number of their castles' (Freeman 1944, 623). He was succeeded on 26 November by his son Garret Óg, the ninth earl of Kildare.

O'Byrne (2002,15) has observed that the machinations of Garret Mór Fitzgerald marked the turning point in the struggle between the colonial community and the O'Byrnes. He further commented that the earl's campaigns reduced the O'Byrnes to 'vassalage' by 1505 and that Theobald Walsh of Carrickmines was a leading player in the lord deputy's strategies and actions. In tandem with their kinsmen from Shanganagh and Kilgobbin, the Walshes of Carrickmines had proved to be a bulwark against the Irish forces that lay to the south of the Pale.

Theobald Walsh was married to Eleanor Marward (TCD MS 1212, 38). A son, James, was subsequently recorded (*ibid.*, 45). In two inquisitions, dated 24 January and 30 January 1538, James 'Mareward', baron of *Scryn* (Skreen, Co. Meath), was recorded as having on 5 February 1525 named his aunt Eleanor 'Mareward' and her 'heirs male' as amongst his beneficiaries. Her 'heirs male' had been fathered by, firstly, John Dowdall and, secondly, 'Tybbot Walche' (alternatively 'Walsh') (Griffith 1991, 58, 59).

Eleanor was the daughter of Walter Marward, titular baron of Skreen, and his wife Margaret, the third daughter of Sir Christopher St Lawrence, second baron of Howth, and his wife Elizabeth (a.k.a. Anne and Amy) Bermingham (Lodge and Archdall 1789, III, 186; Cokayne 1910–59, VI, 606). Back in 1459 the baron of Howth had been tasked, along with the abbots of St Mary's and St Thomas's and the prior of Kilmainham, to prepare a report on 'the conduct of the Walshes of Carrickmines which was regarded in very diverse lights' (Ball 1902–17, V, 50). Lodge and Archdall (1789, III, 186 fn.) maintained, erroneously, that Eleanor Marward was married to Robert Walsh, a son of Theobald (see below).

THE PALE

The 34th act of Poynings's 1494–5 parliament legislated 'for ditches to be made about the English Pale', primarily to prevent the 'making of preys' by raiding parties coming from, for example, the Wicklow Mountains. The obligation was placed on the resident landholders to conduct the construction work.

The eastern enclave, known as 'the Four Obedient Shires', had become a geopolitical reality by the latter decades of the fifteenth century. The '*Maghery*' (plain) encompassed the English-settled parts of counties Dublin, Kildare, Meath and Louth. An act passed by a parliament sitting in 1488 in Drogheda defined the bounds of the *Maghery* as then constituted: 'From Merrion inclusive, to the water of the Dodder, by the new ditch to Saggart, Rathcoole, *Kilhell* [Kilteel], Rathmore, and Ballymore [Eustace]'. The bounds looped around Naas, travelled up to Clane, proceeded northwards to Athboy, on to Kells and north-eastwards to Ardee, Dundalk and the sea (D'Alton 1838, 34). The south-eastern part of the 'Shire of Dublin' included the towns of Dalkey, Carrickbrennan (adjacent to Monkstown), Rochestown (by Sallynoggin), Clonkeen (Kill of the Grange), Thorncastle (by Ringsend), *Ballyboteer* (Bootherstown) and Bullock (*ibid.*). The precise route that the Pale Ditch followed through south County Dublin is undetermined. To complicate matters, it was not a static boundary. Ball and Hamilton (1895, 8) conveyed an account of its trajectory identified by the Revd George T. Stokes: 'The Pale began at Dalkey, and followed a south-westerly direction towards Kilternan; then turning northwards passed Kilgobbin, where a castle still stands, and crossed the Parish of Taney to the south of that part of the lands of Balally now called Moreen, and thence in a westerly direction to Tallaght, and on to Naas in the County of Kildare'. He also noted the presence of a stretch of the ditch extending from Clongowes Wood College to Clane (*ibid.*, 237).

Goodbody (1993, 28–32) identified a section of the ditch to the immediate west of Carrickmines Castle at Ballyogan (in the townland of Jamestown). The 500m in evidence was shadowing the marshy banks of the river that flows past Kilgobbin and

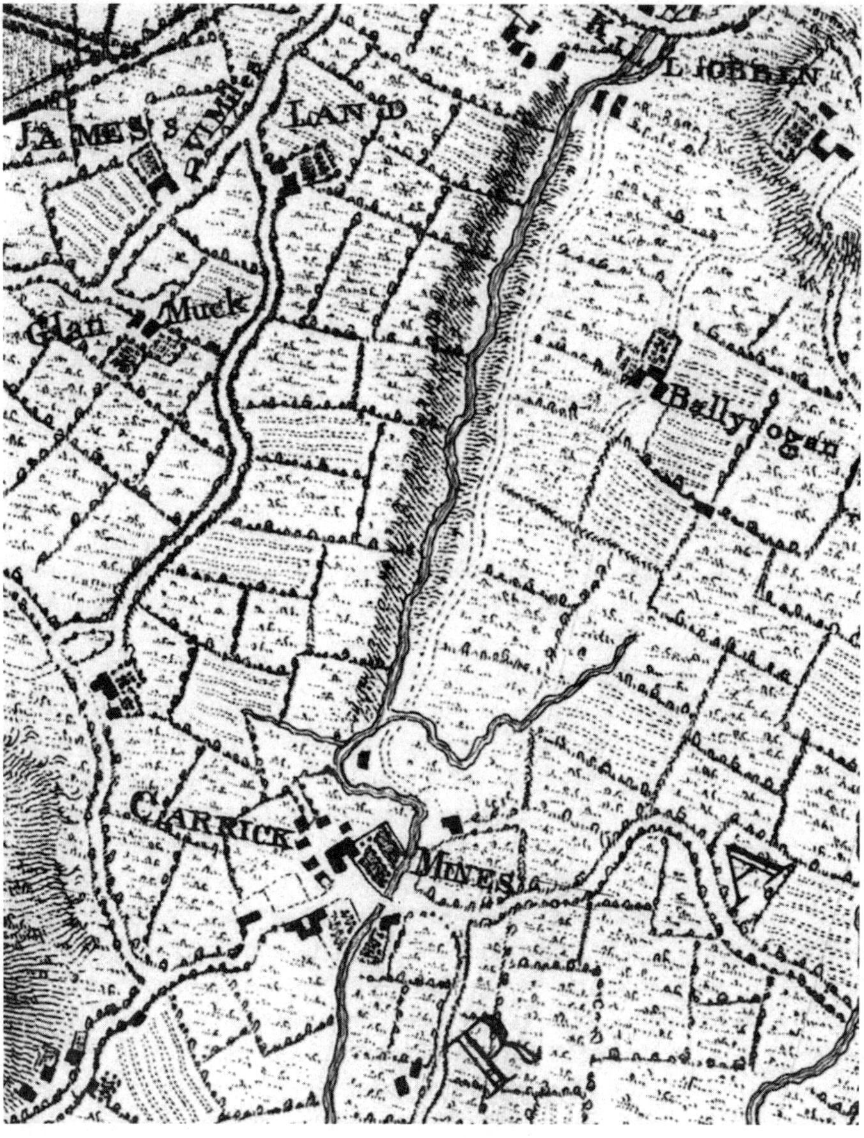

Map 4—John Rocque's map of County Dublin (1760). The Pale Ditch shadowed the course of the river between Kilgobbin Castle and Carrickmines Castle.

Carrickmines castles (Map 4). A deed dating from January 1621/2 mentions 'the ould ditch bancke extending from the lands of *Carrickmaine* along the south side of a low "bogg or meddowe" directly to the lands of *Mullghanstowne*' (Mulchanstown) (McEnery and Refaussé 2001, 306). Given the responsibility of landholders to build the sections of the ditch in their own areas, it is reasonable to suggest that the Walshes were the sponsors of this section of the Pale Ditch. The section at Balally may also have fallen within the family's remit.

The protection of the *Maghery* had steadily evolved. Beyond the core area lay the marchland, with its castles and fortified bridges. Men were employed to act as watchmen along the frontier and to light beacons to warn of approaching danger. Their wages were levied as a tax called 'smokesilver' (Berry 1914, 665; Lydon 1973, 132). The *Maghery* was well populated, and its many villages formed a lattice of mutual protection. Some defensive earthworks had already been dug (Ellis 2011, 16). The passing of an act of parliament in 1429 had stimulated the construction of castles in the shires of Dublin, Louth, Meath and Kildare. A subsidy of £10 was made available for the construction of a tower-house measuring '20 feet (in length) by 16 feet (in breadth) and 40 feet (in height)' within ten years (Berry 1910, 35). Leask (1941, 77) advanced Donore in County Meath as a possible example of a £10 castle, while observing that in the main the towers are 'more ambitious, of larger dimensions and more liveable'. McNeill (1997, 202) has stated that there are no known examples conforming to the specified dimensions.

It was no coincidence that the newly enhanced fortified area was named 'the Pale'. Poynings and his cohort had only recently been transferred to Dublin from their previous posting in the Pale of Calais (Ellis 2017, 332).

The act of 1495 specified that the Pale Ditch should consist of a bank with an external and an internal fosse. The bank should be 'six foot' in height. In recent years data garnered from archaeological excavations have generally corroborated the documentary evidence. At Jamestown, to the west of Carrickmines, the bank was 4m in width and at least 2m in height. The external fosse was 2.2–2.4m wide and 1.2m deep, while the internal fosse was 1.8–2.2m wide and 1.1m deep (O'Carroll 2003). At Balally the bank survived to a height of 1–1.2m. It was 6m wide at the base and 3–4m on top. The two flanking fosses were *c.* 2m in width, and the original depth was exposed to 0.3m (Healy 1978). The bank was traceable for 222m. It probably extended *c.* 50–60m further northwards but here had been flattened to create a late eighteenth-century carriageway. The absence of the flanking fosses in the latter stretch may be explained by the decidedly marshy terrain, which would have rendered them unnecessary (Clinton 2002).

Ellis (2017, 332) has described the Pale as the earl of Kildare's 'principal achievement'.

GARRET ÓG FITZGERALD

After a decade of ruling the sept, Cahir Mac Dunlaing was assassinated by a kinsman in 1500, and the O'Byrnes almost disappear from the records for the next twenty years. The O'Tooles were not raiding either. The controlling hand of the Fitzgeralds must be sensed here. Indeed, the ninth earl, Garret (Gearóid) Óg, was more assertive than his father in imposing suzerainty. He planted family members in key locations, for example his brother Sir James in Hollywood and the Three Castles and another brother, Richard, in Powerscourt and Fassaroe (O'Byrne 1998a, 74).

At an inquisition held on 22 April 1529 before the barons of the exchequer it was established that the heir to Theobald Walsh of *Carrykmayn* was his son James. It was also recorded, however, that James had died on 15 December 1512. The absence of a lineal heir might suggest that he had died relatively young. He was married to the daughter of 'McWadok', a native of 'O'Byrne's country' (Ken Nicholls, pers. comm.). James's 'nearest heir', his brother Robert, thereupon 'intruded' and took possession of the estate (Griffith 1991, 22). Robert Walsh's tenure cannot have been lengthy, as his successor was in possession within five years. His widow was recorded as holding Ballycorus and Ballyman in south-east County Dublin in 1540–1. It was further noted that *Balmacorus* and '*Glanmonder alias Ballyman*' were located 'in the *Walsshmanslands* in the marches of Dublin' (White 1943, 90, 118). Ballycorus borders Ticknick (part of the Carrickmines estate), while Ballyman lies between Phrompstown and Old Connaught. Thus there was an almost contiguous tract of land stretching from Kilgobbin to Shanganagh held by the Walsh family, and hence 'Walshmanslands'.

The next occupant of the *Carykmane* estate was an Edmund Walsh. At the request of William Hasard, the sub-prior of Holy Trinity Church, Edmund renounced his claim to the lands of *Ketingsland* and *Prioursland* 'near' Carrickmines (McEnery and Refaussé 2001, 112). A 'court of arbitration' declared that the said lands were the property of Holy Trinity and that Edmund owed them '4 marks in respect of all arrears of rent' but that he could hold the said lands for eleven years at an annual rent of 20s. and two hens at Christmas (*ibid.*, 228).

Keatingsland, *alias* '*Kiltekerah*', was described in two seventeenth-century deeds as being situated 'near *Carrickmaine*, or in the fields of *Carrickmaine*' (*ibid.*, 319, 345). The additional information provided is detailed but frustrating in that the places named are now unknown. If one were to equate Keatingsland approximately with the townland of Carrickmines Little, however, the descriptions would make sense. We are informed that 'The Commons of *Brenanstowne*' was called '*Dromin*' and that it lay to the east of Keatingsland. The townland of Brenanstown lies to the immediate east of Carrickmines Little. The southern boundary of Keatingsland was described as consisting of a 'fence', 'hedge' or 'ditch'. This feature was said to have extended westwards 'from the corner of *Dromin*' (where the road leading to 'the entrance' to *Carrigmaine* was located). This would align quite well with the known section of the Pale Ditch extending through Jamestown to the immediate west of Carrickmines (see above) (Map 3). The designation of 'the land of the Grange of Clonkene'—or, more specifically, land 'of the Dean's Grange' called '*Cronmore*'—as marking the northern boundary of Keatingsland again tallies. The western limits of Keatingsland were identified as *Monolough* (or *Monnelough*) to the north and *Drinanmore* (or *Drynamore*) to the south. The former was described as a common belonging to the grange of Clonkene and the latter as 'formerly a shrubby pasture' (*ibid.*). Another seventeenth-century deed recorded the existence of a '*loughe*' in '*Ballinlower*' (i.e. Leopardstown) (*ibid.*, 306). A lough to the west of Carrickmines is of potential relevance to the place-name evidence on display in *Monolough*. The only solid piece of evidence regarding the location of Priorsland is that it was situated 'on the south side of the lane from

Coinerscourt to *Carrigmaine*' (*ibid.*, 319). The document bearing this information dates from 1639. The thoroughfare, illustrated on John Rocque's map of 1760, running from Cornelscourt to Carrickmines can be advanced as a close representation of the 1639 'lane' (Map 4). Dromin (*Dromming*) had been in the possession of Holy Trinity since July 1186 (*ibid.*, 37).

Henry Walsh had a documented brother named 'Esmund' who was recorded as being active in 1465 (Berry 1914, 399). Given that over half a century had passed, the Edmund documented in 1519–20 (McEnery and Refaussé 2001, 228) would probably be another son of Theobald's, i.e. a grandson of Henry's.

Garret Óg was summoned to London by Henry VIII in January 1519 (he had previously been summoned in 1515). After 1514 Cardinal Thomas Wolsey was the king's chief adviser and his animosity towards Fitzgerald was ill disguised almost from the beginning (MacCurtain 1972, 7). It was decided that Thomas Howard, the earl of Surrey, should be assigned to Dublin. This order was executed on 10 March 1520. The subsequent offensive that he launched against Leinster brought home to the Gaelic chieftaincies the reality that there was a greater power than the Geraldines looming on the horizon (Maginn 2005, 28). Surrey enjoyed the active support of Piers Butler and Turlough O'Toole, the head of his sept. Nevertheless, he was under-resourced and the objective of strengthening royal authority in Ireland was unsustainable (Cosgrove 2011, 147). The O'Byrnes renewed raids on the Dublin marches in the autumn of 1520, possibly at the prompting of the earl of Kildare (Maginn 2005, 34–5). In March 1522 the earl of Surrey was permitted to return to England (O'Byrne 1998a, 76).

Sir Piers Butler was appointed lord deputy after Surrey's departure. An act of parliament passed on 21 December 1521 declared him to be the 'true and lawful heir' to James Butler, the late earl of Ormond (Hamilton 1860, 4). Despite the support of the Irish chieftains of the south-east, he was in reality too far removed from Dublin (the seat of power), from which he was cut off by the intervening hostile Geraldines, to be effective in office.

The animosity between the Butlers and the Fitzgeralds, and their respective efforts to attract the support of the Gaelic chieftains of south Leinster, only served to increase instability in the country. Sir James Fitzgerald, the brother of the earl, was involved in the murder of Robert Talbot, the sheriff of Dublin (O'Byrne 2003a, 155). As Talbot was a client of Butler's, retribution was not slow in coming. Fitzgerald was driven from his lands and the castles of Hollywood and Three Castles occupied (*ibid.*).

The disorder and growing chaos could not be tolerated for long. The earl of Kildare was once more appointed to the top office in May 1524, but all was not resolved. The king summoned both earls to London in August 1526. The stand-in appointment, Richard Nugent, twelfth Baron Delvin, was openly anti-Kildare. This prompted Garret Óg to signal his followers to wreak havoc (*ibid.*, 157). The king responded by reappointing Butler in August 1528. All this chopping and changing had broken the spell of the Geraldines and the *status quo* was shaken. The Gaelic lordships were now truly ensnared in the enticing possibilities of *realpolitik*.

Henry VIII had little choice but to explore fresh ideas. In June 1529 he made his natural son (by Elizabeth Blount) Henry, duke of Richmond, lieutenant of Ireland (MacCurtain 1972, 14). Sir William Skeffington was dispatched to review the military position. The consequence was that Tudor government would now become an ongoing political reality in Ireland. The more experienced Skeffington was appointed lord deputy on 12 June 1530 (Morrin 1861–2, I, 2).

A new thorn in Fitzgerald's side was John Allen, the archbishop of Dublin and lord chancellor. He personally answered to Thomas Cromwell, who was now the king's chief adviser, and he was tasked with keeping London informed of the earl's activities. A veritable swarm of Fitzgerald's enemies kept Allen awash with intelligence of varying degrees of credibility (MacCurtain 1972, 15). To compound matters, Allen himself revived archiepiscopal claims to estates in south County Dublin, County Kildare and County Carlow. Should the claims prove successful, the loser would be the House of Kildare (Maginn 2005, 40). Garret Óg did not succumb to the threat. Almost incredibly, the king, yet again, had a change of mind. In July 1532 Fitzgerald was duly reappointed lord deputy. He arrived and received the sword of state from Skeffington in August (O'Donovan 1854, V, 1412 fn. w). The pressure on Allen was already mounting. In a letter to Thomas Cromwell dated 19 March 1531 the archbishop had pleaded for royal funding to recruit 'a dosyne yemen archors'—a dozen yeoman archers—to protect him from his Irish enemies and 'Inglishe *rebelles*' when he was in residence in the church lands he held in the marches (State Papers 1830–52, III (2), 159). These enemies and adversaries of his are more clearly identified in a gloss in Archbishop Allen's register: 'These five septs, viz. Harrolds, Walchmen (the Walshes), Archbads (Archbolds), O'Bryn (O'Byrnes) and O'Tolls (O'Tooles), have wasted everything' (McNeill 1950, 172 fn. 16).

By the early sixteenth century many of the Walshes were closely tied to the House of Kildare, exemplified by their being amongst the recipients of annual gifts—in the form of horses and hackneys—from the earl. The Walshes in question were settled in counties Kildare and Dublin but, frustratingly, nearly all the individuals identified are not geographically placed. The Christian names are very familiar family ones: Oliver, Richard, William, Howell, Maurice, Walter, Nicholas, Henry, Gerrot, Piers and Robert. In 1513, 1515, 1523, 1526 and 1530 an Oliver Walsh received a horse (of varying colours—a black, a grey and a dun). In 1515 there were two references to Oliver, in both of which he is refined as 'son of James'. He apparently received both a grey and a 'sorell' (a sorrel, a reddish-brown horse). This Oliver reappears in 1526. The Oliver mentioned in 1523 was described as being 'of *Moybealla*' (i.e. Moyvally, to the west of Enfield in County Kildare). One may surmise that we are dealing with either one or two individuals (MacNiocaill 1992, 319, 323, 324, 335, 345, 346). A William Walsh accepted gifts in 1513, 1514, 1517, 1523, 1525 and 1530. The gifts varied from a dun and two hackneys (a horse for general use) in 1513 to a grey in 1514 and 1523, a hackney in 1517 and 1525, and a bay in 1530 (*ibid.*, 321, 322, 328, 329, 335, 336, 343, 347). A Richard Walsh appears under 1513, 1516 and 1530. In 1526 the full given name is Richard Boy Walsh. There is a reference to a 'Richard Walshes son of *Shanganaghe*' in 1525 (*ibid.*, 321, 325, 342, 345, 347). There are no references to an

Edmund while there are two to a Robert in these records, i.e. the contemporaneous Walsh heads of households at Carrickmines. William did not inherit until after 1537. In 1525 the Robert Walsh in question received a 'haberion' (a habergeon—a sleeveless coat or jacket of mail), while in 1530 he received a 'don' (dun) (*ibid.*, 340, 347). These two dates would not, however, be compatible with the Robert of Carrickmines. The indications are, therefore, that Carrickmines was independent of the Geraldines. The Shanganagh offspring may well have been domiciled elsewhere and living within the orbit of the earl. Ellis (1995, 137), it should be noted, has written that 'it is not clear how these gifts should be interpreted'. The same writer has calculated that on average the earl dispensed about 65 chief horses every year to his relatives, servants, horsemen, important border chieftains, the chief landowners of the lordship, leading gentry in the County of Kildare and some individuals in England (*ibid.*, 137–8). Whilst the financial outlay was *c.* £800 a year, the earl was drawing from a very impressive herd of close on a thousand horses (*ibid.*).

An event of great portent took place in England in May 1533 in the wake of Henry VIII's clandestine marriage to Anne Boleyn: the break with Rome. Religion henceforth would increasingly become a new dividing factor in Ireland.

In the interim, unsurprisingly, back in Ireland the Butlers were not content with their lot. They encouraged their aligned O'Byrne septs to harry the Geraldine lands. An audacious raid on Dublin Castle by Edmund Óg O'Byrne of the Downs branch in 1533 caused public outcry (Maginn 2005, 41–2). Once more the king was obliged to summon Piers Butler and Garret Óg Fitzgerald to London (O'Byrne 1998a, 85). Prior to his delayed departure—very likely deliberately so owing to a feeling of foreboding (MacCurtain 1972, 15)—in the following spring, Garret entrusted the administration of the country to his eldest son, Thomas (called 'Silken Thomas'), Lord Offaly.

THE INSURRECTION OF 1534

Thomas was instructed to convene a meeting of the privy council. He has the reputation of having been a very headstrong individual (MacCurtain 1972, 16; Cosgrove 2011, 149) but this is probably unwarranted: rash and impetuous, yes, but not much more so than most youthful men suddenly thrust into great power (see Brady 2017, 391). Hence the renowned incident of his riding to Dublin on 11 June 1534 and throwing down the sword of state before the assembled council in St Mary's Abbey. The key piece of information in understanding his theatrical actions is that he had been secretly instructed to behave so by his father (O'Byrne 1998a, 85; 2003a, 161; Cosgrove 2011, 149). There was a time when this rash conduct and the subsequent display of military strength would have caused the king to yield to an expedient resolution, but that time was now past (Maginn 2005, 43).

Sir William Skeffington was ordered to prepare to leave for Ireland at the head of an army. Meanwhile, the Geraldine forces and their allies overran most of the Pale;

only Dublin city, Fingal and the County Louth border area offered resistance (Ellis 1995, 221). On the 'laste day of July' Archbishop Allen attempted to flee the country but was caught by associates of Kildare. The official report stated that the archbishop had boarded a ship to depart for England but had been seized and brought before the earl who had him, 'in hys syght, by hys cummaundement', 'cruelly and shamefully murderyd' (State Papers 1830–52, III (2), 201). According to the Annals of Ulster *s.a.* 1534, Allen had boarded a ship at Howth (to the north of Dublin) but Kildare's men had arrived and seized him. He was brought to the castle at Artane, closer to the city. The earl was sent for and made great haste to get there. Upon his arrival 'he put to his people to do a prodigious, unprecedented, unmerciful deed', i.e. he had the archbishop murdered (Hennessy and MacCarthy 1887–1901, III, 594–5). Piers Butler's forces were routed at Tullow and Thomastown and he had to seek sanctuary in Waterford (O'Byrne 1998a, 86). Fingal was raided as far as Howth and Malahide by the Fitzgerald-allied septs of the O'Byrnes and O'Tooles (Maginn 2005, 44). Garret Óg Fitzgerald, the ninth earl of Kildare, died in London on 2 September 1534. 'Silken Thomas' accordingly became the tenth earl. It should be noted in passing that the 'silken' sobriquet is a later invention (Brady 2017, 388). The tide, however, was turning. Even his uncles, Sir James and Richard Fitzgerald, were now fighting against him. Skeffington and his forces finally landed in October, and Kildare's allies started to slip away. Ellis (*ODNB*, IX, 849) judged that the tenth earl had 'acquitted himself well militarily' but was overwhelmed by political difficulties that would have 'taxed even the most experienced politician'.

REALIGNMENTS

William Walsh was identified as the son and heir of Theobald of Carrickmines in an inquisition dated 20 June 1537. He had been aged sixteen at the time of his father's death. The family holdings were listed as the manor of *Carrickmayn* (held in chief by knight service), twenty acres in *Ballycnomppe* (i.e. Phrompstown) held of the king's manor of Rathdowne, and 'divers' lands etc. in Oldcourt, Co. Wicklow, held from the earl of Ormond (Griffith 1991, 63). The date of his marriage to Margaret Fitzwilliam (TCD MS 1212, 26, 80) is unknown. Her branch of the family had moved their seat from Dundrum Castle to Baggotrath before finally settling in Merrion (Ball 1902–17, II, 68).

This marriage was a highly advantageous union. Margaret's father, Thomas, had served as sheriff for the county of Dublin in 1511. Her mother was Eleanor Dowdall. Margaret had three brothers and at least one sister. Her sister Alison was first married (in 1524) to Christopher Ussher, an alderman who had served as mayor of Dublin from 1516 to 1517. He died in 1526. Her eldest brother, Richard of Baggotrath, was a 'trusted adherent' of Garret, the ninth earl of Kildare, and later served as a gentleman of the bedchamber to King Henry VIII. In 1527 he was appointed 'seneschal for life' of the king's manors at Newcastle near Lyons, Esker, *Tassagard* and *Cromlin*. He was married to Catherine Bathe of *Kepoke* (i.e. Cappoge), Co. Dublin. They had three recorded sons, Thomas, Michael and John. Whilst their eldest, Thomas, was described as 'of *Meryon* and *Baggotrath*', Michael was seated at '*Donamore* or *Dunore*' in County Meath (Lodge and Archdall 1789, IV, 312). Michael Fitzwilliam served as surveyor general of the Crown lands during the reigns of Edward VI, Mary and Elizabeth. An Elizabethan fiant dating from 1560–1 records the leasing of a parcel of lands to Michael. These included *Donamore, Woodtown, Moghoreston, Roberston, Bulleston, miche Felenston, littell Fellenston* and *Archerston* (*DKR 11* (1879), 62). To the south and south-east of Ashbourne on the Meath/Dublin border can be found a cluster of townlands now known as Donaghmore, Wotton, Muckerstown, Robertstown, Bullstown, Fleenstown Great, Fleenstown Little and Archerstown. Michael Fitzwilliam was married to Mary Preston, the daughter of Jenico, third Viscount Gormanston. Among their five children was Eleanor, more of whom anon.

Margaret's second eldest brother was Sir William Fitzwilliam. It is reasonable to assert that Sir William forged a remarkably successful career for himself. Amongst the positions he held were chief gentleman of the privy chamber in the household of Prince Edward (1547–53), keeper of Windsor Great Park (by 1552) and member of the privy council of Ireland (1554–6), and in February 1555 he was designated deputy chancellor in Ireland. It was John Dudley, duke of Northumberland, who during the minority of King Edward VI (i.e. from 1549 to 1553) was the most powerful man in England, who appointed William as lieutenant of Windsor Castle and keeper of the Great Park. As a gentleman of the privy chamber he was involved in the obsequies for King Edward VI in August 1553. It was Edward's successor, Queen Mary, who sent Sir William to Ireland. He had not lost contact with family and home and was in possession of an estate at Kildrought, Co. Kildare. In the autumn of 1555 he was given temporary custody of the great seal. His detailed investigation of Irish affairs resulted in the exposure of the apparent misconduct in office of the lord deputy, Sir Anthony St Leger. In 1558 Fitzwilliam was granted a 21-year lease on the estate of Donaghmore as a reward for his work in Ireland. This land augmented his considerable holdings in England. Sir William was married to Jane Roberts of the prominent family in Cranbrook, Kent. A daughter of theirs married the lord viscount of Gormanston. Sir William was elected to the first parliament of Queen Elizabeth but died on 3 October 1559. He is buried in St George's Chapel in Windsor Castle.

Margaret and Sir William's youngest brother, Nicholas, held the position of treasurer of St Patrick's Cathedral, Dublin. He was described as 'Nicholas Fitzwilliams, late Treasurer' in an inquisition held in Lusk on 17 January 1547 (Mason 1820, 35; Genealogical Office MS 48, 10; Bindoff 1982, I, 141–2; O'Flanagan 1870, I, 235; Lodge and Archdall 1789, IV, 311).

The collective influence, contacts and political allies of his wife's three brothers and their spouses' families can only have been of enormous potential benefit to William Walsh. It is worth observing that Sir William and Nicholas Fitzwilliam both clearly embraced the Reformation. Whether Richard or Alison followed suit is unknown. Given the religious affiliations of their son and heir, it is unlikely that

Margaret converted.

It was without doubt a time of change. The execution of Thomas Fitzgerald, the tenth earl of Kildare, alongside five of his uncles (including the innocent Sir James and Richard), at Tyburn on 3 February 1537 marked the end of an era. A succession of English-born lord deputies would be appointed to serve in Ireland over the ensuing two decades. The void created by the collapse of the House of Kildare needed to be filled urgently, and almost by default the government had to 'step into those shoes'. Of immediate concern to the inhabitants of the southern marches of the Pale were the now-unfettered O'Tooles and O'Byrnes. The leading protagonist amongst these chieftaincies was Turlough O'Toole. The O'Byrnes of Gabhal Raghnaill were also definitely on the rise. The territory of the Gabhal Raghnaill extended from the area of Rathdrum and Glenmalure to Shillelagh close to the Carlow border (Long 1998, 250). Leonard Grey, Viscount Grane, the lord deputy from 1536 to 1540, made several sorties against them during his tenure. Grey was recalled to England in April 1540. The administrative hiatus in Dublin in the wake of his departure was soon to be exploited by Turlough O'Toole, who proceeded to burn the Pale in tandem with the O'Connor Falys and the O'Mores (O'Byrne 2005, 20).

In 1539 King Henry VIII dissolved the monasteries. As was the case in England, the local landed gentry in Ireland instantly recognised the great opportunities suddenly available for land acquisition. The Dublin authorities, however, on 12 December 1539 recognised that the Holy Trinity community, 'having been secular at its foundation', should continue to enjoy the benefits of its holdings. The newly constituted dean would therefore continue to hold the temporalities due from (amongst others) the estates in *Dalkeya* (Dalkey), *Killeny* (Killiney), *Balliloghan* (Ballyogan), *Ballybrenan* (Brenanstown), *Priorsland* and *Ketingsland* near *Carrickmayne*, and the churches of (amongst others) *Carrickmayne*, *Tullaghe* (Tully), *Stalorgan* (Stillorgan) and *Dalkeya* (Dalkey) (McEnery and Refaussé 2001, 115). The lands in Brenanstown, Priorsland and Keatingsland would naturally have concerned the young William Walsh. He may have had aspirations to obtain full ownership, but that ambition would now have been stymied. Killiney had appeared a year earlier in a deed dated 8 August. The prior of Holy Trinity had leased 'the town of *Kyllenyn*' to a 'William Walche otherwise called William Mc. Howell, of *Kyllenyn*' for 31 years at a rent of £1 6s. 8d. (*ibid.*, 234). The transaction was documented again in January 1565–6 (*ibid.*, 262).

Grey's successor, Sir Anthony St Leger, pursued a less militant policy known as 'Surrender and Regrant', whereby Irish chieftains could surrender their lands, adopt English mores and subsequently be regranted the lands, often accompanied by a conferred title (O'Byrne 2003a, 168). Turlough O'Toole submitted under this policy in November 1540. He was accordingly confirmed in his expanded holdings (Hamilton 1860, 57) and thus secured the key castles of Powerscourt and Castlekevin. The latter of these two castles was subsequently occupied by his brother, Art Óg (Maginn 2005, 65). Turlough, in the words of Emmett O'Byrne (2005, 19), had become a master of 'pillage, parley and pardon' and had thus exploited the English system to the hilt. On 9 August 1541 William Walsh of Carrickmines served as a commissioner tasked with determining the extent of Castlekevin and Fertire (Griffith 1991, 92). A fellow commissioner was Edward Basnet, dean of St Patrick's Cathedral. In years to come William's daughter Joan, prior to her marriage, would be Basnet's concubine (Ken Nicholls, pers. comm.). Maginn (2004, 136) has observed that the exclusion of the marchers from the 'Surrender and Regrant' policy 'best illustrates their status as English subjects'.

O'Toole threw sand in the eyes of his hosts while visiting England. His stay in London included a meeting with King Henry VIII to be formally confirmed in his tenurial rights. He was adamant that Imaal had always been part of the deal, but in reality it had never been St Leger's intention to include the territory of Imaal as, for one thing, this would create problems with Peter Talbot, who had already been granted land there. The king did not want O'Toole's formal submission to unravel and it was quickly decided that Talbot should be compensated elsewhere, at the expense of the Walshes (Maginn 2005, 67). The Imaal question, however, was not resolved. The branch of the O'Tooles that occupied the territory was not about to roll over, nor was the lord deputy willing to resign himself to conceding the point.

On 26 June 1541 St Leger dispatched a short but succinct report to London: 'Parliament has met. Act passed for Henry VIII to be King of Ireland' (Hamilton 1860, 59). The monarch's wishes had been fulfilled. Ireland had hitherto functioned as a lordship, founded in the twelfth century. The reputed legal basis for the lordship rested on an elusive papal document issued in 1155 by Pope Adrian IV known as *Laudabiliter*, whose entire or partial authenticity has long been debated without an agreed conclusion. One aspect is certain and that is that Henry could no longer tolerate one of his realms remaining under the status of 'by gift of the Pope'.

An insight into the condition of the marches at this time is provided by a bill introduced on 7 December 1542. It instructed all landowners to physically dwell in their homesteads and to defend the land 'against the spoil and waste of the rebels' (Hamilton 1860, 65).

The chieftaincy of the O'Byrnes in the late sixteenth century would be rotated between the four principal houses of Newrath, Kiltimon (Culteman), the Downe and Croneroe (Nicholls 1998a, 23). Tadhg O'Byrne of Kiltimon held the chieftaincy in 1536 when he entered into formal agreement with the lord deputy, Leonard Grey (*ibid.*, 25). His branch was to maintain cordial relations with the Dublin administration for most of the remainder of the sixteenth century. This period of *détente* created land acquisition opportunities for the more ambitious marcher families. William Walsh of Carrickmines leased lands in '*Kilpeter*, in O'Byrnes country' in August 1541 (*Fiants*, I, No. 246, 30). This holding (modern Kilpedder, East and West), to the west of Kilcoole in east County Wicklow (Map 5), was acquired for a 21-year lease at an annual rent of 26s. 8d. Formerly the property of the Hospital of St John of Jerusalem, it lay to the south of the Three Trout Stream, which marked the northern border of Críoch Branach (Nicholls 1998a, 7).

Turlough O'Toole lost his patience while waiting for the agreed extended holdings to come fully under his control. He decided to take possession of Imaal

Map 5—South Dublin and east Wicklow.

without any further delay and in early 1542 advanced on the territory. On arrival, however, he was ambushed and killed by the local branch of the O'Tooles (O'Byrne 2003a, 170; Maginn 2005, 71).

A patent of lease to William Walsh of Carrickmayne 'of the lands and tithes of *Kylpole* in the country of O'Byrne' dates from 17 August 1542. It notes that the land was lately in the possession of the Hospital of St John of Jerusalem. The lease was for 21 years at an annual rent of 6s. 8d. (*Fiants*, III, No. 6794, 631). An inquisition dating from 1544–5 detailed the composition of the property: an old hamlet called *Ballma Kygll*, described as 'part of the vill of *Kylpole*', twelve messuages and cottages, and 620 acres (Griffith 1991, 107). Kilpoole lies to the south/south-west of Wicklow town and thus within the borders of Críoch Branach (Map 6). It should be noted that as recently as 1540–1 the property had been described as impossible to value 'at present', as it lay 'among the Irish'. In fact, it had not delivered a profit 'for a long time past' (White 1943, 91). On 12 April 1542 all the lands of Walter Walsh of Shanganagh, a minor, had been granted to William for a sum of money partly paid upfront, with the residual amount to be paid upon the marriage of Walter to William's (aforementioned)

Map 6—South Dublin, Kildare and Wicklow.

daughter Joan. The estates would subsequently be placed at the disposal of Walter and Joan's male heirs 'for ever' (*ibid.*, 130). Walter's holdings included *Connaghe* (Old Connaught), *Corkagh* and *Kiltuke* (Kiltuck was a subdivision of Shanganagh) (*ibid.*).

These various acquisitions were not without a cost. On 12 May 1543 William appeared before the court of chancery to acknowledge a bond of 100 marks in respect of land deeds (Morrin 1861–2, I, 96).

William served as a juror in an assessment of an inquisition held on 7 February 1545. The jury was tasked with ruling on the extent and composition of the lands formerly held by the Abbey of the Blessed Virgin Mary at Kiltiernan (*Cal. Pembroke*, No. 222, 72). Serving alongside William on the jury were his relatives Walter Walsh of Shanganagh, James Walsh of Brenanstown and Bene Walsh of Monkstown. Two other named individuals, Patrick Óg and Gerald O'Byrne, may have been servitors from Carrickmines. Richard, William's son and heir, was nominated to be a beneficiary of a grant from Dean Edward Basnet of 'the town and fields of *Kyltyernan*, County Dublin, and the church and rectory of the same'. This was agreed on 29 January 1546 (see below). William was present when the deed was delivered to Thomas FitzWilliam (*ibid.*, No. 227, 74). In January 1546 he was granted custody of the Balally estate of his late cousin Thomas Walsh during the minority of his son and heir, John. He was also granted the 'wardship and marriage' of the boy, and 'the value of his marriage, should he decline when he shall be thereunto required by William' (Morrin 1861–2, I, 120). A plum acquisition came to Willliam in 1548: the lease of the prebend of Rathmichael, with its manse, land and tithes, 'also all tithes of corn and hay of the prebend extending to the towns of Rathmichael, Shankill, *Balmacorus* [Ballycorus], *Ballyrowgan*, Shanganagh, *Quorke* [i.e. Cork Great/Little], and *Ballygelonan*' (there is a hill called Carrickgollogan in the south-west sector of the townland of Shankill), and 'all tithes and altarages' of the parish. The lease was for 21 years, at a rent of £22 *per annum*. The only obligation was for William to find a suitable chaplain for the church (*Fiants*, I, No. 214, 107–8).

It was not all plain sailing. 'William Walsh, of *Carrickmayne*, *alias* William Walshe, of *Olde Courte*' was granted a pardon in April 1549 for some unspecified misdemeanour (Morrin 1861–2, I, 177). Then on 24 August his son Richard was pardoned of all intrusions at Kiltiernan. Richard and Geoffrey Walsh, and others, appeared in the 'King's Chancery' on 26 August to become sureties for Edward Basnet of Dean's Rath (*Cal. Pembroke*, No. 234, 77). The relationship between Richard and Geoffrey is unknown.

It was about this time that the power and prestige of the O'Byrnes of Gabhal Raghnaill became manifest. From their base at Ballinacor, at the mouth of Glenmalure, these O'Byrnes presided over a growing 'business empire' that was predominantly financed by 'extortion and timber' (O'Byrne 2005). Contemporary sources indicate that the main residence at Ballinacor was a wooden building surrounded by an earthwork and not a stone-built castle (Long 1998, 251). In keeping with this more traditional and antiquated style of abode, bards played an important role in life at Ballinacor. Indeed, Feagh O'Byrne and his second wife, Rose, were also known for their hospitality. The wine and music flowed generously (*ibid.*, 257, 258). The branch from the mid-1500s would be led by the very able Hugh Mac Shane O'Byrne (Nicholls 1998b, 110).

The growing strength and influence of the Gabhal Raghnaill O'Byrnes discommoded the Butlers of Ormond, who had territorial ambitions in east Leinster. In July 1548 they pitched Tibbot (Theobald) Walsh (see below), constable of Arklow Castle, supported by the O'Byrnes of Críoch Branach (who were located to the west of Wicklow town), against the Gabhal Raghnaill. Reeling under the onslaught, Hugh and his father Shane appealed to Sir Edward Bellingham, the lord deputy (since May), to intervene. This call was answered, as overall stability was obviously of prime concern to Dublin (O'Byrne 2003a, 178).

Once at the helm, Hugh Mac Shane continued to consolidate his dynastic position in Leinster. The plantation of Leix and Offaly in the mid-1500s would create a multitude of dispossessed nobles, many of whom would find succour at Ballinacor (O'Byrne 2005, 20). Hugh also found that marriage was a very useful agency when it came to forging his network of contacts and allies. His eldest son Feagh first married Sadhbh, the daughter of Donal Mac Cahir Kavanagh of Garryhill, Co. Carlow. Feagh's second marriage was to Rose, daughter of Feagh O'Toole of Castlekevin. His daughters Margaret, Elizabeth and Honora were married respectively to Rory Óg O'More of Leix, Brian Mac Cahir Mac Art Kavanagh of St Mullins in County Carlow and Robert Walsh of Ballynalour (modern Leopardstown) in south County Dublin (Nicholls 1998b, 111–12). Robert was the third son of William Walsh of Carrickmines. The marriage of Robert and Honora was recorded in a 'Visitation of the County of Dublin' conducted by Daniel Molyneux, Ulster King of Arms, in 'Anno Domini 1610' (Genealogical Office MS 48, 20).

On 22 February 1554 the dean of Christ Church, Sir Thomas Lockwood, leased the parsonage of *Kyllehurler* (Killahurler) near *Ortelow* (Arklow, Co. Wicklow) to Walter Peppard of *Kilkaye* (Kilkea, Co. Kildare) and Morgh Kavanagh. The agreed annual rent of 'nine fat beeves' was to be delivered at *Carrick Mayne* (McEnery and Refaussé 2001, 248). It is apparent from this arrangement that Carrickmines had the facilities to handle livestock professionally. Ball (1901, 198) made the point that the reason why Carrickmines was chosen was that 'it seems not improbable that fairs were then held there'.

The dean and chapter of Holy Trinity concluded a new land agreement with William Walsh on 28 October 1555. He would be leased 'the town and lands of *Ballybrenan* (and) *Priorsland* and *Ketyngesland* in the fields of *Carrickmayne* for 51 years'. The rent would be 20s. a year for the lands in Carrickmines and 16s. 8d. a year for the lands in *Ballybrenan*. A penny of Edward VI date struck at York was found to the immediate south of the castle at Carrickmines (Pl. 14). William was obliged to 'mow the meadow and gather the tithes of *Ballybrenan* to the usual place known as the *Holy Stood*' (McEnery and Refaussé 2001, 249). Clare (2005, 19) has written that from the fourteenth century the grange of Clonkeen had a wooden pillar called 'the holy stood'. This was a formal ceremonial place, of particular importance given the illiteracy

Pl. 14—Silver penny of Edward VI, minted at York, 1550–3.
Obverse: central Tudor rose. Inscription: E DG ROSA SINE SPINA ('Edward by the Grace of God a rose without a thorn').
Reverse: quartered royal arms over long cross fourchée. Inscription: CIVITAS EBORACI ('City of York'). (Photo: Sara Nylund)

of the vast majority of the population, where formal transactions could take place. Between 1552 and 1561 William was involved in several other land transactions in partnerships with James Goodman of Rochestown, Richard Caddell of Harbartston, Christopher Marten of Gormanston, Robert Mayneringe of Naas and William Forster, a merchant in Dublin (Griffith 1991, 175). Sir John Travers of Monkstown was a key player in these deals (*ibid.*, 175–7, 181, 183). One of the properties that featured in these transactions was Three Castles in County Wicklow. It was granted in October 1561 on a 30-year lease to Tibbot (son of Maurice) Walsh, the former constable of Arklow Castle (*ibid.*, 176 fn. 2). A related deed, dated 20 April 1599, was witnessed by, amongst others, a Robert Walsh (*ibid.*, 313 fns 2 and 3) (see below).

THE WALSHES OF THREE CASTLES

In July 1548 the Gabhal Raghnaill branch of the O'Byrnes made complaints against Tibbot (the son of Maurice) Walsh, constable of Arklow Castle. They alleged that the constable had been confiscating their goods and imposing 'coign' (billeting and quartering) on them (Maginn 2005, 90). These nefarious enterprises may well have contributed to Tibbot's need for the pardons that he was granted on 26 May 1549 (*Fiants*, I, No. 323, 122) and in 1550 (*ibid.*, No. 560, 146). A second recipient in the latter pardon was Charles McMoryce (i.e. son of Maurice), who may well have been a brother of Tibbot.

The feud was to prove long-running. An alliance composed of Feagh Mac Hugh of the Gabhal Raghnaill O'Byrnes, one of the sons of Teige Óg O'Byrne of the Críoch Branach branch of the O'Byrnes, some of the Kavanaghs and the O'Tooles of Imaal launched an attack on Tibbot (son of Maurice) Walsh of Three Castles in August 1564

(Hamilton 1860, 244; Maginn 2005, 113). Walsh was driven from his lands (O'Byrne 2003a, 183). Not that he was yet without blemish; indeed, he had to procure another pardon from the authorities that same year (*Fiants*, II, No. 660, 75). Three Castles is located to the north-east of Blessington in County Wicklow on the banks of the River Liffey (Map 6).

Henry Walsh of *Arcloo* was pardoned in 1582 (*ibid.*, No. 3991, 553). On 28 August of that year a pardon was granted to Henry Walsh of Three Castles, establishing that the family reoccupied the lands after their earlier eviction. Along with Henry (the son of Tibbot?), the pardon also extended to James Walsh and his wife Katherine Fitzwilliams, and to Edward Walsh and Nicholas Walsh, all of Three Castles. In addition, it also covered Maurice Walsh of *Calliaghton* and Robert Walsh of *Skallardston*. The relevant document made two specific observations: it noted that all the 'Walshes aforenamed are brethren', and it made it clear that 'none of them' were 'of the houses of *Carrikmayn* or *Arclo*' (*ibid.*, No. 4016, 557). In 1601 a pardon was issued to a Robert 'McTibbot' of Three Castles (*DKR 17* (1885), 256), possibly indicating the integration of the branch into Gaelic society.

A NEW ORDER

The coronation of Queen Mary in 1553 had, predictably, been joyfully celebrated by the Catholic majority in Ireland. Two key subsequent developments should not be overlooked, however. First, the pope was persuaded to recognise Henry's 1541 proclamation of the kingdom of Ireland. As MacCulloch (2003, 395) has written, 'Mary was not going to lose that title'. Needless to say, neither would her successors, regardless of their religious persuasion. Second, it was the Catholic Queen Mary who first implemented plantation on a large scale in Ireland. In 1556 'orders for *Leix*' were issued. The territory would be divided between the 'English and Irish' (Hamilton 1860, 134). The following year the queen and king wrote to the lord deputy (Sussex) requesting 'for the third time a draft of an Act for assuring of *Leix* and *Offaley*' (*ibid.*, 138). Queen's County and King's County were accordingly formed, named in honour of Mary and her husband, Philip of Spain (MacCurtain 1972, 56–61).

One of the top priorities for the new lord lieutenant upon his arrival in Ireland in the spring of 1556 was to break the power of the McDonnell-controlled Hebridean Scots who ruled in the Glens of Antrim. Sir Thomas Ratcliffe, soon to be earl of Sussex, was primed to implement the policy objectives of the new monarch, Queen Mary, and the 10,000 fighting 'Redshanks', as the Scots were called, were an obvious obstruction that had been brewing for almost half a century (Curtis 1936, 152). A call to arms was sounded, the order to rally being issued on 12 June (HMC 1897, 3). In the marches of the county of Dublin, 'all the Walshemans country, Haroldes country, and the Archeboldes' were obliged to contribute twelve horsemen and sixteen kerns. While the O'Byrnes were expected to send twelve horsemen and 23 kerns, the O'Tooles were exempt, as their lands were 'waste' (*ibid.*, 14).

An unqualified pardon was apparently difficult to obtain in the case of the murder of one Peter Talbot. A document dating from 1558, while confirming the pardoning of William (son of Theobald) Walsh of Carrickmines and some of the Archbolds, specifically excluded those 'concerned in the murder of Peter Talbot' (*Fiants*, I, No. 275, 325). A marginally earlier document, dated 6 December 1557, isolated Theobald Walsh from a general pardon granted to an assortment of Palesmen and Wicklow Irish owing to his 'connection with the death of Peter Talbot' (*ibid.*, No. 187, 315). This Theobald could possibly be a brother of William, given the chronology and circumstances. William's loyalty, despite his occasional transgressions, was still acceptable to the Dublin authorities. In July 1560 he was listed amongst those dependable to call upon 'to take the muster and array of the county Dublin, and its crosses and marches, to call before them all the subjects of each barony, and assess them in warlike furniture of weapons, arms, horses, horsemen, and footmen, according to the manner and quantity of their lands and chattels, as the instructions of the Lord Lieutenant, and the customs and laws of the realm require' (*Fiants*, II, No. 260, 27). The three appointments for the barony of Rathdown were Sir John Travers (the dean of Christ Church), Patrick Barnewall and 'William Welshe of *Carrickemayne*' (HMC 1897, 86). The assembly date was set for 13 July, and all men 'being of th'age between sixtene yeres and threschore yeres' were eligible for service (*ibid.*, 84). While most areas had to provide carts or wagons to transport the army, in the marches they were exempt. Under 'Marche cariage' it was specified that from 'the Welchmens countree and the Archebolds' they expected twelve horsemen and sixteen kerns. The O'Byrnes had to provide twelve horsemen and 24 kerns. Again, as in June 1556, the O'Tooles were exempt owing to their territory still being 'waste' (*ibid.*, 89).

The heir to Hugh O'Byrne's domain was his eldest son, the (aforementioned) Feagh. He, like many young contemporaries, was heavily influenced by the wave of Counter-Reformation priests returning from the Continent. In fact, many of the Gaelic lords now sent their sons to mainland Europe for their education. Feagh was thus gradually imbued with an anti-Protestant, anti-government spirit (O'Byrne 2003a, 182).

Outbreaks of violence were still occurring along the borders of the marches. A report to the queen from the lord lieutenant dated 22 September 1563 noted that in general the O'Byrnes, the O'Tooles and the Kavanaghs were 'obedient'. There had, however, been an incident in which a number of the Talbots were killed by elements of the O'Byrnes or the O'Tooles (Hamilton 1860, 222). Feagh Mac Hugh O'Byrne was now, in effect, recruiting and training a private army (O'Byrne 2003a, 183). His main protagonist would be yet another lord deputy, Sir Henry Sidney, who was to serve three terms extending (with gaps) from 1565 to 1578 (Maginn 2005, 117, 136). One of his first major acts was to appoint Sir Francis Agarde as seneschal of the O'Byrnes and O'Tooles (*ibid.*, 118). Seneschals were intended to function as the district law-enforcement officers.

The offence recounted on 26 November 1560 as having been committed by William Walsh of Carrickmines, James Goodman of Rochestown, Robert Manneringe of Naas and Christopher Marten of Gormanstown could be described as a misdemeanour. On 28 October 1562 it had been found that they had granted 'the manor of *Karrickbrenan* (*alias* Monkstown), ten castles, 100 messuages, one watermill and 449 acres in Carrickbrenan, Newtown, Cornelscourt, the Three Castles, Buttlerscort, *Ballore alias Ballygoore*' (and seven other locations) to Richard Luttrell of Luttrellston 'without royal licence' (Griffith 1991, 175–6). The grant had been reciprocated with 'a sum of money' (*ibid.*, 311). Fifty acres of the land was described as being covered with furze (*ibid.*, 312 fn. 1).

The lease on the lands of Kilpoole (see above) was renewed on 4 July 1562 at Westminster. This time an Owen Walsh is named as the co-grantee along with William. Their obviously close relationship is not defined. A fiant dated 1570/1, however, has an Owen Walsh residing in *Ballebrenan* (Brenanstown). He is referenced in association with two sons of William, Robert of *Ballenelowre* (modern Leopardstown) and Edmund of *Frompstone* (Phrompstown) (*Fiants*, II, No. 1783, 240). William had a son named Howell. It has been suggested that Owen and Howell are one and the same (Ken Nicholls, pers. comm.). A deed dated 28 November 1572 recorded the leasing of Priorsland and Keatingsland by Sir John Garvey, dean of Holy Trinity, to Owen Walsh of *Ballybrenan*. '*Keatinges land alias Kylltekeare*' was leased for 81 years at a rent of 40s. Under the terms of the agreement Owen was obliged to plant '20 ashes, oaks, or such like timber' every year in *Ballybrenan* (Brenanstown) (McEnery and Refaussé 2001, 267). Worth noting is the fact that this parcel of lands, including Brenanstown, had been leased to William Walsh of Carrickmines in 1555 (*ibid.,* 249) (see above). A document dating from 1574 has Richard Walsh of *Carrickmayne* and 'Ouin' Walsh of *Ballybrynane* appearing together (*Cal. Pembroke*, 87). The accompanying tithes were listed as '2 coples of oats'. The lease was for 21 years at an annual rent of £4 9s. 4d. A stipulation was that the lessee had to maintain two able English horsemen on the property. A further stipulation made it clear that none of the holding could be 'set to any persons not English by both parents' (*Fiants*, II, No. 466, 52).

The rising level of violence was causing concern in Dublin. Sir Nicholas Bagenal, lord marshal, observed in March 1566 that he had never known 'the country so out of order'. 'Robbing, stealing, and killing' were endemic throughout the Pale. The situation in the southern marches was particularly bad owing to the reciprocal pillaging being conducted between the O'Byrnes, the O'Tooles, and the Walshes (Hamilton 1860, 289). The following month the lord deputy informed the privy council that the 'countries' of the Walshes, the Archbolds and the Harolds had been committed to the charge of Thomas Fitzwilliam of Merrion (*ibid.*, 296). In September he was granted the office of seneschal. His territory was delineated as 'the whole marches of Dublin, that is to say the barony of Rathdowne, the nations of the Walsches, Asspoles (Archbolds) and Harolds' (*Fiants*, II, No. 933, 109). The lord deputy, Sir Henry Sidney, had already issued instructions to Matthew King, clerk of the cheque, regarding the deployment and discharging of troops. His dispatch was dated 8 March 1566 and was issued from *Carrigmayne* (Hamilton 1860, 292). Local disturbances inevitably continued. A pardon was granted in February 1566/7 to, amongst others, Richard and

Nicholas Archbold of *Kylrelyn* and Phelim O'Toole of Powerscourt, and to Richard the son of Robert Walsh of Carrickmines (*Fiants*, II, No. 994, 119). This Robert was married to Honora O'Byrne, the daughter of Hugh Mac Shane.

THE WALSHES OF SHANGANAGH

Undoubtedly the Walsh holding that would ultimately rival Carrickmines in terms of extent and wealth was Shanganagh (Pl. 15). The initial holding would have been secured to install an offspring from the Carrickmines nucleus. On 2 March 1447 Edmund (sometimes Esmund) Walsh leased 80 acres of arable land in Shanganagh from the 'Vicars of St Patrick's Cathedral' (Mason 1820, 90). Edmund was still the occupant in 1473 when the vicars lodged a petition with parliament maintaining not only that his lease had expired but also that he owed them six marks. Furthermore, he was unwilling to either vacate the land or pay them any rent. This aggressive stance was not an isolated incident. A fellow lessee in Shanganagh was Thomas Lawless. In fact, he was

Pl. 15—Shanganagh Castle, Co. Dublin, as painted by Gabriel Beranger. A tower-house of early fifteenth-century date, it was in the possession of the Walsh family by the mid-fifteenth century (National Library of Ireland).

in place prior to Edmund's arrival and is credited with building the tower-house *c.* 1408 (Turner 1983, 85; Corlett 1999, 163). A descendant of his, Richard Lawless, pleaded before parliament that he could not gain access to or possession of his late father's estate. Actually, 'he dare not for Esmund Walsh, gent, and Johan his wife, and their great number of men that they have with them from day to day' (Berry 1910, 489). And Lawless was not just talking about the family holding in Shanganagh. Also barred to him were their 'lands and tenements with the appurtenances' in Old Connaught, Cork (Great/Little), *Raulynstown* and *Clementstown*. The Walshes were ordered to present themselves before parliament with proof of title and legal rights to the land, otherwise they were to vacate it (*ibid.*, 491). According to Turner (1983, 85), Johan (Joan) was the daughter of Aveline and John Lawless.

Somehow the Walshes got the better of the Lawless family, as in 1482 we find Charles Walsh in possession of Shanganagh (at the least) (McEnery and Refaussé 2001, 96). The power of the Carrickmines hub may have influenced the final outcome. Ellis (1995, 41) has observed that 'the growth of a marcher society habituated to war exacerbated the government's difficulties in keeping control and maintaining law and order'. In other words, by this point in time the Walshes were of more use to the Dublin authorities than an apparently unsupported Richard Lawless.

An inquisition taken on 20 June 1537 indicates that the holding of which the late Richard Walsh was seised had grown slightly overall (one messuage and 60 acres in Shanganagh) and that the Old Connaught land (40 acres) was still in their possession. The document held that his son and heir Walter was only four years of age at the unspecified time of Richard's death but was now married to a Talbot. It is further revealed that a John Walsh, a brother of Richard(?), held the estate for ten years (presumably during Walter's minority); he too had died prior to 1537 (Griffith 1991, 63). Walter's second marriage, *c.* 1542, was to Joan, the daughter of William Walsh of Carrickmines (*ibid.*, 130).

A jury was convened on 7 February 1545 to assess an inquisition previously held to define the extent and value of former church holdings in Kiltiernan. Walter Walsh of Shanganagh was a member of the jury (*Cal. Pembroke*, No. 222, 72). Walter's 'son and heir' John was to be a beneficiary of the sharing out of the holdings agreed on 29 January 1546 courtesy of Dean Edward Basnet of St Patrick's Cathedral, who had been confirmed in his grant of the lands at Kiltiernan of the dissolved abbey of the Blessed Virgin Mary in Dublin on 7 February 1545 (for a consideration of £57) (*ibid.*, No. 227, 74; No. 223, 73).

Walter Walsh died on 3 September 1551. He was seised of a castle, seven messuages and cottages and 60 acres in Shanganagh (held of Peter Talbot of the manor of Rathdown); a castle, four messuages and cottages and 120 acres in Old Connaught; and eight messuages and cottages and 160 acres in Cork (Great/Little) and in *Kiltuke* (a subdivision of Shanganagh) (*ibid.*, 130). This tally represents a significant increase in the size of the Walsh estate. According to the inquisition, his son John was a baby, just six months old at the time of Walter's death. The problem here is that a son named John was extant in 1546 (see above). Furthermore, a pardon was issued on 20 August

1550 to John, the 'son and heir of Walter Walsh of *Shanganaghe*', who had been charged with 'intrusion and alienation' (*Fiants*, I, No. 542, 145). A pardon was also issued to a Charles Walsh of Shanganagh and Edmonde, his kern, on 30 November 1552 (*ibid.*, No. 1104, 205). John Walsh, 'the son and heir of Walter Walsh of Shanganagh', served alongside Richard Walsh of Carrickmines as a trustee in 1553 (Griffith 1991, 141). John collected another pardon on 23 May 1566. There had been two incidents involving William, the son of Shane Walsh of *Corkagh* (Cork). In the first case, William and his kern 'Neil O'Donyll' (O'Donnell?) had robbed a widow living in Glencullen. They made off with a brass pan (worth 26s. 4d.), two gallons of butter (worth 18d. per gallon), three sheep (worth 2s. each), one nightgown (worth 10s.), two women's gowns (worth 20s. each) and one cloak (worth 5s.). Arrested by George Stokes, the sub-sheriff for the county, they were on their way to justice when a party of Walsh's relatives set upon the law officer. This successful rescue took place 'on the King's highway by *Shangan*' (*Fiants*, II, No. 856, 93). The rescue party consisted of John Walsh of Shanganagh, Charles Walsh of *Newton* and Edmund Walsh of *Corkagh* (a brother of William?). Clearly these Walshes of *Corkagh* were an offshoot and thus closely related to the Shanganagh branch. Amongst the Walshes (and others) who were granted a 'pardon in general terms' on 7 December 1574 was John Walsh of Shanganagh (*Cal. Pembroke*, No. 265, 87). He was pardoned again on 10 September 1577 for 'intrusions' at Kiltiernan (*ibid.*, No. 270, 89). A further pardon came in 1577. John is described as 'late Sheriff' of the county. Gerald Walsh, a brother(?), was also pardoned in this reprieve (*Fiants*, II, No. 3151, 429). Yet another pardon was granted to John in 1582. Again he was in the company of relatives: Theobald Walsh (of Killincarrig, Co. Wicklow), Oliver Walsh (of Merrion), Henry Walsh (of Arklow) and Edmund Walsh (of *Ballyvan*, Co. Dublin) (*ibid.*, No. 3991, 552–3).

The Walshes of Shanganagh still held their interest in transactions involving the former church holdings in Kiltiernan in September 1577 (*Cal. Pembroke*, No. 266, 88). That same month John, in tandem with Richard Basnet of Kiltiernan, had to post a bond to the value of £1,200 in favour of Thomas FitzWilliams of Merrion (*ibid.*, No. 268, 89). On 30 January 1575 John Walsh of *Sanganaghe* had been a beneficiary, along with Sir Thomas FitzWilliams, of a grant of a castle and lands by James Goodman of *Laghnanston* (Loughlinstown) (Griffith 1991, 284, 402). Witnesses to a will made by Goodman on 14 February 1589 included Walter Walsh and Gerrod Walsh (*ibid.*, 285 fn. 3).

It was not all negative as far as the authorities in Dublin were concerned. In 1574 John Walsh was amongst the luminaries of the county commissioned 'to muster and array the inhabitants of the County Dublin' (*Fiants*, II, No. 2444, 323). He was called upon to repeat the service in 1583 (*ibid.*, No. 4148, 580) and again in 1585–6 (*ibid.*, No. 4820, 726). The privy council on 12 May 1581 registered a recognisance of £100 in the case of Roland Goodman, and £50 each by his guarantors Apoloner Talbot and William Goodman. Roland was to keep the peace towards all men 'but particularly towards John Walsh of the *Shanganah*' (Prendergast and Quinn 1967, 118). In 1596 John was listed as being amongst the leading men of the barony of Rathdown (Brewer and Bullen 1867–73, III, 189). 'Walshe of *Shaunogherghe*' appeared amongst the 'Men of name in (the) Countie' in 1598 (Hogan 1878, 38). John died in 1600 (Ball 1902–17, III, 89). He had been married to Rose (*Reix*) Goodman of Loughlinstown (Griffith 1991, 466), who died in July 1609 and was buried in Rathmichael graveyard. They had eight children: Walter, Symon, James, Edmunde, Joan, Margerie, Margaret and Marion. Joan (a.k.a. Jane) married Gerald Fitzgerald of *Allon* in County Kildare, Margerie married John Delahide of *Belantrie* and Margaret married Henry, the eldest son of Theobald Walsh of Killincarrig. Marion was unmarried in 1609 (Genealogical Office MS 66, 16, 92).

Walter and Symon, the two eldest sons, would appear to have died in the time of their father. Walter was married to a Mary Cartye (*alias* 'Garvy', *alias* 'Tole', i.e. O'Toole) (Griffith 1991, 466). On 1 May 1593 Barnabas O'Toole of Castlekevin in County Wicklow had made a grant of a sizeable inventory of lands to Peter Walsh of *Kilgobane*, Theobald Walsh of *Killenecarig* (Killincarrig) and Walter Walsh of Shanganagh. A deed made by O'Toole was witnessed by, amongst others, a Gerald Walsh (*ibid.*, 306 fn. 1). Another deed by O'Toole was witnessed by a John Walsh (*ibid.*, 306 fn. 4).

It was thus John's younger son James who inherited Shanganagh in 1600 (Hardiman 1826–9, I, Car. 1, No. 29). At the beginning of the seventeenth century James Walsh was seised of 'the inheritance' of one castle, ten messuages, one watermill, 173 acres of arable land, ten acres of meadow, and 30 acres of pasture in Shanganagh and *Kilturke* (held from Peter Talbot of the manor of Rathdown); one castle, ten messuages, 140 acres of arable land, twenty acres of woodland, five acres of meadow and 40 acres of pasture in *Conagh* (Old Connaught); ten messuages, 70 acres of arable land, six acres of meadow and ten acres of pasture in '*Corke alias Corcagh*' (Cork); and three messuages, 24 acres of arable land and ten acres of pasture in Little Bray (held of the manor of Bray)—a very impressive estate built up over the preceding century (even allowing for the inevitable claims, in this instance from Patrick Barnewall of Shankill, the vicars choral of St Patrick's Cathedral and Patrick Archbold of *Kenleston*, i.e. Kindleston in County Wicklow) (Hardiman 1826–9, I, Jac. 1, No. 16).

THE WALSHES OF BALALLY

On 11 March 1400 the Crown granted 'Henry Adamesone' of *Cairykmayn* parcels of lands in *Baulyhaule* (Balally), *Balyhamond* (Edmondstown), *Balytyr* (Balinteer) and *Balymargy* (*Cal. pat. rolls, Henry IV*, 237). His son William was confirmed in these lands (minus *Balymargy*) on 29 October 1407, 'before the Feast of St Martin'. The annual rent was set at six marks (Hunter 1834, 45). A subsequent patent, dated 27 April 1431, establishes that the name of William's son and heir was Henry. The original document was referenced and the annual rent of six marks reiterated. The three place-names were rendered *Ballyhawly*, *Ballyhamond* and *Ballytir*. An interesting aspect of the latter document is that it reveals how William had committed himself to constructing a 'fortalicio', a fortalice or fortress (i.e. a castle), on the land at Balally but that it was unfinished (*sed non finito*), as he had died within three years of undertaking the work. Finally, it indicated that a Howell Walsh would be in the line of succession to Henry (Tresham 1828, 249).

Work on the fortalice was eventually completed after 'a considerable time (had) elapsed' (Ball 1902–17, II, 74). In 1481 Ballally was still being listed as a holding of the Walshes of Carrickmines (see above). Its autonomy would appear to have been gained, or more likely granted, by the time William Walsh inherited Carrickmines in 1537. The first documented incumbent, Thomas Walsh, must have been a very close relative of William—perhaps a brother(?).

A jury was convened on 9 August 1541 to determine the extent of Castlekevin and Ferter, and one of the jurors was Thomas Walsh of *Bunolawley* (Griffith 1991, 92). On 8 February 1543 Thomas Walsh of *Balawle* again served as a juror, on this occasion in a case dealing with the properties of the 'Nunnery of Hogges' (*ibid.*, 98 fn. 3). St Mary de Hogges had been founded in 1146 under the patronage of Diarmait MacMurrough, king of Leinster. It was sited 'without the walls', to the immediate east of Dublin city. Its location would be in the vicinity of the more recent St Andrew's Church. This confiscated Augustinian house was granted by King Edward VI in 1552 to James Segrave (Wilson 1786, xvii; Warburton *et al.* 1818, I, 369–70).

An inquisition dating from 11 July 1545 documented the extent of the Balally estate: a castle, three messuages and eight acres in Balally, and one messuage and 80 acres in *Ballyhammond* (Edmondstown). The latter property had been leased to a Peter Talbot in 1543. It was recorded that Thomas Walsh died on 10 August that year (Griffith 1991, 108). As his son and heir John was only six years old, 'all the manors, lands, and possessions', the wardship and marriage rights of John were placed in the custody of his cousin William Walsh of Carrickmines. William was also to receive 'the value of (John's) marriage' should he decline the proffered prospective bride(s) (Morrin 1861–2, I, 120).

John received livery of his lands in *Ballaule* and *Balliemon* in 1561. The fine was set at £3 6s. 8d. (*Fiants*, II, No. 357, 40). John (of *Balleawle*) was pardoned along with a number of Walsh kinsmen in February/March 1570/1 (*ibid.*, No. 1783, 240).

John Walsh of *Ballawlie* was named as a leading citizen of the barony of Rathdown in 1596 (Brewer and Bullen 1867–73, III, 189; Hogan 1878, 38 fn.). He granted *Ballawly* and *Edmondston* to Peter Barnewall of *Drumnigh*, 'to certain uses', on 10 November 1605 (Griffith 1991, 387). John had two encounters with the authorities in 1611. On 12 May Thomas Hibbotts received a grant 'of all intrusions or alienations, without licence, and wardships heretofore committed or done, or due to the Crown out of or by reason of any of the lands and hereditaments of [amongst many others] John Walshe of *Ballawlie* in Dublin county' (*Cal. pat. rolls chancery*, 176). Again, on 1 October it was found that John owed the exchequer £3 6s. 8d. (Brewer and Bullen 1867–73, VI, 116). The sum of money is noteworthy (see above).

John died on 10 May 1615. He had been married first to Joan, the daughter of Theobald Archbold of Templecarrig. They had three children, James, Richard and

Margaret. He subsequently married Elizabeth Rochfort (Genealogical Office MS 66, 49). By 1615 James was 34 years old and married, and his son and heir was identified as Henry (Griffith 1991, 387).

MUNSTER

The province of Munster was to be riven by the First Desmond Rebellion, which erupted in the summer of 1569. The *de facto* leader was James fitz Maurice Fitzgerald, the cousin of Gerald fitz James, fifteenth earl of Desmond. James purported to be acting on behalf of the earl but in fact was placing him in mortal danger. The earl had been held in the Tower of London since December 1567 and his attempts to return home now looked doomed. It is no exaggeration to say that only the queen's belief in his innocence and loyalty saved him from the gallows that summer (Edwards 2017, 345).

On 17 June the mayor and officers of Cork wrote to the lord deputy requesting 'speedy succour' from the 'malefactors' (Hamilton 1860, 409). They wrote to him again on 20 June. The rebels were threatening both Cork and Kinsale and there were many rumours of help arriving for them from Spain. In 1571 James fitz Maurice took Kilmallock. His followers thoroughly plundered the town, demolished houses of wood and stone and set fire to the ruins. The devastated town became the abode of wolves (O'Donovan 1854, V, 1654–5). The mayor noted that the Butlers were now part of the confederation (Hamilton 1860, 409). The State struck back hard. Humphrey Gilbert adopted a scorched-earth approach, destroying all the corn and slaughtering all the cattle in the surrounding territories; his forces alone took 30 Desmond castles (Brady 1997, 140). The Annals of the Four Masters, *s.a.* 1569, credited the 'great hosting' led by Sir Henry Sidney as eventually returning home 'after victory and triumph' (O'Donovan 1854, V, 1632–3). Fitz Maurice's pleas for Continental aid to support his Catholic crusade came to naught.

In early 1573 the earl of Desmond finally convinced Elizabeth of his full commitment to her cause. He did not make his declarations lightly. When he departed for Dublin he left behind his only son. The toddler, James fitz Gerald, had been born in London and would now reside in the care of Robert Dudley, earl of Leicester, then the queen's favourite (Edwards 2017, 346).

James fitz Maurice finally submitted to Sir John Perrot, the president of Munster, in February 1573 (Hamilton 1860, 496; O'Donovan 1854, V, 1664–5). Desmond's return to Munster in November quenched the embers of fitz Maurice's cause. Crucially, fitz Maurice had been deprived of his sound economic bases and with the return of the earl was now denied any access to broader resources. He departed for the Continent in March 1575. Desmond had dutifully reported his cousin's imminent departure to the relevant authorities (Edwards 2017, 357–8).

LEINSTER

In Leinster Sir Edmund Butler, Ormond's brother, had joined in the fray largely as a reaction to the audacious attempt by Sir Peter Carew to lay claim to his castle and estate at *Cloghgrenan* (Clogrennane) in County Carlow (Hamilton 1860, 420; Maclean 1857, 87). With the support of his brothers Piers and Edward, he conducted a devastating campaign in south Leinster. On 2 June 1569 Edward Langham wrote to the lord deputy to report that Sir Edmund had spread the story that not only had his brother the earl been put to death but so had the queen! This was his ploy to increase support. Carlow town was now under threat but he, Langham, would organise its defence (Hamilton 1860, 410). On 1 July Francis Cosbie wrote to the lord deputy from Stradbally, Co. Leix. He reported that Sir Edmund and his brothers had on the previous night torched the town and some others in the area (*ibid.*, 412). Sir Peter Carew, taking advantage of his military commission in the rebellion, laid siege to and took Clogrennane Castle from Butler's garrison in July 1569 (Maclean 1857, 92–3).

Ormond himself was in a bind but ultimately chose the path of discretion. In order to protect the family's assets, interests and future, he threw in his lot with the lord deputy. Sir Edmund duly surrendered in September 1569 and was imprisoned in Dublin Castle. When all seemed lost, he was daringly assisted by Feagh Mac Hugh O'Byrne and managed to escape. He would die while still on the run in 1602. The destructive exploits of the Butler brothers undoubtedly did no favours to the family's ambition to exploit the fall of the Fitzgeralds. The O'Byrnes of Ballinacor, for one, were not slow to take advantage of the resulting power vacuum.

An inquisition dated 14 April 1570 recorded that William Walsh had died on 29 September 1569. Emmett O'Byrne (2003b, 251) has suggested that he may have lived until 1573 on the basis of a government document dated 29 December 1572 that portrays William Walsh of Carrickmines and his sons, along with their relatives in Brenanstown, Kilgobbin, Ballaly and Shanganagh, as being in league with the mountain chieftains (*ibid.*, 250). William's holdings at the time of his death included the manor of Carrickmines (containing an estimated 310 acres and a watermill), one messuage and 40 acres in *Anowdan* (including the vill of *Ballerowe*), all 'held in chief by knight's service'; 73 acres in Oldcourt (held from the earl of Ormond); and 36 acres in *Ballycrompe alias Crompeston* (Griffith 1991, 196).

Sir Francis Agarde, seneschal of the O'Byrne and O'Toole territories, died in 1577 and was replaced by his son-in-law, Sir Henry Harrington (Maginn 2005, 136). In the eyes of the Dublin authorities Agarde had not lived up to the job, a government report relating how he had given the Gaelic chieftains 'so much liberty, being seneschal of them, that now he cannot command them' (Mahaffy 1912, 597). Harrington was a nephew of Lord Deputy Sidney and related by marriage to two other deputies, the earl of Sussex and Sir William Fitzwilliam (Nicholls 1998a, 33). He was more brutal in his approach, employing martial law and methods to the hilt (Donovan 1998, 134). Harrington and his son, who succeeded him, were to effectively rule in their dominion for almost half a century (Nicholls 1998a, 38).

Richard, son and heir of William Walsh of Carrickmines, was of full age and married when his father died in 1569 (Griffith 1991, 63). On 29 January 1546 Edward Basnet had granted to Richard ('and others') the castle, twenty messuages and cottages, and 120 acres of *Glancullyn* (Glencullen) and *Mangan McTyre*; 120 acres of 'stony mountain' in *Kyltiernan* (Kiltiernan); and the 'Old Grange of *Kylcullyn*, *Betaghton*, and *Ballycakan*, all parcels of *Kyltiernan*, and the church and rectory of *Kyltiernan*', all to be held 'in chief by knight service' (*ibid.*, 141). William Walsh had put this deal in place for his young son (*Cal. Pembroke*, No. 227, 74). The Edward Basnet in question was the (aforementioned) dean of St Patrick's Cathedral, who, it would appear, died during the suppression of the cathedral in the first year of the reign of Queen Mary (31 January 1554). It should be recalled that Richard's sister Joan had been his concubine. The value of these holdings was 160s. a year (Mason 1820, 151 fn. m). The Carrickmines-centred holdings held by his father (see above) were later also held by Richard (Griffith 1991, 254). He received livery on 12 November 1572. The fine was set at £5 10s. (*Fiants*, II, No. 2166, 277). On the available evidence, he would appear to have been less expansionist than his father in terms of land acquisition. He was apparently involved in some low-profile transgressions. He was pardoned, along with Thomas Fitzwilliam of Merrion, James Goodman of Loughlinstown, his cousin John Walsh of Shanganagh, and his brothers Robert Walsh of *Ballenelowre* (Leopardstown) and Owen (Howell) Walsh of *Ballybrenan* (Brenanstown). Edmund Walsh, Philip O'Byrne and others were also included in the pardon, dated 7 December 1574 (*ibid.*, No. 2534, 336). Richard did have a brother Edmund but it is not clear whether this was the man in question. Thomas Fitzwilliam of Merrion would have been a first cousin of Richard. The nature of the transgression was unspecified. The pardon was classified as being 'in general terms' (*Cal. Pembroke*, No. 265, 87). Another pardon, granted on 10 September 1577, described him as 'Richard Walshe, son and heir of William Walshe, late of *Karrickmayne*'. The 'late' must pertain to William, as Richard was to live another three years. His cousin John Walsh of Shanganagh (see above) was also pardoned. Along with Thomas Fitzwilliam (see above), Richard Basnet of Kiltiernan and Edward Barnewall of *Dromnagh* (Drimnagh), they had been indicted for 'intrusions and alienations' of the lands and rectory of Kiltiernan (*Fiants*, II, No. 3098, 420). Richard and his cousin John of Shanganagh still held an interest in the former church lands at Kiltiernan in September 1577 (*Cal. Pembroke*, No. 266, 88). When the paperwork was being processed on 6 September there was an Oliver Walsh in attendance, possibly Richard's son.

Nevertheless, William retained his good standing with the government. In 1573 he was amongst the leading men called upon 'to take the muster and array of the inhabitants of the county Dublin' (*Fiants*, II, No. 2345, 307). It is in this context that we should view the 'footman' he retained at Carrickmines. The man in question, Nicholas Archbold, probably served in a military capacity rather than in a domestic role. A contemporary member of the household in 1577 named Owen fulfilled a more aesthetic role: he was a piper (*ibid.*, No. 3151, 429). It is possible, however, that Owen may have played a dual role because in 1566 he was described as a kern, i.e. a fighting man (*ibid.*, No. 856, 93). In that light the group of individuals listed in *Fiants* No. 3151 could be interpreted as a

Walsh fighting group. The pardon in question was granted to John Walsh of Shanganagh, who is described as a former sheriff of the county, along with (a brother?) Gerald Walsh and Nicholas and Shane McHugh, two other residents of Shanganagh. The latter pair, along with Owell Boy of Little Bray and Hebbart McMorish of *Connogher* (Old Connaught?), in addition to the (aforementioned) Nicholas Archbold and Owen Piper could all have served as kerns.

Richard was married to Eleanor Eustace of Clongowes Wood (TCD MS 1212, 26) in County Kildare, from a branch of a distinguished old settler family. She was also referred to as Elizabeth (*ibid.*, 93). His brothers Howell and Edmund were married to Esmay Talbot (of Belgard) and Isobel Talbot (of *Cromlin*) (Genealogical Office MS 48, 20). According to a pedigree of the Talbot family of Belgard, a brother of Esmay (who it is confirmed was married to 'Howell Walshe of the house of *Carrickmayne*') named Polymer was married to a Margaret Walsh, also of the house of *Carrickmayne* (*ibid.*, 33). This would strongly suggest that Howell and Margaret were siblings. It should be noted in passing that Margaret, the eldest sister of Esmay and Polymer Talbot, was married to Felim O'Toole of Powerscourt (*ibid.*). Richard's sisters Katherine and Joan were married respectively to John Walsh of the Kilgobbin branch (Genealogical Office MS 66, 68) and Walter Walsh of the Shanganagh branch (Griffith 1991, 130). A fourth sister, called Elizabeth, was married to William Seagrave of Cabragh (Genealogical Office MS 47, 19). All these families were of old settler stock. In stark contrast, their brother Robert was, as noted above, married to Honora (a.k.a. Margaret), the daughter of none other than Hugh Mac Shane O'Byrne (Nicholls 1998b, 111). Robert and Honora were domiciled at *Ballynalour* (modern Leopardstown), Co. Dublin. 'His male issue by her [were] all extincte' by 1610 (Genealogical Office MS 48, 20). Howell and Esmay set up home in the adjoining (to Carrickmines) townland of Brenanstown. They 'begate many daughters' (*ibid.*). Edmund and Isobel were living on the family holding in Phrompstown. Ball (1902, 125) noted that a fortified dwelling occupied by a member of the Walsh family stood there in the sixteenth century. It can be seen that the family did not stray from settler stock in terms of bloodline and geography except for the clearly expeditiously arranged tactical marriage of Robert to a very well-connected O'Byrne. A privy council record dated 3 May 1582 referred to Eleanor Eustace as the 'late wife of Richard Walshe' (Prendergast and Quinn 1967, 128). Richard died on 10 July 1580 (Griffith 1991, 255).

At 28 years of age Theobald Walsh, the eldest of Richard and Eleanor's seven sons (the others being Oliver, Henry, Maurice, Edward, Gerrot and William), inherited the Carrickmines manor on the death of his father. Theobald, to judge by the extant documentation, would appear to have lived a relatively quiet life at Carrickmines despite the ongoing turbulent situation in the nearby Wicklow Mountains and beyond. Not that he was immune from trouble. In 1574 a Tybbot (i.e. Theobald) Walsh was indicted on a charge of 'riot', along with Richard Flynn, John Garrahall 'and others'. On 5 May Tybbott 'and fifteen others' were acquitted 'with allowance of costs'. On 14 May there was a renewed order for their discharge (HMC 1905–9, I (1), 2). This may well be Theobald of Carrickmines, but one must allow for the fact that Theobald Walsh of

Killincarrig was to be granted a pardon eight years later in 1582 (*Fiants*, II, No. 3991, 552). He received a pardon again in 1578, along with Thomas Fitzwilliam of Merrion (*ibid.*, No. 3495, 481). On 10 April 1581 Theobald Walsh of Carrickmines and William Barnewall, a merchant from Dublin, legally guaranteed the appearance before the lord deputy of Mary Peppard of *Glascarrick* in County Wexford by entering into a recognisance of £100 each. This recognisance was cancelled before the lord deputy and council on 25 November 1584 (Prendergast and Quinn 1967, 114). Mary was the wife of Anthony Peppard, whose father, Walter Peppard of Kilkea, Co. Kildare (Fitzgerald 1896, 12), also held properties in counties Leix, Dublin and Wexford and had acquired the monastic estate of Glascarrig in 1550 (Hore 1900–11, VI, 147). Walter had become embroiled in financial complications and died in October 1565 (Hamilton 1860, 277). His son Anthony petitioned the privy council on his own behalf and on behalf of his mother for leave to take legal proceedings against those who 'did spoil them of £4,000' (*ibid.*, 306). The amount of money involved gives a good insight into the scale of the family's commercial dealings, which included mining (*ibid.*, 209, 236). It is possible that the recognisance entered into by Theobald Walsh in 1581 is an indication that the Peppard's financial disputes were long-running. How Theobald knew the family is not revealed. A John Eustace pledged security for Walter Peppard in 1562 (Fitzgerald 1896, 12), and given the Walshes' many connections with the Eustaces it was possibly through this family that the association originated.

Like his father and grandfather before him, Theobald was regarded as one of the loyalists who could be called upon to 'take the muster and array of the county', i.e. to raise and provide troops for the Dublin authorities, as he was called to do in July 1584 (*Fiants*, II, No. 4462, 630).

Theobald's wife, Eleanor Fitzwilliam, was described in 1610 by Daniel Molyneux (Ulster King of Arms) as the daughter of Michael Fitzwilliam of *Donamore*, the 'Surveiour of the Queenes landes' (Genealogical Office MS 48, 21). The lord deputy in December 1552 referred to Michael Fitzwilliam as general surveyor of Ireland (Hamilton 1860, 129), and in July 1571 he is referred to as surveyor of her majesty's lands (*ibid.*, 491). The *Donamore* in question is Donaghmore, Co. Meath (see above). Theobald and Eleanor were second cousins.

In addition to the six brothers already named, Theobald had three sisters, Joan, Anne and Margaret (Genealogical Office MS 48, 21). The marriages of the ten siblings provide an invaluable insight into the political and cultural affiliations of the Walshes of Carrickmines during this period. Oliver was married to Anne Eustace of the house of Rosberry, Co. Kildare (located to the north-west of Newbridge), while his sister Joan was the wife of the Honourable Edmund Eustace of Baltinglass, Co. Wicklow. Maurice was the husband of Mary Fitzgerald of 'Newton [Newtown] near Harolds Grange', and Edward was married to Elizabeth Booth from Dunham in Cheshire. Gerrot was married to Thomasina, the daughter of Richard Rownswell, who served two terms as mayor of Dublin (1578–9 and 1586–7), and Anne to Robert Barnewall of Shankill Castle. Robert had 'a base sonne' named Nicholas who married Honora, the daughter of Edmund Walsh of Shanganagh (Genealogical Office MS 48, 14; Griffith 1991, 299). The marriages of

Theobald's other two brothers stand in stark contrast. While Henry was married to Dorothy, the daughter of 'Mac Ô More' of the county of *Weysford* (Wexford), his brother William was married to Mary, a 'base' daughter of Sir Henry Harrington, the English-born government-appointed seneschal of the O'Byrnes' and O'Tooles' territories. A Phelim Mc Da More is recorded in north County Wexford in 1611–13 and again in 1614, with a Redmond Mc Da More also being documented in the latter year (Griffiths 1890, 280; Hickson 1884, II, Appendix C, 273). A Henry 'Welshe' of *Clonrawne* received a pardon in 1601 (*DKR 17* (1885), 255–6). Henry Walsh of *Clonranye* was listed as one of 'the Gentlemen of *Gwery*' in July 1608 (Carew MS 600, 136). He was scheduled to lose 90 of his 220 acres in the plantation scheme of 1614 (Hickson 1884, II, Appendix C, 273). Cloneranny, in the barony of Gorey, is located in north-east County Wexford, close to the Wicklow border. Theobald's youngest sister, Margaret, was documented in the genealogical record of her mother's death (Genealogical Office MS 66, 42). It is interesting to note that there had been a shift in marriage partner selection from the previous generation. While the old English settler stock is still well represented by the two Eustaces, Fitzgerald, Barnewell and Fitzwilliam, and there was one marriage to a woman of an Irish background, there were two marriages (if not three) to individuals with distinctively 'new' English lineages. Elizabeth Booth was the daughter of Sir William Booth and his wife Elizabeth Warburton. Her brother, Sir George, was the grandfather of George, a prominent supporter of parliament but ultimately a player in the restoration of Charles II. He was to be created first Baron Delamere at the coronation of the king (Ormerod 1819, I, 402–3). Moreover, Elizabeth Booth and most likely Thomasina Rownswell were Protestants, and the natural daughter of Harrington was possibly Protestant, depending on the background of her unnamed mother. Edward and Elizabeth were settled in Clonmannan, Co. Wicklow. Their holding consisted of 825 acres 'besides bog' (*DKR 19* (1887), 36). Clonmannan is on the coast to the south of Newcastle and to the north of Wicklow. It was located within Críoch Branach and, importantly, within the administrative zone of the father-in-law of Edward's brother William, i.e. the seneschal Sir Henry Harrington.

The year of Richard's death at Carrickmines witnessed the next major upheaval in the region. Hugh Mac Shane O'Byrne had died in 1579, leaving his son Feagh in full control of the Gabhal Raghnaill sept. That same year the second Viscount Baltinglass also died. James Eustace, the third viscount, despite an education in England, was heavily influenced by the Counter-Reformation, and a trip to Rome heightened his zeal (Maginn 2005, 154). The outbreak of rebellion in Munster was the impulse that was needed.

THE SECOND DESMOND REBELLION

The Second Desmond Rebellion broke out in July 1579 with the return of James fitz Maurice Fitzgerald accompanied by an expeditionary force of papal troops. On 16 July Sir Owen O'Sullivan had reported the appearance of 'six ships well appointed' off the coast (Hamilton 1867–90, II, 172). He subsequently reported that fitz Maurice had landed on 18 July at 'the Dingle'. By 22 July the earl of Desmond had written to the lord justice declaring that he was ready to take immediate action against the invaders and simply awaited instruction (*ibid.*, 173). Fitz Maurice had laboured hard to secure assistance on the Continent. Pope Gregory XIII had finally been swayed by his intercessions, and the expedition of four ships had set forth from Galicia, followed by an additional two ships. The trouble for the earl was that, besides the Spanish, Italian and Basque soldiers, fitz Maurice was accompanied by Dr Nicholas Sander, an English Catholic priest and scholar and the papal envoy to the Irish rebels (Tait 2007, 130). He had been a long-time vocal critic and antagonist of the queen, and his movements and associations on the Continent had been closely monitored (Hamilton 1867–90, II, 172; Tait 2007, 133). His arrival in Ireland electrified the government and guaranteed a determined and vicious response. As nobody seemed inclined to express sufficient confidence in the earl, it was inevitable that he would be sidelined in the forthcoming conflict (Edwards 2017, 372).

Sir John Fitzgerald and Sir James Fitzgerald, brothers of the earl, joined the rebellion at the beginning of August (Hamilton 1867–90, II, 178). By 23 July fitz Maurice had been killed in a skirmish (*ibid.*, 182). The hunt for the 'papistical arrogant traitor Sander' continued (*ibid.*, 190); he was to die of exposure in the winter of 1581–2. Edwards (2017, 368) has written that the tipping point for the government was probably Desmond's failure to disband his private army. This had been one of the 'Articles to be observed by the earl' laid down back in January 1573 (Hamilton 1860, 492). Proclaimed a traitor on 2 November, he was in truth pushed into rebellion (Edwards 2017, 376).

In July 1580 Feagh Mac Hugh O'Byrne and Viscount Baltinglass rose in support of Munster. On 12 August Arthur Grey, fourteenth Baron Grey de Wilton, the new lord deputy, landed in Ireland with a sizeable army of over 2,000 troops (Maginn 2005, 158–60). His attempt to quickly remove the Leinster rebels from the conflict ended disastrously on 25 August at the Battle of Glenmalure. O'Byrne and Baltinglass routed the government force, which lost around 800 men (O'Byrne 1998b). This success was followed by sporadic raiding and clashes—for example, O'Byrne burned Rathcoole and Coolmine close to Dublin on 19 October (Hamilton 1867–90, II, 263)—but no other significant victories were to follow.

The massacre of 500–600 of the papal troops who had landed at Smerwick in September effectively turned the tide in Munster. Amongst the English officers was one Captain Walter Raleigh, who reportedly was employed in the executions (Carey 2007, 84). The colonel in charge of the papal troops, Sebastian da San Giuseppe, was kept alive, along with 20–30 of his officers, and allowed to return to Spain to dissuade any others from coming to Ireland (Hamilton 1867–90, II, 267). The scorched-earth policy adopted by Grey resulted in famine, disease and death across Munster. Sir Warham Sentleger, provost marshal of Munster, wrote in April 1582 to the queen to express his deep reservations about the policy. He reported the deaths of more than 30,000 people across the province from famine (*ibid.*, 361). In 1581 Elizabeth had concluded that a general pardon would be less expensive than wide-scale repression. She instructed Grey not to incite any costly trouble. In effect his efforts were being neutralised. As a result, his recall in 1582 did not disappoint or upset him (*ODNB*, XXIII, 807). In reality, however, his work was done: the rebellion collapsed.

The Annals of the Four Masters *s.a.* 1581 presented an overview: 'The English and the Geraldines were at war and strife with each other; nor was there a truce of one night, or a friendship of one month, between them, from the commencement of the war to this time. No account, enumeration, or description of the injuries done between them can be attempted' (O'Donovan 1854, V, 1754–5). Baltinglass fled to France in late October 1581 (Maginn 2005, 175). His brother Edmund fled to Scotland in June 1583 (Hamilton 1867–90, II, 451). The earl of Desmond, after a long time on the run, was cornered on Monday 11 November 1583 in a hut in a cavern in the Glanageenty Woods near Castlemaine in modern Kerry. The five-man patrol from the nearby garrison was commanded by Owen Mac Donnell O'Moriarty. Upon discovery the earl was beheaded, it is believed, by the reward-seeking Daniel O'Kelly. The earl of Ormond displayed no signs of regret: 'So now is this traytor com to the ende I have longe looked for, appointed by God to dye by the sword to ende his rebellion' (Hamilton 1867–90, II, 478; O'Donovan 1854, V, 1794–5, 1794 fn. a; *ODNB*, XIX, 810). Feagh Mac Hugh O'Byrne had submitted in November 1582 (O'Byrne 2003a, 207).

The fall of the Eustaces of Baltinglass would have had some impact on the Walshes of Carrickmines. The main victim would have been Theobald Walsh's sister Joan. She was married to the viscount's brother Edmund, who, as noted above, had fled to Scotland and she would accordingly have lost her home. She was a survivor, however, as is evident by the fact that she remarried. Her second husband was Dermot Mac Maurice Kavanagh of *Knockangarw* (described by Molyneux in 1610 as 'current') (Genealogical Office MS 48, 21). The suggestion of a third husband by Hussey Walsh (1900–1, 218) is confusing. In the paper in question he is identified as Kavanagh of *Knockangan*, while her second husband is named as Dermot Fitzmaurice! These 'two' men are therefore probably one and the same. An Elizabethan fiant dating from 1592 refers to a holding in County Wexford bearing the name '*Knockanegall*' (*Fiants*, III, No. 1994, 192). Knockangall is a townland in the barony of Forth in Wexford. Joan's mother was a Eustace of Clongowes Wood, Co. Kildare, who lived until 1616 (Genealogical Office MS 66, 42). This branch was an offshoot of the Castlemartin line (Devitt 1899–1902, 211). According to a manuscript compiled by a Brother Eustace, Alexander Eustace of Clongowes Wood was married to a Mary O'Byrne, while his two sons were married to an O'Toole and a Kavanagh respectively. Despite these connections the Clongowes Wood Eustaces apparently took little or no part in the rebellion. This is suggested by the fact that they suffered no confiscations in its wake (*ibid.*, 212). Joan's brother Oliver was married to Anne Eustace of Rosberry, Co. Kildare. The second wife of Theobald Walsh of the Killincarrig branch was Jane Eustace of Ballymore (Eustace) (Genealogical Office MS 66, 103).

In 1591 the Walshes were listed along with their 'cousins german' the Fitzwilliams (of Merrion) and other families considered to be the 'men of power' in Leinster and Meath. They were the only listed family, however, that came with a caveat. Some of the Walshes, it was noted, were 'matched in marriage with the Byrnes and Toohels (O'Tooles)' and thus 'bear secretly with them' (Mahaffy 1912, 597). Which branch of the family was under suspicion was not specified. Theobald Walsh of Carrickmines passed away at the age of 41 on 17 November 1593 (Griffiths 1991, 296). The inquisition that recorded his death also indicated that the 'manor of *Carrickmaine*' had diminished in size: 310 acres in Carrickmines (including a watermill), two messuages and 40 acres in *Annondan* and *Ballinrowe*, a watermill in Oldcourt (held from Thomas, the earl of Ormond) and 66 acres held in '*Balli* [...] *alias Crompeston*' (*ibid.*, 295–6). This reduced estate was to be inherited by Richard, the eldest son of Theobald and Eleanor.

Richard was a minor when he came into his inheritance. According to a chancery inquisition he was only ten years of age (and 'unmarried') (Hardiman 1826–9, II, No. 20). His 'wardship and marriage' and the 'custody of his lands' were accordingly awarded to Peter Barnewall of Lispopple in north County Dublin (it lies to the north-east of Kilsallaghan) on 8 November 1595. The rent on the land during Richard's minority was £7 (Irish). The fine was £15 (English) (*Fiants*, III, No. 5966, 261).

THE WALSHES OF KILGOBBIN

Kilgobbin was held by the Harolds from the Hackets from the early years of the thirteenth century (Mills 1894, 166; Curtis 1910, 118). Other tenants appeared later. In February 1440 a raiding party led by Thomas fitz Maurice Fitzgerald and 'Brian O'Brynne' swooped on *Kylgoban*. Fitzgerald, later to become the seventh earl of Kildare, was then in dispute with the authorities. The second named individual was very likely Bran O'Byrne, the contemporary O'Byrne chieftain (Nicholls 1998a, 22). The raiders burned the wheat and corn stored 'in haggard and stacks'. The aggrieved owners of these goods were 'Murgh McHarry, James Walsh Adamesson and Richard O'Brothyr' (Curtis 1932–43, III, 119). The shared ownership and order of names suggests that the Walshes had not yet achieved dominance in Kilgobbin. The suffix to his given name, Adamesson, would indicate a Carrickmines connection for James Walsh. The founder of the dynasty at Carrickmines was 'Henry Adamesone' (Stamp 1927, 69). Could James and Henry have been brothers? If correct, this would confirm James as the founder of the Kilgobbin branch of the Walsh family.

A pedigree charted in 1610 originates with Maurice Walsh of *Kilgoban*, who was succeeded by his son 'Pierce or Peter' (Genealogical Office MS 48, 22). In 1476 an attack led by 'O'Byrne the King's Irish enemy' and Esmond Tibbot O'Toole rased more than half of the castle of Jamestown to the ground. This was the property of 'Morice Walshe of *Kilgoblin*' (Pl. 16). Jamestown is immediately adjacent to Kilgobbin along its eastern flank and this could have led to the designation. Maurice appealed for financial aid to rebuild the castle, claiming that he simply could not afford it. He was

Pl. 16—Kilgobbin Castle, Co. Dublin, as drawn by George Petrie. A tower-house of fifteenth-century date, built by the Walsh family.

duly awarded the levy of 'every ploughland' in the barony of Rathdown to achieve this aim (Morrissey 1939, 517). Amongst the men who entered into bonds with Holy Trinity on 27 March 1482 was 'Morice Walsh of *Gylgoban*' (*DKR 20* (1888), 96). It has been suggested that this Maurice was a 'servant' to the earl of Kildare (O'Byrne 2003b, 246 fn. 78). The root source of this suggestion, however, is not site-specific (Berry 1914, 445), and the Maurice referred to might not be the man from Kilgobbin but rather one of the Walshes of County Kildare.

A pardon was granted to the Walshes of Carrickmines and 'Thomas Walsh of Kilgobbin' in 1466 for 'divers offenses, trepasses and injuries' (*ibid.*, 399). Thomas, the son of Maurice Walsh of Kilgobbin, 'with all his sons' and many others were granted pardons in 1468/9 for 'divers and many extortions, oppressions, larcenies, robberies and taking of pledges' (*ibid.,* 445). On the basis of the dates, Thomas could have been an older brother of Piers/Peter who died before he could inherit Kilgobbin.

Piers/Peter was the occupant of Kilgobbin in 1509 (Ball 1902–17, III, 67). He was succeeded by his son Richard, who was married to Margaret, the daughter of John Harold of *Kilmahioke* (i.e. Kilmashogue in south County Dublin). On 8 February 1543 Richard (of *Kilgobban*) served, alongside Thomas Walsh of Balally, as a juror in an assessment of the extent of the nunnery of St Mary de Hogges (Griffith 1991, 98 fn. 3). He took advantage of the availability of church lands and in June 1547 leased the rectory of Kilgobbin with two acres and the tithes of corn, etc., extending to the 'towns' of Kilgobbin and Jamestown. The 21-year lease was at an annual rent of £3 1s. 4d. (*Fiants*, I, No. 47, 92). In April 1549 he was granted a pardon (*ibid.*, No. 268, 115). Richard and Margaret 'begat divers sonnes' but only the youngest son, John, survived. The others all died 'without legitimate issue' (Genealogical Office MS 48, 22).

John married Katherin, the daughter of William Walsh of Carrickmines. Patrick 'Archepoll' (Archbold) held the manor of *Bree* from the Crown. Financial need apparently obliged him to mortgage his lands in June 1560 to John Walsh of *Kilcobban* and James Goodman of *Ballylaghaan* (Loughlinstown) (Griffith 1991, 172). Patrick stipulated that his wife, Margaret Walsh, should have use of the lands in 'the *Breyes*' (i.e. Much Bray to the south and Little Bray to the north of the Bray River, the modern Dargle) for life (*ibid.*, fn. 1). The possibility must exist that Margaret was a sister of John Walsh. On 22 March 1576/7 John was appointed a commissioner, along with Sir Thomas Fitzwilliam, Sir William Sarsfield and others, to 'survey and make enquiry of all countries, territories, towns and vills, lying in the parts of Leinster from the Barrowe to the sea South and East'. We are told that all of the enclosed territory was 'in effecte waste and desolate other than inhabited with a fewe idell and evell-disposed persons'. The completed work of this commission would define the extent and boundaries of the new county of Wicklow (*Fiants*, II, No. 3003, 401).

John and Katherin had four sons and two daughters: Pierce, Nicholas, Christopher, Thomas, Anne and Margaret. The marriages of these offspring are notable (Genealogical Office MS 48, 22–3).

John died on 17 May 1578. He was 'said' to have held 'of the Queen', 'service unknown'. His son 'Piers' was aged eighteen and 'married' (Griffith 1991, 244). The Kilgobbin/Jamestown estate consisted of 300 acres at the time of his death. Peter/Pierce, his son and heir, was described as being eighteen years of age and unmarried ('*non maritat*') at the time (Hardiman 1826–9, II, No. 35) (see above). On 14 July 1578 a Christopher Wrenne was granted the wardship, marriage rights and custody of 'Piers' (Pierce). Wrenne was also granted custody of the Kilgobbin estate (*Fiants*, II, No. 3366, 461).

Pierce first married Elenor, the daughter of James Goodman of *Langhnanston* (Loughlinstown), and secondly Margaret, daughter of James Flatsbury of Johnstown, Co. Kildare. The Flatsbury family, long established in the county, also owned the adjacent land in Palmerstown (O'Hart 1887, 443). Pierce received a pardon in 1598–9 (*Fiants*, III, No. 6274, 332).

Nicholas, the second son, who was domiciled in Dundrum, was also married twice, firstly to Joan, the daughter of John Malone, an alderman in Dublin. Joan died in childbirth, as did their firstborn. His second wife was Ursula, the daughter of Captain Thomas Henshaw of Henshaw Hall, Siddington, Cheshire. Captain Henshaw served with the army in Ireland. He was garrisoned in *Knockfergus* (Carrickfergus, Co. Antrim) in October 1588 and July 1589, possibly continuously (Hamilton 1867–90, IV, 57, 226). In October 1591 he was appointed as seneschal in County Monaghan, with 100 soldiers at his service. Monaghan had been divided into eight chief lordships with 280 freeholders (*ibid.*, 428). On 30 December 1591 the lord deputy, William

Fitzwilliam, reported to Lord Burghley (the queen's chief adviser) that Monaghan was 'quiet … under Captain Thomas Henshaw' (*ibid.*, 446). In August 1598 Henshaw fell in battle at the Yellow Ford. He had commanded a company of English soldiers in the expeditionary force of 4,000 foot and 350 horse led by General Sir Henry Bagenal, who was also killed (Atkinson 1893–1905, VII, 224).

Ursula had also had an interesting first husband. On a blustery March day in 1597 a shipment of gunpowder was being unloaded at Wood Quay in Dublin. The wooden city crane, which was positioned above the Custom House, was transferring the last load of the 140 barrels of gunpowder from the boat to the quay when there was an enormous explosion. The clocks had just struck one o'clock and many people had already adjourned to the taverns of Winetavern Street or strolled home for some mid-day nourishment, and thus many lives were saved. Nevertheless, the death-toll of men, women and children came to 126 (76 citizens and 50 others). Structural damage at the junction of Wood Quay, Merchant's Quay and Winetavern Street was extensive; 20–40 houses were levelled, and the city crane and the Custom House (along with the family of the crane operator, Stephen Sedgrave, who lived on the premises) were blown to pieces (Lennon 1995, 29; 2001, 46).

In the aftermath the 'blame game' got into full swing. John Allen, clerk of the munitions storehouse, had been in charge of the operation. On 28 February the lords justices Loftus and Gardener, the earl of Ormond and the rest of the council had written to the privy council in London to request that John Allen be supplied with the necessary munitions and 'sent with all convenient speed' back to Ireland (Atkinson 1893–1905, VII, 65). While the shipment was being unloaded, however, Allen and Alderman Nicholas Barran had adjourned to share a pot of ale (Lennon 1995, 30). To compound this dereliction of duty there was also the issue of a disgruntled workforce. When the mayor, Michael Chamberlain, conducted hearings on 20 March, it emerged that 'divers porters' had been working whole days under duress with little or no pay from Allen (*ibid.*, VI, 245). Whilst John Shelton and Alexander Pallas, the sheriffs of the city of Dublin, could testify to legitimate purchases of munitions, a search of Allen's house uncovered gunpowder and armour that may well have been on its way to private buyers (*ibid.*, 246; Lennon 1995, 32). Given that there was an ongoing war, this money-making under-the-counter dealing was totally unacceptable. Allen was duly imprisoned in Dublin Castle. The horror of the aftermath of the explosion and the shock of the raid on their home cannot have pleased his wife, Ursula Henshaw.

Ursula and her second husband Nicholas Walsh had two children, Luke and Katherin.

Christopher, the third son of John and Katherin Walsh, married Marion, the sister of Robert Talbot of Templeogue. Christopher received a pardon on 12 March 1602/3 (*Fiants*, III, No. 6772, 622) and another on 17 February 1613 (*Cal. pat. rolls chancery*, 239).

Thomas, the fourth son, was credited with being 'the father of divers bastardes' (Genealogical Office MS 48, 23).

The eldest daughter, Anne, was married to Christopher Garvey, son of the Revd

John Garvey. John Garvey was born in 1527 in Kilkenny and received a doctorate in Divinity at Oxford University (Crawford 1993, 46). He progressed through the ranks of the church, becoming dean of Christ Church in 1565. By 1573 he was a member of the Irish privy council. He was appointed archbishop of Armagh in 1589 while still being allowed to retain the deanery of Christ Church Cathedral (Coleman 1900, 328). Archbishop Garvey was known as being completely loyal to the monarchy (Crawford 1993, 456).

John and Katherin Walsh's younger daughter, Margaret, was married to John Mey of County Kildare.

The backgrounds of the spouses of John and Katherin's children may be described as predominantly Old English settler stock. Henshaw was 'new' English and Protestant, while the religious affiliation of Garvey, the archbishop's son, is unquestionable!

By 1596 'Peter' Walsh of Kilgobbin was listed amongst the leading citizens of the barony of Rathdown (Brewer and Bullen 1867–73, III, 189; Hogan 1878, 38 fn.). Peter Walsh of *Kilgobban* was seised of Jamestown, containing three messuages and 75 acres, held of the king by knight service. On 10 June 1619 Peter and his son and heir, John, and James Flatsbury of Palmerstown, his feoffee, transferred the lands to William Archbold of *Crookeston* (Crookstown, to the north-east of Athy) in County Kildare 'without licence' (Griffith 1991, 405). In a chancery inquisition dating from 1633 he was described as William Archbold *de Tyrnall in co' Kildar* (Hardiman 1826–9, II, No. 34).

Simpson (2003, 302) has drawn attention to the ongoing problems encountered by the Archbold family in proving title to their lands in the early seventeenth century. The disputes resulted in the holding of many inquisitions. It is in this context that the claim staked by 'Peter *alias* Pierce Walsh *de* Kilgobbin' on 10 April 1627 should be considered. The argument was based on a lease from Patrick Archbold. The inventory of lands was extensive: *Kenlyeston* (Kindlestown), containing one castle, ten messuages and 300 acres; *Balldonogh* (Ballydonagh), containing 40 acres; *Delgany alias Templedelgin* (Delgany), containing six messuages, a watermill and 200 acres; and *Coolegaddin* (Coolagad), containing 40 acres (Hardiman 1826–9, I, No. 4). This cluster of lands lies to the west of Greystones in north County Wicklow. Patrick's son Edward, a minor at the time of his father's death in 1624, divested the 'manor, castle, town and lands of Bray' to the earl of Meath. As Scott (1913, 148) noted, Patrick had left the estate 'hopelessly mortgaged'. The earl soon obtained possession of Kindlestown, Delgany and Coolagad (*ibid.*) simply by again buying up all the relevant mortgages (*ibid.*, 228).

THE NORTH

The short, uneasy peace in Ireland was again shattered by the unfolding events of 1593, 1594 and 1595. The northern Gaelic lords—Hugh O'Neill of Tír Eoghain (Pl. 17), Red Hugh O'Donnell of Tír Chonaill and Hugh Maguire of Fermanagh—were to the fore in the growing conflagration. The interests and futures of these three men were 'inextricably linked' (Morgan 1993, 139) (Map 7). Again, at the heart of the

Pl. 17—Hugh O'Neill (1550–1616), earl of Tyrone. (Lord Dunsany)

Map 7—General map of Ireland.

conflict were the rumbling twin causes of discontent: government infringements on local authority and the suppression of religious liberties.

O'Neill had in his youth been under the wardship of Giles Hovenden and his family in Leix (*ibid.*, 93) and was consequently regarded as being loyal and reliable. Although the parliament of 1585 decided to confer the earldom of Tyrone on him (*ibid.*, 102), his main objective was to be recognised as The O'Neill, the overlord of all the O'Neills. He finally achieved this aim in the autumn of 1595 (Foster 1988, 4; Morgan 2007, 115). The military build-up that followed was systematic and thorough (Hayes-McCoy 2011, 161). O'Neill recruited mercenaries and imported muskets and ammunition from abroad. All these preparations were made in collaboration with his close ally Red Hugh O'Donnell.

The lord deputy, Sir William Fitzwilliam, had meanwhile being toying with the idea of imposing a provincial president. To compound O'Neill's difficulties with the creation of such an office, the preferred candidate was Sir Henry Bagenal, a personal enemy of O'Neill's (Morgan 1993, 47, 60). Between 1589 and 1590 the government transformed the Oriel lordship into the county of Monaghan. Fitzwilliam arrested and hanged the ruling MacMahon chieftain (Morgan 2007, 107). Moves were also made against the O'Farrells of Longford and the O'Reillys of west Breifne. O'Neill and O'Donnell could only interpret these events as a tightening of the noose.

It was Hugh Maguire who made the first move. In 1593 he expelled Captain Humphrey Willis, the sheriff, from Fermanagh (*ibid.*, 108). O'Neill initially stood aside, still angling to secure the presidency of Ulster for himself. Queen Elizabeth opted to maintain her support for the reliable Bagenal. O'Neill responded by launching an attack on the English stronghold on the River Blackwater.

The government counter-attacked only to suffer a string of defeats, including the battles of Clontibret (March 1595) and the Yellow Ford (August 1598) (Morgan 1993, 179, 218). Henry Bagenal was amongst the many who fell in the latter engagement. The stunning victory at the Yellow Ford inspired an island-wide rebellion. The Pale remained loyal, however, despite overtures on religious grounds.

Elizabeth was determined to regain lost ground. Robert Devereux, the second earl of Essex and sometime favourite of the queen, was dispatched to Ireland at the head of an army 17,000 strong. Despite great fanfare, the expedition achieved nothing (managing to chalk up another defeat at the battle of the Curlew Pass) and Essex negotiated a truce with O'Neill. He returned, unsummoned, to London in 1599 and was executed after a move against the queen.

His replacement was Charles Blount, eighth lord Mountjoy (ably assisted by Sir George Carew and Sir Arthur Chichester). By the summer of 1601 Carew had quelled the rebellion in Munster.

A sea landing near 'the Derrie' under Sir Henry Docwra brought the war home to Ulster. This force, later to be augmented by dissident O'Donnells, could not be ignored (McGurk 2007, 122–3). Mountjoy attempted to exploit their deployment but was repulsed at the battle of Moyry Pass in the late autumn of 1600.

When the long-hoped-for help from Spain finally arrived in 1601 it landed at the wrong end of the island. O'Neill and O'Donnell were forced to march all the way to Kinsale in County Cork to relieve the besieged Spanish force of 3,500 troops. The ensuing encirclement of Mountjoy's army of 7,000 would have ultimately forced their surrender but O'Donnell opted to force the issue. The planned surprise attack was, however, routed by Mountjoy's cavalry. The Ulstermen's siege collapsed and the Spaniards surrendered.

The retreat to the north further weakened the Ulster forces through deprivation and appalling weather. Red Hugh O'Donnell departed for Spain to seek further aid. He was dead by 1602. Meanwhile, back in Ulster the food shortages resulting from the ongoing destructive sweeps by the government had resulted in widespread famine (McGurk 2007, 123).

O'Neill surrendered on 30 March 1603. Queen Elizabeth, unbeknownst to him, had died on 24 March. The signing of the Treaty of Mellifont marked the end of the war.

Pl. 18—Killincarrig Castle, Co. Wicklow, a fortified house of late sixteenth/early seventeenth-century date. Built by the Walsh family, it featured two storeys and an attic. (Courtesy of the National Monuments Service)

THE WALSHES OF KILLINCARRIG

According to Albone Thomas Preston, Ulster King of Arms, in a pedigree dating from January 1634, the Walshes of Killincarrig were 'descended of the family of the Walshes of *Ballauly* (Balally) and consequently of the Walshes of *Carrickmayne*' (Genealogical Office MS 69, 69).

Killincarrig lies to the immediate south and south-west of Greystones in east County Wicklow (Pl. 18). According to a 1594 inquisition, the alternative name of the place was *Suttonston* (Griffith 1991, 292). It occupied the coastal northern banks of the Three Trout Stream and thus lay to the immediate north of Críoch Branach.

The first documented Walsh in Killincarrig was Henry. On 1 March 1565/6 'Henry Wallshe of *Suttoneston*, in the marches of Dublin', was leased some properties in Dalkey by the dean of Holy Trinity. These included 'a cottage place near the east gate … with land belonging thereto'; three houses and a ruined house and the land attached to these premises located 'on the south side of said town'; a further three houses with attached gardens on 'the north side of the town'; and a small plot of ground 'north of the priest's gardens and Dalkey churchyard'. The lease was for 61 years with the rent set at 22s. 4d. The lessee was also obliged to pay for 'four couple of watch hens at Christmas' and to supply the 'best beast' to Holy Trinity 'as a herthell' on the death of the lessee or his successors (*DKR 24* (1892), 162). At the time of his death on 26 September 1570 Henry was still in possession of extensive holdings in the port town of Dalkey. These included two castles and several houses (Smith 1996, 33). An inquisition dating from 1594 found that at the time of his death he was in possession of one messuage and 40 acres in *Killencargye*, held of the queen by service unknown, and two castles and five and a half acres 'in two small fields' in *Dalkie*, held of the archbishop of Dublin by rent. It was recorded that 'the tenure of the lands has long been concealed from the queen and her predecessors' (Griffith 1991, 292). He was described as 'late of *Killencarge*' in a fiant dating from 24 October 1595 (*Fiants*, III, No. 5961, 260). Livery to his son and heir Theobald (and a set fine of £6 10s.) was recorded in the same fiant. Theobald had been pardoned along with some other Walshes in 1582 (*Fiants*, II, No. 3991, 552). Giles Allen, an alderman, granted a house in Dublin city to Theobald Walsh of *Killinkaricke* on 28 June 1582 (Griffith 1991, 337). The erection of the Jacobean-style house at Killincarrig has been attributed to Henry (Grogan and Kilfeather 1997, 192; Corlett 1999, 153) but chronologically it is more likely to have been built during Theobald's tenure.

Theobald was married twice. His first wife was Anne Allen of Palmerston, Co. Dublin (Genealogical Office MS 66, 103), whose father, William, was a native of Cotishall in Norfolk (Genealogical Office MS 48, 32). They had six children: Henry, William, Michael, Katherine, Anastace and Margaret. His second wife was Jane Eustace of Ballymore (Eustace), Co. Kildare (Genealogical Office MS 66, 103). 'Margery', his daughter, married Oliver, the son of Richard Luttrell of Portlester, to the immediate east of Ballivor, in County Meath (Genealogical Office MS 69, 10). Richard was a grandson of Sir Thomas Luttrell of Luttrellstown Castle, Co. Dublin, chief justice of the common pleas (Ball 1902–17, IV, 8).

A deed of mortgage made by Barnabas O'Toole, dated 24 November 1593, assigning lands in 'the *Fartree*' to Edward Archbold of *Tamplecarge* (Templecarrig) was witnessed by, amongst others, Theobald Walsh of *Killenecargy*. A second deed, dated 3 February 1598, made Theobald the beneficiary (Griffith 1991, 306 fns 2 and 3). In 1596 Tibbot (i.e. Theobald) Walsh of *Killegarge* was ranked amongst the leading men of the barony of Rathdown (Brewer and Bullen 1867–73, III, 189). In that year he was also named in 'a perambulation of the Pale' as 'Walshe of *Killegarge*' (Hogan 1878, 38 fn.).

FEAGH MAC HUGH O'BYRNE

David Edwards (1998, 214) has argued convincingly that Feagh Mac Hugh O'Byrne was integrally involved from the beginning in the conspiracy that led to the widespread revolt in the early 1590s. It would appear that he resorted to arms in conjunction with Maguire and O'Donnell. Undoubtedly the major achievement of his efforts was to split the government's ability to respond to the escalating hostilities. The threat to the southern flank of the Pale—and, indeed, to Dublin itself—was sufficient to tie down significant manpower that would otherwise have been directed solely against Ulster.

Feagh's contributions to Red Hugh O'Donnell's successful escape from Dublin Castle and safe return to Tír Chonaill were pivotal. On 6 January 1592, on his second attempt, Hugh managed to make it to Ballinacor. When fully recovered from the winter ordeal, and with help from O'Neill, he returned home in triumph (MacCurtain 1972, 84). This event alone would have consolidated the trust, co-operation and comradeship between the three men.

The fears of the Dublin administration were exemplified in the omission of Sir Henry Harrington from the full muster of Crown forces at Tara in the autumn of 1593. Sir Henry was held in reserve to protect the Pale from the expected attack from the Wicklow Mountains. Feagh was both cautious and skilfully duplicitous in his dealings with the Dublin authorities. The burning of Ardree Castle near Athy, Co. Kildare, could be blamed on Walter Reagh Fitzgerald (Feagh's lieutenant) and his brothers (Hamilton 1867–90, V, 227). The fact that three of Feagh's sons were also present while the occupants—including the owner, Sir Piers Fitzjames, and his wife—burnt to death was glossed over. Martial law was reluctantly reintroduced on 15 August (Edwards 1998, 228). To temper its effect, prevent abuses and avoid alienating otherwise loyal factions, the earl of Ormond, trusted by the queen, was to be the sole martial law commissioner.

Elizabeth announced the appointment of Sir William Russell as lord deputy, replacing Sir William Williams (Hamilton 1867–90, V, 238). He was to prove to be a much more worthy match for Feagh Mac Hugh O'Byrne.

On the night of 16 January 1595 the new lord deputy launched a surprise assault on the O'Byrne heartland. Deepest winter was not a normal time to make forays into the mountains. As Edwards (1998, 229) has observed, the suggestion that this was an unprovoked attack 'makes little sense'. The results were spectacular. Feagh had to abandon Ballinacor, which was subsequently seized and garrisoned by Russell's forces (Hamilton 1867–90, V, 292, 299). In the region of 500 troops, based mainly at Enniscorthy, Newcastle McKynegan, Castlekevin and Ballinacor, were now strategically garrisoned around the O'Byrne territories (Edwards 1998, 231; O'Byrne 2003a, 225). Russell pressed home his advantage. On 7 April Feagh's right-hand man (and son-in-law) Walter Reagh was cornered and captured on information received. He was tortured, forced to confess and executed (Hamilton 1867–90, V, 311; Edwards 1998, 232; O'Byrne 2003a, 226). Ironically, it was the son of the occupant of the torched Ardree Castle, in concert with a rival O'Byrne, who had supplied the key intelligence. Rose, Feagh's wife, was captured on 28 April, along with her sister, and they were imprisoned in Dublin Castle (Brewer and Bullen 1867–73, III, 230; Hamilton 1867–90, V, 319). On 26 June Rose was found guilty of treason and on 27 June was sentenced to be burned—a sentence ultimately never carried out. Hostilities petered out, as the Wicklow Mountains, no longer an impregnable haven, were awash with double agents and spies.

Hugh O'Neill's timely intervention in the war reduced the pressure on the

O'Byrnes. The seizure of Monaghan Castle and the defeat at Clontibret refocused the government's attention. The truce negotiations of October 1595 brought further respite.

The attention of all parties was now focused on Spain. Would the anticipated invasion happen? Where? And when? In mid-September the Jesuit James Archer, a fervent Counter-Reformation adherent, landed at Waterford with the news of an imminent Spanish arrival (Edwards 1998, 241). A reinvigorated Feagh impelled himself back into the fray by storming and razing the government fortress at Ballinacor to the ground. The campaign was relaunched with a vengeance, but all was to be in vain.

The Venetian ambassador to Spain, Agustino Nani, kept the doge and senate informed of developments in the royal court of Philip II. On 10 October 1596 he reported that 'great preparations' were being made in Lisbon. Embarkation of supplies and weapons had already commenced (Brown 1897, 233). A follow-up report, dated 25 October, noted the presence of an Irish bishop and many of his fellow countrymen (including their wives and families). Their presence had led local opinion to deduce that Ireland was the intended destination of the expeditionary force (*ibid.*, 235). In a dispatch dated 3 November Nani informed the doge that the king had ordered the fleet to sail at once despite the protestations of the captains, who feared the 'obvious risk of being shipwrecked', given weather forecasts. The king still insisted that they sail; his order was obeyed on 23 October. They headed for Vigo in Galicia. The fleet did 'not exceed one hundred sail', with 12,000 men on board (including Irish defectors from the English navy) (*ibid.*, 239). The following dispatch (dated 12 November) reported that the feared storm had struck on the night of 27 October. The fleet had come to grief off Cape Finisterre. The *adelantado* (commander-in-chief) survived, but over 2,000 infantrymen were lost and at least twelve ships had sunk, with another eighteen missing (*ibid.*, 240). There would be no help coming for the foreseeable future.

Feagh had played his last ace and could do nothing now but gamely fight on. He was willing to talk terms, even to travel to England to address the queen (Hamilton 1867–90, V, 510), but the authorities were not willing to listen. This was made clear when Captain Thomas Lee tried to assassinate him during a false parley in August 1595 (Atkinson 1893–1905, VI, 81–2).

Throughout early 1597 Feagh's closest friends and associates were picked off one by one (O'Byrne 2003a, 235). Lee hunted them down in the wooded valleys and mountain redoubts. Cattle and horses were seized and settlements and homes were burnt to the ground, the noose ever tightening. The circumstances of Feagh's death are clouded. The official government line was that Sir William Russell, the lord deputy, 'upon some espial' (i.e. sightings) quickly advanced south into the Wicklow Mountains, where he came upon 'that ancient and cankered traitor Feagh McHugh' (Atkinson 1893–1905, VI, 286–7). Some further clarification came in a letter from Loftus, the lord chancellor, to Lord William Burghley wherein he reported that Feagh had fallen 'into the hands of Captain Lee's company, whose sergeant … slew him' (*ibid.*, 288). The lord general, Sir John Norreys (no friend of Russell, it should be stressed), was not convinced. In a letter to Sir Robert Cecil he wrote that 'how Feagh McHugh came to his end is diversely reported [...]' (*ibid.*, 298). The account of the event from Russell's personal journal is therefore insightful: 'Sunday [8 May]. Early in the morning our foot entered the Glynnes and fell into the Quarter where Feagh McHugh lay; coming several ways on him [...] being so hardly followed ... run out of breath and forced to take (refuge in) a cave, where one Milborne, sergeant to Captain Lee [...] cut off Feagh's head with his own sword' (Brewer and Bullen 1867–73, III, 258; Price 1932, 170).

Price (*loc. cit.*) drew attention to the fact that both the seventeenth-century historian Philip O'Sullivan Beare and the Annals of the Four Masters attributed Feagh's discovery to treachery. O'Sullivan (Byrne 1903, 97) used the term 'removal by treachery', while in the AFM it was written that he had been 'treacherously betrayed by a relative' (O'Donovan 1854, VI, 2018–19). The allegation of treachery is corroborated by the line in Russell's journal noting that the soldiers came 'several ways on him'. This certainly sounds like a party of soldiers acting on very precise information. The location of the place of death is given as *Fanenerin* in a chancery inquisition dated 4 May 1616 (Hardiman 1826–9, I, No. 10). Captain Lee was amply rewarded with three payments from the Irish concordatum fund, receiving a total of £256 7s. 4d. The Leinster rebellion continued but a new leader of the calibre of Feagh Mac Hugh O'Byrne was not forthcoming.

THE AFTERMATH

It does not appear that Feagh's death resulted in a fraught succession contest. His eldest son Turlough was already dead. Apparently seriously disliked by his siblings, he had been handed over to the Dublin authorities by Feagh to earn a reprieve for the imprisoned Rose. His subsequent execution occurred on 18 July 1595 (Nicholls 1998b, 113). It was thus Phelim who succeeded Feagh, and in close association with his brother Redmond he continued with the war. In the interim, Turlough's widow Dorothy married James Walsh of the Balally branch in County Dublin (*ibid.*). According to Thomas Preston, King of Armes, in a document dated 22 January 1634, the Walshes of Balally were an offshoot of the Carrickmines family (Genealogical Office, MS 69, 69).

Phelim and Redmond were fired by the same avid religious fervour as their father (O'Byrne 2003a, 236). To avoid endless pursuit, they escaped north to join Hugh O'Neill (Atkinson 1893–1905, VI, 322), who gave Phelim, along with Brian Riabhach O'More of Leix and Murchadh Mac Murrough-Kavanagh of Wexford, command of the fort on the Blackwater (*ibid.*, 345). They lost possession of it in July 1597. O'Neill wanted the Leinster front to be reactivated. With that objective in mind, he dispatched Brian Riabhach, Redmond O'Byrne and 1,000 fighting men to the south-east in August (O'Byrne 2003a, 238). The O'Byrne brothers were definitely on the government's radar. An overview dating from May 1599 described Phelim as 'the wolf of the mountain'. Redmond was named as being amongst the leading 'traitors' in the land (Atkinson 1893–1905, VIII, 51). Brian Riabhach was already dead. In June 1598 Ormond had launched an assault against Leix. In a fierce engagement, O'More was wounded and died soon afterwards (O'Donovan 1854, VI, 2058–9). He was supplanted by his half-brother, Uaithne Mac Ruaidhrí O'More.

In a letter dated 13 June 1599 to Sir Robert Cecil (the son of William, Lord Burghley, and later earl of Salisbury), chief minister to the queen since the previous year, John Clifford observed that there was a detachment of cavalry based at Carrickmines—'Threescore horse and upwards'. Their commander was identified as the earl of Southampton, but it was not made clear whether or not he was there in person (Atkinson 1893–1905, VIII, 63). The date of their arrival or departure is unknown. It was a raid on the night of 12 June that earned the garrison a mention in the letter. Again, there is an ambiguity in the wording: 'Last night the enemy came thither, and took away the prey of the town, and burned it, and went away without any harm, the horsemen being all in the town' (*ibid.*). Prey, in the context of being burnable, was clearly perishable, very possibly corn, but then why take it away and burn it? By 'town' we must assume 'castle'. The 'prey', therefore, was apparently stored outside the main building/compound, probably in barns or outhouses.

The key to understanding why the detachment of cavalry was stationed at Carrickmines would appear to lie earlier in Clifford's letter to Cecil. He noted that, prior to embarking on an expedition to the south, 'His Lordship took as great care of the borders and all other parts as might be, both for the defence of the subject and for the offence of the rebels' (*ibid.*, 62). Carrickmines was clearly a logical choice of place in which to leave a garrison that would 'take care' of the border of the Pale/marches (and its subjects). The 'offence of the rebels' aspect of the plan was the tasking of Sir Henry Harrington to 'prosecute Feagh Mac Hugh's sons and the rest of the rebels about the mountains' (*ibid.*).

Presumably the cavalrymen—and Southampton?—were welcome at Carrickmines Castle. The earl was certainly present in Arklow and Wicklow in June 1599 (Brewer and Bullen 1867–73, III 312). While 'certain of the Walshes' had joined the rebellion about this time (Atkinson 1893–1905, VIII, 51), there is no available evidence to suggest that the sixteen-year-old Richard Walsh was one of them. His two uncles, Maurice and William, were not so loyal, however, but were presumably living elsewhere. A report for the council dated January 1600 calculated that 'many of the Welshes and Harrolds' had boosted rebel numbers by 'near 100' (*ibid.*, 437). The fact that Richard's wife (or wife-to-be) Eleanor was a Eustace does not establish that she was necessarily anti-government. Not all the branches of the Eustace family had been involved in the Baltinglass rebellion.

The earl of Southampton would have been a fascinating dinner guest. Henry Wriothesley became the third earl of Southampton at an early age, when he was around seven years old. He thus became a royal ward under the custody of Sir William Cecil, Lord Burghley, chief minister to the queen (Stopes 1922, 17). He was a mere seventeen years of age when he made his first appearance at court. There he was taken under the wing of Robert Devereux, the second earl of Essex (*ibid.*, 35). He also formed a close friendship with William Shakespeare and became a patron of the poet, who dedicated at least two poems to him ('Venus and Adonis' in 1593 and 'The Rape of Lucrece' in 1594) (*ibid.*, 52, 64). In his early twenties the earl became engaged in a furtive relationship with Elizabeth Vernon, a lady-in-waiting to the queen. Marriage became a necessity and—predictably—when this became known the news sent the queen into a prolonged rage (*ibid.*, 122).

Southampton had previously accompanied Essex on military expeditions to Cadiz and the Azores (*ibid.*, 98, 110), but Essex's decision to recruit Wriothesley for his new regime in Ireland was not to go down at all well with the aggrieved monarch.

In the meantime, Southampton had been engaged in some actions. A note made by the army at the Battle of the Curlews (on Sunday 5 August) recorded that the earl's troop had suffered three casualties (two fatal) (Atkinson 1893–1905, VIII, 114). He was also involved in some skirmishes with O'Neill in Louth. A parley held between Essex and O'Neill on 7 September 1599 at the Ford of Bellaclinthe on the River Lagan was closely observed by Southampton (this was the parley that led to the six weeks' cessation of hostilities) (*ibid.*, 146).

As early as 10 June the privy council had notified Essex that the queen had now become aware of the fact that he had employed Southampton as 'General of Horse'. She was furious with the appointment, given that she had explicitly prohibited it in the first place (*ibid.*, 61). Southampton was still serving in the army in Ireland on 21 August (*ibid.*, 127). It would appear that he was there purely for the adventure. A report on him dated September 1599 observed that he 'came over to see if there would be a conclusion of the wars; which, if it fell out, he purposed to sue for leave to seek some other war' (*ibid.*,165).

An alarming event, from the government's perspective, took place on 9 April 1600. A parley that went wrong led to the capture of the earl of Ormond by Uaithne Mac Ruaidhrí O'More. He was held at the castle of Gortnaclea on the Gully River in County Leix, where he was subjected to three weeks of attempted indoctrination by the Jesuit James Archer (O'Byrne 2003a, 239). In the meantime, the earl of Tyrone was attempting to have Ormond transferred into his custody in the north, but the O'Mores were not agreeable (Atkinson 1893–1905, IX, 127). Eventually, on 16 June, in return for a ransom of £3,000 and hostages, Ormond was released (*ibid.*, 237). Essex had failed to defeat the rebels and returned to England without permission. This move proved fatal. His replacement was the more dynamic and militarily adroit Charles Blount, Lord Mountjoy. Heavy fighting was reported back to London throughout the summer of 1600. Uaithne O'More was one notable fatality. On 24 August Domhnall Spáinneach MacMurrough-Kavanagh surrendered (he was the last of the kings of Leinster). Phelim O'Byrne was resolved to seek a truce, but on the night of 6 December Mountjoy launched a surprise attack and seized Ballinacor. It was the final straw and in the following March Phelim and Redmond surrendered before the council in Dublin (Atkinson 1893–1905, X, 240). Phelim O'Toole of Castlekevin followed suit. They were rewarded with pardons.

Domhnall Spáinneach MacMurrough-Kavanagh was pardoned in May 1601; this pardon was confirmed on 16 October 1602 (Hamilton 1915, 113). Amongst his many confederates who were also pardoned were 'Morrysh' (Maurice) and William Walsh of *Carrickmayne* (*Fiants*, III, No. 6517, 453). These were brothers of Theobald Walsh. It should be noted that Domhnall Spáinneach's daughter Elinor was or would be the wife of Edmond Walsh of Clonmannan, Co. Wicklow (Ken Nichols, pers. comm.). Nicholas Walsh of Kilgobbin, a cousin, was later granted a general pardon in 1603 along with Phelim O'Toole of Castlekevin. Interestingly, Nicholas was domiciled in their adjoining property in Jamestown (*Cal. pat. rolls chancery*, 33). Henry Walsh of Dalkey had been pardoned in June 1602 (*Fiants*, III, No. 6660, 570). These pardons were resignedly and genuinely accepted. The fighting was thus finally finished. As Edwards (2018c, 48) put it plainly, 'the country was conquered'.

PART 3

Theobald Walsh: a time of peace, politics and foreign adventures

The world in which Theobald Walsh would grow up was on the cusp of a radically new era. For the first time in living memory and beyond, peace—albeit uneasy—had descended on the land. People could now live their lives and get on with ordinary pursuits. And it was not a bad place to be. A contemporary writer described the county as 'a very plentifull County both in corne and catell, abounding also with game for pleasure'. On the deficit side, 'their greatest want is fuell, which is a heavie turfe or English sea-coale'. The inhabitants were described as a 'people of a stately port and garbe, in gentile neatnesse and carriage surpassing all the rest of Ireland'. To the south lay the mountains, with 'many hollow valleyes over-run with trees'. The whole county was described as 'Neptunes neighbour' (G.N. 1642, 14). It was further related that 'a little higher where the River Bray disburdens into the Sea, is seene Oldcourt, the possessions of the Walshes of *Carickmain*, who are a large and ancient stocke' (*ibid.*, 14–15). This description was clearly drawing on an earlier tract (see below).

Theobald was born about the year 1605 (Genealogical Office MS 48, 23) and was the eldest son of Richard Walsh and Jane Eustace (of Confey, Co. Kildare).

Richard had been born in 1583 (Hussey Walsh 1900–1, 219). On 8 November 1595 a grant of 'the custody, wardship, and marriage of Richard Walsh of *Karrickmayne*' was awarded to Peter Barnewall (Morrin 1862, 322), who accordingly became Richard's guardian (Ball 1901, 198). A patent roll recorded that 'Livery of Seisin and Pardon of Intrusion' were conveyed and granted to Richard Walsh on 22 January 1609. The 'fine' (i.e. fee) paid was £10 10s. (Irish) (*Cal. pat. rolls chancery*, 127). Richard had five confirmed siblings, William, Thomas, Robert (also known as John), Mary and Elizabeth. A probable sixth, Walter, was also documented (see below).

AFTER-EFFECTS OF THE TREATY OF MELLIFONT

The formal cessation of hostilities was marked by what became known as the Treaty of Mellifont. Hugh O'Neill, earl of Tyrone, and Charles Blount, eighth baron Mountjoy, agreed to meet at Mellifont, Co. Louth, at the home of an intermediary, Sir Garret Moore. There on 30 March 1603 they agreed terms. Unbeknownst to O'Neill, Queen Elizabeth had died on 24 March. O'Neill may not have appreciated being kept in the dark, but the death of the queen in fact enabled Mountjoy to be more independent and generous in the terms granted. O'Neill, despite having engaged in a prolonged rebellion and despite his defeat, would be confirmed in the earldom of Tyrone and would be allowed to retain most of his vast estates. He and all those involved in the rebellion would be pardoned. Likewise, Rory O'Donnell would be confirmed in the earldom of Tyrconnell and would retain his lands (Beckett 1966, 24).

The devil, however, was in the detail. The Ulster lords now held their estates from the monarch. Furthermore, their fiefdoms would henceforth be subject to English common law.

Sir John Davies, eventually to become attorney-general, arrived in Ireland in November 1604. He had studied at Oxford and was called to the bar in 1595. Besides his legal work, Davies was a highly regarded poet. In *c.* 1594 he published *Nosce Teipsum*, his sententious and wily poem on the immortality of the soul. On the queen's death in March 1603, Davies joined Sir Robert Carey, later to be created the first earl of Monmouth, in his rush to the court of King James VI of Scotland. The meeting went very well, not least because James was delighted to meet the author of *Nosce Teipsum*. Unsurprisingly, the king advanced his appointment as solicitor-general to Ireland in September 1603. He was promoted to attorney-general on 29 May 1606 (*ODNB*, XV, 378). The task of implementing English common law in Ireland thus rested on his shoulders. Committed and competent, he proved to be relentless in the task.

In 1604 Davies and Sir Edmund Pelham, the chief baron, had completed a legal circuit about seven shires in Leinster. In all shires they 'found many civil and substantial gentlemen and freeholders' to serve on the juries, who all 'understood and dispatched their business in every way' as thoroughly and efficiently as any of their counterparts in England (Russell and Prendergast 1872–80, I, 158). Again, on 7 August 1607 he reported to Robert Cecil, the first earl of Salisbury and secretary of state, that he had visited the counties of Meath, Westmeath and Longford, along with King's County and Queen's County, and that it was 'almost a miracle to see the quiet and conformity of this people' (*ibid.*, II, 250). These were the private observations of an astute lawyer to a mentor and thus carry weight. Davies took pride in the fact that he and Sir Edmund Pelham were the first 'Justices of Assise' that ever sat in Tyrone and *Tirconnell* (Davies 1747, 262).

It has been suggested that the earls of Tyrone and Tyrconnell could not adjust to the status of land magnates since until recently they had been 'independent princes' (Clarke 2011, 164). Canny (1970–1, 396, 398) argued that, while O'Donnell and

Maguire indeed could not adjust to their new lives, O'Neill was making the transition, but that on the cusp of the departure of the others he panicked, possibly having realised the optics and their implications, and joined the others and their families at Lough Swilly.

More recently the uncovering of key information in the Spanish sources has revealed not only that O'Neill had been planning to depart from Ireland for a long time but also that he had been involved in an ongoing conspiracy involving Spain. On 22 October 1602 King Philip III added a marginal note to a council of state report. He wrote that they would help the Catholics in Ireland with 'money, arms and munitions, and with 30,000 ducats', and that the correspondence with the 'Earl of *Tiron*' should be continued (Kerney-Walsh 1986, 146). Hugh O'Neill wrote to the king on 24 December 1602 pleading for help. He concluded that, should the king choose not to send aid, then 'we beg you to send a warship to the northern part of Ireland so that we may be conveyed to you, safe from the fury of our enemies' (*ibid.*, 147). On 23 December 1604 the conde de Villamediana, ambassador of Spain at the court of St James, wrote to the king. He reported that 'four or five nights ago Irish Earl Odonel, whom they call Tirconel, came to see me in the greatest secrecy. On behalf of the Earl Onel, his brother-in-law, whom they here call Tiron, and on his own behalf.' The bottom line was that they were willing to remain in place for the next two years to serve the Spanish cause, but should the king 'have no need of this service' they wished to leave, 'if Your Majesty will send a ship to a place which they will name'. There 'they will embark, [and] leave their country' (*ibid.*, 152).

The end result was that O'Neill, O'Donnell, Maguire and more than 90 members of their families and followers boarded a ship on 3 September 1607 at Rathmullan on Lough Swilly in County Donegal. They sailed to the Continent and never set foot in Ireland again.

The following January, the lord deputy (Sir Arthur Chichester), Sir John Davies and their fellow commissioners arrived in Ulster to inspect the escheated lands. Davies's main mission was to indict the fugitive earls. A second and a third commission followed, in 1609 and 1610 respectively, the objective being to formulate the plantation of Ulster. Davies was granted 5,500 acres by the king as a token of thanks for his tireless work on the endeavour (*ODNB*, XV, 379).

The final upheaval in Ulster had come in the spring of 1608. The ruler of the Inishowen Peninsula, Sir Cahir O'Doherty, was a mere twenty years of age. He had hitherto been very loyal and actively supportive of the Crown forces and had a good personal relationship with Sir Henry Docwra, the governor of 'the Derrie'. In 1606, however, Docwra was succeeded as governor by Sir George Pawlett, who within a short space of time had proved himself to be of a very different character. In the opinion of Sir Arthur Chichester, Pawlett 'was hated by those over whom he had command, and neither beloved nor feared by the Irish, his neighbours' (Russell and Prendergast 1872–80, II, 481).

Pawlett certainly managed to alienate Sir Cahir O'Doherty. In fact, according to the Annals of the Four Masters, he had not only insulted but had also struck him

(O'Donovan 1854, VI, 2360–1). This insult could not be forgiven. The reconstituted fort of Culmore lay 7km downstream from 'the Derrie' on the western shore of Lough Foyle. On 18 April 1608 it was seized by O'Doherty's men by means of a ruse. Earlier that day the commander of the fort, Captain Henry Hart, his wife and young son had arrived as invited guests at O'Doherty's home in Buncrana. A pleasant afternoon and dinner followed. As they were about to depart, however, they were informed that they were prisoners. Mrs Hart was escorted back to Culmore while her husband (and little boy?) were held hostage under threat of death. She called on the warders to open the gates for her, and when they complied they were rushed by O'Doherty's kerns (Colby and Larcom 1837, 237; Russell and Prendergast 1872–80, II, 481).

An hour before dawn on 19 April, O'Doherty with 'a hundred men or thereabouts' slipped into 'the Derrie' and 'surprised the little city'. Pawlett was quickly dispatched into the next life, along with 'all others that made resistance': The town was looted and set alight. It burned to the ground (Russell and Prendergast 1872–80, II, 480–1).

But there the rebellion stalled. Sufficient support was not forthcoming from any quarter. Sir Cahir fell in battle on 18 July. His remaining followers scattered (Beckett 1966, 45).

Chichester was clear as to where the blame lay. In a letter to the earl of Salisbury, he wrote that 'that which he ever feared since Sir Henry Docwra's departure from the Derrie and Sir George Pawlett's coming to be governor there, is come to pass' (Russell and Prendergast 1872–80, II, 483). Sir Henry Dillon also wrote to Salisbury. He credited the fall of the fort to 'no other cause than the deficiency of the Governor'. He did add, however, that 'the indiscretion of the justices of assizes' employed in the region over the past two years had reduced Phelim Reagh McDavid, O'Doherty's foster-father, to such dire circumstances that it was he who had encouraged Sir Cahir to rebel (*ibid.*, 485–6).

The knock-on effect of this relatively minor uprising was seismic. The plans for a limited introduction of settlers into Ulster were now shelved in favour of a full-scale plantation (Clarke and Dudley Edwards 1976, 196). In the summer assizes of 1608, 'almost all of the land' in the counties of Armagh, Cavan, Coleraine, Donegal, Fermanagh and Tyrone was judged 'to be in the King's hands' (*ibid.*, 197). All in all, over 3.6 million statute acres were confiscated in Ulster (Edwards 2018c, 60). Moreover, the salutary lesson for the Catholic Irish was that, no matter how 'on side' they remained, they were always hovering on the brink of their own destruction. O'Doherty had done almost everything that he could do to stay 'on side'; for example, he acted as foreman of the jury that sat on the indictment of the fugitive earls convened by Davies, and he even applied 'to be admitted as one of the gentlemen of the Prince [of Wales's] Privy Chamber' (Russell and Prendergast 1872–80, II, 414, 481). Yet all his work was undone owing to his negative encounters with one conniving duplicitous individual. His Achilles' heel was his religion. There was no escaping the fact that Catholicism was the religion of the rivals and enemies of England.

The continued unease, the rapid change and the 'Derrie' episode that was to affect day-to-day life in the first decade of seventeenth-century Ulster were not overtly manifest elsewhere on the island.

The Old English of the Pale would have followed the saga in 'the Derrie' and environs with interest, not least because O'Doherty's wife was a sister of Lord Gormanston (Russell and Prendergast 1872–80, II, 481). They would also have been following the antics of Lords Howth and Delvin, who had been flirting with 'treasonable conspiracies' (*ibid.*, 254, 327).

Smaller-scale plantations took place outside Ulster. In County Wexford a royal claim based on a fourteenth-century title was used to confiscate land (Beckett 1966, 54). The instigators were New English entrepreneurs. The two rules of thumb for the enterprise were that only 25% of an estate should be planted and that those with holdings of less than 100 acres should be exempt; needless to say, avarice often clouded the percentages (Clarke and Dudley Edwards 1976, 219; Butler 1915, 422, 424). Initially, in 1611, the detailed scheme was stymied by legal challenges, mostly lodged by pertinacious Old English landowners. On 16 April 1613 the king wrote to Lord Chichester. He named two of the leading 'turbulent spirits' in the opposition, 'one Henry Walsh and one Hoare', and directed Chichester to mete out 'due punishment' and basically get on with the plantation (Russell and Prendergast 1872–80, IV, 337–8). The completion of the task fell to his successor, Sir Oliver St John. Despite vigorous opposition, including some physical actions taken against the new colonists, by 1620 the operation had been completed and order re-established (Beckett 1966, 54–5).

The leadership of the O'Byrnes and O'Tooles in Wicklow must have been keeping an anxious eye on proceedings in Wexford. They were right to be vigilant, given that Viscount Falkland, the lord deputy, was recalled in 1629 on the grounds of dubious practices in relation to a failed attempt to dispossess the O'Byrnes (Beckett 1966, 61; Foster 1988, 48n.). The plantation of Ranelagh had occurred in 1628. All the lands of the O'Byrnes of Knockrath in County Wicklow were granted to Sir Adam Loftus of Rathfarnham (Nicholls 1998c, 276–7).

In south County Dublin the extended Walsh family continued to enjoy the peace. A description of their environment penned about 1598 by an English official gives us an insight into their world (Hogan 1878, vi):

> 'Dublin is a good corn country, abounding in all sorts of game, but so bare of wood in many parts that they are forced to burn turf or English pit-coal; it is well stocked with towns and inhabitants, surpassing the rest of Ireland in improvements, and in a peculiar neatness. Where the little river Bray falls into the sea, a little higher up one sees *Ould Court*, an estate of the Walshes of *Carrickmain*, of ancient nobility and numerous in these parts' (*ibid.*, 298).

In an addendum added between 1603 and 1607 (*ibid.*, vi), amongst the 'men of name in the Countie' were 'Walshe of *Carrickmayne*' and 'Walshe of *Shaunogherghe* (Shanganagh)' (*ibid.*, 38).

On 12 November 1606 Richard Walsh of *Carrickmayn* was ordered to appear before the court of chancery, under threat of a penalty of £100. Amongst the other parties summonsed were 'William Rocheford of *Breningston*' and his wife Margaret Walsh (McEnery and Refaussé 2001, 297). In 1610 it was recorded that the couple were still residing at *Ballybeenan* (Brenanstown). Margaret was described as the daughter of Howel Walsh of said place, which confirms that Rochfort had acquired the estate by marriage. It was also recorded that his first wife had been Margery Walsh, the daughter of John Walsh of *Litle Bre* (Genealogical Office MS 48, 36). Ball (1902–17, I, 105) observed that William 'doubtless' belonged to the Rochforts of Kilbogget, a townland to the immediate east of Brenanstown. The estate of Henry Rochfort of *Kilbogoge* was declared forfeit in the late 1650s (O'Hart 1887, 248). Price (1940, 130–1) stated that Kilbogget 'should be written *Kilbegog*'. Austin Cooper recorded that a circular part of Brenanstown Castle was still standing in July 1780 (Price 1942, 54). It is striking that, of the additional five couples summonsed to appear before the court of chancery in 1606, four of the five women bore the maiden name of Walsh. Is it possible that these four women—Rita, Katherine, Ismay and Ieneta—were Margaret's sisters? In other words, that these were the 'many daughters' 'begate' by Richard's great-uncle Howell and his wife Esmay Talbot (see Part 2)? Interestingly, the remaining woman (and the first named) in the summons was an 'Ismay' Talbot, whose husband is named as William Eustace of *Dudingston* in County Dublin. Could this be the same Esmay Talbot, i.e. the mother of the five girls, with her second husband?

According to Hawkins (1721, 63–4), *Gulielmus* (William) was the eldest of Richard Walsh's male siblings and died without issue (*obiit sine prole*). In 1610 Molyneux had described him as 'deade without issue' (Genealogical Office MS 48, 21). Yet in Richard's will, made in December 1619, there is a reference to 'his brother William Walsh of *Ballinadroght*, gent' (Griffith 1991, 447). Ballymadrough lies to the north-east of Swords, on the estuary of the conjoined Ward and Broadmeadow rivers. There was a William Walsh of *Ballmadrought/ Ballinadrought* 'indicted of treason' in 1641 and again in 1642 (Gilbert 1882–91, III, 385), possibly either an aged William or a son of the same name.

Richard had two sisters, Mary and Elizabeth. The girls' marriage prospects had been facilitated by their father, Theobald, who in 1592/3 had allocated a '£200 marriage portion for Mary', to be followed by a £200 marriage portion for the younger Elizabeth. The money was to come from the revenue generated by their lands in Carrickmines, *Amboane* (Annodan?) and Phrompstown (Griffith 1991, 296). Mary married John Allen of Bishopscourt, Co. Kildare (Genealogical Office MS 48, 21). The adjoining townlands of Bishopscourt Lower and Upper lie to the immediate north of Kill, to the north-east of Naas. Elizabeth, it appears, may not have married, judging by the data from 1610 and 1619.

The remaining two brothers, Thomas and Robert (a.k.a. John), are of particular interest. Both departed for the Continent, never to return. Richard, the eldest of the three, was born in 1583, so we can conjecture that the two boys were born before *c.* 1590. Therefore they could not have gone abroad prior to approximately 1605 at the earliest. We do know—or at least Molyneux recorded—that Thomas was 'thought' dead by 1610 (Genealogical Office MS 48, 21). Hawkins (1721, 63) noted that Thomas, 'the 3rd son', was '*in Germani am migravit*'. Hussey Walsh (1900–1, 218) had him still active 'in the German Service in 1610'. Unfortunately, there is no clarification as to which 'German Service' was in question. There was a multiplicity of German principalities at the time. In May 1608 the Protestant Union, a military alliance of over two dozen of the Protestant principalities and cities, was formed under the leadership of Frederik IV, the elector of the Palatinate. The powerful elector of Saxony stood aside, however, which weakened the alliance. The following year, in July, some of the Catholic German states formed their own alliance, the Catholic League, under the leadership of Maximilian I, duke of Bavaria. Thomas Walsh could have entered the service of any of these constituent armies. In the wake of the signing of what has become known as 'the Twelve-Year Truce' between the Dutch and Imperial forces in the Spanish Netherlands on 9 April 1609, a lot of foreign soldiers moved east in search of new employment (see Part 4).

The remaining brother, Robert (or John), had also gone abroad. Molyneux described him as 'Walshe now *liurnze*'(?). Hawkins (1721, 63) had him married to an unnamed '*filia Domini de Carras*'. The unnamed spouse has also been described as the daughter of Robert, seigneur de Carras (Hussey Walsh 1900–1, 218). Hawkins (1721, 64) continued the descent. Their son *Jacobus* (James) married a Maria McDonagh, clearly the daughter of another emigrant. In turn, their son, Robert Walsh, also married the offspring of an Irish emigrant, a daughter of a James Irwin. They had three sons: Philip, the youngest, who died in the West Indies; Edward, the eldest, who married a Brigida Plunket, thus keeping up the family tradition of marrying a member of the Irish diaspora; and Lucas, the second son, who served as an adjutant in an Imperial division in the State of Hanover.

The departure of these two young men to the German States in a time of peace at home is striking. Did they go for adventure, or was it a case of financial necessity?

Finally, it should be noted that there would appear to have been an additional son, named Walter, who died young (Griffith 1991, 296). He did not appear in Molyneux's chart of 1610. The third wife of a William Browne (d. 27 February 1623) was Mary, the daughter of Walter Walsh of *Carickmain* (Genealogical Office MS 68, 12; TCD MS 1216, 25).

THE PARLIAMENT OF 1613

There had not been a parliament held in Ireland since 1585. In truth, for most of its history it 'was more of an event than an institution' (Potter 2013, 14). Only four parliaments had been held in Ireland between 1543 and 1613. The corresponding figure for England was approximately twenty (MacCurtain 1972, 120).

The plantation of Ulster—and, to a lesser extent, Munster—had changed the political landscape. The extension of English common law over the entire island clearly necessitated new legislation.

The decision to hold a parliament was taken in the autumn of 1610 but the complexities of its composition meant that it would be May 1613 before it convened. Prospective representation was of primary concern to the government and to both the 'new' English and the Old English. The latter had always controlled parliaments in Ireland and were not about to relinquish that monopoly. The government's agenda was succinctly summarised by Thomas Leland (1773, 441): their objective was that this parliament should 'support the arrangements lately made; remove real grievances; repress causeless discontents' and 'secure the administration against all attempts of turbulence and disaffection'. The engrafting of anti-recusant legislation was to be of paramount importance.

The refusal of the lord deputy to divulge the agenda in advance stirred the Old English into action. On 25 November 1612 six of the leading temporal lords—Viscount Gormanston and the lord barons of Slane, Killeen, Dunsany, Trimleston and Louth—wrote directly to King James. The language employed was designed to make them sound as loyal and as reasonable as possible while getting their message of discontent across. They complained about 'the matters therein to be propounded not made known unto us and others of the nobility'. They respectfully pointed out that, under the terms of a statute dating from the time of King Henry VII, they, (belonging) to 'the grand council of the realm', 'should join with the governor of this kingdom, in certifying thither, what acts should pass here in parliament' (Leland 1773, 443; Curtis and McDowell 1943, 135).

Their objections, complaints and anxieties were brushed aside. The solution to the problem of a non-compliant parliament had by then been identified and implemented by Sir George Carew. His plan was simple. To achieve the necessary majority, an array of new boroughs would be created, especially in the north. It was ironic that Ulster, which had been the core of Gaelic resistance, would become the foundation stone of the new order. The Protestant nature of all new boroughs, not least the University of Dublin, which was to elect two burgesses, was implicit (Russell and Prendergast 1872–80, IV, 340). Between November 1612 and May 1613, 40 new boroughs were created (Potter 2013, 15). When parliament finally convened, there were 132 Protestant and 100 Catholic members present in the House of Commons. Proportional representation in the House of Lords was a foregone conclusion, as the twenty Protestant bishops automatically guaranteed a majority.

What followed in the House of Commons could be described as a farce. The Old English faction held the majority of the Catholic seats; in fact, the Gaelic Irish only held eighteen seats (MacCurtain 1972, 120). They refused to accept the validity of the representatives of the new boroughs. As the lords had put it in writing, these men, they argued, were the representatives of 'places that can scantly pass the rank of the poorest villages' and/or 'places consisting of some few poor and beggarly cottages' (Leland 1773, 444-5; Curtis and McDowell 1943, 134–5). The pro-government members withdrew from the chambers. The Old English seized their opportunity and elected Sir John Everard as Speaker. The pro-government members were outraged to discover this manoeuvre upon their return. When they failed to eject Everard from the chair, they physically lifted their candidate, Sir John Davies, the attorney-general, onto his lap. After a scuffle and an exchange of intemperate language, it was now the turn of the Catholic members to withdraw from the chamber. A couple of days later the temporal lords followed suit.

Parliament was prorogued on 17 June. Further rounds of intrigue, lobbying and letter-writing ensued. In a letter to the king the Old English overplayed their diplomatic hand by making a reference to the 'rebellious discontented of this nation abroad' taking advantage of the turmoil to 'procure the evil affected at home' (Leland 1773, 450). This was not well received in London and so a delegation was dispatched to make personal representations to the king.

In August 1614 King James delivered his final judgement, which was more conciliatory than his sharp verbal pronouncements to date. All those boroughs that had received their charters after the writ of summons to parliament had been issued were now excluded. As a result, the Protestant camp lost 24 members while the Catholic party lost only two members while gaining an additional four. The Protestants now had only a majority of six and that was not workable. Indeed, given the rate of absenteeism, the Catholic party found themselves in the majority as often as not. All bills of a decidedly anti-recusant nature were quietly dropped when parliament reconvened (Moody 1939–40, 59).

Ten statutes in all were passed after the two sessions. They included the recognition of the king's title to the crown of Ireland and acts for the attainder of the earls of Tyrone and Tyrconnell, the trial of pirates and the repair of highways. A bill of subsidy for the king was also processed. This was a fraction of the legislation that had been envisaged back in the heady days of 1610 (*ibid.*, 60–3). Nevertheless, the king was pleased and conveyed his congratulations to parliament (Leland 1773, 457).

There was much to be quietly satisfied about in royal circles. On a functionary level, the boroughs that had recently been excluded would be perfectly valid at the next parliament. On the macro level what had been achieved was seismic. The Old English party, who had controlled the Irish parliament since its very inception, would henceforth be effectively reduced to the party of opposition. And what was even better from a Westminster perspective was that they were willing to continue participating in the functioning of the kingdom. This was essential, at least in the short term, for the stability of society. Chichester dissolved the parliament on 16 May 1615 (Clarke and Dudley Edwards 1976, 216, 219).

CRISIS OF CONSCIENCES

Aidan Clarke (1966, 10–11) has observed that 'the union of Catholics in Ireland was, from first to last, a Protestant achievement, not a Catholic one'. The alienation of the Old English by the authorities in England and Dublin was unnecessary, if not irrational. It was rooted in an inability to accept that a Catholic subject could be totally loyal to a Protestant monarch. This fear was compounded by the undeniable fact that all of England's real and potential enemies were Catholic states.

The Oath of Supremacy—or, specifically, the failure to embrace it—became a major impediment. As Sir John Bath, an Old English landowner in counties Meath and Dublin, explained to some leading politicians in England in the summer and autumn of 1625, in the old days the legal profession was 'the only livelihood' available to 'the younger sons of the English Pale' (*ibid.*, 31). With this end in mind, many of them were educated in England. Whilst there, they would inevitably have become immersed in mainstream English culture and society and be thoroughly refreshed in their customs and ways. Other offices available to them on their return would have been administrative posts, judgeships and, if extremely fortunate, the privy council (*ibid.*).

The embargo on Catholics who declined to take the Oath of Supremacy removed the impetus to have an English education. The Continent, and the southern Catholic states in particular, became the only viable alternative. An education gained there was unlikely to extol the virtues of a Protestant monarch or society. In reality, the Counter-Reformation ethos prevailing in those countries could only exacerbate the differences and difficulties when the scholars returned home.

It is interesting to observe the different attitudes to the Oath of Supremacy in Catholic circles in Ireland and in England. A key objective in the introduction of the oath in 1606 was to separate those Catholics who believed in the right of the pope to depose a secular ruler from those who did not—that is, to identify those who could be trusted and those who could not (Patterson 1997, 124). The wording of the oath had been prepared by Richard Bancroft, bishop of London, assisted by Christopher Perkins, a former Jesuit (Tierney 1839–43, IV, 70). The pressure from Rome was intense. In 1600 Pope Clement VIII had issued two papal bulls addressed to the English Catholics in which he specifically instructed them not to submit to non-Catholic monarchs (*ibid.*, 59). Pope Paul V succeeded Clement in May 1605. He unreservedly condemned the oath in a brief published on 22 September 1606, yet many Catholics in England were willing to take the oath to display their loyalty to the king. George Blackwell, for example, had been appointed as archpriest in charge of the Catholic mission to England on the authority of Pope Clement. He thus had authority over all the secular priests in England. Blackwell took the oath and by doing so convinced many other Catholic clerics and laity to follow suit. Another prominent cleric, Thomas Preston, a leading Benedictine monk charged with the revival of the order in England, not only embraced the oath but produced many treatises in its support (*ibid.*, 72). The same crisis of thought does not seem to have manifested itself in the hearts and minds of the Old English in Ireland. It would be reasonable to suggest that this may have been due to the Continental Counter-Reformation background of the majority of the clergy in Ireland.

King James had dithered over anti-recusant measures, although he had made some efforts. For example, in June 1605 he issued a proclamation ordering all priests—and particularly Continental seminary priests—to leave the kingdoms; they were to be gone before Christmas (MacCurtain 1972, 127). In December of that year the

'Nobility and Gentry of the English Pale' presented a petition to the lord deputy to be forwarded to London. In it they declared their absolute loyalty to the king, regardless of their adherence to the Catholic faith. They pleaded with the monarch not to discriminate against them. Amongst the signatories of the petition were a James Welsh, a Thomas Walsh and a Richard Walsh of County Dublin (Russell and Prendergast 1872–80, I, 362–3). The Richard is probably of Carrickmines, the James probably of Shanganagh and the Thomas possibly of Kilgobbin. The overriding factor for King James, however, was to be the quest for a prospective bride for his son and heir. It would not have looked good if he was actively persecuting Catholics in his three kingdoms while trying to arrange the nuptials of his son to a Catholic princess. All prospective brides for the heir to the throne had to be considered in terms of strategic and political value. While the choice of a Protestant princess would be both logical and popular domestically, internationally the many advantages of a political alignment with either France or Spain were very alluring and not lost on James.

An Anglo-Spanish marriage arrangement had been on the cards since the formal end of hostilities between the two countries in 1604 (Patterson 1997, 315). The Treaty of London was signed in August of that year, ending a conflict that had started in 1585. The first envisaged marriage was to be between Henry, Prince of Wales, and the *Infanta* Anna, daughter of King Philip III. This plan came to an abrupt end with Henry's death in November 1612. That same year Anna became engaged to King Louis XIII of France. The two fourteen-year-olds married in 1615.

The quest remained the same as far as James was concerned. The only difference was that the bridegroom would now be Charles. The initial contacts were with France and by early 1614 the prospects were looking good for a marriage. In January Sir Thomas Edmondes, the English ambassador to France and Flanders, arrived in London with a firm offer from the French (Bellamy 2002, 62). The prospective bride was Christine Marie de Bourbon, the third child of King Henry IV (by his second wife, Marie de Médicis). By 1614 she would have been eight years old. To James's utter chagrin, the House of Commons in the failed parliament of that year made it absolutely clear that they would not countenance the marriage of the heir to the throne to a Catholic princess from France (Redworth 2003, 15). Christine would later marry the duke of Savoy.

The lessons learnt by James were that all future negotiations should be as discreet and private as possible, and that parliament would not tolerate any marital union that was conditional on granting generous concessions to the Catholics of England, Ireland or Scotland. Undeterred, he now set his sights on a Spanish match for Charles. The intended bride this time was to be the *Infanta* Maria Anna, the younger daughter of the Spanish king.

James was not a Puritan. In his first speech to the English parliament, on 19 March 1604, he spoke about his hopes for reconciliation between the Christian churches. To advance this 'generall Christian union in Religion' he was willing to help organise and participate in an ecumenical council (Patterson 1997, 36). A better insight into the thinking of the king emerged in a May 1603 conference held between

Edward Bruce, Lord Kinloss, a Scottish member of the English privy council, and Giovanni Carlo Scaramelli, the Venetian representative in England. Lord Kinloss made it clear that Catholics would not be persecuted 'as long as [they] remain quiet and decently hidden' (*ibid.*).

The Gunpowder Plot of 1605 did anything but advance the Catholic cause. And yet, once the individuals involved had been dispatched, there was no full-blown concerted campaign waged against their co-religionists. It was not kindness or magnanimity that prevented James from launching a violent response; rather it was simply political expediency. Plainly put, prolonged collective retribution was incompatible with his foreign ambitions and thus policy.

Two players above all other participants shaped the course of the epic negotiations. John Digby served as ambassador to Spain from 1610 to 1618. While he was not enthusiastic about the marriage of the heir to the English throne to a Catholic, as a skilled diplomat he could appreciate the advantages. Besides the political benefits of a close relationship with a major power, there was also the enticement of a healthy dowry—the latter dimension being very important to the perpetually cash-strapped James. The king tasked Digby with squeezing £500,000 from the Spaniards. One can therefore imagine James's delight in April 1618 when Digby managed to negotiate for £600,000 to go on the table (Redworth 2003, 17; *ODNB*, XVI, 148).

Digby's counterpart on the Spanish side was Diego Sarmiento de Acuña, count of Gondomar. He had been appointed ambassador to England on 21 August 1612 and arrived the following year. His refusal to lower his colours upon entering Portsmouth harbour attracted the attention of the king, who granted him an exemption (*ODNB*, XLVIII, 987). This was the opening chapter in what proved to be a long and remarkably harmonious personal relationship (*ibid.*, 989). This close relationship between monarch and ambassador was perfectly duplicated in Madrid between Philip IV (who succeeded his father in March 1621) and John Digby.

Gondomar was very well versed in and informed about events in Ireland. The Spanish Embassy in London was a natural magnet for Irishmen fleeing to the Continent. The embassy gave them refuge, money and the necessary contacts in either Flanders or Spain, and during their stay these men would have been thoroughly questioned by the staff. Thus Gondomar kept himself up to date on affairs in Ireland (*ibid.*, 988). Yet Spain was happy to use Ireland as a pawn in negotiations. In return for non-interference in their operational zone and harsher treatment of pirates, Gondomar promised London that Spain would not interfere in Ireland (Redworth 2003, 14–15).

The opening round of negotiations ground to a halt in 1617 with James baulking at granting freedom of conscience to the Catholics of his three kingdoms. The plan was not, however, allowed to wither on the vine. Indeed, the match was of such importance to James that he was willing to sacrifice Sir Walter Raleigh, highly popular with the public, for its advancement.

In 1616, after twelve years of confinement in the Tower of London, Raleigh was granted a reprieve. He had been sentenced to death for allegedly plotting against the king, but his sentence was subsequently commuted to life in prison. He was permitted to lead a second expedition to South America in search of fields of gold but was warned not to interfere with the Spanish. The fleet of fourteen ships set sail from Plymouth on 12 June 1617. A violent storm struck and forced the thirteen surviving vessels into Cork Harbour. Repairs kept them there until 19 August (*ONDB*, XLV, 855). After a traumatic crossing of the ocean, Raleigh was laid low with a fever. An exploratory force led by Captain Lawrence Keymis was sent up the Orinoco River. They came upon the Spanish settlement of Santo Thomé and, against orders, stormed and burned it. Raleigh's son Walter was killed in action. Sir Walter was so distraught that Keymis, full of remorse, committed suicide (*ibid.*, 856). The bedraggled and demoralised remnants of the expeditionary force arrived back in England in mid-June 1618. Gondomar demanded satisfaction and Raleigh was arrested. His death sentence was reactivated. He was executed on the morning of 29 October 1618 at Westminster. He held his courage to the end, quipping to the executioner while touching the edge of the axe that this was 'a sharp medicine, a physician for all diseases' (*ibid.*, 857).

By February 1622 the marriage plan was firmly back on the agenda. Digby's efforts earned him elevation to the earldom of Bristol on 15 September 1622 (*ODNB*, XVI, 148). Once again progress was good but the conferring of freedom of religion remained the unresolved sticking point. Nevertheless, James approved the terms of the marriage contract. What was to happen next remains one of the great surprises in European history. On 7 March 1623 two strangers arrived in the English ambassador's residence in Madrid, announcing themselves as John and Tom Smith. Their names were as false as their beards. To Bristol's amazement, he found himself face to face with the prince of Wales and the marquess of Buckingham, the favourite and close adviser of King James. They had arrived to collect Charles's intended bride, the *infanta* (Redworth 2003, 82).

Beyond all the ensuing diplomatic flurries, proclamations and confusions lay one insuperable consequence totally unforeseen by Charles and Buckingham. The Spanish court was fully convinced that Charles's clandestine arrival could mean only one thing: that he was now ready and willing to convert to Catholicism.

In the interim, Catholics across the kingdoms of England, Ireland and Scotland rejoiced at their imminent religious liberation. Many now rashly began to practise their religion openly. In County Cavan there was even an attempt to take possession of an old parish church (*ibid.*, 89). The release of large numbers of 'recusants' from prisons in England in early 1622 increased the fervour. Inevitably, the more confident and public the Catholics became in their religious practice, the more the anxieties and adverse reaction of the Protestants grew. They need not have feared, for Charles had no intention of converting to Catholicism. By now, however, he realised that he was stuck in Madrid and not in a position to offend his hosts. Indeed, Francis Cottington, an English diplomat with extensive experience in Spain, had warned King James that the Spanish would be tempted to up the stakes with the prince of Wales in their hands (Patterson 1997, 321–2). There was the further complication of obtaining a dispensation from Rome for the marriage to proceed.

Both the English and the Spanish sides were obliged to placate the powers that be in Rome. The papacy during the relevant time-frame passed from Clement VIII (1592–1605) to Leo XI (1605), to Paul V (1605–21), to Gregory XV (1621–3) and to Urban VIII (1623–44). Neither Clement VIII nor Leo XI (who lasted a mere 27 days) played any significant role in the marriage negotiations. Paul V was very legalistic in his approach to his role as head of the Church, undoubtedly the result of his legal training. Gregory XV was also a law graduate and a great proponent of Catholic missions abroad. In order to advance, streamline and co-ordinate the myriad of participating parties he founded the *Congregatio de Propaganda Fide* in 1622 (giving the world a new descriptive term for the hard sell). Yet he was in general not anti-English and quite in favour of the proposed marriage.

James was still well intentioned towards the match. In a letter dated the 'fifth day of August' 1623 he informed his 'sweet Boys', Prince Charles and the now duke (since 18 May) of Buckingham, in Madrid that 'to be short, I have given order to put in execution, all that I have promised, and more; as themselves confess, and had been done before this time, if themselves, by new unreasonable motions, had not hindered it … [including] a discharge of all debts already owing to me by recusants; and therefore, if they cast up now the great dowry that they are to give, remember that, by this deed, I quit six and thirty thousand pounds of good rent, in England and Ireland; which, in good account, will strike down the third part at least of their dowry' (Hardwicke 1778, I, 445).

Gaspar de Guzmán, count of Olivares, duke of Sanlúcar la Mayor and grandee of Spain, had by 1621 become the royal favourite of King Philip IV. He was to serve as prime minister until 1643. An Anglo-Spanish marriage alliance did not suit his vision of closer harmony with the related Habsburgs of the Holy Roman Empire. Olivares was facilitated in his policy objective by bureaucrats in the service of the Church. The long-awaited papal dispensation finally arrived on 24 April 1623 but with some new technicalities added by the officials. It was now required of James that promulgations reflecting the content of private agreements be made public in England. In the secret treaty it was 'stipulated that no law, affecting the religion or the conscience of Catholics, should thenceforth be executed' (Tierney 1839–43, V, 138). Interestingly, Pope Gregory and Philip IV were content that Catholic worship should be tolerated only 'in private houses, through the whole of the three kingdoms of England, Scotland, and Ireland'. Crucially, the king was now obliged to convince parliament to repeal all existing anti-Catholic statutes (*ibid.*). In his heart James knew that parliament would never consent to these demands. A final insurmountable hurdle was that the Spanish side now expected the privy councils of England, Scotland and Ireland to vote individually in support of the repeal of the anti-Catholic laws (Redworth 2003, 118).

Charles and Buckingham arrived back home to a tumultuous public welcome on 6 October 1623. The absence of a Spanish bride and the prince's fidelity to the Protestant faith only served to increase the popular acclaim (Patterson 1997, 335). The recriminations began. In an interrogation of the earl of Bristol conducted the following year, he was questioned as to whether or not the prolongation of the marriage negotiations was merely a ploy to coerce the king into granting 'an absolute toleration of religion in his dominions, and a restoration of the rebels and fugitives of Ireland to their estates' (Hardwicke 1778, I, 510).

Although Charles would be the first to marry (in 1625), he may well have been slow to forgive the *Infanta* Maria Anna for her perceived rejection, which would later be compounded by her marriage in 1631, as Olivares had hoped, to her first cousin, the future Ferdinand III of the Holy Roman Empire. This was the man upon whom in 1627 would be conferred the kingship of Bohemia. His predecessor, the leading Protestant Frederick V of the Palatinate, who was married to Charles's sister Elizabeth, had been ousted in 1620. All this, in the wake of Charles and Buckingham's prolonged and latterly enforced stay in Madrid, ensured that public opinion in England—not to mention the future king—would be firmly set against the Spanish and their Habsburg kinsmen in Austria for the foreseeable future.

RICHARD WALSH, SOLDIER OF FORTUNE

It was Valentine Hussey Walsh (1900–1, 219) who first published details of the Continental military career of Richard Walsh of *Carrickmayne*. He also drew attention to the conflicting records. An *Inquisition Post Mortem*, taken at Bray in May 1620, registered 5 January 1619 as the date of death of Richard Walsh (*ibid.*). There is also an entry in the Genealogical Office manuscripts recording his death on 6 January 1619 (Genealogical Office MS 66, 87). This evidence is totally at odds with the body of material relating to the family preserved on the Continent. Hussey Walsh's contention was that the information contained in the 'Austrian sources' had to be more accurate and reliable, as it had been used in the exacting process of both a son and grandson of Richard establishing their *bona fides* at court in Vienna. The fact that there were so many fellow immigrants from Ireland working in official circles at the time meant that a fraudulent pedigree would quickly have been exposed and denounced.

Hussey Walsh noted that the Austrian sources record that Richard and his two sons, Theobald and Oliver, were in the imperial service of the Emperor Ferdinand II 'as far back as 1622' (*ibid.*). Similarly, Barker (1982, 52–3) wrote that Richard Walsh (Wallise) of *Karighmain*, owner of 'extensive lands', arrived in 1622 with his sons Theobald and Oliver. Worthington (2004, 151 fn. 26) recorded the date of arrival as 'either 1612 or 1622', while Clark (2010, 183) advanced 1612 as Richard's date of arrival.

The visitation conducted by Daniel Molyneux in 1610 described Richard as 'now of *Carrickmaine*' (Genealogical Office MS 48, 21). The pedigree drawn by Molyneux establishes that in 1610 Richard was married to Jane Eustace of Confey and that they had four children. There is a reference in his will to a deed he had executed on 9 June 1619. The will itself was made on 27 December 1619 (Griffith 1991, 446). The making of a will would make sense in the context of an imminent departure to war. Significantly, in the will it is also established that Richard and Jane had three additional children between 1610 and 1619. It would be difficult, therefore, to sustain the argument that Richard departed for the Continent in 1612.

When Richard's son Theobald is taken into consideration, the argument against the earlier date is further strengthened. According to Molyneux, Theobald was only five years of age in 1610. By 1622 he would therefore have been seventeen years old and ready for military service. Furthermore, the collapse of the Dutch–Spanish cessation of hostilities in 1621 brought an end to the Twelve Years' Truce between the two countries. The demand for foreign volunteers once again blossomed on the Continent. Catholics from Ireland would naturally have been drawn to the opportunities now available in Spain, France and the Holy Roman Empire.

There were great opportunities for foreign soldiers to achieve rank and status in the Empire. Indeed, they became a mainstay of the army as the seventeenth century progressed. They came from all over, for example from the various Italian states, the southern German states, Scotland, Lorraine, Venice and Ireland (Barker 1982, 15). Prominent amongst the Irish families were the Taaffes, the Browns and the Butlers (Silke 1976, 609).

Ferdinand II succeeded as emperor in 1619. In the preceding year the revolt in Bohemia had ignited what was to become the Thirty Years' War. The Bohemian phase, however, was over two years later. During the night of 7–8 November 1620, the Bohemian army led by Christian von Anhalt and an imperial force commanded by Johann Tserclaes, Count Tilly, confronted one another at the White Mountain (Bílá Hora) to the immediate west of Prague (Mann 1976, 143–4). Battle was joined at first light on a wet, cold winter's morning and the fighting was over within the hour (Pl. 29). The Protestant revolt in Bohemia collapsed. The victory at White Mountain was hailed by the Catholic powers across Europe. There have been many suggestions that the philosopher and mathematician René Descartes was an official observer on the day, but this is not certain (Gaukroger 1995, 126).

In the aftermath of the defeat the Protestant population of Bohemia suffered a reign of terror. Twenty-seven of their leaders were executed in June 1621, their mutilated remains left to rot on Charles Bridge in Prague. Hundreds of landowners were dispossessed. The *Verneuerte Landesordnung* officially ended diversity of religious practice in Bohemia in favour of Catholic exclusivity (Ingrao 1994, 34–5).

By 1622 Count Tilly and his forces were operating on the River Rhine. The pursuit of the deposed king, Frederick V, had progressed westward from Bohemia into the Upper Palatinate and to the Lower Palatinate. Geographically, the imperial army was now more conveniently placed to recruit soldiers of fortune from the western parts of Europe, including Ireland. Silke (1976, 610) has observed that the first contingents of Irishmen to serve in the imperial army probably came from Flanders to serve under Tilly. Exactly where it was that Richard Walsh and his sons enlisted is impossible to say, but the Lower Palatinate seems like a strong possibility. Nevertheless, the fact that Richard had one brother (presumably still alive) domiciled in Germany must be borne in mind. He could simply have initially joined him wherever it was that he and his spouse were located. It can be said, however, that within a few years Richard was rising rapidly through the imperial ranks.

Map 8—The German theatre (1618–32).

Pl. 19—Albrecht von Wallenstein (1583–1634), duke of Friedland, duke of Mecklenburg, prince of Sagen and general of the Holy Roman Empire. (Wikimedia Commons)

Tilly was kept busy in the Rhineland. He suffered heavy losses in a clash with Count Ernst von Mansfeld's army of mercenaries on 27 April 1622 at Mingolsheim (Wilson 2009, 334). There was a narrow victory over Georg Friedrich, margrave of Baden-Durlach, south of Wimpfen on the River Neckar on 6 May 1622 (*ibid.*, 334–5). Christian of Brunswick was defeated on 20 June at Höchst on the River Main. The war against Frederick V and the Palatinate was over and won by the end of the year (Map 8). It is not known how long Richard Walsh served under Count Tilly, if the thesis is correct, or when he entered the service of Albrecht Wenzel Eusebius von Wallenstein.

Wallenstein was a Bohemian landowner who accumulated great power and wealth throughout his 41 years. His eventual collection of titles included those of duke of Friedland, duke of Mecklenburg and prince of Sagen (Pl. 19). Born and raised a Protestant, he later converted to Catholicism. Two marriages brought him the bulk of his fortune. He approached the emperor with proposals to raise a self-supporting army, leading to prolonged discussion and negotiations. On 21 June 1625 the deal was struck at the castle of Cardinal Dietrichstein at Nikolsburg in Moravia (Mann 1976, 269). It was agreed that the army should have an initial strength of 24,000 men. Wallenstein was raised to ducal status as a reward.

His first major test came in April 1625 when he rushed his army to Dessau Bridge, a strategic crossing on the River Elbe about 65km north of Leipzig, where he encountered the Danish army under the command of von Mansfeld (Mann 1976, 285;

Pl. 20—Gustavus Adolphus (1594–1632), king of Sweden. (The Royal Armoury, Sweden)

Birely 2014, 162). The battle raged for six hours on 25 April. Wallenstein's forces held firm and repulsed the Danish forces. The fugitive von Mansfeld later died in Venice on 14 December.

Wallenstein and his army spent 1627 driving the Protestant forces from Silesia. The following year he played a supporting role to Count Tilly in Mecklenburg. This northern duchy on the Baltic Sea had supported the intervention by King Christian IV of Denmark. Success in the campaign led to Wallenstein's second ducal title and possession of the dukedom. In truth he was granted Mecklenburg by Ferdinand II in lieu of monies owed (Mann 1976, 427). Nevertheless, his reforms and administration improved many aspects of life in the duchy. For example, almshouses and hospitals were set up in all towns and parishes (*ibid.*, 426).

The intervention in 1630 of King Gustavus Adolphus of Sweden gave a dramatic turn to the ongoing conflict (Pl. 20). Within six weeks Saxony had entered the fray as his ally, and other states would follow over the coming months (Ingrao 1994, 45). Ferdinand summoned a conference of the electors at Regensburg. Their co-operation was made conditional on the emperor's dismissal of Wallenstein, whose power and predominance was a constant irritant to them.

Tilly took command of all forces. He was roundly defeated at Breitenfeld outside Leipzig by a Swedish/Saxon force of 42,000 troops on 17 September 1631. The contribution made by soldiers of fortune at the time is illustrated by the fact that only about 20% of the army were native Swedes (Lee 1991, 44). This victory encouraged other German states to rebel (Birely 2014, 231). On 15 April 1632 the Swedish forces crossed the River Lech near Rain and entered Bavaria. Tilly was wounded in the resulting battle and died two weeks later. Ironically, his injury prompted the imperial army to withdraw and thus escape the lethal encirclement planned by the Swedish king (*ibid.*, 244).

THE BATTLE OF LÜTZEN

Ferdinand had little option but to recall Wallenstein. The duke rallied and advanced into Saxony with the intention of subjugating the electorate (Mann 1976, 640). Gottfried Heinrich, Graf zu Pappenheim, having been uncontactable for weeks, finally arrived in Leipzig with an 8,000-strong supporting force on 6 November (*ibid.* 647). Gustavus Adolphus quickly recognised Wallenstein's design and realised its potential serious negative effect on his German allies. He advanced as fast as his army could move and arrived on the River Saale. His forces took Naumburg on 10 November (Wilson 2009, 507).

Wallenstein and Pappenheim advanced as far as Weissenfels, about an hour's march from Naumburg and also located on the River Saale (Mann 1976, 648). As Gustavus did not sally forth to meet them, they withdrew on 14 November to Lützen, about 20km south-west of Leipzig.

On the morning of 15 November Major-General Rudolph Colloredo led a detachment of Croats and dragoons back in the direction of Weissenfels. Simultaneously, Pappenheim led his eight regiments towards Halle, with the prime objective of driving the Swedes from the castle of Moritzburg (Geijer 1845, I, 279). He occupied Halle later that afternoon. Meanwhile, Colonel Melchior von Hatzfeld and a further four regiments headed for Eilenburg, to the north-east of Leipzig (Mann 1976, 649).

Colloredo reached the River Rippach close to its confluence with the River Saale. There was localised flooding in the area but that was not his primary concern, as he found his small force confronting not scouting parties but the vanguard of the Swedish army on the march.

When Wallenstein received word from Colloredo, he began the process of digging in at Lützen. Estimations of the strength of his army on the day vary. According to Wilson (2009, 507), he had at his disposal 8,550 infantry, 3,800 cavalry and twenty pieces of heavy artillery. Mann (1976, 654) put the figure at 8,200 foot, 7,500 horse and 21 heavy guns. He calculated the Swedish force as being between 18,000 and 19,000 strong (*ibid.*). Colloredo fulfilled his duty by delaying the Swedish advance, holding them at a narrow pass close to the hamlet of Poserna (Geijer 1845, I, 283).

Wallenstein dispatched an urgent message to Pappenheim to rejoin him as fast as humanly possible. Resistance at Poserna finally ended at about 4 o'clock in the afternoon and the Swedish army began pouring through the pass. It was now too late for the two armies to engage that day.

Reinforcements for Wallenstein continued to arrive throughout the night of 15

Pl. 21—The Battle of Lützen in Saxony (16 November 1632). (Nationalmuseum of Sweden)

November. Lützen, a small town of about 300 houses and a castle, lay along the road from Naumburg to Leipzig. To the immediate north of the town the road curved to the east before curving again and heading off to the north-east. It was here, using the castle and town as his right flank, that Wallenstein established his front. The road featured broad, deep ditches on both sides and the imperial army positioned itself behind the 'northern' side of the road. The front was approximately 2km long. On either flank detachments of cavalry and musketeers were interspersed. Fourteen quarter-cannon were positioned on a hill topped by four windmills close to the town to support the right wing; seven more were positioned between the centre and the left flank. The left wing of the army was manned mostly by Hungarians, Croats and Poles. The centre was to be held by four brigades of infantry, each consisting of several regiments (Geijer 1845, 280). All through the night the imperial dragoons and pioneers laboured non-stop; trees were felled, earthen banks were raised and ditches were deepened (Geijer 1845, 280; Mann 1976, 654).

Gustavus Adolphus, naturally, would have liked to attack at dawn but 16 November broke in a dense fog—*Lützen-dimma* in Sweden to this day. It did not break properly until towards noon. The Swedish army spent the time in prayer. They then sang Luther's psalm 'To us our God is a strong tower' and listened to Gustavus's rendition of 'Jesus Christ our Saviour, death He did overpower'. A break in the fog about 10 o'clock prompted the opening up of the artillery (Geijer 1845, 281). The Swedish troops had been gradually moving forward since 8 o'clock and towards noon battle was finally joined (Pl. 21).

Gustavus led the attack on the left flank and broke the imperial line, his cavalry jumping over the abandoned ditches. Then suddenly to the rescue came Pappenheim and his 2,300-strong force of cavalry, having ridden 35km through the night (Wilson 2009, 510). The imperial front was thus restored, but in the execution of the counter-attack Pappenheim was hit by a molten projectile, and possibly by a musket-shot, and killed (Geijer 1845, 283; Mann 1976, 655 fn.). The counter-attack faltered. All would have been lost had not a division of Croats circumvented the Swedes and attacked the rear, necessitating a distracting redeployment.

Bernard von Weimar led an attack against the imperial right flank. Wallenstein had the town torched, and the combination of swirling smoke, heavy artillery fire and a counter-charge led by Wallenstein himself threw the Germans back. In trouble, they appealed to Gustavus. The king came galloping across the field of battle. Towards the centre he became separated from his Smålander cavalry and was hit in the left arm by a musket-shot. He blundered into a party of the enemy and was cut down by a fusillade of pistol-shots. His body was stabbed repeatedly and robbed of all valuables.

Octavio Piccolomini, who had taken command of the left flank in the wake of Pappenheim's death, led charge after charge against the Swedish lines. Just as their right wing's struggle against the imperial front stagnated, those Swedes and Germans fighting on the left experienced a dramatic change of fortune. The effort to retrieve the fallen king's body turned into a general advance. The imperial trenches were overrun, as was their artillery battery not long afterwards. Still their centre and the revitalised left held. With darkness approaching, time was about to bring a halt to the day's proceedings.

As the night drew in, Pappenheim's infantry finally arrived after their long forced march from Halle: five regiments with an overall strength of 3,000 men (Wilson 2009, 510). Wallenstein used them to cover the withdrawal of his army. By morning, to the Swedes' surprise, they were gone. On the field of battle lay over 9,000 dead, the ratio being almost two to one in favour of the imperialists (*ibid.*). The battered and bloody body of Gustavus Adolphus had been recovered by Finnish troops under the command of Colonel Stalhandske and brought to the hamlet of Meucken (Geijer 1845, I, 283). Stalhandske is also credited with the slaying of Pappenheim (*ibid.*).

The imperial forces withdrew to Leipzig, where they remained for 24 hours. When they departed, they left about 1,160 wounded in the city (Mann 1976, 664; Wilson 2009, 510), and amongst these was Richard Walsh of Carrickmines.

It is reasonable to suggest, given his rank and previous appointment, that Richard was in command of a regiment at Lützen. He had attained the rank of colonel (*Oberst*) of infantry by the late 1620s and had served as governor (*Statthalter/Kommandant*) of Szatmárnémeti on the frontier with the Ottomans (Worthington 2004, 151 fn. 26). It would be intriguing to know whether he had fought on the left or the right flank or in the centre at Lützen. The latter position had seen particularly intense fighting between the respective infantry regiments. The Swedes had committed their élite Blue and Yellow regiments to this theatre of the battle; both suffered devastating losses (Geijer 1845, I, 281; Mann 1976, 660).

There can be little doubt that Richard's second wife, Countess Barbara Schlick of Bohemia, was instrumental in his rise through the ranks (Worthington 2004, 151 fn. 26). She was the daughter of Carl Maximilian, count of Bassano und Weisskischen (Hussey Walsh 1900–1, 219), lord of Welichau near Karlsbad (Barker 1982, 53). Richard was to serve as an imperial chamberlain (*Kammerherr*) and as a member of the imperial war council (*Hofkriegsrat*) (*ibid.*).

The fact that Walsh ended up in Wallenstein's service is unsurprising, as the great generalissimo had built his army group on foreign manpower. He raised men up through the ranks irrespective of nationality or religion, and also practised a system of substantial rewards. A regimental colonel received a wage of 500 florins per week in addition to extensive powers—not least the 'ownership' of the regiment (Worthington 2004, 146), which included control of recruitment (*ibid.*, 147 fn. 11). These substantial rewards attracted many upwardly mobile hopefuls from abroad. Indeed, the position of *Inhaber* (regimental 'owner') was an 'instrument of social mobility' (*ibid.*, 150).

According to the Wallis Family Archive (*Rodinny Archiv Wallisu*) stored in the Moravian Regional Archives in Brno/Brúnn, Richard Walsh was accompanied to the Continent by his sons Theobald and Oliver (Worthington 2004, 151 fn. 26; Barker 1982, 53, 205 fn. 58). Hussey Walsh (1900–1, 219) argued that these records had to be accurate, as they contained documents and pedigrees that formed the basis both of Oliver Walsh's appointment as chamberlain to the Emperor Leopold I in 1665, i.e. his 'sixteen quarterings' (*seize quartiers*), and of his son Georg's 'thirty-two quarterings' (*trente-deux quartiers*), also necessary for promotion.

Oliver Walsh is somewhat problematic. His absence from the pedigree drawn up by Molyneux in 1610 could be explained either by his absence (although surely Molyneux would have described him accordingly) or by assigning him a post-1610 date of birth. That would mean that he would have been only twelve at the projected date of his father's departure to the Continent, although he could, of course, have followed his father and older brother at a later date than 1622. He is, however, absent from the will made by Richard on 27 December 1619 (Griffith 1991, 446), which is difficult to explain unless there had been an estrangement. He is also absent from a 1619 document in the Genealogical Office manuscripts that recorded Richard's death and listed his seven children (Genealogical Office MS 66, 87). Clark (2010, 184) described him as being 'of the same breed' as Richard, giving his date of birth as 1600 and his place of birth as *Carrighmain*. His time of arrival on the Continent is assigned to the beginning of the Thirty Years' War. Silke (1976, 610) described Oliver as being 'related' to Richard.

If Richard did well in the imperial world, his achievements were surpassed by Oliver. He was created the first Baron von Wallis in 1642, was raised to the position of *Herrenstand Bóhmen* (Bohemia) on 28 June 1645 and to *Herrenstand Máhren* (Moravia) in 1650, before being appointed chamberlain to the emperor in 1665. He was colonel and *Inhaber* of the Wallis Regiment of infantry. Further senior positions were to follow: he was appointed commander-in-chief of the forces to the east of the River Theiss and of his father's old command at Szatmárnémeti in eastern Hungary.

Oliver married Maria Agnes, daughter of Heinrich Lorenz, Count von Guttenstein. They had four children, Georg, Franz Ernst, Jane Elizabeth and Anna Barbara. It may be of significance that, unlike the other three children, the eldest daughter bore an 'Anglo' name; Jane was the name of Richard Walsh's first wife, Elizabeth the name of his sister. The eldest son, Georg, the second Baron von Wallis, was born in 1621. He served as a lieutenant-colonel in the von Wallis regiment. A very successful military career culminated in promotion to *Feldmarschall Leutnant* and commander-in-chief of imperial forces in Upper Hungary and on the River Rhine (Hussey Walsh 1900–1, 219–20). His five sons all followed military careers. His son Franz Paul rose to the rank of *Feldmarschall* in 1737 (*ibid.*, 221). Their descendants were to enjoy many further major achievements (Hussey Walsh 1900–1, 221–4; Clark 2010, 197; Barker 1982, 53–6).

The length of the wounded Richard's stay in Leipzig is unknown. The available documents all record that he finally passed away in Magdeburg in late 1632 (Hussey Walsh 1900–1, 219; Worthington 2004, 151 fn. 26; Clark 2010, 183). This city, which lies over 120km to the north/north-west of Leipzig, was a miserable place in which to die. It had been stormed and torched on 20 May 1631 by out-of-control soldiers under the command of Tilly and Pappenheim. A contemporary account by Otto von Guericke described the event as 'naught but beating and burning, plundering, torture, and murder' (Robinson 1904–6, II, 211). Approximately 20,000 of the 30,000 citizens were slain. Their bodies were cast into the River Elbe.

THEOBALD WALSH

Barker (1982, 53) suggested that improved conditions under King Charles I prompted Theobald to return home to *Karighmain*. Presumably he had soldiered under the command of his father Richard throughout his stay on the Continent. Given his subsequent marriage to Maria Hoare and the projected age of their two sons, it would appear that he had returned to Ireland prior to the Battle of Lützen. Indeed, the implication in a report compiled by Archbishop Lancelot Bulkeley in the early months of 1630 was that Theobald at the time was in residence at his 'mansion house' in *Carrickmayne* (Bulkeley 1869, 158; Ronan 1941, 82). This suggestion is advanced by his appearance in a deed pertaining to the Walshes of Shanganagh and dated to March 1631 (see 'The Walsh cadet houses', below).

Ball (1901, 199; 1902–17, I, 101) noted Hussey Walsh's placing of Theobald in the 'Austrian service'. He observed that 'a payment made by the great Earl of Cork in 1630 to the owner of Carrickmines' on instructions received from 'a foreigner called Pompeio Calandrino' might have been related to Theobald's foreign service. The 'Lismore Papers' were named as the source of the data referred to here.

The full quote in the Lismore Papers reads: 'This day I receaved lettres from pompeio calandrino to pay Mr. Walsh of *carrickmayn*, upon Mr. Burlymachies bill of exchange 169 *l.* sterling' (Grosart 1886, III, 43). This entry was dated July 1630. In a second entry, dated September of the same year, however, the earl clarifies that the payment went to 'one Mr. Edward Walsh of *Carrickmayn*' (*ibid.*, 52). The man in question would most likely be Richard's uncle Edward, born at Carrickmines but living in Clonmannan, Co. Wicklow, by 1630. He was still alive and described as being 'eighty years old, blind and bed-ridden' in 1641 (*DKR 19* (1887), 36) and would thus have been around 70 years of age in 1630.

A scenario worth considering is that, with Richard away on the Continent, Edward was acting as the head of the family. Richard's father, Theobald, had died in November 1593. A further question to be addressed, however, is that of who exactly had earned the £169 sterling. Was it Theobald or Richard or, indeed, a son of Edward's? Theobald was apparently back home at this point, but possibly deferring to Edward as the senior member of the family.

The two gentlemen mentioned in the document further complicate the picture. Pompeo Calandrini and his older brother Julian had inherited their share of their father Giovanni's banking house after his death in 1623 (Grell 2011, 111); their brother Philip also played an important role in the business (*ODNB*, VIII, 865). Their sister Elizabeth was married to Philip Burlamachi, the co-founder of the merchant banking house in London with their father Giovanni (Grell 1989, 62).

The Calandrinis and the Burlamachis had been domiciled in Lucca in Italy until the 1560s. Their adherence to the Reformed Faith had led to their expulsion from their homeland. The Calandrinis remained very committed to their faith. Another brother of Pompeo's, Cesar, was a Calvinist minister, a 'puritanical theologist' by profession (*ibid.*, 64). He formed a close friendship in London between 1623 and 1626 with James Ussher, the future archbishop of Armagh (*ibid.*, 65).

The Burlamachi–Calandrini merchant bank became a major player in the financial affairs of the English royal family. Philip Calandrini personally pawned jewels for Charles I in Amsterdam (*ODNB*, VIII, 865). Between 1620 and 1628 Philip Burlamachi advanced the wages and financed the supplies of Protestant forces fighting in the Thirty Years' War to the grand total of £700,000. He also covered the expenditure of the English and Scottish troops serving in Germany, the United Provinces and Denmark (Grell 2011, 111). Covering the operations in the Lower Palatinate alone in 1624 required a sum of £20,000 to be raised (*ODNB*, VIII, 866). Julian Calandrini was officially described in February 1631 as 'paymaster of the army beyond seas' (Bruce 1858–69, IV, 504). Pompeo remained working at home in the London office (Grell 2011, 111).

On 29 August 1629 a commission was granted to Philip Burlamachi for the sale of 4,000 tons of iron ordnance to the Dutch (Bruce 1858–69, IV, 44). On 30 June 1630 it was agreed that he should be paid for all monies owed for covering the household expenses of the exiled king and queen of Bohemia (*ibid.*, 295). A state document, dated provisionally to 1630, concerns payment to a Sir John Radcliffe 'for service in the Low Countries', according to the 'accounts of Burlamachi and Calandrini' (*ibid.*, 432). The dating of this document is close to the time of the Carrickmines monetary transaction. There is, it is quite apparent, no evidence to support the proposition that the

Burlamachi–Calandrini merchant bank had any financial dealings with the Holy Roman Empire, i.e. the employers of Richard Walsh and his sons. In fact, their military involvements were exclusively with the Protestant cause. A remaining question, therefore, is whether there was a son of Edward Walsh of Clonmannan fighting on the Protestant side in either the Netherlands or the north German States at the end of the 1620s.

Theobald was the eldest of the seven (or eight, including Oliver) children of Richard Walsh and Jane Eustace. He was born in 1605, according to the pedigree drawn by Molyneux (Genealogical Office MS 48, 21). His other siblings were Eleanor, Mary and Katherin (born before 1610) and Michael, Margaret and Anne (born after 1610).

Oliver, with all the attendant complications relating to him, has been discussed above. The only information available on Michael is that he was alive in 1619 and was to be left £100 in his father's will (Griffith 1991, 446). Katherin married George Archbold of Kingston (Hussey Walsh 1900–1, 219). Eleanor appeared in an entry relating to her father in 1619 (Genealogical Office MS 66, 87). A pedigree of Henry Walsh of Killincarrig, Co. Wicklow, who died in 1634, recorded that his eldest son John had married 'Eleanor daughter of Richard Walsh of *Carrickmayne* in the County *Dublyn* Esq' (Genealogical Office MS 69, 69).

In the will drawn up on 27 December 1619 Richard arranged to leave £20 each to his daughters 'Ellenor, Mary, Kate, Margaret and Anne'. As his instructions relating to future marriages are exclusive to Eleanor and Mary, the inference is that the other three girls were married by that date. While we know (see above) that Eleanor did marry, we lack marital information on Mary and Anne. Some information contained in the Civil Survey must also be considered. It relates that about the year 1635 or 1636 Theobald had to mortgage some land 'for the maintenance of his sisters' (Simington 1931–61, VII, 271). This would imply either that not all his sisters married or that one or more were widowed and left dependent on the support of the Walsh family, or perhaps that one or more were financially challenged members of a religious order.

Margaret married James Hoare, a scion of Kilsallaghan Castle in north County Dublin. His father, Philip, inherited the castle and estate from his father, also Philip, in 1630. The estate consisted of over 700 acres of quality land and two townhouses in Dublin. The close ties between the two families were further strengthened by the marriage of James Hoare's sister Maria to Theobald Walsh himself (Clinton 2005, 26–7).

When Richard Walsh drafted his will (see above), he appointed four men as his trustees: John Fagan of Feltrim in north County Dublin, Nicholas Eustace of *Confie* (Confey), Co. Kildare, John Allen of Bishopscourt, Co. Kildare, and Richard Barnewall of *Lespopple* (Lispopple) in north County Dublin (Griffith 1991, 447). It should be noted that Fagan was described as his 'uncle' and both Eustace and Allen as his 'brothers' (*ibid*., 446). Richard's wife, Jane Eustace, was the daughter of Marie Fagan, hence the Fagan relationship. Nicholas was a brother of Jane's and thus brother-in-law to Richard. John Allen was married to Richard's sister Mary and thus was also a brother-in-law. In May 1623, when Theobald was *c.* eighteen years of age, i.e. still legally under age, the lease on the Walsh lands was acquired from the trustees by John Finglas of *Tobberton* (Toberton, to the west/north-west of Balbriggan in north County Dublin). The Walsh estate was described as consisting of one castle and 300 acres in *Carrickmayne*; *Ballinrowe* and *Glannermucke* (Glenamuck) (60 acres); and *Frompston al' Crompston* (66 acres) (Hardiman 1826–9, II, No. 54).

On 30 November 1621 the 'tithe corn of *Carrickmayne*, *Pryorsland* and *Keatingsland*' had been granted by Randal Barlowe, the dean of Holy Trinity, to William Wolferston of *Rabo* in the county of Dublin for a term of 21 years (McEnery and Refaussé 2001, 306). Wolferston was still in possession of these corn tithes in 1633, along with neighbouring lands in Tipperstown, Ballyogan, Mulchanstown and Stillorgan (*ibid.*, 312).

CONFESSIONAL CONTRADICTIONS

Given the amount of grief, duplicity and misunderstanding that had ensued from Prince Charles's courtship of the *Infanta* Maria, there was almost something perverse about the fact that King James would once again embark on a duplicate quest. France was as Catholic a country as Spain and complications were clearly inevitable. A marriage of the heir to the throne to a suitable Protestant princess from northern Europe would have been a resoundingly popular move with parliament and people. Yet securing a Habsburg or Bourbon marriage alliance was the golden prize for James, despite its being an open invitation to trouble.

In Ireland hopeful eyes turned once more towards the Continent. The prolonged negotiations with Spain had tempered anti-Catholic activities at home. It was reasonable, therefore, for people to have similar expectations in relation to the French courtship. The problem, however, was that there was now an increasing divarication in the policy agenda of the different arms of the State. While the monarch and his court might favour one set of objectives, there was no longer a guarantee that either the parliament in London or the administrations in Dublin or Edinburgh would comply. This resulted in many compromises and much gamesmanship. For example, when the king, towards the end of his reign, issued a proclamation ordering all Catholic priests to leave before 14 June 1624, he did so to deflect criticism from parliament (Patterson 1997, 352).

James I died on 27 March 1625 at the age of 59. Charles was crowned king of England at Westminster Abbey on 2 February 1626. He was 24 years of age.

George Villiers, the newly created duke of Buckingham, greatly favoured an alliance with France. In geographical terms alone, it was perfectly placed to counter the Habsburg axis of Spain and the Holy Roman Empire (*ibid.*, 353). Henry Rich, soon to be earl of Holland, was dispatched to Paris to sound out the French court in February 1624. He proved a very good choice socially but quite inept politically. He intrigued with Marie de Médicis and had an affair with Marie de Rohan, the duchesse de Chevreuse. The reports to London were overly optimistic and ultimately misleading (*ODNB*, XLVI, 665).

The English negotiating team in London thought that the French would accept the terms of the proposed marriage to Princess Christine back in 1616, which would have confined religious toleration to the bride's household. To their dismay, their French counterparts presented them with a document containing thirteen articles. Basically, they were emulating the Spanish demands, including a universal removal of restrictions against the Catholic population of the three kingdoms (Patterson 1997, 353).

The primary prerequisite, naturally, was that Princess Henrietta Maria's personal adherence to her religion should be unimpeded and remain sacrosanct. The religion of her children, up to the age of thirteen, was also a key issue. Other demands covered such considerations as the abolition of the anti-Catholic penal laws and the revocation of 'the Oath of Allegiance' (Freist 2011, 39). As in the *Infanta* Maria affair, the procurement of a dispensation from Rome was obligatory. The suspicion that the French side would bend this process to their advantage was foremost in the minds of the English negotiators (Hardwicke 1778, I, 526, 537).

A furious James Hay, first Lord Carlisle, wrote from Paris to the duke of Buckingham on 16 February 1625. He accused the French of attempting to 'impose a new treaty upon us, after a perfect treaty concluded, signed, and sworn by his Majesty', and all based on the 'Pope's borrowed name' (*ibid.*, 552). The long-hoped-for dispensation from the pope had been issued by Rome. Carlisle was putting all new demands down to French gamesmanship. The new demands were for a 'public notification' of full toleration of Catholicism in 'all his Majesty's kingdom'. Both King James and Prince Charles would be obliged to confirm toleration by oath and to dispatch a written copy of the commitment to the pope (*ibid.*). Again, the Spanish agreement was used as a precedent in that they were insisting that 'something must be granted in favour of our Catholics, for the facilitating of the dispensation' (*ibid.*, 553).

It had already been finally decided that the formal wedding contract would be supplemented by a secret covenant to be approved by the pope. The '*Escrit Secret*' basically promised all that the French king and court, and the pope, would want to hear. The terms of the covenant had been agreed by the ambassadors of England and France on 18 November 1624. Catholics were promised enhanced liberty and franchise ('*de jouir de plus de liberté & franchise*') regarding their religion. They would be left alone 'in their persons and goods' ('*personnes & biens*'). They would be obliged to practise their religion 'modestly' ('*pourveu tout es fois qu'ils en usent modestement*') and to 'render obedience as good subjects of their King' ('*rendent l'obisance que de bons & vrays subjects doivent á leur Roy*'). Lords Carlisle and Holland signed on behalf of King James (*ibid.*, 546–7). The 'public' marriage agreement was also signed in November and ratified in the parliament in December.

English resolve hardened on the contract as previously agreed. The French accepted. There was then a delay owing to the untimely death in March of King James.

Henrietta Maria was obliged to write personally to Pope Urban VIII to give him her word that her children would be baptised into the Catholic Church and that she would do her utmost to bring succour to the Catholic population. The letter was written in Paris and dispatched on 6 April 1625 (Freist 2011, 39 fn. 27).

A proxy marriage took place in May in Paris, with the duc de Chevreuse standing in for Charles. Henrietta Maria, accompanied by her entourage and escorted by the duke of Buckingham, landed in England in June.

On 1 May Charles had signed a proclamation stating that he had been 'moved, in contemplation of his marriage with the Lady Marie [...] to grant to his Roman Catholic subjects a cessation of all pains and penalties by reason of their recusancy. His will is, that the Lord Keeper should give warrant and direction to all Judges and other officers to forbear all manner of proceedings against His Majesty's Roman Catholic subjects' (Bruce 1858–69, I, 16).

The good intentions quickly evaporated. To appease an agitated parliament, the secret accord was quietly discarded and the anti-Catholic laws renewed with vigour (Freist 2011, 41). After Buckingham was assassinated in 1628, Henrietta Maria and Charles finally developed a close relationship. She was to remain 'a symbol of hope and an icon of Catholicism, piety and devotion' (*ibid.*, 5) to the 'recusants' throughout the 1630s.

THE GREAT ASSEMBLY

The diplomatic manoeuvring between England and France resulted in some benefit, albeit temporary, for Ireland. Whereas in January 1624 Henry Cary, first Viscount Falkland, the lord deputy, had been given the authority to issue an edict against Catholic priests and to enforce the anti-recusant laws with vigour, by February he had been told to put the operation on hold, and within a year was instructed to cease all operations (Clarke 1976b, 233). The preparations for war against Spain further improved the possibility of positive change in Ireland. It was decided in London that defence of the island would be the financial responsibility of the indigenous loyal population, in practical terms the Old English. This was the sort of opportunity that the latter needed to display their loyalty to the king, regardless of their religious affiliations. Their expectations were dashed when the plan of organising local militias was scuppered by the Dublin administration backed by the new Protestant settlers (*ibid.*, 234), who viewed control of the army as an integral factor in the protection of their interests (Clarke 1966, 35).

The need to defend Ireland, England's back door, from a Spanish invasion remained. Aidan Clarke (1976b, 235) has encapsulated the attitude of the Old English representatives thus: 'they were not prepared to trust Charles unless he was prepared to trust them'. Why pay for the maintenance of an army when they could form a self-financed home guard themselves at no cost?

It was decided to hold a 'great assembly' in Dublin in mid-April 1627 in an attempt to resolve all the conflicting interests. Whilst the Old English attended with their set of grievances, so too did the New English. In their case the issue was the unwelcome meddling of central government. They resented the prospect of the formal ending of the payment of recusancy fines (although the payment of these had been in abeyance for some years) or any redaction of the Oath of Supremacy. A levelling out of obligations and privileges would in effect remove their higher standing in law and society. The fact that it was being flagged that they too would be expected to contribute to the defence fund only increased their discontent (*ibid.*, 236). The denouncement of any relaxation of anti-recusant measures from the pulpit of Christ Church Cathedral inflamed the resentment (Clarke 1966, 39). After a lot of to-ing and fro-ing, including a reasoned interjection by Archbishop Ussher, Falkland decided to bring proceedings to a close on 2 May, having achieved practically nothing (*ibid.*, 41).

None of this was of any use to a cash-strapped Charles. He decided that 'money-raising expedients' were the way forward, even if this meant granting concessions. Recusancy fines, religious tests for inheritance, office-holding and the practising of law would all be put on offer (MacCurtain 1972, 130–1). These 'matters of grace and bounty' were later to be commonly called the 'Graces'. Despite his personal wishes, Falkland allowed representatives from the four provinces to go to London to negotiate directly with the king. In May 1628 an agreement was finally reached. Three annual subsidies, of £40,000 *per annum*, would be delivered into the royal coffers (Beckett 1966, 59).

Falkland attempted to convene a parliament in late 1628 but in his haste contravened Poyning's Law on procedure. He was obliged by the English privy council to abandon the attempt and start the process again (Clarke 1976b, 239–40). The resultant backlash in Ireland did at least lead to the Court of Wards dropping its insistence on the taking of the Oath of Supremacy in all cases, and many Catholic heirs quickly availed of and benefited from this change in policy (*ibid.*, 240).

Viscount Falkland, in the wake of the death of his patron, the duke of Buckingham, in August 1628, found his star to be on the wane. By 13 April 1629 he was writing to the king from Dublin Castle, bemoaning his recall. He suggested that, pending the appointment of his successor, 'in the meantime the sword be placed in the hands of the justices' (Mahaffy 1900–1, I, 447).

This course of action was adopted, and Richard Boyle, earl of Cork, and Adam Loftus, the chancellor, were duly invited to form a joint leadership as lord justices (Clarke 1976b, 241). They took office in October. It did not take long for attitudes to harden. Back on 1 April Falkland had issued a proclamation 'forbidding the exercise of all ecclesiastical jurisdictions derived from Rome, and ordering that all colleges and monasteries of the Catholic orders shall dissolve and separate upon pain of seizure and expropriation' (Mahaffy 1900–1, I, 445). By 5 April he was able to report to the privy council that the measure had enjoyed 'very good results'. To his knowledge, there was 'hardly a Papist left in Dublin' and all their 'houses' were locked up. An amusing point of information is that he reported that 'the Jesuits and Franciscans each said the others were deserving of repression, and that they themselves were humble poor souls who might have been exempted from the process'. Curiously, he observed that he felt sure 'that the laity and moderate and secular priests are in sympathy with our action' (*ibid.*, 446). Before he could take his policy any further he was packing to leave for England, but the diktat was not rescinded.

On St Stephen's Day 1629 'the Government suppressed by peaceful means several priests and nun's houses and schools, and seized some priests'. The raids and arrests were conducted by 'the Archbishop, the Mayor, the Sheriffs', assisted by 'some pursuivants and officers'. The operation, however, was not without setbacks. The archbishop and mayor were set upon by a stone-throwing mob and had to take refuge. Several officers were 'severely hurt'. The justices and other officials had to rush from their respective church services to rescue them (Mahaffy 1900–1, I, 500). The event prompted a hard-line response from the State. All known religious houses were seized and closed. This policy was then extended to the entire island. Within a year the justices were proudly announcing that they had terminated the public observance of Catholicism in Ireland. The leasing of property by the religious orders now also became difficult (Clarke 1976b, 242).

The solution for the Gaelic and Old English Catholic gentry was simple. They could organise church services within the privacy of their own homes.

In his report on the diocese of Dublin in the year 1630 Archbishop Lancelot Bulkeley noted that 'every gentleman thereabout [Bray] hath a priest or a friar for their domestic chaplain and maintains and abetts them'. In this context he referred to Theobald Walsh of *Carrickmaine*. He wrote that Theobald 'doth relieve and abett one Turlough Reily, a Mass-priest, and one Patrick Comin, a friar, who celebrate Mass, and execute their function in his mansion house of *Carrickmayne*'. Bulkeley added that the religious services were 'frequented by neighbouring towns publicly' (Bulkeley 1869, 158; Ronan 1941, 82). The small church of Balally, close to the Walshes' castle, upon whose grounds it stood, was also in use. A John Cawhell (Cahill), priest, 'commonly' said Mass there and in Dundrum (Ball and Hamilton 1895, 14).

THE WALSH CADET HOUSES

Francis Erlington Ball (1902–17, II, 74) provided a brief summary of the lineage of the Walshes of Balally: 'In 1546 Thomas Walsh, who was then in possession of three houses and eighty one acres in Balally, was succeeded by his son, John, then a minor; in 1597 William Walsh was in possession, and in 1641 James Walsh was seized of the castle and lands, as well as those of Edmondstown, near Rathfarnham'. Thomas and his son John have been addressed in detail in the previous chapter (see Part 2). John was certainly still in possession in 1596 (Brewer and Bullen 1867–73, III, 189). The William noted above by Ball under the year 1597 was in fact William Walsh of Carrickmines, who was to administer the estate during John's minority. John Walsh of *Ballawly* died in May 1615. He was succeeded by his son James (Griffith 1991, 387). The death of Dorothy, the wife of James Walsh 'of *Balaunely*' in County Dublin, occurred on 7 September 1623 (Genealogical Office MS 68, 29; MS 79, 111). Dorothy was the daughter of

Murrough McEdmund O'Byrne of Kiltimon (TCD MS 1216, 27), the leader of the pro-government faction of the O'Byrnes. James was Dorothy's second husband; her first had been Turlough McFeagh McHugh O'Byrne, who had been executed on 18 July 1595 (Nicholls 1998b, 113). A deed dating from 1605 records the name of James's son and heir as Henry (Griffith 1991, 387). A survey of the 'Half-Barony of Rathdrum, in the County of Dublin', conducted by order of Charles Fleetwood, the lord deputy, in October 1654, recorded that in 1641 James Walsh was the proprietor of *Bellawly*. He was described as an 'Irish Papist' whose 220 acres consisted of twelve acres of meadow, 108 acres of arable and 100 acres of rocky/pasture land, with a revised valuation of £90. Along with the land, James was in possession of a thatch-roofed castle, the walls of a chapel and several houses. Arnold (1993, 154) credited James with 552 acres based on the data contained in the Dublin volume of the Quit Rent set of Books of Survey and Distribution.

Katherin Walsh of Kilgobbin died on 5 August 1617 (Genealogical Office MS 68, 23; MS 66, 68). Her eldest son, Pierce, had seven children by his second wife, Margaret Flatsbury of Johnstown—three sons (John, Richard and Edward) and four daughters (Katherin, Mary, Margaret and Elizabeth). By 1610 the eldest son, John, was married to Margaret, the daughter of Sir William Synnott of '*Bolmfernocke* in the county of *Weysford*'. William Synnott of *Bolefernock* in County Wexford was knighted by Sir Arthur Chichester, the lord deputy, at Dublin Castle on 22 June 1606 (Shaw and Burtchaell 1906, II, 140). There are two townlands named Ballyfarnogue in County Wexford, one of which lies to the north-north-east of Castlebridge and to the south-west of Blackwater. In the Civil Survey of 1654 it was rendered as *Bolefarnoge* (Simington 1931–61, IX, 63). John's sister Katherin was married to Theobald, the eldest son of Edward 'Archpole' (Archbold) of *Templecarge* (Templecarrig, to the north-west of Greystones, in the barony of Rathdown, Co. Wicklow) (Genealogical Office MS 48, 23). She died on 20 June 1622 (Genealogical Office MS 68, 2; TCD MS 1216, 25). Her mother, Margaret Walsh (née Flatsbury), died on 2 June 1623 (TCD MS 1216, 25b; Genealogical Office MS 79, 109).

According to Ball (1902–17, III, 65), Kilgobbin Castle was 'a strongly built oblong structure, two storeys over the basement in height'. A court was held there on the instruction of the exchequer during the tenure of Pierce/Peter Walsh (*ibid.*, 67). Peter Walsh died on 16 May 1633. Interestingly, although his son and heir John was 40 years of age and married, the estate was taken into the custody of James Flatsbury of Johnstown, Co. Kildare (Hardiman 1826–9, II, No. 34), Peter's father-in-law. The estate was described as consisting of one castle, ten messuages and 200 acres in Kilgobbin, and six messuages and 100 acres in Jamestown. The hamlets of *Bally-Edmonduffe* and *Ballybrack* were also mentioned (*ibid.*). The lands of Kilgobbin and Jamestown were in the possession of Sir Adam Loftus of Rathfarnham by 1640. The estate contained the castle (with a thatched roof), a garden plot and the walls of the parish church (Simington 1931–61, VII, 274). Joyce (1921, 164) ruminated on whether the Walsh family had lost the property 'by forfeiture or otherwise'.

Theobald Walsh of Killincarrig, Co. Wicklow, died on 11 January 1620

(Genealogical Office MS 66, 103) and was succeeded in the estate by his son and heir Henry. Henry had married Margaret, the daughter of John Walsh of Shanganagh. They had seven sons—John, Michael, Walter, Richard, Ambros, Francis (changed from Thomas) and William—and five daughters, Katherin, Rose, Begnet, Anne and Mary. The eldest son, John, married Eleanor, the daughter of Richard Walsh of Carrickmines. Interestingly, the fifth son, Ambros, 'dyed unmarried in the Lowe Countryes'. It is not unlikely that he was in military service there. Only two of the five daughters were married by the beginning of 1635. Katherin, the eldest daughter, was married to John O'Byrne of *Courtfoile* in County Wicklow, while her sister Rose was married to Edmund O'Byrne of *Tenaughpkey* in the same county (Genealogical Office MS 69, 69). Both Courtfoyle (to the south-south-west of Newcastle, north-north-east of Ashford) and Tinnapark Demesne (to the west of Kilpedder) lay within Críoch Branach. The tenures of the two O'Byrnes would have coincided with a profound shift in the administrative status and control of the territory. The effective rule of Críoch Branach for the half-century following 1580 was to lie in the hands of the New English adventurer Sir Henry Harrington, followed by his son William; the territory became in effect 'a private lordship' (Nicholls 1998a, 38, 39). The marriages of the two Walsh women to O'Byrne men had been preceded by that of their aunt Anastace, who had married James O'Byrne of *Ballinarin*. The townland of Ballynerrin lies to the immediate south of Killincarrig. Anastace died on 25 May 1622 (Genealogical Office MS 68, 1; TCD MS 1216, 24). Her sister Katherin, who died on 5 June 1616, had been the wife of William Harold from County Kildare (Genealogical Office MS 66, 55).

In June 1611 the king regranted the Shanganagh estate to James Walsh. The full inventory consisted of the castle, ten messuages, a watermill, 170 acres of arable land, ten acres of meadow and 30 acres of pasture in Shanganagh and *Kilturke*; a castle, ten messuages, 140 acres of arable land, twenty acres of woodland, five acres of meadow and 40 acres of pasture in *Connagh*; ten messuages, 70 acres of arable land, six acres of meadow and ten acres of pasture in *Corke alias Corkagh*; and three messuages, 24 acres of arable land and ten acres of pasture in *Little Brea*. No rent was reserved; it was 'to hold for ever' (*Cal. pat. rolls chancery*, 198). Two deeds, dating from March 1631, provide valuable insights into the lives of the Shanganagh branch of the Walshes in the early seventeenth century. The first, dated 10 March, records the terms of an agreement made between the head of the family, James Walsh, and Sir Robert Kennedy, chief remembrancer of the exchequer. It covers the dowry paid by the Kennedys to the Walshes in relation to the marriage of Sir Robert's daughter Mary to James's son John. Apparently £200 had already been paid, with another £600 now to follow. It was stipulated that the money would be reserved for the provision of dowries for James's daughters. He was to put most of his lands in Shanganagh in John and Mary's hands by the following Easter. The lands were to be stocked with '300 English ewes, 300 English lambs, 20 cows, 10 heifers & a plough of garrons with harness' (a garron is a small, sturdy horse). The animals were to be of a 'good breed'. Mary was also to receive £100 a year for life. The settlement of a property on Ale[...] Walsh (née Devenish), James's wife, for her lifetime was guaranteed after his death. Ultimately John would inherit the entire estate. There were, however, provisions made for 'Litle' (*sic*) Walsh (the second-eldest son) of £100 and for Dominick (the third son) of £200; the daughters were allocated a minimum of £200 each. The overseers of the agreement, including Theobald Walsh of *Carrickmayne* and John Walsh of Kilgobbin, were, however, authorised to increase Rose's (the eldest girl's) dowry to £500, Mary's to £400 and Kate's to £300. Should any daughter join a religious order she was to be granted £200 only (Griffith 1991, 461). An inquisition held in January 1643 clarified that James's second son was called *Lucas* (Luke). It also claimed that his daughters were named Margaret and Begnet (Hardiman 1826–9, II, No. 73).

Sir Robert Kennedy, besides holding the position of chief remembrancer of the exchequer, was also a member of parliament (representing the borough of Kildare). He held lands in counties Dublin (in the Lucan area) and Wicklow, including Ballygarney, now renamed Newtownmount-Kennedy (Ball 1902–17, IV, 78). He was married to the English-born Constance Silyard. Their son Richard entered Lincoln's Inn in 1638. He would in time be knighted, appointed baron of the exchequer and elected to represent Mullingar in parliament (Ball 1926, I, 347). This was a very influential and powerful Protestant establishment family, a very good marriage alliance for the Walshes of Shanganagh.

The deed also identifies other landholdings of the family. In fact, in the first deed James is described as being of *Conogh* (i.e. Old Connaught) in the county of Dublin. Money and Newrath in County Wicklow are mentioned. Newrath is located to the immediate north-east of Rathnew in the barony of Newcastle. The conjoined townlands of Money Big and Money Little are located to the south-south-east of Arklow. There is also reference to Kilclone *alias* Kilclonagh in County Meath. Kilclone is located to the north of Maynooth, just inside the County Meath border.

The second deed, dated 20 March 1631, denotes the core holdings of the family, i.e. Shanganagh, Kiltuck (a subdivision of the previous townland), *Conagh* (Old Connaught), Cork *alias Corkagh* and Little Bray (Griffith 1991, 462). This deed identified Edward as the son and heir of John (the son of James). The name of James's fourth son is revealed as Francis. Other Walshes are named: Richard Walsh of *Little Brea*, Piers Walsh of Dublin (merchant) and his brother Charles. An Oliver Walsh of Shanganagh, Theobald Walsh of *Carrigmayne* and John, the son of Henry Walsh of Killincarrig, are also mentioned. The exact relationship between these men and James Walsh of Shanganagh is not specified. Oliver of Shanganagh was not listed amongst the sons of John Walsh; he may therefore have been a brother(?). Piers and Charles were identified as being brothers; this would tend to preclude that relationship with James. Richard Walsh of Little Bray, owing to the land occupancy, was clearly a close relation. Two of the witnesses to the deed were a Luke Walsh and an Edward Devenish (clearly a relative of James's wife Ale[...]).

James had a sister named Margaret who was married to Henry Walsh of Killincarrig, Co. Wicklow (Genealogical Office MS 69, 69). He also had a brother named Edmund, mentioned in their father John's will (Griffith 1991, 46). Edmund was identified as the 'second brother to the House of *Shanganaugh*' (Genealogical Office

MS 79, 107)—'second brother' as in 'then alive'. He was the father of Giles, who was married to Edward Archbold of Templecarrig, Co. Wicklow (Genealogical Office MS 68, 20; TCD MS 1216, 25), and Honora, who was married to Nicholas Barnewall. The will illustrates the extended nature of the family by this point in time; it mentions a Gerald Walsh of Rathmichael (deceased), his two sons Richard and Thomas, a Pierce Walsh of Dublin, his brother Charles and his three sons Edmund, Richard and Robert, and a Nicholas Walsh of *Little Brea* (see the deed of 20 March above).

The chancery inquisition of January 1643 (see above) recorded that James Walsh of Shanganagh died on 10 November 1641. It also detailed leasing arrangements between James and other individuals, including Thomas Allen, an alderman in Dublin city, concluded in March 1631. The inventory of properties listed a castle, ten messuages and two carucates in Shanganagh/Kiltuck, 120 acres in *Corke alias Corcagh* and a castle, six messuages and 200 acres in *Conagh*. An additional four messuages and 30 acres at an unnamed location (presumably in Little Bray?) were identified. A second concordat concluded the same month involved, amongst others, Walter Ussher, another alderman in the city, Sir William Parsons and his son, Richard, and John Pue, later to be mayor of Dublin (Hardiman 1826–9, II, No. 73). Ussher was married to Mary, the daughter of George Kennedy, an alderman in the city. He died on 3 April 1636 (Wright 1889, 31, 263).

THOMAS WENTWORTH, EARL OF STRAFFORD

Thomas Wentworth, born on 13 April 1593, was the eldest son of Sir William of Wentworth-Woodhouse and Anne Atkinson of Stowell in Gloucestershire (Pl. 22). He married Margaret Clifford, the daughter of the fourth earl of Cumberland, in October 1611; on 6 December he was knighted (*ODNB*, LVIII, 142).

Wentworth entered politics and served Yorkshire as a knight of the shire in the parliament of 1614. He represented the shire again in 1621. His wife died the following year (Knowler 1739, II, 430). His own health suffered at the time and he was seriously ill from fevers in both 1622 and 1623. His appointment as sheriff of Yorkshire in 1625 effectively precluded him from sitting in parliament. That year he remarried, his new wife being Arabella, second daughter of John Holles, first earl of Clare, and a sister of Denzil Holles, 1st Baron Holles, a childhood friend of King Charles.

On 21 July 1628 Wentworth was granted the baronies of Wentworth-Woodhouse and Newmarch and Oversley (Bruce 1858–69, III, 222). In December of that year he was raised from baron to viscount. He was appointed president of the council of the north on 25 December 1628 (*ODNB*, LVII, 145).

In a warrant signed on 30 December 1630 the king instructed the attorney-general to prepare a bill that would facilitate the granting of named offices to Thomas, Viscount Wentworth, i.e. bailiff of the franchise of Richmond, steward of the same, chief forester of the forest and keeper of the castles of Richmond and Middleham in Yorkshire (these had previously been held by the late earl of Sunderland) (Hamilton

Pl. 22—Thomas Wentworth (1593–1641), 1st earl of Strafford, lord lieutenant of Ireland. (National Portrait Gallery: NPG 1077)

and Crawford Lomas 1897, 388).

October 1631 witnessed the death of his wife Arabella. A year later he was married for a third time, this time to Elizabeth Rodes.

LORD DEPUTY OF IRELAND

It came as no real surprise to the members of the royal court when Wentworth was announced as the new lord deputy of Ireland in January 1632; in February preparations for his arrival in Ireland began in earnest. On 4 February Sir William Parsons, master of the wards in Ireland, wrote to him to declare his loyalty and support (Knowler 1739, I, 64–5). Wentworth persuaded the English privy council on 17 February 'that good men be put in as Bishops in Ireland' and 'that they be made members of the Irish Privy Council'. His rationale was that service in Ireland, in general, should be promoted as a guarantee of later advancement in England (Mahaffy 1900–1, I, 647).

The lord justices of Ireland (Adam Loftus and Richard Boyle) wrote to the lord deputy regarding 'His Majesty's Castle of Dublin'. They reported that it was 'much decayed, and very ruinous, especially in the Parts thereof which are used for the Deputy's Habitation' (Knowler 1739, I, 68). On 21 February the king had instructed the lord justices to provide funds for the restoration of Dublin Castle, as it was 'much decayed'. They were also to deliver 'our house the Phoenix near *Kilmaignham*' to George Hull, the man responsible for all preparations for the lord deputy's arrival (Mahaffy 1900–1, I, 648).

Wentworth finally arrived in Dublin on 24 July 1633. Captain Sir Richard Plumleigh reported to the secretary to the admiralty Sir Edward Nicholas that he had landed the lord deputy on that day. The Sword of State was conferred on him 'on St James' Day' (i.e. 25 July). Whilst Wentworth 'rode to church in great magnificence', in private he was, Plumleigh reported, 'affable' and 'very friendly'. Amusingly, he discovered that the 'concealed lady' who had long been in residence in Dublin Castle was 'the Lord Deputy's wife', Elizabeth Rodes (Mahaffy 1900–1, II, 15). Sir George Radcliffe confirmed that 'her ladyship' had travelled 'with me into Ireland' back in January (Knowler 1739, II, 430).

The lord deputyship of Ireland had never been an undemanding role. Nevertheless, the tasks that faced the new appointee in 1633 were even more onerous than any hitherto encountered. There had long been the displaced and/or discontented old Gaelic order to confront, but now the increasingly disappointed and distrustful Old English were shifting—or, to be more precise, were being shifted—towards the ranks of the disaffected.

The watchword that would guide and frame Wentworth's policies in Ireland was 'Thorough'. References to 'Thorow and Thorowout' may be found in his correspondence with his friend and confidant Archbishop Laud of Canterbury (Knowler 1739, I, 298, 329). He was not impressed with the regime that he found ensconced in Dublin on his arrival. By August he was writing to the lord treasurer with the observation that 'I find them in this Place, a Company of Men the most intent upon their own Ends that ever I met with [...]' (*ibid.*, 96). The omens for a harmonious administration were not good.

Wentworth did not arrive unprepared. He had, in truth, been pulling the diplomatic strings for the previous eighteen months. Collection of the final subsidy payments may have been imminent, but his physical absence had not diminished his political input. He was very aware that October 1632 was the financial deadline. To fulfil the needs of the Crown in the shortest possible time-span, it was decided on his prompting that the administration should once again put the word about that its munificence was 'for sale' (Clarke 1966, 65). And once again, not unsurprisingly, the Old English would be expected to lean towards the inclination to take the bait. The Graces, they had to believe, would be confirmed, and thus their position as loyal and trusted, and finally contented, subjects could finally be assured.

Obtaining money from the Old English Catholics was not an insurmountable problem for Wentworth. He knew that basically the only realistic choice that faced them was to become subject to unlimited 'Recusancy Fines', as advocated by the chief justices, or to make fresh voluntary payments—in short, to extend the subsidies. But it

Pl. 23—Richard Boyle (1566–1643), 1st earl of Cork. (Bridgeman Art Library)

could not be expected that they would be rushed into any rash final binding agreement. Trust was the key issue. He would have known that in their view they had been hoodwinked before.

In November 1632 the dissident vice-treasurer of Ireland, Francis Annesley, Lord Mountnorris, finally managed to arrange a general meeting of the nobility and gentry. Dangled before them was a letter from Wentworth written on 16 October. Simply put, it contained an offer of a confirmation of the Graces in exchange for a continuation of 'the Contribution'. Furthermore, the threat of the recusancy fines would be removed. Yet the pervading hostility of the Dublin government to the Catholic parties could not be ignored. This was encapsulated by the dogmatic attitude of Richard Boyle, the earl of Cork (Pl. 23).

In a notable November confrontation between the Old English lords and the council over access to a letter of clarification from the king, it was the former who for once achieved the upper hand. They got to read the letter despite Cork's trenchant opposition, and they magnanimously announced that they would agree to advance half a subsidy over the following year as a gesture of goodwill (Clarke 1966, 71).

On 12 December the lord justices were instructed by the king to halt all proceedings concerning recusancy (*ibid.*, 73). The New English Protestants were not at all pleased. There was active resistance in counties Cavan and Fermanagh to the 'new Applotment of Monies [...] for the Army' but it was brushed aside (Knowler 1739, I, 147, 150).

The discontent displayed by the Protestant faction could only encourage the Old English to trust and believe even more in the lord deputy. It was 'a hope born of credulity, and weaned on deceit' (Clarke 1966, 77). Indeed, King Charles and Wentworth were brewing up a plan that was simple but brutal: divide the parliament into two sessions, get all they wanted in the first session and promise to deliver everything desired in return in the second. In a letter to Secretary Coke the lord deputy outlined the strategy: 'So as, if they without Condition supplied the King [the subsidies], they might be sure his Majesty would go along with them in the next Meeting' (Knowler 1739, I, 277). Of the latter they had no intent.

There was a further nasty surprise awaiting the Old English and Gaelic representatives. Wentworth had arrived at the conclusion that he could invert the established application of Poyning's Law and thus turn it to his advantage. His interpretation was that it was solely the right of the Dublin administration to submit and thus determine prospective legislation to the privy council in London. If his view held, then the parliament in Ireland would not be legally entitled to introduce any legislation in its own right and would accordingly be reduced to merely making recommendations (Clarke 1966, 79). Wentworth would keep this manoeuvre under wraps during the first session (*ibid.*, 83).

As in the previous parliament, composition would be pivotal. The rewards of the gerrymandering initiated in the past could now be reaped. The representation would comprise 142 Protestant members and 112 Catholic members, of whom 94 belonged to the Old English; of the eighteen Catholic members who bore Gaelic surnames only eight represented areas under native influence (Clarke 1976c, 247–8). The key factor was that about 50 of the Protestant members were aligned with the administration (Beckett 1966, 66).

THE PARLIAMENT OF 1634

With great pomp and ceremony, the parliament of 1634 was inaugurated with a service in St Patrick's on 14 July. The parade to the church was in strict order of rank. The dignitaries were preceded through the streets by companies of horse and foot accompanied by trumpeters; next came the barons, followed by the knights, bishops and viscounts; the earls were followed by the archbishops and, finally, the primate of all Ireland, the lord chancellor and the lord deputy, surrounded by all the paraphernalia of state (Mahaffy 1900–1, I, 59–62). This day also witnessed the assembling of the parliamentary representatives from all parts of Ireland in Dublin Castle (*ibid.*, 62–7).

Wentworth had reasoned that a self-sufficient, prosperous Ireland would be of enormous benefit to the monarchy. The major challenge, however, was that in order to achieve his objective he would have to attack 'the interests of every important group in Ireland' (Clarke 2011, 168).

The lord deputy addressed both houses of parliament on 15 July. He revealed that the 'Debts of the Crown were an hundred thousand Pounds Irish'. More importantly for many in attendance, he declared that the only way currently available to them to pay the army was 'by levying the twelve Pence a Sunday upon the Recusants' (Knowler 1739, I, 287). There was, he declared, an alternative strategy, however, and that was to extend the Contribution for a further year. The king envisioned holding two sessions of parliament. The first would be 'for the Crown', the second for his subjects and their wellbeing (*ibid.*, 288)—or, as Wentworth put it in his report to Secretary Coke, 'the one for himself' (i.e. the king), 'the other for them' (*ibid.*, 277).

On the morning of 17 July, the Catholic side of the house sought a ruling on the question of 'Non-Residency'. Their objective was to 'purge' the parliament of as many Protestant members as possible. Resolution of this issue was quickly and cleverly referred to the committee of privileges. As the committee was controlled by the administration, no problems would be created for the lord deputy (*ibid.*). After prolonged internal debate that evening Wentworth resolved on an immediate course of action. The next morning the 'Gift of six Subsidies' was sprung on the parliament. It was passed unanimously, both sides unwilling to gift any credit to the other. As Wentworth later wrote, the money was in the bag before 'Twelve of the Clock'! He further confided to Secretary Coke that for the rest of the first session he 'spun them out in Discourses' while preventing them 'from concluding any Thing' (*ibid.*, 278). It amused Wentworth to observe the two opposing sides in parliament, 'one watching the other lest their Fellow shou'd rob them' (*ibid.*, 274).

By 21 August Wentworth was in a position to report to the judges of assize on the overall progress made to date. First, the 'quarterly Payments of £20,000 a Year' would be extended to the end of December. Secondly, the king would send over 'a Commission of Grace for Confirmation of the defective Titles'. Thirdly, His Majesty would moderate all 'Excess in the Fees of his Officers and Ministers of Justice'. Fourthly, the archbishops and bishops had been instructed to 'forbear questioning any for clandestine Marriages and Christenings', which had been leading to 'a great Burthen and Charge'. Fifthly, 'Cattle, Corn, and other Commodities' were free to be exported. Sixthly, all outstanding laws enacted in England over the past 'hundred years' were now to be adopted in Ireland (*ibid.*, 292–3). The parliament was adjourned until 4 November (*ibid.*, 279).

There can hardly have been anyone in Ireland who didn't expect the 'Graces' to dominate the second session of parliament in November. Both the Protestant and Catholic parties were intent on the 'Graces' being confirmed by statute. The Catholic side were being advised and directed by, amongst others, the lawyers Patrick Darcy and Richard Martin, and the former agents Sir Henry Lynch, Sir Edward Fitzharris and Sir Thomas Luttrell (Clarke 1976c, 248). A leading light amongst the Protestants was Richard Jones, third Viscount Ranelagh. He was a son of the former archbishop of Dublin and the son-in-law of Richard Boyle, the earl of Cork (Beckett 1966, 66).

The Old English would be coming back with a vengeance. Wentworth had realised that there was no point in keeping up the pretence. On 19 August the council informed the various representatives that only a few of the less important 'Graces' would be addressed by legislation (Clarke 1976c, 249). Articles 16 and 17 (relating to the court of wards), Articles 2 and 44 (relating to control of the army) and Articles 24, 25 and 26 (the king's title to land) were to be placed out of bounds (Clarke 1966, 87).

Parliament reconvened as planned on 4 November. The Old English immediately launched into trenchant opposition. A bill against bigamy was defeated as a warning shot across the lord deputy's bow. While the frustration of Catholic expectations and demands should have endeared Wentworth to the Protestant landowners, it transpired that they were more animated by his efforts to curb their own power and thus he ended up with the support of neither camp (Canny 1996, 169). The wily Wentworth knew that he had to placate the Protestant side of the house. To achieve this objective, he realised that he would have to give ground on the 'Graces'. The king's claims against defaulting planters in Ulster (Article 26) were dropped; in fact, legislation to confirm their estates would be tabled. In all, now only two of the 'Graces' would not be addressed by legislation: the statute of limitations guaranteeing land titles of 60 years' standing, and a confirmation of land titles in Connacht (Beckett 1966, 67; Clarke 1976c, 250). The lord deputy made all this explicitly clear to parliament in a speech delivered on 27 November (Knowler 1739, I, 350). The Catholic side of the house was incandescent. Wentworth, in a report to Secretary Coke written on 16 December, observed that 'the refusing [of] their two darling Articles' resulted in their being 'wrought up to a strange insolent Frowardness, refusing and rejecting all which came from the State' (*ibid.*, 347). Ultimately, however, beyond the odd irrelevant victory in parliament (owing to Protestant absenteeism) there was to be no redress. The second session ended on 15 December, and after a third session parliament was dissolved on 18 April 1635.

The resulting enduring hostility of the Gaelic nobility and the Old English did not cause Wentworth undue concern. In fact, since his arrival in Dublin he had not hesitated to take on any factions that stood in the way of his policies. The king's best interests were paramount in his attitude to people, no matter who they were. Viscount Charles Wilmot, lord president of Connacht, was taken to task in 1635 regarding alleged alienation of the king's manor of Athlone. The lord deputy insisted that he must 'restore the Crown to the Land', noting that it was 'richly worth five hundred Pounds a Year'. Wilmot's defence he judged to be 'bad, very bad' (*ibid.*, 399). But Wentworth's real targeted adversary was the avaricious Richard Boyle, the earl of Cork. It transpired that the earl had been engaged in the misappropriation of church lands and properties. If the Church of Ireland were to have a dynamic future, it would naturally need to be in full possession of its assets. That future was important to both Wentworth and his ally the archbishop of Canterbury. It was inevitable that they would be active in its pursuit.

There was no option other than to force the earl to relinquish his church holdings. Proceedings were launched and brought before the court of castle chamber. As Wentworth reported to Secretary Coke on 16 December 1634, 'the Gauntlet is thrown down' (Knowler 1739, I, 347). The bishops of Cork and Waterford were made parties to the suit (*ibid.*). The archbishop of Canterbury had voiced his opinion of the bishop of Waterford the previous year: 'I have known the Bishop of Waterford long, and when he lived in the College, he would have done any Thing, or sold any Man for six Pence Profit' (*ibid.*, 212). The final outcome was that the earl had to surrender much of the church property in his possession and pay a fine of £15,000 (Beckett 1966, 68).

There was also the matter of the highly contentious tomb that the earl had erected for his wife in St Patrick's Cathedral. Its specific position had offended Wentworth. As far as he was concerned, it was as if the congregation at a service were 'crouching to the earl of Cork and his lady' (Clarke 1976c, 252). Archbishop Laud shared Wentworth's displeasure at the site chosen for the tomb in the cathedral. He responded to representations from the earl on 21 March 1633: 'It is very true that I have taken Exception to the Monument [...] the Tomb was built in the Place where the High Altar stood, and the Communion Table should now stand'. He also refuted the suggestion that it was the lord deputy who had lodged the official complaint. As a final riposte, he observed that it had been said that 'you have not been a very good Friend to the Church in the Point of her Maintenance' (Knowler 1739, I, 223). The matter was concluded to the satisfaction of Wentworth and Laud. On 1 May 1634 the former received word from London that 'no letter will come hence to stop your Purpose of removing of my Lord of Cork's Monument, for I hear that the King hath refused to sign it, and hath forbidden it ever to be offered him again' (*ibid.*, 243).

Francis Annesley, first Lord Mountnorris, was an early source of information for Wentworth on State affairs in Ireland. The incoming lord deputy was particularly interested in material relating to previous holders of the office (Merritt 1996, 115). Mountnorris facilitated contact with the Catholic parties in Ireland (Clarke 1966, 66–7) and supported efforts to have the king's letter of late 1632 published (*ibid.*, 71). Relations between the two men soured, however, owing to the vice-treasurer's hampering of the lord deputy's personal style of financial administration. Complaints made to London fell on deaf ears (Beckett 1966, 63). Mountnorris's complaint to the king regarding his management of the customs prompted Wentworth to act (Clarke 1976c, 255). The fact that Mountnorris held a captaincy in the army (like other officials) was used to try him by court martial. The charge was mutiny, which Beckett (1966, 68) deemed 'far-fetched'. Idle social talk, possibly fuelled, had led to his being accused of traducing the lord deputy. He was condemned to death and, more importantly to Wentworth, was obliged to relinquish public office. His control of the exchequer thus came to an end. In truth, there was no real intention of carrying out the sentence. Wentworth informed Secretary Coke in a letter dated 14 December 1635 that 'myself and all the Captains will become most humble Suitors to his Majesty to pardon him the Punishment of Death' (Knowler 1739, I, 498).

Slowly but surely the lord deputy altered the composition of the privy council to one that generally met with his approval (Clarke 1976c, 252). He kept a constant eye out for fresh talent to augment the team that had accompanied him from London (notably Sir George Radcliffe and Christopher Wandesford). Sir Adam Loftus was one such discovery. In a letter to Secretary Coke, dated 6 October 1634, Wentworth wrote: 'I see no Man on this Side, that can weigh against him, having equal Sufficiency with the ablest amongst them'. He requested Loftus's advancement (Knowler 1739, I, 306). In a second letter to Coke, dated 16 December, he wrote: 'Those who have carried themselves in the Commons House without Comparison with most ability, and best Affections, are, the Lord Dillon, Sir Adam Loftus, the Master of the Rolls, and Sir George Radcliffe'. He described the latter pair as his 'intimate Friends' who had 'done remarkable Service'. One particular individual from the 'Higher House' who caught his attention was the young lord of Ormond: 'I hold him a Person of Consequence, and fit to receive some Mark of his Majesty's Favour [...] he is young, but take it from me, a very staid Head' (*ibid.*, 352). Already by 31 January 1635 Coke was noting that 'now his Majesty hath conferred the Office of Vice-Treasurer upon Sir Adam Loftus' (*ibid.*, 513). Wentworth now had his own man in charge of the exchequer.

CHURCH REFORM

The Church of Ireland was not in good shape. The root problem had long been that the government was invariably totally preoccupied with political affairs. As a result, a consistent pursuit of evangelisation amongst the Old English population was decidedly lacking. Inevitably, therefore, that community remained mostly Catholic (Canny 1996, 162), while the Calvinistic tendencies of the church in Ulster were nurtured by the close connections with Scotland (MacCurtain 1972, 135).

Wentworth was very clear in his ambition: he wanted all Catholics and Dissenters to convert or adjust to Protestantism as defined by Laud (*ibid.*, 171). He held both Catholics and Presbyterians in low esteem. In relation to Ireland, he firmly believed that 'so long as this Kingdom continues Popish, they are not a people for the Crown of England to be confident of. Whereas if they were not still distempered by the Infusion of these Friars and Jesuits, I am of Belief, they would be as good and loyal to their King, as any other Subjects' (Knowler 1739, I, 351).

The hitherto random and sporadic interest afforded the Church of Ireland was transformed under Wentworth and Laud. In fact, they brought 'sustained attention' and 'unprecedented interference' to bear upon the institution (McCafferty 1996, 192). Disappointingly, Trinity College had not made any significant inroads into the overall poor quality of the ministry in Ireland (*ibid.*, 188). The 'asset-stripping' already mentioned was not helping in the recruitment of more qualified candidates.

Wentworth's primary aim for the Convocation of 1634 (the first since 1615) was basically to bring the Church of Ireland into conformity with its sister church in England. This objective would rely heavily on the imposition of the 39 English Articles and the sidelining of the Irish Articles (*ibid.*, 192). His principal agent in the business was John Bramhall. This cleric had accompanied the lord deputy to Ireland as chaplain and in 1634 was appointed bishop of Derry (Clarke 1976c, 257). Bramhall was also highly instrumental in reclaiming the sources of revenue of the church (MacCurtain 1972, 136). Many Protestant and, indeed, Catholic landowners were called before a tribunal and had their holdings of church land removed from them (Canny 1996, 171).

By 13 July 1635 the secretary Sir Francis Windebank was drafting a letter to the lord deputy for the earl of Cork, in which he wrote: 'The King is moved to accept Lord Cork's surrender of everything which he holds from the Church, and his fine for any offences he has committed' (Mahaffy 1900–1, II, 108). An error in the lord deputy's reckoning, however, was his appointment of Archbishop James Ussher to head the Convocation. Ussher's personal aim was to 'preserve the broader more Godly base' of the Irish church and to manifest some independence in the Canons (McCafferty 1996, 199). Compromise was the almost inevitable result. There would be no bowing to the name of Jesus, the Book of Canons would be a hybrid but the auricular (i.e. privately into the ear) confession would be adopted. The latter would be anathema to Dissenters and, indeed, the broader Protestant church, which believed that God alone has the power to forgive sins. There would now also be a commonality in the behaviour of the ministry, in marriage regulations and in the format of churches and services (*ibid.*, 208). Nevertheless, a rather sarcastic Archbishop Laud declared to Bramhall: 'God bless your free Church of Ireland, though for my part I do not think the Canons of the Church of England would have shot any of the freedom of it' (*ibid.*, 198).

THE THREAT OF CONFISCATION

Satisfied with his successful manipulation of the parliament, Wentworth decided to press ahead with a plantation in Connacht. Here he revealed the true motivation behind his withholding of the 'two darling Graces': to make the required land available it would be necessary to confiscate vast tracts of the province. At the heart of Wentworth's thinking was the desire to embroider Crown rule into the fabric of Irish life. The introduction of new Protestant settlers into Connacht would advance this vision.

The key to the plantation of Connacht lay in a royal claim dating from the time of King Edward IV (Knowler 1739, I, 454–5) and based on the marriage of Elizabeth de Burgo to Lionel, duke of Clarence. The claim had never been pursued but was still good in law (Beckett 1966, 70).

The first county to attract the lord deputy's attention was Roscommon. He duly set up court in Boyle Abbey on 9 July 1635 (Knowler 1739, I, 442). The legal breakthrough was mentioned almost as an afterthought to a rapturous endorsement of 'bonneyclabber' (*bainne clábair*, thickened sour milk). In his letter to Francis, Lord Cottington, he declared the beverage to be 'the bravest freshest Drink you ever tasted […] the Drink of the Gods all the while'. He then added that 'the best is, we have found his Majesty's Title to the County of Roscommon' (*ibid.*, 441). Thus fortified, Wentworth rode roughshod over the convened jury. They succumbed and accepted the king's title.

The lord deputy's entourage 'departed from thence to the County of Sligo, and so from thence to the County of Mayo' (*ibid.*, 451). The hearings were heard in Sligo town and Ballinrobe respectively, and in both counties the selected juries found in favour of the king's title. This was largely achieved by 'organised intimidation' (Clarke 1966, 93). They then moved on to Galway, where they 'apprehended more difficulty' (Knowler 1739, I, 451–4).

Controversially, Wentworth's entourage took possession of a fortified house in Portumna belonging to Richard Burke, the fourth earl of Clanricarde. It was in the hall of this house that the court of inquiry, starting on 14 August, was held.

Richard Burke was highly regarded by King Charles. He had served the Crown loyally throughout the Nine Years War. He was married to Frances, the daughter and heir of Sir Francis Walsingham, secretary of state to Queen Elizabeth. She had previously been married to Sir Philip Sidney and to Robert Devereux, the earl of Essex (Lodge and Archdall 1789, I, 134).

Wentworth was clearly stretching the bounds of his authority and power. Merritt (1996, 129) has referred to his 'audacity' in setting up the court in the earl's house. Letting his horses graze in the best meadows and killing the private deer at will may well have been intended as calculated insults to the earl. It has been recounted that he never bothered to remove his riding boots while reposing on the expensive linen and coverings of the beds (Clarke 1966, 97).

The Catholic party at court lobbied furiously against the proposed plantation of the Clanricarde lands (Canny 1996, 179). Unlike his counterparts in the three other counties, the sheriff, Martin Darcy, ignored the directive from Dublin and chose his own jury. They cleverly delivered a verdict that recognised the king's title only to those lands that had reverted to the Crown upon the death of William de Burgo (Clarke 1966, 95). Wentworth could not tolerate this challenge to his authority, and the king was obliged to support him. The lord deputy brought the jury to trial on 27 May 1636. In April 1637 a second jury was convened; they duly accepted the king's full title (*ibid.*, 104).

During this tussle, Richard Burke had died on 12 November 1635 at the age of 72. Many at court held Wentworth 'morally responsible' for his death (Clarke 1976c, 255). His embittered son and heir, Ulick Burke, the fifth earl of Clanricarde and second earl of St Albans, renewed the struggle and his persistence ultimately paid off. On 26 October 1640 the earl wrote to Secretary Windebank, recounting that he had just had a blazing row (a 'very sharp encounter') with the lord deputy 'in his Majesty's presence' which 'lasted above two hours'. At its conclusion he was able to relish the fact that he had 'recovered all my tenures and chiefries' (Hamilton 1873–93, XVII, 197). As Jane Ohlmeyer (1996, 221) has observed, Clanricarde had 'skilfully torpedoed' the entire plantation of Connacht by getting County Galway excluded from the enterprise. By 1640, not least owing to an absolute dearth of prospective settlers, nothing tangible had been achieved anywhere in the province (Clarke 1966, 108).

LIFE AT CARRICKMINES

Theobald Walsh, along with his relatives, friends and neighbours, would undoubtedly have been following closely the proceedings of the recent parliament and the subsequent events. One first-hand source of information available to him would have been Thomas, Viscount Fitzwilliam of Merrion, whose attendance at the opening of parliament was documented on 14 July 1634 (Mahaffy 1900–1, II, 60). Although, like Clanricarde, he was a Catholic, he remained totally loyal to the king and committed to the Dublin administration (Lodge and Archdall 1789, IV, 316). He would have been Theobald's third cousin once removed, but whether he had any influence at all on his Carrickmines cousin is unknown.

The attempted plantation of Connacht would have reverberated throughout the Old English community. The earl of Clanricarde was as 'true blue' as any 'Gentleman of the Pale'. As Clarke (1966, 97) put it, 'if the personal possessions of the premier catholic peer of Ireland were not free from petty abuses, and the earl himself from petty indignities', then what could everybody else expect? As MacCurtain (1972, 134) asked, 'who would be next?'

Theobald Walsh would have been relatively secure in his tenure. Whilst there is no indication that he was in imminent danger of having any of his land titles declared defective, he would nevertheless naturally have harboured concerns. He held land from three disparate entities: Christ Church Cathedral (formerly the Priory of the Holy Trinity), the earldom of Ormond and the Crown. There had to be a gnawing concern that, as all lessors were Protestant, the day would come when all lessees would be required to follow suit. Yet Clanricarde's success in resisting the plantation of his lands—and, indeed, the committed participation of individuals such as Viscount Fitzwilliam in political affairs—would have nurtured the belief that there was still a place for a loyal Catholic of English or Cambrian descent within the structure of the State and in the culture of the kingdom.

There was also the cold comfort that Wentworth's plan for Connacht was restricted to 25% of each holding, or 'Quarters', as he termed it (Knowler 1739, I, 421), although that would have been tempered by the fact that rents or levies on the remaining 75% of a holding would be increased.

Those Walshes with holdings in County Wicklow had more immediate concerns. As previously noted, members of the Walsh family of Killincarrig were married to O'Byrnes of Críoch Branach, while the Walshes of Shanganagh held lands in that fiefdom. On 17 June 1635 the earl of Carlisle wrote to the lord deputy in relation to Wicklow. He described how he had been approached at court by a gentleman who insisted that he had it on good authority that the lord deputy was resolved 'to make a Plantation in the Birne's Country for the King'. Carlisle had taken 'Umbrage at any such Report' (*ibid.*, 434), but his indignation was misplaced.

An inquisition was held on 29 March 1636 in Wicklow town. The sittings were conducted under the auspices of Sir William Parsons, Sir George Radcliffe, Sir Adam Loftus and others. This investigation was into the king's titles in relation to *Feartry* and to Castle Kevin, both of which were in the possession of the O'Tooles. It was determined that King Henry VIII had been seised of the whole territory of '*Feartry*, alias *Ferter*' and its castles (Mahaffy 1900–1, II, 127). This territory was variously called

Fartir, *Fartire*, *Fartry*, *Fertir* and *Fertyr* in the Wicklow inquisitions, *tempore* Charles I (O'Hanlon 1875, VI, 82 fn.172). More relevant to the Walshes was the subsequent declaration that the king's title to 'the Territory of the Birnes' had been 'found'. This event is recorded in a letter from the lord deputy to the king dated 5 June 1638 (Knowler 1739, II, 175). By 18 May 1639 Wentworth was in a position to inform Secretary Coke that 'the Territory of the Birnes [is] now ready, to be settled according to his Majesty's former Appointments' (*ibid.*, 343). These inquisition-determined expropriations were, as in the case of Connacht, for the purposes of putting more new Protestants on the ground and raising more money for the Crown. The fact that no change of occupation took place was purely due to changing circumstances as opposed to any changes in policy. Nevertheless, the entire process would undoubtedly have seriously unsettled the O'Byrnes and their tenants.

Theobald Walsh was clearly committed to his faith. That he retained not only a 'Mass-Priest' but also a friar in his house at Carrickmines has been noted above (Ronan 1941, 82). It is unfortunate that the order to which the friar belonged is unknown, as some orders were decidedly more fired by the Counter-Reformation than others. We do know that his son Richard was away at school in 1641 (Carte MS 154, fols 54–5), and there is a strong likelihood that the school or college in question was on the Continent. Given Theobald's Catholic credentials, it is likely that this institution of learning was in France or Spain, although there is always the outside possibility that he had been placed in the care of his uncle Oliver Walsh in Vienna. Clearly the Carrickmines branch of the Walsh family was unlikely to embrace the Reformation in the short term.

Economically, there are intimations that Theobald Walsh enjoyed a comfortable lifestyle. Whilst he had mortgaged his land in neighbouring Glenamuck (100 acres), this was not exceptional. This transaction occurred *c.* 1635/6 (Simington 1931–61, VII, 271). The selling or mortgaging of property, while retaining occupancy, proved tempting to many freeholders at the time, the opportunity for raising immediate cash not easy to scorn (Clarke 1976a, 170). It was from his livestock and crops that Theobald would have made his living.

A good insight into the number and composition of Theobald's livestock can be obtained from the 1631 deed pertaining to Shanganagh (Griffith 1991, 461; see above). The stocking level was listed as 300 ewes, 300 English lambs, twenty cows and ten heifers. These would have been sustained on ten acres of meadow, ten acres of pasture and 380 acres of arable land (Simington 1931–61, VII, 274). The pasturelands could have been used for the grazing of the cows and heifers. The meadows would have produced hay to feed them during the winter. The arable land, all 380 acres of it, probably also served as post-crop pastures for the sizeable flocks of ewes and lambs. The stubble left after the harvest would have been available to them (Foster 1988, 19), for example, as would the surrounding weeds and all pre-sowing natural growth.

Theobald had even more land at his disposal than his cousins. Between Carrickmines, Glenamuck and Phrompstown he was in possession of 44 acres of meadow, 234 acres of pasture and 324 acres of arable land (Simington 1931–61, VII,

270, 271, 278). The leases to Priorsland and Keatingsland were restored to him in May 1639 by Henry Tilson, the dean of Holy Trinity (McEnery and Refaussé 2001, 319). There was also his estate at Oldcourt, Co. Wicklow. According to the notation on the relevant Down Survey map, Oldcourt contained 241 acres. The Walsh estate may have accounted for 103 acres of the total, judging by an inquisition of 1593 (Griffith 1991, 295–6). In May 1620, 60 acres of his holding there were described as *arabilis* (arable). The watermill was apparently operative (Hardiman 1826–9, I, No. 20). It is reasonable to propose, therefore, that his herds and flocks were greater than those of his cousins at Shanganagh. The 234 acres of pasture (probably a lot more, depending on the class of land available at Oldcourt) are particularly noteworthy. The presence of the bawn at Carrickmines, noted in the Civil Survey (Simington 1931–61, VII, 270), indicates the capacity there to corral livestock.

Both Carrickmines and Shanganagh were in possession of sizeable areas of arable land. Excluding the unquantified Oldcourt, the arable land held by Theobald accounted for just over 50% of his holding. This percentage would have been below the regional average, which was *c.* 75% of agricultural land (Murphy and Potterton 2010, 348). There was a reference to a plough and horse in the 1631 deed and to a mill at Shanganagh in the Civil Survey. The presence of a watermill at Carrickmines was recorded in 1570, *c.* 1580 and 1593 (Griffith 1991, 196, 254, 295); its absence from the Civil Survey inventory may have been an oversight or evidence of its redundancy. The inquisition from 1593 also credited Theobald with a watermill at Oldcourt (*ibid.*, 295–6). A patent roll dating from 1612 documented the presence of 'a water mill' at Shanganagh (*Cal. pat. rolls chancery*, 198). What crops could they have been growing? Corn was grown predominantly in Ulster and in County Wexford (Clarke 1966, 52). Nonetheless, the sowing of oats, barley and rye would have been geographically widespread, where the soil quality allowed (Foster 1988, 19; Clarke 1976a, 173). Wentworth's administration spent £1,000 pounds on flax seed in the spring of 1636. Specialist workers were brought in from the 'Low Countries'. The lord deputy was determined to establish a viable linen industry in Ireland (Knowler 1739, II, 19–20). The growing of flax was therefore becoming increasingly widespread. Potatoes are another possibility. There is no doubt that by Theobald's time they would have been an established crop in Ireland. In all the speculation about just how and when the plant arrived in Ireland, it is a fact that in the late 1590s *Capsicum annuum* was growing in the garden of the botanist and herbalist John Gerard (Jackson 1876, 29) at Holborn, near London, and knowledge of the benefits and attractions of the crop cannot have been very long in crossing the Irish Sea.

The availability of generous crops of potatoes led to a pronounced expansion in pig-farming (Foster 1988, 20). Significantly, there was no mention of pigs in relation to Shanganagh, nor of goats, which may reflect the situation at Carrickmines.

There were two orchards at Shanganagh and one at Carrickmines. Both had 'garden plotts'. Fruit and vegetables were thus available, probably just for domestic consumption. The apples may also have been used to produce cider.

Ireland's leading exports were 'cattle, meat in cask, hides, tallow, wool and fish'.

Pl. 24—Pastry jigger. 'Consisting of a stem with a wheel at one end that leaves a zigzag pattern and a jagged cutter at the other, these objects were part of the tool kit of the pastry chef from around the sixteenth century. Now associated with pasta-making as well as with the cutting and decorating of pastry, they would have been used to make elaborate pies and other pastry creations to impress the lord and lady of the house or their guests. This example, found in the destruction layer of the revetted fosse that defined the south-eastern enclosure, probably dates from the seventeenth century and appears unbroken, perhaps indicating that it was lost or mislaid rather than discarded'—Dr Sharon Greene. See Finlay 2014 for further information. (Photo: Sara Nylund)

The removal of licensing controls would further increase the profit margins (Clarke 1966, 52). With the probable exception of fish (unless the Oldcourt holding was engaged), it is fair to argue that Theobald Walsh was profiting from most, if not all, of these elements of the market-place. The export market for live cattle was not just confined to England but also included the new colony of Virginia (Clarke 1976a, 177). Indeed, judging by the size of the flocks of sheep at Shanganagh, and more than likely at Carrickmines, wool was clearly a very important economic asset of the Walshes. As far back as 1622 it was reported that 'carding, spinning, weaving, working, dressing, and dyeing cloth' was providing work for 'many poor people' near Dublin (Russell and Prendergast 1872–80, V, 361). While the number of sheep exported had risen to 35,000 by 1640 (Clarke 1976a, 178), it was wool itself that remained the prime export (*ibid.*, 179). The final curbing of piracy on the Irish Sea facilitated this growth of all aspects of the expanding trade (Knowler 1739, II, 19).

All in all, day-to-day life at Carrickmines at the close of the 1630s would appear to have been more than reasonably acceptable to its residents (Pl. 24).

THE PARLIAMENT OF 1640

On 12 January 1640, to the sound of trumpets and drums, the lords, having met in the council chamber, proceeded to the Presence Chamber, 'the Earls of Newcastle, Cleveland, and Clare carrying the insignia, and Lord Wentworth being supported by the Earl of Northumberland and the Marquis of Hamilton' (Hamilton and

Crawford Lomas 1897, 616). Thomas Wentworth had finally realised his long-cherished ambition: he had just been created earl of Strafford and Baron Raby.

What should have been the pinnacle of his endeavours was, however, flawed by a totally unnecessary contrivance. The second title chosen by Wentworth, i.e. Baron Raby, was believed by Sir Henry Vane (the elder) to be an honour that rightfully belonged to him. The earl of Clarendon, writing in the 1640s, described Wentworth's choice as 'an act of the most unnecessary provocation' (Hyde 1826, I, 266). On 3 February Vane replaced the ageing Sir John Coke, who had become the scapegoat for the misfortunes in Scotland, as secretary of state. Wentworth had resisted the appointment, with animus and in defence of his friend, 'with great earnestness', but Vane enjoyed the active support of the queen, who had no fondness for the newly appointed earl of Strafford (*ibid.*, 222, 265). Wentworth had made a powerful and entrenched enemy who was to retain an 'implacable hatred of him' (*ibid.*, 245). Their enmity was rooted in the turmoil of the First Bishop's War against Scotland (Burnet 1852, 220).

Clarendon (Hyde 1826, I, 265) observed that 'The Earl of Strafford had for the space of almost six years entirely governed Ireland, where he had been compelled, upon reason of State, to exercise many acts of power'. These 'acts of power' had by now alienated every influential group on the island.

The composition of the new parliament was to comprise 68 members representing the Old English, six members representing the Gaelic Irish and 163 members representing the Protestants/New English (Clarke 1966, 126; MacCurtain 1972, 137).

Parliament met on 16 March 1640. Wentworth arrived from England two days later (Clarke 1976d, 273). By 23 March the Irish privy council was able to report to London that 'a vote for four subsidies was passed unanimously', with the prospect of more to come (Mahaffy 1900–1, II, 239), but when the parliament reconvened on 1 June, after a two-month adjournment, it quickly descended into a grudge match. The Catholics and a substantial number of the New English Protestants formed an unlikely alliance, united in their opposition to Wentworth (Clarke 1966, 129). The Nonconformists in the north, for example, had compiled a list of 44 grievances in relation to church affairs (Clarke 1976d, 277). The Court of High Commission also received criticism (*ibid.*). At the heart of the joint opposition was 'a shared hostility towards a governmental attitude that regarded its own convenience as sufficient' (*ibid.*). The current reality was that an individual could lose his property, his representation, his religious freedom and his legal rights at the total discretion of one man and his government.

The inherent danger, however, for the Old English and Gaelic Irish in adopting this political stance was that by opposing the king's man they were in effect challenging the king. The struggle was to be defined in terms of a conflict between executive government and the law of the land. In Ireland the Old English were the masters of legal procedure and parliamentary precedence. Indeed, MacCurtain (1972, 138) has described the gathering as a 'lawyer's parliament'. The New English dissidents quickly realised that they should simply follow their lead. The cruel irony was that by restoring the powers of parliament to the detriment of Wentworth's administration the Catholic parties were ultimately weakening the power of the throne, i.e. the very power upon which their community had long relied.

TWO PARLIAMENTS IN ENGLAND

Wentworth had been appointed chief political adviser to King Charles in late 1639. This appointment regularly brought him back to England. With the support of Archbishop Laud, he strongly urged the king to call the first parliament in eleven years to raise funds for renewing the struggle against the Scots. Eventually their advice was accepted and on 13 April the 'Short Parliament' convened. The king addressed the lords and commons on the opening day (Hamilton 1873–93, XVI, 25). Strafford fell ill at Chester and thus his arrival was delayed (*ibid.*, 42). The parliament earned its name owing to the brevity of its sitting. In short, Charles wanted them to approve funding for the renewal of hostilities but the members were determined to have their many grievances against State and church policies addressed first. Ship Money, to take one contentious issue, was an unpopular tax devised to finance the Royal Navy. The king had imposed the tax on the country without parliamentary approval. On 17 April Sir John Pym made an impassioned speech encapsulating the widespread discontent (*ibid.*, 46–8). Charles was willing to offer some concessions, but at a price: the Ship Money tax would be relinquished 'absolutely' if parliament supplied him with twelve subsidies (*ibid.*, 115). When they demurred, the king responded by dissolving parliament on 5 May (*ibid.*). Strafford's high hopes that the compliant parliament in Ireland, as manifested in its March sittings, would prompt and encourage its counterpart in London to embrace the template had been dashed. The June sittings of the Irish parliament further deflated him, their non-compliance stark. His health was not good either; a bout of dysentery was followed by a bad chill (*DNB*, LX, 280; *ODNB*, LVIII, 153).

The ensuing defeat in the Second Bishop's War in August (see Part 4) effectively deprived Charles of any room to manoeuvre. The Scottish Covenanters' army now occupied the six northern counties of England. Not only were they not going home, they were also demanding the funds necessary to maintain the army of occupation.

The English and Scottish commissioners duly convened at Ripon, north Yorkshire, on the 'forenoone' of 2 October 1640. John Digby, the earl of Bristol, headed the English negotiating team, which included Robert Devereux, Robert Rich and Henry Rich (the earls of Essex, Warwick and Holland respectively), and William, Lord Paget (Bruce 1869, 2). John Campbell, first earl of Loudoun, led the Scottish delegation (*ibid.*, 3). Haggling over the maintenance money was prolonged. The Scots were initially insisting on £40,000 a month (*ibid.*, 22) but dropped the price to £30,000. Eventually, on 15 October the earl of Bristol proposed £850 a day (*ibid.*, 37), describing the offer as 'a very good Contribution for a great Army'. The earl of

Loudoun countered that it was 'a good Contribution, but not a Competencie' (*ibid.*, 39). The £850-a-day offer was accepted by the Scots on 17 October (*ibid.*, 45). Finally, on 26 October 1640 the Treaty of Ripon between England and Scotland was concluded (*ibid.*, 68; Hamilton 1873–93, XVII, 197).

The difficulty for Charles was that only parliament would be in a position to raise the necessary funding. The Scots were also insisting on parliament's approval of the recently negotiated treaty (Hamilton 1873–93, XVII, 247). The Long Parliament was thus convened on 3 November. King Charles led the royal procession 'from Whitehall by water to Westminster Stairs, and thence on foot'. Archbishop Laud's prayer for the occasion invoked God to 'give the King a heart of judgement' and to grant the parliament 'a heart of duty' (*ibid.*, 242). Again John Pym, the veteran parliamentarian and fervent opponent of Rome and Arminianism (High Church Anglicanism), played a pivotal role. He in effect determined the course of the proceedings by securing an act forbidding the dissolution of parliament without its own consent.

Pym, like many others, believed that the king was a good man badly misguided by malevolent advisers. The parliamentarians accordingly lost little time in making their moves against the detested 'King's men'. It has been written that Archbishop William Laud's misfortune lay in 'attempting as he did to force upon the many the religion of the few' (*DNB*, XXXII, 192). It is hard to avoid the conclusion that Laud was tactless and irritable and that his self-righteousness deprived him of any useful allies (*ODNB*, XXXII, 669). On 18 December he was impeached by order of the House of Commons, and by 1 March 1641 he would be committed to the Tower of London. Thomas Wentworth, earl of Strafford, was to be next on their list.

Strafford was portrayed as the root of all miseries afflicting the kingdom (Kilburn and Milton 1996, 234). By this time he was known throughout the land as 'Black Tom Tyrant' (*ODNB*, LVIII, 153). Indeed, popular opinion played an increasingly important role in the campaign of vilification being conducted against him. His impeachment in November 1640 was built around charges that he had assumed regal powers in Ireland and in the north of England, that he had conspired against the parliament and turned the king against the good of his people (Kilburn and Milton 1996, 233). The parliamentarians had not calculated on Strafford's cleverness and mental agility, however, and the impeachment proceedings faltered. Changing tack rapidly, they instigated charges of treason before the lords could dismiss the initial case. The cornerstone of the new charge was that he had planned to deploy the army of Ireland against the people of England. This was basically a distortion of the plan to deploy the army against the Scottish Covenanters. The key witness was Strafford's old nemesis, Sir Henry Vane. The law, however, required a corroborating second witness. The prosecutor, John Glyn, invoked '*Vox Populi*'—hardly legal, but effective (*ibid.*, 236). A wave of pamphlets calling for Strafford's execution swept across the land (*ibid.*, 237). Against such a choreographed tidal wave the king could do nothing to save him. On the morning of 12 May 1641 he walked past the window of Laud's quarters in the Tower of London. The archbishop fainted while attempting to give him a final blessing as he passed (*ODNB*, XXXII, 666–7). On the scaffold he refused a blindfold. What the parliamentarians had envisaged as a high-profile public showcase for their new England turned into high theatre, with Strafford not only taking the leading role but also acting as stage director. It was at his signal that the executioner struck, and he was beheaded. There was no doubt that he faced death with 'great calm and courage' (*ODNB*, LVIII, 154).

THE DRIFT TOWARDS CONFLICT

Ireland was a rapidly changing place. Strafford's absences and final departure had created a power vacuum in the political landscape. It was a void that was not to remain vacant for long.

On 15 December 1640 Charles appointed Robert, Lord Dillon of Kilkenny West, and Sir William Parsons as chief justices for Ireland (Mahaffy 1900–1, II, 248). Dillon had been close to Strafford; his son, Sir James, was married to the lord deputy's sister (Carte 1851, I, 237). As far back as 1634 the lord deputy in a dispatch to Secretary Coke had described Dillon as 'one of the ablest Men of this Council' (Knowler 1739, I, 259). A year and a half later he wrote that 'an honester or an abler Gentleman you shall seldom have the Opportunity to mention' (*ibid.*, 495). In December 1640 these words of praise would have done Dillon no favours. Even the fact that he had experience in the office, having served as lord justice during Wentworth's absences in 1639–40 (Clarke 1966, 137 fn. 3), counted for nothing. Within weeks the king, responding to the negative reaction in Dublin, replaced Dillon with Sir John Borlase (Mahaffy 1900–1, II, 248).

In 1602 William Parsons had succeeded his uncle, Sir Geoffrey Fenton, as surveyor-general of Ireland (*ODNB*, V, 42, 941). His wife, Elizabeth Lany, was a niece of Sir Geoffrey and thus a cousin. Another of Parsons's cousins, Catherine Fenton, was married to Richard Boyle, the earl of Cork. He also enjoyed the early political backing of Buckingham. His appointment in late 1622 as master of the court of wards (Carte 1851, I, 100; Mahaffy 1900–1, II, 248) put him in a key influential role regarding the shaping of Irish society. The Protestant upbringing of parentless aristocratic children was designed to slowly erode the critical mass of the Catholic nobility. To succeed to their estates these future heirs would be obliged to take the Oath of Supremacy (*ODNB*, V, 42, 942). According to Carte (1851, I, 382), Parsons was 'plodding, assiduous, and indefatigable, greedy of gain, and eager to raise a fortune'. Strafford had never taken to him; in August 1633 he remarked in a letter to Secretary Coke that 'first and last I found him the dryest of all the Company' (Knowler 1739, I, 99). Dry he may have been but over the years he fervently accumulated a sizeable land-bank in Ireland. Amongst his holdings was an estate of 2,000 acres in Ranelagh (in the O'Byrnes' country) and over 2,000 acres in Fermanagh (Carte 1851, I, 384) (Pl. 25).

Sir John Borlase had been appointed master of the ordnance in 1633. Wentworth's letter to Coke, dated 6 October, had noted that '[Borlase] is now fully settled' into the job. He had been instructed by the lord deputy to inspect and quantify

Pl. 25—Sir William Parsons (c. 1570–1650), 1st baronet of Bellamont, lord justice of Ireland. (National Portrait Gallery)

all military stores on the island (Knowler 1739, I, 307). Foster (1988, 83 fn. v) has observed that, as he was 'bred a soldier and little else, [he] left much of the work to Parsons'. Curtis (1923, 243) labelled Borlase and Parsons as 'Puritans and Parliament men'. Lecky (1913, I, 42) had previously expressed a similar view regarding Parsons's political leanings, and elaborating that 'he was one of the most unprincipled and rapacious of the land-jobbers'. Both Bellings (Gilbert 1882–91, I, 14) and Lecky (1902, 42) drew attention to Parsons's extensive landholdings in County Wicklow: 'Parsons who was charged to have acquired much of the great estate he possessed in that county by sinister means'; 'He had been the chief agent in the scandalous proceedings against the O'Byrnes'. Beckett (1966, 78) portrayed Borlase and Parsons as 'neither in ability nor in character' 'suited for the difficult task' that awaited them. Clarke (1966, 137) dryly observed that to describe Borlase as ineffectual would find general agreement amongst historians in Ireland.

The articles of impeachment against Strafford had been significantly structured on information brought by commissioners dispatched to London by the Irish parliament (Beckett 1966, 77; Foster 1988, 83). By now individuals and parties on both sides of the Irish Sea were incrementally inching towards the designs and wishes of either king or parliament. This was a seismic shift in basic belief and concept. The very notion that loyalty to the monarch could be conditional—or, indeed, ultimately optional—had not been so overtly manifest in an aeon. A taboo had been broken. The cause of this transformation in fundamental thought was rooted in the two recent disastrous wars against Scotland. There was no disguising the fact that the king had lost on every front—militarily, politically and, more importantly, morally. The inevitable outcome was that all quarters saw opportunity in the resultant flux. In Ireland, with its clearly defined groupings, this was particularly true. The New English expected the weakened king to be more compliant in the realisation of their aggressive ambition, especially in the wake of the demise of the restraining Strafford. The Old English wanted their long-standing privileges and prominent position in society restored, while also enjoying freedom of conscience. The Irish yearned for a return to a Gaelic Catholic Ireland.

All-out war in October 1641 was to be preceded by a period of opportunistic looting, the dispossession of the new settlers and, in the case of Ulster, widespread bloodshed (see Part 4).

THE CONFLICT AND CARRICKMINES

Theobald Walsh inevitably became involved in the fray, although his degree of willingness or enthusiasm is debatable.

There were various and possibly conflicting factors at play. Not least would have been the peer pressure exerted by relatives, friends and neighbours. All three sectors are represented in the testimonies provided by victims of the violence both during and after the conflict. These depositions are invaluable in that they are neighbourhood accounts peopled by local participants.

John Brakenbury (1641 Depositions, TCD MS 809, fols 249r–249v), late of Dean's Grange in the County of Dublin, testified that 'aboute the 15th of December [1641]' the rebels had 'deprived, robbed, and despoyled' him of 'Cowes & other Cattle to the vallew of £150' and 'Horsses and maires & plow Garronns to the vallew of £80'. The raiders had also helped themselves to household goods and farming implements, and corn both threshed and unthreshed. The total value of his losses he put at £733. In a second deposition (TCD MS 810, fols 198r–198v) he testified that 'at the beginning of January [1642]' the rebels had taken the remainder of his stock, consisting of '3 Cowes and 5 bullockes'.

William Wharme, late of 'James Towne' (*ibid.*, fols 103r–103v), testified that 'about the 1st of December [1641]' he had been robbed of 'horses, Cowes & other Cattle' (value £420) as well as 'Corne & hay' (value £70). Also taken were 'household goods, wood, Turffe, ffaggotts & winter provision'. He estimated the value of his losses at £890.

Thomas Foxe of *Butterston* (i.e. Booterstown) alleged the loss of 'sixscore faire English Cowse … in horsses and Mares fifteene … howshould stuffe Brasse and pewter and other goods' with a total value of £462 sterling (*ibid.*, fols 147r–148v). The raid was reported to have occurred 'about the first of December, Last past 1641'. Foxe was slain later in the conflict (*ibid.*, fol. 344v).

All three deponents named 'Theobald Walsh of *Carrickemayne*' as a participant in the raiding parties. His partners in the enterprise included some relatives. John Brackenbury identified Henry Walsh and Edmond Walsh of *Clonmarninge* in County Wicklow. Thomas Foxe named Edmond Walsh of *Clonnanyn* and Edward Walsh of *Clonnanyne* in County Wicklow as being amongst his assailants. These place-names are variations on Clonmannan, a coastal townland to the north of Wicklow town. It would have been sited within Críoch Branach. Ball (1901, 199; 1902–17, I, 51) described Edward Walsh as the 'second son of the owner of Clonmannan'.

The founder of the Clonmannan branch was Edward Walsh of Carrickmines, the fifth son of Richard and Eleanor (née Eustace). In Molyneux's 1606 visitation it is recorded that he 'dwelleth at *Clonmanin* neere Wicklow and hath to wife Elizabeth Booth of the house of Dunham in Cheshire' (Genealogical Office MS 48, 21).

Elizabeth was the daughter of William Booth and Elizabeth Warburton of Dunham Massey in Cheshire. Her father was the sheriff of Cheshire in 1571 (Wooton *et al.* 1771, I, 27). Her brother George was created a baronet in 1611; he was to be high sheriff of Cheshire twice and high sheriff of Lancashire twice. Her great-nephew George was to be created first Baron Delamere in 1661; his first wife was Catherine Clinton, daughter of the fourth earl of Lincoln. Elizabeth's first husband was William Basnet of Eaton, Denbighshire, in Wales. Her second marriage was to Edward Walsh of Carrickmines (*ibid.*, 28; Burke 1866, 60). Her introduction to Edward most likely occurred in Ireland. Her first husband was of the same family as Edward Basnet, the dean of St Patrick's at the time of the Reformation. The latter's first appointment was as vicar of Swords in May 1536, and he went on to serve as a privy counsellor under both Henry VIII and Edward VI (Kippis 1778–93, I, 672). It would thus appear that William Basnet brought his wife with him when he joined his relatives in Ireland.

It is ironic that the son of a woman with such a solid English Protestant establishment background should marry the daughter of a Gaelic king. Edmond Walsh, the son of Edward and Elizabeth (Ken Nicholls, pers. comm.), married Elinor, the daughter of Domhnall Spáinneach MacMurrough-Kavanagh, the last king of Leinster. Domhnall had surrendered to Lord Mountjoy on 24 August 1600 (O'Byrne 2003a, 240) and thereafter resolved to be a loyal subject of the monarch until his death in 1632 (*ibid.*, 242).

If Edmond was the eldest son and Edward the second son (see above), it is probable that 'Henry Walsh of *Clonmarninge*' was a younger brother. The three sons and their father would later be 'indicted of treason' (Gilbert 1882–91, III, 385–6).

The third Walsh identified by Brackenbury was Pearse Walsh of Shanganagh. Piers Walsh, a merchant resident in Dublin, was a contemporaneous member of the Shanganagh branch (Griffith 1991, 462) but not a leading member.

John Brakenbury, after referring to Theobald Walsh of Carrickmines, named 'James Hore of the same'. The simple explanation is that James was Theobald's brother-in-law, twice over! James was married to Margaret Walsh and Theobald was married to Maria Hoare. James's permanent abode was in Kilsallaghan Castle in north County Dublin (Clinton 2005, 24–35).

Brakenbury provided the interesting fact that Theobald had been accompanied by one Hugh Murphy, his 'cook and servant', on the raid on Dean's Grange (1641 Depositions, TCD MS 809, fols 249r–249v). It is possible that Murphy survived the conflict. On 25 January 1653 a Hugh Murphy of Loughlinstown was brought before the high court of justice to give evidence regarding details of his participation in the hostilities, specifically information concerning the hanging of a William Beaton (see below). This Hugh Murphy was by then about 31 years of age and living in the immediate area of Carrickmines; he could well have been the former employee of Theobald Walsh.

Theobald was also in the company of some of his influential neighbours on the forays. Robert Barnewall of Shankill took part in the raid on Dean's Grange and was also implicated in a raid on lands held by a William Cooke near Powerscourt, Co. Wicklow (*ibid.*, fols 263r–263v). There was a family connection. Barnewall was a second cousin of Theobald's (his grandmother being Theobald's great-aunt, Anne Walsh). James Walsh of Old Connaught accompanied Barnewall on the raid on Cooke's estate. The tenants of the two men were also members of the raiding party. Old Connaught was part of the Shanganagh holdings. James apparently did not live much longer, as he is described in the Civil Survey as having 'died in the beginning of the Rebellion' (Simington 1931–61, VII, 276). Notably, also participating in the raid were Luke O'Toole of Castle Kevin and a Luke O'Byrne, possibly Luke or Feagh McRedmond of Killacloran, who was indicted in 1642 (Nicholls 1998b, 113).

The Goodmans were very active in the fray. James Goodman of Loughlinstown participated in the raids on *Butterston* (Booterstown) and Dean's Grange. In the latter raid both father and son ('the elder' and 'the younger') were present. At Dean's Grange they were accompanied by Rowland Goodman of *Bulloge* (Bullock), a man involved in fisheries there, Christopher and James Goodman of *Cronerow* in County Wicklow and their brother, a Rowland Goodman of *Ballentilley* in County Dublin. Cronroe, Co. Wicklow, is located to the south-west of Ashford and to the north-west of Rathdrum. Thomas White and Patrick Phelim, servants to the Goodmans of Loughlinstown, were also present. The raiders at Booterstown included James Goodman of *Ballentlea* (Ballinclea, to the south-west of Dalkey), Alexander Rochford of Rochestown (in the same area) and Henry Warren of Glenamuck (see Simington 1931–61, VII, 261).

Unlike their brethren in, for example, County Louth, the Old English of south County Dublin did have some discretion as regards the level of their involvement in the escalating hostilities. This is exemplified in the behaviour of certain families, not least the Walshes of Shanganagh. The Fitzwilliams of Merrion remained totally loyal to the State throughout the ensuing warfare. The Wolverstons of Stillorgan did their best to stand aside. James, the son of George, died in 1609 and was succeeded by his son and heir, William Wolverston. It has been written of William that he was 'one of the most prominent residents, and the most striking personality, in the southern portion of the County Dublin' (Ball 1902, 118). Although married to a Barnewall of Shankill, he assiduously 'kept himself clear from any overt act of rebellion' (*ibid.*, 119). This did not, however, fully protect him later from false accusations (see below) and from being indicted for his 'adherence to the Irish' by the Commonwealth (Simington 1931–61, VII, 264). The extent of the Wolverstons' estate is apparent in the 1650s Civil Survey: Stillorgan (176 acres), *Little Newtowne* (the modern Newtown Park, Newpark and Galloping Green North) (95 acres), Hackettsland (37 acres), Leopardstown (100 acres), Ballycorus (to the east/south-east of Kilternan) (160 acres) and a moiety of Little Bray (twenty acres) (*ibid.*, 264, 269, 271, 275, 277).

THE LEVEL OF PARTICIPATION BY THEOBALD WALSH

The three documented raids involving Theobald Walsh were clearly bloodless affairs. The homesteads in question were apparently neither damaged nor destroyed. Indeed, the most insightful event in these episodes was the reaction of John Brakenbury in the wake of the second raid on his holding. Hearing that the rustlers had driven the remainder of his livestock to Carrickmines, he went there, apparently alone. Upon arrival, he entered the 'house' and found 'ould Mr Fagan' sitting by the fireside. Brakenbury complained to Fagan about his losses. He remained with him for about an hour. Theobald returned and entered the room. He informed Brakenbury that 'there was 3 or 4 off the Irishe Captains to dyne with him and thatt they would nott like [him] being there'. Brakenbury took this advice and departed. On his way out of the building he recognised some of the other guests who were arriving, including James Goodman of Loughlinstown and Thomas Cheevers of Monkstown. Both were later 'indicted of treason' (Gilbert 1882–91, III, 350, 364). They were in the company of 'divers of the Country gentlemen' and the Gaelic captains. What is particularly noteworthy is that John Brakenbury was not afraid to go alone to Carrickmines, nor was he fearful of entering the Walsh stronghold. It is equally clear from the account that Theobald was both unthreatening to him and mindful of his safety.

The use of Carrickmines as a 'clearing house' for the rustled livestock was logical, if not inevitable. As the venue for four annual fairs, Carrickmines would have possessed all the necessary infrastructure and experienced personnel to handle the stolen livestock. The Fair Days were listed, particularly the two double-day events, in nineteenth-century publications as 12 January, 14 and 15 April, 24 June, and 14 and 15 October (Archer 1801, 52; Lewis 1837, I, 275; D'Alton 1838, 15–16), and undoubtedly most, if not all, had been held since time immemorial.

The third recorded episode involving Theobald was more random in nature. A certain James Wharme of *James Towne* (Jamestown, to the immediate west of Carrickmines) was out riding with his servant, John 'Rely' (Reilly), around 1 December 1641 when they were set upon and pursued by a party of 'souldiers' led by 'Tibbot Walsh of *Carreckmaine*' and Matthew Talbot of Kilgobbin. Wharme managed to outride his pursuers but Reilly was captured. A subsequent raid on Wharme's property cost him an estimated £890 in stolen cattle, horses, household goods and winter fuel (1641 Depositions, TCD MS 810, fols 103r–103v).

Matthew Talbot had become a neighbour of Theobald's when he leased Kilgobbin Castle. The Walshes had by then relinquished their interest in the castle to Sir Adam Loftus of Rathfarnham. Thus it was Loftus who had let the property to Talbot (Ball 1902–17, III, 67).

Matthew Talbot was very active in capitalising on the insurrection, leading the lord justices to offer £400 for his head (D'Alton 1838, 827). Besides the raid on Jamestown, he was also instrumental in launching raids on Murphystown (to the immediate north-west of Carrickmines). About 26 October 1641 the holding of Alice Hogg, an English-born Protestant widow, was looted of 'Cowes & horses [...] hay [...] houshouldstuffe [...] in all amounting to One Hundred and twentye pounds ster'. Significantly, Talbot was accompanied on the raid by Luke O'Toole of Castle Kevin, 'Banabye' (Barnaby) O'Toole of *Carrogroe* (Cronroe) 'and their wicked leud and rebellious companye' (1641 Depositions, TCD MS 810, fols 153r–154v). Alice Poore, also of Murphystown, had her holding looted by soldiers acting on the orders of Matthew Talbot. Her losses of 'seaven horses and Mares' cost her an estimated £30 sterling. A more alarming event occurred on 'St Thomas's Day 1641' (i.e. 21 December), when Talbot's men set upon her and violently took her horse. In addition, 'Tenn shillings six pence in money' was removed from her pocket. Fearlessly she proceeded to Kilgobbin Castle, where she confronted Talbot. He was in the company of his mother, his sister Katherin and a priest. Poore knelt before Mrs Talbot and begged for the return of half the cash to enable her to 'buy some corne' for herself and her children. She described Mrs Talbot as 'a woman not moved with compassion'. The subsequent looting of her winter fuel by Katherin Talbot and some companions compounded her difficulties (*ibid.*, fols 248r–249v).

Talbot's presence in the locality did not last much longer. On 20 January 1642 a party of horse from Dublin took Dundrum Castle and then proceeded to Kilgobbin Castle. There, to their surprise, they were fired on from within the building. Two of their horses died, and one man was mortally wounded. The cavalry withdrew and regrouped and then made a second approach, but they found the occupants gone. It was reported that Luke O'Toole and Hugh O'Byrne had been on the premises (1641 Depositions, TCD MS 840, fols 007r–010v). Of meaningful insight into the thinking of the army command in Dublin, especially in the light of subsequent events, was the fact that the castle was neither torched nor damaged, even though it could not be occupied at that time. The same was also true of the above-mentioned Fitzwilliam castle at Dundrum (Ball 1902–17, II, 68), although Kilgobbin Castle was certainly occupied by August 1642 (HMC 1895, 136).

When John Brakenbury entered Carrickmines Castle he had met, as mentioned above, 'ould Mr Fagan of Feltram'. In 1524 Thomas Fagan married Amy Nangle, daughter of the baron of Navan. He thereafter acquired considerable estates in both the city and county of Dublin, including Feltrim. His son Richard was both high sheriff of the county (1575) and lord mayor of the city (1587); he married Cecily

Holmes of Manchester. When Richard died in March 1610 he was succeeded by his son John. A sister of John's, Mary Fagan, married John Eustace of Confey, Co. Kildare. Their daughter Jane married Richard Walsh of Carrickmines. These were Theobald's parents.

The adjective used by Brakenbury in relation to 'Mr Fagan of Feltram' is evidential. 'Ould' would not have been applicable to Christopher Fagan, Theobald's contemporary. As Christopher's father, Richard, had died in August 1622 (Burke 1835–8, IV, 628), the reference must therefore be to John, his grandfather, who was alive in 1637, when he obtained possession of lands in County Wexford (D'Alton 1838, 216). John Fagan was thus Theobald Walsh's great-uncle.

THE WALSHES OF WICKLOW

Whilst, as observed above, the Old English of south County Dublin had some alternatives as regards their prospective stance in the escalating conflagration, this leeway would not have been available to their kindred in County Wicklow. The O'Byrnes, followed by the O'Tooles, were in rebellion from 12 November, and the news of the uprising had reached Dublin by the following day (Mahaffy 1900–1, II, 347). It quickly became clear that all those who were not allied with them would inevitably be swept away, or at least have their properties ransacked or expropriated.

The involvement of three of the sons of Edward Walsh of Clonmannan in the early raids in south County Dublin has already been noted. Closer to home, they featured in an occurrence in a far more benevolent manner. John Pugh of *Newragh* (Newrath, to the immediate north-east of Rathnew) was visited in his home on 16 November 1641 by a party of the O'Byrnes, including Edmund McArt O'Byrne of Monduff. Edmund took Pugh aside for a quiet word. He told him that the whole county would soon be in full revolt under the leadership of Luke O'Toole, Luke O'Byrne and Caher McPhelim O'Byrne. The latter, a grandson of Feagh Mac Hugh O'Byrne, would later be executed by the Commonwealth (Nicholls 1998b, 116). It was suggested to Pugh that he had two choices: if he 'would goe to Mass, and do as they did', i.e. convert and assimilate, he could stay; otherwise he had better get out. Pugh chose the latter option and rode north-eastwards to Edward Walsh's house in Clonmannan (about two miles away), where he stayed that night. The next morning he set out for Dublin, escorted by 'foure of the said Mr Walsh's … sonnes', two of their men and James Byrne, 'a Masse Priest'. The party had only proceeded about four miles when they encountered about 100 of 'the poore plowmen and labouring men of those partes'. These men, armed only with 'Clubbs, Pitchforkes, staves and Dungforkes', were led by Edmond O'Byrne of the Downs (armed with a pistol and a pike) and 'Leifetennant' Cahir McArt O'Byrne of Ballyronan (armed with a 'fowling Peece'). Other than searching the two carts carrying provisions for Pugh's children in Dublin for weapons, the O'Byrnes did not prevent or impede his progress (1641 Depositions, TCD MS 811, fols 166r–167v). It is apparent that the escort of Walshes had conferred immunity on John Pugh. His property, however, did not enjoy the same protection and was duly ransacked and looted by a raiding party led by Teige Óg O'Byrne of Ballinavalley and Dowling McCahir O'Byrne of Toberaviller. This information was later relayed to Pugh in Dublin by his saddler and employee Walter Ash (*ibid.*, fols 132r–132v).

Henrie Brabazon of '*Ranowe* [Rathnew?] in the parish of Wickloe' had his home looted by neighbours 'about the xth daie of November An. 1641'. Having made a break for Dublin, he suffered a second blow when his livestock was seized on the road. He found himself (by design?) 'at the dore of a farme house of Edward Walsh of *Crunnakerry*' (Cronykerry, the adjacent townland to the west of Clonmannan). This would have been the home of Edward the younger, second son to Edward, the elder, of Clonmannan. Brabazon found no safety here either, as 'the Rebells' appeared and took from him 'a downe feather bed withall things belonging to it [...] pewter [...] and brasse to the value of £20'. This brought his estimated losses to a total of £140 15s. 8d. There are no mentions of Edward Walsh the younger or his brothers being involved in any of the three incidents of robbery. Edward Walsh (the elder) of Clonmannan was described in the account as 'being a landed man of great meanes' (*ibid.*, fols 030r–030v).

The Clonmannan holding consisted of 825 acres 'besides bog'. The title to the property was disputed by Sir William Parsons, forcing Edward to repurchase it. By 1641 he was 'eighty years old, blind and bed-ridden'. Curiously, he was residing 'in the house of Lord Esmond, a Protestant, one of the Privy Council in Limerick' (*DKR 19* (1887), 36). Sir Lawrence Esmonde was by 1622 major-general of all the king's forces in Ireland and the governor of Duncannon Fort on Waterford Harbour. He was raised to the peerage as Lord Esmonde, baron of Limerick in the county of Wexford (Burke 1845, 376). He was referred to as a member of the privy council by Charles I in a letter to the lord deputy dated 1629 (HMC 1895, 85). Limerick is located to the north of Gorey. Edward's place of residence may have been connected to the fact that he had been in the service of Thomas Butler, tenth earl of Ormond, in the time of Queen Elizabeth (*DKR 19* (1887), 36). Esmonde was married to Ellice Butler, the daughter of Walter, fourth son of James, the ninth earl (Lodge and Archdall 1789, IV, 28).

The Walshes of Clonmannan appear in a more negative guise in an account relating to the siege of Wicklow Castle, albeit again in a non-combatant role. Thomas Molineux of Brittas decided, 'about the beginning of the month of November [1641] last', that for his own safety it would be best to take himself northwards to Wicklow Castle. In his absence his 'goodes and chattells', including his crops of 'peaze and oates', were looted. His servant John Finnagh later informed him that the main perpetrator was Teige Óg O'Byrne of *Bollinvillin*. Teige Óg (see above) was of the Ballinavalley O'Byrnes (Nicholls 1998b, 117).

Molineux assumed some authority in the command of Wicklow Castle alongside the under-keeper, John Joyce. About the '10th of November' (Molineux's dates appear to be slightly out), Barnaby O'Byrne, son-in-law of Luke O'Toole, led a party of insurgents to the gate to demand the surrender of the castle. Their request was denied.

This prompted the launching of a series of attacks, none of which succeeded.

The besiegers then adopted a new tactic. Letters began to arrive addressed to both Molineux and Joyce. In a letter delivered to Molineux from Teige Óg O'Byrne an offer of land was made to the two men, but only if they would 'reconcile your selves to our profession'. Another letter arrived, dated 31 December, from the brothers Edward and Henry Walsh, purportedly on behalf of their father, Edward (the elder) of Clonmannan. They stressed the hopelessness of the defenders' situation, given the forces now massing in the town. A free passage to either Dublin or Wexford was offered to him (1641 Depositions, TCD MS 811, fols 154r–157v). The offer was ignored.

John Walsh of Killincarrig was listed, along with over 80 other men, by a Robert Fox as being 'in Rebellion in County Wickloe' (*ibid.*, fols 141r–141v). In a deposition dated 4 January 1642 Robert Welden, a tenant of John Walsh of *Killicarrick* whose holding had been located 'in the parrish of kilcool in the Barony of new castle' (this is the area that lies to the immediate south of Killincarrig/Delgany), recorded the theft of his cattle, horses, corn and 'howsestuffe'. The raid had occurred 'upon the thirde of November last' and had cost him an estimated total of £637 15s. He placed the blame on the O'Byrnes and the O'Tooles (including Luke O'Toole). Furthermore, he alleged that John Walsh of Killincarrig, 'gentleman', who was his landlord, subsequently 'rebelliously & forceibly seized upon and taken possession of this deponents howse and farme & taketh the proffits thereof & plowed & sowed the same with this deponentes owne corne and keepeth himself and his family there' (*ibid.*, fols 106r–106v). One should note that Elizabeth Lison's deposition (see below) testified that John Walsh had been in residence at his own home in Killincarrig during that period.

John Lison of Delgany was hanged at *Ballygarney* (i.e. Mount Kennedy Demesne) 'about a month before Christmas' by 'the Rebells'. His widow, Elizabeth, named Morgan McEdmond and 'Brian of the Kellory' as the perpetrators. She fled her home and took refuge with 'John Walshe of *Killnicargie*'. She stayed with him and his wife until about three weeks before Easter. During the Walshes' absence, Morgan McEdmond, John Fynne and two others came to the house and seized Mrs Lison. She was brought to *Ballygarney* and there questioned by a 'Captaine Toole a Comaunder of the Rebells' (Luke O'Toole?) and a George Hackett, 'their Marshall'. She was then transferred to Arklow Gaol, from where she managed to escape and make her way to Dublin (*ibid.*, fols 152r–153v, TCD). John Walsh had sheltered Elizabeth Lison for several months while dispossessing his tenant Robert Welden; his approach to the insurrection could be said to have been a nuanced one. Nevertheless, he was later 'indicted of treason' (Gilbert 1882–91, III, 385). John Walsh's wife, Eleanor, was a sister of Theobald Walsh of Carrickmines.

Curiously, there is a reference in a deposition dated 4 March 1642 to 'the howse of Mrs Welsh of *Ould Coates*' in County Wicklow. The implication in the deposition is that 'the howse' had been used as a repository for looted goods. John Hayes, an English-born Protestant, had been an innkeeper in Bray. He testified that about a fortnight before Christmas he had been robbed of his cattle, horses, sheep, hay, corn,

Pl. 26—Oldcourt Castle, Co. Wicklow, as painted by Gabriel Beranger from an original by Major John Corneille. A hall-house of late fifteenth-century date, it stood on an outcrop above the Swan River. Only the service tower survives. (National Library of Ireland)

fuel and household goods to an estimated value of £130 sterling. He identified the perpetrators as Luke O'Toole's 'Companie' and others 'belonging' to Luke O'Byrne. He also recognised Garrett 'Ashpoole' (Archbold) of '*great Bray*'. The Manor of Great Bray consisted of Bree and Little Bree (Simpson 2003, 366). This area is now represented by the townlands of Bray and Little Bray. It may be no coincidence that another of those held responsible was 'James Hore sometimes of *Ould Coates*' (1641 Depositions, TCD MS 811, fols 057r–057v).

The will of Richard Walsh, Theobald's father, was drawn up on 27 December 1619. One clause acknowledged that 'the town, mills & lands of *Oldcourte*' would be delivered on his death to his wife Jane (née Eustace) 'as jointure' (Griffith 1991, 446). What was understood by 'jointure' was the property settled on a woman at marriage that was to be enjoyed by her after her husband's death. But who exactly was this Mrs Walsh of Oldcourt, mentioned in 1642? It was hardly Theobald's mother Jane, given both the passage of time and the fact that Richard had apparently remarried. The alternative interpretation would be that the reference was to Theobald's own wife, Maria, and that she, for reasons unknown, was domiciled there on a regular basis. Apparently her residency was prolonged enough for her brother James to be described as semi-resident there (Pl. 26).

By no stretch of the evidence can the rising in Wicklow and its environs be described as a pogrom. While there were fatalities, such as in the case of John Lison, there was nothing remotely approaching the scale of what was going on in Ulster.

Five weeks or so into the insurrection, all English people—men, women and children—who lived in the neighbourhood of Clones, Co. Monaghan, were ordered to gather about the high cross in the town. There they were robbed of all possessions, stripped naked and banished into the December night. The alternative on offer was death (Mac Cuarta 2007, 164). As Armagh City burned, the corpses of the slain Protestants were stripped and had Bibles placed on their 'privy parts' (*ibid.*, 171).

THE LOCAL THEATRE

Nothing resembling the excessive behaviour on display in Ulster was evident in the south County Dublin or Wicklow area. There were, however, isolated incidents of graphic violence. The Reverend Simon Swayne, the vicar of Rathmichael, testified that on 3 December, about '9 of the clock at night', with only his son John and two female companions (Ellenor Oliverson and Jane Evans) at home, his house was ransacked and looted. Swayne named the leaders of the raiders as Edward Barnewall and Edward Stokes of Shankill; they had been accompanied by other residents of Shankill and about 60 men from County Wicklow. Another raid followed on 10 December. The Reverend was left in no doubt that he was the prize that they sought. One of the intruders had professed that they would rather have found him at home than find 'a horseload of gold and silver' (1641 Depositions, TCD MS 809, fols 329r–329v).

The Reverend Swayne clearly decided that his security needed to be expeditiously improved. He and his family and their retainers took up residency in Lehaunstown Castle. His instincts were correct. An attack was launched 'about 10 of the Clocke in the night' by a force numbering about 100. He identified the 'cheefe leaders' as Robert Barnewall of Shankill and James Goodman the younger of Loughlinstown. There followed 'many shotts on both sides'. Eventually the besiegers managed to set the castle on fire. Five of the defenders had been slain and another one was now 'burnt [...] to ashes'. Swayne himself survived but 'the violence of the fire [had] burned one of his eyes out of his head [and he had been] fearfully burned [on] his hands, haunches, and leggs' (1641 Depositions, TCD MS 810, fols 183r–183v).

The Reverend John Wilson, the vicar of Killiney and Dalkey, had fled his parish out of fear of an attack by the insurgents. His wife Susan testified that the loss of his £80 *per annum* position in addition to their property had left them totally bereft in the city of Dublin. Wilson fell ill and was dead within a few months (*ibid.*, fols 191r–192v).

A third case involving a Protestant clergyman implicated William Wolverston of Stillorgan. The Reverend Joseph Smithson of the parish of Clonkeen (Kill of the Grange) testified that on 'Innocents Day' (i.e. 28 December) his homestead had been raided and looted of household goods, hay, pigs and poultry (hens, geese, ducks and turkeys). More alarmingly, but interestingly referred to in the said chronological order, was the fact that his wife had been abducted. The alleged perpetrators were Philip 'Malene' (Malone?) and John Garvey of Rochestown, servants of Nicholas Rochford, accompanied by James Goodman of Ballinclea, Alexander Rochford of Rochestown and Patrick Keenan of Kill of the Grange. The manner of her abduction was violent. Her apron was pulled off and she was dragged out of the house by 'the hayre of her head'. Her arms were bound, and she was set upon her horse bareback with 'her Clothes pluckt from under her'. The deposition alleged that she was thus brought to the home of William Wolverston in Stillorgan. He was said to have promptly instructed the abductors to hang her but 'not upon his landes'. Accordingly, she was put back on her horse, again in the 'same manner', and forced to ride an additional '20 miles'. Smithson testified that he had been 'crediblie informed that the said Rebells have most barbarouslie and crewellie hanged his said wife till shee dyed and a servant woman of hers alsoe' (1641 Depositions, TCD MS 809, fols 327r–328v).

The basic thrust of the Reverend Smithson's account was partially corroborated by John Heyes, the innkeeper, late of Bray (see above), but with notable differences. He testified that about 6 January 1641 a Katherine Sherlock, also late of Bray, had informed him that Mary Smithson had been 'carried away in a very unseemly manner' by 'the Rebbells' to *Portscorte* (Powerscourt) and thence to *Kilmacannock* (Kilmacanogue) in County Wicklow. Heyes testified that it was there that the abductors had received written instructions from William Wolverston 'that they should by noe means spare the said Mrs Smithson's life'. Heyes further stated that he 'hath since credibly heard that the said Rebbells have putt both the said Mrs Smithson and her maide to death' (1641 Depositions, TCD MS 811, fols 062r–062v).

Most of the above testimony would seem to have credibility. Borlase (1680, 114 App.) accepted the veracity of the story, writing that Mrs Smithson was brought to *Stellorgan*, then to Powerscourt, 'and there she and her servant hang'd'. Another published account, however, raised the ante in graphic detail. Daniel Harcourt, a commissioner appointed by the king to investigate grievances (mostly) in Ulster, reported that the insurgents had 'stript her of her apparell, setting her naked astride upon a leane jade, tying heavy weights at her heeles' (a jade was a worthless horse). He further related that after being tortured and mutilated she was hanged alongside her maid 'upon one bough' (Pamphlet 30).

There is, however, a further account. Josuah Bishop, of the 'City of Dublin', testified that he was present when William Wolverston was questioned regarding the above accusations, the interrogation being conducted by Sir William Reeves in the presence of the Reverend Smithson. When it was put to him that he had played a part in the death of Mary Smithson he denied it. Furthermore, he requested that he be brought before a commission where he would prove his innocence. And this he would achieve by bringing forth Mary Smithson alive (1641 Depositions, TCD MS 809, fols 248r–248v)! The veracity of this account is supported by the fact that Bishop was a witness hostile to Wolverston. The available evidence, therefore, would suggest that, while Mary Smithson had been abducted in an abusive and humiliating fashion, neither the reports of her death by hanging nor William Wolverston's involvement were substantiated.

As in the case of John Lison, not all the reported isolated incidents of violence against Protestants in the south County Dublin area involved clergymen and/or their families. William Beaton, an English-born Protestant, had lived in the Dean's Grange area and later in Loughlinstown (1641 Depositions, TCD MS 810, fols 370r–370v). Before the harvest of 1642 he had been brought to Bray and hanged from a willow tree. Hugh Murphy of Loughlinstown (see above) subsequently buried his body there. Murphy testified that Beaton had been hanged on the orders of James Goodman the elder of Loughlinstown. Goodman, he reported, had then been acting as 'Marshall' to Hugh McPhelim O'Byrne (*ibid.*, fols. 366r–367v). Goodman, then aged about 60, later pleaded that he had been acting on the orders of Lieutenant General Hugh McPhelim, a grandson of Feagh Mac Hugh O'Byrne (Nicholls 1998b, 115). He gave evidence that Beaton and another unnamed man had been convicted on a charge of pillaging (1641 Depositions, TCD MS 810, fols 373r–374v). Goodman was subsequently executed by the Commonwealth 'for murther done' during the insurrection (Simington 1931–61, VII, 270).

CARRICKMINES CASTLE

When John Brakenbury entered Carrickmines Castle in early January 1642 he had found John Fagan of Feltrim and Bullock sitting by the fire. One can only imagine the number and length of the fireside conversations that Fagan held with Theobald between the preceding November and the following February. The older man certainly did spend time there. His servant John Coppinger recounted how his employer had arrived unexpectedly at Bullock Castle, with no provisions stored on the premises. Rather than wait around hungry, John Fagan had gone straight to Carrickmines to avail of the hospitality of his great-nephew, and resided there 'for about a weeke'. The Thursday before Christmas, Coppinger journeyed there to report to him that all was finally ready in his Bullock abode. Still Fagan lingered at least another day. As noted above, he was back in residence at Carrickmines in early January. About eight to ten days after Christmas he had sent a consignment of fish thence (1641 Depositions, TCD MS 810, fols 199r–200v). There can be no doubt that the major topic around the fireside on those winter days and nights would have been the evolving drama of the insurrection. The key question, however, is whether the conversation was driven by ideological concerns or by self-preservation.

Judging by their recorded activities and the testimonies of others, both friend and foe, the Walshes do not seem to have been involved in any killings, woundings, abductions, physical humiliations or acts of arson. Indeed, the limited looting and petty theft in which, for example, Theobald Walsh had engaged would, judging by all legal precedents, have ultimately resulted in fines being imposed and a pardon being granted. This had been the way of the world for countless generations. Why would it be any different this time around, once peace had been re-established under the restored authority of the king? In other words, was Theobald Walsh treading a carefully thought-out fine line, one that would see his family and estates through the tangled mesh of allies and opponents and their conflicting expectations of him? Inevitably, most writers have referred to the fact that in the Civil Survey of the 1650s Theobald is recorded as having 'acted in the Irish Army, as Captaine of a foote Company' (Simington 1931–61, VII, 270, 278), but there is no evidence to establish when he took up this appointment. In all contemporary references to him he is called either 'Mr Walsh' or simply by his given name. Never is he referred to as 'Captain Walsh'. It could well be the case that Theobald's active military service only began after the calamitous events of March 1642.

Carrickmines Great and Lehaunstown are adjoining townlands. Lehaunstown Castle lay a mere 1.5km to the south-east of Carrickmines Castle. There is little chance that the rising flames from the torched Lehaunstown Castle were not observed from the upper levels of Carrickmines Castle. Theobald's non-participation in the Barnewall- and Goodman-directed attack is therefore worthy of some attention and certainly raises questions. Was Theobald informed of the planned attack? Did he decline to participate or was he kept in the dark? Wherever the truth lies, it is reasonable to suppose that he may well not have approved or, indeed, might have been perceived as potentially disapproving.

It is important to note that, if the dates in the depositions concerning Theobald are accurate, the Jamestown and Booterstown incidents occurred prior to the formal involvement of the Old English in the insurrection. Similarly, the raid on Dean's Grange took place about 15 December, just over a week after the second and conclusive meeting between the Gaelic Irish and the Old English leaderships. The first meeting took place on the Hill of Crofty (south of Bellewstown) about 3 December, the second on 7 December on the Hill of Tara (Gilbert 1882–91, I, 36–40; Clarke 1966, 180–3). The implications would be, therefore, that the three raids involving Theobald Walsh, his kinsmen and neighbours were purely localised affairs with no connections to a nascent strategic design.

There is an intriguing report of an encounter that occurred 'about the xxiiith of May' 1642. The venue was 'the Castle of the Deanes Grange'. This is likely to have been the building described in the Civil Survey as a 'Castle, slated' (Simington 1931–61, VII, 266). Four individuals, including the unnamed 'good wife of the house', were up 'on the Topp of the Castle', keeping watch for any approaching insurgents. One man armed with a musket advanced towards the building and demanded that the

Pl. 27—Bullock Castle, Co. Dublin, as drawn by George Petrie. The tower-house is of probable fifteenth-century date. The attached eighteenth-century three-storey house was demolished in modern times. In the seventeenth century the castle was owned by the Fagan family of Feltrim.

'English Captaine' whom he believed to be inside should come forth. The woman of the house denied that there were any soldiers within. Another of the watch, one Murtagh Bredon, recognised the musketman as a 'sometimes' servant of the previously mentioned Mr Brakenbury. Bredon shouted that he should 'follow his trade' and not the insurgents. The man retorted that he had 'cause to curse my Maister Brakenburie who sent mee with Powder unto Welsh of *Carrigmain* for since that tyme I never durst shew my head' (1641 Depositions, TCD MS 810, fols 201r–201v).

Ball (1902–17, I, 51) interpreted this episode as evidence that Brakenbury had dispatched 'powder to the rebels at Carrickmines', but it would be strange if John Brakenbury, having twice been looted by the insurgents, were subsequently to supply them with gunpowder. It is possible, of course, that he was acting under duress, perhaps buying insurance on a *quid pro quo* basis. But whom exactly was his servant trying to placate? Who were the people to whom he was afraid to 'show his head'? The slaying or capture of an English captain would hardly have endeared him to the Dublin authorities. The logical alternative, therefore, is that he was hoping to make amends to the insurgents. This would suggest, in turn, that the gunpowder delivery had not been for them in the first place but was a personal transaction between Brakenbury and Walsh. Could this consignment of powder not simply have been for the protection of the castle against any renegade elements? These were, after all, very unstable and unsettled times. Had the private transaction incurred the displeasure of the insurgents, thus causing the Brakenbury servant's anxiety to redeem himself with them?

One final piece of evidence in the attempt to determine Theobald Walsh's mind-set in the early months of 1642 is to be found in the saga of the cannon. On 'the Thursday before Christmas', while John Coppinger was *en route* to Carrickmines Castle, a messenger from there arrived at the Fagan castle in Bullock (Pl. 27) and relayed his purpose to Coppinger's wife. A 'piece' (cannon) that had 'for many years past lay on the Battlement of the Castle of Bullock' was now to be shipped to Carrickmines Castle. It was accordingly 'carried unto Carrickmines, the same night', and remained there till about 'Candlemas', i.e. 2 February (1641 Depositions, TCD MS 810, fols 199r–200v). John Brakenbury noted the presence of the cannon at Carrickmines in early January, describing it as a 'small horse peece called a slinge piece' and identifying it as the gun formerly sited at Bullock Castle (*ibid.*, fol. 198r). As noted above, the cannon was returned to Bullock in early February, having been 'sent home by the said Mr Walsh'. The time-line must have a key bearing. The clearance attacks on Dundrum Castle and Kilgobbin Castle occurred on 20 January and were followed by other operations in the south-west of the county. The news of these attacks would have reached Carrickmines almost immediately. There was no ignoring the fact that the attacks were part of a growing litany of reversals. The attack on Kilgobbin in itself must have had a negative psychological impact. This was a castle that had until very recently been a Walsh possession, and had been for centuries. More portentously, it lay less than 3km away. Theobald Walsh was a former professional soldier. He would hardly have dispensed with his best piece of ordnance in these circumstances if he had any intention of physically defending Carrickmines Castle.

And so the days would have passed. Early February witnessed a significant defeat in the field for the insurgents at Dean's Grange. The conjoined townlands of Dean's Grange, Galloping Green South, Walterstown and Foxrock constitute the historic Dean's Grange (Ball 1902–17, I, 47), and thus the scene of the battle was not much more than a few kilometres away from Carrickmines. Retreating elements of the defeated army may well have streamed past the gates of the castle. The mood within the walls cannot have been lifted. All that Theobald Walsh could do now was to wait.

PART 4

Sir Simon Harcourt and the fall of Carrickmines Castle

Bonfires burned on the hilltops surrounding Dublin Bay on the last day of December 1641. They had been lit in response to an event anticipated for many weeks: the arrival of a fleet transporting soldiers from England. The ships now sailing towards Dublin port were carrying the regiment of Sir Simon Harcourt (seven companies with a total complement of 1,100 men, including officers) (Pamphlets 1 and 2).

The bonfires were lit by the insurgent forces who had maintained a loose siege around the city for many weeks past. What effect they had on the besiegers was not recorded, although it may be assumed that it was a mixture of alarm and disappointment. Indeed, many within their ranks may well have hoped that help for the beleaguered city would never be dispatched by the king to whom they had professed loyalty. The psychological impact on the authorities and citizens of Dublin was naturally the complete opposite. The fears of the inhabitants had been fuelled since early November by an almost daily arrival of refugees from the surrounding countryside and from as afar afield as Ulster. The northern refugees, in particular, would undoubtedly have derived a certain amount of *schadenfreude* from the fact that the newly arrived soldiers from England immediately set about raiding 'Masse Houses', from which they took 'Pictures and broke them al to pieces' (Pamphlet 2).

Sir Simon Harcourt arrived in Dublin with very precise personal expectations. As far as he was concerned, he had the backing of king and parliament. In a letter to his wife Anne sent from Chester, dated 16 December 1641 and dispatched while he awaited transport to Ireland, he wrote: 'That I have undertaken this employment, beeinge thereunto called by both houses of Parliament; I did it, confidently beeleevinge yet what they did was by his Majesties direction & abrobation' (Harcourt 1880–1905, I, 159). His latter assumption is corroborated by a letter from Charles I dispatched to Frederik Hendrik of Nassau, prince of Orange (Sir Simon's employer), dated 20 December 1641, which advocated that, while Harcourt's services were required in Ireland, his temporary absence from his duties in the United Provinces (the

Pl. 28—Sir Simon Harcourt (1603–42) by Gerrit van Honthorst. (Courtesy of the Courtauld Institute, London)

Netherlands) should not 'be to his prejudice, but that he may still retain his command during his absence' (Hamilton 1873–93, XVIII, 209).

King Charles I would have first encountered Simon Harcourt at his knighting on 26 June 1627 at Whitehall (Shaw and Burtchaell 1906, 192). A more personal relationship would have developed during the Scottish or 'Bishop's' War of 1639. The royally sanctioned attempts by Archbishop William Laud of Canterbury, member of the privy council and chief religious adviser to the king, to impose Anglican forms of worship in Scotland had aroused such entrenched resistance that open conflict erupted in that kingdom (Fissel 1994, 3). It is possible that Harcourt was recruited on the recommendation either of the archbishop or of Charles's sister, Elizabeth Stuart, the titular queen of Bohemia (see below). On 11 March 1636 she wrote to Archbishop

Laud, extolling the virtues of Sir Simon and noting how highly he was held in the esteem of the prince of Orange (Bruce 1858–69, IX, 266; Akkerman 2011, II, 389–90). The archbishop duly promised to 'give him all the assistance that is in my power' (Bruce 1858–69, IX, 338; Akkerman 2011, II, 401). To fully appreciate how it came to pass that the name and reputation of a relatively obscure young knight from the English midlands came to the attention of some of the leading figures of seventeenth-century western European society one must return to his origins (Pl. 28).

FAMILY BACKGROUND

The Harcourt family had a long and distinguished history. Robert de Harcourt served as sheriff of Warwickshire and Leicestershire in 1199 and 1201. He succeeded to his father Ivo's estate in 1202 and married Isabel de Camville. This marriage brought the lordship of Stanton in Oxfordshire into the family (Harcourt 1880–1905, I, 18). The lordship of Stanton (henceforth Stanton Harcourt) formed part of the royal demesne of Woodstock (*ibid.*, 20). The fortunes of the family flourished throughout the following centuries.

Simon Harcourt's father, Robert, led an adventurous life. In time he obtained 'letters patent' from James I to plant a small area in South America. This led to the establishment in 1608 of a colony on the River *Wiapoco* (the Oyapock or Oiapocque) (Markham 1888, 385), which forms most of the border between modern Brazil and French Guiana. Robert was following in the footsteps of Sir Walter Raleigh, who in 1595 had led an expedition to the Orinoco River in search of 'Eldorado'. Raleigh had published an account of this journey in 1596 (*The discoverie of Guiana*; see Lorimer 2006) and had formed personal relationships with some of the indigenous population, one of whom lived with him in England for three or four years. When Robert Harcourt settled on the *Wiapoco* he contacted this man, who had by then returned home but still bore great affection for Raleigh (*ibid.*, lxv fn. 2). Harcourt's colony was still extant in 1610 (*ibid.*, 292 fn. 3). In 1613 he published an account of his exploits, *Relation of a voyage to Guiana*. He had, however, invested a vast sum of personal money into the enterprise, fitting out three vessels, including the 80-ton *Rose*. In addition, there was a costly building programme under way at Ellen Hall in Staffordshire. The end result was that he had to sell both Ellen Hall and Whitham in Berkshire to cover some of his losses. These two properties had been in the possession of the family since the time of King John (Harcourt *et al.* 1806, 28). It has been stated that Robert's brother Michael had accompanied him to Guiana and remained there when Robert returned to England after a three-year sojourn (Markham 1888, 385). Elsewhere it is recorded that Michael served as a ship's captain under the command of Sir Walter Raleigh (Harcourt 1880–1905, I, 247). His sister Elizabeth served as maid of honour to Queen Anne, wife of James I (*ibid.*).

Sir Robert was married twice, first to Elizabeth FitzHerbert and then to Frances Vere, daughter of Geoffrey, the youngest son of the fifteenth earl of Oxford. They had three sons and four daughters, Simon (born *c.* 1603) being the eldest. Robert died in 1633 (Akkerman 2011, II, 390 fn. 1). The most important and influential figure in Simon's life proved to be his maternal uncle, Horatio, Lord Vere of Tilbury, who has been described as 'the most revered English commander of his day' (Cust 2013, 130).

As has been noted, Sir Robert's life of adventure on the high seas had done the family fortunes no favours. Simon, therefore, could only look forward to inheriting what has been described by Robert Dunlop as a 'somewhat embarrassed estate' (*DNB*, XXIV, 321). Thus at the age of sixteen he embarked on what transpired to be a lifetime of professional soldiering.

Horatio Vere, first Baron Vere of Tilbury, led a long and illustrious military career. He had gained invaluable experience with the English forces sent to aid the Dutch in the ongoing struggles between the embryonic United Provinces (the Netherlands) and the Spanish forces set on crushing them. After many years of military service, he returned to England in the wake of the Battle of Mulheim (9 October 1605). In 1607 he married Mary Tracy of Gloucestershire. There were to be no more military opportunities for the ensuing decade or more, as Spain and the United Provinces began the 'Twelve Years' Truce' in 1609.

The festering religious divide in Europe caught fire in 1618. The Thirty Years' War had begun. The Protestant people of Bohemia attempted to free themselves from the Catholic Habsburgs. They offered the kingship to one of the leading advocates of the Protestant cause in Europe, Frederick V, elector palatine of the Rhine and director of the Protestant evangelical union. He duly accepted their offer in 1619 but his reign proved to be short-lived.

These clouds of war in central Europe cast shadows on England. Frederick V of the Palatinate, recently crowned Frederick I of Bohemia, was married to Elizabeth Stuart, daughter of James I. Popular opinion in England was clamouring for the king to intervene on her side in the struggle against the Habsburgs. James I accordingly permitted Count Dohna, the Bohemian envoy, to recruit volunteers and appeal for financial aid. Sir Horatio Vere was appointed English commander. The expeditionary force of 2,200 men set sail from Gravesend for the Netherlands on 22 July 1620. Sir Horatio was accompanied by his sixteen-year-old nephew, Simon Harcourt.

THE PALATINATE

Habsburg forces had already engaged the Bohemian rebels in the campaign to reimpose imperial and Catholic rule. The crucial battle would be fought on 8 November 1620 at Bílá Hora (White Mountain) to the west of Prague (Lee 1991, 2) (Pl. 29). The Protestant rebellion was crushed and King Frederick I was deposed. There followed a wave of executions, land confiscations and the expulsion of all Protestants from the kingdom. Frederick's situation worsened with the invasion of his homeland, the Palatinate, by a combined force of Spanish and Bavarian troops.

Upon landing in the United Provinces, the English expeditionary force was

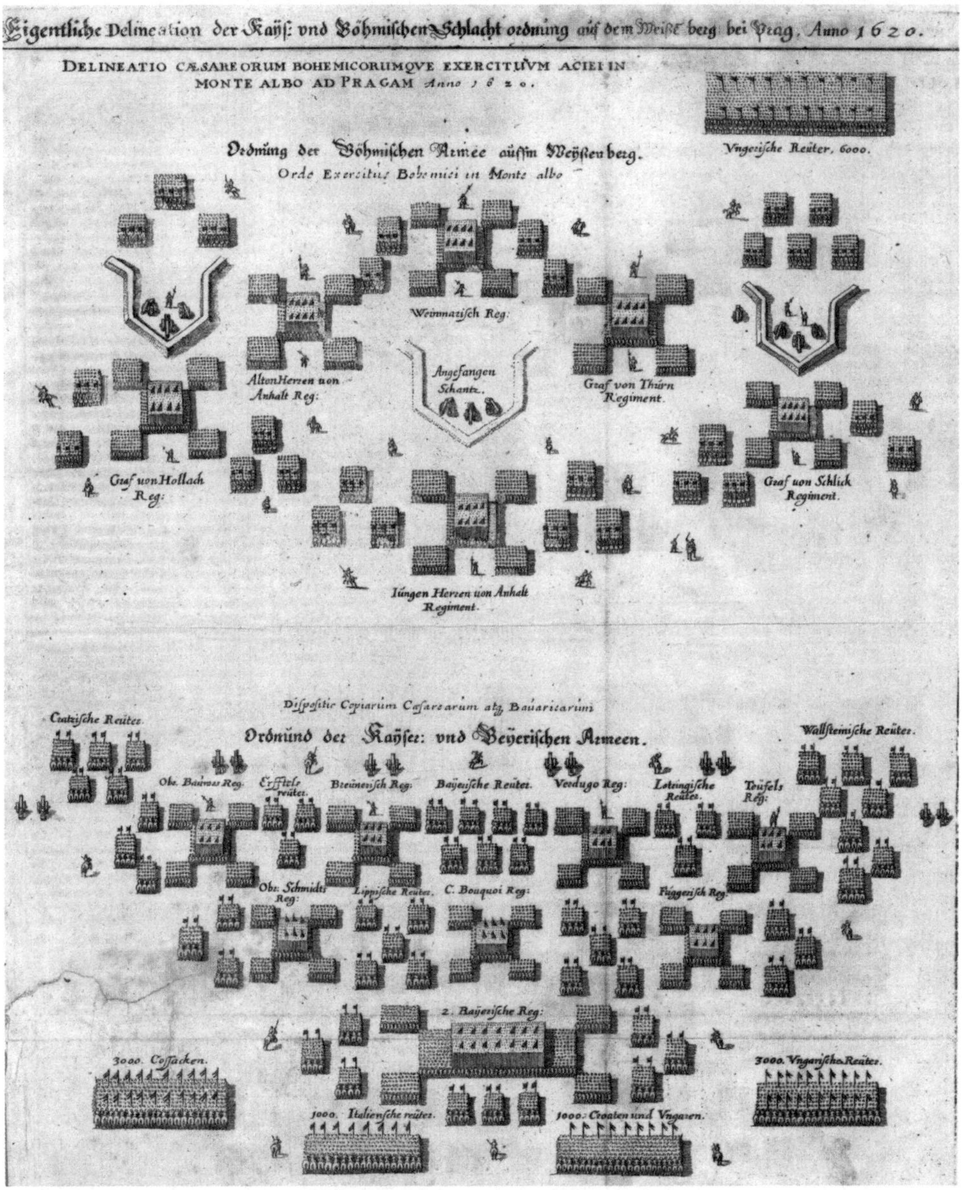

Pl. 29—The Battle of Bílá Hora (White Mountain) in Bohemia (8 November 1620). (www.arkivkopia.se)

joined by Dutch cavalry under the command of Frederik Hendrik, younger half-brother of Maurits, count of Nassau, prince of Orange. Vere led the force eastwards into the Rhineland, playing cat-and-mouse with the Spanish army under Don Ambrogio Spinola, first marquis of the Balbases, who attempted to block his progress. As his German allies fell away, the Elector Frederick found his position increasingly desperate. The English troops soon found themselves garrisoning three towns. Vere was in command of Mannheim, where he was visited in 1622 by Frederick and his wife Elizabeth. This would have been the young Simon Harcourt's first encounter with the 'Winter Queen'.

The siege of Mannheim tightened and the English garrison, having set light to the town, were confined to the citadel. With no hope of relief, surrender was arranged at the end of October 1622. Vere negotiated with Johann Tserclaes, Count Tilly, for the right to march out of Mannheim with flags flying, matches burning and musket-balls in mouth. With the 'honours of war' secured, Lord Vere, at the head of his 1,500 men, baggage train (including 30 'tuns' of wine and 200 sacks of flour) and two falconets, proceeded to Frankfurt and thence back into the Netherlands (Hinds 1911, 501).

THE LOW COUNTRIES

It is impossible to say with certainty how many engagements Simon Harcourt was involved in during his long military service in the Netherlands. One can attempt to follow his career by tracking the progress of the regiment of Sir Horatio Vere (and later his successor, Colonel George Goring). Harcourt, Vere's nephew, was just one of a generation of young English officers whose careers were nurtured by the veteran soldier.

In the late sixteenth century sympathy with the Protestants of the Netherlands had manifested itself in the rallying of English volunteers to their nascent revolt against Spanish rule. A peaceful, unarmed protest march was organised in April 1566 by about 200 nobles in Brussels in order to present a petition to the governor of the territory, Margaret of Parma, half-sister of Philip II of Spain. The protestors were described as beggars by a court official and consequently called themselves the *Geuzen* (beggars). As a result of the presentation of the petition, extant religious decrees were temporarily suspended pending a formal response from Madrid. This window of religious freedom led, however, to widespread attacks on Catholic Church property by a predominantly Calvinist iconoclastic movement. This wave of attacks became known as the *Beeldenstorm*.

The king reacted badly and sent Fernando Álvarez de Toledo, third duke of Alva, to the Netherlands at the head of a 10,000-strong army to restore his autocratic rule. The leading lights of the 'revolt' were subsequently either executed or exiled. Alba's Council of Troubles, installed to try all those involved in the movement, soon became known as the 'Blood Court'. William of Orange fled to his father-in-law's territory in Saxony. His attempts to stage a comeback were faltering when the 'Sea Beggars' suddenly seized the port town of Brill on 1 April 1572 (Markham 1888, 29). These seafaring adventurers were a mixture of dispossessed noblemen and freebooting outlaws. The fall of Brill signalled a general uprising in the towns of Holland and Zeeland. The 'Eighty Years' War' had begun (Bindoff 1950, 247–8).

Queen Elizabeth of England finally climbed down from the diplomatic fence in 1585. The assassination of William, prince of Orange, in 1584 and the encirclement of

Antwerp by the army of Alessandro Farnese, the duke of Parma, in the summer of 1585 signalled the imminent collapse of the Dutch revolt. It was time to act and by the end of the year Elizabeth had deployed the earl of Leicester and a force of 6,000 troops to the Low Countries (Wilson 1970, 86). Spain's displeasure would soon lead to the Spanish Armada.

The arrival of English volunteers had begun in April 1572. Thomas Morgan and 300 men had mustered at Greenwich before the queen. Their destination was Flushing, where they would join the garrison (Markham 1888, 42). This first detachment was followed by Sir Humphrey Gilbert and 1,500 men (*ibid.*, 43). Besides allowing volunteers to go to the Netherlands, Queen Elizabeth was also making personal loans to the Dutch; between 1577 and 1581 she advanced them at least £284,000 (*ibid.*, 52).

Under the terms of the June 1585 Treaty of Nonsuch between England and the United Provinces, the former would financially maintain its army in the field in return for the latter temporarily placing two towns under English control. The towns would be returned upon repayment of all debts owed by the Dutch. The so-called 'Cautionary Towns' were Flushing (along with the castle of Rammekens) and Brill. Markham (1888, 69) noted that Ostend was a later addition. Elizabeth issued a formal declaration (in several languages) in November (Wilson 1970, 86).

The commander of the expeditionary force was Robert Dudley, the earl of Leicester, long-time confidant and intimate of Queen Elizabeth. Sir Thomas Cecil was appointed governor of Brill, Sir Philip Sydney was given charge of Flushing and the castle of Rammekens, while the garrison of Ostend was placed under the command of Captain Errington. Flushing, the first of the towns, was occupied by December (*ibid.*, 90). Sir Philip, Dudley's nephew, was wounded in action in September 1586 during the Battle of Zutphen; he later died of septicaemia. He was the older brother of Robert Sydney, the first earl (reactivated) of Leicester.

By December 1587 the earl of Leicester had departed for home. His expeditionary force had not performed exceptionally well in the field during the course of the campaign, although it succeeded in drawing off the heat from the tottering forces of the Provinces. Philip II's attention now refocused on England. The relatively short passage to the launching of the 1588 Grand Armada against England was now under way. This breathing space, at the end of the day, would save the Dutch State. Leicester's departure, however, did not mark the end of the war for all the Englishmen now fighting in the Low Countries, who effectively became fully fledged units of the army of the United Provinces.

Francis Vere had signed up as a volunteer in Colchester in December 1585. He excelled at his duties and by November 1586 had been promoted to the rank of captain (of a company of 150 men at Bergen-op-Zoom) (Markham 1888, 98). It was the start of a stellar career. By July 1601, as governor of Ostend, he had to defend the city against a force led by the Archduke Albrecht that was three times his strength. The 3,000-strong garrison was composed of Dutch and English troops (Lawrence 2009, 329). Supplied from the sea, they were to hold out for the next three years (*ibid.*, 330).

Map 9—The Low Countries (1620–40).

Vere held his command in Ostend for the first eight months of the siege. He was transferred, along with his brother Horace, on 7 March 1602. The town held out until 20 September 1604; by then it was a smouldering heap of ruins (Markham 1888, 331).

Horatio Vere had joined his two older brothers on active service in the Netherlands in 1590. He began his military service in the infantry company commanded by Francis. Their brother Robert was commanding his own troop of horse (*ibid.*, 157). By the beginning of 1592, while Sir Robert Sydney was governor of Flushing, Horatio had acquired command of his own company of infantry (*ibid.*, 181). His career was to reach the same heights attained by his brother Francis. He played a pivotal role in such engagements as the Battle of Nieuwpoort (1600) and the aforementioned siege of Ostend, where he commanded eight companies of battle-hardened English troops. When Francis retired from the army in 1606 Horatio succeeded him in his command. Francis passed away peacefully at home in England in August 1609.

A truce signed in April 1609 between the Dutch and the Spanish was to last for twelve years; both sides were exhausted and had more or less fought each other to a standstill. The 'Cautionary Towns' remained under English control and were accordingly garrisoned by English troops. Horatio succeeded Francis as governor of Brill in 1609.

The fragile peace was almost broken in 1614. Motivated by the aspirations of the Counter-Reformation movement, the Spanish occupied extensive territory in the Lower Rhineland region, making the eastern flank of the United Provinces increasingly vulnerable. Maurits, prince of Orange, ordered Lieutenant Colonel Frederik Pithan, governor of Jülich, to broaden the Dutch pocket centred on the town (Israel 1997, 35).

By May 1616 the Dutch had repaid their debt and the 'Cautionary Towns' were returned to their control.

The treaty was finally broken in 1621. A Spanish army under Spinola quickly positioned itself at Wesel to thwart any advances from the heartland. Simultaneously a second Spanish force under Count Hendrik van den Bergh swept into the duchy of Jülich, rolling up all resistance in their path. Jülich itself was besieged in September 1621. The garrison of Dutch and Brandenburger troops surrendered after five months (Israel 1997, 35–6; Wilson 2009, 331; van Nimwegen 2006, 19).

When Horatio de Vere withdrew his expeditionary force from the Palatinate at the beginning of November 1622 and re-entered the Netherlands he was returning to his home from home. So was his teenaged nephew Simon Harcourt, although he would not have known it at the time (Map 9).

THE SPANISH SIEGE OF BREDA

The town of Breda in the North Brabant featured formidable defences. The walls incorporated fifteen bulwarks and five hornworks. The rivers Merk and Aa-of-Weerijs united before the walls, separated to fill the moat and joined again to form a harbour (Markham 1888, 425). Ambrogio Spinola, marquis de los Balbases, commander of the army of Flanders, laid siege to the town on 28 August 1624. The garrison of Dutch, English and Scottish troops was commanded by Justin of Nassau, a natural son of William I, prince of Orange.

Spinola encircled and sealed off the town with deep entrenchments. The aim was to use famine to force an eventual surrender (Cannon 1839, 90–1). In pursuit of this objective, Francisco de Medina occupied the village of Ginneken (de Mesa 2014, 72). The Irish *tercio* of Tyrone was part of the forces at de Medina's disposal.

On 16 September the garrison sallied forth but were repulsed by Captain Garrett Barry's company initially, joined soon afterwards by the companies of Captains Walter Delahyde and Edmund O'More. The involvement of the companies of Captains Thomas Preston and George Fitzgerald in blocking a further Dutch advance brought the number of Irish units involved in this engagement up to five (*ibid.*, 73).

The death of Maurits, prince of Orange and stadtholder, occurred during the siege. His half-brother and successor Frederik Hendrik resolved to make another attempt to relieve the town. On 17 May 1625 Sir Horatio Vere was ordered to advance with 70 ensigns of foot to attack the besiegers' defences at the village of Terheyden (Cannon 1839, 93). Two entrenchment forts manned by Italians were taken but the attack ran out of steam and casualties were heavy. Vere's cousin, the earl of Oxford, was wounded in the arm; he died in The Hague a few months later (Markham 1888, 428). The garrison in Breda capitulated on favourable terms on 5 June (Cannon 1839, 94). The loss of the town was a blow to morale in the United Provinces (Israel 1997, xiv).

On 25 July 1625 Sir Horatio was created Baron Vere of Tilbury in recognition of his services.

THE SIEGE OF OLDENZAAL

In 1626 Spanish attention became focused on building a fortified canal that would not only facilitate water traffic but also form a strong line of defence. Frederik Hendrik saw an opportunity to quickly invest the fortified town of Oldenzaal in the province of Overijssel. A force of 7,000 under the command of the prince and his cousin Ernest Casimir, count of Nassau-Dietz and stadtholder of Friesland, accordingly arrived at the town on 24 July 1626 (Pl. 30). The garrison of less than 1,000 men was under the command of Guillermo de Verdugo, who commanded Spanish forces in the Lower Palatinate from 1623 to 1628 (Polisensky and Snider 1978, 69). Spinola did not have the necessary reserves to come to the assistance of the town (Israel 1997, 55) and it surrendered on 1 August, a mere eight days after the siege had begun. A detachment of English soldiers served in the siege (Cannon 1839, 96). According to the official history of the regiment, 'some companies' of English troops were detached from the siege to set upon 'Broeckhuise Castle', which they captured in two days (*ibid.*).

THE SIEGE OF GROLL (GROENLO)

The following year the forces of Frederik Hendrik descended on the eastern town of Groll in the province of Gelderland (Pl. 31). Adopting the strategy used by Spinola at Breda in 1624, his forces constructed an earthen wall, embellished with fortifications

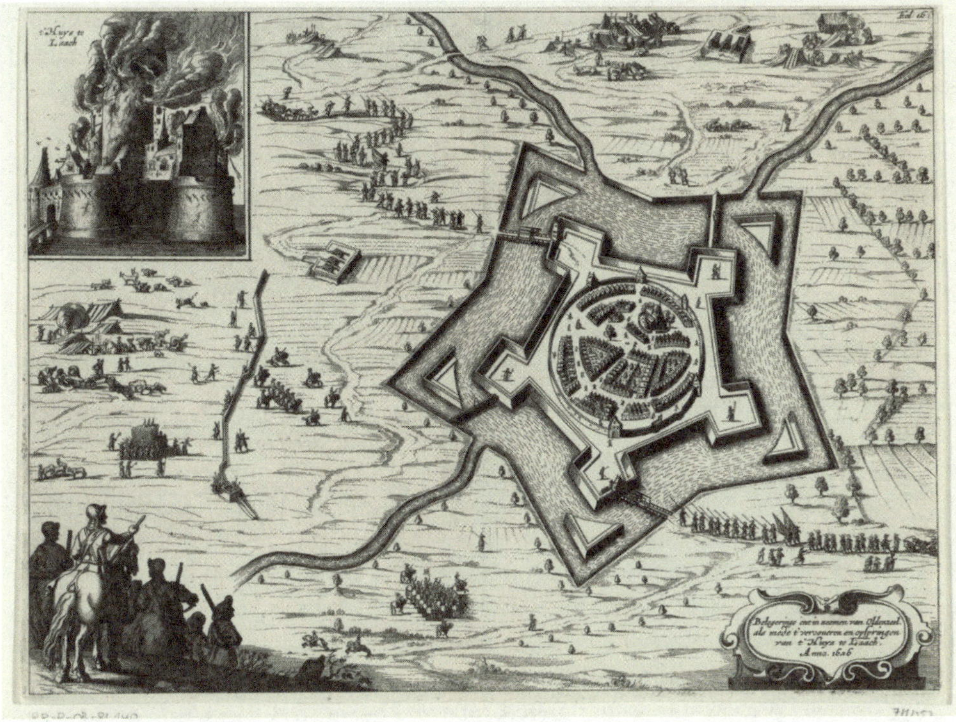

Pl. 30—The siege of Oldenzaal in the Low Countries (24 July–1 August 1626). (Geheugen van Nederland)

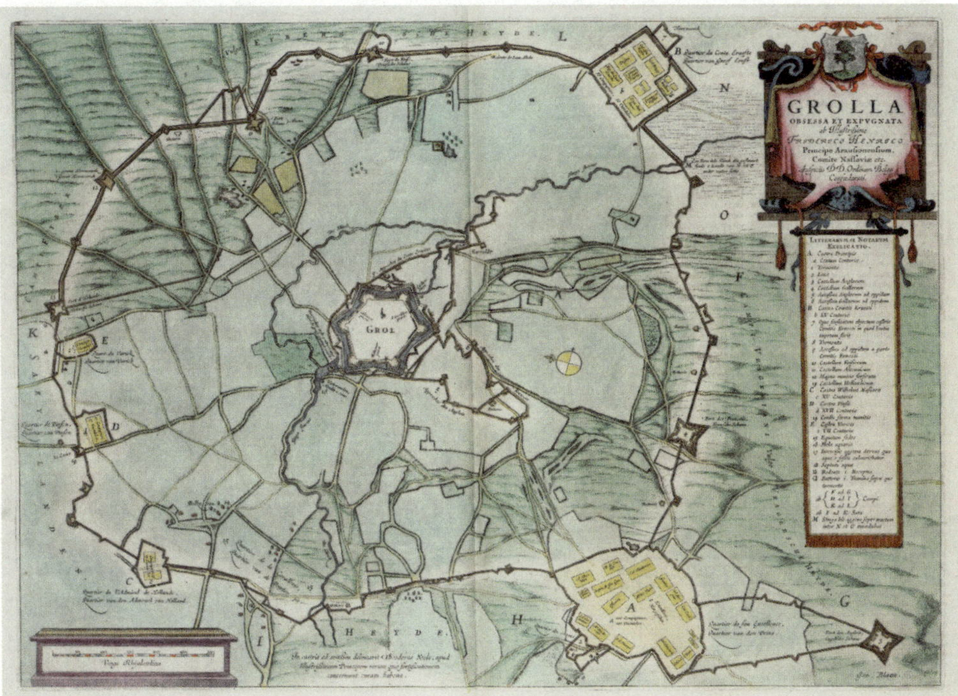

Pl. 31—The siege of Groll (Groenlo) in the Low Countries (20 July–19 August 1627). (Rijksmonument)

and entrenchments, around the town. These earthworks were positioned beyond the range of the garrison's artillery. While work was still in progress, the Spaniards sallied out against the line but after intense fighting were repulsed by 'some' Scottish companies who were on guard (Kay 1795, 19).

The Dutch army was truly an international force. This was clearly manifest at Groll (the modern Groenlo), where major roles were assigned exclusively to the respective national groupings. Approaches were dug, in standard zigzagging patterns. The English were first to reach the defensive canal. Eventually a combination of drainage and dam-building, all done under constant fire, enabled the besiegers to get to the walls. The tide could well have turned with the arrival of a Spanish relief army under the command of Hendrik van den Bergh, a cousin of Frederik Hendrik. He attempted to destroy a large supply convey approaching the town but lack of co-operation between the Italian and Spanish elements of his army botched the operation (de León 2009, 248–9). He thereupon launched a full assault on the Dutch circumvallation but was repulsed by a Scottish regiment under the command of Captain Morrey. Van den Bergh withdrew from the field and the siege continued. The English managed to set a mine beneath the outer defensive wall and charged through the resulting large breach. Three times they were beaten back by intense musket fire, taking heavy casualties. Nevertheless, the commander of the garrison, Matthijs Dulken, his ammunition running low, realised that now was his moment to negotiate from relative strength. A cease-fire was arranged, followed by satisfactory terms. The garrison and citizens, with their goods and possessions, were granted full permission to leave.

Lord Vere was on active service with his regiment for most of 1627 and 1628 (Markham 1888, 433).

THE SIEGE OF 'S-HERTOGENBOSCH (BOIS-LE-DUC)

In September 1628 the Dutch gained a major victory at sea over the Spanish. The battle, which took place in the Bay of Matanzas off the coast of Cuba, resulted in the capture of sixteen ships bearing a huge haul of 90 tons of gold and silver and quantities of exotic trading goods. This booty would finance the war back home for many months to come.

Frederik Hendrik was determined to capitalise on this success. Lord Vere was summoned to The Hague to participate in the council of war. It was decided to launch an attack on the town of 's-Hertogenbosch (Bois-le-Duc) in the southern Netherlands (le Blond 1759, 111), known to the English as *Busse* (Hexham 1630). Vere departed from The Hague on 24 April 1629. His regiment included his nephew Simon Harcourt, his son-in-law John Holles (Lord Haughton), his cousin the nineteenth earl of Oxford, and the young Thomas Fairfax, a future son-in-law and leading parliamentarian general.

The army advanced past Arnhem and crossed the River Waal by Nijmegen and the River Meuse near Grave, 56 troops of horse and 286 companies of foot crossing

Pl. 32—The siege of 's-Hertogenbosch in the Low Countries (1 May–14 September 1629). (Rijksmuseum)

the latter river by the bridge. Heeswijk Castle surrendered once the defenders caught sight of the size of the advancing army (on 'the last day of April'). The night was spent camped by the River Aa. On May Day the army passed through Gemonde and crossed the River Dommel. Having reached Vught, they separated into their allocated quarters (Hexham 1630, 6; Markham 1888, 436). Four English companies, led by Vere, Edward Cecil (Viscount Wimbleton), Colonel Morgan and Sir Edward Harwood, had formed the rearguard on the advance. Upon arrival, the prince instructed his sappers and a force of labourers to commence work on a full circumvallation (30 miles in length) around the town. He had them divert the rivers Dommel and Aa into an outer canal to secure his defences against the approach of a relief army (Hexham 1630, 7; Kay 1795, 19; le Blond 1759, 116) (Pl. 32).

The prince gave his permission for several women, children, nuns and maidservants to leave the town (le Blond 1759, 119). Work on the outer defences completed, the English and French companies started digging 'approach trenches' on 27 May. The French dug towards Fort Isabella while the English objective was Fort St Anthony. Bombardment of the defences intensified as the batteries of 24-pounders, twelve-pounders etc. were moved into advance positions. On 1 June, and again on 3 and 4 June, the defenders sent signals by means of lit fires on the top of the steeple (*ibid.*, 122). The English and French trenches continued to make progress towards the town's defences. Waterlogging and flooding caused endless problems and thousands of fascines (bundles of small branches) were used to counteract them.

Count Hendrik van den Bergh assembled an army of 25,000 foot and horse at the town of Turnhout. Part of an Irish *tercio* was attached to this relief force (de Mesa 2014, 76). Hugh Albert O'Donnell, count of Tyrconnell, a captain of lancers, was to serve with distinction in the campaign (*ibid.*, 22). Van den Bergh began his advance towards 's-Hertogenbosch on 23 June and arrived on 28 June (*ibid.*, 127–8). Hexham (1630, 10) estimated his forces as 7,000 horse and 20,000 foot. They set up camp at Buxill. The garrison had already sallied out on ten occasions and now van den Bergh launched a full assault on the lines of the besiegers. The careful preparations made by the Dutch paid off, however, and the relief attempt failed. Thereafter van den Bergh set about an ongoing campaign of harrying the Dutch besiegers. As Hexham (1630, 11) wrote, '[they] made the nights our dayes, and the days our nights'. This strategy was employed over the course of 23 nights before Van den Bergh broke camp and departed. He adopted a policy of widespread harassment in an attempt to lure Frederik Hendrik's forces away from the siege. While the Dutch did dispatch a shadowing force the siege went on.

On 18 July the French took Fort Isabella ('the great Sconce') and on the following night the English, led by Colonel Harewood, stormed Fort St Anthony ('the little Sconce'). They pressed on towards the main defences with renewed vigour.

A letter delivered to the prince on 20 August was the cause of great delight in the camp. 'Newes comes from heaven', was how Hexham (1630, 14) put it. Baron Otto van Gendt, lord of Dieden and Oyen, was one of the commanders shadowing the Spanish forces in the field. Information was brought to him that temporary construction work at Wesel on the Rhine had rendered the fortress vulnerable. He acted on this intelligence immediately. Guided by some locals to the key location, the foot broke into the town, taking the slack garrison completely by surprise. A local blacksmith brought down the drawbridge and the horse galloped in. Wesel was theirs within hours. Dieden wrote his letter to the prince in the small hours of Sunday 19 August, 'a little before sunne rising'.

The capture of Wesel was of great significance, as it had served as a major supply depot for the army of Flanders. Amongst the booty were approximately 50 cannons and enough muskets, firelocks and pikes 'for to arme five thousand men', 1,000 barrels of powder, general provisions, food supplies etc. (*ibid.*, 18). The 1,600 foot and eight troops of horse in Dieden's force did not come away empty-handed either: 'The souldiers fell a plundering, gott into the Spaniards shops, the officers houses, and the bitterest Papists and Jewes houses, Ransacks the cloisters [...] and got an incredible booty' (*ibid.*, 17). Also taken was the personal plate (i.e. platters, bowls, cups and utensils, all made of gold or silver) of Count Hendrik and the 'riches' of many other officers and nobles. The loot was divided amongst the victors. There had also been attacks on the local Catholic churches, where 'Images' were broken.

At Busse the siege dragged on. Lieutenant Colonel Sir Edward Vere was inspecting the trenches late in the night of 18 August. He was walking alongside Sir Thomas Conway but, being the taller of the two, became the target for a Spanish sniper. A musket-ball hit him in the back of the head and he died four days later. The earl of Oxford took his place. On the night of 9 September, into the morning of 10 September, a massive mine was set and blown beneath the ravelin (an earthwork opposite the curtain wall) before the Vught Gate (le Blond 1759, 139). Sir Simon Harcourt's company, augmented by 30 musketeers, were commanded to launch an all-out attack on the earthwork. After an intensive exchange of gunfire, he was further strengthened with an additional 50 musketeers and a number of pikemen. The Spaniards held their ground and the fighting within the ravelin or half-moon was bitter and at close quarters. The Spaniards finally broke and retreated into the walled town. Harcourt's men held the captured earthwork until 'it began to be light'. They were relieved soon afterwards. The defenders of the town had now been driven back within its walls.

Harcourt had been at the heart of the engagement. Hexham (1630, 30) recorded that in the course of the fighting he had been 'five times thrust, and shot thorow his cloathes'. A series of narrow escapes would be a reasonable summation.

The governor of 's-Hertogenbosch, Anthonie Schetz, baron of Grobbendonck, had had enough. A parley was arranged. On Friday 14 September, at about four o'clock in the afternoon, the terms of capitulation were settled between the baron and the prince of Orange. On 17 September the garrison marched out before a formal review group including the prince and princess of Orange, the exiled king and queen of Bohemia and the prince of Denmark. The company then retired to a celebratory dinner along with the nobles and army officers.

The siege of 's-Hertogenbosch had been an expensive affair. The final cost was in the region of 18,000–19,000 guilders ('t Hart 2014, 26).

THE CAPTURE OF VENLO, STRALE AND ROERMOND

Four English and three Scottish regiments took part in the capture of Venlo, Strale and Roermond (Cannon 1839, 99). On 1 June 1632, 120 soldiers, including 80 from Lord Vere's regiment, initiated work on the approaches before Venlo in the province of Limburg. The town, situated on the River Meuse, was garrisoned by about 300 men. On the first night Ensign Willoughby had his leg shattered by a 'Sling Bullet'. On 2 June a battery was positioned in the French approaches and two 'halfe cannons' opened up on the town. By 4 June the magistrates wished to parley and a cease-fire was arranged. The magistrates negotiated their own 'quarter and conditions' with no reference to the garrison. When the news of this concord reached the town, shooting recommenced. Negotiations were soon resumed, however, and a new agreement concerning burghers and soldiers was quickly reached. The garrison duly marched out with 'flying colours', 'bag and baggadge'. The citizens of the town were guaranteed their rights and religious freedom. This guarantee extended to the clergy, cloisters and nunneries (Hexham 1633, 4–5).

Strale, located nearby, surrendered 'upon the first summons'. On 5 June the army marched on towards Roermond in a continuous downpour, an 'abundance of rayne'. The Count Earnest, lord marshall of the field, while 'viewing of the grounde' before the town had been hit by a 'firelocke bullet' from the town and died. A Scottish officer, Captain James Morrey, had also been mortally wounded (*ibid.*, 37). The magistrates, burghers and soldiers of Roermond sent messages to the prince of Orange 'intreating him to give them good quarter'. There was great trepidation that, owing to the death of Count Earnest, the besieging force would be set upon launching a violent assault on the town without 'any quarter'. The prince, however, was content to grant terms and the next day the garrison of approximately 300 soldiers marched out.

THE SIEGE OF MAASTRICHT

The next military objective to be chosen was Maastricht in the province of Limburg, located on the River Meuse at its conjunction with the River Jeker in the south-east of the Netherlands (Pl. 33).

The army arrived before the town on 10 June 1632. The prince and Lord Vere set up their headquarters close to the centre of the line opposite the Brussels Gate. They were thus dug in to the west of the city, with the English entrenchments stretching towards the river (Markham 1888, 441). Work began on two zigzagging trenches. These would extend to the walls of the town and were manned respectively by the English and French contingents.

When Edward William Harcourt published *The Harcourt papers* between 1880 and 1905, he included an excerpt from the journal that Sir Simon had kept during the First Bishop's War in Scotland. Whilst the entries from 22 April to 24 May 1639 do indeed concern events on the Scottish border, the ensuing entries from the '9th of May' (*sic*) to 'ye 23rd' do not. It will be argued here that these latter entries relate to the siege of Maastricht, covering the period from 9 June to 23 June 1632.

Under Friday 13 (June) Harcourt recorded that the army, having arrived at 'ye Towne', was divided into five parts and deployed around the town (Harcourt 1880–1905, I, 134). The prince's camp contained 88 companies, 'The Lord of *Bredroes*' had 48 companies, 'The Count *Solloms*' 32 companies, 'The Count *Morris*' fifteen companies and 'The Lord *Deedems*' eighteen companies. Count Everard Solms and Lord Floris de Brederode had served at the siege of 's-Hertogenbosch (Hexham 1630, 7). Hexham (1633, 8) clarified elsewhere in his account on Maastricht that the 'Count *Morris*' in question was 'Count Maurice of Nassau'. This would be John Maurice, count of Nassau-Siegen.

In his diary Harcourt assigns the date of 16 June to the commencement of work on the 'aproch' trench, 'Collonell Hollis' in command (probably Sir Thomas Holles).

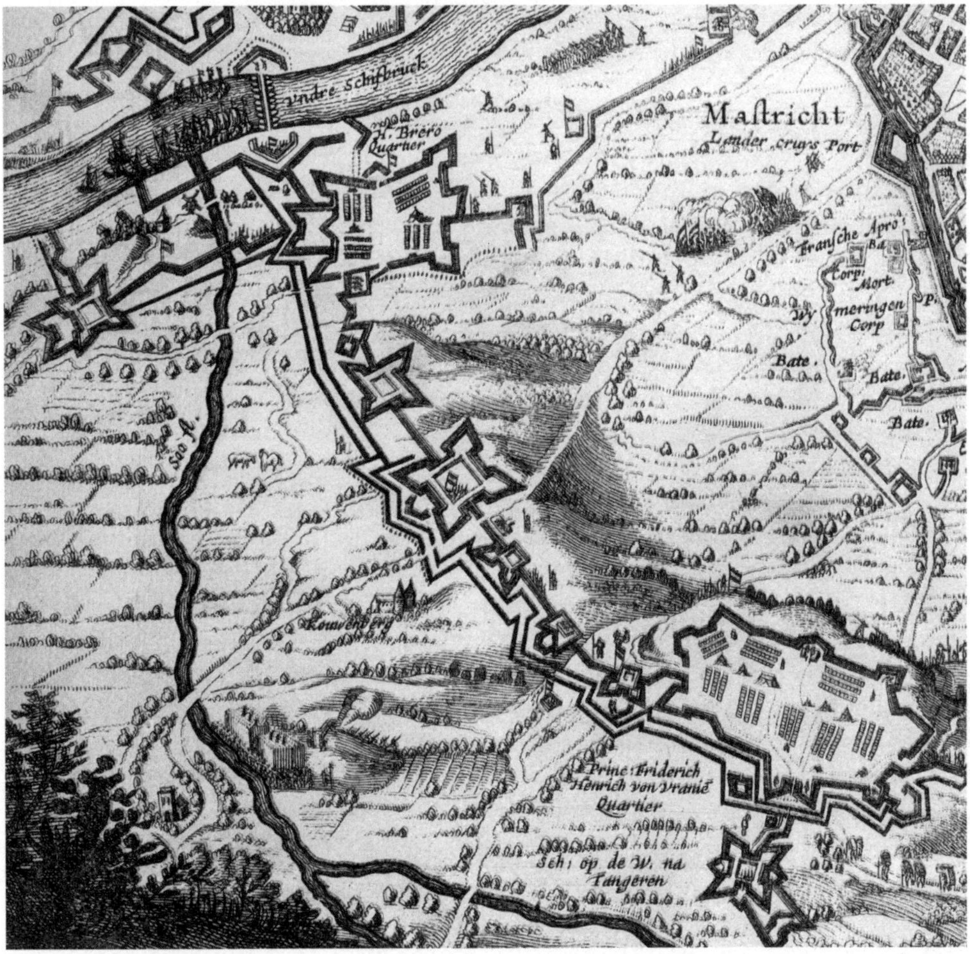

Pl. 33—The siege of Maastricht in the Low Countries (10 June–22 August 1632). (https://commons.wikimedia.org/wiki/File:Maastricht_map_from_Dankaerts_Historis.tiff)

The key passage in assigning these entries to the siege of Maastricht appears under 17 June: 'Collonell Broge commandinge in ye Aproches, haueinge more than double ye number of workmen then before, aduanced somme 500 pases, makinge thereon 2 courts of gard, without any looss'. Under 17 June, in his account of the siege of Maastricht, Henry Hexham (1633, 9) wrote: 'This night the Scotch Colonell Brogue his Regiment beginning, tooke their turnes to watch in the approaches [...]'. A Colonel Brog commanded a Scottish regiment at Maastricht (Murdoch and Grosjean 2014, 61).

Harcourt's entries are concise and factual. There are details here that were omitted from Hexham's account. Under 18 June he recorded that the artillery, based on 'Chappell Hill' by the prince's quarter, had become operative. The progress of the approach trench was impressive: 500 'pases' on 18 June and 120 'pases' on the following day. A sergeant of Lord Leicester's regiment fell that night (Harcourt 1880–1905, I, 135). Under 22 June he has 'Coll. Pagnam commandinge' as they began work on a new earthwork from the right flank of the approach, a hornwork being the objective. Hexham (1633, 9) had 'Colonell Pakenham' commanding in the trenches under 23 June. What Harcourt omitted was that 'Pagnam' was 'shott in his face' during that night's tour of duty. A Colonel Sir Philip Pakenham was wounded at Maastricht. Elizabeth Stuart wrote that his 'whispering is almost spoiled he is shott in the face but without danger' (Akkerman 2011, II, 108).

On 1 July about 800 men from the garrison launched a sortie from the town and fell upon the English 'works'. As Hexham (1633, 11), quartermaster to the regiment of the Lord General Vere, noted, 'it was doubtfull for a while whether ours or the Enemyes men should carry it'. Sir Simon Harcourt rushed in with reinforcements to bolster the stand being made by Captain Roockwood's men. 'The fight grew hott, by reason the Enemy shott so much among our men, and diverse were slayne and hurt [...] Captain Roockwood, his arme shot in pieces.' He wasn't the only officer hit: Harcourt was 'shot through his cheeks by the Pallate of his mouth'. More seriously, 'his thigh [was] sorely torne with a granadoe'. These men were carried off the field of battle.

This was not the only sortie made by the Spanish defenders. There was particularly fierce fighting close to the wall of the town on 17 August. Remarkably, a patched-up Harcourt was evidently fit enough to be back at the front, as his presence was noted that day. Late in the evening Robert, the nineteenth earl of Oxford, was mortally wounded by a shot to the head (*ibid.*, 26).

The siege continued. By 20 August a mine was in position under the wall. It was detonated at 9 o'clock in the morning and a large section of the wall collapsed into the moat. The English soldiers clambered up over 80ft of debris and poured over the collapsed wall. After intense hand-to-hand fighting they were ordered to withdraw by Vere, who was worried by the prospect of increasing casualties. The effort, however, had been enough. The next day Maastricht surrendered (Markham 1888, 445).

The Vere family had paid a high price. Besides the earl of Oxford, another fatality was his kinsman Lieutenant Edward Vere. It is believed that he was probably the son of Sergeant-Major John Vere, a natural son of Horace's eldest brother John (*ibid.*, 384, 385 fn.1). Amongst the injured were Captain Avery Vere and Lieutenant Peter Vere. Hexham (1633, 35) listed 'Sr. Symon Harecourt, Sar.Maiour' and Lieutenant Colonel Holles in the company of the cohort of the wounded.

This engagement had been a notable success for the Dutch. They had not only overcome the garrison but also seen off attempts at relief by the armies of Don Gonzala Fernandéz (24,000 strong) and Count Pappenheim (16,000 strong), who had arrived in July and August respectively. The four English regiments under Vere had played a pivotal role. The French had also played a major part and three Scottish regiments (under Colonels Brog, Buccleuch and Balfour) had been in action too (Murdoch and Grosjean 2014, 61). Fighting had lasted from 10 June until 22 August 1632.

LIMBOURG, ORSOY AND RHEINBERG

On 8 September 1632 Dutch forces took Limbourg (van Nimwegen 2010, 234; Cannon 1839, 102). This fortified town occupied a hill strategically looped by the Vesdre (Weser) River. According to Griffiths (1844, 12), an English regiment led by the veteran Sir Charles Morgan was involved in the action. This operation was followed by a surprise attack in November on Orsoy, on the west bank of the River Rhine. The Dutch almost won the day but were beaten off despite having gained access to and fought on the streets of the town (Israel 1997, 42).

A second fortress, in proximity to Orsoy, was located at Rheinberg on the Rhine. Frederik Hendrik began his summer campaign of the year 1633 by laying siege to the fortress. The 1,700 defenders held out for 22 days and surrendered on 2 June (van Nimwegen 2010, 235). The capture of this key bastion and (on the second attempt) of Orsoy ended Spanish 'hegemony' in the German borderlands (Israel 1997, 43). Trade on the Rhine was reopened, and the war taxes imposed by the Spanish on the provinces of Gelderland, Overijssel and Upper Guelders were lifted ('t Hart 2014, 26; Frijhoff and Spies 2004, 31). The financial and commercial aspects of the campaign had been a significant motivation in the targeting of Rhineberg. Frederik Hendrik knew that the merchants of Dordrecht and Rotterdam, key players in the 'peace faction' within the United Provinces, would be politely sidelined by the delivery of this mercantile prize into their laps. The political and pecuniary gains for the leadership of Gelderland and Overijssels were also not unforeseen by him (van Nimwegen 2010, 235). The English regiments employed in the campaign had been directed against the northern defences of Rheinberg (Cannon 1839, 102). The fourteen-year-old Prince Rupert, son of Frederick and Elizabeth of Bohemia, was initiated into the military life under the tutelage of Frederik Hendrik during this siege (Grossman 2007, 299). Another victory followed with the capture of Fort Philippine, four miles to the north-north-west of Sas-van-Ghent in Flanders, by Willem of Nassau (Salmon 1745, 180; Playfair 1808–14, II, 66; Hubner 1748, 779).

THE SIEGE OF TIENEN (TIRLEMONT)

On 18 April 1634 a treaty was signed between the United Provinces and France. In return for seven years of subsidies from France, the Dutch committed themselves to maintaining their hostilities against Spain for the following year. Cardinal Richelieu was hopeful that King Charles would align England with the pact but met only with obfuscation (Poot 2013, 119). Frederik Hendrik was anxious that the French should become more proactive. After intense negotiations, he managed to arrange the signing of an offensive–defensive pact on 8 February 1635 (*ibid.*, 120). On 19 May France finally declared war on Spain.

Horatio, Lord Vere, had retired to England. His soldiering days were over. His three eldest daughters had already married and the fourth, Anne, was now engaged to

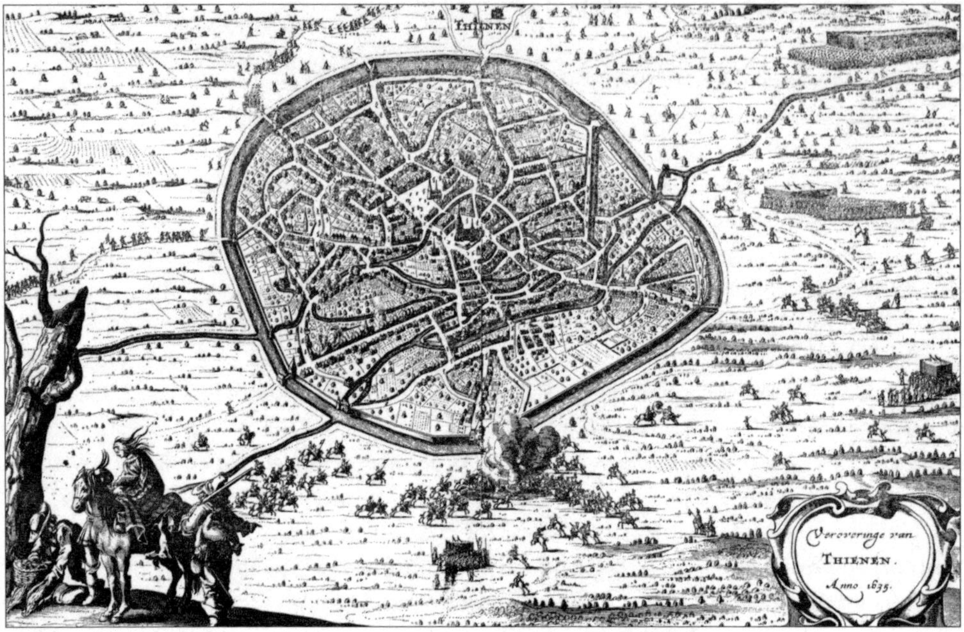

Pl. 34—The siege of Tienen (Tirlemont) in the Low Countries (8–9 June 1635). (https://commons.wikimedia.org)

Thomas Fairfax. While having dinner with his friend Sir Harry Vane on 2 May 1635 he collapsed and died.

Sir Simon Harcourt had served under Vere for almost twelve years. From *The commentaries of Sir Francis Vere* (Vere 1657, viii) we learn that as serjeant-major he was ranked in third place in the regiment (below the earl of Oxford and Lord Fairfax) and above fifteen captains. Upon Vere's retirement, Harcourt continued his service with the regiment in the United Provinces. Colonel George Goring took command, Harcourt again serving as serjeant-major (Hexham 1637, 10).

A combined Dutch and French army advanced on Tienen (Tirlemont in French documents) in the Flemish province of Brabant. Upon their arrival on 8 June 1635, Frederik Hendrik dispatched a messenger to call for the surrender of the town (van Nimwegen 2010, 246). The safety and liberties of all citizens were promised to the burghers. The Spanish commander, Don Martino de Los Arcos, had 1,200 men at his disposal and sufficient supplies (Sabbe 1933, 233). He felt that it would be beneath his honour to surrender without a shot having been fired. The following day saw two more attempts to achieve a peaceful surrender. Both failed. Frederik Hendrik, in his official account of the operation to the States General (of the Netherlands), insisted that he had given the town four or five opportunities upon which to surrender on reasonable terms but that he had been rebuffed (*ibid.*). In the early afternoon the artillery opened fire, and this was followed by an assault of 6,000 men. After several hours of exchanging fire, de Los Arcos agreed to throw in the towel. Unfortunately, he left the prince of Orange waiting for him for over half an hour to receive the confirmation of the terms of surrender. This proved fatal, as in the lull Dutch and French troops managed to force entry into the town. Anarchy ensued, resulting in full-scale destruction (Cannon 1839, 104). The brutality of the sacking of Tienen prompted a wave of contemporaneous publications (Arblaster 2014, 176). The bulk of these tracts laid the blame on the French troops, e.g. 'dese barbarische Fransche Calvinisten' ('these barbaric French Calvinists'), who were responsible for the '[…] Pilleringhe … moorden … verkrachten van dochtes … ende schoffieren van vrouwen … werd de gansche stad in brand gestoken […]' (Vanderheijden 1933, 115)—in other words, for the pillaging, murdering, raping of the daughters, insulting of the women and the setting on fire of the whole town. The further implication was that the king of France had unleashed the Huguenots on the Catholics of Flanders! Yet the handwritten account by Anna Wielant (1982), the mother superior of the convent of Annunciates in Tienen, credited the French soldiers with escorting the nuns from the town on the morning of 11 June before plundering what was left in the convent. She contrasted their behaviour with that of the Hollander and Frisian soldiers, who had ransacked and plundered the night before while beating and insulting the nuns (Sabbe 1933, 233; Kuijpers 2015, 137–8). While it is confirmed that there were English troops involved in the assault on the town, no accusations of abuse are directed against them in the contemporaneous literature (Pl. 34).

SCHENKENSCHANS

Both sides were capable of the most egregious tactical blunders. Schenkenschans was a notable fortress positioned on the narrow isthmus created by the subdivision of the Rhine into the Waal and Lower Rhine rivers. Its strength, both natural and built, was matched only by its strategic location. Whoever held it held the key to the province of Gelderland and the heartland of the United Provinces (de León 2009, 189; Israel 1997, 73; Poot 2013, 138) (Pl. 35).

The strength of its defences was due to the diligent work performed by Dutch and English detachments under the supervision of Martin Schenk (whose name it bore—the 'sconce of Schenk'). The earl of Leicester had been instrumental in the work, undertaken back in the late 1580s (Markham 1888, 88).

It is therefore difficult to comprehend why such a pivotal prize should be garrisoned with a mere 60 or so defenders, and lax ones at that. In a period of high tension, when the Dutch army and their French allies had withdrawn from the siege of Louvain and were anxiously awaiting the counterstroke by the Spanish and imperial forces, it is astonishing that a key fortress should be left in such a vulnerable state. Suddenly, on 28 July 1635, a force of 500 Spaniards swooped and took the fortress without a struggle. The 60 hapless defenders were put to death (van Nimwegen 2010, 248). The night attack had been launched on the personal initiative of a local commander from Gelder (de León 2009, 189).

Pl. 35—The siege of Schenkenschans in the Low Countries (31 July 1635–30 April 1636). (https://commons.wikimedia.org))

In July the English regiment of Colonel George Goring was encamped in the vicinity of Roermond (Memegalos 2007, 50) in expectation of the Spanish advance. There is no evidence to suggest that Sir Simon Harcourt was not serving with the regiment at that time.

The shock and dismay in the United Provinces was matched only by the elation in Spanish quarters. Don Gaspar de Guzmán, count-duke de Olivares, *valido* (chief minister) and favourite of King Philip IV of Spain, considered Schenkenschans to be more important than Antwerp and Maastricht combined (*ibid.*). He accordingly put great effort into preparing the fortress for the anticipated counter-attack.

It duly came. At the beginning of August, the Dutch army arrived and began digging trenches on the landward side (van Nimwegen 2010, 248). It quickly became apparent to them that the water-saturated terrain was totally unsuitable for the standard siege trench warfare. One alternative was to starve out the garrison, but as the attack was well anticipated the defenders' stocks were good. The Cardinal-*Infante* Ferdinand of Austria, son of Philip III of Spain, had provisioned the élite 1,500-man garrison with sufficient supplies for seven months (Israel 1997, 71).

During August and September Spanish and imperial forces occupied the German duchy of Cleves on the Dutch border, thus increasing the pressure on the United Provinces (*ibid.*). After the relief of Louvain, the army of Flanders was divided into three army corps, each of which contained an Irish *tercio*, led respectively by Thomas Preston and Tyrconnell (in one corps) and by Tyrone and Owen Roe O'Neill in the others (de Mesa 2014, 81).

Throughout these months the Dutch army besieging Schenkenschans had opted for a continuous bombardment of the fortress. The importance of the target to Frederik Hendrik was emphasised by the decision to continue the siege throughout the winter months, a very atypical strategy for the time. Incredibly, the Spanish commanders in the field did not respond in kind. As winter set in, the officers quietly removed themselves to Brussels and Madrid, as had been their custom. Schenkenschans was gradually deprived of officers of rank. Bizarrely, the officer who had seized the fortress was derided by his peers for threatening their winter social routine (de León 2009, 189). The dereliction of duty was contrary to royal instructions and the stringent urgings of Olivares to hold, but even the cardinal-*infante* himself adjourned to Brussels (*loc. cit.*).

The relentless bombardment from land and river-based batteries continued. Finally, on 30 April 1636 the 600 bedraggled survivors emerged from the smouldering ruins and surrendered (Cannon 1839, 104; Israel 1997, 73). The Spaniards had undoubtedly lost an invaluable opportunity to win the war.

Frederik Hendrik had maintained a strong military contingent around the fortress throughout the nine months of the siege. The English regiments would have done their tours of duty but none of the horse or foot contingents would have played any significant role in the actual onslaught. The artillerymen won this contest of arms practically unaided.

The crumbling French army had been of little use in the affair. Sickness, hunger, lack of money and desertion slowly but surely reduced their numbers by two thirds (van Nimwegen 2010, 249). They eventually limped back home to France.

THE DUTCH SIEGE OF BREDA

The destruction of Tienen and the abuse of its citizens inflicted serious damage on the attempt to woo the mass population of the Spanish Netherlands over to the cause of the United Provinces (Kay 1795, 25–6). The fall-back plan, as agreed in the pact of May 1635, was for the Dutch and the French to carve up the southern provinces between them (Poot 2013, 122). The campaign in the field was not a runaway success either. On 20 May 1635 the French defeated the Spanish army of Flanders at the Battle of Les Avins, south-south-east of the village of Huy in the bishopric of Liège, although this victory was hardly surprising, given their three-to-one numerical advantage ('t Hart 2014, 27). There was heated debate between the allies in the spring of 1637 as to what the prime objective for that year's campaign should be. The French, with good reason, argued that it should be Dunkirk, as in those days it served as a major port in the region, but Frederik Hendrik had his eyes on Breda in North Brabant for a number of reasons. The town was of historical significance to his regime, having been the *caput* of his family up to the time of his late father, William of Nassau, prince of Orange. It had changed hands on three occasions, most recently in June 1625, when the Dutch had surrendered it to the Spanish general Don Ambrogio Spinola after a grinding nine-month siege. In military terms the town was very strategic in that it lay on the main north–south road.

The weather may have favoured Frederik Hendrik's plans, as inclement conditions and rough seas seriously curtailed the movement of maritime traffic. The main Dutch army, nevertheless, was giving the impression that a push into Flanders was on the cards. To the astonishment of its inhabitants, the Dutch suddenly appeared before the gates of Breda on 21 July 1637. Count Henry Casimir, governor of the province of Friesland, had rapidly advanced south at the head of 55 companies of foot and 38 troops of horse (Memegalos 2007, 54). The sudden appearance of the cavalry had prevented cattle and provisions from the neighbouring districts from being brought into the town, and the success of the manoeuvre encouraged the Dutch to believe that supplies in the town would thus be low. This, however, did not prove to be the case (van Nimwegen 2010, 254). The main Dutch army, with Frederik Hendrik at its head, arrived two days later.

Breda was no easy objective. The walls of the town had fifteen bastions surrounded by hornworks, all encircled by a moat beyond which lay a counterscarp wall (Memegalos 2007, 55). The Dutch came well prepared. Thousands of farmers had arrived in the wake of the army and were now set to work on digging a ditch around the entire circumference of the town, and beyond that an outer defence against an external counter-attack. As a final touch, rivers were dammed and the surrounding countryside flooded. The siege had begun. The precautionary measures adapted by the Dutch proved to be very wise, as on 2 August the cardinal-*infante* and his cousin, Margaret of Austria (sister of Emperor Ferdinand II), arrived at the head of a 20,000-strong Spanish army (van Nimwegen 2010, 254).

Remarkably, the Spanish relief force never attempted any serious attack on the Dutch army surrounding the town. In fact, on 15 August, after maintaining a counter-siege for only two weeks, the cardinal-*infante*'s forces withdrew. On the previous night elements had already broken camp, literally, and set it alight. The following morning the main Spanish army marched towards *Loone* (Hexham 1637, 9). According to an eighteenth-century source, *Loon* was a village in the province of Brabant, situated to the south-south-east of *Ravenstein* (Robinson 1794, LO). Neerloon lies to the immediate south-south-east of Ravenstein. This would indicate that the army advanced to the north-east. According to Hexham, they hoped to draw the prince of Orange away from Breda. In pursuit of that objective, they moved towards 'the Sconce of the Vorne, and *Theil*'. Teil is on the northern bank of the Waal in the province of Gunderland. In the eighteenth century it was described as being on 'a small island'. There was a strong citadel in its immediate vicinity in the 1600s (Robinson 1794, TH). Downriver the Waal draws very close to the course of the Meuse/Maas. A nineteenth-century source described *Voorn* as 'a fort of the Netherlands' in Gelderland, sited on 'a small island formed by the Waal and the Meuse' (Brookes 1820, VOU). It was described as 'a small island with a fort, situated at the east of *Bommelwaert*', in the eighteenth century (Robinson 1794, VO). Bommelerwaard is a district surrounded by the Maas, the Waal and the Afgedamde Maas River in the west. Vorn is located to the immediate north-west of Heerewaarden. Hexham (1637, 9) related how a detachment of the Spaniards had marched against these two places. Upon reaching the *Maze* (i.e. the Maas), they commandeered boats and moved 'over the river' into 'the Island of the *Vorne*'. They were expected, however, as a deserter, 'a Boore', had warned the defenders. It would appear that a 'man of warre' was also employed in the defence of the fort. The Spaniards retreated, leaving their 'Scaling ladders' behind. The main force had arrived by then (*ibid.*, 10) but, having lost the element of surprise and given the strength of the resistance, it was apparently decided to call off the action.

In the interim, the prince of Orange, rather than give pursuit, had proceeded with the attack on Breda. He did, however, dispatch 'Coronell' Wyne-bergen and Sir Simon Harcourt ('Sariant Maiour to Coronell Gorings Regiment') at the head of '25 companies out of every regiment'. Their orders were 'to attend the Ennemy'. Judging by the path followed by this force, their purpose was to shadow the cardinal-*infante*'s army. They marched north-north-west to *Ghetrudenberke* (i.e. Geertruidenberg) on the night of 14 August. Thereafter they altered course to the north-east and proceeded 'to *Hemersward* by Heusden'. While the identity of the latter town is clear, the former, *Hemersward*, is problematic. Could it be Heerewaarden? This would make geographical sense.

In a letter dispatched from The Hague by Sir William Boswell, the English ambassador, to Sir William Feilding, first earl of Denbigh, courtier and soldier, it was intimated that 'a good part of [the] Cavallerie under Stakenbroeck' took part in the operation (HMC 1879, 222). Hexham, however, makes no mention of the cavalry taking part in the operation—nor, indeed, of any involvement on the part of 'the Lord of Stakenbroecks', whom he identified as lieutenant general of the horse (Hexham 1637, 2).

Wyne-bergen continued to advance with fourteen companies, while Harcourt and eleven companies remained in garrison. New orders arrived from the prince on 18 August and Harcourt advanced as instructed to the fortified town of Grave, *c.* 11km to the south-south-west of Nijmegen, 'for the securing of that Towne' against the marauding Spanish army. Harcourt held the town for 'ten, or twelve daies', and by then the army of the cardinal-*infante* was marching away to the south-east in the direction of Venlo and Roermond on the River Meuse. Fresh orders had Harcourt move into Nijmegen, whereupon he embarked his troops on boats and began the voyage to *Wesell* (i.e. Wesel, upriver on the River Rhine in the duchy of Cleves). Before his flotilla had reached its destination, he was ordered to disembark and return to Breda. His detachment rejoined the siege on the night of Tuesday 15 September. In the meantime, Venlo had fallen to the Spanish army on 25 August and Roermond on 3 September.

Goring had returned to The Hague early in 1637 after a sojourn at home in England. He was now also serving as King Charles's envoy to the prince of Orange (Memegalos 2007, 52). Towards dawn on 27 August he had a close call at Breda. He had just visited the forward positions when two Spaniards armed with 'long firelockes' crawled up to the edge of the trench and opened fire. Both the work master and one of the sappers fell 'starkdead' (Hexham 1637, 17). His luck ran out, however, on 1 September. While leading from the front in an operation that led to the damming of the moat, his left leg was struck by a sling bullet. His ankle was shattered, and the surgeons were insisting that the leg be amputated. Goring would not hear of it, despite the real fear of infection and gangrene. His stubbornness paid off and he kept his leg. Needless to say, he never walked unimpeded again, and to alleviate the pain, as his adjutant Sir Richard Bulstrode later recorded, he 'strangely loved the bottle' (Memegalos 2007, 63 fn. 2). Hutton (1989, 9) accepted that Goring's renowned drinking bouts could be attributed to his being 'ravaged by pain' from the ankle wound.

On 7 September the prince of Orange was present in the approaches to give the order for the blowing of two mines, which breached the defences of the 'horneworke'. The English, led by Captain George Monck, charged into the breach. Monck was followed by twenty musketeers and ten pikemen. Captain Hammond, Ensign Paget and a full company of men brought up the rear. Soon the hornwork protecting the Ginneken Gate was in Dutch hands (*ibid.*, 27–9).

New volunteers arrived from England about this time. These included Lieutenants Woodhouse and Roberts and Ensign Washington, who were assigned to Colonel Goring's company (*ibid.*, 31). About 11 September Sir Faithfull Fortescue, a captain of a troop of horse in the king's service in Ireland, arrived in camp; he was accompanied by a Mr Byron. When Harcourt returned to camp on 15 September he would have been introduced to his new comrades-in-arms Woodhouse, Roberts, Washington and Fortescue. As noted above, Paget (Thomas) and Hammond (Thomas?) were already in camp.

Once driven back into the town, the Spaniards lost heart. About seven o'clock on the morning of Tuesday 6 October the garrison called for a parley (the drummer having approached the English approach-trench). The terms of surrender were agreed, the garrison duly marched out and the prince of Orange entered the town. He had repossessed the ancient inheritance of his family (*ibid.*, 46) (Pl. 36).

THE BATTLE OF KALLO

The Dutch and the French agreed a strategy to be implemented in 1638: the former would assault a major objective while the latter would draw off the Spanish forces. Frederik Hendrik chose the strategic port of Antwerp. As he led his forces towards the port, he dispatched an advance force under the command of his cousin, Willem van Nassau-Siegen. This 5,700-strong force was composed of a mixture of Dutch, German

Pl. 36—The siege of Breda in the Low Countries (21 July–6 October 1637). (https://commons.wikimedia.org)

and Scottish troops. Their main objectives were three key fortresses on the River Scheldt close to the city. The operation was initially successful, but on 20/21 June a counter-offensive led by Don Felipe da Silva, the commander of the Antwerp garrison, overwhelmed the Dutch forces near the village of Kallo and they fled in panic. This was probably the worst defeat suffered by the Dutch in the course of the war; 400–500 of their men died, over 2,000 were taken captive and many were wounded. Willem lost his only living son, Count Maurits-Frederik. In addition to the human losses, the Dutch also lost their artillery and horses and about 80 barges. The remainder of the advance force fled into the fortress of Liefkenshoek (Guthrie 2003, 190; van Nimwegen 2010, 256). It was to cost the Dutch 150,000 guilders to ransom their men.

The English companies had remained with the main army battle group, approximately 16,300 combined foot and horse under the overall command of the prince of Orange. They accordingly saw little serious action (Cannon 1839, 105). According to Kay (1795, 29), the main army, including the four English regiments, were in the vicinity of Bergen-op-Zoom (to the north of Antwerp).

The French fared no better that year. Their diversionary siege of Saint-Omer was a fiasco. They surrounded the town on 1 June, capturing a number of outlying strong

Pl. 37—Lady Anne Harcourt (1605–61) by Peter Lely. (Courtesy of Sotheby's)

points. A fundamental flaw in the plan was that the French commander, Gaspard de Coligny, Maréchal de Châtillon, only had 10,000 foot and 3,000 horse at his disposal. By his own calculations this was an insufficient number of men to invest the town (Parrott 2001, 128). His reckoning was correct and the French encirclement was so deficient that the Spaniards managed to slip in reinforcements on 8/9 June. At last the French high command grasped the inadequacy of their preparations and rushed the full corps of Maréchal de la Force to support Châtillon. King Louis XIII himself arrived in Amiens and Cardinal Richelieu moved up to Abbeville. But it was too late: on 12 July the Spanish boldly marched a second relief force into the 'besieged' town. The two maréchals agreed that the situation had become hopeless and accordingly lifted the siege (*ibid.*).

It should be noted that the *tercio* of Owen Roe O'Neill had taken an active part in the Spanish relief of the town. In one operation his men used barges to supply the town (de Mesa 2014, 85). Irish losses in Flanders in 1638 prompted the Spanish authorities to actively seek replacements from Ireland (Stradling 1994, 25).

It is almost certain that Sir Simon Harcourt was on active duty with his regiment that year. Indeed, on three occasions, 17, 21 and 27 September, he wrote three short letters from Nijmegen to Monsieur de Zulichen requesting a pass to go to England, as he was suffering from a 'quartan ague' (a fever with recurring paroxysms) (*Cat. hist. documents*, 11). Whether he was granted leave or not, on 6 October he was in The Hague. He wrote to the 'Right Honourable Lady Leticea Pagett' concerning the arrangements for his wife Anne's imminent childbirth. Lady Letitia (Lettice) Paget, Anne's mother, was the daughter and co-heir of Henry, the eldest son of Sir Francis Knollys. An averred Protestant, Sir Francis had escaped to the German states during the reign of Queen Mary. He was later a privy councillor and knight of the garter under Queen Elizabeth. His wife, Catherine Carey, was a first cousin of the queen. His daughter Lettice was married first to Walter Devereux, first earl of Essex, and then to Robert Dudley, first earl of Leicester. His granddaughter Lettice Knollys married William Paget, fourth Baron Paget of Beaudesert (Cokayne 1910–59, X, 284). In his letter to Lady Paget, Simon informs her that 'I am as yet, by the Prince of Orrange', denied leave. A letter to Anne dated 6 December was written in London, confirming that Harcourt finally made it back to England that year. Philip, his son, had been born and was to be baptised on 15 December (Henning 1983, 489). In the letter, addressing Anne as 'My dear Soule', he wrote that 'My joye was unspeakable at ye newes of thy safe delivery'; he expressed the hope that 'God grant yet [the child] may live' and signed himself 'thy faithfull, now most joyeouse, affectionate husband' (Pl. 37).

SCOTLAND

It is one of history's ironies that a Stuart king should lose the throne of England largely owing to his policies on Scotland. Religion was the spark that ignited the conflict and a growing resentment fanned the flames. At first glance it would appear that Charles was determined to coerce the Presbyterian Church of Scotland into becoming a northern equivalent of the Church of England. To compound the perceived travesty in Scottish minds, this was the Laudian High Church version of the Church of England, a brand increasingly redolent of Rome. Kim (2011, 30) has argued convincingly that what Charles actually had in mind was something different—in effect a revised liturgy for both kingdoms, starting in Scotland, with England to follow. The fact that the end result would have borne more than a passing resemblance to the liturgy of the Church of Rome may or may not have been the intention.

The introduction of a revised Prayer Book in Scotland on 23 July 1637 finally blew the lid off the hornets' nest. The Scots regarded this move as 'ecclesiastical imperialism' (Seel 2005, 2). Violent demonstrations and public disorder met any attempted outings for the text. A National Covenant had been organised by the following spring (*ibid.*). The Scots' loyalty to the old Kirk was non-negotiable.

Charles, with the approval of William Laud, archbishop of Canterbury, and encouraged by Queen Henrietta and Thomas Wentworth, made no attempt to placate the Scots, whose grimly held views were not to be accommodated in the slightest. The decision by the Covenanters to abolish bishoprics in Scotland only increased the king's determination to yield not an inch.

One of the king's principal advisers on Scottish affairs was James Hamilton, third marquess and first duke of Hamilton. His failure to coax any concessions from the Covenanters at the Glasgow assembly led him immediately to advocate a military solution rather than renewed diplomacy. Neither side was for turning.

Charles had been a sickly child. He had not walked until the age of seven, and the solitude of his teenage years had also left its mark on him. He put great effort and energy into becoming an assertive young man (Ashley 1998, 650). On 25 March 1625 he was crowned king, and by 13 June he was married. Henrietta Maria de Bourbon was fifteen years of age when she stood at the altar. The first few years of the marriage were fraught. Her French retinue of over 100 attendants, including ladies-in-waiting and a spiritual contingent of about a dozen and a half clerics, not least Daniel du Plessis, the bishop of Mende and her confessor, did not encourage intimacy. Their dismissal by Charles a year later was ultimately beneficial and helpful to the marriage. Her devotion to Catholicism and her firm belief in the divine right of kings were neither constructive nor helpful in the growing crisis. The assassination in 1628 of George Villiers, duke of Buckingham, hitherto Charles's most intimate associate, further bonded the royal couple together.

Charles, Wentworth, Randal McDonnell, first marquis of Antrim, and others drafted a detailed plan of action to wage war against the Scots without the approval or participation of parliament—something which had not occurred since 1323 (Seel 2005, 5). Charles, after all, had not summoned a parliament since 1629. Absolute rule had become second nature to him. According to John Rushworth, the contemporary historian, lawyer and politician, the plan of action was composed of five key elements that were to be implemented simultaneously.

- The England-based part of the army would place garrisons of 2,000 men in Berwick and 500 men in Carlisle.
- James Hamilton was to serve as general of forces in Scotland. He was to land in the north of Scotland with 5,000 troops and link up with George Gordon, second marquis of Huntly.
- A fleet operating from the Firth of Forth would impede all Scotland-bound vessels.
- Lord Antrim would land with a force of 10,000–12,000 men in Argyllshire in the west of Scotland.
- The earl of Strafford and the army from Ireland would sail in a fleet into the 'Firth of Dunbritton'.

The lord general of the army would be Thomas Howard, earl of Arundel; Robert Devereux, third earl of Essex, would be lieutenant general, and Henry Rich, first earl of Holland, would be the general of horse.

This plan was to be treated as classified information. 'The secret of this design was communicated to none without reserve, save [the archbishop of] Canterbury, [the marquis of] Hamilton, [the earl of] Arundel, Sir Henry Vane [treasurer of the household], and "by letters" [the earl of] Strafford' (Rushworth 1703–8, III, 2).

The lord lieutenants of the shires were to be instructed to 'muster … all the Arms and Train'd Forces within their Counties' (*ibid.*, 5). One major problem was that the king only had £200,000 at his personal disposal and of course he was unwilling to call a parliament to seek the necessary additional funds. It was also resolved to head-hunt in the Low Countries (*ibid.*, 6). This is fully understandable, given that this was where the most experienced and battle-hardened English officers and men available could be found. The earl of Essex, for example, was a veteran of the Palatinate and the Netherlands. Many others would follow.

The 500 men of the Carlisle garrison were veterans drawn from the standing army in Ireland. They arrived at the beginning of April under the command of Sir Francis Willoughby (Little 2018, 245–6).

THE CAMPAIGN

Harcourt had entered active service for the king by 18 April 1639. In a letter of that date to Secretary Windebank he stated: 'According to the time appointed I came to this town [Yarmouth], where I met with the deputy lieutenants, and according to my commission I have received the full number of 1,700 men' (Hamilton 1873–93, XIV, 56). He found the men to be 'generally well-clothed and able bodied' but their 'arms are very faulty, and many altogether unserviceable'. The breakdown of armaments was not encouraging: the muskets were 'old ship-muskets' too heavy to carry, the corselets 'old fashioned', the helmets 'indifferently good' and the pikes 'of unequal length and decayed'. The men, 200 of them from Cambridgeshire, were also untrained—basically raw recruits. He and his officers were training them as much as possible in the limited time available. The men were boarded and ready to go by the time Harcourt embarked on the *Henrietta Maria* on 21 April. The captain of the ship was Vice-Admiral Sir Henry Mainwaring (Harcourt 1880–1905, I, 129), a pardoned former pirate.

On 22 April 1639 the fleet of 28 ships, under the command of James Hamilton, set sail from Yarmouth in Norfolk. Hamilton was a Scottish royalist but in retrospect a rather vacillating and indecisive commander. The fleet consisted of eight naval ships—the *Rainbow* (under Admiral John Pennington), the *Henrietta Maria* (under Mainwaring), the *Boneadventure*, the *Expedition*, the *Roe Buck* and the *Antelope*, plus two others—and twenty colliers (bulk cargo ships used to carry coal). Two hundred and fifty soldiers were packed into each of the dank and dark colliers. The naval ships themselves were not exactly in prime condition. Pennington had informed Hamilton that there were 'many defects in the vessels that are now to attend you' (Thrush 1990, 366). In reality, the *Rainbow* was springing leaks as early as 1625 (*ibid.*, 335).

Harcourt kept a log of the voyage. On 24 April they reached Flamborough Head on the Yorkshire coast, having sailed '35 leages' (Harcourt 1880–1905, I, 130). The living conditions turned nastier on 25 April, when a 'Northwesterly winde' turned the sea 'contrary and stormie'. By 26 April they had to drop anchor off Scarborough (*ibid.*, 131). What Harcourt didn't record is that he had suffered from severe seasickness (Fissel 1994, 83). Alexander, earl of Stirling, informed Secretary Windebank that a dispatch had been sent by Hamilton from Scarborough notifying them of the delay owing to 'evil weather' (Hamilton 1873–93, XIV, 88, 99). The journey was resumed on the following day, when the wind shifted to a south-south-westerly. It was now relatively calm, although rainy. Harcourt noted that one person aboard died that day. On 28 April, after ten days at sea, anchor was dropped at Holy Island, about thirteen miles to the south-west of Berwick-upon-Tweed. Finally, on 29 April Hamilton announced to his senior officers his actual role in the mission and that their final destination in fact lay to the north of the border. The following day the fleet departed for the Firth of Forth. On 1 May anchor was dropped close to the Douglas castle at Tantallon. The fleet had reached the mouth of the Firth. The following day they weighed anchor and proceeded a further two leagues to the east of the Bass Rock. On 3 May the fleet arrived off the town of Leith.

Hamilton opened communications with the leading Covenanters in Edinburgh (Hamilton 1873–93, XIV, 126), conveying messages and entreaties from the king. The arrival of the English fleet had agitated the Scots. Beacons burned on the hilltops and soldiers had shadowed them since they first came close to the shore. Yet there was no intention to land troops. This was reiterated in an order issued by the king in council at Durham on 1 May (*ibid.*, 104).

On 5 May Harcourt was ordered to land his full regiment on Inchcolm. The operation was completed by the following day (Harcourt 1880–1905, I, 132). Sir Thomas Morton's regiment also went ashore (Hamilton 1873–93, XIV, 127). In a simultaneous operation, Sir Nicholas Byron's regiment was landed on Inchkeith (*ibid.*). These two islands lay to the north-west and north-east respectively of Leith/Edinburgh (Map 10).

These landings must have come as an enormous relief to the thousands of soldiers of the three regiments. It does not take much imagination to appreciate how difficult the previous two weeks had been for these men. The conditions aboard ships that were built to carry coal were bad enough, but the onset of the storm and the inevitable seasickness in such cramped quarters would have been vile. It is little wonder that men had begun 'to sicken and die apace' (*ibid.*). To compound their misery, there was an outbreak of smallpox (*ibid.*, 140). The open air of the two islands and their supply of fresh water were undoubtedly wonderfully welcome, although the Covenanters had managed to poison some of the springs on Inchcolm (*ibid.*, 127), resulting in a restricted supply. All was to be quiet for the following six days.

On 13 May Hamilton held a conference on Inchcolm with two commissioners

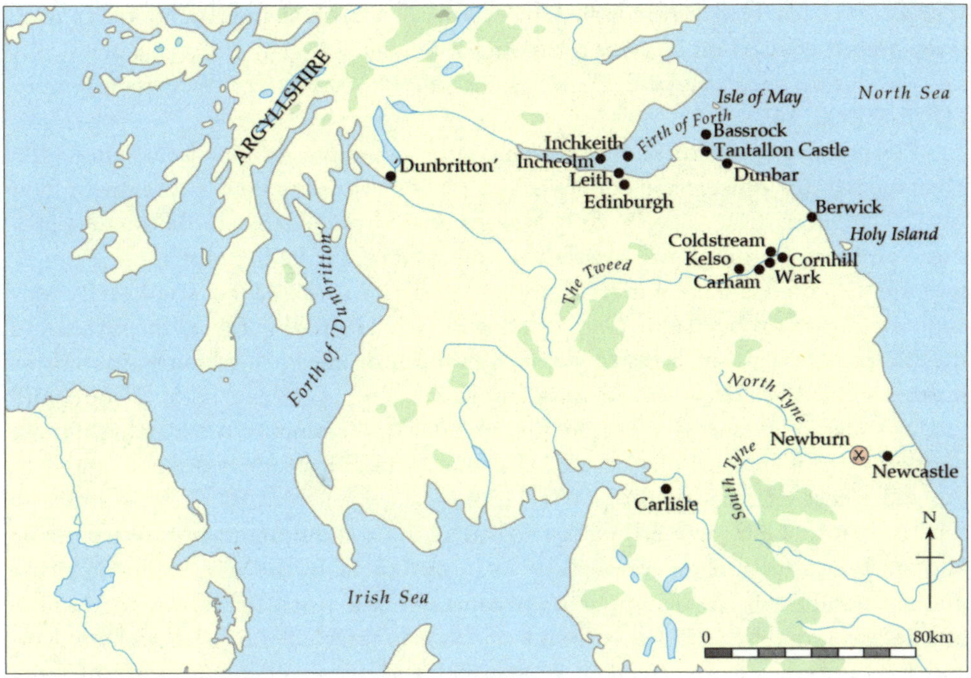

Map 10—The Scottish campaigns (1639–40).

from the assembly of Covenanters. At about 'four of the clock' an individual called 'Eliaser', whom Harcourt described as 'one of ye most zealous and obstinate', delivered letters which did not please the marquess. In short, no accommodation was forthcoming.

The presence of the English fleet made an impact on the importation of weapons and ammunition into Scotland. Two of the Covenanters' main sources were Sweden and the United Provinces. The Danes played a curious role—half-facilitators and half-interceptors. The Danish navy seized many shiploads of arms in the Sound (the strait that separates Sweden from the Danish island of Zealand), yet, in response to a request from Queen Christina of Sweden, the Danish authorities allowed Colonel Robert Monro as well as two regiments of Scottish veterans, their arms and munitions to pass through unobstructed (Murdoch 2010, 194). Alexander Leslie, who was to serve as lord general of the Covenanter army, had served as a field marshal in the Swedish army.

The storm of late April that had battered Hamilton's fleet also forced a number of Scottish ships into harbours loyal to the king. It was reported that one full of arms had come from the Netherlands. In a dispatch to Edward, second Viscount Conway, it was observed that many believed that the 'Low Countries' was the source of 'most of their arms and ammunition' (Hamilton 1873–93, XIV, 98). The fact that the English had facilitated the shipment of men and their ongoing wages from Spain to the Spanish army of Flanders had not endeared them to the House of Orange. The Dutch accordingly allowed the Scots to borrow money, acquire weapons and ship them home

(Furgol 2002, 35). Harcourt recorded the capture of a 'Flemish hoye' (a hoy was a small sloop-rigged coaster) on 20 May (Harcourt 1880–1905, I, 133). It was not their only success; during their stay the English ships seized Scottish vessels 'with impunity' (Thrush 1990, 14).

The time spent on Inchcolm had been put to good use. Admiral John Pennington observed that the officers had conducted exercises to train the men 'in the use of their arms' (Hamilton 1873–93, XIV, 200). Nevertheless, the deficiency in the water supply was a problem. Hamilton had demanded fresh water from Leslie, who, unsurprisingly, told him to 'come and fetch it' (*ibid.*, 180). The garrison vacated the island on 21 May and moved towards Inchkeith. On the following day Hamilton ordered them to sail to the Isle of May. This small island lies at the mouth of the Firth of Forth, towards its northern coastline. They arrived on 23 May, there to water and lie at anchor until further orders. Harcourt went ashore the next day to reconnoitre the island. Although he found 'divers springes', he decided that these would not supply enough water for the entire fleet (Harcourt 1880–1905, I, 133).

Alexander Leslie, first earl of Leven, had a long and distinguished military career. He had begun his foreign service, like so many others, in the Vere regiment in the Netherlands. In 1605 he held the rank of captain. Three years later he switched to the Swedish army and by 1628 held the rank of colonel (Terry 1899, 17). Ironically, in May and July 1631 he had engaged in correspondence with and subsequently met the marquess of Hamilton regarding campaigning against the Habsburgs (*ibid.*, 23–4). There was further correspondence between them in 1636, by which time Leslie had risen to the rank of field marshal (*ibid.*, 34). In a further irony, in May of that year he had offered his services to King Charles (*ibid.*, 37). By the time he sailed to Scotland in a small barque in October 1638 he had 30 years of military service behind him (*ibid.*, 39).

Events in Scotland were moving along. It may have been the astute Leslie's decision, but the army of the Covenant had made their move—not against Hamilton, whom they now apparently realised was not the main threat, but rather marching towards Berwick on the border (Hamilton 1873–93, XIV, 210). Henry de Vic, a member of Charles's circle (Bray 1827, 213 fn.), was aboard the *Rainbow*. In a letter to Secretary Windebank dated 25 May, he reported the departure of the main part of the Scottish army towards the frontier and that they had already reached Dunbar. He advised Windebank that Lord Hamilton had decided to dispatch the greater part of his fleet towards that town with the objective of drawing off some of the army bearing down on the king (Hamilton 1873–93, XIV, 228–9). In a follow-up letter dated 26 May, dispatched from the *Rainbow* as it sailed towards the Isle of May, he informed Windebank that they had received the king's orders and that two regiments (3,000 men) under the command of Harcourt and Morton would proceed with haste to join the army at Berwick (*ibid.*, 233). Two days later they were 'four or five miles [off shore] but intend to come in with the next tide'. They duly landed at Holy Island and subsequently marched to the king's camp (*ibid.*, 242–3). In the meantime, Colonel George Goring had led 600 horse into Scotland to publish the king's proclamation.

By 28 May Charles had assembled the core of his army on a hill called 'Birks', 'Birkhill' or 'Brickhill', to the south-west of Berwick-upon-Tweed (Fissel 1994, 23). Harcourt described the location of his camp as 'Hurtley fields, by Berwicke' (Harcourt 1880–1905, I, 144). The 8,000 troops already in camp were to be augmented by the 3,000 arriving under Harcourt and Morton and 5,000 *en route* from Yorkshire and the bishopric of Durham (*ibid.*).

Harcourt settled into camp. He would have felt quite at home, being again in the company of Dutch veterans such as Goring, Henry Wilmot and undoubtedly many others. It is very likely that Goring would have introduced Simon to his brother-in-law Richard Boyle, Viscount Dungarvan. The viscount, eldest son of the earl of Cork, commanded a troop of horse (Little 2018, 246). He was definitely present in the camp in late May and early June (*ibid.*, 248).

Harcourt's post caught up with him. Six letters from Anne were delivered, largely concerned with their ongoing financial struggle. In response he did manage to send her some money but 'had I been able, I would have sent thee more' (*ibid.*, 140–2). It is clear that the feeling in the camp was that the Scots would reach an accommodation without bloodshed. Harcourt informed Anne in a letter dated 31 May that they were expecting 'Lord Humes, one of the cheefest of the covenanters', to lead 'a great party' into the camp to submit to the king (*ibid.*, 140). This was presumably Sir James Home of Cowdenknowes, third earl of Home. His leanings towards an accommodation can be seen in his later service to the king in the Civil War.

The king himself was not really displaying any great enthusiasm for giving battle to the Covenanter army (Robertson 2014, 46). In the short term, however, matters were to conclude in a most unsatisfactory way. On 4 June 1639 the earl of Holland advanced towards Kelso, where the Scots had dug in. According to Sir John Coke, secretary of state, he was at the head of 1,000 horse and 3,000 foot (Hamilton 1873–93, XIV, 277). Sir Henry Mildmay, writing to Secretary Windebank, put the numbers at 1,200 horse and 2,000 foot (*ibid.*). He noted that the infantry were exhausted by the long march and the hot weather. They ground to a halt and lay down by the wayside. Edward Norgate, clerk of the signet, in a letter to his cousin Robert Read dated 5 June, described how events unfolded. The horse troops had kept going forward. They observed a party of pikemen, who retreated before them. The English cavalry fell for the ploy and, led by Holland, Goring and Wilmot (Memegalos 2007, 72), pursued them. They found themselves flanked by a river to their left and a morass to their right, with entrenchments before them. Suddenly there were flying colours all about and they found themselves confronted by thousands of Scots. It was alleged that a 'trumpet' was dispatched to the English force to advise them to withdraw, which they promptly did (*ibid.*, 277, 281). Basically, the Scots had let the English cavalry escape rather than butcher them. The king, suitably unnerved, concluded the 'Articles of the Pacification' at Berwick with the Covenanters on 17 June. It was signed on the following day (*ibid.*, 322).

INTERLUDE

The Pacification of Berwick brought the First Bishop's War to an unsatisfactory conclusion (Robertson 2014, 52). When Charles had set out from London on 27 March, accompanied by 100 Horse Guards, an artillery train of 100 heavy guns (Cressy 2015, 172) and his trailing retinue, he would have carried with him great expectations that had now failed to be realised. In truth, the First Bishop's War was little more than 'a military stand-off' that had 'resolved nothing' (Seel 2005, 2).

The Scots had displayed vision and commitment and had enjoyed good fortune. The clarion call to the professional soldiers of the diaspora had been timely and had met with a resounding response. The two Scottish regiments, for example, that had been allowed to sail through Danish waters were major players in the capture of Edinburgh Castle a mere four weeks later (Murdoch 2010, 195). The capture of the castle had not been easy. It was only with 'Victuals, Ammunition spent, water fail'd, most soldiers dead' (Rushworth 1703–8, III, 182) that the remnants of the garrison surrendered.

The 'grand design' devised by Charles and his advisers to crush the Scottish resistance failed practically on all counts. Strafford's army never arrived from Ireland, nor did Antrim's forces make the short crossing across the narrow seas into Argyllshire. There was derisory action in the north of Scotland that achieved nothing. Hamilton's fleet lay at anchor in the Firth of Forth and was then ordered to dispatch a significant contingent from its ranks to join the king at Berwick.

The leadership was lacking in guile and executive skills. The queen's circle, including the earl of Holland and George Goring, were favoured. Henry Rich, the earl of Holland, has been described as 'rather frivolous' (Memegalos 2007, 70). By all accounts Essex would have been a better choice as general of horse.

Whatever the causes, the bottom line was that the signing of the Pacification resolved none of the quarrels that had led to the conflict in the first place (Terry 1899, 83).

THE SECOND CAMPAIGN

It has been maintained that Sir Simon Harcourt also played an active role in the Scottish campaign of 1640 (*DNB*, XXIV, 321; *ODNB*, XXV, 131). That is hardly unexpected, given his exemplary performance in the 1639 war. The king himself had written to congratulate him while he was still based on Inchcolm (Hamilton 1873–93, XIV, 179). They subsequently met while they were both based at the English camp near Berwick-upon-Tweed and, given the confined circumstances, presumably on several occasions throughout the month of June. In a letter to his wife Anne dated the 'last of May', he wrote that 'his Majesty is very gratious to me' (Harcourt 1880–1905, I, 141). He would also still have enjoyed the favour of Charles's sister Elizabeth, queen of Bohemia, and in turn of her confidant the archbishop of Canterbury. Neither did

Harcourt's excellent chances of a renewed commission rely exclusively on royal patronage. The king had formed a council of war in December 1639 (Hamilton 1873–93, XV, 188). Amongst the dozen members were the marquess of Hamilton, whom Harcourt had served diligently in the previous campaign, Sir Nicholas Byron, alongside whom he had served in the Firth of Forth, and Lord Conway. Edward Conway, second Viscount Conway, was eventually appointed as commander of the horse and *de facto* leader of the army that marched north in August 1640. Conway, like his uncle Thomas, had served under Vere in the Netherlands (Vere 1657, vi). His mother's sister Mary had been married to the late Sir Horace Vere. In fact, Conway was a nephew ofVere's by marriage, while Harcourt was a nephew by birth. Then there was the earl of Holland, who had served as general of horse in the First Bishop's War. Sir Simon's wife Anne had a brother, William Paget (fifth Baron Paget), who was married to Lady Frances Rich, the daughter of Henry Rich, first earl of Holland. Harcourt mentions him in two letters to Anne as being a source of assistance (Harcourt 1880–1905, I, 146, 148). A further boost to Harcourt's job opportunities came on 6 February 1640, when Colonel George Goring, his old regimental commander in the Netherlands, was added to the council of war by the express wish of the king (Hamilton 1873–93, XV, 431). There is no doubt that Harcourt was offered a position during the preparation for war in late 1639/early 1640. In a letter to Sir Thomas Roe dated 10 January 1640 and dispatched from Westminster, Sir Richard Cave reports under 'Court news' that 'Sir Nicholas Byron, Governor of Carlisle, (…it is said) shall be Sergeant-Major-General of the Army', while 'Sir Simon Harcourt may have employment if he will' (*ibid.*, 321). There is, however, no solid evidence that Harcourt actually accepted a command in the Second Bishop's War of 1640.

It was not a glorious war for England. At every turn the Scots proved themselves to be in control of events. The English preparations were fractious, piecemeal and in many quarters half-hearted. There were many who felt that the Scots were simply protecting their faith and liberties. In truth, those anti-episcopal leanings were not confined to north of the border. The distrust between king and parliament was also growing by the day. Nor was there any reason to believe that the poorly performing soldiers of 1639 would prove to be any better in the forthcoming campaign. The fact that the commander-in-chief of the army in the field, Algernon Percy, tenth earl of Northumberland, was apparently a defeatist was the *coup de grâce.* A convenient illness prevented him from ever actually joining the forces in the field.

In a letter from Sir John Conyers, dated 21 August 1640, to Secretary of State Francis Windebank, it was reported that 'the Scots have now come over with their army at Cornhill, all but their cannon, which cannot yet pass because of the high water' (Hamilton 1873–93, XVI, 614). Indeed, the main body of the army crossed at Cornhill. The river was swollen from heavy rainfall and two soldiers drowned (Terry 1899, 108). Cornhill and the two other crossing points on the River Tweed, i.e. Wark and Carham, are located to the south-east and south-west of the town of Coldstream. Having crossed the Tweed, the Covenanters advanced southward across Northumberland.

Charles had not left London until 20 August. He reached York two days later. He did not know it, but events were quickly overtaking him as he journeyed north.

The army of the Covenant was advancing towards the River Tyne. The order was finally given to 'cast up works' at three fords, including Newburn (Hamilton 1873–93, XVI, 634).

Viscount Conway decided to advance out of Newcastle to meet the approaching threat. He had at his disposal 'all the horse and 2,000 foot' (*ibid.*). On Thursday 27 August a party of English officers riding from Newcastle encountered 'a Drummer' (i.e. a messenger) from General Leslie, who had been reappointed as the Scottish commander. The messenger bore letters for those in authority in Newcastle. Sir Jacob Astley, who was present, explained that as the letters were sealed it would not be lawful for him to receive them. He dismissed the 'Drummer' but sent his regards to General Leslie (Terry 1899, 112–13)!

On the same Thursday evening the Covenanters encamped at Heddon. Below in the valley lay the village of Newburn, and across the river the English positions protecting the ford (*ibid.*). Two 'sconces' or earthworks had been prepared on the southern bank. Alexander Leslie, displaying the skills he had developed on foreign shores, positioned his ordnance on the high ground in the village and along the wooded, sloping northern banks of the Tyne. The steeple of Newburn church was used to house some Swedish guns (Rushworth 1703–8, III, 199–200).

There are a number of accounts of the events of 28 August. Both Sir Henry Vane, the treasurer of the household, and Captain Thomas Dymock sent reports to Secretary Windebank. Lord Conway, James Gordon (parson of Rothiemay in Banffshire) and Covenanter Sure Newis also recorded some of the events. The most vivid and detailed account was by John Rushworth, historian and politician, who was present during the engagement. A synthesis of the various reports gives us a good impression of the day (Terry 1899, 131–8).

Lord Conway had set out at about 2 o'clock on the afternoon of 27 August. Later in the evening he arranged his forces on Stella Haugh, an even meadow that stretched southwards from the ford. It was there that he also established his headquarters and stationed the cavalry. The two earthworks were each manned by 400 musketeers and the limited ordnance. The men were drawn from the Durham levies (*ibid.*, 114).

The morning of Friday 28 August was curiously quiet. Neither side made a move. Occasionally one or other of the Covenanters would casually come down to the river to water their horses, but there were no provocations or taunts given by either side. One Scottish officer, wearing the standard Covenanter blue hat but embellished with a black feather, took his turn. He rode his horse into the water. While the horse was drinking, one of the English musketeers reached the conclusion that the officer was surreptitiously surveying their positions. He fired a shot and, whether it was his intention or not, it hit the officer, who fell wounded into the Tyne. The Scottish musketeers opened fire and were soon followed by the ordnance.

The English earthworks were soon taking a pounding from the carefully positioned Covenanter guns. Colonel Thomas Lunsford displayed courageous leadership in the larger of the two earthworks, and only his resolve prevented the men from breaking. Nevertheless, the loss of some officers and the relentless barrage eventually caused the men to flee their positions. A detachment of the Scottish cavalry now began to cross the river. A counter-charge from the English cavalry, which had positioned themselves in the meadow close to the ford, forced the Scots to retire. The English cavalry were led by Henry Wilmot, commissary general for the cavalry and a veteran of Breda in the Netherlands (Memegalos 2007, 70), where he had been shot in the cheek (Knowler 1739, II, 115). The Scottish cavalry counter-attacked in strength. Captain Vane, who had led the first charge, was dislodged from his wounded horse but recovered and departed from the field. According to Treasurer Vane, the English cavalry were not entirely courageous and many fled from the battlefield (Hamilton 1873–93, XVI, 645). The Scottish horse, commanded by Sir Thomas Hope, and two regiments of foot, commanded by Lord Crawford Lindsay and Lord Lowdon, were now on the southern banks of the Tyne and there was danger of a general rout. The ordnance, however, made a successful withdrawal and headed for Newcastle. Their retreat was organised and covered by the actions of Lieutenant Colonel George Monck. He lined the hedges with his firelocks ('the Infantry Musquets'), who provided covering fire (Skinner 1724, 18; Wortley 1838, 15). Remnants of the cavalry under Wilmot, Sir John Digby ('a Recusant') and Daniel O'Neill ('an Irishman') provided protection for the retreating foot (Rushworth 1703–8, III, 200).

The ordnance and foot withdrew to Newcastle, but the cavalry didn't stop until they reached Durham to the south-east. After resting their horses, they continued to *Darnton* [Darlington], a further '12 miles southward' (Hamilton 1873–93, XVI, 645). The king was even further to the south-south-east at Northallerton. His hastily conceived plan was to withdraw with the regrouped army to York.

Newcastle was soon to fall to the Covenanters without a struggle. By then the defenders, including the 'Train of Artillery', had fled south. The loss of Newcastle, besides being a military débâcle, also had economic implications: as Rushworth (1703–8, III, 202) noted, 'at this time the Coal Mines there, which were wont to imploy 10,000 persons all the year, were utterly forsaken'. Hitherto the coal had been shipped by sea to supply London and other urban centres.

So where was Harcourt? He was almost certainly still in the Netherlands. It would appear very likely that he was refused permission to leave by the prince of Orange. It is clear from his letters to Anne that permission to leave was by no means automatically granted. If he had really wanted to take up a command in England, he could have formally quit his post in the service of the United Provinces. George Monck had served for almost ten years in the Netherlands, at first under the command of the earl of Oxford and latterly under George Goring. In 1638 he had led the forlorn hope in the assault on one of the outer fortifications at Breda. He was a captain of his own company before he was 30 years of age (Skinner 1724, 14), but his service came to an abrupt end. Having been assigned winter quarters in Dortrecht in the province of South Holland, a dispute arose with the burghers over who had authority over some disorderly soldiers. When the prince of Orange failed to support him in the dispute,

Monck quit the service and returned to England. He quickly gained employment in the artillery wing on the recommendation of his kinsman the earl of Leicester. There he served under the earl of Newport, general of the ordnance.

According to the Harcourt papers (Harcourt 1880–1905, I, 125), Frederick, Simon and Anne's second child, was born in the Netherlands. In fact, it was only in 1648 that he was 'adjudged deemed and taken to be a natural freeborn Subject of this Kingdom of England' (*JHL*, X, 416). Might his Christian name have been a 'tip of the cap' to the prince? The child apparently did not enjoy good health. In his letter dated 24 December 1641 Simon asked Anne how the children were faring. He enquired specifically about 'little Frederick' and said that he would 'be glad to heare [he] were well' (Harcourt 1880–1905, I, 162). In an entry in her diary in June 1649 Anne recorded that 'My children, beeinge both very sickly, have bin often recovered and preserved by God' (*ibid.*, 170). Frederick may not have lived a long life; he certainly did not leave any children (Brydges 1812, IV, 443; Burke 1835–8, II, 223). The assertion in the Harcourt papers is interesting in that it would place not only Simon but also Anne in Holland in the latter part of 1640.

Had Harcourt been at Newburn it is very possible that he would have been in the company of his former commanding officer George Goring. There is, however, some confusion as to whether Goring was even present at the battle. In a letter dated 28 June 1640, Viscount Conway reported to the earl of Northumberland, the lord general, that 'I hear that Colonel Goring is gone into the Low Countries' (Hamilton 1873–93, XVI, 354). This suggestion contradicts the eyewitness account of the historian John Rushworth (1703–8, III, 199), who named 'Sir Jacob Astley and Colonel Goring' as being present at the meeting with the Scottish 'Drummer' on 27 August. It is, however, fair to say that, whether Harcourt was involved in the Second Bishop's War or not, he clearly did not see any action. In other words, he would have gone through two successive wars against the Scots without having fired a shot—quite a contrast to his previous experiences on the Continent.

The outcome of the Second Bishop's War was disastrous for King Charles. The army, no matter how poor their performance, still had to be paid. The Scots encamped in the north-east of England had to be bought off before they would go home. To raise the necessary funds, Charles had no choice but to summon parliament—the last thing that he wanted to do. His fears were quickly realised when the parliament was called. Not only would the members not confine their deliberations to Charles's financial agenda but they also ultimately refused to adjourn. The Long Parliament was born. The Scottish 'problem' had now in effect become the English 'problem'.

FINAL CAMPAIGNS IN THE NETHERLANDS

There is a dearth of information regarding Harcourt's movements in the wake of the conclusion and signing of the 'Articles of Pacification' on 18 June 1639. He had written to Anne on 25 March 1640 from The Hague, explaining to her that 'as yet I cannot obtaine my leave, which doth soe much discontent me' (Harcourt 1880–1905, I, 145), and also alluding to 'ye losse of employment in ye Kinges Service'. The impression he gives is that if his legal problems—and consequently his financial worries—could be resolved, he would be in a position to retire from the service of the United Provinces. Unfortunately for Simon and Anne, the legal problems were to drag on.

Colonel George Goring had retired from active service in the Netherlands after the bad injury he received at Breda. He was appointed governor of Portsmouth in January 1639. His regiment, however, remained in existence. Two of its officers, Captain Peter 'Apsaley' and Captain Abrahall, were travelling to rejoin the regiment on 9 May 1639 (Hamilton 1873–93, XIV, 142). Sir Allen Apsley, the lieutenant of the Tower of London, was married three times. By his second wife, Ann, the niece of Sir George Carew, he had a son named Peter. By his third wife, Lucy St John, he had a son named Allen. Thus, Peter and Allen Jr were half-brothers (Hankey 1889, 15). The old regiment therefore continued to function and to serve as Harcourt's home from home.

The next published letter, dated 27 July 1641 (Harcourt 1880–1905, I, 156), bears no address or location—just a stark 'from Ye Army'. He does, however, inform Anne of '[...] ye assured newes of a parly which began yesterday about 1 a clocke; on Monday or Tuesday they are to march out of ye ffort' (*ibid.*). The fortress of Gennep, in the province of Limburg, fell to the Dutch on 27 July 1641. This fortress and town, located on the River Niers, a tributary of the Maas, had been under siege since 8 June (de Mesa 2014, 88). Elizabeth of Bohemia had kept the English court informed of developments there through her correspondence with the diplomat Sir Thomas Roe (Hamilton 1873–93, XVIII, 6, 11, 51). She announced its surrender in a letter dating from 19–29 July and observed that the prince of Orange had only lost 'two officers of note' during the siege (*ibid.*, 55).

The spirited defence of the town had been conducted under the auspices of the commanding officer, Thomas Preston. The defenders had fought hard, launching a series of sallies and *encamisadas* (nocturnal attacks). The besieging army in turn had launched five assaults (de Mesa 2014, 88). This border fortress, which controlled the significant volume of passing traffic on the river, was highly prized by the Spaniards. The cardinal-*infante* described it as 'one of His Majesty's best plazas in the Netherlands, more easily supplied and of incomparably greater importance than Fort Schenkenschans' (de León 2009, 276). Thomas Preston, who was later to command the insurgent forces in Leinster, was either an uncle (Clarke 1966, 215–16) or a brother (Beckett 1966, 90) of Nicholas Preston, the sixth Lord Gormanston. According to some observers, Preston was peculiarly jaunty upon the formal surrender of Gennep, given that supplies and manpower were still sufficient to maintain the defence (de León 2009, 276) (Pl. 38).

The English presence at Gennep is confirmed by the personal account of John Evelyn, who visited the town in the immediate aftermath of its surrender. He had visited the queen of Bohemia in The Hague before serving for a week as 'a volunteer

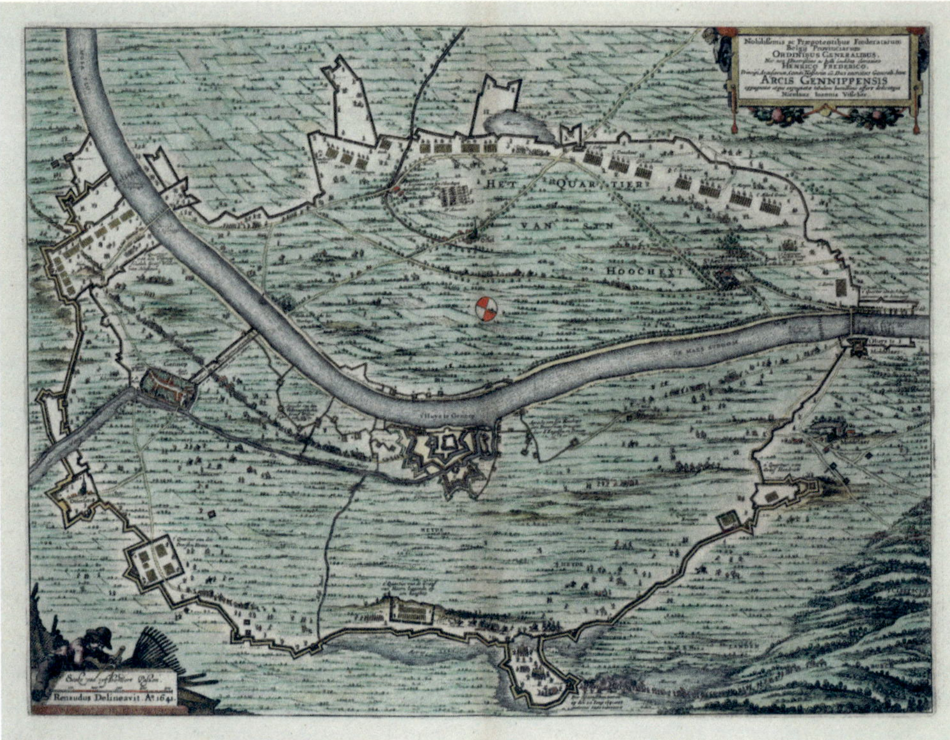

Pl. 38—The siege of Gennep in the Low Countries (8 June 1641–27 July 1641). (https://commons.wikimedia.org)

in Captain Apsley's Company' (Hone 1833–43, I, 273). Captain Peter Apsley served as an officer in Goring's regiment. It is reasonable, therefore, given the cumulative evidence, to deduct that Sir Simon Harcourt served at the siege of Gennep from 8 June to 27 July 1641.

The fact that Evelyn attached himself to Captain Apsley's company is interesting in that it happened in the wake of a visit to the court of the 'Winter Queen'. One of her closest ladies-in-waiting was Elizabeth Apsley, a distant cousin of Peter's. Her mother, Lady Eliza Apsley, was in regular correspondence with the queen.

Evelyn (*ibid.*) noted in his account that he had taken his turn to stand watch 'on a horn-work' until 'the fortifications were repaired'. Upon the completion of the reconstruction work, the English regiments sailed down the River Maas in small boats.

The history of the regiment records that they were subsequently employed in the operations being conducted by the French in Flanders (Cannon 1839, 106). Basically, the English regiments were used in an attempt to divert the Spaniards. The French had employed these tactics the previous year. Feints against Béthune and Aire-sur-la-Lys had successfully drawn troops from Arras, whereupon a combined force led by the Maréchals de Châtillon and de la Meilleraye swooped down on the town on 13 June 1640. The ensuing siege was to last for months. The determined resistance was led by the governor of the town, Colonel Owen Roe O'Neill (de Mesa 2014, 87). Louis XIII of France joined his besieging troops to add his support. The Spaniards mounted a counter-siege as hope for the defenders faded, but a supply train broke through on 2 August. O'Neill launched a desperate attack on 8 August to break the siege but was beaten back into the town. He surrendered the next day.

On 27 July 1641 the Maréchal de Meilleraye seized the town of Aire-sur-la-Lys. The Spaniards were determined to take the town back and laid siege to it after driving the French forces from the area. The French garrison held out until 7 December. It would appear that the French had hoped that the arrival of the English regiments in the region would draw off at least some of the besiegers. It is in this light that the English encampment near the strongly fortified San-van-Gent (Cannon 1839, 106) on the River Ley might be considered. Their final movements for the year were to proceed to the fort of St Philippine, where they embarked and set sail for Bergen-op-Zoom in North Brabant. There they were distributed into garrisons for the winter (*ibid.*).

It is impossible at present to say whether Sir Simon Harcourt remained with the regiment until they went into their winter quarters. It was not his intention to do so but he would have been at the disposal of the prince of Orange. In a letter to Anne dated 27 July he said that he hoped to see her in 'about 7 or 8 dayes hence, if I can gett leave' (Harcourt 1880–1905, I, 156). What we do know is that by 26 November he was in Coventry. He had finally been granted leave of absence by Frederik Hendrik and was back in the service of King Charles. The parliament in London had ordained that '12 antient Commanders' be appointed to the committee overseeing the forthcoming military campaign in Ireland. Included among these were 'Sir Simon Harcocke', Sergeant-Major Berry, Lord Wilmot, Lord Conway and Captain Atkins (Pamphlet 28). A second account described 'Sir Simon Harcot' as 'Colonel over the first Regiment' and noted that Sergeant-Major Berry would command '300. Men with fire-locks' (Pamphlet 34). Harcourt, Berry, Viscount Wilmot, Viscount Conway and Captain Jonathan Atkins were all to see active service in Ireland (HMC 1895, 128, 132).

On 26 November it was announced before the king in council that Sir Simon Harcourt was raising 1,100 men for service in Ireland (Hamilton 1873–93, XVIII, 181). The 'word on the street' was that Harcourt was to raise 'eleven thousand and three hundred Horse' (Pamphlet 36).

A letter to Anne, dated 26 November, is illuminating in a number of ways. In the first place it gives his route from London to Chester. Secondly, it is clear that Harcourt was not riding at the head of a full regiment. In fact, it is very plainly stated not only that he is recruiting as he travels north but also that it is not going very well. A mere twenty recruits had been the result of three days of 'beating the Drummes' in Coventry and *Daintry* (Harcourt 1880–1905, I, 157). Daventry, a town in Northamptonshire, lay to the south-east of Coventry. Even more revealing is Harcourt's statement that if he doesn't 'gett upp my Regiment' he will have no choice but to 'presse'. In other words, he would press-gang men into the king's service. In the interim he would spend 'four or five days' recruiting in Lichfield before proceeding to Chester.

On a personal level, Harcourt sent his 'most respective love' to his 'Bro: and Sister Erby' (*ibid.*, 158). Anne's sister Catherine was married to Sir Anthony Irby, a member of the House of Commons who represented Boston in Lincolnshire on a number of occasions, including the Short and Long Parliaments of 1640. He also assured his 'Cozen Hammon' that her son was in good health. This confirms the presence of Ensign Robert Hammond on the journey north.

CHESTER

Harcourt was to spend most of the month of December in Chester. At that time the town was engaged in more overseas trade than the port of Liverpool. Its final decline was not to come until the 1700s, when the inner estuary of the River Dee seriously silted up. This process had begun as early as the fourteenth century (Woodward 1970, 2; Willan 1938, 180). Indeed, in the sixteenth century New Haven was constructed ten miles downstream at Neston. Smaller boats would transport goods and passengers to and from the town. The largest ships would anchor off Hilbre Island at the mouth of the Dee (Woodward 1970, 3). During the reign of Charles I business boomed in Chester largely owing to a huge expansion in the importation of livestock from Ireland. The 1638–9 period witnessed the arrival of a record 470 ships (*ibid.*, 127 fn. 3). Consumer goods—e.g. coal, cloth and wine from the Continent—were the main exports. Passengers, both civilian and (increasingly) military, also contributed to the commerce of the port. As a port town and gateway to Ireland it would have been awash with reports from across the water. Many travellers would have been arriving and undoubtedly fuelling the rumour machine. Amongst them were the wives of the Dublin leadership. Sir George Rawdon, in a letter written in November to Lord Conway, observed that 'this town is full of ladies and women of fashion from Ireland with their trunks and stuff'. He identified Lady Borlase, Lady Parsons 'with her children', Lady Ware (the wife of Sir James), Lady Wentworth (wife of Captain John), Lady Meredith (wife of Captain Adam), Lady Osbaldeston (wife of the late attorney general Sir Richard) and others (Mahaffy 1900–1, II, 345). Clearly their spouses were not overly confident regarding the outcome of the insurrection. The taverns of Chester were natural venues for contact between sailors, travellers, locals and, inevitably, soldiers. Given human nature, tales of terror and outrages would have been eagerly told and retold.

The Gaelic lords of Ulster had lost control of their followers within weeks of the outbreak of the uprising in late October 1641. An accusation raised by one commentator was that, while the male perpetrators 'were bad', 'the women were worse' in their despoliation of settler families (Pamphlet 26). Looting quickly turned into indiscriminate killing. Many writers have commented on the torrent that was unleashed. Beckett (1966, 83) stated that there was 'no doubt that great brutalities were committed', while Forkan (2007, 206) described the unfolding events as 'an orgy of sectarian violence'. Cunningham (2018, 73) attributed the 'many murders and some large-scale massacres' to a collapse in the social order. It has been observed that a principal strand in the preaching of the Catholic Church in Ulster from the early 1600s onwards was to 'cleanse' Ireland of the Protestant creed (Mac Cuarta 2007, 166, 168, 170). The Franciscans, with their well-established links to the Continent, were to be the foremost in the inculcation of this aim, whatever the consequences (*ibid.*, 157, 162, 169). Priests reportedly encouraged their brethren to take up arms with the promise that those who fell in the fray 'would avoid Purgatory and go straight to Heaven' (Tait 2005, 19). Even before a deluge of pamphlets set about sensationalising the already gruesome events, verbal accounts would have been rapidly circulating throughout the two islands. The flood of refugees that followed would not have underplayed the trauma of their experiences in the slightest. Never in the history of mankind has accuracy got in the way of improving on a powerful story; 'imaginary persons and places' (Nicholls 2007, 182) and invented 'battles and outrages' (Foster 1988, 90) peppered the purple prose. The dispersed settlements beyond the walled towns in Ulster proved particularly vulnerable. Whatever about the hyperbole that is to be found in the 1641 Depositions (taken from those who had found themselves embroiled in the conflagration), there is 'more than enough', as Foster (*ibid.*, 86) puts it, 'coincidence in the evidence' to document the horror. The number of victims is unknown. The late nineteenth-century historian William Lecky (1902–3, I, 79), having evaluated previous credible estimations, arrived at a total of between 4,000 and 8,000. Foster (1988, 85) has judged this figure to be excessive and has proposed a more conservative ballpark figure of 2,000. The alleged numbers doing the rounds in the winter of 1641–2 were many, many multiples of these estimates (Tait *et al.* 2007, 13). The dead don't talk, however, and it was the testimony of thousands of refugees, who had lost their homes and possessions and many of whom had been stripped naked and left to struggle through the harsh wintry landscape in search of safety, that inflamed the public outrage in Dublin and across the Three Kingdoms. Many more didn't survive the ordeal (Beckett 1966, 83). The weather that winter was 'unusually inclement' (Lecky 1902–3, I, 50). The litany of atrocities was accordingly elevated to widely extravagant levels (Foster 1988, 85; Forkan 2007, 205).

This was the age of the Europe-wide death struggle between the Protestant and Roman Catholic worlds. In the early decades of the seventeenth century the overt hostility towards Catholics in England and Scotland had begun to ease with the growing view that they should be regarded as more of a niggling residual than an overt threat. Charles's marriage in 1625 to Henrietta Maria, a French Catholic princess, the opening of the Catholic Chapel Royal in London and the divisive ecclesiastical policies of Archbishop William Laud had, however, resulted in rising alarm within traditional Protestant circles, arousing fear of a slide back towards Rome. Laud's attempts to enforce new canons and a revised version of the Book of Common Prayer in Scotland had the effect of ending religious tolerance north of the border and of heightening tensions in England. The same reluctant tolerance had not been extended to Ireland, where the sheer imbalance in the numbers rendered the situation fraught.

Once hostilities erupted, the conflict inevitably evolved into what Kenneth Nicholls (2007, 191) has termed 'an ethno-religious conflict'.

A vicious backlash was probably unavoidable. It was only a matter of time. Once English troops, gorged on a cascade of Gothic horror stories, set foot on the shores of Ireland there would be serious bloodletting. Revenge would be the watchword. Whether deliberately or not, many of the commanders would exhibit 'as little control over their troops as the Irish leaders had over their followers' (*ibid.*, 190). The common English foot-soldier would be only too willing to inflict retribution on the local population. And what of the officers? Harcourt is not exactly very forthcoming on the subject, judging by his personal correspondence. In three letters to Anne, dated 16, 18 and 24 December, he does not mention the Irish insurgents once. A later letter, sent from Dublin in February, does provide insights but one can only wonder whether the views portrayed were long held or had been recently acquired from his new peer group in Ireland. In the letter in question he says that 'no creddитt' should be given to 'soe base an enemy'. In the context of the desperate situation of the besieged garrison in Drogheda, he suggests that 'they should make their conditions by a capittulation'. He believed, however, that 'they would never be kept' by the insurgents (Harcourt 1880–1905, I, 149). Still, one wonders whether Harcourt was more tolerant of Catholics than many of his colleagues; in 1609 his father Robert had been prosecuted and fined for his recusancy (i.e. refusal to attend Anglican services) (*DNB*, XXIV, 321).

In Chester Harcourt had other matters on his mind. By day he would have been very busy preparing for the forthcoming expedition. As he had done in Yarmouth and on Inchcolm in the preparations for the First Bishop's War, there would have been intense drilling and training of the recruits. Twenty years of military experience had taught him that instilling a strict battle-ready discipline into his regiment was a prerequisite to victory in the field.

In his free time his thoughts were concentrated on his usual worries, in addition to a few new anxieties. In his letter to Anne dated 16 December, his main preoccupation was with the information which she had conveyed to him that he had incurred the 'Kinge's displeasure' (Harcourt 1880–1905, I, 158). This news had perplexed him; he could not think of anything that he had said or done that might have displeased Charles. He instructed Anne to see what she could find out, as this news could mean trouble in store for him. If necessary, he was willing to resign his commission, but the 'way of doeing it must advisedly be thought on'. He asked her to seek advice from their connected friends. By 18 December (when he penned his second letter) his concern about the king's demeanour had diminished and he wondered whether it had been but a false report. In the third letter, dated 24 December, he was more or less of the mind that he had not in fact incurred the king's displeasure (*ibid.*, 161).

These three letters also dealt with their ongoing legal difficulties and financial concerns, the root cause of which lay in the improvidence of Simon's father, Robert, whose South American speculations had cost the family dearly. Properties were sold off to clear his debts. In 1611 he had settled the manor and estate of Stanton Harcourt on his wife Frances (née Vere) in jointure. In 1612, however, he reneged on this arrangement and apparently sold the property. There were three subsequent owners. Robert Harcourt died in 1630. In 1633 the legality of the 1612 sale was challenged, and two years later the Court of Wards determined that Simon, as his mother's heir, was the legal successor to Stanton Harcourt under the terms of the settlement of 1611 (Crossley and Elrington 1990, 274). The most recent 'owner' of the estate, Nicholas Roberts, challenged the verdict on the grounds of collusion between Harcourt and the officers of the court. In the course of the proceedings Robert was described as 'a man that would say or do anything for a little money …' (Hamilton and Crawford Lomas 1897, 496). The saga therefore dragged on, and the ongoing costs and dearth of assets left Simon and Anne in a permanent state of financial stress. Simon's prolonged absences on the Continent, in Scotland and in Ireland probably did not help to expedite the legal disputes, as his brother Francis told him in a letter dated 28 October '1639' (*recte* 1632) (Harcourt 1880–1905, I, 165–7). It is clear from these three letters that Simon had entrusted Anne with handling their legal case and with acting publicly and in court on their behalf. He encouraged her 'sollissitinge', 'although it may prove somewhat troublesome unto you at present', that in the end 'it will be for your greater contentment and satisfaction' (*ibid.*, 158).

Anne was also to confirm with the 'Prince of Orringe and the States' (i.e. the Netherlands) that his leave of absence was still acceptable to them. As regards money, if his lieutenant had arrived in England she was to collect £50 from him as arranged, in addition to the £40 that Harcourt had borrowed on his behalf from 'a merchant att Rotterdam' (*ibid.*, 162). He also had £40 to send to her from Chester at the earliest opportunity, and would send more 'as often as I can spare any' (*ibid.*, 160). To add to Harcourt's financial worries, it would appear that his brother Vere was overspending again from the family's limited funds and Simon resolved to have a word with him (*ibid.*). His sister Dorothea was no longer an additional anxiety, given her marriage to Thomas Chetwynd of Staffordshire (Grazebrook 1885, 83).

There is tenderness in the letters between all the worldly concerns. He assures her that he lives 'still in thy loveinge and effectionate thoughts of me […] which of all other is yet I most valew, and shall ever be most wellcome unto me', and that 'for yourself my prayers shall be, yet God would bless and preserve you in health, untill he make us happy by a comfortable meeteinge […]'. Elsewhere he expressed his disappointment that he hadn't heard from her. There are also family concerns. He enquires after 'little ffrederick's' health (both Frederick and his older brother Philip were sickly children) (*ibid.*, 160, 161, 162).

In the letter dated 18 December Harcourt declared that he was 'now in readiness', his 'Regiment beeinge compleate and havinge Armes and all things necessary' (*ibid.*, 160). Now they were just waiting for a favourable wind. In fact, the lord justices and council had been awaiting Harcourt's arrival since 3 December (HMC 1903, 32). They would have to wait. Simon promised Anne that he would look after his 'cozen Rob: Hammon' (Robert Hammond) and asked her to assure Robert's mother of that promise. He made it clear that he would advance Hammond's position when the opportunity arose (Harcourt 1880–1905, I, 160). Two of these three letters to Anne were posted to *Chercy/Chercey*, where she was staying; Chertsey in Surrey was the home of the Hammond family (Malden 1911, III, 406–8).

Finally, the winds were favourable, the regiment embarked and the journey across the Irish Sea began. They sailed into Dublin Bay on New Year's Eve 1641. The bonfires on the hilltops that greeted them more than likely reminded Harcourt of the 'greeting' that had awaited them along the shores of the Firth of Forth.

IRELAND

The lord justices and council confirmed the arrival of Harcourt and his regiment to the lord lieutenant. They noted that 300 additional men were still at sea. A second reference implied that they had come ashore but bore no arms (HMC 1903, 56). A letter dispatched from Dublin on 1 January reported that 1,400 men had landed but 'with arms only for 1,100' (HMC 1905–9, I, 158).

The reality of the political situation that Harcourt faced in Dublin caused him considerable dismay. Prior to his departure from England, he had been appointed governor of Dublin and was given command of Dublin Castle, but on arrival he was denied both positions. In a letter to Anne dated 3 January 1642 he wrote: 'My Deare Hart, I am, I prayse God, safely arrived with my Regiment at Dublin, where I shall make noe longe staye, if I am not righted in ye wrongs I now suffer; for I find another established by the Lord Justices as governor here' (Harcourt 1880–1905, I, 146). The lord justices calmly but firmly explained in correspondence with the earl of Leicester that the governorship of the city had already been conferred on Sir Charles Coote on 2 December and that they were disinclined to reverse the appointment (HMC 1903, 57). As an afterthought, they also informed Leicester that Sir Francis Willoughby had been given the command of Dublin Castle (*ibid.*, 58) on 23 October. The subsequent failure of the lord lieutenant—and, for that matter, the king—to override the lord justices in these matters only further strengthened localised authority. Harcourt was not taking the setback lying down. He urged Anne to travel to London to lobby her brother, 'Lord Pagett', to 'presse for a speedy answer yet I may knowe on what leggs I stand'. As previously noted, William Paget, fifth Baron Paget, was married to Lady Frances Rich, daughter of the earl of Holland. It would appear that Harcourt's men were billeted about the city. A Norris Mulys, in a letter to her brother Sir Philip Percival dated 12 January, complained that there were twelve of them residing in her house, and she was not happy with the 'ill language' of one trooper (HMC 1905–9, I, 160).

The former lord lieutenant, Thomas Wentworth, the earl of Strafford, had been executed on 12 May 1641. His death, after his highly proactive approach in Ireland, had created a power vacuum that was increasingly and voraciously filled by the lord justices, Sir William Parsons and Sir John Borlase. The non-arrival of the new lord lieutenant, Robert Sidney, the earl of Leicester, the outbreak of the insurrection in

October and the failure of the authorities in England to immediately dispatch significant commanders and forces to Ireland led to an administrative isolation that could only compound the growing authority of the lord justices. The failure to send an army to Ireland was a by-product of the increasing mistrust between king and parliament. The former did not wish to be too closely associated with the Roman Catholic insurrection (nor simultaneously to completely negate their potential usefulness) while the latter remained unconvinced of the short-term viability of intervention (Beckett 1966, 86).

Robert Sidney, second earl of Leicester, was stuck in limbo. His appointment as lord lieutenant in 1641 came at a time when politics were uncertain at best. In effect, he had to please two conflicted masters. He summed up the impossible ongoing situation in which he found himself in a letter to his sister-in-law Lucy Percy, the countess of Carlisle: 'The Parliament bids me go presently; the King commands me to stay till he dispatch me. The supplyes of the one, and the authority of the other, are equally necessary, I know not how to obtain them both, and am more likely to have neither …' (Blencowe 1825, xxi). Harcourt would have expected more of Leicester as a fellow veteran of the campaigns in the Netherlands, and informed Anne that he had written to him seeking redress. He was perplexed as to why Leicester had not pressed his case home upon the lord justices. In fact, he was getting a little suspicious as to what exactly was going on and vowed that 'if I find there hath binn by dealinge [i.e. underhand dealings], you shall have me speedely with you'.

It was thus a disgruntled Harcourt who semi-settled into life in Dublin in January 1642. He did have the welcome company of his comrades and relatives Captain Thomas Paget (Anne's brother) and Lieutenant Robert Hammond (his cousin). Captain Michael Woodhouse had soldiered by his side since the siege of Breda in September 1637. He mostly missed his wife: 'My deare lett me here often from thee, for thy lovinge lines must and ever shall be ye most wellcome and acceptablest present can be sent unto Thy most faithfull and affectionate husband' (Harcourt 1880–1905, I, 147).

SWORDS

Neither was luck running on Harcourt's side. On 11 January 1642 an attack was launched on an insurgent force entrenched in the village of Swords. Lots were cast to determine whether Harcourt or Coote would lead the assault, which would include elements of Sir Simon's regiment; Coote won (HMC 1903, 62–3). According to Sir Paul Davys in a letter to Sir Philip Percival dated 11 January, Harcourt accompanied Coote on the operation. He identified the commander of the insurgents as Luke 'Nettirvill' (HMC 1905–9, I, 159). Both Borlase (1680, 52) and Carte (1851, I, 173) indicated that Coote led the operation alone. Contrarily, the report received in London intimated that both officers had been present (Hamilton 1873–93, XVIII, 264). The encounter was short but hard fought and resulted in a decisive victory for the Dublin forces. While Sir Lorenzo Cary (son of Lord Falkland, a former lord lieutenant) and eight to ten soldiers (according to the lord justices) or four soldiers (by Captain Edmund Verney's own personal witness reckoning) (HMC 1879, 436) were lost on the government side, the insurgents reportedly suffered significant fatalities (HMC 1905–9, I, 159–60). According to one account, the inhabitants of the village were put to the sword, and neither 'man, woman, or childe therein' was spared. Significantly the killing was attributed to the 'new English Souldiers' (Pamphlet 31). Edmund Verney had been commissioned as captain of a company of 'one hundred foot' in the regiment of Sir Simon Harcourt by the lord lieutenant on 18 November 1641 and was expected to raise the company in Gloucester himself (HMC 1891, 495).

The victory at Swords undoubtedly raised morale in Dublin. Save for an expedition by Coote into County Wicklow, there had been only a limited number of minor engagements in the weeks leading up to Christmas 1641 and no significant encounters since the battle at Julianstown, Co. Meath, on 29 November, when a government force of 600 foot and 50 horse, led respectively by Sergeant-Major Christopher Roper (brother of Lord Baltinglass) and Sir Patrick Weames, had suffered a resounding and potentially calamitous defeat (Gilbert 1882–91, I, 32–4; III, 334–6).

WICKLOW

On 27 November Sir Charles Coote had set forth at the head of 500 foot and 80 horse. Marching south, they arrived without incident at Bray (interestingly, their route would have brought them past Shanganagh and close to Carrickmines Castle). On 28 November (a Sunday) Newcastle McKynegan was garrisoned and two accused spies taken and hanged from the castle walls. The following day brought the expeditionary force to Wicklow town, resulting in the relieving of its castle (the besiegers simply melting away). It was recorded that 'some men and women' were captured and executed (Gilbert 1882–91, I, xxxii). Later that same day, two insurgents were apprehended in the general area and subsequently hanged; a third individual was apparently shot by Coote himself. On 30 November three of the townspeople were charged with having received looted goods and were executed. The army group thereupon set out on the return journey to Newcastle. The alarming events at Julianstown on 29 November had caused near panic in Dublin, and a troop of horse had been sent after Coote with orders for an immediate return in order to defend the city against an anticipated assault. Accordingly, on 1 December the full expeditionary force set out for Dublin from Newcastle. They were, however, 'ambushed' at Kilcoole, Co. Wicklow, by a strong party of insurgents led by Luke O'Toole. Despite their advantage in terms of timing and terrain, O'Toole's men failed to make any impact on Coote's forces and, indeed, suffered 27 losses as opposed to none on the government side. After an all-night forced march, the expedition arrived back in Dublin. Later that day, 2 December, Sir Charles Coote was appointed governor of the city (Clarke 1966, 177). It should be noted at this point that the number of people executed during the

Pl. 39—Sir Charles Coote (c. 1581–1642), 1st baronet. (*Paintings in Ballyfin Demesne* by Christina S. Keddie)

incursion into County Wicklow was eight specified and perhaps between six and twelve additional personages, depending on one's definition of the word 'some' (see above). These statistics do not qualify as a pogrom. Emotive talk about a woman in Wicklow town being executed for allegedly receiving looted goods despite being 'great with child' or about the individual shot by Coote being a 'simple man' (Bellings, in Gilbert 1882–91, I, 35) must be pondered. The number of instances in the contemporary literature of slain females being 'great with child' indicates that it was a formulaic device. Carte's recounting of Coote's having been entertained during the Wicklow foray by the sight of 'a poor babe' on the end of a soldier's pike (Lecky 1902–3, I, 84 fn. 3)) may well be equally apocryphal (Pl. 39).

CLONTARF

December was marked by limited actions to the immediate north of Dublin. On 15 December Coote, with 400 foot and 100 horse, moved against Clontarf on the orders of Ormond (as instructed in turn by the lord justices). Although the castle there was the home of George King, a prominent member of Old English society and active amongst the gentlemen of the Pale then formulating their strategy, it would seem that it was the seizing of a barque in the immediate vicinity by looters that had prompted government action (Bellings, in Gilbert 1882–91, I, 43).

Given the precedent set at Drogheda, it would have been an ongoing concern of the authorities that there might be an attempt to block the entrance to the harbour at Dublin. It is possible that they viewed the seizing of the barque and the garrisoning of the castle at Clontarf by insurgents in this light (*ibid.*; Gilbert 1882–91, I, xxxiii). Alternatively, the 'first light' attack on Clontarf Castle and village may have been prompted by its proximity to the city. One report alleged that Coote, at the head of a force of '1500 horse and foot', 'the week before Christmas' cleared a force of insurgents from the 'town', took a number of prisoners, hanged a few stragglers and set the castle alight. It was reportedly burning for three or four days afterwards. His soldiers pillaged the settlement before returning to the city (Pamphlet 1).

SANTRY AND FINGLAS

The government's move against Clontarf was soon to be countered by the insurgents, who were now bolstered by an alliance with the Old English, the latter having finally taken the fateful plunge and openly entered the conflict. Two forward positions were established at Santry and Finglas. Santry had previously suffered a raid by a troop of approximately 40 horse from Dublin in which four armed Catholics, described as 'strangers', had been apprehended and hanged. This incident had upset the Old English gentry and was referenced in their dispatches to the lord justices (Gilbert 1882–91, I, 41). What had transpired was that 'about the first of December' 'some loose country fellowes', taking advantage of the turmoil created by the insurrection, had engaged in a spate of petty robberies. What upset the gentry was that a number of innocent villagers were also slain (*ibid.*, 43). On Wednesday 22 December Coote marched against the outpost at Santry with '1000 foote and two troopes of horse' (*ibid.*, xxxiii). The insurgents, with banners flying, came out to meet him but were dispersed by an advance guard led by Captain Prime[iron] Rochford. While Coote was bearing down on Santry, a second force consisting of 500 foot under the command of Colonel Lawrence Crawford had advanced towards Finglas. The insurgents there, once strengthened by their retreating cohorts from Santry, launched an attack on Crawford. The fighting, however, was derisory and ended at the approach of Coote, who, in the interim, had set Santry village alight after hanging two captives (*ibid.*, xxxiv). The insurgent forces withdrew north towards *Feildston*. Given that Fieldstown lies to the immediate north of Kilsallaghan (see below), it might be suggested that this was their actual destination.

To describe Sir Charles Coote as a harsh operative, coldly determined in his prosecution of the campaign against the insurgents, would be deemed an understatement in many quarters. According to Carte, he was of 'rough and sour temper' and 'an hotheaded and bloody man' (Carte 1851, II, 178; Hickson 1884, I, 175). The charge of premeditated genocide, however, does not stand. The genesis of his evil reputation is based on his conduct in the small number of engagements noted above and on the assertion that he had vigorously advocated before the privy council for the total elimination of all Catholics (Lecky 1902–3, I, 84 fn. 3; Clarke 1966, 184). The latter charge—and, indeed, its sentiments—was completely rejected by the lord justices (Gilbert 1882–91, I, 242), although whether they were being politically astute, deceitful or simply telling the truth has been the subject of an ongoing discourse. It might be suggested, however, that the charges against Coote were at least gilded, if not fabricated, by Roger Moore (a.k.a. Rory O'More) as a crucial and integral element of his highly emotive and persuasive speech to the assembled Old English gentry of the Pale at the Hill of Crofty near Duleek, Co. Meath, about 3 December. The rousing reception accorded to this speech effectively delivered the harassed Old English into the insurgent camp (Bellings, in Gilbert 1882–91, I, 35; Clarke 1966, 181). It is therefore a distinct possibility that Coote's intrinsic nature and his unpopularity in Old English circles suited the political requirements of the Irish insurgents and their wily advocate at the crucial moment in the evolving turmoil and were used accordingly, with cataclysmic results in the long run for the old order.

Charles Coote the elder has long remained one of the most divisive figures in Irish historiography. He was certainly successfully avaricious in the accumulation of extensive properties and public offices (Forkan 2007, 207). During the course of the hostilities, was he, at best, simply prone to an 'over-zealous application of martial law', as Forkan (2007, 217) has reflected, or is there some truth in the possibility that he was gripped by a psychosis (Tait *et al.* 2007, 22)? Or, indeed, was he a murderous 'notorious anti-Catholic bigot', as maintained by Ó Siochrú (1999, 37)?

MUNSTER

Having lost out to Coote in obtaining command of the expeditionary force dispatched against Swords, Harcourt soon found himself operating in County Cork. Given his suggested involvement in the engagement at Swords on 11 January, he would have to have sailed in its immediate wake. How his deployment came to pass is undocumented. There is, however, a very plausible explanation.

Richard Boyle, first earl of Cork, had arrived in Ireland decades earlier with little money but great ambition (Pl. 23). By exploiting 'every opportunity of profit', often in 'a not very scrupulous' manner, he built up 'a vast estate', including several towns in Munster (Beckett 1966, 62). His 'grandeur was unequalled, north or south' (Foster 1988, 70). He was also 'influential in London' (*ibid.*, 14). At his peak, *c.* 1640–1, he was probably the wealthiest landowner in the Three Kingdoms, certainly in Ireland (Edwards and Rynne 2018, 13; Edwards 2018c, 62). It has been advanced that Boyle is 'possibly best understood as an entrepreneur or tycoon in a colonial setting' (Edwards and Rynne 2018, 16). The earl of Cork was a former lord justice and a keen opponent of the late earl of Strafford (Beckett 1966, 68).

Boyle's first marriage, in November 1595, was to Joan Apsley, whose dowry lands proved to be the foundation stone of his future vast financial success (Edwards 2018a, 170). Joan was the daughter of Captain William Apsley and his wife Annabel Browne (*ibid.*, 167). Annabel's father, John Brown, was a key figure in the administration of Garret Fitzgerald, the fifteenth earl of Desmond (*ibid.*, 168). William was the son of Nicholas Apsley and his wife Mary Dawtrey, who resided at Old Place, Pulborough, Sussex (Hankey 1889, fig. 1). His brother John was the father of Sir Allen Apsley Sr, whose second wife, Ann Carew, was the niece of Sir George Carew, the lord president of Munster (*ibid.*, 13, 15). She was the daughter of Sir Peter Carew the younger, who died at Glenmalure on 25 August 1580 (O'Byrne 2003a, 211).

Boyle had fifteen children by Catherine Fenton, his second wife, and he made great efforts to secure them all prestigious marriages. His daughter Lettice married the dashing but spendthrift George Goring. In fact, it was Boyle who bought Goring his regiment in the Netherlands in 1632 for £4,000 (Memegalos 2007, 41). Apparently, Wentworth had expectations in October 1633 of being able to persuade the earl to write off the £2,000 that Goring still owed him for 'the procuring [...] [of] my Lord Vere's Regiment in the Low Countries [...]' (Knowler 1739, I, 119). When the insurrection broke out in Munster, who better to send for than his son-in-law's former right-hand man, now conveniently positioned in Dublin? Although the earl was a financial supporter of the king, he was not without considerable influence at Westminster (*ibid.*, 30, 80). The lord justices may have regarded Harcourt's departure to the south as affording them a brief respite from his frustrated expectations. The journey would appear to have been undertaken by sea, given the perilous state of the countryside throughout Leinster and Munster.

Sir Simon's exploits in the south of Ireland are of broader significance in that there exist detailed accounts pertaining to his tactical style and operational approach in the campaign. The taking of Kinsale in mid-January would seem to clarify his policy regarding the treatment of captured foes. An 'English Gentleman' described the scene in the 'Church and Churchyard', where all males over the age of thirteen who had been apprehended were dispatched from this world: 'such pitiful clamours and mortal groanings I never heard before, and hope I shall never hear again' (Prendergast 1875, 57). On Sunday 16 January it was learned that a force of insurgents led by the recently risen Dominic McCarthy was *en route* to the town and castle of Inishannon, approximately 15km north-west of Kinsale, with a view to supplying and reinforcing the garrison. Harcourt set out to engage this force with a complement of 200 horse, 1,500 foot and five small field pieces. Prior to departure he prayed to God for 'dispensation for breach of the Sabbath' (Pamphlet 1) (Map 11).

The two armies met at the ford of Inishannon. The insurgents numbered approximately 400–500 horse and 2,000 foot. The estuary was broad at the point of engagement, but the water was shallow and the bottom a hard chalky clay. Harcourt opened hostilities with a cavalry charge. The cavalrymen were described as seasoned soldiers and the horses as well fitted 'as ever were horses, that went out of England',

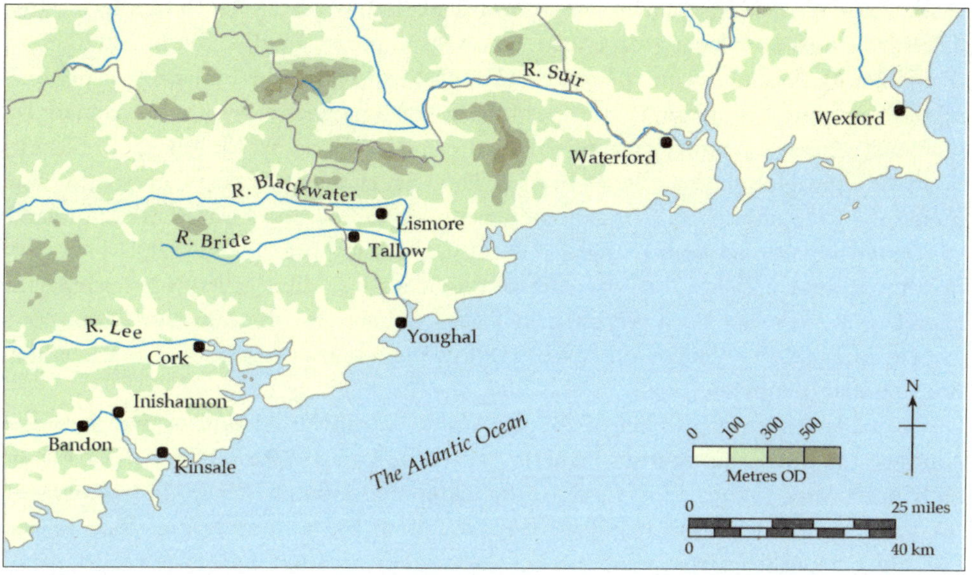

Map 11—Counties Cork and Waterford (1642).

indicating that these men were not local recruits. McCarthy's men held firm on the opposite strand and their fire broke the charge. The insurgents used the high sandy banks behind the strand as repositories for their supplies, which kept them well resourced. Harcourt pulled the cavalry back and ordered his infantry to advance into the water, but only for a short distance. From a range that proved advantageous to the attackers but which was described as being beyond the range of the defenders (indicating a disparity in weaponry), the government side maintained a steady fire on the insurgents. After suffering significant casualties, the latter withdrew into the dunes and sandbanks. The advantage was now pressed, with the reintroduced cavalry following hot on the heels of the advancing infantry. The banks were overrun and the insurgents routed with considerable losses. Dominic McCarthy and 'his two bastard bretheren' were beheaded and their heads carried towards Inishannon on poles. The town offered no resistance but the garrison in the castle refused to surrender. The siege was short-lived, as Sir Simon simply directed his five field pieces to blow down the gates. Once this was accomplished, the castle was stormed and the 30 defenders within were seized and hanged (some of them over the castle walls and others in different parts of the town). Both available accounts of this engagement are almost verbatim and bear the authority of having been written by Robert Pickering, private secretary to Sir Simon Harcourt. Pickering had accompanied him to the south and his accounts were written in the field (Pamphlets 3 and 4).

Having garrisoned and stocked Inishannon Castle with supplies, Harcourt's forces returned to Kinsale on Monday 17 January. Within days they had advanced eastwards into County Waterford.

Their first objective was to defend the west County Waterford town of Tallow against an encroaching detachment of insurgents led by Sir Denis Butler. In a letter dated 20 January Pickering described Tallow as 'a pretty Market Towne all English' (Pamphlet 4). In the interim, the town of Youghal had been overrun by the insurgents, who thereupon laid siege to the castle. The castle garrison was commanded by Harcourt's current patron, Richard Boyle, the earl of Cork. Sir Simon was reluctant, however, to dislodge his forces from Tallow, as Butler's exact whereabouts and intentions were unknown. Consequently, a muster of 500 Scots under the command of Lieutenant Colonel John Douglas were dispatched towards Youghal while Harcourt held his ground at Tallow. The presence of the Scottish soldiers is very interesting; it is feasible that they had been recruited in Ulster, possibly on the initiative of the lord justices in late 1641 (Stevenson 1981, 51), but their transportation to Cork was not documented (see below).

Douglas's attempted relief of Youghal Castle was thwarted *en route* and the siege continued. A further letter from Pickering, dated 28 January (Pamphlet 4), relates how an Irish footman to the earl of Cork by the name of Dominick managed to swim from the castle to dry land and make his way to Tallow. He arrived at 9 o'clock in the evening, personally briefed Harcourt on the current situation and, after a hasty meal, insisted on proceeding to Lismore, where the earl's son, Viscount Dungarvan, was based. In response to the earl's appeal for help, a relief force under the joint command of Dungarvan and the earls of Kildare and Barrymore advanced towards Youghal. David Barry, the earl of Barrymore, was married to Lady Alice Boyle, while George FitzGerald, the earl of Kildare, was married to Lady Joan Boyle, both ladies being daughters of the earl of Cork. Harcourt, at the head of 300 horse, accompanied the expedition, while Sir Thomas Temple and a reserve of 200 additional horse remained at Tallow with orders to follow should the need arise.

Having advanced to within a mile and a half of Youghal, the approaching army was confronted by a force of insurgents reportedly in the region of 6,000 strong (probably an inflated number). Considering that the defeat of Colonel Douglas's attempted relief had been in no small part due to finding himself fighting on boggy ground, it is not surprising to learn that Harcourt declined to launch a cavalry attack. He elected to form the foot into a solid formation and directed them to advance to a specified distance, whereupon they were to open fire with their first volley directed against the insurgent lines. This manoeuvre was repeated until the third volley, at which point the insurgents' resistance began to waver. At this juncture a heated debate erupted between Sir Simon and Captain Thomas Paget. These two men had soldiered together since the Netherlands and were brothers-in-law. The captain had earlier assured Harcourt that he was familiar with the terrain and that the precaution of not employing the cavalry was unnecessary. Now he again urged Harcourt to launch a cavalry charge, given that the enemy were on the verge of breaking. Harcourt overruled Paget's counsel and once more ordered the infantry to advance, this time to the point where the vanguard (with 200 horse on the flank) were almost 'up to the very beards' of the insurgents. At this stage the defence collapsed and a retreat quickly turned into a rout, whereupon Harcourt finally unleashed the cavalry. They rapidly bore down on the fleeing insurgents, causing great slaughter. The pursuit was only maintained for half a mile on Harcourt's orders, as he did not trust the terrain and was not willing to risk the possibility of the cavalry being lured into a bog. It is noteworthy that despite the designated command structure the earls were apparently content to defer to Harcourt's professionalism when it came to tactical decisions in battle. Dungarvan would inevitably have been made aware of his international reputation when they were both stationed in the king's camp outside Berwick-upon-Tweed in the early summer of 1639.

Amongst the notable casualties on the defeated side were Sir Patrick Roche (second son of Lord Roche), 'O'Donnell Swillian' (known as 'the White Knight') and a member of the Barry family. Unfortunately for Barry, although mortally wounded he was still alive when he fell into government hands. He was brought to the now-abandoned Youghal, where he was hanged before the gates. The body was then beheaded and quartered, the head placed on the castle gate and the body parts about the town. The earl of Cork informed the relieving force that Sir Denis Butler had actually been in Youghal and had maintained the siege on the castle until he perceived that all was lost, at which point he withdrew his forces. The town of Youghal was thus back in government hands within three days of being taken by the insurgents.

Sir Simon Harcourt apparently remained in Youghal from 23 to 28 January. He had sailed back to Dublin by 30 January. A month had now passed since his arrival in Ireland.

The question of the presence of active Scottish troops in Munster is intriguing. The received wisdom is that the Scottish army did not land in Ireland until early April 1642 (Beckett 1966, 210), the regiment of Major-General Robert Monro being the first to arrive on 3 April (Stevenson 1981, 69). By the end of the month the numbers had risen to just under 3,000 (*ibid.*, 72). Yet we have, for example, letters from Sir John Lucas, later to be promoted to commissary-general of the horse, and Viscount Dungarvan, a son of the earl of Cork, referring to their earlier presence. Lord Dungarvan wrote on 30 January that Sir Simon Harcourt had taken 'divers Forts and Castles' from the insurgents and kept 'the same well manned with good Garrisons'. He noted the presence of Scottish troops amongst Harcourt's forces (Pamphlet 32). Lucas, writing on 24 February, recounted how, on arrival, his regiment was 'happily joyned' 'to the forces under command of that right valiant and worthy Captain Sir Symon Harcourt'. When describing a victory gained by the government forces over the insurgents in Munster, he observed that the commander of the relevant English forces was Lord Dungarvan while, remarkably, he maintained that the commander of the Scottish forces engaged was 'General Lesley' (Pamphlet 27). While Lucas, as a military participant, is a qualified and credible source, the absence of any corroborative testimony from his contemporaries in the field would suggest that the renowned General Alexander Leslie's presence in Munster in January 1642 is highly questionable. What Lucas may have meant is that the Scottish troops' 'ultimate' commander was Leslie.

As the Covenanter army in Scotland had just disbanded, there would have been a considerable body of men available for military employment (Stevenson 1981, 51). There is also the question of volunteers. There are no figures available regarding how many Scots crossed the sea in the early months of the insurgency to come to the aid of their co-religionists (*ibid.*). The earl of Cork may well have used his considerable personal assets to procure the services of several hundred of these experienced officers and men. This may be the explanation for the early presence of the sizeable force of Scottish soldiers in Munster.

Edwards and Rynne (2018, 17) have observed that the insurrection of 1641 seems to have caught the earl of Cork off guard. Consequently, most of his estates, with the exceptions of Lismore and Youghal, quickly fell to the insurgents. This widespread collapse was all the more surprising given that as early as 1602 Boyle had set about employing farmer-soldier tenants to protect his assets (Edwards 2018b, 228–9). In a report submitted by the vice-president of Munster, Sir Richard Morrison, in October 1611, it was stated that Sir Richard Boyle had paraded 80 horse and 400 foot before him (*ibid.*, 240). Boyle's muster book of that year establishes that the actual number of foot was 442 (*ibid.*). This body contained 186 pikemen and 250 men armed with guns and powder (*ibid.*, 241). By the early 1620s Boyle was maintaining two armies of comparable strength, one based in west Cork and the other in Tallow, Co. Waterford. Within half a decade the eastern force was composed of 215 horse and 720 foot (*ibid.*, 243). The fact that by 1641 there were increasing numbers of both Old English and Irish men serving in the ranks inevitably raises the question of loyalty once hostilities had broken out (*ibid.*, 244). The need to import troops from abroad, for example from Scotland, may thus have been sudden and imperative.

We do know that the necessary shipping was available. On 3 January the lord justices had responded to letters from the earl of Northumberland, the lord high admiral. They acknowledged the dispatch of the *Swallow*, by order of parliament, to protect the coastline of Ireland. Reference is also made to the *Hart*, a pinnace (a small boat, typically with sails and oars), serving as a tender. But they urgently requested that more ships be allocated to serve in Irish waters (HMC 1903, 58–9). It was shipping that was employed to keep Drogheda supplied (*ibid.*, 63, 79). Reference was also made to the *Phoenix* and its tender/pinnace, the *Swan* (*ibid.*, 78).

SOUTH COUNTY DUBLIN AND COUNTY KILDARE

Harcourt's return to Dublin may well have been precipitated by the decision of the lord justices to finally allow the earl of Ormond to take the field (Pl. 40). At the head of an army consisting of 2,000 foot, 300 horse and five small field pieces, the earl set forth on 31 January 1642 (HMC 1903, 70; Carte 1851, II, 174–5). Besides Harcourt, Ormond was also attended by Lord Charles Lambart, Sir Charles Coote and Sir Thomas Newcomen (Pamphlet 5). The latter officer, attached to the lieutenant general's regiment, was deceased within a few months (HMC 1895, 131, 139). The expedition had been prompted by the reported presence of a large and active muster

Pl. 40—James Butler (1610–88), 12th earl of Ormond, 1st duke of Ormonde. (National Gallery of Ireland)

of insurgents in the south-west County Dublin/north County Kildare area (Map 12). The first target was Newcastle (*Novum Castrum de Leuan*) in south-west County Dublin, which lay *c.* 25km from the town. There 'six or seven old castles' and 'many thatched houses' were in the possession of the insurgents (HMC 1903, 70). The forces in this area were under the command of Martin and Thomas Scurlocke, the sons of the local member of parliament Patrick Scurlocke (O'Sullivan 1986, 35). All three were outlawed for high treason (Gilbert 1882–91, III, 380). Newcastle was taken without any notable resistance and used as quarters for the night. The following

Map 12—North-east Leinster.

morning (1 February) the army set out for the market town of Naas in north County Kildare. In their wake they left the ruins of Newcastle, which had been burnt to the ground. The village and castle of Lyons and the Scurlockes' castle at Rathcreedan met with a similar fate. The 'roofes of the castles' were specifically targeted for firing (Pamphlet 5). Undoubtedly this policy was also employed at the castle of Oughterard, which was taken later that morning. It was home to Edward and Richard Allen, both of whom also featured on the list of persons outlawed (Gilbert 1882–91, III, 341).

Naas had lately been used as a headquarters by the insurgents and was thus viewed as a strategic objective. Colonels Hugh McPhelim O'Byrne, Roger Moore (alias Rory O'More) and Nicholas Sutton of Tipper were amongst the senior commanders of the garrison there. At the approach of Ormond's expeditionary force, however, the insurgents fled from the town and thus the Dublin detachments were deprived of any significant encounter or, indeed, a decisive outcome. The personalised element of the campaign that had already claimed the seats of the Scurlockes and Allens was further exemplified by the destruction of the Suttons' castle to the east of Naas at Tipper.

Naas was used as a billet for the night and on the following day a further thrust to the south-west saw attacks launched on Kilcullenbridge and Castlemartin. As the assaults on these locations would have involved a round trip of approximately eighteen miles, it is probable that the operation was conducted exclusively by the cavalry. In fact, a letter sent from Dublin noted that it was 'our English horse' that had journeyed there (Pamphlet 6). Whether Harcourt was thus employed or not is unknown. The personalised hostility continued with the burning of two castles on the advance to Kilcullenbridge. Mullacash and Newland were homes to the Eustaces. The list of persons outlawed in 1642 included Walter, Thomas and Richard Eustace of *Mullaghcash*, and Christopher, John and William Eustace of Newland (Gilbert 1882–91, III, 359). The holdings of Maurice and Edmund Eustace (*ibid.*) probably prompted the assault on Castlemartin. 'Eustace of Castlemartin' had co-commanded (with Rory O'More) an insurgent army based at Rathcoole in late December (Clarke 1966, 191). A number of minor characters from Kilcullenbridge appear on the list of outlawed persons, e.g. Barnaby Bardan, George Missett and Robert Ryan (*ibid.,* 342, 372 and 378). The tavern owned by Edward Orde (*ibid.,* 375) was also undoubtedly visited prior to its being torched (Map 6).

Ormond balanced necessity and strategy by authorising his soldiers to loot and pillage but not to destroy the town of Naas. The town, which contained 'many slated and thatched houses and castles' (HMC 1903, 70), having served as the main base of operations of the insurgency forces in the Dublin–Kildare border zone, would have contained badly needed provisions and hardware, which would have been a godsend to the half-starved and poorly dressed government soldiers. Ormond obviously appreciated the psychological benefit of allowing these soldiers to help themselves to whatever they could lay their hands on, while by insisting that the town be left standing he was planning for its future occupation. On Thursday 3 February, Ormond, Harcourt *et al.* led the army, laden with booty, back to Dublin. Along the way they torched Johnstown and Kill (Pamphlet 5). Meanwhile, the town of Naas was quickly reoccupied by the insurgents. Indeed, overall the expedition might be described as an unspectacular success. Neither side had suffered any notable losses in battle but neither had there been any significant engagements. The hand of Coote might be evident in the fact that the only significant statistic in human terms was the hanging of 'fourscore rogues' captured during the campaign (Pamphlet 6). This perfunctory cruelty, however, almost unravelled the very fabric of the ruling regime upon the return of the expeditionary force to Dublin. Fr Higgins, a Franciscan friar who had served in Naas, had earned a reputation as a charitable man who had provided succour for Protestant citizens of the town dispossessed during the early stages of the insurgency and, indeed, had prevented a number of them from being murdered. He had been arrested on Ormond's orders during the brief occupation and brought back to Dublin as a prisoner by the returning army. Ormond was therefore disgusted to hear that the friar had soon afterwards been hanged on Coote's orders. The outraged earl insisted that the lord justices dismiss Coote immediately. To his intense chagrin, they not only refused this demand but also chose to endorse Coote's conduct in general (Carte 1851, II, 177–8; Lecky 1902–3, I, 98). Ormond threatened to resign his commission as commander-in-chief of the army, but this proved to be an empty threat. The hanging of Fr Higgins was not an isolated incident, as is attested by the memoirs of the earl of Castlehaven: 'It was certainly a miserable spectacle, to see every day numbers of persons executed by martial law, at the discretion, or rather caprice of Sir Charles Coote, an hotheaded and bloody man, and as such accounted even by the English and Protestants. [These executions] he performed with delight, and a wanton kind of cruelty' (Carte 1851, II, 178).

RATHCOOLE, SAGGART AND ARTANE

This first major excursion by the government's forces was book-ended by two minor localised forays. In late January Captain Thomas Armstrong led a raiding party of 200 horse against the villages of Rathcoole and Tassaggart (modern Saggart) in south-west County Dublin. They engaged a party of insurgents at Rathcoole and killed sixteen of them (HMC 1903, 70; Carte 1851, II, 174). Part of the village of Rathcoole and all the village of Tassaggart were burnt to the ground. It should be mentioned here that a detachment of 200 horse sallied forth from the captured Newcastle on 31 January and burnt 'what was left' of Rathcoole (Pamphlet 7). On 10 February the insurgents were dislodged from Artane Castle and a garrison installed in their place (Pamphlet 8). The castle at Artane was home to Christopher Hollywood and his son Nicholas Hollywood, both of whom were indicted for treason (Gilbert 1882–91, III, 366, 367). Young Hollywood had attended the meetings of the gentry of the Pale on the Hill of Tara and later at Kilsallaghan in early December (*ibid.*, I, 272, 282).

THE BATTLE OF DEAN'S GRANGE

Government activity to the south of Dublin city had been limited since the outbreak of hostilities in the Wicklow Mountains on 12 November 1641 (Clarke 1966, 169, 175). The clinically lethal operation conducted with success by Coote at the end of November had not been subsequently exploited militarily. His relief of Wicklow

Castle on 29 November and the rout of an insurgent force led by Luke O'Toole on 1 December were thus strategically of little or no value. The accompanying executions of civilians had done the government cause no favours either, given the unsettled mentality prevalent in the Pale. The only government activity of note in the area since Coote's all-night march back to Dublin on 1–2 December was a successful foraging raid conducted in mid-January. This outing of 700 horse and foot combined had gone 'a cow-catching into Wicklow amongst the mountains and bogges' (Pamphlet 9) and had resulted in a haul of 500 or 600 head of cattle and 2,000 or 3,000 sheep. The expedition was led by Colonel Lawrence 'Crafford' (i.e. Crawford) and returned to Dublin on 20 January. There was 'great joy' in the city at the arrival of 'fresh-meate', it 'being wondrous scant'. The current prices had reached ten shillings for 'a quarter of small mutton' and 'egges two pence a piece'.

On 11 February the authorities in Dublin were alerted to an imminent threat on their southern flank. Since late December the O'Byrnes and O'Tooles had been manoeuvring in strength to within three or four miles of the city (Clarke 1966, 191). Three extant accounts refer to the receiving of an intelligence report that was to precipitate immediate action. An account by Adam Loftus of the privy council relates how an insurgent force of about 1,000 men led by Sir Morgan Cavanagh had entrenched themselves at Dean's Grange (Pamphlet 35). It should be noted that two extant sources place the encampment at Loughlinstown (*Laughlinston* and *Soughing Towne* respectively) (Pamphlets 7 and 8). The latter, however, was described as being 'some 6 miles' from Dublin. The fact that Dean's Grange is approximately five–six miles from the city while Loughlinstown is in the region of nine miles away would seem to support the placing of the encampment at the former location. There is no doubt, however, that the two accounts in question are descriptions of the 'small battell' (Pamphlet 8) that occurred on Saturday 12 February. An otherwise fantastical description of the encounter may throw some light on the nature of the 'intelligence' received. William Philips, a merchant resident in Dublin, described in a letter how one of the insurgents had slipped away from his companions and arrived at a city gate 'about 11. of the clock at night' ... 'upon Saturday, the Twelfth of February'. He asked to see the governor of the city, Sir Charles Coote, and was duly escorted to the latter's bedchamber once he had been 'chained with Fetters of Iron'. He revealed that the plan of the assembled insurgent force was to launch a surprise attack in the morning when all good citizens would be at church. Sir Charles, it is reported, immediately rose from his bed and sent word to Sir Simon Harcourt, who joined him shortly afterwards. Both gentlemen then proceeded to the lord justices and the city was put on full alert. The letter by Philips to his friend in London (Pamphlet 10) goes on to maintain that a massive nocturnal attack was thereafter launched against the insurgents 'about two and three of the clock in the morning', resulting in their total rout. The details of the battle provided by Philips are a complete exaggeration and in fact a distortion of the known facts. His allegation of its having been a defector who brought news of an imminent attack by the insurgent army may, however, be close to the truth. All available accounts do suggest that action was taken on very short notice. In fact, Loftus specifically states that it was on Saturday itself that they 'received intelligence', i.e. on the day of the battle (Map 12).

Whatever about the exact time of the engagement, there is no doubt as to its course and outcome. Lord Charles Lambart sallied forth with a complement of 800 foot and 100–200 horse (HMC 1903, 82; Pamphlet 11). They would appear to have taken the force of approximately 1,000 insurgents by surprise. Their commander, Sir Morgan Cavanagh, had reportedly departed to visit Art Cavanagh at Three Castles in County Wicklow three days prior to the attack and had not returned (Pamphlet 5). The insurgent forces were described as being drawn from counties Wicklow and Wexford (Pamphlet 6). Included in the list of 'Persons Outlawed for Treason' in 1641–2 was Sir Morgan Cavanagh of Clonmullen, Co. Carlow (*Catherlogh*) (Gilbert 1882–91, III, 350). The fighting was short-lived and ended in the rout of the insurgents. The consensus from the available accounts puts the government casualties at one wounded and no fatalities. Losses on the opposing side were in the region of between 70 and 100, including a number of officers (at least one if not two captains fell in battle). Between a dozen and twenty prisoners were taken. One account noted that amongst the captives was a 'Rebel Captaine' (Pamphlet 8). Only one report actually names him as Edward Walsh, 'second son of old M. Walsh of *Clonmanim*' (Pamphlet 5). The same writer added that Walsh and his comrades would soon be hanged and was of the opinion that it would be no less than they deserved. The deposition by John Cliffe of *Courtowne* in County Wexford identified the Walsh captured at Dean's Grange as 'Edmund Walsh, son to Edward Walsh of *Clonmanin*' (1641 Depositions, TCD MS 818, fols 107r–109v). The list of 'Persons Outlawed for Treason' does not resolve the issue, as it contains Edmond Walsh (gent.) and Edward Walsh (esq.) and Henry Walsh (gent.) of *Clonmanen* in County Wicklow (Gilbert 1882–91, III, 385, 386). The depositions by John Brackenbury of Dean's Grange name Henry Walsh and Edmond Walsh of *Clonmanige* as being amongst the insurgents active in the area (1641 Depositions, TCD MSS 809, fol. 249, and 810, fol. 67b), while the deposition by Owen Deane names Edmund Walsh and Edward Walsh of *Clonnangin* as active insurgents (*ibid.*, MS 810, fol. 147). The presence of either Edmund or Edward at Dean's Grange might be better understood by the fact that Edmund was married to Elinor Cavanagh of Clonmullen (Ken Nichols, pers. comm.). Clonmullen, Co. Carlow (*Catherlagh*), was the named abode of Sir Morgan Cavanagh (see above), the commander of the insurgent force at Dean's Grange. Given the testimony of John Cliffe and the relationship by marriage, it is likely to have been Edmund (Walsh) who was captured at Dean's Grange.

Significantly, according to Cliffe's deposition (1641 Depositions, TCD MS 818, fols 107r–109v), 'Edmund' did not die on the gallows. John Cliffe had fled his leased properties near Courtown at the start of the insurrection. He named Sir Morgan Cavanagh as a leading 'actor' in the subsequent looting of his holdings. Cliffe was clearly well connected, for no less a personage than Sir William Parsons instigated the hiring of a boat that would transport his fleeing party to Dublin. The boat duly sailed from Arklow but was struck by 'a furious storme' off Bray Head. Forced to put into port in Wicklow, those on board were arrested by men in the service of Luke O'Toole.

The prisoners were sentenced to death and were to be hanged. Cliffe attributed their rescue to divine intervention. He recounted how in the wake of the battle of Dean's Grange 'Edmond Walsh, son to Edward Walsh of *Clonmanin*', was taken prisoner and brought to Dublin. The insurgents suggested to Cliffe that, should he be able to convince the Dublin authorities, they would be willing to make an exchange of prisoners. Thus it came to pass that 'after 16 weeks imprisonment' the lord justices and council approved the deal. John Cliffe and his companions were given safe conduct by Luke O'Toole and made their way by road to Dublin. 'Edmond' Walsh was set free. He was fortunate, for in general the other prisoners taken at Dean's Grange were hanged.

On 12 February Simon started on a lengthy letter to Anne. It is wide-ranging in subject-matter. The weather has been so stormy that no ships have been able to put to sea. He is aware of her growing concerns when she doesn't hear from him: 'I know your feares for me are great, concidderinge ye times heare, which I beeleeve are made more dangerous by report than in truth they are, for were our supplyes of horsse and foote come out of England, I am of opinion yet ye great danger of this rebellion were past' (Harcourt 1880–1905, I, 148). He indicates that the relief of Drogheda is uppermost in their minds. They have been receiving dispatches from the governor of the town and from some of his officers, pleading for aid and reporting the dearth of supplies at their disposal, 'having nothinge left them but herringes and malt and rye, and of these not for above 8 dayes'. 'The garrison is sickly, and the cavalry's horses are been driven out of the town as there is no fodder to feed them. The authorities in Dublin are considering whether to relieve them by sea or by road but the weather is so bad that all is at a standstill' (*ibid.*, 149).

His thoughts are still dwelling on their personal legal struggles and he wishes her well in her 'endeavours therein'. He dreams of 'a retiringe place, where I may at last finnish my dayes in peace and quiet, and in ye comfortable enjoyment of thy deare selfe'. He enquires after her health and that of the children. As for his own health, he 'never enjoyed it more perfectly' (*ibid.*, 150). He had arranged with her brother 'Tom' (Paget) for £50 to be advanced to her in England (*ibid.*, 151). It is apparent from this letter that their plan was for Anne to join him in Dublin. This may well have rested on his obtaining and holding the long-term governorship of the city, as originally promised. To that end he encouraged her to try and ascertain the time of arrival of the lord lieutenant in Ireland, 'for matters here will never be put into a right frame till then' (*ibid.*). With her arrival in mind, he has already been accumulating household goods from the spoils of war: 'a very good basin and eawer [ewer], 2 fflaggons, a salt, sugar-box, and 2 wine cupps of silver, some 2 dossen of pewter dishes, and a good store of ordinary househould linnen'. This haul came from the sacking of Lyons on 1 February. The owner of the castle in question, 'Banesly Britton', a '*Barkeshire* man', had hitherto 'stoode neuter' but was now in rebellion. This was followed by 'ye pilliageinge' of *Nesse* (Naas). The looting of captured castles and towns should be considered against the background of sporadic pay and poor conditions. Harcourt put it to Anne that 'If I continue here I shall be nessesseated to turne begger unto some of my friends in England, to helpe me unto a good serviceable horsse or 2, for I am in very great want, beeinge forced to borrowe whensoever I goe abroade on service' (*ibid.*, 152). He was also lacking in personal attire: 'A small supply of linnen woolde be very wellcome, as half a dozen bands, cuffes, and many paire of hooses, and some pritee small laces, but not great prized ones: for I will spare your pursse as much as may be'. Most of all he misses her 'most desired and sweete company and conversation'. He promises to tell her of 'some other wants' that he has, 'ye cheefe of which cannot be supplyed without your presence, which in all my lifetime I never more desired' (*ibid.*, 152–3).

There were, however, some payments made. The lord justices and council issued a number of 'orders and warrants' to Sir Adam Loftus, the vice-treasurer and general receiver in Ireland. On 5 January £800 had been advanced to Sir Simon, 'to be deducted from future pay to his regiment'. Again, on 8 January '£200 more' was allocated to him, followed by £300 on 17 January (Mahaffy 1900–1, II, 777, 778, 779). By 1 March, nevertheless, several military men were in debt to the 'inhabitants of Dublin', including Lieutenant Colonel Gibson and Captains Woodhouse and Vane (*ibid.*, 782).

THE BATTLE OF KILSALLAGHAN CASTLE

On 20 February—an ominous day for the insurgents—a proclamation personally signed by King Charles finally arrived in Dublin. It had actually been issued on 1 January, but inclement weather had caused the undue delay in its arrival. The contents were quite clear: all those under arms were to be regarded as rebels and traitors, and failure to surrender immediately would bring full retribution in time (HMC 1903, 81; Clarke 1966, 201). As word of its contents spread, the illusion of legitimacy of action would have been dispelled from Old English hearts. Undoubtedly, had there been a more approachable administration in Dublin at this point in time there is every possibility that a trickle of submissions from that quarter would have turned into an unbridled flow. The lord justices, however, were not in the slightest way inclined to accept any attempts at *rapprochement*, for, as if they weren't trenchant enough in their views, that same portentous tide on 20 February brought further reinforcements from England, under the command of Lieutenant Colonel George Monck and Sir Richard Grenville. These two men, related by marriage (Grenville's sister-in-law Grace was Monck's aunt), were veterans of the wars in the Netherlands and Scotland and no doubt well known to Harcourt. Monck was heading his kinsman's outfit, the lord lieutenant's regiment of 1,500 foot, while Grenville was in command of 400 horse. Landings continued on 21 February (HMC 1903, 79).

These reinforcements finally alleviated the siege mentality of the Dublin government. As they arrived with neither cash nor provisions (Carte 1851, II, 183), however, the resources of the city were now severely overstretched and consequently the bad conditions deteriorated even further. The 'scorched-earth' policy of the lord justices had exacerbated the inevitable deprivation of the besieged city. Not only were there the citizens and the increasingly large army to sustain but also the great influx of refugees. The obvious solution was to dispatch the army, or at least a sizeable proportion of it, into the field.

The objective chosen (on the basis of information received) was to prove more problematic than was apparently anticipated. This may have been a result of shortcomings in intelligence evaluation, which appears overall to have been notably deficient. The root cause of this deficiency may have lain in the almost pathological reluctance of Borlase and Parsons to give any credibility to Old English sources, no matter what their rank or social status. The identification of the objective was, however, motivated by the perception of an imminent direct threat against the city.

Kilsallaghan Castle lay approximately nine miles north-north-west of Dublin city (Map 12). This turreted tower-house was still 'inhabited and in good repair' when visited by Austin Cooper in the late 1770s (Price 1942, 42–3). In 1642 it formed the centrepiece of a highly defensive position adopted by an insurgent force under the command of 'divers of their best commanders' (HMC 1903, 82), including Hugh Byrne and Mac Thomas (Carte 1851, II, 185). Byrne was a Flanders veteran (having served in the *tercio* of Owen Roe O'Neill) and had co-commanded at Julianstown (Clarke 1966, 157, 177). The reported number of insurgents encamped at Kilsallaghan varies from 500 (Gilbert 1879–80, I (1), 21) to 3,000 (HMC 1903, 82). Considering the biased nature of both accounts, there might be more credibility in Harcourt's own professional estimate of 'nere upon 2000' (Pamphlet 12). This figure tallies well with a report written by an Ed. Loftus (Pamphlet 8). In a letter to Anne dated 21 March, Harcourt gave the estimated strength of the insurgents as 'some 1,500 or 2,000, stronge as any as I have yet seene in Ireland' (Harcourt 1880–1905, I, 154). On 23 February or immediately thereafter a government force consisting of 2,500 foot, 300 horse and four field pieces left the city and advanced towards Kilsallaghan. Leading the force was the earl of Ormond, attended by Sir Simon Harcourt, Lord Charles Lambart, Sir Charles Coote and Sir Thomas Lucas. The topography of the locality was of prime importance in its defence. The government correspondence described it as 'a place of very great strength in regard of woods, and many high ditches' (HMC 1903, 82). To Harcourt's military eye it was truly impressive and obviously well chosen: 'The setuation of the place [was] as naturally strong as I have seen any castle in Ireland, having moorish and boggy ground on the one side, the other invironed with thick woads, quick-set hedges, high bancks and deep Ditches [inaccessible]' (Pamphlet 12). The castle stood 'in the middle' of the woods and was only approachable by one avenue, which the insurgents had blocked with 'a Traverse or Barricadoe'. The adjacent churchyard had also been occupied. The assault began with pioneers, covered by musketeers, forging a way towards the castle. The barricade was quickly taken, thus opening up the approach to the castle. At this point, however, Harcourt ordered Captain Francis Congrave to take 100 musketeers and launch an assault on the defended churchyard. He had planned to personally lead an additional 500 of his own regiment as a second wave but this proved unnecessary (Harcourt 1880–1905, I, 154–5). The fall of the churchyard prompted a general retreat, with the insurgent detachments breaking for the woods and marshland. Those who headed for higher ground were pursued, on Harcourt's orders, by Lord Borlase's troop of horse. As a result, some 60 or 70 of the insurgents had their throats cut. Meanwhile, the infantry was in pursuit of those who had fled into the woods, resulting in the death of 'about as many more'. The camps of the defeated battalions were torched in the aftermath of the battle. Losses on the government side were minimal—only eight, including five or six of Harcourt's own regiment and Captain James Rochford (of Coote's regiment, who had led the 'Forlorn Hope'), having fallen (Pamphlet 12). One account of the battle described it as having lasted two hours and resulting in the death of 80 insurgents and seven on the government side, including Captain Rochford. The author added that there would have been considerably more casualties on the insurgent side 'but that the wood defended them, so that the Trees tooke off all that was sent to them' (Pamphlet 8). He described Harcourt's regiment as having 'behaved themselves Valliantly'.

The engagement at Kilsallaghan would have been a complete success had it not been for one notable defect: the failure to take the castle itself. It was clearly not an easy objective. The available evidence suggests that it featured four towers, one set at each corner. The projecting aspect of the two recorded turrets is remarkably similar in design to the nearby Dunsoghly Castle, a notable bastion (Clinton 2005, 24–35). Although Harcourt credited the garrison with including 'some of their best men', he specifically explained that the government side's inability to take the castle was a result of not having any 'pieces of Battery' (Pamphlet 12) but only 'field peeces' with them (Pamphlet 8)—a predictable deficiency but frustrating to a professional of Harcourt's calibre. The question that remains unanswered is whether there were no heavy guns available to them in the city or whether they had neglected to bring one with them.

THE RELIEF OF DROGHEDA AND ITS AFTERMATH

The new-found confidence and growing authority of the Dublin administration were soon manifested in a series of decisive political acts. On 23 February the lord justices issued a proclamation defining the terms of engagement with the enemy. These were extreme, to put it mildly. Not only were all insurgents and their supporters to be killed and their houses and property to be destroyed but also the male inhabitants of any area or town supportive of their cause were to be executed and their property laid waste (Carte 1851, II, 185–6). It could be argued that the new directive made no practical difference in the field and that the individual commanders continued to operate under personal determinations: Ormond with a somewhat *laissez-faire* approach, Harcourt, Lambart *et al.* more or less according to the military handbook for Ireland, and Coote with his usual decidedly *laissez-aller* attitude. Borlase and Parsons suffered one setback while flexing their new-found powers: an attempt to deprive Ormond of command of the forthcoming major military expedition was resolutely resisted and ultimately thwarted by the indignant earl (*ibid.*, 189–90). Significantly, his place was to have been taken by Sir Simon Harcourt. This enhanced favour with the lord justices was confirmed when Harcourt was finally appointed to the privy council on 3 March (HMC 1879, 436). The appointment was long overdue and still fell well short of his original expectations. There is a distinctly cynical edge to the words of Captain Edmund Verney on the subject in a letter home to England: 'My colonel was last night sworn a Privy Councillor, and lives in mighty esteem here, and I think not without desert; it is wondered that ye have not yet settled him in his government of Dublin, or in some other place of as great honour and worth' (*ibid.*).

When the major hosting eventually sallied forth, it turned out to be rather anti-climactic in terms of military success. On the morning of Saturday 5 March Ormond rode out of Dublin at the head of an army consisting of 3,000 foot and 500 horse (HMC 1903, 86; Carte 1851, II, 188). Amongst those attending him were Sir Simon Harcourt, Sir Thomas Lucas and Sir Robert Farrer (Pamphlet 11; Carte 1851, II, 188, and V, 300–3). Harcourt laconically described the expedition as intending to 'make a visit unto the Lords and Gentry of the Pale' (Pamphlet 12). The lord justices had given them strict instructions not to cross the River Boyne. Sensibly, they had adopted a more logical policy of not destroying crops or assets within a five-mile radius of Dublin, and this also formed part of their issued instructions (Carte 1851, II, 189).

In the end, the reluctance of the insurgents to give battle and the limited set objectives of the lord justices in effect reduced the campaign to a walkabout. There were, however, a number of minor achievements. Kilsallaghan Castle, the home of the Hore family, was probably occupied on, if not before, 7 March (HMC 1903, 94). It was clearly not destroyed, as there is a record of its being garrisoned on 17 August (HMC 1895, 136). Having taken and garrisoned the castle without encountering any resistance, the army 'burnt the houses about it'. The same fate befell *Filston* (Fieldstown lies to the immediate north of Kilsallaghan) and probably *the Navue* (the Naul) (Pamphlet 29). Of interest is the reported capture of 'Con Magenis' at *Care* and 'Rory Magwire' at the town of *Clogham* (Pamphlet 25). There are two townlands called Cloghran in north County Dublin.

Sir Con Maginnis had led the insurgent forces into County Down. He thereupon issued a declaration to the government commanders in the county: '... we desire no blood to be shed, but if you mean to shed our blood be sure we will be as ready as you for the purpose' (Beckett 1966, 83). The full-scale attack that he led against Lisburn towards the end of November, however, had failed with considerable losses (*ibid.*, 84). Rory Maguire was a brother of Connor, Lord Maguire of Enniskillen (a leading figure in the formulation of the insurrection), and had been active in opposition in the Commons (Clarke 1966, 156). Appointed a captain, he served initially in County Fermanagh. On entering the church in Newtownbutler, he reportedly tore up the Bible and scattered its pages (Mac Cuarta 2007, 171). It was maintained in the relevant pamphlet that the arresting English officers had subsequently collected the reward money on offer from the lord justices for the apprehension of these 'principal conspirators, and actors in the Rebellion' (Pamphlet 25).

The village of Garristown (*Garrett's Towne*) was occupied by 9 March. Garristown in north County Dublin was the abode of Patrick Cusack, who was outlawed for high treason (Gilbert 1882–91, III, 349). He had commanded a company of soldiers at Kilsallaghan back in December 1641 (*ibid.*, I, 283). As the weather had turned wretched, it was decided to encamp the infantry at Garristown (Pamphlet 13). Within days word was arriving of the collapse of the siege of *Tredagh* (Map 12).

The town of *Tredagh* (Drogheda) had played a pivotal role since the outbreak of hostilities in late October 1641. Reinforcements had been dispatched to *Tredagh* even before the earl of Ormond had arrived in Dublin to assume command of the army. This decisive act on the part of the lord justices was totally at odds with an emerging policy otherwise characterised by military inertia, save for a desperate attempt to withdraw all other elements of a widely dispersed army back to Dublin. The fate of those loyal citizens whose safety depended on the local garrison was of little concern to the panicking authorities in Dublin. Sir Henry Tichborne had personally raised a regiment of 1,000 foot in Dublin (Bellings, in Gilbert 1882–91, I, 32). These men were largely, if not completely, drawn from the ranks of the refugees who were streaming in on a daily basis (Clarke 1966, 169; Corish 1976, 292). In one contemporary account Dublin is described as 'our City of Refuge' (Lecky 1902–3, I, 65). On 3 November Tichborne marched out of Dublin with his recently levied regiment and reached Drogheda safely. In the interim, Captain Seafoule Gibson and Michael Burnell had both been authorised to raise companies of 100 men apiece in the town and environs of *Tredagh* itself (HMC 1895, 123). Captain Gibson was thereafter to serve in the regiment of Lord Charles Moore (*ibid.*, 124, 140). Sir Henry's arrival in the town was timely. An insurgent army of the Irish of Ulster had captured Dundalk on 31 October (Clarke 1966, 164); this was followed, as reported by a member of the privy council, by the taking of the mid-Louth town of Ardee (Pamphlet 14). Given the sizeable Old English community resident in Drogheda, it is reasonable to suggest that the town would more than likely have surrendered to the insurgents soon after, had it not been for the arrival of Tichborne and his regiment. The following two and a half weeks witnessed little action. On 21 November, however, Lord Moore's residence at Mellifont was attacked and looted (Clarke 1966, 175). As it lay a mere five miles from Drogheda, it was clear that the noose was tightening. Tichborne, who had been confirmed as governor of the town, was alert to the danger and requested further reinforcements from Dublin. No doubt Lord Moore would also have been quite animated by the growing crisis. On 27 November a detachment of 600 foot, under the command of Sergeant-Major Christopher Roper, and a troop of 50 horse led by Sir Patrick Weames, a brother of Lord Baltinglass and a veteran of Ormond's troop (HMC 1895, 120), departed from Dublin (Bellings, in Gilbert 1882–91, I, 32). The inexperience of the infantry was immediately apparent in their appalling progress, which brought them only to Swords by nightfall, a distance of no more than eight miles. The following day proved to be equally unimpressive, as the expedition only managed to cover *c.* ten miles before camping at Balrothery. In the interim, a body of insurgents had crossed the River Boyne with the specific intention of intercepting the Roper and Weames detachment (*ibid.*, 33). A dispatch from Dublin brought news of this alarming development to the expeditionary force but the report seems to have made little impact on its commanders. Sir Henry Tichborne, appreciating the threat, had in the meantime led a small force of men south from Drogheda with the intention of rendezvousing with the Dublin detachment, but having failed to make contact returned to the town. The third day again began at a leisurely pace and the expedition only passed by the home of Lord Gormanston (Nicholas Preston) at about 7 o'clock in the morning. Roper paid a courtesy call on his lordship, whereupon he was instantly informed of the Ulster army now blocking their way. Bellings suggests that Roper did not even bother to impart this intelligence to his fellow officers (*ibid.*, 33), but this is contradicted by the contents of a letter from Weames to the earl of Ormond (*ibid.*, III, 334) in which he makes it clear that he had been personally and directly informed by Lord Gormanston, whose display of loyalty is worth noting in the context of the line being peddled in Dublin regarding the affiliations of the Old English.

Again, there are contradictions in the accounts of the march north from Gormanston. Bellings states that Roper dispatched only three scouts north (*ibid.*, I, 33), whereas Weames insists that he personally dispatched 'severall scouttis' upon receipt of the information. Bellings writes that at least one of Roper's scouts took himself off to an alehouse 'not farr from the roade', from where his horse was stolen, while Weames insists that his 'several' scouts returned having seen no sign of the enemy. No sooner had the Dublin party crossed the bridge over the River Nanny at Julianstown, however, than they ran straight into the Ulster force. The two sides quickly arranged themselves in battle formation. The Dublin troops adopted a simple arrangement of cavalry to the front with the infantry drawn up behind. The Ulster force formed into five great bodies ('fyve gret bodyes') of infantry, with their cavalry positioned on both flanks. They were also equipped with two field pieces. Weames reported that he fully intended to charge the Ulster lines, which had begun to advance, but upon his trumpeter's sounding the attack he discovered that the infantry had taken to their heels! He stressed that his men were still willing to charge but that he saw little point in such a potentially suicidal manoeuvre (*ibid.*, III, 335). Bellings is dismissive of any such suggestions of willingness or, indeed, intention to fight on the part of the government side, and rather laconically describes Weames's cavalry as advancing without pause until they reached the gates of Drogheda (*ibid.*, I, 34). Later in the day Sergeant-Major Roper, two of his captains and about 100 of the foot struggled into the town. The rest of the detachment and all of the supplies, weapons and ammunition were lost. The operation, in short, had been a military disaster. Furthermore, and more significantly, the rout had the political ramification of nudging the Old English closer to an alliance with the Ulster insurgents, as much out of fear as out of a growing desperation born of the increasing hostility of the State.

The roads to Drogheda were now effectively closed. The siege itself, however, was not conducted along classic military lines. In the first place, the besieging army was totally bereft of the requisite ordnance with which to breach the walls of the town. Secondly, as may be noted throughout the government dispatches, the weather was particularly inclement for the time of year. The tactic adopted, therefore, was to deploy in strength in all of the surrounding villages in the immediate area. Sir Phelim O'Neill, commander of the insurgent forces at Drogheda, did attempt one major assault on 20 December (Clarke 1966, 200), but this only served to emphasise the deficiencies in the weaponry of the besiegers. The only option left to the insurgents was to starve the town into submission. There was one major shortcoming in this plan, however, and that was the fact that the town lay towards the mouth of the River Boyne and thus had access to the Irish Sea. The tidal channel to the open sea was approximately four miles in length. The insurgents were not long in laying a crude barrier (probably of sunken boats) across the river at the entrance to the harbour (HMC 1903, 64, 65). Given that they had no other options, the Dublin authorities decided to attempt a relief effort by sea despite the inherent dangers. A pinnace (a small vessel with oars and sails) under the command of Captain Thomas Stutvill accordingly set sail and arrived in Drogheda on 11 January (*ibid.*, 63). The difficulty of the voyage would have been compounded by the prevailing westerly winds. It seems that a favourable tide enabled the pinnace to ease across the barrier and reach the safety of the town despite concerted musket fire from the banks. Having delivered the supplies, the return journey was attempted on Thursday 13 January but the good luck the sailors had hitherto enjoyed almost immediately ran out. The pinnace ran aground before she could make the open sea and soon came under attack. Being too far removed from the town, she could expect no assistance from Sir Henry Tichborne (Pamphlet 15). It would appear that the pinnace had some small ordnance piece(s) on board, but owing to the angle at which she was lying these proved to be of no use. As the water in her immediate vicinity was only knee-deep, it did not take the insurgents long to discover that it was possible to wade out to the vessel (HMC 1903, 64). A party of about 100 armed with pickaxes and iron crowbars launched an attack with the intention of totally disabling the vessel. Captain Stutvill managed to repel the assault by throwing a number of 'Grannadoes' amongst their ranks. Having thus suffered heavy losses, the attacking party withdrew to the shore. The only fatality on board the pinnace was Lieutenant Sparke. Of note is the fact that he was a member of Captain Edmund Verney's company and thus belonged to Sir Simon Harcourt's regiment (Pamphlet 15). The vessel remained aground until the following Monday, when the crew finally managed to refloat her, but there had been no further serious attacks. On 18 (or 19) January the pinnace arrived back in the port of Dublin.

Sir Phelim O'Neill, although undoubtedly disappointed that the relief vessel had got through to Drogheda, quickly saw an opportunity of turning the setback to his advantage. It must be remembered that at heart the town was a bastion of the Old English, and at this point in time the citizens in question were committed to an alliance with the besieging army. At first light on the morning of 12 January, a party of the townspeople, taking advantage of the post-celebration mood in the town, set about unblocking an old door in the walls from the inside. A party of approximately 300 insurgents were waiting and quietly entered through the opened door, but either the alarm was raised or the party was inadequate in number to overcome resistance. Tichborne led the spirited defence and the attack was repelled, although a part of the incursive force managed to seek shelter about the town (HMC 1903, 65). O'Neill thereafter reverted to his policy of forcing capitulation through starvation.

The worsening conditions in the town remained in the minds of the Dublin authorities and a second relief effort by sea was attempted in late January. Three of the 'King's Pinnaces' duly set sail but at once encountered atrocious weather. In fact, so bad were the conditions that one of the vessels was shipwrecked on the coast of Wales (Pamphlet 6), having fallen victim to the prevailing westerly winds. The other two pinnaces limped back to Dublin. The next attempt to relieve Drogheda was made a few weeks later. Once again Captain Thomas Stutvill was tasked with the enterprise (HMC 1903, 79), which on this occasion was a more ambitious one, given that both supplies and reinforcements were involved. On 12 February Stutvill set sail with a fleet of nine small vessels. On board were 'victualls and munition and 400 men' (Pamphlet 6). The dispatch of the fleet may have been partly due to the direct intercession of Tichborne, who had sent Captain William Cadogan to Dublin. He had arrived in the town on 5 February and sailed back immediately prior to the dispatch of the fleet (Pamphlet 7). The insurgents had in the interim improved on their original barrier at the entrance to the harbour. A string of boats with a massive chain slung across them now blocked access to the river and town (HMC 1903, 79). The expedition was equipped with devices to undo the blockade, but this proved to be unnecessary. For once the foul weather proved to be an unlikely ally. A 'very great storm' arose which scattered the boats in the barrier and snapped the chain. Just at the time when the prevailing winds could have had a disastrous effect on the approaching fleet, the direction of the wind changed and thus facilitated rather than hindered a smooth and rapid passage up the river to Drogheda. Unsurprisingly, the garrison in the town and the privy council back in Dublin interpreted this timely stroke of good fortune as a sign of God's favour (*ibid.*, 79). The reinforcements and desperately needed supplies were unloaded on 14 February. The only casualties on board were two men killed and fourteen wounded by a shot from a field piece, another manifestation of the improved blockade of the harbour. O'Neill again launched an attack but it had little or no effect on the town (Clarke 1966, 202) and was probably mounted with an ebbing conviction.

The arrival of the supplies of food and ammunition in addition to the 400 fresh soldiers had a galvanising effect on Tichborne and the commander of the horse, Lord Charles Moore. In effect the initiative now passed irretrievably to the defenders of the town. The latent insurgents and sympathisers in the town were expelled, while Lord Moore instigated a series of cavalry forays against the surrounding village encampments (*ibid.*).

Finally, when news of the trajectory of the earl of Ormond's major expeditionary force reached the ears of Sir Phelim O'Neill and his officers on 5 March, the decision was quickly taken to abandon the siege. Within hours the insurgent army was withdrawing northward. The siege of *Tredagh* was over.

The fallout and its implications for the insurgency were negative indeed. In stark contrast, had the insurgents succeeded in capturing the town, the combined forces of the army of Ulster and its Old English augmentations would have been instantly made available for a concerted effort against Dublin. In that endeavour they would have been operating in concert with the Irish of counties Wicklow, Wexford, Kildare and Carlow and their Old English neighbours. The fall of Dublin would have enabled the Old English, presumably with the tacit support of the Irish, to enter direct negotiations with the king and thus bring about an end to all hostilities—if only temporarily, given the likely opposition of the English parliament. Instead, Drogheda and Dublin were now totally safe while the army of Ulster was in full retreat. Almost inevitably, cracks in the unity of the coalition were not long in appearing.

As Ormond, Harcourt and their fellow officers sat in their rain-drenched headquarters in Garristown a steady trickle of visitors began to arrive. The progressive retreat of the Ulster army from the Pale when combined with the effects of the dissemination of the contents of the proclamation issued by King Charles (wherein he declared that all those under arms against the government were to be considered rebels) (Borlase 1680, 52–3) was having a not-unpredictable reaction in Old English circles. On Wednesday 9 March Lieutenant Colonel Sir John Reade and Patrick Barnewall of Kilbrew, Co. Meath, presented themselves at Ormond's quarters. They assured him that the insurgent army had now completely withdrawn from the Drogheda area (Carte 1851, II, 190). Patrick Barnewall had served as a member of the parliament of 1640, where he had represented County Meath (Clarke 1966, 258). His sister was married to Rory O'More (*ibid.*, 179). Barnewall was one of those entrusted by the lords of the Pale to organise the Old English contingents into a functioning army. His powers even extended as far as the authorisation to coerce contributions of horses and funds from recalcitrant elements of that society (Gilbert 1882–91, I, 282, 283). He had been an active participant at the key meetings held on the Hill of Tara and at Kilsallaghan Castle (*ibid.*, 272). In 1639 Sir John Reade had been sent to Ireland by the king; his mission was to assist the earl of Antrim (the head of the Irish branch of the MacDonnells) in the preparation of resources that might be used against the Scots. He had remained in Ireland to take up a commission in the new army. After the outbreak of hostilities, he was offered a senior position under the command of Lord Gormanston but had declined (Clarke 1966, 187). He was willing, nevertheless, to personally deliver letters from the lords of the Pale to the king and queen, and furthermore to impart verbal messages of their loyalty and willingness to serve (*ibid.*, 190). When Reade presented himself to Ormond at Garristown he was carrying a letter from Viscount Nicholas Nettirvill which requested safe passage for a delegation (including Reade) that would go and investigate the authenticity of the king's recent proclamation. The letter further stated that, should the rumoured contents of the document prove to be true, the call to lay down their arms would be obeyed (*ibid.*, 205). Ormond received Barnewall, Reade and the lawyer Richard Birford (who had presented himself on the previous day) cordially enough. He sent Reade and Birford to Dublin but allowed the 66-year-old Barnewall to go home in order to make some preparations prior to his journey to the town.

Ormond, Sir Simon Harcourt, Sir Thomas Lucas and Sir Robert Farrar, having listened to the situational reports delivered by Barnewall, Reade and Birford and believing them to be true, now adjourned to evaluate the evolving military position. They were unanimous in the opinion not only that they should now proceed into Drogheda but also that they should, with whatever reserves the town could afford, immediately thereafter pursue the enemy north, advancing initially as far as Newry. Their collective military analysis was then dispatched post-haste to the lord justices in Dublin (Carte 1851, II, 190).

On 11 March Ormond rode into Drogheda at the head of the cavalry and was made 'very welcome' by a jubilant Sir Henry Tichborne and Lord Charles Moore (Pamphlet 13). He noted the weak defences of the town and was even more impressed at its defence (Carte 1851, II, 193). The main objective of the lord justices, to 'perhaps ... beat off the rebels' from *Tredagh* (HMC 1903, 86), had in fact been achieved with little or no effort on Ormond's part. A joint conference between Ormond, Harcourt, Lucas and Farrar and the town's commanders, Tichborne and Moore, came to the same conclusion as had been reached in Garristown: that the expanded army should march north without delay. Tichborne calculated that he could spare 1,000 foot and 100 horse (Carte 1851, II, 191). Ormond would thus be in a position to pursue O'Neill with 4,000 foot and 600 horse at his disposal. A letter signed by all six officers was immediately dispatched to Dublin, again urging the lord justices to approve the advocated advance northwards (*ibid.*, V, 300–1). As it happened, the lord justices' response to the first letter arrived that night while the military commanders were still gathered together in the town. Borlase and Parsons (the latter in particular, no doubt) absolutely forbade the army from storming towards Ulster and reiterated that the River Boyne was to be observed as the delimitation of its current manoeuvres. A rather disappointed Ormond returned on 12 March to Garristown, where he was joined by Lord Charles Lambert and Sir Richard Grenville, who arrived from Dublin. Another 'council of war' was convened, with Sir Simon Harcourt, Sir Thomas Lucas and Sir Robert Farrar again in attendance (*ibid*,, II, 196). Yet again the unanimous opinion of these professional soldiers was that there should be an advance made at least as far as Dundalk. A letter to this effect was accordingly signed by those officers present (and by Grenville as a postscript) and dispatched to Dublin (*ibid.*, V, 301–3). To alleviate the inactivity, the army moved eastward to Balrothery and burnt it (Pamphlet 13). Ormond had independent evaluations of the current fighting capabilities of the northern army presented to him by Tichborne and Lord Moore, but it was all to no avail. Against the advice of all their leading military experts, the lord justices refused to alter their original directive: the army was not to cross the River Boyne, never mind advancing on Ulster! Ormond concluded that there was no point in further argument; Borlase and Parsons were not for turning. The army therefore swung to the south and, leaving a garrison of 200 in Malahide, arrived back in Dublin on 17 March. They had spent eleven days in the field.

On 21 March Simon again wrote to Anne from Dublin. He thanked her for her recent correspondence and assured her that he availed of all opportunities to write home, 'for there's nothinge in this world I aime at or studdy more than thy content, and to be a comfort to thee; which to ye utmost of endeavours I shall expresse in all ye wayes yet it's possible, or may be in ye power of a loveinge husband [...]' (Harcourt 1880–1905, I, 154).

The lack of a potent lord deputy, and preferably one with a military background, was sorely felt at this point in the conflict. Simply put, the king's best interests were not being served. What was the logic in recalling a body of 3,500 men to a town suffering from hunger and sickness? Neither the town nor the army were under any direct threat. Surely it was preferable to let them go foraging in enemy territory than to add to the burden of hungry mouths back in Dublin? And what of the military potential? A successful push to Dundalk or Newry would have effectively put the Ulster army and its adherents on the defensive. An ensuing political accommodation with the Ulster Scots would probably have brought the insurgency in the north to an end. Many years ago, Thomas Carte's (1851, II, 198–9) analysis of the political machinations of Borlase and Parsons led him to the conclusion that their hidden agenda was to prevent a 'speedy suppression of the rebellion'. To support this evaluation of their motives one need look no further than the fate of the 66-year-old Patrick Barnewall, who had in the interim made his way to Dublin. In late March he was subjected to torture on the rack (Gilbert 1882–91, I, xxxiv). Sir John Reade had already suffered a similar fate on 22 March. It is possible that the harsh treatment of these prisoners, superficially employed to elicit information and confessions, may have been prompted by an ulterior motive. The subliminal message, if there were one, would have been explicitly clear to the leadership of the Old English: this is the fate that may well await you all. In the face of such malicious intransigence they had little option but to fight on. Any lingering doubt that remained as to the intentions of the lord justices was quickly dispelled when an overture to initiate a virtual end to the conflict arrived from the leading lords of the Pale (Gormanston, Slane and Nettirvill) (*ibid.*, 302). The letter, delivered to James Touchet, earl of Castlehaven, an English Catholic who had remained loyal, was duly passed on to the Dublin authorities (*ibid.*, 302–3). In their reply to Castlehaven he was severely admonished for having had any contact with the insurgents and for not placing the bearer of the lords' letter under arrest. There was no mention of the possibility of a speedy end to the war (*ibid.*, 303–4). Amongst the signatories to this letter from the privy council to the earl of Castlehaven, dated 24 March 1642, was Sir Simon Harcourt. It was to be his last official act in Dublin.

Perhaps in an attempt to placate or possibly alleviate the obvious frustration of the military, the lord justices did approve a proposal whereby the Drogheda reserves would be permitted to undertake a limited foray northward. Sir Henry Tichborne, with 800 foot, and Lord Charles Moore, accompanied by 'some horse' (HMC 1903, 100), moved against *Atherdee* (Ardee) in late March. Their progress was blocked by a party of insurgents consisting of 1,100 foot and 100 horse. These were quickly defeated and suffered significant losses. A number of the insurgents may have been drawn from the encampment at Greenmount, some five and a half miles east-north-east of Ardee (Leslie 1908, 20). Having taken Ardee, Tichborne and Moore found it in such a 'ruinous' state that they thought it more convenient to capture a 'strong castle' nearby and garrison it with 100 foot and some 40 or 50 horse (Carte 1851, II, 201). The castle in question may have been Roodstown (Leask 1941, 78, 107); it fits the description and lies about two and a half miles east-north-east of the town. The advance then proceeded onward towards Dundalk, which was defended by approximately 1,200 insurgents (HMC 1903, 100). After several hours of fighting it too was taken. Tichborne recorded in his 'Narrative of the Siege of Drogheda' that for months afterwards 'neither man nor beast' was to be found in the sixteen miles between the two towns of Drogheda and Dundalk (Leslie 1908, 30–1). When a request to Dublin for reinforcements to facilitate the garrisoning of the town was refused, they held on to the town regardless (Carte 1851, II, 201–2). In fact, it is reasonable to propound that the overall plan of action as devised by Ormond, Harcourt and their fellow officers at Garristown did have every chance of bringing the war in the north-east to a successful conclusion. The outright rejection of the plan by the lord justices on the implied reasoning of its being too hazardous was therefore logically a nonsensical decision and ultimately a totally unjustifiable one in military terms.

COUNTY KILDARE

The regiments of Sir Charles Coote and Colonel Lawrence Crawford had remained in barracks in Dublin during Ormond's expedition into north County Dublin. It was rumoured in the city that upon the return of Ormond's expeditionary force it would be the turn of Coote and Crawford to sally forth (Pamphlet 13). The perceived trajectory of the foray would lead them to *Leaslip* (Leixlip), *Kilkock* and on into County Kildare, with *the Queenes Countrey* (Laois) as the final destination. In reality, the manoeuvre against Maryborough (in Queen's County) was deferred until early April.

Inevitably, there were many minor manoeuvres and engagements that went unrecorded. As William Guy, coronet to Sir Richard Grenville, observed in a letter home to his brother, 'We are every day upon some march or service'. In the same dispatch, dated 10 March, he mentioned a skirmish at *Lunderston* between the insurgents and a Lieutenant Colonel Hurclifft. There is a Lunderstown, but it is to the south of Duleek in County Meath. One wonders whether he meant Luttrellstown, near Clonsilla, Co. Dublin. His regiment was garrisoned at Lyons in south County Dublin and was departing to march to Kildare town. Matters became more serious when word reached them of a major advance by the insurgents from *Caterlaff* (Carlow) led by 'Lord Dulon'. The identity of this individual is unclear, but it might have been James Butler, Lord Dunboyne, who had been active in the County Kilkenny area under the command of Richard Butler, Lord Mountgarrett (Clarke 1966, 197). Intelligence reports observed that the insurgents were advancing in the direction of *Woodstocke*. This would be the area of Woodstock Castle on the River Barrow to the immediate north of Athy, Co. Kildare (Map 6). The government forces encamped that Monday night at *Clanmor*, while the insurgents reached *Bolton*. Bolton Castle is located to the north of Castledermot. At 3 o'clock on the Tuesday morning orders arrived from Sir Simon Harcourt instructing Grenville to advance with haste to Kildare town.

The detachment of 1,300 foot and 180 horse set off immediately from their overnight camp. By 8 o'clock a fresh intelligence report had arrived, informing them that the insurgent army, now reportedly 6,000 (horse and foot combined) in strength, had also been on the move under the cover of darkness. Alarmed by the news, Grenville ordered his men to adopt defensive positions 'at a place of advantage' within a mile of the town. A dispatch received at 8.30 a.m. brought word of reinforcements in the form of two companies and two pieces of ordnance that were drawing near. These two contingents were led by Captain Thomas Paramour (of the lord lieutenant general's foot) and Sergeant-Major Berry. With confidence thus restored, the army marched into Kildare town. In the interim, the insurgent forces were entrenching at *Water Town*, 'four miles distant'. This would be Walterstown to the south of Kildare. Grenville decided to take the initiative and advanced out of the town. At 4 o'clock in the afternoon the enemy were sighted.

Captain John Marrowe and a troop of horse, accompanied by the company of foot commanded by Sergeant-Major Berry, led the first attack. Within half an hour of battle having commenced, a sudden deluge of rain rendered conditions very difficult. The insurgents thereupon withdrew into woodland close to *Water Town*. At 7 o'clock in the evening Berry's firelocks began to unleash a sustained fusillade into the body of the woods; his men were soon joined by the remainder of the army and before long the insurgents broke cover. The retreating force was hotly pursued in the direction of Woodstock, but the chase was abandoned at *Bernee*. This was most likely Nurney, given the trajectory. In the final brief skirmish, Grenville personally captured a kinsman of the 'Lord Dulon'. Amongst the other prisoners taken was a Lieutenant FitzJames. The booty from the baggage-train included 'three pieces of Iron Ordinance' and wagons of ammunition and weapons. More importantly from the ordinary soldiers' point of view, they had also captured 'seven wagons of Bread, Cheese, and Butter', with which, Guy reported, upon their return to Kildare they 'merrily cheer'd our bellies'. It is interesting to note that the baggage-train was also said to include '700. cattell, 3,000. sheep and about 200. swine'. Whatever about the numbers, this would indicate that the insurgent army drove its meat supplies along on the hoof.

It is unclear when the government forces returned to their quarters at Lyons. William Guy did not write his letter until the (following?) Monday. The sortie had been a complete success. According to Guy, besides the windfall of booty they had managed to inflict losses of about 1,000 on the enemy and to (on the word of FitzJames) badly wound the 'Lord Dulon' with a shot to the thigh. Their own fatality list totalled 97 in all, including an officer, Lieutenant Cannock. Other casualties were Captain Marrowe's quartermaster and, from Guy's own company, Will Parker and the company cutler (knife-maker and repairer). The coronet ended his letter on a personal note with a plea for news from his home in Bristol, and especially for word from his mother (Pamphlet 16).

Further payments had been sanctioned by the lord justices and council. On 2 March £50 was issued to Harcourt 'for the inferior officers of his regiment'. A further £8 10s. 8d. was paid out for the same purpose on 5 March (Mahaffy 1900–1, II, 782,

783). On 24 March Sir Simon, the nine captains and the junior officers of his regiment were awarded £80 19s. 3d. The privates of the regiment were granted £144 (*ibid.*, 785). Finally, on 26 March £42 6s. 6d. was allocated to Sergeant-Major Berry 'for the officers and men of the 400 firelocks' (*ibid.*, 787).

CARRICKMINES CASTLE

Early on the morning of Saturday 26 March 1642 Sir Simon Harcourt led a detachment of horse out through the gates of Dublin and headed south. Within a couple of hours he found himself at the perimeter of Carrickmines Castle.

There are several possibilities as regards the events that precipitated a siege at the castle. The *least* convincing argument is that Sir Simon and his troop of cavalrymen simply chanced upon the castle and spontaneously decided to launch an assault on it. Edmund Borlase (1680, 72), however, has proposed that it was simply restlessness that had spurred Harcourt to venture forth with his 'small party of men' towards County Wicklow, and that they had thus found the insurgents in strength in possession of *Carrickmain*. A stronger case could be built on the suggestion that it was the arrival of an intelligence report that had prompted the Dublin authorities to take immediate action (as it had in the case of Dean's Grange). In fact, there are two accounts that specifically attribute the sortie to the receiving of intelligence. The account by William Owen (Pamphlet 17) relates how the Dublin authorities had received word of a meeting of insurgents at *Careggmayne Castle* and thereupon dispatched Harcourt to deal with them. As noted previously, councils had been held at Carrickmines in the past (see Part 3). The second account (Pamphlet 18) is a little more informative in that it relates that the intelligence was received on the Friday night, that the insurgent muster consisted of 'some 3. or 400. Rebels' and that they had taken possession of the castle on that very day.

Interestingly, it is only in an official government document that the assertion is made that the assault on Carrickmines Castle was a premeditated event. In fact, the privy councillor Sir John Temple, in a personal letter to his brother (a pastor in Battersea in London), only goes so far as to state that Harcourt had intended 'only to view' (Pamphlet 19) the castle on that fateful morning. In contrast, the letter from the lord justices and council to the earl of Leicester, dated 31 March, outlines and suggests a far more deliberate sequence of events. It portrays Harcourt's expedition as a planned response to the occupation of 'several old castles' by the insurgents from County Wicklow, the attested plan being that if they were dislodged from one of these castles they would abandon the others. The account is somewhat self-contradictory in that it maintains that Harcourt was unprepared 'at finding that there were a number of rebels lodged [at Carrickmines]' (HMC 1903, 99). The absence of infantry—and particularly artillery—in his detachment is especially noteworthy. This omission would be exceptional for an officer of Harcourt's calibre, and particularly so in the light of his recent experience at Kilsallaghan Castle, where Ormond, Harcourt and Coote, despite winning the overall engagement decisively, had failed to take the castle owing, in Harcourt's own words (Pamphlet 19), to their 'having no pieces of Battery'. It seems almost inconceivable, then, that Sir Simon specifically set out to take Carrickmines Castle on that fateful morning. Furthermore, the very fact that it was a Saturday morning is relevant. If Carrickmines Castle was known to the Dublin authorities as, for example, 'a place as well by art as nature fortified' (Pamphlet 18), there was every possibility that the taking of the castle might have required more than one day. Fighting on a Sunday was generally unacceptable on religious grounds to many of the Dublin leadership. Harcourt's personal feelings on the subject were exemplified in the context of the encounter at Inishannon, Co. Cork, on 16 January (see above). There he had 'desired of God dispensation for breach of the Sabbath, and after some short prayers, and recommending ourselves unto God', had only then engaged the enemy (Pamphlets 1 and 3). The quoted report on the latter engagement was first-hand information written by Robert Pickering, Sir Simon's private secretary.

The conduct and design of the general campaign also argue against interpreting the attack on Carrickmines as a preconceived strategic operation. The sparse attention paid to the south County Dublin theatre by the Dublin administration throughout the December–March period is striking. Expeditions against Clontarf, Santry, Finglas and Swords were followed by a switch to the south-west and action at Rathcoole and Saggart, followed by Lyons, Newcastle and Naas. The clearance of the castles of Dundrum and Kilgobbin was a one-day affair. The battle at Dean's Grange on 12 February was a pre-emptive strike against a perceived threat prompted by an intelligence report. There was no follow-through in the south county area, and in fact the battle was book-ended by the encounters at Artane and Kilsallaghan, i.e. to the north and north-west of the city respectively. This 'neglect' of the south County Dublin theatre is demonstrated by the fact that following the arrival of the reinforcements led by Grenville and Monck on 20/21 February the main effort was again directed towards the north and north-west of the city, i.e. Kilsallaghan Castle, Garristown, *Tredagh* (Drogheda) and Balrothery. To emphasise the apparently spontaneous nature of the siege of Carrickmines Castle, it should be further noted that in the wake of the engagement the government forces immediately withdrew from this hard-fought-for prize. No damage to the castle would have been authorised by Lieutenant Colonel Richard Gibson had it been a preordained military objective. On the contrary, it would have been held and garrisoned. Finally, it must be significant that the major expeditionary force that marched forth a mere five days after the fall of Carrickmines headed straight for Rathcoole and then Naas before proceeding as far afield as Maryborough in Queen's County. In the short term, therefore, the capture of Carrickmines Castle was strategically meaningless. It is difficult to find any convincing arguments in favour of the thesis that Sir Simon Harcourt intended to launch an assault on Carrickmines Castle when he rode out with his detachment of cavalry early on the morning of Saturday 26 March 1642.

What exactly did happen, then, on that day which led to the siege of the castle? There are two principal scenarios worthy of consideration. One is that Harcourt had specifically ventured to Carrickmines with the sole purpose of reconnaissance but had been almost immediately drawn into a full-scale engagement. Alternatively, it could be proposed, based on a number of reports, that it was a chance encounter in the field with a body of insurgent horse that had initiated what rapidly escalated into a major confrontation at the castle.

According to the Revd Rodger Puttock, one of the most prominent ministers in the city of Dublin, writing in April 1642, a force of insurgents had advanced from the Wicklow Mountains towards the city on Friday 25 March. He reports that 'very early' on Saturday morning a troop of cavalry moved against them. The insurgents took flight and were pursued. He maintains that approximately 300 of the retreating party subsequently took refuge in 'the Castle of *Carrigmayne*' (Pamphlet 20). By 'nine of the clock' in the morning messengers had arrived in Dublin requesting 'two peeces of Ordnance, to batter the castle'. Puttock's account alludes to time-wasting and delay in dispatching the necessary reinforcements. He obliquely attributes the blame to one individual, the '*conctator maximus*', which might suggest Sir William Parsons, who was reportedly the more dominant of the two lord justices (Corish 1976, 292; Beckett 1966, 78). An assault on Saturday therefore proved impossible and the besieging force had to maintain their position until Sunday morning. The Revd Puttock laments that the unnecessary delay meant that the engagement had to be extended into 'the Lord's day'. A second account (Pamphlet 21) has Sir Simon Harcourt and his cavalry having a chance encounter on the morning of Saturday 26 March with a party of insurgents while riding through the south Dublin countryside 'toward the County of *Wicklowe*'. He gave pursuit and they took refuge in the 'Castle of *Kilgobbon*' (*sic*), whereupon a siege was laid 'that none should get forth'. He then sent a dispatch to Dublin for reinforcements. A third account details a chance encounter leading to the taking of 'a great Castle called *Carricke Mayne*' (Pamphlet 22). In this account, however, the government force was led by a Captain Scontes (or Scout?), whose troop was out on a foraging mission when they encountered 'a great party of the Rebels'. Pursuit was given so vigorously that the insurgents were obliged to take refuge in the castle. It is further erroneously maintained that Sir Simon and 'Captayne Berry' did not arrive until 'the 27. of March on the Kings day'.

Whether or not Harcourt encountered the insurgents in the field and whatever time he arrived at Carrickmines, why did he embark on the siege of a strong castle when all he had at his disposal was a detachment of horse? The castle and its occupants were obviously not going anywhere, and logic would have demanded that he return to Dublin and reappear on Monday morning augmented with infantry and, crucially, artillery. The answer would appear to be that he was in fact provoked into the assault. There are no fewer than three accounts of deliberate provocation on the part of the occupants of the castle. What form this incitement took is unclear; while the anonymous W.P. simply noted that 'the Rebels dared our men' (Pamphlet 22), Sir John Temple recorded that Harcourt was 'extremely provoked by the Rebels within' (Pamphlet 19). The most insightful account comes from Edmund Borlase (1680, 72), who wrote that 'they began to brave [i.e. defy] him from within, and to use reproachful signs from the top of the Castle, thereby to express their contempt and scorn of him. This his spirit was not well able to brook [...]'. It is important to note that the now-obsolete meaning of the word 'reproachful' was 'disgraceful', far more potent in meaning and connotation. Thus we can take it that the 'signs' were clearly of a very offensive nature. After all, as far back as Roman times the middle digit was referred to as the 'impudent' or 'obscene' finger (Morris 1977, 199).

The question of who exactly it was within the castle that goaded Harcourt into unpremeditated action remains unanswered. Nevertheless, there must be a strong likelihood that it was the possibly unexpected guests who had either arrived on Friday night or were pursued there by Harcourt on Saturday morning. The triumphal mockery might in fact make more sense in the context of the latter scenario. They, after all, were the only variable in the equation. Whilst the castle and possibly its inhabitants would still have been there on the following Monday (unless the Walshes had thought it expedient to temporarily abandon their home and their unmovable worldly goods), the insurgent horse would most likely have been long gone. Therefore Harcourt, if he was now determined to punish them for their insolence, could not even temporarily withdraw to the city and thereby allow them to escape.

Once Sir Simon had decided on a course of action, he would naturally have turned his attention to the necessary military requirements. Heavy guns, obviously, would have been top of the list, in addition to supporting infantry. A dispatch rider was sent with speed to Dublin while the temporary stalemate continued. The rider would have reached Dublin within two hours and the requested reinforcements, had they been immediately mustered, could have been in position by early afternoon. The most structured account of the subsequent supply and deployment of detachments was written on 2 April 1642 by William Owen (Pamphlet 17), who maintains that 800 foot did arrive at *Careggmayne Castle* in the afternoon. Approximately half of this complement would have consisted of Sgt-Major John Berry's firelocks, who had arrived in the recent past from England (Pamphlets 19 and 21). There is an outside possibility that Berry and his firelocks had not come from the city but rather from Grenville's quarters at Lyons, some sixteen miles along the foot of the Dublin–Wicklow Mountains to the west-north-west. They certainly would appear to have retired there in the very recent past in the wake of the fighting near Kildare town (see above). Harcourt, naturally, would have been aware of Berry's whereabouts and would have dispatched a messenger accordingly. The remaining 400 or so of the arriving foot very possibly consisted of from two to four companies of Sir Simon's own regiment, depending on whether or not Lieutenant Colonel Richard Gibson's company was amongst them. The strength of the horse was also augmented that afternoon and now stood at 250, but there was still no sign of the crucial ordnance. It can be stated with some certainty that the guns were not employed elsewhere and thus their non-arrival is initially puzzling, although it might be speculated that the consistently overcautious hand of Sir William Parsons is in evidence here. While the lord justices would have had little difficulty with Harcourt riding out with a troop of *c.* 120 horse, the situation that was now developing at Carrickmines would have caused them (on their previous record) to dither. The Revd Puttock's account (see above) would tend to confirm this explanation for the non-arrival of the artillery. It should, however, be observed that demi-culverins were cumbersome to move: up to sixteen oxen per gun could be required. Depending on the quality of the roads, progress could have been slow (Clinton *et al.* 2007, 198).

As dusk faded into night at Carrickmines, both sides would have had the opportunity to reflect on the events of the day. If there had been any casualties, they would probably have been on the government side and more than likely the result of the accuracy of a noted marksman in the castle. These possible losses, however, would not have exceeded more than one or two, given that the besiegers would quickly have removed themselves out of musket range. The bravado displayed by the insurgents in the morning would have long passed, as the reinforcements arrived and the siege cordon tightened. Harcourt was undoubtedly frustrated by the non-arrival of the ordnance, given that he had been waiting since early on the Saturday morning. None of the available accounts make any reference to the weather and thus we may infer that it was unremarkable and typical for that time of year. While the majority of the besiegers settled about their campfires, others remained deployed about the castle. Edmund Borlase noted that Harcourt 'took special care for the surrounding of the castle' to prevent any sallies and employed 200 firelocks in this service (Borlase 1680, 72). William Owen's report recounts that the tactic employed was to place a 'Musketteer between each Horse, and in that posture, stood all night' (Pamphlet 17). It is possible, therefore, that approximately 400 soldiers (infantry and cavalry combined) remained on active duty throughout the night.

The brightest fire burning that late March night may not have been in Harcourt's camp, for it is further reported by Owen that the insurgents 'made a fire upon the Battlements of the Castle' which (alarmingly for the besiegers) was 'answered by another fire from the Mountaine'. The fire on the battlements would naturally have been interpreted as a signal for help, and consequently a rider was dispatched to Dublin requesting an additional 400 foot. Given that Harcourt already had sufficient soldiers with which to assault the castle, it may be surmised that the final reinforcements sought were a precautionary measure against a counter-attack emanating from the Wicklow Mountains.

The stalemate of the preceding (almost) 24 hours was finally violently broken at dawn on the Sunday morning. Daybreak proved to be the signal for an attempted break-out from the castle. The combination of the deployed firelocks and cavalry proved, however, to be too robust and the attempt failed. One pro-government account acknowledged the efforts of one 'brave daring Fellow upon a White horse' who rode into the ranks of the besieging line and discharged his pistol (Pamphlet 22). Whether or not he broke through the line and escaped is not recorded. The break-out may have been thwarted but the price paid by the besieging force was a costly one. Lieutenant Richard Cooke of the firelocks was shot dead and his commanding officer, Sgt-Major John Berry, was badly wounded (Pamphlets 17, 21 and 22) by a musket-ball in his side. He was to die in Dublin city eight days later (Borlase 1680, 72).

The rest of the morning was spent 'in exchange of Shott' (Pamphlet 17). Eventually, at noon, the requested ordnance in the form of '2. Demy Culverings' finally arrived (Pamphlet 22). The delay may have been due to the dearth of draught horses. In a letter dated 4 March from the lord justices and council to the earl of Leicester (the lord lieutenant), it was reported that 'it is not possible to get draught horses here for drawing ordnance with the army'. Harcourt was amongst the signatories (HMC 1903, 87). It is also possible, as noted above, that draught oxen were employed as a substitute (Clinton *et al.* 2007, 198). It is not clear whether the cannons were accompanied by the final complement of 400 foot or whether these arrived separately. With his forces fully assembled, Harcourt was finally ready to launch an attack on Carrickmines Castle.

According to Sir John Temple, Harcourt's initial manoeuvre was to position his 'Musquetiers' within close firing range of the castle. Their instructions were to maintain an intense fusillade, particularly on the windows of the building. This they achieved with such efficiency that hardly 'any durst peep out to discharge upon them' (Pamphlet 19). Next on the agenda was the placing of the two demi-culverins or 'Great Peeces', as Borlase (1680, 72) termed them. John Hallowes noted that they were positioned 'within halfe a musket shot of the castle' (Pamphlet 23). More topographically interesting, however, are the specific details of Sir Simon's ordering his two cannons to be lodged in the immediate vicinity of—if, indeed, not within the walls of—a 'little thatched house' or 'Irish house' (Pamphlets 19 and 22). It was while he was at the back or, more likely, to the side of this building, overseeing the placing or 'levelling' of the guns, that Harcourt was hit 'with a shanker-bullet out of a long Peeice, which fell him to the ground' (Pamphlet 17). One source observed that he was operating 'within musket shot' of the castle (McNeill 1943, 155). While two sources maintain that he was hit in the left shoulder (Pamphlets 21 and 22), the consensus of the other descriptions is that the wound was made in the right side of the chest, just 'under his neck bone' (Borlase 1680, 73; Pamphlet 19). Temple's identification of the wound as being in the right chest area is of key importance, given that he visited the ailing Sir Simon on Monday 28 March.

The badly wounded Harcourt, unable to walk unaided, was assisted from the field by two comrades (Pamphlet 17) and brought 'into a little Cabine hard by' (Pamphlet 19). He insisted that the officers leave him and attend to their duties. Temple's account, largely based on a first-hand report that he had received from Harcourt's ensign, Lieutenant Robert Hammond, on the day before his time of writing, would suggest that Sir Simon remained lucid long enough to enquire about the progress the battery was making on the walls. On hearing that it was having little effect, he issued his final order that the besiegers should switch their main effort into the storming of the gates, a tactic that he had employed successfully in the taking of Inishannon Castle, Co. Cork.

The preceding account by Temple is indirectly corroborated by both Cole and W.P., who note, respectively, that '21. shot' and '22. shot' were discharged by the artillery with little or no effect on the walls of the castle (Pamphlets 21 and 22). More specifically, there are the additional descriptions of the ordnance having made 'little or no entrance' on the castle (Pamphlet 18) and of the soldiers becoming 'impatient of the Battery' (Pamphlet 17).

What happened next would appear to be quite clear. Captain Michael Woodhouse selected a group of men and, equipped with 'Hatchets and Timber' and/or 'Croes and Axes', they rushed up to and broke open 'the Bawne gate' (Pamphlets 22 and 18). Resistance persisted as the attackers, clearly in vengeful mood, approached 'the doore, and broke it downe' (Pamphlet 19). The party that broke down the door of the main building was led by Captain Woodhouse, Lieutenant Robert Hammond, Lieutenant Thomas Maritt of the ordnance and Captain Francis Congrave (who had been 'mentioned in dispatches' at the battle of Kilsallaghan) (Pamphlets 19 and 22). Hammond, as Harcourt's cousin, friend and ensign, and Maritt, a subordinate of Christopher Price, a 'Gentleman of the Ordnance' who had also fallen in battle, would appear to have been particularly enraged. The defenders, 'with great obstinacy and violence', continued to fire from 'the Garrets above, and from the Cellars below' (Pamphlet 19). According to Temple, there were only about '12. Musquetiers' present amongst the insurgent defenders of the castle. It has also been recorded that they were not equipped with 'moulds to cast Bullets in' and consequently were soon reduced to improvisation. In fact, the projectile that hit Harcourt was described as 'a slug of Leade' (Pamphlet 22). Considering these limitations, the defenders could be said to have performed in an exceptional manner.

Nevertheless, surrender quickly followed the forced entry into the main building. Captain Congrave thereupon 'called for the Master of the house' and was surprised when 'his Son appeared' in his stead. Congrave demanded that the notable marksman from the battlements be produced—that is, the man responsible for the grievous wounding of Sir Simon and others. The description given for this man—'the fellow in greene'—corresponds with the observation by Owen of the 'notable Marks-man' who was identifiable 'by his habit' (Pamphlets 19 and 17). Congrave's demand was initially refused by young Mr Walsh on the grounds of 'I know not whom you meane', but on being further threatened he complied. When young Walsh reappeared accompanied by the green-clad marksman, Captain Congrave produced a brace of pre-charged pistols and shot them both dead on the spot.

The execution of young Walsh and the 'man in green' signalled the start of a killing spree that was only to end with the deaths of all the occupants of Carrickmines Castle; neither 'man, woman, nor childe' was spared, such was the vehemence of the besiegers and their desire for retribution.

One description recounts the subsequent discovery of a priest hidden in 'an empty Pipe Caske' that had been sealed prior to the fall of the castle (Pamphlet 22). Mistaking the heavy pipe as being full of 'good Beare', the soldiers made a breach in its flank. When no liquid came out, they cut off 'the Hoopes' and discovered the priest. It is not impossible that this was either Fr Turlogh Reily or Friar Patrick Comin, whose presence at Carrickmines was recorded in Archbishop Bulkeley's report on the Dublin diocese in 1630 (Bulkeley 1869, 158; Ronan 1941, 82). The priest was immediately slain and allegedly dismembered 'as small as Flesh to the pot' (Pamphlet 22). The source for this information gains credibility given that the writer was a neighbour of the officer to whose house in the city Harcourt was finally brought.

There has been suggestion that an agreement was dishonoured during the course of the siege. Ball (1901, 202 fn. 1) wrote that 'it seems not improbable that there was some breach of faith on the part of the besiegers'. The pro-royalist tract 'An Aphorismical Discovery of Treasonable Faction', apparently written between 1652 and 1660 (Gilbert 1879–80, I, vii), relates how Sir Simon, impressed by the strength of resistance, 'caused a parley to be sounded', whereupon the occupants of the castle were offered 'a faire quarter' and to 'marche away armed'. When, however, an appointed emissary from the castle appeared before Harcourt he had him hanged (*ibid.*, 24). This is an interesting interjection, the parley, offer of quarter and honourable departure being typical of the many sieges in which Harcourt had taken part in the Low Countries; the hanging of the emissary would not make sense. Clarendon (1720, 343) attributed the bad faith to Lieutenant Colonel Richard Gibson, accusing him of having granted quarter but subsequently putting all within the castle to the sword. On the other hand, in the account by John Hallowes (Pamphlet 23) it is alleged that it was the insurgents who had acted in bad faith. He claims that once the ordnance had commenced firing the insurgents immediately requested quarter, but 'as a Gentleman was going to receive the Castle from them, he was shot'. In this context it is relevant to recall, as noted above, that Mr Christopher Price, a 'Gentleman of the Ordnance', was slain 'at the assalte of the Castle of Carrigmayne' (Roberts 1647, 225). It may also be recalled that it was one of Price's gunner's mates, Thomas Maritt, who had reportedly been to the forefront of the furious assault on the castle door. Clarendon further asserted that a Colonel Washington had endeavoured to save a 'child of seven years of age' from the onslaught but had failed, 'which was a principal Motive of his quitting that Service' soon afterwards (Clarendon 1720, 343). The only soldier of that surname on record is a Captain Henry Washington of the lord lieutenant general's regiment (HMC 1895, 128, 139). He had arrived in Ireland with Lieutenant Colonel George Monck and the regiment on 20 or 21 February 1642 (see above). His movements are generally traceable during the relevant period; for example, he was in Dublin city on 3 May (*ibid.*, 132), at *Leslepp* (Leixlip) in August (*ibid.*, 136) and back in Dublin (mustered on Oxmontowne Green) on 29 November (*ibid.*). Again, he was garrisoned in Dublin on 18 January 1643 (*ibid.*, 142). It can thus be established that he did not quit the service. As there are no other sources that place Washington at Carrickmines, his presence there is by no means certain. If Clarendon erred in relation to Washington, his damning charge against Gibson would need to be treated with caution.

Apart from the (aforementioned) fantastical account of the engagement at Carrickmines entitled 'An Aphorismical Discovery' (Gilbert 1879–80, I, 24–5), there is one other pro-insurgent written version of what transpired on that weekend in late March 1642. Walter O'Byrne of Newrath, an insurgent who was active in the area, informed John Joyce, the vice-constable of the Black Castle of Wicklow, of the fall of

Carrickmines Castle. In a letter dated 8 April he informed Joyce that the taking of the castle by the English had resulted in the deaths of '14 men that were wardes [i.e. garrisoned soldiers] there […] many women children' (1641 Depositions, TCD MS 811, fol. 149v). This information may well represent the most accurate account of the exact number of military fatalities on the side of the defenders/occupants of the castle. Significantly, the figure tallies very closely with the number advanced by Temple (see above). It is the non-combatant figures that are difficult to quantify. There is a marked consistency in the records of the opposing side. In fact, there are no fewer than seven sources that quantify the fatalities as being in the region of 200–350. At the top of the scale it was advanced that 'six hundred' were 'put to the sword' (HMC 1900, 151). It should be noted that according to the 'Aphorismical Discovery' tract the total number of deaths in the castle was two (*ibid.*, 25), which is patently ridiculous. Nevertheless, the broadly accepted figures are problematical. The individuals within the castle would have fallen into three categories: the inhabitants, local refugees and the sheltering insurgents. Given the sudden appearance of Harcourt's cavalry and the immediate setting of the siege, it is unlikely that significant numbers of refugees from the area could have gained late access. The relative stability of the general area in the months preceding the siege would also have militated against a large influx of local civilians. It thus remains impossible to either quantify or identify the true number of civilians present. While some notable figures are known to have visited the castle in late December, such as Edmund O'Byrne of Tinnapark, Co. Wicklow, and John Fagan of Feltrim in north County Dublin, there is no evidence available that places them there at the time of the siege (1641 Depositions, TCD MS 810, fol. 199). Edmund O'Byrne was married to Rose Walsh of the Killincarrig Castle branch of the family in County Wicklow (Genealogical Office MS 69, 69). The mother of Theobald Walsh of Carrickmines was the daughter of John Eustace of Confey and his wife Maria Fagan, formerly of Feltrim. Besides their distant relationship, there are firm indications that Theobald and John Fagan were good friends. There is no evidence, however, to suggest that either man was present.

One of the most notable aspects of the siege was the absence of Theobald, the master of the house. The identification of the young Mr Walsh who had appeared before Captain Francis Congrave in his father's stead is unresolved. The eldest son of Theobald and his wife Maria, according to Hussey Walsh's (1900–1, 219) family history, was Richard. Richard Walsh 'of *Carrigmaine*' was still alive in 1666 (E. Edwards 2005, xliii) and therefore clearly was not present during the siege. In fact, in a late petition he states that he was away at school (Carte MS 154, fols 54–5). In the list of Walshes attainted in '1642', however, we find Theobald and John of Carrickmines (D'Alton 1860, II, 215). John Walsh of *Carrigmayne* was 'outlawed' at Kilmainham on 18 November 1643 (Simington and MacLellan 1966, 345). The 'outlawing' of deceased individuals was not unknown, as information was scant and varying in accuracy. As Theobald had no brother named John, it is not impossible that this John Walsh was a younger brother of Richard and was the one who died at the fall of the castle. Another unresolved question is whether Theobald's wife Maria was still living at Old Court, as she apparently had been (see above). Theobald had two unmarried sisters, Mary and Anne. Again, the odds are that they died that day.

In the account of the anonymous W.P., a writer who, as stated above, had a first-hand source of information, there is a reference to a 'Welch woman' dying of her wounds (Pamphlet 22). It is further qualified that she was a sister to one of the insurgents who had taken refuge in the castle early on Saturday morning and that she had acted as 'a servant in Master Welch his house'. Her exact identity is unknown.

The non-Walsh family casualty list included the (aforementioned) noted marksman, 'the man in green', who unfortunately otherwise remains nameless. Reputedly there was also the priest, tentatively identified as either Fr Reily or Friar Comin. There is one more potentially nameable victim: Hugh Murphy, who had acted as 'cook and servant' to Theobald (1641 Depositions, TCD MS 810, fol. 67b). The key question, of course, is whether he had departed with Theobald or remained at home. There is evidence to suggest that he may have survived (see Part 3).

The final act in the fall of Carrickmines Castle was the destruction of the principal building. It is not known whether this happened in the immediate wake of the executions, later in the day or, indeed, on the following morning. The building would first have been thoroughly searched and undoubtedly looted. The extent of the destruction is unknown. Two accounts record that the castle was 'blown up with powder' (HMC 1903, 100; Pamphlet 21); a further two reports record that it was 'blown up' (Pamphlets 17 and 19). The remaining supplies of powder from the artillery probably provided the necessary material. The evidence would seem to suggest that the shell of the building remained standing for a considerable time afterwards. The Civil Survey of 1654–6 described the premises as containing 'the Walles of a Castle, an Orchard, and garden plot [and] a Bawne' (Simington 1931–61, VII, 270), which is practically identical to A Survey of Rathdown, carried out in 1654 on the order of Charles Fleetwood, the lord deputy (Lodge 1772, II, 551), in which 'the wall' of a castle was the term employed. The terrier (i.e. the written record) accompanying the relevant mid-seventeenth-century Down Survey map noted the presence of 'only the Walls of a Fayre Stone House'. The cartographical evidence corroborates the suggestion that there were standing remains, given that the Down Survey map indicates a fanciful winged structure at Carrickmines (Map 13; Pl. 41), while a bracket-shaped building was denoted on John Rocque's map of 1760 (Bowen 1947–8, 118) (Map 4). Judging by the former illustration, if it is taken as representative, by the mid-seventeenth century the castle at Carrickmines had been supplanted by a fortified dwelling. By April 1781, however, when Austin Cooper visited Carrickmines, the built elements of the structure had been reduced to the fragment that stands to this day (Pl. 42). The site was by then occupied by 'a Farmer's House, with a few Cabbins' (Price 1942, 59). The medieval drystone-built revetment that delineated a rectangular enclosure was identified by the Ordnance Survey cartographers in the early 1800s (Map 1), while the presence of the earlier moated or ringwork-like earthen enclosure was determined by Patrick Healy in the early 1980s (Healy 1983, 2) (Map 2). There is no reason to believe that either of these two sizeable enclosures were part of the seventeenth-century

Map 13—The Down Survey map of the parish of Tully (1650s).

Pl. 41—Theobald Walsh's 'Mansion House at Carrickmayne', as represented on the 1650s Down Survey map. (Painted representation by Ruth Clinton)

Pl. 42—Standing remnant of Carrickmines Castle, featuring a north-facing splayed embrasure. (Photo: Mark Clinton)

defences at Carrickmines. Given their overall dimensions, it would have required a serious deployment of armed personnel to defend either enclosure, never mind both. There is absolutely no evidence to support the presence of such a sizeable garrison.

It is unclear when the government forces withdrew to Dublin. One thing that is certain is that they did not establish an outpost, and thus the area would have reverted into the control of the insurgents. It is almost beyond doubt, therefore, that Lieutenant Colonel Richard Gibson had led the forces back to Dublin by Monday evening at the latest. The regiment returned to the area on 30 April, when they raided Bullock and Bray, 'killed some, and brought into the City eighteen Rogues, who are committed to Prison' (Pamphlet 37).

It is known that the bodies of Lieutenant Richard Cooke and Mr Christopher Price of the ordnance were brought back to the city. Price was afterwards interred in St Patrick's Cathedral. He was the eldest son and heir of Captain Samuel Price from County Longford and had recently married (Roberts 1647, 225). On 28 March, £8 8s. had been credited to him; the money was collected by his father (Mahaffy 1900–1, II, 788). Cooke was buried in St Michan's Church with full military honours on 29 March (Ball 1901, 202 fn. 5). The register of the church, containing any additional information, was burnt (P. Parfrey, parish administrator, pers. comm.) in the destruction of the records stored in the Four Courts in 1922. Sgt-Major John Berry died of his wounds in Dublin city, having lingered on in a fever for eight days (Borlase 1680, 72). His place of interment is unknown. Of the rank and file, it was recorded that Gibson's,

Pl. 43—Tully Church, Co. Dublin (*Tulach na nEaspag*, 'The hill of the bishops'), an early medieval foundation. The foundations of an early nave survive, along with a thirteenth-century chancel arch. The graveyard was the traditional burial ground of the Walshes of Carrickmines. (Chris Corlett)

Woodhouse's and Vane's companies lost one soldier apiece and that Berry's firelocks lost two men. Half a dozen men were wounded (HMC 1895, 131). It is not known what happened to the bodies of the fatalities, but it might be speculated that they were brought back to Dublin and given a Christian burial in some unmarked plot.

Given that the area surrounding Carrickmines Castle would have been clear of government forces within a day or two of its destruction, it is inconceivable that its ruins were not visited by all concerned parties, not to mention the curious. It is highly unlikely that the remains of the deceased members of the Walsh family were left to wither amongst the rubble and debris, given the number of kith and kin that they had in the general area. Shanganagh Castle, another Walsh holding, for example, was only three miles away. The husband of Theobald's sister Elinor was the son of a Shanganagh Walsh. John Walsh of Shanganagh was described as an 'Irish Rebel', even though the same document noted that he had died 'half a year before the rebellion' (Lodge 1772, 559)! Other centres of active compassion would have been found at Balally (residence of James Walsh, who lived until 1648), which lay less than three miles to the north-west, and at Corke (immediately north of Bray), which was also a Walsh holding at the beginning of the insurgency and no more than four to four and a half miles away. One must, of course, also believe that Theobald would have returned to Carrickmines at the earliest opportunity—a forlorn pilgrimage to his now-destroyed home, the place of his birth and the root of his heritage. One can only imagine the horror that awaited him. It is almost certain, therefore, that the slain members of the Walsh family were later interred in the ancestral family plot at Tully Church (Pl. 43). Many of the household staff and estate workers would probably have been from local families and thus their remains would also have been removed for formal burial. It is equally likely that some (at least) of the insurgents who took refuge in the castle were strangers to the place. Given the scale of casualties, many of these would have had to be given very perfunctory burial. It is thus not surprising that the majority of the human remains uncovered during the excavations at Carrickmines had been deposited in crude shallow pits (Pl. 44). Two multiple burials contained the remains of a minimum of eighteen individuals. Strikingly, the deceased, where sex could be determined, were mostly female, some very young (Fibiger 2003). Identified wounds had largely been inflicted from behind. The victims, therefore, were apparently being pursued or were in a prone position. The discovery of twelve silver coins (three shillings and nine sixpences) in one of the mass graves would indicate that the bodies were clothed when interred and that at least one of the individuals had the coins hidden upon his or her person (Pls 45 and 46). The fact that the bodies were not stripped would indicate the extremely bloodied condition of the clothes (Clinton *et al.* 2007; 2013).

While the fighting had still been raging on the previous Sunday afternoon, it was decided to transport the gravely wounded Sir Simon back to Dublin city. He was laid out on a cart and the torturous journey began. The jolting of the cart proved to be

Pl. 44 (opposite)—A mass burial dating from 1642 at Carrickmines Castle. (Photo: Mark Clinton)

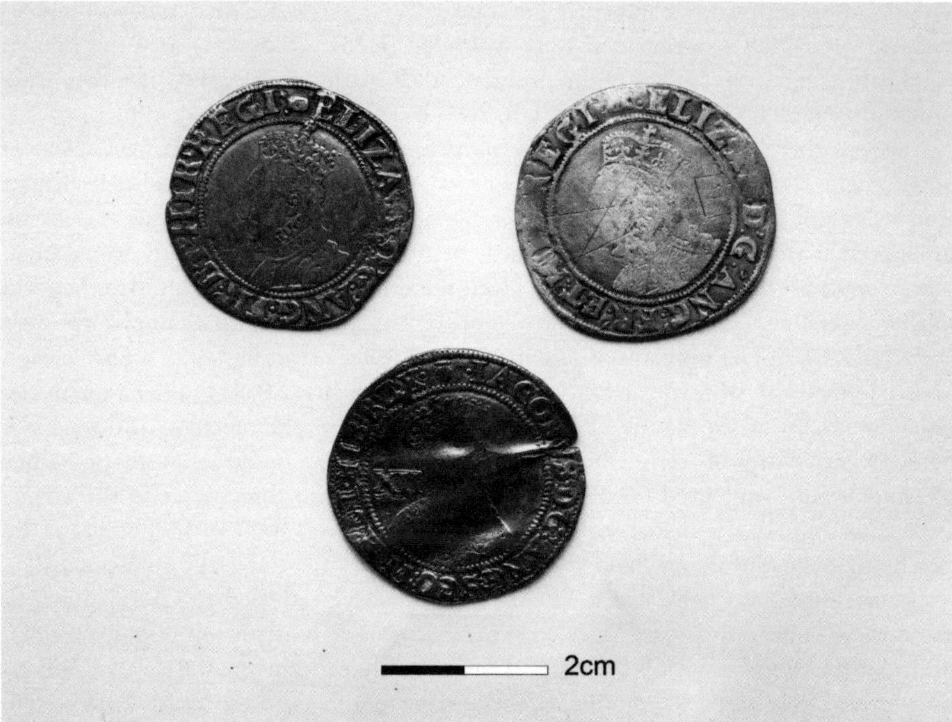
2cm

2cm

Pl. 45 (left)—Three silver shillings recovered from a 1642 mass grave at Carrickmines, obverse (top) and reverse (bottom).

Top row: two coins of Elizabethan date. The obverse of both coins features a crowned bust facing left and bears the inscription: ELIZAB[ETH] D.G. ANG', FR', ET HIB REGI[NA] ('Elizabeth, by the Grace of God, Queen of England, France, and Ireland'). One of the coins has 'Z E' scratched into its surface, possibly somebody's initials. The reverse of both coins features the royal coat of arms (quartered three lions and three fleur-de-lis) over a long cross fourchée and bears the inscription: POSUI DEU'. ADIUTORE[M] MEU[M] ('I have made God my helper').

Bottom row: one coin of Jacobean date. Obverse: crowned bust facing right, with a value of XII stamped to the left of the portrait. Inscription: IACOBUS. D.G. ANG. SCO. FRA. ET HIB. REX ('James, by the Grace of God, King of England, Scotland, France and Ireland'). Reverse: shield (centred), divided into four sections—at the top left and lower right (quartered) are the three lions of England and the three fleur-de-lis of France; at the top right is the Welsh dragon and at the bottom right the Irish harp. Inscription: EXURGAT. DEUS. DISSIPENTUR. INIMICI ('Let God arise and His enemies be scattered'). A thistle mint-mark indicates a 'first coinage' date, i.e. 1603/4. (Photo: Sara Nylund)

Pl. 46—Five silver sixpences recovered from a mass grave at Carrickmines.
A total of nine sixpences were recovered, their condition varying from good to very poor. The obverse of all the coins (where apparent) features a crowned bust facing left and bears the inscription: ELIZABETH D.G. ANG' FR' ET HI[B]' REGINA ('Elizabeth by the Grace of God Queen of England, France, and Ireland'). At least four of the coins feature a rose behind the head. The reverse of all the coins (where apparent) features the royal coat of arms (quartered three lions and three fleur-de-lis) over a long cross fourchée and bears the inscription: POSUI DEU. ADIUTORE M: MEU. ('I have made God my helper'). On five of the coins there is a date above the shield—1571, 1574, 1582, 1585 and 1593. (Photo: Mark Clinton)

impossible to bear, however, and it was decided to stop at Lord Fitzwilliam's castle at Merrion. It was there that Sir John Temple visited him on the following day. He found him in a very poor condition, 'his spirits so spent, as he was able to say little to me'. Sir Simon had in fact 'passed the night in most extreame paine' (Pamphlet 19). He had managed nonetheless to reiterate his initial request that 'all he had' should go to his wife Anne and 'left his children to be provided for at her discretion'. His initial words on the matter had been uttered to his fellow officers on being struck down at Carrickmines. He again sought God's favour on his soul. Within a few hours of Temple's return to the city word arrived of Sir Simon's death.

Apparently, the initial plan was to have the body embalmed and transported to his home in 'Staffordshire' (Pamphlet 22), but owing to a lack of the necessary aromatic drugs it was decided that he was to be buried in Christ Church Cathedral (Finlayson 1878, 74). A full-scale military funeral followed. In a letter from Thomas Richard to his cousin in London, it was related that 'Sir Simon Harcourt was honourably interred, here in this Towne, by the Lord Generall, and all the Chevalry: the solemnity being ended with 3000 shot in three vollies, besides Ordnance' (Pamphlet 24). In the south corridor of the former Harcourt residence at Nuneham House in England there hung a portrait of Sir Simon Harcourt. Beneath it the inscription read:

> 'Holland first prov'd his valour,
> Scotland stood his trembling
> And Ireland drank his blood'.

THE EPILOGUE

Theobald Walsh died in Spain sometime before May 1664. He had served there as a captain under the command of Sir Walter Dungan (Carte MS 154, fols 54–5). In the wake of the war in Ireland over 30,000 of the men under arms had departed to the Continent (Clarke 2011, 173).

Sir Walter Dungan, armed with letters of recommendation from the king, had presented himself to the marquess of Ormond in 1645. Given the prevailing 'cessation', there was little employment then available. Ormond, however, did find him a position with Thomas Preston, who was then engaged in reducing pockets of resistance in, for example, Roscommon (Carte 1736, II, 285).

According to a petition submitted by Theobald's son Richard, prior to his departure Theobald had been 'plundered and robbed' by 'Owen Roes party', the depredation having taken place during a cessation of hostilities negotiated by Ormond (Carte MS 154). Given the desolation at Carrickmines, it is more than likely that Theobald was residing at his castle in Oldcourt during this time (Pl. 26). The period of the depredation is impossible to determine definitively, given that Ormond negotiated a 'cessation' and two peace agreements in the 1640s. All these moratoriums were basically motivated and driven by the king's more pressing interests and needs in England. Charles accordingly initially commissioned Ormond on 23 April 1643 to treat with the Irish parties (Gilbert 1882–91, II, 267). The articles of cessation were finally concluded on 15 September at Sigginstown, Co. Kildare (*ibid.*, 365).

On 18 November the marquess of Ormond was handed the sword of state, marking his appointment as lord lieutenant of Ireland (Mahaffy 1900–1, II, 387). Simultaneously, bail was granted to Sir William Parsons, Sir John Temple, Sir Adam Loftus and Sir Robert Meredith of the privy council (*ibid.*, 388), all four of whom had been imprisoned to facilitate the negotiation of the cessation of hostilities. The first treaty negotiated by Ormond was concluded in March 1646 and the second in January 1649 (Beckett 1966, 97, 100; Arnold 1993, 28).

The raid on Theobald's property may have occurred in late 1646. Giovanni

Battista Rinuccini, archbishop of Fermo and papal nuncio to Ireland, had managed to persuade Thomas Preston, the general of the Catholic forces in Leinster, to abandon the first treaty and join his counterpart from Ulster, Owen Roe O'Neill, in an attack on Dublin. Preston had returned from the Continent in September 1642, while O'Neill had preceded him in late July (Clarke 2011, 172). Both of these men had almost 40 years of military experience in the service of Spain (Corish 1976, 296). Their combined forces were lodged about Lucan by late October of that year. It was already known that O'Neill was not averse to letting his men 'help themselves' whilst on campaign. The excesses that they had inflicted on counties Westmeath and Longford while 'refreshing' themselves in the wake of their victory on 5 June at Benburb had infuriated Preston, a large proportion of whose forces were drawn from that region (Gilbert 1882–91, V, 32). It is known that 'the undisciplined conduct of the Ulster army' was an embarrassment to their self-proclaimed patron Rinuccini (Beckett 1966, 99). In a letter sent by Preston to the mayor of Kilkenny, dispatched from Lucan on 24 November, he explained that when they pitched camp about Lucan they had brought only sufficient supplies for one week but were based there for five. He reported that consequently the surrounding countryside had been 'all plundered by the Ulster armye within twenty myles of this place' (Gilbert 1882–91, VI, 163). Theobald's property at Oldcourt, which lay within this radius, may thus have been ransacked and looted at that time. The planned attack on Dublin ultimately failed to materialise owing to the mistrust and long-standing mutual dislike between the commanders. Sir Walter Dungan, while serving under Preston, was still answering to the lord lieutenant. He was credited as having influenced Preston to reach an accommodation with Ormond (Carte 1736, II, 285). Nevertheless, on 19 June 1647, frustrated by Rinuccini's machinations, Ormond surrendered Dublin to Michael Jones and the parliamentarian forces (Cunningham 2018, 85). When the marquess departed in July he instructed Dungan and his serving relatives to remain active and quietly loyal. Upon his return in late September 1648 he was joined by a regiment of horse commanded by Sir Walter. Dungan was wounded in action and taken prisoner. Upon release he was appointed commissary-general of the horse. In the wake of the final collapse of the royalist cause he transported himself and his men to Spain (*ibid.*).

In the aftermath of his dismissal and imprisonment by Ormond on the instructions of the king, Sir William Parsons made his way to London, but on his arrival in December 1646 he was decidedly disappointed by the indifferent reception he received. He did, however, secure a pension of £500 *per annum* and was to participate in matters concerning Ireland. He was buried on 2 March 1650 'with all due honour' in St Margaret's in Westminster (*ODNB*, XLII, 943). Sir John Borlase ended up in London by the summer of 1645. He, too, was to be engaged in advising parliament on Irish affairs. Towards the end of his life he was financially embarrassed. In March 1648 his wife had to approach parliament to pay for the cost of his funeral (*ODNB*, VI, 662). Back in May 1642, in the course of an engagement at Trim, Co. Meath, Sir Charles Coote had been hit by a stray round. The fatal shot had apparently been fired by one of his own lieutenants (Forkan 2007, 213; Tait 2007, 141). It is reasonable to suggest that had he still been alive, and given his recent elevation to the privy council, Harcourt at that point would have finally secured the promised governorship of Dublin.

The petition submitted by Richard Walsh was lodged by June 1666 at the latest. The document lists his late father's holdings prior to the conflict: 'the Townes and Lands of *Carrigmaine*, *Ballinroe*, *Glanemuck*, *Ticknick*, *Fromstowne*, and *Kilbabog als Anadan* in the County of Dublin and *Ould Court* in the County of *Wicklowe*'. The lands of Carrickmines (Great and Little), Glenamuck (North and South) and Ticknick form a contiguous block. Kilbogget is separated from this block by Brenanstown (formerly a Walsh holding) and lies to the east. Phrompstown lies to the south, towards County Wicklow. Oldcourt is located to the immediate south of Bray.

Allowances must be made for the expansion and contraction of these lands over the years. According to the Civil Survey conducted in the 1650s, Theobald had been in possession of 466 acres in *Carrickmayne*, 100 acres in *Glanmucke* and 36 acres in *Prompstone* (Simington 1931–61, VII, 270, 271, 278). The contemporary Down Survey parish map of Tully credits him with 844 acres of 'Meddowe, Pasture, Arable and Rock Furzy Mountaine' in *Carrickmaine* and *Glanmuck*. The parish map of *Connough* credits him with a further 100 acres and three roods of arable and pasture lands in *Prompstown*. The Down Survey map featuring *Oldcourt* indicated that it contained 241 acres. The only reference to *Kilbegog* in the Civil Survey was to 55 acres formerly in the possession of Henry Rochford, the tithes belonging to Christ Church (*ibid.*, 278). Arnold (1993, 114, 154) credited Theobald with an estate of either 'nearly' 900 acres or 944 acres based on the data available in the Dublin volume of the Quit Rent set of Books of Survey and Distribution. The modern acreage of these lands as recorded in the census of 1851 was: Carrickmines (Great and Little), 670 statute acres, three roods and sixteen perches; Glenamuck (North and South), 371 statute acres, two roods and two perches; and Phrompstown, 199 statute acres, one rood and fifteen perches. Oldcourt contained 316 statute acres and 26 perches, while Kilbogget contained 331 statute acres, three roods and 33 perches. Ticknick was credited with 204 acres and 38 perches. This makes a grand total of 2,094 statute acres and ten perches (one Irish or Plantation acre = 1.62 statute acres).

The fact that Richard Walsh described *Kilbagog* as '*als Anadan*' is significant. *Annodan* was part of the original grant to Henry fitz Adam Walsh at the beginning of the fifteenth century (D'Alton 1838, 836) and its exact location is otherwise undocumented. As noted above, amongst the properties forfeited in the late 1650s was Henry Rochford's land in *Kilbegog*. In *Leabhar Branach* (the Book of the O'Byrnes) a poem dedicated to 'Aodh mac Seaáin of the Gabhal Raghnaill' branch of the family contains the line '*Corcach is Cill Beagóige*' (Mac Airt 1944, 71). The modern manifestation of the former is Cork (Great and Little). Price (1940, 130–1) observed that Kilbogget should be correctly written Kilbegog. There is also the intriguing 1598 reference to 'Walshe of *Kilbegan*' amongst the 'men of name' in County Dublin (Hogan 1878, 38).

The restoration of the monarchy in 1660 naturally aroused the hopes of both the old and the new landholders in Ireland. The old order, given their consistent loyalty to the Crown, and the new Cromwellian wave of settlers, considering their *de facto* possession and firm support in the English parliament, all harboured inflated expectations. Inevitably, the only result could be a collective disappointment. The supply of land simply did not match the demand. As the duke of Ormonde, in an often quoted remark, exclaimed: '[...] there must be new discoveries made of a new Ireland, for the old will not serve to satisfy these engagements. It remains then to determine, which party must suffer in the default of means to satisfy all; or whether both must be proportionately losers' (Carte 1736, II, 240).

An Act of Settlement, passed in May 1662, represented an attempt to square the circle. Under its terms a Court of Claims was established, which opened its hearings on 13 January 1663 (Arnold 1993, 53). It was abolished on 4 January 1666, when a second Court of Claims opened its procedures (*ibid.*, 97), but before its closure it was to hear hundreds of cases. The result was that 566 Catholic and 141 Protestant claimants argued their cases successively (Foster 1988, 115). Thousands of other individuals were now excluded, not least amongst the native Irish. Unsurprisingly, confusion and conflict abounded. In response, an Act of Explanation was finally passed in December 1665 (Arnold 1993, 91), a critical aspect of which would be the taking of one third of their holdings from large numbers of the new settlers. This land would be used to accommodate others dislodged by the successful claimants who were found 'innocent' before the Court of Claims. It was still not enough to satisfy the requirement. No more, however, would be done. Catholic landowners had effectively been reduced from possessing three fifths of the land in Ireland prior to the conflict to occupying one fifth in its wake (Beckett 1966, 120–1; Simms 2011, 177). In County Dublin, however, the Catholic landowners regained possession of nearly two thirds of their former holdings, a percentage clearly not realised anywhere else (Arnold 1993, 141).

Richard Walsh had applied to the Court of Claims on 14 May 1664. As no decision seemed forthcoming and he was 'disabled' 'by his poverty', he had repaired to England (Carte MS 154). Richard would therefore not appear to have received any succour from his cousins. This is curious, as not all branches of the family had fallen on such hard times as their Carrickmines brethren.

James Walsh of Balally was listed amongst the 'Old English Catholic Proprietors' of 1641. D'Alton (1838, 792–3) noted that after 1641 'Walsh of Ballyawly forfeited Edmondstown', the just over 112 acres being subsequently granted to Gerald Archbold, Sir Henry Talbot and John Borr. James was credited with an estate of 552 acres by Arnold (1993, 154). He died in 1648, having mortgaged the property to Henry Warren (Lodge 1772, 536; Simington 1931–61, VII, 260). James's son, Henry, soon afterwards sold the estate for £700 to John Borr of Dublin (Ball 1902–17, II, 74), the son of a naturalised Dutchman who had become a highly successful merchant (Arnold 1993, 55).

On the list of 'Old English Catholic Proprietors' in 1641 we find a John Walsh holding 400 acres and a James Walsh of Old Connaught holding 697 acres (Arnold

1993, 154). This entry probably represents the Shanganagh estate. The 697 figure tallies precisely with the acreage given for John Walsh in the 1663–9 period (*ibid.*,158). The lands of Shanganagh were restored to John Walsh by the commissioners of settlement (Ball 1902–17, III, 89). In the decree issued in response to John's petition he was declared to be 'an innocent Protestant' (Arnold 1993, 60). He was one of only half a dozen claimants to be fully restored to their estates in County Dublin (*ibid.*, 110). John was only a youth but he had influential connections. His great-grandfather was Sir Robert Kennedy and his great-uncle Sir Richard Kennedy. Sir Robert served as chief remembrancer of the exchequer and as member of parliament for the borough of Kildare. He was created a baronet after the Restoration (Ball 1902–17, IV, 78). It was Sir Robert who represented the 'claimant', submitting his pedigree as 'John Walsh, son of Edward, son of John', the former 'proprietor' (*DKR 19* (1887), 64). Sir Richard enjoyed a successful fifteen-year innings at the Irish bar before being appointed a baron of the Irish exchequer (Ball 1902–17, IV, 79; 1926, I, 268). When John died on 7 May 1671 he was in possession of the Shanganagh estate, in addition to *Killturke*, *Connagh*, Cork and *Little bray*. These lands were held directly from the king by military service. Given the short time-span until his death and the fact that he fathered a child, it is apparent that John was close to his majority at the time of the Restoration. John's son and heir, Edward (Hardiman 1826–9, I, No. 2), died without issue. His brother John accordingly inherited the estates. He was married to Jane Forde of Coolgreany, Co. Wexford (Burke 1835–8, IV, 190). John Walsh of *Shagnogh* was on a list of Catholics licensed to carry arms on 30 March 1705. He was permitted to own a sword, a case of pistols and a gun (HMC 1895, 477). It was in John's time, *c.* 1712–13, that a private act was passed by the Irish parliament enabling the sale of the Shanganagh and Cork or *Corcagh* 'parcels' to pay off his debts (D'Alton 1860, II, 216).

Edward Walsh, the son of Edward senior, 'late of *Clonmayning*' (i.e. Clonmannan), had been listed for transplantation but 'refused to go'. No action was taken against him. The Walsh holding had, in the interim, been acquired by a Dr Yarner (*DKR 19* (1887), 36). The lands forfeited in County Wicklow had been set aside for the benefit of the '49 Officers, i.e. those military men who had served in Ireland prior to 5 June 1649. Dr Abraham Yarner, a 'chirurgeon' (surgeon), was one of these officers and had accordingly been granted lands in Wicklow in 1658 during the Commonwealth (Price 1951, 106). He obtained 800 acres in the Newcastle area (Arnold 1993, 144). On 13 April 1659 he successfully petitioned to retain his Irish 'servants and others' 'upon his lands in the County of Wicklow', claiming that none of them were native to the said county (Dunlop 1913, I, clii; II, 694–5). This ruling was indicative of the failing of the enforcement of mass transplantation. In January 1661 Lieutenant Colonel Abraham Yarner held the position of commissary general of the musters in the kingdom of Ireland (E. Edwards 2004). Edward Walsh fought hard to be restored to the family estate. On 30 November 1660 he obtained a letter of royal support, and another on 7 June 1661. A certificate in his favour followed (*DKR 19* (1887), 36), and yet Yarner's grant was confirmed under the Act of Explanation passed in December 1665 (Price 1951, 106).

Richard Walsh's circumstances by June 1666 were not good. He pleaded that 'his sufferings have been many greate and grevious not only from the adverse party of the Irish but also from the late usurpers who sequestered all the estate belonging to [his] father'. The latter part of that statement is somewhat contradicted by his observation that his late father's possessions 'were not set forth to Adventurers or soldiers'. Was he implying, therefore, that Cromwellian squatters of some description were exploiting the Carrickmines estates? As the Commonwealth came to an end in 1659 there were five English-born people residing in Carrickmines (Hardinge 1865, 10; Ball 1901, 203). Richard's sense of injustice was exacerbated by the fact that he had been 'a Boy at schoole' when the insurrection began back in October 1641. The likelihood is that his school was on the Continent. In other words, he had no hand, act or part in the conflict.

Ormonde noted that it had been 'intended' to add Richard Walsh to those innocents 'nominated in the Act Explaining the Act of Settlement', but that owing to a 'multitude of other affairs' his 'name was forgotten'. The duke thereupon endorsed Richard's claim to 'the said Lands which were his fathers or such part' as may be 'judged fit'. The order was dated 26 June 1666 (Carte MS 154, fol. 55v; E. Edwards 2005).

According to Hussey Walsh (1900–1, 219), Richard had married Maria, the daughter of Simon Browne of *Belracan*, and died *sine prole*. In the petition, however, Richard does refer to his 'disconsolate family'.

In the wake of Sir Simon Harcourt's death Sir John Temple had impelled the Irish privy council to lobby the parliament in England to procure 'a large proportion of land to be settled upon [the] wife and children' of the fallen soldier. The privy council thought it appropriate that the 'particular proportion of land whereon he lost his life' should be allocated to the family. The present owner was identified as 'one Welsh' and the quality of the land was deemed 'very good, worth five hundred pounds per annum'. Temple added that he considered this grant alone as insufficient (Pamphlet 19).

In January 1645 the House of Lords found that the late Sir Simon Harcourt had died in the service of parliament and left behind him a 'personal estate far short of his debts'. As a result, his 'Lady and children are left in a distressed condition' (*JHL*, VIII, 101). In 1646 Anne Harcourt petitioned for assistance. Parliament, both lords and commons, ordered the immediate payment of £2,000. It was observed that a vote had been passed in the House concerning the granting of 'the Castle and Lands belonging to one Welch' (i.e. Carrickmines) to Anne and the children. It was further noted, however, that this estate had ended up in the possession of the earl of Meath. Accordingly, it was now proposed to settle the 'Town and Lands of Corballis in the County of *Dublyn*' on the Harcourt family. This estate had been held by the insurgent Luke Nettirvill, 'deceased'. In addition, all other lands and holdings of the said Luke should be awarded to Anne and the children. The calculated annual income was £400. Sir John Temple and Sir Anthony Irby were tasked with implementing the edict (*JHC*, V, 509; *JHL*, X, 416). Sir Anthony Irby was the husband of Catherine Paget, Anne's sister (Harcourt 1880–1905, I, 137).

On 28 March 1648 a draft order was made to pay £2,000 to Lady Anne Harcourt (HMC 1879, 18). On 3 August the House of Lords issued a draft ordinance that Lady Harcourt was to be granted £400 a year from the income of the estate of Luke Netterville. The grant was made 'in recognition of the services of her husband, Sir Simon Harcourt, in Ireland' (*ibid.*, 41). Again, on 8 August Colonel Jones, the governor of Dublin, was instructed to 'put Lady Anne Harcourt' 'in possession of the lands settled upon [Sir Simon's] heirs' 'by ordinance of Parliament' (*ibid.*, 51).

Anne Harcourt kept a journal. In June 1649 she enumerated the 'many mercies' that she had 'receaved from God'. She recorded that she had been given 'an honest and kind husband', 'children very hopefull', enough property to provide an income and 'the love of my husband's kindred and friends'. The recent recovery of Stanton had finally guaranteed financial security. Her husband Simon, she affirmed, was 'a usefull and much desired man' who had 'dyed in an unquestionable quarrell'. She was thankful for the kindness of others: 'God has stirred me up some good people to be my friends, though unknown to me formally' (Harcourt 1880–1905, I, 170).

On 13 April 1652 she remarried. Her second husband was Sir William Waller, son of Sir Thomas Waller, constable of Dover Castle, and Margaret, a daughter of Lord Dacre (*ibid.*, 167). Waller was a leading parliamentarian officer in the initial phase of the Civil War. Like Harcourt, he had served on the Continent. He and Ralph Hopton had led the party that escorted the deposed queen of Bohemia through the snow to safety (*ODNB*, LXVI, 986). He was a highly regarded tactician. His troop deployment at the battle of Cheriton, on 29 March 1644, for example, was said to have vindicated his reputation as the best 'shifter and chooser of the ground' amongst his contemporaries (Gardiner 1910, I, 324). His enthusiasm for the struggle was tempered by finding himself opposing former comrades and friends from his Continental days. In a letter to Sir Ralph Hopton, now an adversary in the field, he noted the 'sad sense' he carried with him 'upon this service'. He described the conflict as a 'war without an enemy' (*ibid.*, 168). His espousal of the Presbyterian cause led to a three-year incarceration without trial. He was arrested on 12 December 1648 and not released until early 1652 (*ODNB*, LXVI, 989). His marriage to Anne was a success. He described the pair of them as 'not only one flesh, but one spirit; one in our affections, judgements, wayes, ends, (as if wee had been cut out of one and the same peece)' (*ibid.*). He eventually became involved in the restoration of the monarchy. Anne's son Philip Harcourt later married Anne, Waller's daughter from a previous marriage.

In the Civil Survey of 1654–6 it was documented that Anne was the holder of half a dozen properties formerly belonging to Colonel Luke 'Netterfield' of the Irish army. These properties formed two clusters: Cottrelstown, Grallagh, Jordanstown and Palmerstown in the environs of Oldtown (Simington 1931–61, VII, 52, 36, 53), and Corballis and *Kilcraugh* (i.e. *Cill Chreach*, Kilcrea) to the immediate south of Donabate (*ibid.*, 50). These holdings amounted to 973 acres: 603 of arable, 255 of meadow and pasture, ten of furzes, twenty of bogs, 45 unprofitable and 40 'a cunnybery' (i.e. a cony/rabbit burrow). Except in the case of the minor holding in Grallagh, where Anne is referred to as Lady Harcourt, she is referred to in the entries as Lady Waller.

Neither Richard Walsh nor Anne Harcourt secured long-term possession of the Carrickmines estate. As noted above, it was the earl of Meath who gained the property and at an early stage. How this came to pass was not documented, and what became of Richard and Maria Walsh is unknown. After the Restoration, Oldcourt was granted to the Edwards family (Scott 1913, 135).

Harcourt's ensign and cousin Robert Hammond had returned to England in the wake of the assault on Carrickmines Castle. He had certainly departed by May 1642 (HMC 1895, 133). He subsequently served with the parliamentary forces in the Civil War and by 1645 was a colonel of foot (*ONDB*, XXIV, 961). As the war progressed, he became increasingly uneasy about the growing friction between parliament and the army. A convenient exit strategy presented itself with his appointment as governor of the Isle of Wight on 31 August 1647 (*ibid.*, 962). Robert's uncle, Henry, served as a chaplain to the royal court. His influence, and a cordial meeting between the king and Robert during the summer, persuaded the monarch and his companions to flee to the Isle of Wight in mid-November. Robert, however, remained loyal to parliament and the army and duly imprisoned the king at Carisbrooke Castle, although he was not overjoyed at the task (*ibid.*). Oliver Cromwell, wary of Hammond's wavering in his duty, dispatched a short series of letters to him. On 3 January he expressed his concerns about subterfuge at the castle: 'you should do well, if you have anything that may discover juggling, to search it out, and let us know it' (Carlyle 1904, I, 290). He also let Hammond know in April that they had 'eyes' about the place, informing him that they were aware of the king's recent attempted escape (*ibid.*, 302). There were also rewards: for example, £500 a year was settled on Hammond and his heirs (*ibid.*). Largely, though, the letters were solicitous and evangelically driven: 'I know thou hast long been under trial'; 'Dear Robin, beware of men, look up to the Lord. Let Him be free to speak and command in thy heart' (*ibid.*, 393, 398). Cromwell made it clear that he believed that the army was 'a lawful power', 'called by God to oppose and fight against the King upon some stated grounds […]' (*ibid.*, 396). The use of Hammond's byname emphasises the familiarity between the two men. Sir Simon had also referred to him as 'Robin'. Ordered to report to St Albans, Hammond departed the island in November 1648. His role as the king's gaoler had been terminated. To his relief, he was retired from active service the following January. On 27 August 1654, however, his career was reactivated by Cromwell and he was appointed to the Irish council with an annual salary of £1,000. That autumn, when he again stood on Irish soil, almost twelve years had passed since he had landed with Harcourt and his other old comrades. Ironically, he was taken ill and was dead by early October. Thus he too was laid to rest in Ireland (*ODNB*, XXIV, 962).

The other old comrades had soldiered on together. The regiment was still intact, with practically all the leading players still serving in December 1642. On 22 December £165 12s. was issued to Colonel Richard Gibson, Lieutenant Colonel Thomas Paget, Sergeant-Major Michael Woodhouse, Captains George Vane, Edmund Verney, Robert Croft, Michael Bidulph and Francis Congrave, Captain Denne and Sir

Thomas Meredith. The money was to be divided between 'their sergeants, drummers, corporals, and men' (Mahaffy 1900–1, II, 790). On Captain Verney's evidence we know that the soldiers who had engaged in the assault on *Cariggmaine* Castle back in March were earning 8d. a day (HMC 1879, 435). Amongst the ranks of the '49 Officers on record are Colonel Richard Gibson, Captain Francis Congrave, George Vane, Captain Robert Crofts and Sir Edmund Verney (O'Hart 1887, Appendix X, 388, 379, 381, 409), all members of the regiment. Verney had been knighted on 9 December 1643 (Shaw and Burtchaell 1906, II, 217). A Captain Flood had also served with the regiment and amongst the '49 Officers listed were both an Anthony and a Jenkin Flood (O'Hart 1887, Appendix X, 387). A Sir Michael Woodhouse was also listed (*ibid.*, 411).

As noted above, Edward Brabazon, the second earl of Meath, had come into possession of Carrickmines by 1646. The earl, when sailing from Ireland to England, was drowned on 25 March 1675 along the north Anglesey coast between Holyhead and Beaumaris (Lodge and Archdall 1789, I, 278; Burke 1845, 672). The Glenamuck portion of the old estate ended up in the hands of Roger Jones. Arnold (1993, 114, 181–2, fn. 21) has provisionally identified Jones as an attorney and a sub-commissioner to the trustees of the '49 Officers. His services would have been employed during the sittings of the second Court of Claims. In 1670 Jones sold Glenamuck to Thomas Corker, who in turn sold the property to Christopher Johnson, possibly a native of Durham (*ibid.*, 136). About 1680 Sir Joshua Allen, a successful businessman and former lord mayor of Dublin, purchased Carrickmines from William Brabazon, third earl of Meath, and Stillorgan from the widow of the restored but now deceased James Wolverton (*ibid.*, 135–6). By 1798 the site of Carrickmines Castle was in the possession of the Mooney family, as is attested by the evidence presented during the court-martial of two soldiers (Shiels 2001) who were based at the army camp at Lehaunstown (Murray 1944–5, 32). Privates Brennan and McPeake of the 5th Dragoons were duly convicted of attempting to loot and burn down the farmhouse of James Mooney. The Mooney family were to remain in possession of Carrickmines until the year 2000.

Philip Harcourt and his wife Anne Waller (see above) named their son, who was born in December 1661, Simon. He was to serve as solicitor-general (1702) and attorney-general (1709) in England, and was created Viscount Harcourt of Stanton Harcourt on 24 July 1721. He and his wife, Rebecca Clarke, also named their son, who was born in 1684, Simon. He married Elizabeth Evelyn and their son, another Simon, was born in 1714. As his father had died in 1720, it was the younger Simon who succeeded his grandfather in 1727 as the second viscount. He held several prestigious positions, such as ambassador to Paris.

In 1749 he was created first earl of Stanton-Harcourt, and he served as lord lieutenant from 1772 until 1777. His service in Ireland was later recognised by the naming of a Dublin street in his honour. The name of the street, in turn, prompted the naming of the new railway line that terminated at its southern end. The Harcourt Street Line, which opened in July 1854, was to serve many of the suburbs between

Dublin and Bray. One of its stations was located at Carrickmines, a few hundred metres from the ruins of Theobald Walsh's castle, where the earl's great-great-grandfather, Sir Simon Harcourt, had fallen mortally wounded during the course of the siege back in March 1642.

A LOYAL LOVE-LETTER (FROM A MAID)

A seventeenth-century ballad

[Bodleian Library, Oxford, MS 40 Rawl. 566 (fol. 216)]

The long nights spent around the hearths within, or the campfires without, would have been lifted by many a song. Yearnings for home and loved ones were only to be expected. Here is one of the ballads of the time.

No comfort I can have
while absent thou remains:
Thy company would more rejoice,
my heart, than gold or gains,
With fears I am possest
and terrors for thy sake:
Both day and night I am distrest
no rest that I can take.

Full many a pensive hour,
my self I do retire:
Into some lonesome shady bower,
near to the winged quire,
My thoughts for to divert,
when grief doth me assail:
With thinking of my own sweetheart
yet all will not avail.

Sometimes I am afraid
that on some foreign shore,
Thou should be cast, and then my eyes
shall see thee no more;
Or that some dreadful shot
should cut thee off in twain,
And so should we divided be,
and never meet again.

Therefore my onely sop,
let mercy give with speed,
A letter from thy own dear hand
or else my heart will bleed:
For why I long to hear
the truth of thy welfare,
That God thee bless with happiness
it shall be all my prayer.

GENEALOGICAL TABLES

THE WALSHES OF CARRICKMINES

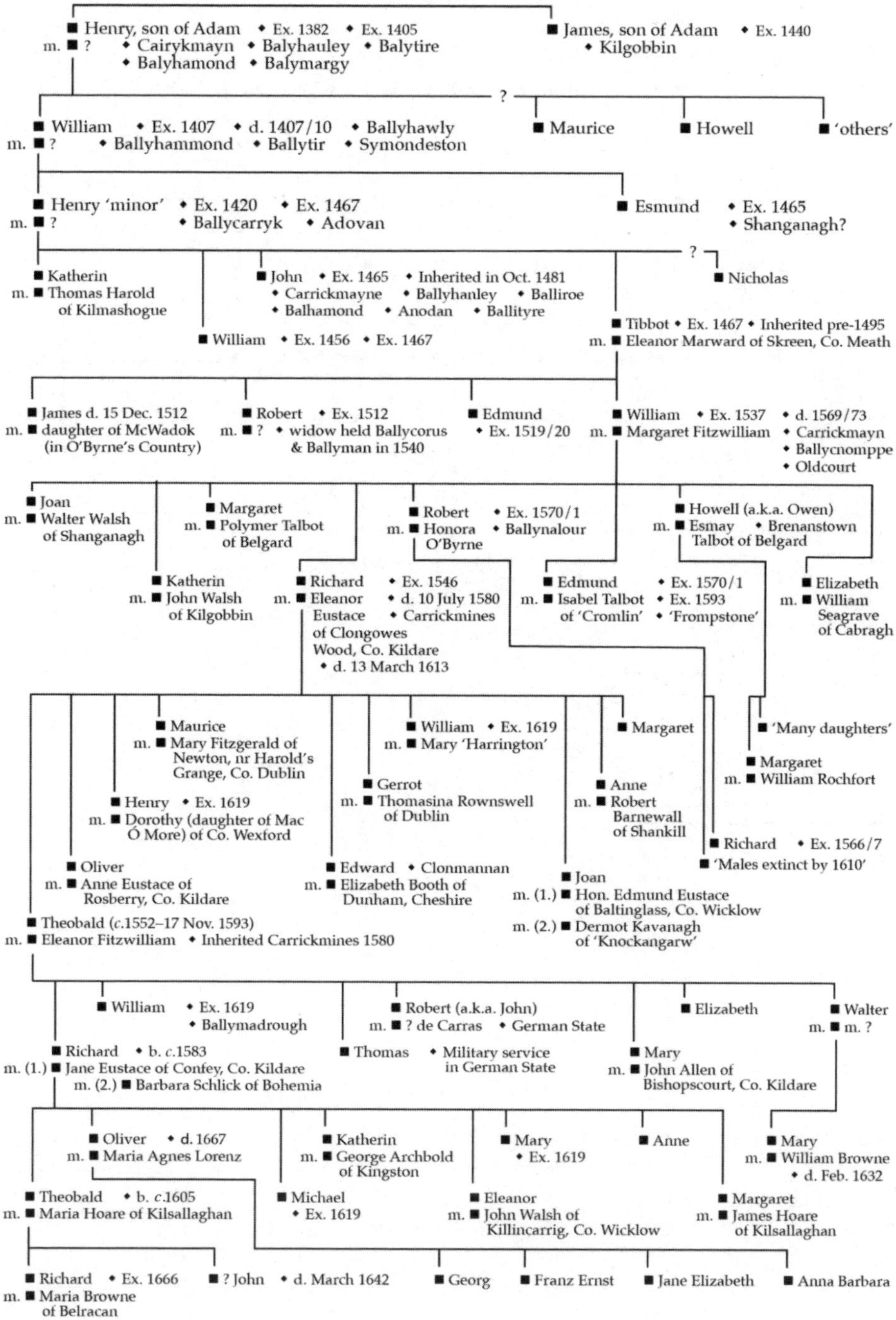

THE WALSHES OF SHANGANAGH

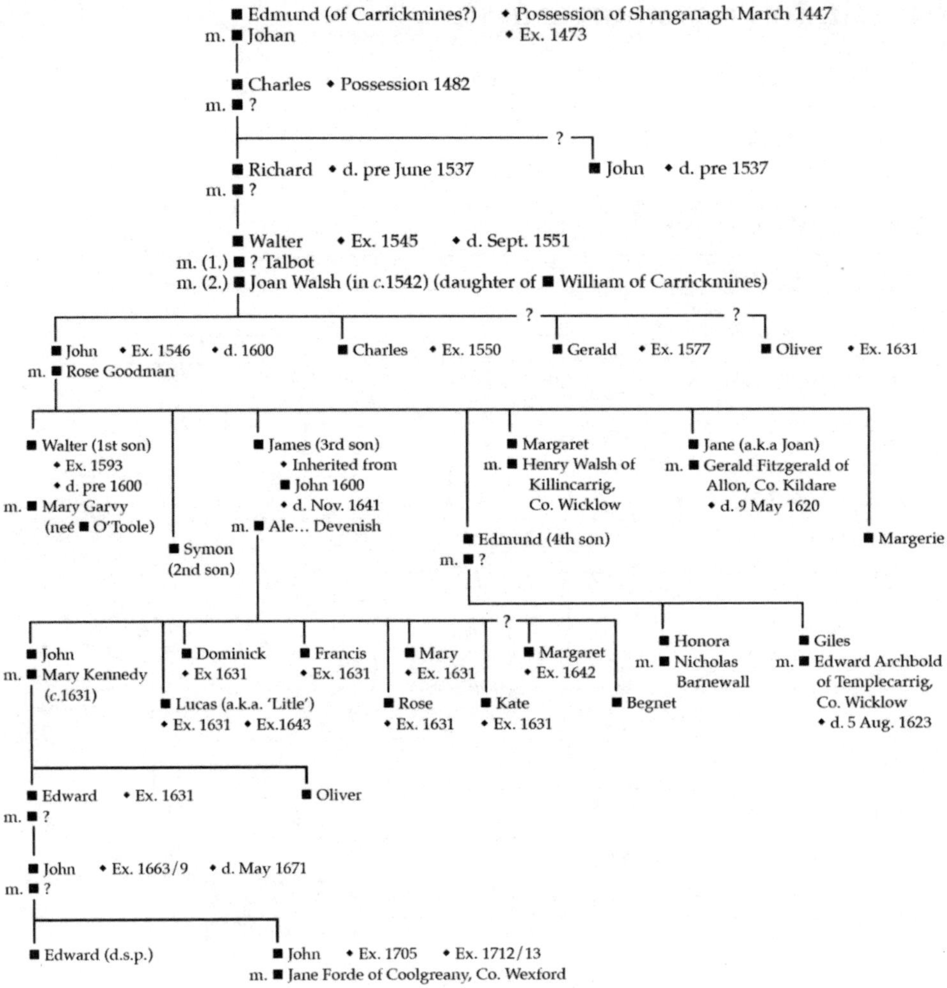

THE WALSHES OF KILGOBBIN

- James, son of Adam ◆ Ex. Feb. 1440
  - Maurice of Kilgobbin & Jamestown, m. ? ◆ Ex. 1476
    - Thomas ◆ Ex. 1465/6
    - Pierce/Peter ◆ Ex. 1509, m. ?
      - Richard ◆ Ex. 1543, m. Margaret Harold of Kilmashogue
        - John ◆ d. May 1578, m. Katherin Walsh of Carrickmines ◆ d. Aug. 1617
          - Pierce ◆ *c.*1560–May 1633, m. (1.) Elenor Goodman of Loughlinstown; m. (2.) Margaret Flatsbury of Johnstown, Co. Kildare ◆ d. June 1623
            - John, m. Margaret Synnott of 'Bolmfernocke', Co. Wexford
            - Richard
            - Edward
            - Katherin, m. Theobald Archbold of Templecarrig, Co. Wicklow ◆ d. June 1622
            - Mary
            - Margaret
            - Elizabeth
          - Nicholas of Dundrum, m. (1.) Joan Malone of Dublin; m. (2.) Ursula Henshaw of Siddington, Cheshire
            - Luke
            - Katherin
          - Christopher ◆ Ex. 1613, m. Marion Talbot of Templeogue
          - Thomas 'father of divers bastardes'
          - Anne, m. Christopher Garvey of Dublin/Armagh
          - Margaret, m. John Mey of Co. Kildare
        - 'Other sons all died' (*sine prole*)
        - ? Margaret ◆ Ex. 1560, m. Patrick Archbold of the Manor of Bree

THE WALSHES OF BALALLY

■ Henry Adamson of Carrickmines and 'Balyhauley'
 • Grant of March 1400

■ William of C. & 'Ballyhawley'
 • Inherited in Oct. 1407

■ Henry of Carrickmines
 • Ex. 1420 • Ex. 1467

■ John of C. and 'Ballyhauley'
 • Inherited in 1481

■ Thomas of Balally
m. ■ ? • d. Aug. 1543

■ John • b. *c.*1537, • d. May 1615
m. (1.) ■ Joan Archbold of Templecarrig, Co. Wicklow
m. (2.) ■ Elizabeth Rochfort

- ■ James • b. *c.*1581 • d. 1648
  m. ■ Dorothy O'Byrne • d. Sept. 1623
  of Kiltimon, Co. Wicklow
  - ■ Henry • Ex. June 1605 • Ex. 1648/9
- ■ Richard
- ■ Margaret

THE WALSHES OF KILLINCARRIG

[Carrickmines]

[Balally]

■ Henry • Ex. 1565/6
m. ■ ? • Suttoneston a.k.a. Killincarrig
• Dalkey • d. Sept. 1570

■ Theobald • Ex. 1582 • d. Jan. 1620
m. (1.) ■ Anne Allen of Coteshall, Norfolk
m. (2.) ■ Jane Eustace of Ballymore, Co. Kildare

- ■ Henry • d. Dec. 1634
  m. ■ Margaret Walsh
  of Shanganagh
  - ■ John • Ex. 1631
    m. ■ Eleanor Walsh
    of Carrickmines
  - ■ Michael
  - ■ Walter
  - ■ Richard
  - ■ Ambros
    • Died, unmarried
    in Low Countries
  - ■ Francis
    (a.k.a. Thomas)
  - ■ William
  - ■ Katherin
    m. ■ John O'Byrne
    of Courtfoyle,
    Co. Wicklow
  - ■ Rose
    m. ■ Edmund O'Byrne
    of Tinnapark,
    Co. Wicklow
  - ■ Begnet
  - ■ Anne
  - ■ Mary
- ■ Michael
- ■ William
- ■ Katherine • d. June 1616
  m. ■ William Harold
  of Co. Kildare
- ■ Anastace • d. May 1622
  m. ■ James O'Byrne
  of Ballynerrin, Co. Wicklow
- ■ Margaret
  m. ■ Oliver Luttrell
  of Portlester,
  Co. Meath

BIBLIOGRAPHY

ABBREVIATIONS

Cal. close rolls = *Calendar of the close rolls preserved in the public record office: Edward I (1279–88)* (London, 1902); *Edward II (1323–7)* (London, 1898).

Cat. hist. documents = *Catalogue or an invaluable and highly interesting collection of unpublished manuscript historical documents* (London, 1825).

Cal. pat. rolls = *Calendar of the patent rolls preserved in the public record office: Edward IV (1461–7)* (London, 1897); *Edward IV, Henry VI (1467–77)* (London, 1900); *Henry IV (1399–1401)* (London, 1903); *Richard II (1391–6)* (London, 1905).

Cal. pat. rolls chancery = *Calendar of the patent rolls of the chancery of Ireland* (Dublin, 1800).

Cal. Pembroke = *Calendar of ancient deeds and muniments preserved in the Pembroke estate office, Dublin* (Dublin, 1891).

DIB = J. McGuire and J. Quinn (eds), *Dictionary of Irish Biography* (under the auspices of the Royal Irish Academy) (9 vols) (Cambridge, 2009).

DKR = *Reports of the Deputy Keeper of the Public Records and Keeper of the State Papers in Ireland*: *Eleventh report* (1879); *Seventeenth report* (1885); *Nineteenth report* (1887); *Twentieth report* (1888); *Twenty-fourth report* (1892); *Thirty-sixth report* (1904); *Thirty-seventh report* (1905); *Thirty-eighth report* (1906); *Thirty-ninth report* (1907); *Forty-first report* (1909); *Forty-second report* (1911); *Forty-third report* (1912); *Forty-fifth report* (1913); *Fifty-fourth report* (1927). Dublin and London.

DNB = L. Stephen and S. Lee (eds), *Dictionary of National Biography* (63 vols) (London, 1885–1900).

Fiants = *The Irish Fiants of the Tudor sovereigns: during the reigns of Henry VIII, Edward VI, Philip and Mary, and Elizabeth 1* (3 vols) (Dublin, 1994).

HMC = Historic Manuscripts Commission.

JHC = *Journal of the House of Commons.*

JHL = *Journal of the House of Lords* (London, 1767–1830).

JKAS = *Journal of the Kildare Archaeological Society.*

JRSAI = *Journal of the Royal Society of Antiquaries of Ireland.*
NLI = National Library of Ireland.
ODNB = H.C.G. Matthew and B. Harrison (eds), *Oxford Dictionary of National Biography* (60 vols) (Oxford, 2004).
PRIA = *Proceedings of the Royal Irish Academy.*
RIA = Royal Irish Academy.
TCD = Trinity College Dublin.

PRIMARY SOURCES

(a) Pamphlets held by the Royal Irish Academy and the National Library of Ireland

1. *A true and good Relation of the Valliant Exploits, and Victorious Enterprises of Sir Simon Harcourt, and Sir Charles Coote, with their valliant overthrow, of at least 5000. Rebels, with the burning of three townes, where the Rebels lay incamped neare Dublin: and also the relief of Tragidaugh, and other particulars/related in a letter, dated Jan. 20. 1641, from Mr. Chappell of Dublin [...].* London.
2. *A Perfect Copy of a Letter, sent from Dublin, relating the true Condition of Ireland, as it now stands. With two proclamations, Published by the States there. Brought over by the last post. January, 18, 1642. First printed at Dublin. And re-printed at London, by* G.C. London.
3. *Warranted Tydings from Ireland. Written by Master Robert Pickering, Secretary unto the Right Worshipfull, Sir Simon Harcourt, Sergeant-Major of the Horse Troopes there arrived. From Corke, January 16. 1641.* London.
4. *Gods Providence to the distressed Protestants in Ireland, or, the last proceedings in the Province of Munster. Attested by two Letters sent from Robert Pickering Clerke unto Sir Symon Harcourt, Sergeant Major of all the Horse there arrived. The one dated at Tologh, Jan. 20. The other at Youghall, Jan. 23. 1641. [...] Youghall was taken by the Rebels [...].* London.
5. *The Particular Relation of the Present Estate and Condition of Ireland: as now it stands, manifested by several Letters sent from and to such persons as may give full satisfaction of the truth therof. Published by Authoritie. 1642.* London.
6. *A Proclamation of The Lords Justices for the apprehension of the chiefe Rebels: and The Reward for taking any of them: with the true and last Newes from Ireland, and in what state Dublin stands at this present; sent from an Honourable, and one of the chiefest persons there, to a nephew of his in London. To be sold at the Signe of the Bible in Chancery-Lane.* London.
7. *Two famous Battels fought in Ireland: wherin the Protestants under the command of the Earle of Ormond, Sr. Charles Coote, and Sr. Simon Harcourt, slew great numbers of the Rebels, routing them from one Town to another, and tooke divers prisoners to their great joy and comfort. Faithfully related in a Letter, sent from Mr. Ralph Parsons in Dublin, to Sir William Brewerton, a worthy Member of the House of Commons. [...].* London.
8. *Approved, Good, and happy Newes from Ireland: relating how the Castle of Artaine was*

taken from the Rebels, two of their Captaines kild, and one taken prisoners by the protestants. With the arrival of 2000 foot, and 300 horse from England. Also a great skirmish between the Protestants and the Rebels at a place neere Feleston, wherein the English obtained great renowne and victory. [...]. Printed by Order of Parliament. London.

9. *The Newest Intelligence from the Army in Ireland (in two letters)—(dated in Dublin: 1st Febr. 1642).* London.
10. *Confident Newes from Ireland. Dublin, February 15, 1641. Being a letter sent from Mr. William Philips, Merchant, dwelling in Dublin, to Mr. William Baber, [...] How one of the Rebels flying from his Confederates into Dublin, related to Sir Charles Coot their damnable Designes, who making it known to Sir Simon Harcott [...] they suddenly issued forth [slew 800 of them ...].* London.
11. *A Relation touching the present state and condition of Ireland. Collected by a Committee of the house of Commons, out of severall letters, lately come from the Lords Justices of Ireland and others [...].* London.
12. *A Letter sent from Sr. Simon Harcourt, to a worthy Member of the House of Commons. With a true relation of the proceedings of the English Army, under his command, to this present March. Whereunto is added the many miraculous deliverances, in the Relieving and Defending the City of Tredagh, by the providence of God. Exactly related, by the Minister of the same Town, who was an eye witness thereof, and is still resident there.* London.
13. *The Last True Intelligence from Ireland. Dated in Dublin, 16. March, and received in London 28. March. 1642. Printed for H. Blunden.* London.
14. *The Irish rebellion: or, An history of the beginnings and first progresse of the general Rebellion raised within the kingdom of Ireland, upon the three and twentieth day of October, in the year, 1641: together with the barbarous cruelties and bloody massacres which ensued thereupon. By Sir John Temple Knight. Master of the Rolles, and one of His Majesties most honourable Privie Councell within the Kingdom of Ireland.* London.
15. *Dublin January the 28th. A true and perfect Occurrence of the present state of Dublin. And of every severrall passage betweene the Protestants and the Rebells there. Beeng the substance of severall Letters which was sent from Sir Henry Tichborne, and Captaine Studley, to some friends of theirs now resident heere. [...].* London.
16. *Good Newes for England: or, comfortable tydings from Ireland, to all true hearted Protestants. Being a real relation how Sir Simon Harcourt, Sergeant Major Berry, and Captain Paramore, with the joint assistance of divers other Protestants, obtained a famous Victory over the Rebels at Kildare [...] Sent from the English Quarters at Lyons, within four miles of Dublin by Alderman Guy his son of Bristoll. Cornet to Sir Richard Grenvile.* London.
17. *The last True Intelligence from Ireland. Being a letter sent from Chester: dated the second of Aprill 1642, from Mr William Owen, to a friend of his in London [In which is Related, the taking of Carreggmayne Castle, seven Miles south-east from Dublin, from the Rebels, where Sir Simon Harcott was slain, being shott from the Castle in the side,*

with a shanker Bullet, out of a long piece. Also, Sergent Major Berry, is a mortally wounded in the Flank]. London.

18. *True Intelligence from Dublin, April the 3. Touching those important passages have happened thereabouts. As also the death of Sr. Simon Harcot an honourable Gentleman. Together with a worthy Relation from Deane Barnard concerning several remarkable particulars of Gods mercy towards our forces in the County of Louth, and the taking in of Ardee and Dundalke, two places of great Importance [...].* London.
19. *The Copie of a Letter from Dublin in Ireland, Dated March 29. 1642. By Sir John Temple, Knight, Master of the Rolles, and one of his Majesties privy Councell of that Kingdom, written to D. Temple, D. of Divinity and Pastor of Batersey, neare London: Relating the Manner of taking the Castle of Carrick-Maine, six miles from Dublin, by Sir Simon Harcourt, and some English under his command: Together with the manner of his hurt and death, with some other passages.* London.
20. *Good and true Newes from Ireland being the Copy of a Letter sent from Mr. Rodger Puttock one of the chief Ministers in the City of Dublin, to a Brother of his, a merchant, living in Aldermon-Berrie in London. Shewing in a true and reall Relation, how 400. Foot and 100 horse sent from Dublin, under the command of Sir Charles Coot marched towards Ardee 8.miles from thence [...] slew 1100 men at Dundalk [...].* London.
21. *True Intelligence from Ireland. Dated from Dublin the second of April, and received here the eleventh. Printed for H. Blunden, 1642.* London.
22. *The Last True Newes from Ireland, Being the Copie of a Letter sent from Dublin, to a Gentleman of good Ranke, and now Resident in this City. Wherein is declared many great overthrowes and Defeates given to the Rebels. Likewise the manner how a great Castle called Carricke Mayne (within 6. myles of Dublin) was taken by the English, and the Rebels put to death. Man, Woman, and Child. Also a true intelligence that the Rebels are beaten by Sir Henry Titchburne out of Dundalke.* London.
23. *Aprill the 22nd: New and True Newes from Ireland: Relating these particulars following. 1. The meeting of 6 or 700 Abbots, Monks, Fryars, and Priests, in the West part of Ireland, at least three weeks, with fasts and prayers three days in a week after their Popish manner. 2. Another meeting at Westmeath, for the plotting of the confusion of the Protestants in that Kingdome. 3. Their divelish plot against Dublin and divers other places. [...] With divers other particulars [...].* London.
24. *May the second, 1642. The Warlike, Noble, and prosperous proceedings of the Protestant Army in Ireland. Being the true Copy of a Letter, sent from Mr. Thomas Richard Merchant in Dublin: to Mr. Thomas Andrewes Grocer without Newgate, in the Parish of St. Sepulchres. [...] a very memorable victory obtained by the English, wherein 1800 of the Rebels were hanged, and slaine, 16. Of their Colours taken, [...].* London.
25. *The Truest, most Happy, and joyfull Newes that ever came from Ireland: being sent over in a letter, and read in the honourable House of Commons, Februarie 29. 1641: relating the renowned victory of the Protestant party, in repelling the Rebels from Dublin, under the commands of the Earl of Ormond, Sir Charles Coot, and Sir Simon Harcourt [...] near to the town of Trohedagh [...].* London.
26. *A Briefe Declaration of the Barbarous and inhumane dealings of the Northern Irish*

Rebels, and many others in several Counties up-rising against the English, that dwelt both lovingly and securely among them. Written to Excite the English Nation to relieve our poore Wives and Children, that have escaped the Rebels savage crueltie, and that shall arrive safe among them in England […] By G.S. Minister of Gods word in Ireland. London.

27. *Admirable good Newes againe from Ireland, or, the copie of a Letter written from Sir Thomas Lucas, one of the Commanders of our army in Ireland to a worthy Member of the House of Parliament here in England, bearing date, February, 24. 1641. […] two great over-throwes which was given to the Rebels by the English and Scottish Forces. […]*. London.
28. *Orders from the High Court of Parliament for the setling of these Kingdomes in peace. As also, a Relation of 4000. Redshanks that are sent over into Ireland with Generall Lesley. With the Orders that are taken for their succour […]*. London.
29. *More good and true News from Ireland, sent from Dublin, by Master Robert Cole merchant, to his Brother John Cole here resident in London*. London.
30. *A new Remonstrance from Ireland containing an extract declaration of the cruelties, insolencies, outrages, and murders exercised by the bloudthirsty, Popish rebells in that Kingdome upon many hundred Protestants in the Province of Ulster, and especially of the ministers there, since the beginning of this base, horrid, unnaturall and unparralelled Rebellion October 23. 1641. In which is also particularly expressed the names of such Ministers and others who have been murthered, imprisoned, famished, and otherwayes cruelly used by those barbarous, and inhumane Rebells. By Daniel Harcourt […]*. Ludgate.
31. *A Perfect Relation of the beginning and continuation of the Irish-Rebellion, from May last, to this present 12th of January, 1641. With the place where, and Persons who, did Plot, Contrive, and put in Execution that Romish damnable Designe. […] Whereunto is annexed the Merchants letter who sent the Copy of this Relation: With another letter wherein is truly related, the Battell fought betwixt our English, and the Rebels, on the tenth of January, at a Town called Swords, eight miles from Dublin*. London.
32. *A True Relation of the Miserable estate that Ireland now standeth in. Manifested by a Letter sent from the Lord Dungarvan Son to the Earle of Corke: to Sir Arthur Magennis, a worthy Knight in England. Wherein is shewed the great distresse of the Protestants there inhabiting: Likewise the preparation for Ireland, by assent of both Houses of Parliament. With the great comfort that they daily receive by meanes of the valour of Sir Simon Harcourt. With a list of the ships, men, money and ammunition sent for the present reliefe of the poore distressed Protestants of Ireland. February 9. 1642*. London.
33. *An Humble Petition and Remonstrance presented unto the High and Honourable Houses of Parliament concerning the insupportable grievance of the Farthing Tokens. Printed in the yeare, 1642*. London.
34. *The last and best Newes from Ireland: declaring first the warlike and cruell proceeding of the Rebels who are all papists and fruits of that Kingdome. Secondly, the entrance of some English and Scottish companies into the North parts of Ireland under the command*

of those foure noblemen; the Lord Grandison, the Lord Chichester, the Lord Conway, the Lord Cromwell [...] Ireland's complaint, and England's reliefe sent by the honourable house of parliament, to ayde and assist their brethren, together with the names of those Commanders that are appointed for this religious designe [...]. London.

35. *A Letter sent to Sir Robert King of whom any may have further satisfaction (of the certainty of the Irish occurents) at his House called Cocill or Wimbleton House in the Strand. Adam Loftus. 14th February 1642.* London.

36. *An Order from the Committee, that Eleven Thousand three Hundred Horse should be conducted by Sir Simon Harecolt into Ireland. As also, Letters read in the Parliament, sent from the Mayre of Dublin and other Justices of the Peace, how Tredagh is besieged and Dublin in great feare of the Rebels. As likewise the Spanish Fleet overthrown in the Sea. Going to assist the Rebels in Ireland. [...] how in a suddaine Tempest they were all Drowned in a devouring Sea. [...].* London.

37. *A True Relation of the Chiefe Passages in Ireland [from the 25th of April to this present] — [May the 14th 1632]. [...].* London.

(b) Manuscripts

The 1641 Depositions. Witness testimonies concerning the 1641 Irish rebellion (31 vols). TCD MSS 809–841, Dublin.

The Genealogical Office Manuscripts. NLI, Dublin.

'The Grand Panel of the county of Wexford, as it was returned in the general sessions holden before Sir James Ley, Knight, Lord Chief Justice of the King's Bench, in Ireland, and Robert Oglethorpe, Esq.; Second Baron of the Exchequer, in Ireland, justices of assize and jail delivery in the county of Wexford, the 25th of July 1608.' Carew Manuscripts MS 600, Archiepiscopal Library, Lambeth Palace, London.

'Obits, ([some] pedigrees, marriages etc.) of most of the principal families in Ireland, more particularly in the 16th and 17th centuries.' TCD MS 1216, Dublin.

'Pedigrees of all the Nobility and Gentry of Ireland, traced to the middle of the reign of Elizabeth.' TCD MS 1212, Dublin.

'To his Grace James Duke of Ormond Lord Lieutenant General and Generall Governor of Ireland: the humble petition of Richard Walsh late of Carrigmaine in the County of Dublin Gent.' Appended: Order signed by the duke of Ormonde, dated 'The 26th day of June 1666'. MS Carte 154, fols 54–55, 55v, Bodleian Library, University of Oxford.

William Hawkins (1721), 'Genealogia Lucae Walsh Qui ex Antiqua Domo de Carrickmaine in Comitatu Dubline natus est'. NLI, Dublin.

SECONDARY SOURCES

Akkerman, N. (ed.) 2011 *The correspondence of Elizabeth Stuart, queen of Bohemia* (2 vols). Oxford.

Arblaster, P. 2014 *From Ghent to Aix: how they brought the news in the Hapsburg*

Netherlands 1550–1700. Leiden and Boston.

Archdall, M. 1873 *Monasticon Hibernicum: or, a history of the abbeys, priories, and other religious houses in Ireland* (3 vols), Vol. 2. Dublin.

Archer, J. 1801 *Statistical survey of the County Dublin*. Dublin.

Arnold, L.J. 1993 *The restoration land settlement in County Dublin, 1660–1688: a history of the administration of the Acts of Settlement and Explanation*. Dublin.

Ashley, M. 1998 *British kings and queens*. London.

Atkinson, E.G. (ed.) 1893–1905 *Calendar of the state papers relating to Ireland of the reign of Elizabeth, 1596–1601*. London.

Ball, F.E. 1901 The castle of Carrickmines and its history. *JRSAI* **31**, 195–203.

Ball, F.E. 1902 Rathmichael and its neighbours. *JRSAI* **32** (2), 113–27.

Ball, F.E. 1902–17 *A history of the County Dublin* (5 vols). Dublin.

Ball, F.E. 1926 *The judges in Ireland* (2 vols). London.

Ball, F.E. and Hamilton, E. 1895 *The parish of Taney: a history of Dundrum, near Dublin, and its neighbourhood*. Dublin.

Barker, T.M. 1982 *Army, aristocracy, monarchy: essays on war, society, and government in Austria, 1618–1780*. New York.

Barry, T. 1995 The last frontier: defence and settlement in late medieval Ireland. In T.B. Barry, R. Frame and K. Simms (eds), *Colony and frontier in medieval Ireland: essays presented to J.F. Lydon*, 217–28. London.

Bateson, M. 1903 Irish exchequer memoranda of the reign of Edward I. *English Historical Review* **18**, 497–513.

Beckett, J.C. 1966 *The making of modern Ireland 1603–1923*. London.

Bellamy, A. 2002 *The politics of court scandal in early modern England: news culture, and the Overbury affair, 1603–1660*. Cambridge.

Berry, H.F. (ed.) 1898 *Register of wills and inventories of the diocese of Dublin in the time of Archbishops Tregury and Walton 1457–1483*. Dublin.

Berry, H.F. (ed.) 1907 *Statutes and ordinances, and acts of the parliament of Ireland. King John to Henry V.* Dublin.

Berry, H.F. (ed.) 1910 *Statute rolls of the parliament of Ireland, reign of King Henry the Sixth*. Dublin.

Berry, H.F. (ed.) 1914 *Statute rolls of the parliament of Ireland: first to the twelfth years of the reign of King Edward the Fourth*. Dublin.

Bhreathnach, E. 2000 Kings, the kingship of Leinster and the regnal poems of *laídshenchas Laigen*: a reflection of dynastic politics in Leinster, 650–1150. In A.P. Smyth (ed.), *Seanchas: studies in early and medieval Irish archaeology, history and literature in honour of Francis J. Byrne*, 299–312. Dublin.

Bhreathnach, E. 2014 *Ireland in the medieval world, AD 400–1000: landscape, kingship and religion*. Dublin.

Bindoff, S.T. 1950 *Tudor England*. London.

Bindoff, S.T. (ed.) 1982 *The history of parliament: the House of Commons 1509–1558* (3 vols). London.

Birely, R. 2014 *Ferdinand II, Counter-Reformation emperor, 1578–1637*. Cambridge.

Blencowe, R.W. (ed.) 1825 *Sydney papers consisting of a journal of the earl of Leicester, and original letters of Algernon Sydney*. London.

Borlase, E. 1680 *The history of the execrable Irish rebellion trac'd from many preceding acts, to the grand eruption. The 23. Of October, 1641. And thence pursued to the Act of Settlement, MDCLXII* [Appendices]. Dublin.

Bowen, B.P. 1947–8 John Rocque's maps of Dublin. *Dublin Historical Record* **9** (4), 117–27.

Bradley, J. 2009 Some reflections on the problem of Scandinavian settlement in the hinterland of Dublin during the ninth century. In J. Bradley, A.J. Fletcher and A. Simms (eds), *Dublin in the medieval world: studies in honour of Howard B. Clarke*, 39–62. Dublin.

Brady, C. 1997 The captains' games: army and society in Elizabethan Ireland. In T. Bartlett and K. Jeffery (eds), *A military history of Ireland*, 136–59. Cambridge.

Brady, C. 2017 The myth of 'Silken Thomas'. In P. Crooks and S. Duffy (eds), *The Geraldines and medieval Ireland: the making of a myth*, 379–98. Dublin.

Bray, W. (ed.) 1827 *The private correspondence between King Charles I and Sir Edward Nicholas: also between Sir Edward Hyde, afterwards Earl of Clarendon, and Sir Richard Browne, ambassador to the court of France, in the time of King Charles I and the usurpation* (5 vols), Vol. 5. London.

Brewer, J.S. and Bullen, W. 1867–73 *Calendar of the Carew Manuscripts, preserved in the archiepiscopal library at Lambeth* (6 vols). London.

Brookes, R. 1820 *The general gazetteer: or, compendious geographical dictionary* (7th edn). London.

Brooks, E.St J. 1936 *Register of the Hospital of St John the Baptist without the New Gate, Dublin*. Dublin.

Brooks, E.St J. 1951 The de Ridelesfords. *JRSAI* **81** (1), 115–38.

Brooks, E.St J. 1952 The de Ridelesfords. *JRSAI* **82** (2), 45–61.

Brown, H.F. (ed.) 1897 *Calendar of state papers and manuscripts, relating to English affairs, existing in the archives and collections of Venice, Vol. 9: 1592–1603*. London.

Bruce, J. (ed.) 1858–69 *Calendar of state papers, domestic series, of the reign of Charles I* (12 vols). London.

Bruce, J. (ed.) 1869 *Notes of the treaty carried on at Ripon between King Charles I and the Covenanters of Scotland, AD 1640. Taken by Sir John Borough, Garter King of Arms*. London.

Brydges, E. 1812 *Collins's peerage of England; genealogical, biographical, and historical* (9 vols). London.

Bulkeley, L. 1869 The Diocese of Dublin in the year 1630. *Irish Ecclesiastical Record* **5**, 145–66.

Burke, B. 1866 *A genealogical history of the dormant : abeyant, forfeited, and extinct peerages of the British Empire*. London.

Burke, J. 1835–8 *A genealogical and heraldic history of the commoners of Great Britain and Ireland, enjoying territorial possessions or high official rank, but unvested with heritable honours* (4 vols). London.

Burke, J. 1845 *A genealogical and heraldic dictionary of the peerage and baronetage of the British Empire*. London.

Burke, J. and Burke, J.B. 1846 *A genealogical and heraldic dictionary of the peerages of England, Ireland and Scotland, extinct, dormant, and in abeyance* (3rd edn). London.

Burnet, G. 1852 *The memoirs of the lives and actions of James and William, dukes of Hamilton and Castle-Herald*. Oxford.

Burton, N. 1843 *History of the Royal Hospital, Kilmainham, near Dublin, from the original foundation to the present time*. Dublin.

Butler, R. (ed.) 1842 *Jacobi Grace, Kilkenniensis, Annales Hiberniae*. Dublin.

Butler, R. (ed.) 1845 *Registrum Prioratus Omnium Sanctorum juxta Dublin*. Dublin.

Butler, R. (ed.) 1849 *The Annals of Ireland by Friar John Clyn; together with the Annals of Ross*. Dublin.

Butler, W.F. 1915 Confiscation in Irish history. IV—The Plantation of Wexford. *Studies: An Irish Quarterly Review* **4** (15), 411–27.

Byrne, F.J. 1973 *Irish kings and high-kings*. Dublin.

Byrne, M.J. (trans.) 1903 *Chapters towards a history of Ireland in the reign of Elizabeth, being a portion of the history of Catholic Ireland by Don Philip O'Sullivan Bear*. Dublin.

Cannon, R. 1839 *Historical records of the British Army: the Third Regiment of Foot or The Buffs [formerly designated The Holland Regiment]*. London.

Canny, N.P. 1970–1 The flight of the earls, 1607. *Irish Historical Studies* **17**, 380–99.

Canny, N. 1996 The attempted Anglicisation of Ireland in the seventeenth century: an exemplar of 'British history'. In J.F. Merritt (ed.), *The political world of Thomas Wentworth, Earl of Strafford, 1621–1641*, 157–86. Cambridge.

Carey, V.P. 2007 Atrocity and history: Grey, Spenser and the slaughter at Smerwick (1580). In D. Edwards, P. Lenihan and C. Tait (eds), *Age of atrocity: violence and political conflict in early modern Ireland*, 79–94. Dublin.

Carlyle, T. 1904 *The letters and speeches of Oliver Cromwell with elucidations* (3 vols). London.

Carte, T. 1736 *An history of the life of James Duke of Ormonde, from his birth in 1610, to his death in 1688* (2 vols). Dublin.

Carte, T. 1851 *The life of James, Duke of Ormonde; containing an account of the most remarkable affairs of his time, and particularly of Ireland under his government* (6 vols). Oxford.

Clare, L. 2005 The Kill and the Grange of Clonkeen: two early settlements in south County Dublin. *Dublin Historical Record* **58** (1), 17–30.

Clarendon, E. 1720 *The history of the rebellion and civil wars in Ireland, with the true state and condition of that kingdom before the year 1640; and the most material passages and actions which have since contributed to the calamities it hath undergone*. London.

Clark, G.B. 2010 *Irish soldiers in Europe: 17th–19th century*. Cork.

Clarke, A. 1966 *The Old English in Ireland, 1625–42*. Dublin.

Clarke, A. 1976a The Irish economy, 1600–60. In T.W. Moody, F.X. Martin and F.J.

Byrne (eds), *A New History of Ireland* (9 vols), Vol. 3, 168–86. Oxford.

Clarke, A. 1976b Selling royal favours, 1624–32. In T.W. Moody, F.X. Martin and F.J. Byrne (eds), *A New History of Ireland* (9 vols), Vol. 3, 233–42. Oxford.

Clarke, A. 1976c The government of Wentworth, 1632–40. In T.W. Moody, F.X. Martin and F.J. Byrne (eds), *A New History of Ireland* (9 vols), Vol. 3, 243–69. Oxford.

Clarke, A. 1976d The breakdown of authority, 1640–41. In T.W. Moody, F.X. Martin and F.J. Byrne (eds), *A New History of Ireland* (9 vols), Vol. 3, 270–88. Oxford.

Clarke, A. 2011 The colonisation of Ulster and the rebellion of 1641: 1603–60. In T.W. Moody and F.X. Martin (eds), *The course of Irish history* (5th edn), 163–75. Dublin.

Clarke, A. and Dudley Edwards, R. 1976 Pacification, plantation, and the Catholic question, 1603–23. In T.W. Moody, F.X. Martin and F.J. Byrne (eds), *A New History of Ireland* (9 vols), Vol. 3, 187–232. Oxford.

Clinton, M. 2000 Settlement patterns in the early historic kingdom of Leinster (seventh to mid-twelfth century). In A.P. Smyth (ed.), *Seanchas: studies in early and medieval Irish archaeology, history and literature in honour of Francis J. Byrne*, 275–98. Dublin.

Clinton, M. 2002 Site No. 203: Balally, County Dublin. In I. Bennett (ed.), *Excavations 2000: summary accounts of archaeological excavations in Ireland*, 65–8. Bray.

Clinton, M. 2003 The preliminary report on the excavation of Carrickmines Castle, 2000–2002. Unpublished report.

Clinton, M. 2005 *The history and archaeology of the parish of Kilsallaghan: past, present and future.* Swords.

Clinton, M., Fibiger, L. and Shiels, D. 2007 Archaeology of massacre: the Carrickmines mass grave and the siege of March 1642. In D. Edwards, P. Lenihan and C. Tait (eds), *Age of atrocity: violence and political conflict in early modern Ireland*, 192–203. Dublin.

Clinton, M., Fibiger, L. and Shiels, D. 2013 The archaeology of the 1642 siege of Carrickmines castle. In C. Corlett (ed.), *Unearthing the archaeology of Dún Laoghaire–Rathdown*, 147–52. Dún Laoghaire.

Cokayne, G.E. 1910–59 *The complete peerage of England, Scotland, Ireland, Great Britain and the United Kingdom* (13 vols) (new edition, revised and enlarged by V. Gibbs). London.

Colby, T. and Larcom, T.A. 1837 *Ordnance Survey of the County of Londonderry*, Vol. 1. Dublin.

Coleman, A. 1900 *Historical memoirs of the city of Armagh by James Stuart* (revised and rewritten). Dublin.

Connolly, P. 1998 *Irish Exchequer payments 1270–1446* (2 vols). Dublin.

Connolly, P. (ed.) 2002 *Statute rolls of the Irish parliament: Richard III–Henry VIII.* Dublin.

Corish, P.J. 1976 The rising of 1641 and the Catholic confederacy, 1641–5. In T.W. Moody, F.X. Martin and F.J. Byrne (eds), *A New History of Ireland* (9 vols), Vol. 3, 289–316. Oxford.

Corlett, C. 1999 *Antiquities of old Rathdown: the archaeology of south County Dublin and north County Wicklow*. Bray.

Corlett, C. 2015 Rathdown slabs revisited. In H.B. Clarke and R. Johnson (eds), *The Vikings in Ireland and beyond: before and after the Battle of Clontarf*, 438–50. Dublin.

Cosgrove, A. 2011 The Gaelic resurgence and the Geraldine supremacy: *c.* 1400–1534. In T.W. Moody and F.X. Martin (eds), *The course of Irish history*, 136–50. Cork.

Crawford, J.C. 1993 *Anglicizing the government of Ireland: the Irish Privy Council and the expansion of Tudor rule, 1556–1578*. Dublin.

Cressy, D. 2015 *Charles I and the people of England*. Oxford.

Crooks, P. 2017 The ascent and descent of Desmond under Lancaster and York. In P. Crooks and S. Duffy (eds), *The Geraldines and medieval Ireland*, 223–63.

Crossley, A. and Elrington, C.R. (eds) 1990 *A history of the County of Oxford: Volume 12, Wootton Hundred (South) including Woodstock. Originally published by Victoria County History*, 274–81. London.

Cunningham, J. 2018 Politics, 1641–1660. In J. Ohlmeyer (ed.), *The Cambridge History of Ireland* (4 vols), Vol. 2, 72–95. Cambridge.

Curtis, E. 1910 The clan system among English settlers in Ireland. *English Historical Review* **25** (97), 116–20.

Curtis, E. 1923 *A history of medieval Ireland from 1110 to 1513* (2nd edn, 1938). London.

Curtis, E. 1924–7 Unpublished letters from Richard II in Ireland, 1394–5. *PRIA* **37**C, 276–303.

Curtis, E. 1932 Richard, Duke of York, as viceroy of Ireland, 1447–1460; with unpublished materials for his relations with native chiefs. *JRSAI* **62**, 158–86.

Curtis, E. (ed.) 1932–43 *Calendar of Ormond deeds* (6 vols). Dublin.

Curtis, E. 1933 Janico Dartas, Richard the Second's 'Gascon Squire': his career in Ireland, 1394–1426. *JRSAI* **63**, 182–205.

Curtis, E. 1936 *A history of Ireland*. London.

Curtis, E. and McDowell, R.B. 1943 *Irish historical documents, 1172–1922*. London.

Cust, R. 2013 *Charles I and the aristocracy, 1625–1642*. Cambridge.

D'Alton, J. 1838 *The history of the County of Dublin*. Dublin.

D'Alton, J. 1860 *Illustrations, historical and genealogical, of King James' Irish army list (1689)* (2 vols) (2nd enlarged edn). Dublin.

Davies, J. 1747 *A discoverie of the true causes why Ireland was never entirely subdued, nor brought under obedience of the crowne of England, until the beginning of His Maiesties happy raigne. Printed exactly from the edition in 1612*. London.

de León, F.G. 2009 *The road to Rocroi: class, culture and command in the Spanish army of Flanders, 1567–1659*. Leiden and Boston.

de Mesa, E. 2014 *The Irish in the Spanish armies in the seventeenth century*. Woodbridge.

Devitt, M. 1899–1902 Clongowes Wood. *JKAS* **3**, 207–15.

Dix, E.R.McC. 1897 The lesser castles in the Co. Dublin. *The Irish Builder* **39**, 75–6.

Doherty, C. 1998 The Vikings in Ireland: a review. In H.B. Clarke, M. Ní Mhaonaigh and R. Ó Floinn (eds), *Ireland and Scandinavia in the early Viking age*, 288–330. Dublin.

Doherty, C. 2000 Cluain Dolcáin: a brief note. In A.P. Smyth (ed.), *Seanchas: studies in early and medieval Irish archaeology, history and literature in honour of F.J. Byrne*, 182–8. Dublin.

Donovan, B.C. 1998 Tudor rule in Gaelic Leinster and the rise of Feagh McHugh O'Byrne. In C. O'Brien (ed.), *Feagh McHugh O'Byrne: the Wicklow firebrand*, 118–49. Rathdrum.

Duffy, S. 1995 Ostmen, Irish and Welsh in the eleventh century. *Peritia* **9**, 378–96.

Duffy, S. 2000 Ireland and Scotland, 1014–1169: contacts and caveats. In A.P. Smyth (ed.), *Seanchas: studies in early and medieval Irish archaeology, history and literature in honour of F.J. Byrne*, 348–56. Dublin.

Duffy, S. 2015 The Welsh conquest of Ireland. In E. Purcell, P. MacCotter, J. Nyhan and J. Sheehan (eds), *Clerics, kings and Vikings: essays on medieval Ireland in honour of Donnchadh Ó Corráin*, 103–14. Dublin.

Dunlop, R. 1913 *Ireland under the Commonwealth: being a selection of documents relating to the government of Ireland from 1651 to 1659* (2 vols). Manchester.

Dwyer, F. 2016 *1348, a medieval apocalypse: the Black Death in Ireland*. Dublin.

Edwards, D. 1998 In Tyrone's shadow: Feagh McHugh, forgotten leader of the Nine Years War. In C. O'Brien (ed.), *Feagh McHugh O'Byrne: the Wicklow firebrand*, 212–48. Rathdrum.

Edwards, D. 2017 Geraldine endgame: reassessing the origins of the Desmond rebellion, 1573–9. In P. Crooks and S. Duffy (eds), *The Geraldines and medieval Ireland: the making of a myth*, 341–78. Dublin.

Edwards, D. 2018a The land-grabbers' accomplices: Richard Boyle's Munster affinity, 1588–1603. In D. Edwards and C. Rynne (eds), *The colonial world of Richard Boyle, first earl of Cork*, 166–88. Dublin.

Edwards, D. 2018b Boyle's private army: the creation of a colonial security force in early Stuart Munster. In D. Edwards and C. Rynne (eds), *The colonial world of Richard Boyle, first earl of Cork*, 223–44. Dublin.

Edwards, D. 2018c Political change and social transformation, 1603–1641. In J. Ohlmeyer (ed.), *The Cambridge History of Ireland* (4 vols), Vol. 2, 48–71. Cambridge.

Edwards, D. and Rynne, C. 2018 Nuancing an archetype: Richard Boyle and his colonial world. In D. Edwards and C. Rynne (eds), *The colonial world of Richard Boyle, first earl of Cork*, 13–26. Dublin.

Edwards, E. 2004 Instructions, by the Lord Justices [of Ireland]. Written from

Dublin, 28 Jan. 1661. Carte Calendar Volume xxxi, January–May 1661. Bodleian Library, University of Oxford.

Edwards, E. 2005 Petition of Richard Walsh, late of Carrigmaine in the county of Dublin. Carte Calendar Volume xliii, January–June 1666. Bodleian Library, University of Oxford.

Ellis, S.G. 1995 *Tudor frontiers and noble power: the making of the British state*. Oxford.

Ellis, S. [G.] 2011 The English Pale: a 'failed entity'. *History Ireland* **19** (2), 15–17.

Ellis, S.G. 2017 The Great Earl of Kildare (1456–1513) and the creation of the English Pale. In P. Crooks and S. Duffy (eds), *The Geraldines and medieval Ireland: the making of a myth*, 325–40. Dublin.

Etchingham, C. 1994 Evidence of Scandinavian settlement in Wicklow. In K. Hannigan and W. Nolan (eds), *Wicklow history and society: interdisciplinary essays on the history of an Irish county*, 113–38. Dublin.

Fellows-Jensen, G. 2015 Through a glass darkly: some sidelights on Viking influence on personal names and place-names in Ireland. In H.B. Clarke and R. Johnson (eds), *The Vikings in Ireland and beyond: before and after the Battle of Clontarf*, 268–83. Dublin.

Fibiger, L. 2003 Report on the human skeletal remains from Carrickmines Great, Co. Dublin. Unpublished report.

Finlay, M. 2014 *Pastry jiggers and pastry prints*. Carlisle.

Finlayson, J. 1878 *Inscriptions on the monuments, mural tablets &c., at present existing in Christ Church Cathedral Dublin*. Dublin.

Fissel, M.C. 1994 *The bishop's wars: Charles I's campaigns against Scotland, 1638–1640*. Cambridge.

Fitzgerald, C.W. 1858 *The earls of Kildare, and their ancestors: from 1057–1773*. Dublin.

Fitzgerald, Lord W. 1896 Kilkea castle. *JKAS* **2** (1), 3–30.

Fitzgerald, Lord W. 1912–14 The priory, or nunnery, of Graney, County Kildare. *JKAS* **7**, 373–81.

Flanagan, M.T. 2005 *Irish royal charters: texts and contexts*. Oxford.

Forkan, K. 2007 Inventing a Protestant icon: the strange death of Sir Charles Coote, 1642. In D. Edwards, P. Lenihan and C. Tait (eds), *Age of atrocity: violence and political conflict in early modern Ireland*, 204–18. Dublin.

Foster, R.F. 1988 *Modern Ireland 1600–1972*. London.

Frame, R. 1981 *Colonial Ireland 1169–1369*. Dublin.

Frame, R. 1982 *English lordship in Ireland 1318–1361*. Oxford.

Frame, R. 1989 Military service in the lordship of Ireland 1290–1360: institutions and society on the Anglo-Gaelic frontier. In R. Bartlett and A. MacKay (eds), *Medieval frontier societies*, 101–26. Oxford.

Frame, R. 1995 Two kings in Leinster: the Crown and the MicMhurchadha in the fourteenth century. In T.B. Barry, R. Frame and K. Simms (eds), *Colony and frontier in medieval Ireland: essays presented to J.F. Lydon*, 155–75. London.

Frazer, W. 1879–88 Description of a great sepulchral mound at Aylesbury-road, near Donnybrook, in the county of Dublin, containing human and animal remains, as well as objects of antiquarian interest, referable to the tenth or eleventh centuries. *PRIA* **16**, 29–55, 116–18.

Freeman, A.M. 1944 *Annála Connacht: The Annals of Connacht (AD 1224–1544).* Dublin.

Freist, D. 2011 Popery in perfection? The experience of Catholicism: Henrietta Maria between private practice and public discourse. In M.J. Braddick and D.L. Smith (eds), *The experience of revolution in Stuart Britain and Ireland: essays for John Morrill*, 33–51. Cambridge.

Frijhoff, W. and Spies, M. 2004 *Dutch culture in a European perspective 1: 1650—hard-won unity*. Assen.

Furgol, E.M. 2002 Beating the odds: Alexander Leslie's 1640 campaign in England. In S. Murdoch and A. Mackillop (eds), *Fighting for identity: Scottish military experience* c. *1550–1900*, 33–60. Leiden and Boston.

Gardiner, S.R. 1910 *History of the great civil war, 1642–1649* (4 vols). London.

Gaukroger, S. 1995 *Descartes: an intellectual biography.* Oxford.

Geijer, E.G. 1845 *The history of the Swedes* (trans. J.H. Turner) (3 vols). London.

General alphabetical index of townlands and towns, parishes and baronies of Ireland. Based on the Census of Ireland 1851 (Dublin, 1861).

Gilbert, J.T. 1865 *History of the viceroys of Ireland, with notices of the castle of Dublin and its chief occupants in former times*. Dublin.

Gilbert, J.T. (ed.) 1879–80 *A contemporary history of affairs in Ireland from 1641 to 1652* (3 vols). Dublin.

Gilbert, J.T. 1882–91 *History of the Irish Confederation and the war in Ireland, 1641 [–1649]: containing a narrative of affairs in Ireland, by Richard Bellings* (7 vols). Dublin.

Gilbert, J.T. 1884 *Chartularies of St Mary's Abbey, Dublin, with the register of its house at Dunbrody, and annals of Ireland* (2 vols). London.

Gilbert, J.T. 1889–1944 *Calendar of ancient records of Dublin* (19 vols). Dublin.

G.N. 1642 *A geographicall description of the kingdom of Ireland, according to the five provinces and 32 counties, together with the stations, creeks, and harbours belonging thereto, fit for gentlemen, souldiers and seamen, as also declaring the right and titles of the kings of England unto that kingdom*. London.

Goodbody, R. 1993 *On the borders of the Pale: a history of the Kilgobbin, Stepaside and Sandyford area*. Bray.

Grazebrook, H.S. (ed.) 1885 *The heraldic visitations of Staffordshire made by Sir Richard St George, Norroy, in 1614, and by Sir William Dugdale, Norroy, in the years 1663 and 1664*. London.

Grell, O.P. 1989 *Dutch Calvinists in early Stuart London: the Dutch Church in Austin Friars 1603–1642*. Leiden and New York.

Grell, O.P. 2011 *Brethren in Christ: a Calvinist network in Reformation Europe*. Cambridge.

Griffith, M.C. 1991 *Calendar of inquisitions formerly in the office of the chief remembrancer of the exchequer prepared from the MSS of the Irish record commission*. Dublin.

Griffiths, F.A. 1844 *The military annual for 1844*. London.

Griffiths, G. 1890 *Chronicles of the County Wexford, being a record of memorable incidents, disasters, social occurrences, and crimes, also, biographies of eminent persons, &c., brought down to the year 1877*. Enniscorthy.

Grogan, E. and Kilfeather, A. 1997 *Archaeological inventory of County Wicklow*. Dublin.

Grosart, A.B. 1886 *The Lismore Papers (First Series) viz. autobiographical notes, remembrances and diaries of Sir Richard Boyle, first and 'great' earl of Cork* (5 vols). Blackburn.

Grossman, M. 2007 *World military leaders: a biographical dictionary*. New York.

Guthrie, W.P. 2003 *The later Thirty Years War: from the Battle of Wittstock to the Treaty of Westphalia*. Portsmouth, NH.

Gwynn, E.J. (ed.) 1991 *The Metrical Dindshenchas* (reprint). Dublin.

Halliday, C. 1884 *The Scandinavian kingdom of Dublin*. Dublin.

Hamilton, G.E. 1915 Fiacha Mac Aodha Ui Bhroin and Domhnall Spáinneach Caomhánach. *JRSAI* **45**, 109–14.

Hamilton, H.C. (ed.) 1860 *Calendar of the state papers relating to Ireland, of the reigns of Henry VIII, Edward VI, Mary and Elizabeth, 1509–1573*. London.

Hamilton, H.C. (ed.) 1867–90 *Calendar of the state papers relating to Ireland of the reign of Elizabeth, 1574–96*. London.

Hamilton, W.D. (ed.) 1873–93 *Calendar of state papers, domestic series, of the reign of Charles I, 1639–49*. London.

Hamilton, W.D. and Crawford Lomas, S. (eds) 1897 *Calendar of state papers, domestic series, of the reign of Charles I. Addenda: March 1625 to January 1649*. London.

Hankey, J.A. 1889 *History of the Apsley & Bathurst families*. Cirencester.

Harcourt, E.W. (ed.) 1880–1905 *The Harcourt papers* (14 vols). Oxford.

Harcourt, G.S., Walpole, H. and Reynolds, J. 1806 *Description of Nuneham-Courtenay in the county of Oxford*. Oxford.

Hardiman, J. (ed.) 1826–9 *Inquisitionum in officio rotulorum cancellariae Hiberniae asservatarum repertorium* (2 vols). Dublin.

Hardinge, W.H. 1865 *Census of Ireland 1659—Dublin County*. Landed Estates Record Office, Dublin.

Hardwicke, P. (ed.) 1778 *Miscellaneous state papers. From 1501 to 1726. In two volumes*. London.

Hayes-McCoy, G.A. 2011 The Tudor conquest: 1534–1603. In T.W. Moody and F.X. Martin (eds), *The course of Irish history* (revised and enlarged edn), 151–62. Cork.

Healy, P. 1978 A report on the importance of an earthwork believed to be part of the Pale ditch at Balally, County Dublin. Unpublished report for An Foras Forbartha Teoranta, Dublin.

Healy, P. 1983 Report on Carrickmines Castle, County Dublin. Unpublished report for An Foras Forbartha Teoranta, Dublin.

Healy, P. 2009 *Pre-Norman grave-slabs and cross-inscribed stones in the Dublin region* (ed. K. Swords). Dublin.

Hennessy, W.M. (ed.) 1871 *The Annals of Loch Cé: a chronicle of Irish affairs from AD 1014 to AD 1590* (2 vols). London.

Hennessy, W.M. and MacCarthy, B. 1887–1901 *The Annals of Ulster* (4 vols). Dublin.

Henning, B.D. (ed.) 1983 *The history of parliament: the House of Commons 1660–1690*. London.

Hexham, H. 1630 *A historicall relation of the famous siege of the Busse, and the surprising of Wesell [...]*. Delph.

Hexham, H. 1633 *A journall, of the taking in of Venlo, Roermont, Strale, the memorable siege of Maastricht, the towne and castle of Limburch under the able, and wise conduct of his Excie: the Prince of Orange, anno 1632. Capt. Henry Hexham, quartermaster to the regiment of the Lord Generall Vere*. Delph.

Hexham, H. 1637 *A true and briefe relation of the famous siege of Breda: besieged, and taken in under the able and victorious conduct of his Highness the Prince of Orange, captaine generall of the States armie, and admirall of the seas, &c.—composed by Henry Hexham quartermaster to the regiment of the honourable Coronell Goring*. The Hague.

Hickson, M. 1884 *Ireland in the seventeenth century, or, the Irish massacres of 1641–2: their causes and results* (2 vols). London.

Hinds, A.B. (ed.) 1911 *Calendar of state papers relating to English affairs in the archives of Venice, Vol. 17: 1621–3*, 501–14.

HMC 1879 *Seventh report, part 1: the manuscripts of the House of Lords, 1–182; of the earl of Denbigh, 196–232; of the earl of Egmont, 232–249; of Sir Harry Verney, Bart., 433–509*. London.

HMC 1891 *Twelfth report, appendix, part IX: the manuscripts of the duke of Beaufort, K.G., the earl of Donoughmore, and others*. London.

HMC 1895 *Fourteenth report, appendix, part vii: the manuscripts of the marquis of Ormonde*. London.

HMC 1897 *Fifteenth report, appendix, part III: the manuscripts of Charles Haliday of Dublin: acts of the privy council in Ireland, 1556–1571*. London.

HMC 1900 *Report on the manuscripts of Lord Montagu of Beaulieu*. London.

HMC 1903 *Calendar of the manuscripts of the marquess of Ormonde*. London.

HMC 1905–9 *Report on the manuscripts of the earl of Egmont* (2 vols). London.

Hogan, E. (ed.) 1878 *The description of Ireland, and the state thereof as it is at present in anno 1598*. Dublin and London.

Hogan, E. 1910 *Onomasticon Goedelicum*. Dublin and London.

Hone, R.B. 1833–43 *Lives of eminent Christians* (4 vols). London.

Hore, P.H. (ed.) 1900–11 *History of the town and county of Wexford* (6 vols). London.

Hubner, J. 1748 *De nieuwe, vermeerderde en verbeterde kouranten-tolk of Zakelyk, historisch—en staatkundig woordenboek*. Leiden.

Hunter, J. 1834 *Rotuli selecti ad res Anglicas et Hibernicas spectantes, ex archivis in domo capitulari west-monasteriensi, deprompti*. London.

Hussey Walsh, V. 1900–1 The Austrian branches of the family of Walsh. *The Genealogist* (new ser.) **17**, 217–24.

Hutton, R. 1989 *Charles the Second, king of England, Scotland, and Ireland*. Oxford.

Hyde, E. 1826 *The history of the rebellion and civil wars in England, to which is added an historical view of the affairs of Ireland* (6 vols). Oxford.

Ingrao, C.W. 1994 *The Habsburg monarchy 1618–1815*. Cambridge.

Israel, J.I. 1997 *Conflicts of empires: Spain, the Low Countries and the struggle for world supremacy 1585–1713*. London and Rio Grande.

Jackson, B.D. (ed.) 1876 *A catalogue of plants cultivated in the garden of John Gerard in the years 1596–1599*. London.

Joyce, W.St J. 1921 *The neighbourhood of Dublin: its topography, antiquities and historical associations.* Dublin.

Kavanagh, J. 2007 Site 599. Church Street, Finglas, County Dublin. In I. Bennett (ed.), *Excavations 2004: summary accounts of archaeological excavations in Ireland*, 139–40. Bray.

Kay, T. 1795 *An historical account of the British regiments employed since the reign of Queen Elizabeth and King James I in the formation and defence of the Dutch Republic particularly of the Scotch brigade.* London.

Kerney-Walsh, M. 1986 *'Destruction by peace': Hugh O'Neill after Kinsale.* Armagh.

Kilburn, T. and Milton, A. 1996 The public context of the trial and execution of Strafford. In J.F. Merritt (ed.), *The political world of Thomas Wentworth, earl of Strafford, 1621–1641*, 230–51. Cambridge.

Kim, J.-L. 2011 The Scottish-English-Romish Book: the character of the Scottish prayer book of 1637. In M.J. Braddick and D.L. Smith (eds), *The experience of revolution in Stuart Britain and Ireland: essays for John Morrill*, 14–32. Cambridge.

Kippis, A. 1778–93 *Biographia Britannica: or, the lives of the most eminent persons who have flourished in Great Britain and Ireland* (2nd edn) (5 vols). London.

Knowler, W. (ed.) 1739 *The earl of Strafforde's letters and dispatches with an essay towards his life by Sir George Radcliffe* (2 vols). London.

Kuijpers, E. 2015 'O, Lord, save us from shame': narratives of emotions in convent chronicles by female authors during the Dutch revolt, 1566–1635. In S. Broomhall (ed.), *Gender and emotions in medieval and early modern Europe: destroying order, structuring disorder*, 127–45. Farnham and Burlington.

Lawlor, H.J. 1908–9 A calendar of the Liber Niger and Liber Albus of Christ Church, Dublin. *PRIA* **27**C, 1–93.

Lawrence, D.R. 2009 *The complete soldier: military books and military culture in early Stuart England, 1603–1645*. Brill.

Leask, H.G. 1941 *Irish castles and castellated houses*. Dublin.

le Blond, M. 1759 *The military engineer: or, a treatise on the attack and defence of all kinds of fortified places*, Part 2. London.

Lecky, W.E.H. 1902–3 *A history of Ireland in the eighteenth century* (5 vols). London and Bombay.

Lee, S.J. 1991 *The Thirty Years War*. London and New York.

Leland, T. 1773 *The history of Ireland from the invasion of Henry II with a preliminary discourse on the antient state of that kingdom* (3 vols), Vol. 2. London.

Lennon, C. 1995 Dublin's great explosion of 1597. *History Ireland* **3** (3), 29–34.

Lennon, C. 2001 The changing face of Dublin, 1550–1750. In P. Clark and R. Gillespie (eds), *Two capitals: London and Dublin 1500–1840*, 39–52. Oxford.

Leslie, J.B. 1908 *History of Kilsaran union of parishes in the County of Louth*. Dundalk.

Lewis, S. 1837 *A topographical dictionary of Ireland* (2 vols). London.

Little, P. 2018 Boyle's war: the first earl of Cork and the First Bishop's War. In D. Edwards and C. Rynne (eds), *The colonial world of Richard Boyle, first earl of Cork*, 245–55. Dublin.

Lodge, J. (ed.) 1772 A survey of the half-barony of Rathdown, in the county of Dublin—by order of Charles Fleetwood, lord deputy, October 4th, 1654. In *Desiderata curiosa Hibernica: or, a select collection of state papers; consisting of royal instructions, directives, dispatches, and letters* (2 vols), Vol. 2, 529–68. Dublin.

Lodge, J. and Archdall, M. 1789 *The peerage of Ireland: or, a genealogical history of the present nobility of that kingdom* (7 vols). Dublin.

Long, H. 1998 Settlement and social life in Feagh McHugh's Ballinacor. In C. O'Brien (ed.), *Feagh McHugh O'Byrne: the Wicklow firebrand*, 249–68. Rathdrum.

Lorimer, J. (ed.) 2006 *Sir Walter Raleigh's Discoverie of Guiana*. Published for the Hakluyt Society [Vol. 15 (3rd ser.)]. London.

Luders, A. *et al.* (eds) 1810–28 *The statutes of the realm: printed by command of his majesty King George the Third, in pursuance of an address of the House of Commons of Great Britain* (11 vols). London.

Lydon, J. 1973 *Ireland in the later Middle Ages*. Dublin.

Lydon, J.F. 1994 Medieval Wicklow—'a land of war'. In K. Hannigan and W. Nolan (eds), *Wicklow history and society: interdisciplinary essays on the history of an Irish county*, 151–89. Dublin.

Lydon, J.F. 2011 The medieval English colony: 13th and 14th centuries. In T.W. Moody and F.X. Martin (eds), *The course of Irish history* (revised and enlarged edn), 123–35. Cork.

Mac Airt, S. (ed.) 1944 *Leabhar Branach: the Book of the O'Byrnes*. Dublin.

Mac Airt, S. (ed.) 1951 *The Annals of Inisfallen*. Dublin.

Mac Airt, S. and Mac Niocaill, G. (ed.) 1983 *The Annals of Ulster (to AD 1131)*. Dublin.

McCafferty, J. 1996 'God bless your free Church of Ireland': Wentworth, Laud, Bramhall and the Irish convocation of 1634. In J.F. Merritt (ed.), *The political world of Thomas Wentworth, earl of Strafford, 1621–1641*, 187–208. Cambridge.

Mac Cuarta, B. 2007 Religious violence against settlers in south Ulster, 1641–2. In D. Edwards, P. Lenihan and C. Tait (eds), *Age of atrocity: violence and political conflict in early modern Ireland*, 154–75. Dublin.

MacCulloch, D. 2003 *Reformation: Europe's house divided 1490–1700*. London.

MacCurtain, M. 1972 *Tudor and Stuart Ireland*. Dublin.

McCutcheon, C. and Meenan, R. 2011 Pots on the hearth: domestic pottery in historic Ireland. *PRIA* **111**C, 91–113.

McEnery, M.J. and Refaussé, R. 2001 *Christ Church deeds*. Dublin.

McGettigan, D. 2016 *Richard II and the Irish kings*. Dublin.

McGurk, J. 2007 The pacification of Ulster, 1600–3. In D. Edwards, P. Lenihan and C. Tait (eds), *Age of atrocity: violence and political conflict in early modern Ireland*, 119–29. Dublin.

Maclean, J. 1857 *The life and times of Sir Peter Carew, kt*. London.

McNeill, C. (ed.) 1943 *The Tanner letters: original documents and notices of Irish affairs in the 16th and 17th centuries*. Dublin.

McNeill, C. (ed.) 1950 *Calendar of Archbishop Alen's register,* c. *1172–1534* (index compiled by L. Price). Dublin.

MacNeill, E. 1981 *Celtic Ireland*. (Introduction with new notes by Donnchadh Ó Corráin.) Dublin.

McNeill, T. 1997 *Castles in Ireland: feudal power in a Gaelic world*. London.

Mac Niocaill, G. (ed.) 1992 *Crown surveys of lands 1540–41 with the Kildare rental begun in 1518*. Dublin.

Maginn, C. 2004 English marcher lineages in south Dublin in the late Middle Ages. *Irish Historical Studies* **34** (134), 113–36.

Maginn, C. 2005 *'Civilizing' Gaelic Leinster: the extension of Tudor rule in the O'Byrne and O'Toole lordships*. Dublin.

Mahaffy, R.P. (ed.) 1900–1 *Calendar of the state papers relating to Ireland, of the reign of Charles I, 1625–47*. London.

Mahaffy, R.P. (ed.) 1912 *Calendar of the state papers relating to Ireland of the reign of Elizabeth, 1601–3, with addenda, 1565–1654, and of the Hanmer papers*. London.

Malden, H.E. (ed.) 1911 *A history of the county of Surrey: originally published by Victoria County History* (4 vols). London.

Mann, G. 1976 *Wallenstein: his life narrated by Golo Mann* (trans. C. Kessler). London.

Manning, J. 1893 Glendalough in the twelfth century. *Irish Ecclesiastical Record* **14** (3rd ser.), 351–66, 636–51.

Markham, C.R. 1888 *The fighting Veres: lives of Sir Francis Vere, general of the queen's forces in the Low Countries, governor of the Brill and of Portsmouth, and of Sir Horace Vere, general of the English forces in the Low Countries, governor of the Brill, master-general of ordnance, and Baron Vere of Tilbury*. London.

Martin, F.X. 2011 The Normans—arrival and settlement: 1169–*c.* 1300. In T.W. Moody and F.X. Martin (eds), *The course of Irish history* (revised and enlarged edn), 104–22. Cork.

Mason, W.M. 1820 *The history and antiquities of the Collegiate and Cathedral Church of St Patrick near Dublin, from its foundation in 1190, to the year 1819*. Dublin.

Memegalos, F.S. 2007 *George Goring (1608–1657): Caroline courtier and Royalist general*. Burlington.

Merritt, J.F. 1996 Power and communication: Thomas Wentworth and government at a distance during the Personal Rule, 1629–1635. In J.F. Merritt (ed.), *The political world of Thomas Wentworth, earl of Strafford, 1621–1641*, 109–32.

Cambridge.

Mills, J. (ed.) 1891 *Account roll of the Priory of the Holy Trinity, Dublin, 1337–1346.* Dublin.

Mills, J. 1894 The Norman settlement in Leinster—the cantreds near Dublin. *JRSAI* **24**, 160–75.

Moody, T.W. 1939–40 The Irish parliament under Elizabeth and James I: a general survey. *PRIA* **45**C, 41–81.

Morgan, H. 1993 *Tyrone's rebellion: the outbreak of the Nine Years War in Tudor Ireland.* Woodbridge.

Morgan, H. 2007 'Slán Dé fút go hoíche': Hugh O'Neill's murders. In D. Edwards, P. Lenihan and C. Tait (eds), *Age of atrocity: violence and political conflict in early modern Ireland*, 95–118. Dublin.

Morrin, J. (ed.) 1861–2 *Calendar of the patent and close rolls of chancery in Ireland, of the reigns of Henry VIII, Edward VI, Mary and Elizabeth* (2 vols). London.

Morrin, J. (ed.) 1862 *Calendar of the patent and close rolls of chancery in Ireland, from the 18th to the 45th of Queen Elizabeth* (2 vols). Dublin.

Morris, D. 1977 *Manwatching: a field guide to human behaviour.* London.

Morrissey, J.F. (ed.) 1939 *Statute rolls of the parliament of Ireland, 12th and 13th to 21st and 22nd years of the reign of King Edward the Fourth.* Dublin.

Murdoch, S. 2010 *The terror of the seas: Scottish maritime warfare 1513–1713.* Leiden and Boston.

Murdoch, S. and Grosjean, A. 2014 *Alexander Leslie and the Scottish generals of the Thirty Years War, 1618–1648.* London and New York.

Murphy, D. (ed.) 1896 *The Annals of Clonmacnoise, being annals of Ireland from the earliest period to AD 1408.* Dublin.

Murphy, M. and Potterton, M. 2010 *The Dublin region in the Middle Ages: settlement, land-use and economy.* Dublin.

Murray, K. 1944–5 Loughlinstown camp. *Dublin Historical Record* **7** (1), 22–34.

Nicholls, K. 1998a Críoch Branach: the O'Byrnes and their country. In C. O'Brien (ed.), *Feagh McHugh O'Byrne: the Wicklow firebrand*, 7–39. Rathdrum.

Nicholls, K. 1998b The genealogy of the Byrnes of Ranelagh. In C. O'Brien (ed.), *Feagh McHugh O'Byrne: the Wicklow firebrand*, 107–17. Rathdrum.

Nicholls, K. 1998c The O'Byrne sept of Knockrath. In C. O'Brien (ed.), *Feagh McHugh O'Byrne: the Wicklow firebrand*, 274–77. Rathdrum.

Nicholls, K. 2007 The other massacre: English killings of Irish, 1641–3. In D. Edwards, P. Lenihan and C. Tait (eds), *Age of atrocity: violence and political conflict in early modern Ireland*, 176–91. Dublin.

Nolan, K. 1939 The ancient church and parish of Kiltiernan, Co. Dublin. *Dublin Historical Record* **2** (1), 38–40.

O'Brien, E. 1992 A re-assessment of the 'great sepulchral mound' containing a Viking burial at Donnybrook, Dublin. *Medieval Archaeology* **36**, 170–3.

O'Byrne, E. 1998a The rise of the Gabhal Raghnaill. In C. O'Brien (ed.), *Feagh McHugh O'Byrne: the Wicklow firebrand*, 40–106. Rathdrum.

O'Byrne, E. 1998b The Battle of Glenmalure, 25 August 1580: cause and course. In C. O'Brien (ed.), *Feagh McHugh O'Byrne: the Wicklow firebrand*, 150–80. Rathdrum.

O'Byrne, E. 2002 On the frontier: Carrickmines castle and Gaelic Ireland. *Archaeology Ireland* **16** (3), 13–15.

O'Byrne, E. 2003a *War, politics and the Irish of Leinster, 1156–1606*. Dublin.

O'Byrne, E. 2003b A much disputed land: Carrickmines and the Dublin marches. In S. Duffy (ed.), *Medieval Dublin IV*, 229–52. Dublin.

O'Byrne, E. 2004 Cultures in contact in the Leinster and Dublin marches, 1170–1400. In S. Duffy (ed.), *Medieval Dublin V*, 111–48. Dublin.

O'Byrne, E. 2005 One world: the community of the southern Dublin marches. *History Ireland* **13** (3), 17–21.

O'Carroll, E. 2003 Site No. 434. Ballyogan, County Dublin. In I. Bennett (ed.), *Excavations 2001: summary accounts of archaeological excavations in Ireland*, 123–4. Bray.

Ó Conbhuí, C. 1962 The lands of St Mary's Abbey, Dublin. *PRIA* **62**C, 21–85.

O'Conor, K.D. 1998 *The archaeology of medieval rural settlement in Ireland*. Dublin.

Ó Corráin, D. 1972 *Ireland before the Normans*. Dublin.

O'Donovan, J. (ed. and trans.) 1854 *The Annals of the Four Masters* (7 vols). Dublin.

O'Flanagan, J.R. 1870 *The lives of the lord chancellors and keepers of the Great Seal of Ireland: from the earliest times to the reign of Queen Victoria* (2 vols). London.

O'Hanlon, J. 1875 *Lives of the Irish saints, compiled from calendars, martyrologies, and various sources relating to the ancient church history of Ireland* (10 vols). Dublin and London.

O'Hart, J. 1887 *The Irish landed gentry when Cromwell came to Ireland, or, a supplement to Irish pedigrees*. Dublin.

Ohlmeyer, J. 1996 Strafford, the 'Londonderry business' and the 'new British history'. In J.F. Merritt (ed.), *The political world of Thomas Wentworth, earl of Strafford, 1621–1641*, 209–29. Cambridge.

Ó Néill, J. 2000 Site 169. Cherrywood, County Dublin. In I. Bennett (ed.), *Excavations 1999: summary accounts of archaeological excavations in Ireland*, 54–6. Bray.

Ó Néill, J. 2013 Excavations at Cherrywood. In C. Corlett (ed.), *Unearthing the archaeology of Dún Laoghaire–Rathdown*, 64–72. Dún Laoghaire.

Ormerod, G. 1819 *The history of the County Palatine and City of Chester: compiled from original evidences in public offices, the Harleian and Cottonian MSS, parochial registers, private muniments […]* (3 vols). London.

Orpen, G.H. (ed.) 1892 *The song of Dermot and the Earl: an old French poem*. Oxford.

Orpen, G.H. 1908 Novum Castrum McKynegan, Newcastle, County Wicklow. *JRSAI* **38** (2), 126–40.

Ó Siochrú, M. 1999 *Confederate Ireland, 1642–1649: a constitutional and political analysis*. Dublin.

O'Sullivan, P. 1986 Placenames, fieldnames and folklore. In P. O'Sullivan (ed.),

Newcastle Lyons—a parish of the Pale, 25–44. Dublin.
Otway-Ruthven, J. 1959 Knight service in Ireland. *JRSAI* **89** (1), 1–15.
Otway-Ruthven, J. 1961 The medieval church lands of Co. Dublin. In J.A. Watt, J.B. Morrall and F.X. Martin (eds), *Medieval studies presented to Aubrey Gwynn*, 54–73. Dublin.
Parrott, D. 2001 *Richelieu's army: war, government and society in France, 1624–1642*. Cambridge.
Patterson, W.B. 1997 *King James VI and I and the reunion of Christendom*. Cambridge.
Playfair, J. 1808–14 *A system of geography, ancient and modern* (6 vols). Edinburgh.
Polisensky, J.V. and Snider, F. 1978 *War and society in Europe 1618–1648*. Cambridge.
Poot, A. 2013 *Crucial years in Anglo-Dutch relations (1625–1642): the political and diplomatic contacts*. Hilversum.
Potter, M. 2013 The greatest gerrymander in Irish history: James I's 40 boroughs of 1612–13. *History Ireland* **21** (2), 14–17.
Prendergast, J.P. 1875 *The Cromwellian settlement of Ireland* (2nd edn, enlarged). Dublin.
Prendergast, J.P. and Quinn, D.B. 1967 Calendar of the Irish council book, 1581–1586. *Analecta Hibernica* **24**, 91–180.
Price, L. 1932 Notes on Feagh McHugh O'Byrne. *JKAS* **11** (3), 134–75.
Price, L. 1940 The antiquities and place names of South County Dublin. *Dublin Historical Record* **2** (4), 121–33.
Price, L. (ed.) 1942 *An eighteenth-century antiquary: the sketches, notes and diaries of Austin Cooper (1759–1830)*. Dublin.
Price, L. 1951 The place-names of the books of survey and distribution and other records of the Cromwellian settlement. *JRSAI* **81** (2), 89–106.
Price, L. 1954 The grant to Walter de Ridelesford of Brien and the land of the sons of Turchil. *JRSAI* **84**, 72–7.
Purcell, E. 2003 Land use in medieval Oxmantown. In S. Duffy (ed.), *Medieval Dublin IV*, 193–228. Dublin.
Redworth, G. 2003 *The prince and the infanta: the cultural politics of the Spanish match*. New Haven and London.
Reeves, W. (ed.) 1850 *Acts of Archbishop Colton in the metropolitan visitation of the Diocese of Derry, AD 1397: with a rental of the see estates at that time*. Dublin.
Reeves, W. 1857 *The life of St Columba, founder of Hy; written by Adamnan, ninth abbot of that monastery*. Dublin.
Roberts, W. 1647 *The booke of entries of the names, commands, offices, families, descents, and former services, of the severall commanders, officers, & gentlemen sent into Ireland, by the most honourable houses of parliament in England, to serve his Ma.tie, against ye Irish rebells &c: begun by William Roberts, Doctor of the Civile Lawe, Ulster, King of Armes of all Ireland, the sixteenth of Aprill Anno Domini 1647*. NLI.
Robertson, B. 2014 *Royalists at war in Scotland and Ireland, 1638–1650*. Farnham and Burlington.

Robinson, J.H. (ed.) 1904–6 *Readings in European history* (2 vols). Boston and London.

Robinson, G.G. and J. 1794 *A gazetteer of the Netherlands. Containing a full account of all the cities, towns and villages, in the seventeen provinces, and the bishoprick of Liège.* London.

Roche, R. 1970 *The Norman invasion of Ireland*. Tralee.

Ronan, M.V. 1941 Archbishop Bulkeley's visitation of Dublin, 1630. *Archivium Hibernicum* (new ser.) **8**, 56–98.

Rushworth, J. 1703–8 *Historical collections from the year 1638 to the year 1641. Abridg'd and improved* (6 vols). London.

Russell, C.W. and Prendergast, J.P. (eds) 1872–80 *Calendar of the state papers, relating to Ireland, of the reign of James I* (5 vols). London.

Sabbe, M. 1933 *Brabant in 't verweer*. Antwerp.

Salmon, T. 1745 *Modern history: or, the present state of all nations* (3 vols), Vol. 2. London.

Sayles, G.O. 1961 The rebellious first earl of Desmond. In J.A. Watt, J.B. Morrall and F.X. Martin (eds), *Medieval studies presented to Aubrey Gwynn, S.J.*, 203–29. Dublin.

Scott, A.B. and Martin, F.X. (eds) 1978 *Expugnatio Hibernica: The Conquest of Ireland by Giraldus Cambrensis*. Dublin.

Scott, G.D. 1913 *The stones of Bray*. Dublin.

Seel, G.E. 2005 *The English wars and Republic 1637–1660*. London and New York.

Shaw, W.A. and Burtchaell, G.D. 1906 *The knights of England: a complete record from the earliest time to the present day of the knights of all the orders of chivalry in England, Scotland, and Ireland, and knights bachelor* (2 vols). London.

Shiels, D. 2001 Transcription of a 1798 court-martial held at Loughlinstown in October 1798 (unpublished).

Silke, J.J. 1976 The Irish abroad, 1534–1691. In T.W. Moody, F.X. Martin and F.J. Byrne (eds), *A New History of Ireland* (9 vols), Vol. 3, 587–633. Oxford.

Simington, R.C. 1931–61 *The Civil Survey, AD 1654–1656* (10 vols). Dublin.

Simington, R.C. and MacLellan, J. 1966 Oireachtas Library list of outlaws, 1641–1647. *Analecta Hibernica* **23**, 317–67.

Simms, J.G. 2011 The restoration and the Jacobite War: 1660–91. In T.W. Moody and F.X. Martin (eds), *The course of Irish history*, 176–86. Dublin.

Simpson, L. 1994 Anglo-Norman settlement in Uí Briúin Cualann, 1169–1350. In K. Hannigan and W. Nolan (eds), *Wicklow history and society: interdisciplinary essays on the history of an Irish county*, 191–235. Dublin.

Simpson, L. 2003 Dublin's southern frontier under siege: Kindlestown Castle, Delgany, County Wicklow. In S. Duffy (ed.), *Medieval Dublin IV*, 279–368. Dublin.

Skinner, T. 1724 *The life of General Monk: duke of Albemarle* (2nd edn). London.

Smith, B. 1999 *Colonisation and conquest in medieval Ireland: the English in Louth, 1170–1330*. Cambridge.

Smith, C.V. 1996 *Dalkey: society and economy in a small medieval Irish town*. Blackrock.

Smyth, A.P. 1994 Kings, saints and sagas. In K. Hannigan and W. Nolan (eds), *Wicklow history and society: interdisciplinary essays on the history of an Irish county*, 41–111. Dublin.

Stamp, A.E. (ed.) 1927 *Calendar of the close rolls preserved in the public record office. Henry IV*, Vol. 1 (1399–1402). London.

State Papers 1830–52 *King Henry the Eighth: Part III. Correspondence between the governments of England and Ireland, 1515–1538* (11 vols). London.

Stevenson, D. 1981 *Scottish covenanters and Irish confederates: Scottish–Irish relations in the mid-seventeenth century*. Belfast.

Stokes, W. (ed.) 1897 The Annals of Tigernach. *Revue Celtique* **18** (3), 267–303.

Stokes, W. (ed.) 1905 *The Martyrology of Oengus the Culdee*. London.

Stopes, C.C. 1922 *The life of Henry, third earl of Southampton, Shakespeare's patron*. Cambridge.

Stout, M. 2017 *Early medieval Ireland 431–1169*. Dublin.

Stradling, R.A. 1994 *The Spanish monarchy and Irish mercenaries: the Wild Geese in Spain, 1618–68*. Dublin.

Sweetman, D. 1999 *Medieval castles of Ireland*. Cork.

Sweetman, H.S. 1875–81 *Calendar of documents relating to Ireland* (4 vols). London.

Sweetman, H.S. and Handcock, G.F. 1886 *Calendar of documents relating to Ireland*, Vol. 5 (1302–7). London.

Swift, C. 2015 Follow the money: the financial resources of Diarmait Mac Murchada. In E. Purcell, P. MacCotter, J. Nyhan and J. Sheehan (eds), *Clerics, kings and Vikings: essays on medieval Ireland in honour of Donnchadh Ó Corráin*, 91–102. Dublin.

Tait, C. 2005 Using and abusing the dying and the dead in early modern Ireland. *History Ireland* **13** (1), 16–20.

Tait, C. 2007 'The just vengeance of God': reporting the violent deaths of persecutors in early modern Ireland. In D. Edwards, P. Lenihan and C. Tait (eds), *Age of atrocity: violence and political conflict in early modern Ireland*, 130–53. Dublin.

Tait, C., Edwards, D. and Lenihan, P. 2007 Early modern Ireland: a history of violence. In D. Edwards, P. Lenihan and C. Tait (eds), *Age of atrocity: violence and political conflict in early modern Ireland*, 9–33. Dublin.

Terry, C.S. 1899 *The life and campaigns of Alexander Leslie: first earl of Leven*. London and New York.

't Hart, M. 2014 *The Dutch wars of independence: warfare and commerce in the Netherlands 1570–1680*. London and New York.

Thrush, A.D. 1990 The navy under Charles I, 1625–40. Unpublished Ph.D dissertation, University College London.

Tierney, M.A. 1839–43 *Dodd's church history of England from the commencement of the sixteenth century to the revolution in 1688* (5 vols). London.

Todd, J.H. (ed.) 1867 *The war of the Gaedhil with the Gaill (Cogadh Gaedhel re*

Gallaibh). London.

Tresham, E. (ed.) 1828 *Rotulorum patentium et clausorum cancellarie Hiberniae calendarium, Vol. 1, pars 1: Henry II–Henry VII*. Dublin.

Turner, K. 1983 *'If you seek monuments': a guide to the antiquities of Rathdrum*. Rathmichael.

Vanderheijden, J.F. 1933 De plundering van Tienen en het ontzet van Leuven in 1635. *Tijdschrift voor Taal en Letteren Jaargang* **21** (2), 111–31.

van Nimwegen, O. 2006 The quest for security: the case of the Dutch Republic. In M. Burgess and H. Vollaard (eds), *State territoriality and European integration*, 17–36. London and New York.

van Nimwegen, O. 2010 *The Dutch army and the military revolutions, 1588–1688*. Woodbridge.

Vere, F. 1657 *The commentaries of Sr Francis Vere being diverse pieces of service, wherein he had command, written by himself in way of commentary*, Part 4. Cambridge.

Walker, S. 1999 Janico Dartasso: chivalry, nationality and the man-at-arms. *History* **84** (273), 31–51.

Walsh, A. 1998 A summary classification of Viking age swords in Ireland. In H.B. Clarke, M. Ní Mhaonaigh and R. Ó Floinn (eds), *Ireland and Scandinavia in the early Viking age*, 222–35. Dublin.

Warburton, J., Whitelaw, J. and Walsh, R. 1818 *History of the city of Dublin, from the earliest accounts to the present; containing its annals, antiquities, ecclesiastical history, and charters* (2 vols). London.

Ware, J. 1809 *Ancient Irish histories: the chronicle of Ireland*. (a) *Collected by Meredith Hanmer, Doctor of Divinity, in the year 1571*, 1–410. (b) *By Henry Marleburrough*, 1–32. Dublin.

Webb, J. 1823 Translation of a French metrical history of the deposition of King Richard the Second, written by a contemporary [Jean Creton]. *Archaeologia* **20** (1), 1–423.

White, N.B. (ed.) 1943 *Extents of Irish monastic possessions, 1540–1541*. Dublin.

Wielant, A. 1982 *Gedenck-weerdige Avonturen, Alteracien ende verstroijingen, jae Martelie, en verwoestinge, die de annunciaten binnen Thienen hebben geleden van de Geusen Anno 1635* (ed. A. Tuerlinckx and R. Poulman). Tienen.

Willan, T.S. 1938 *The English coasting trade, 1600–1750*. Manchester.

Wilson, C. 1970 *Queen Elizabeth and the revolt of the Netherlands*. Berkeley.

Wilson, P.H. 2009 *The Thirty Years War: Europe's tragedy*. Cambridge.

Wilson, W. 1786 *The post-chaise companion: or, traveller's directory through Ireland*. Dublin.

Windle, B.C.A. 1903 *Chester: a historical and topographical account of the city*. London.

Wood, A. 1691 *Athenae Oxonienses: an exact history of all the writers and bishops who have had their education in the most ancient and famous university of Oxford [...] year 1690* (2 vols), Vol. 1. London.

Wood, H., Langman, A.E. and Griffith, M.C. (eds) 1957 *Calendar of the justiciary rolls or proceedings in the court of the justiciar of Ireland I to VII years of Edward II*.

Dublin.

Woodward, D.M. 1970 *The trade of Elizabethan Chester.* Hull.

Wooton, T., Kimber, E. and Johnson, R. 1771 *The baronetage of England: containing a genealogical and historical account of all the English baronets now existing* (3 vols). London.

Worthington, D.C. 2004 *Scots in Habsburg service: 1618–1648.* Leiden.

Wortley, J.S. 1838 *Memoirs of George Monk, duke of Albemarle: from the French of M. Guizot. Translated and edited, with additional notes and illustrations.* London.

Wright, W.M.B. 1889 *The Ussher memoirs; or, genealogical memoirs of the Ussher families in Ireland.* London.

INDEX

Note: Page numbers in **bold** indicate illustrations.

A
Achall, 3
Act of Explanation, 276, 277
Act of Settlement, 276, 278
Adamson, Thomas Maurice, 49
Adrian IV, Pope, 69
Agarde, Sir Francis, 76, 84
Agincourt, Battle of, 46
Alexander III, Pope, 9–10
Allen, Anne, 100
Allen, Edward, 236
Allen, Giles, 100
Allen, John (archbishop of Dublin), 64, 66
Allen, John (clerk, munitions storehouse), 94
Allen, John (of Bishopscourt, Co. Kildare), 112, 132
Allen, Sir Joshua, 281
Allen, Richard, 236
Allen, Thomas, 141
Allen, William, 100
Amlaib Cúarán (Óláfr kváran), 3, 4
Angevin arrival in Ireland, 5–14
Annals of Clonmacnoise, 3, 4
Annals of Connacht, 45, 57, 58
Annals of the Four Masters, 7, 9, 16, 48, 103, 109
    attack at *Leim Ui Bhanain* (Leap), 58
    on Edward Bruce, 17
    s.a. 915, 4
    s.a. 1014, 3
    s.a. 1052, 3
    s.a. 1141, 8
    s.a. 1369, 34
    s.a. 1569, 83
    s.a. 1581, 90
Annals of Inisfallen, 8
Annals of Loch Cé, 17
Annals of Ross, 30, 42
Annals of Tigernach, 8
Annals of Ulster, 2, 3, 17, 57–8, 66
Annesley, Francis (Lord Mountnorris), 144, 148
Annodan, 44, 112, 275
Anodan, 56
Apsley, Sir Allen, 217, 230
Apsley, Lady Eliza, 218
Apsley, Elizabeth, 218
Apsley, Joan, 230
Apsley, Nicholas, 230
Apsley, Peter, 218
Apsley, William, 230
Archbold, Edward, 95, 100, 138, 141
Archbold ('Ashpoole'), Garrett, 169
Archbold, George, 132
Archbold, Gerald, 276
Archbold, James, 38
Archbold, Joan, 82
Archbold, John, 38
Archbold, Nicholas, 78, 85, 86
Archbold, Patrick, 93, 95
Archbold, Richard, 77–8
Archbold, Theobald, 82, 138
Archbold, William, 95
Archbolds, 8, 27, 31, 41, 64, 76, 77
Archer, James, 102
Ardree Castle, Co. Kildare, 101
Arklow, Co. Wicklow, 2, 24, 73, 240
Armstrong, Thomas, 238
Artane, 66, 238, 256
'Articles of Pacification', 216
Ash, Walter, 167
Askulv Mac Turcaill, 7
Astley, Sir Jacob, 214
Atkinson, Anne, 141

B

Bagenal, Sir Henry, 94, 97, 98
Bagenal, Sir Nicholas, 77
Balally, 4, 16, 25, 41, 60, 72, 92, 99, 103, 269, 276
church, 137
the Pale Ditch, 61
Walshes of, 81–3, 137, 288
Balhamond, 56
'*Ballinlower*' (Leopardstown), 62
Ballinteer, 16, 25, 41, 56
Balliroe, 56
Ballityre, 56
Ballybeenan (Brenanstown), 112
Ballybrynane, 77
Ballycorus, 62
Ballycullen, 11
Ballyfarnogue, Co. Wexford, 138
Ballygarney (Mount Kennedy demesne), 140, 168
Ballyhanley, 56
Ballyhawly, 45, 81
Ballymadrough, 112
Ballymaice, 11
Ballyman, Co. Dublin, 10, 62
Ballynerrin, 139
Ballyogan, 20
Ballyroe, 44
Ballyronan, 38
Balyofryn, 20
Bancroft, Richard, 116
Barlowe, Randal, 133
Barnewall, Edward, 85, 170
Barnewall, Nicholas, 87, 141
Barnewall, Patrick, 76, 250, 252
Barnewall, Peter, 82, 91, 107
Barnewall, Richard, 132
Barnewall, Robert, 87, 163, 170
Barnewall, William, 87
Barran, Nicholas, 94
Barry, David, 232
Barry, Garrett, 186
Basnet, Edward, 69, 72, 79, 85, 162
Basnet, Richard, 80, 85
Basnet, William, 162
Bath, Sir John, 116
Bathe, Catherine, 67
Beaton, William, 163, 172
Beaufort, Edward, 48
Bellingham, Sir Edward, 73
Berry, John, 258, 259, 267
Berwick-upon-Tweed, 206, 210, 211, 212
Bílá Hora (White Mountain), Battle of, 122, 180, **181**
Bishop, Joshua, 171
Bishopscourt, Co. Kildare, 112
Black Death, the, 30
Blackthorn, 27
Blackwell, George, 116
Bloody Bank, Battle of the, 45
Blount, Charles (Lord Mountjoy), 98, 105, 108
Boleyn, Anne, 65
Bolingbroke, Henry, 40
Bolton Castle, 253
Bommelerwaard, 201
Book of Howth, 17
Booterstown, 56, 161, 163, 173
Booth, Elizabeth, 87, 88, 162
Booth, George, 88, 162
Booth, William, 88, 162
Borlase, Edmund, 255, 257, 259
Borlase, Sir John, 159, 160, 224, 274
Borr, John, 276
Boswell, Sir William, 201
Boy, Owell, 86
Boyle, Lady Alice, 232
Boyle, Lady Joan, 232
Boyle, Lettice, 230
Boyle, Richard, 136, **144**, 159, 211, 229–30, 232, 234
Brabazon, Edward, 281
Brabazon, Henrie, 167
Brabazon, William, 281
Brackenbury (Brakenbury), John, 161, 162–3, 164, 165, 172, 175, 240
Bramhall, John, 149
Bray, 8, 15, 20, 41, 45, 51, 95, 121, 169, 171, 172
Breda
Dutch siege of, 199–202
Spanish siege of, 185–6
Bredon, Murtagh, 175
Bree (Bray), 15, 51, 93, 169
Brega, 3
Brenanstown, 27, 41, 43, 62, 68, 77, 85, 86, 112, 275
Brodar, 8
Brown, John, 230
Browne, Annabel, 230
Browne, Maria, 278
Browne, Simon, 278
Browne, William, 113
Bruce, Edward, 16–17
Bruce, Edward (Lord Kinloss), 118
Brund (or Brunt), Ralph, 15
Bulkeley, Archbishop Lancelot, 130, 137
Bullock Castle, Co. Dublin, **174**, 175
Bulloge (Bullock), 163
Bulstrode, Sir Richard, 202
Burke, Richard, 151
Burke, Ulick, 57, 151
Burlamachi, Philip, 131

Burlamachi–Calandrini merchant bank, 131–2
Burnell, Michael, 246
Butler, Denis, 232, 233
Butler, Edmund, 84
Butler, Edmund (earl of Carrick), 15
Butler, Ellice, 167
Butler, James (first earl of Ormond), 15–16
Butler, James (fourth earl of Ormond), 47
Butler, James (Lord Dunboyne), 253
Butler, John, 51
Butler, Maurice FitzMaurice, 33
Butler, Piers, 63, 65, 66
Butler, Richard, 16
Butler, Richard (Lord Mountgarrett), 253
Butler, Thomas (tenth earl of Ormond), 167
Butler family, 15–16
Butterston (Booterstown), 161, 163
Byrne, Hugh, 243
Byron, Sir Nicholas, 208, 213

C
Caddell, Richard, 74
Cadogan, William, 249
Calandrini, Cesar, 131
Calandrini, Elizabeth, 131
Calandrini, Giovanni, 131
Calandrini, Julian, 131
Calandrini, Philip, 131
Calandrini, Pompeo, 131
Campbell, John, 157
Carecmayn, 17
Carew, Ann, 230
Carew, Sir George, 98, 114, 230
Carew, Sir Peter, 84, 230
Carey, Catherine, 205
Carey, Sir Robert, 108
Carl Maximilian, count of Bassano und Weisskischen, 129
Carlisle, 206, 207
Carmayn, 15
Carrickemayne, 44, 76, 162
Carrickmayn, 24, 26, 66, 130, 131, 140
Carrickmayne, 56, 68, 86, 99, 106, 111, 132, 133, 137, 275
Richard Walsh of, 77, 112, 121
Theobald Walsh of, 130, 140
William Walsh of, 71, 72, 73
Carrickmines, Walshes of, 40–3
Carrickmines Castle
causeway connection between SE and SW enclosures, **36**
entrance, **36**
map of, **37**
mass burial from 1642, **269**
northern enclosure, **21**, **25**, **26**, **32**
south-eastern enclosure, **32**, **35**
standing remnant, **266**
Carrickmines Great, 173
Cary, Henry (first Viscount Falkland), 111, 135, 136
Cary, Sir Lorenzo, 226
Casimir, Ernest, 186
Casimir, Count Henry, 200
Castledermot, Co. Kildare, 25
Catholic League, 113
Catholicism, 119
Cavanagh, Art, 240
Cavanagh, Elinor, 240
Cavanagh, Sir Morgan, 239, 240
Cave, Sir Richard, 213
Cecil, Edward (Viscount Wimbleton), 189
Cecil, Sir Robert, 103, 104, 108
Cecil, Sir Thomas, 183
Cecil, Sir William, 104
Cellach Cualann, 2
Cernach Sotal, 3
Chamberlain, Michael, 94
Chamburleyn, John, 28
Charles I, King, 130, 133, 135, 145, 157, 158, 159, 177, 195, 206, 221
and the Second Bishop's War, 216
and Sir Simon Harcourt, 178
Charles II, King, 88
Cheevers, Thomas, 164
Cherrywood, 5
Chester, 220–4
Chichester, Sir Arthur, 98, 109, 110, 111, 138
Christian IV of Denmark, King, 125
Christiana de Marisco, 11, 13, 20
Christina of Sweden, Queen, 209
Christine, Princess, 117, 134
Church of Ireland, 149
church property, 24
Cináed ua hArtacáin, 3
Clarke, Rebecca, 281
Clement VIII, Pope, 116, 120
Cliffe, John, 240, 241
Clifford, John, 104
Clifford, Margaret, 141
Clinton, Catherine, 162
Clondalkin, 4, 7
Clones, Co. Monaghan, 170
Clongowes Wood, Co. Kildare, 90
Clonkeen, 24, 28–30, 42, 73
Clonmannan, Co. Wicklow, 88, 106, 131, 162, 166, 167
Walshes of, 167
Clontarf, 227–8
Cogadh Gaedhel re Gallaibh, 3
coins, 18
from 1642 mass grave, **271**
Edward VI penny, 73, **74**

Coke, Sir John, 156, 211
Colloredo, Rudolph, 126
Colton, John, 34
Conall, son of Cú Chongalt, 2
Congrave, Francis, 243, 261, 263
Connacht, plantation of, 150, 152
Convocation of 1634, 149
Conway, Edward, 213
Conway, Sir Thomas, 191
Conyers, Sir John, 213
Cooke, Richard, 259, 267
Cooke, William, 163
Cooper, Austin, 264
Coote, Sir Charles, 224, 225, 226, **227**, 228–9, 234, 238, 239, 243, 253, 274
Coppinger, John, 172, 175
Cork, County, **231**
Corker, Thomas, 281
Cosbie, Francis, 84
Coterel, John, 23
Cottington, Francis, 119
Court of Claims, 276
Courtfoyle, 139
Crawford, Lawrence, 228, 253
Críoch Branach, 69, 139, 162
Crofty, Hill of, 173
Cromwell, Oliver, 280
Cromwell, Thomas, 64
Cronroe, Co. Wicklow, 163
Cronykerry, 167
Cualu, 1–2
Culmore fort, 110
Cusack, Patrick, 245–6
Cynan, the son of Iago, 40

D

da San Giuseppe, Sebastian, 89
da Silva, Don Felipe, 203
Dalkey, 4, 24, 99, 100
Darcy, John, 21, 22, 42
Darcy, Martin, 151
Darcy, Roger, 23
Dartasso (Dartas), Janico, 37–40, 43, 46
Davies, Sir John, 108, 109
Dawtrey, Mary, 230
de Acuña, Diego Sarmiento (count of Gondomar), 118, 119
de Bermingham, John, 17, 21, 22, 33
de Bourbon, Princess Christine Marie, 117, 134
de Bourbon, Princess Henrietta Maria, 206
de Burgh, Elizabeth, 33
de Burgh, Richard, 15
de Burgo, William, 151
de Camville, Isabel, 179
de Clare, Richard FitzGilbert (Strongbow), 6, 7–8
de Cogan, Miles (Milo), 7, 8
de Coligny, Gaspard (maréchal de Châtillon), 204
de Guzmán, Gaspar (count of Olivares), 120, 121, 198, 199
de Karru (de Carew), William, 19
de la Frene, Fulco, 23
de la More, Adam, 24
de la Pole, William, 48
de Los Arcos, Don Martino, 196
de Marisco, Lady Christiana, 11
de Medina, Francisco, 186
de Prendergast, Maurice, 6
de Putot, William, 15
de Ridelesford, Walter, 7, 10, 11, 20, 24, 25
de Ridelesford, Walter II, 11
de Ridelesfords, 11
de Rokeby, Sir Thomas, 30, 41
de Rokebys, 30–7
de St Amand, Amaury, 33
de Toledo, Fernando Álvarez (third duke of Alva), 182
de Troye, John, 31, 33
de Vic, Henry, 210
Dean's Grange, 163, 173, 176, 238–42, 256
Defuble, George, 15
Delahyde, Walter, 186
Descartes, René, 122
Dessau Bridge, 124
Devenish, Edward, 140
Devereux, Robert (second earl of Essex), 98, 105, 151, 157
Devereux, Robert (third earl of Essex), 207
Devereux, Walter (first earl of Essex), 205
Digby, John, 118, 119, 157
Dillon, Sir Henry, 110
Docwra, Sir Henry, 98, 109, 110
Donaghmore, Co. Meath, 87
Donnybrook, 4, 11
Douglas, John, 232
Dowdall, Eleanor, 66
Drake, John, 45
Drinanmore (or *Drynamore*), 62
Drogheda, 244–53
du Plessis, Daniel, 206
Dublin, Viking settlements at, 2–3
Dublin, County, 111, 234–8
maps of, **60**, **70**, **71**
Dublin Castle, 65
Dudley, John, 67
Dudley, Robert (first earl of Leicester), 183, 205
D'Ufford, Ralph, 22, 23
Dulken, Matthijs, 188
Dundalk, 253
Dundrum, 56
Dundrum Castle, 175

Dungan, Sir Walter, 273, 274
Dun-Genainn (Dungannon, Co. Tyrone), 57
Dyflinnarskíri (the shire of Dublin), 2, 3
Dymock, Thomas, 214

E

Edmondes, Sir Thomas, 117
Edward I, King, 11, 17, 42
Edward II, King, 21, 23
Edward III, King, 22, 31, 33
Edward IV, King, 150
Edward VI, King, 67, 82
Edward the Black Prince, 34
'Eighty Years' War', 182
Elizabeth I, Queen, 89–90, 98, 108, 182, 183
Embleton, Robert, 30
Esmonde, Sir Lawrence, 167
Eustace, Alexander, 90
Eustace, Anne, 87, 90
Eustace, Edmund, 87
Eustace, Eleanor, 86, 104, 162
Eustace, James, 88
Eustace, Jane, 90, 100, 107, 121, 132, 166, 170
Eustace, John, 87, 166, 263
Eustace, Nicholas, 132
Evelyn, Elizabeth, 281
Evelyn, John, 217, 218
Everard, Sir John, 114

F

Fagan, Christopher, 166
Fagan, John, 132, 166, 172
Fagan, Maria, 263
Fagan, Marie, 132
Fagan, Mary, 166
Fagan, Richard, 166
Fagan, Thomas, 165
Fairfax, Thomas, 188, 196
Falkland, Viscount (Henry Cary), 111, 135, 136
farming, 14, 55–6, 154
Farnese, Alessandro, 183
Farrar, Sir Robert, 250, 251
Feartry, 152–3
Feilding, Sir William, 201
Fenton, Catherine, 159, 230
Fenton, Sir Geoffrey, 159
Ferdinand II, Emperor, 121, 122, 125, 126
Ferdinand III, Emperor, 121
Fernandéz, Don Gonzala, 194
Fine Ghall, 3
Fingal, 3–4, 34
Finglas, 228–9
Finglas, John, 133
Finnagh, John, 167
First Bishop's War, 212
Fitz James, Gerald (15th earl of Desmond), 83
FitzDavid, Roger, 25–6
Fitzgerald, Garret (Gearóid) Óg, 61–5, 66
Fitzgerald, Garret (Gerald) Mór ('the Great Earl'), 55–9
FitzGerald, George, 186, 232
Fitzgerald, Sir James, 57, 61, 63, 89
Fitzgerald, James fitz Maurice, 83, 88–9
Fitzgerald, Sir John, 89
Fitzgerald, Mary, 87
Fitzgerald, Maurice Óg, 53, 56
Fitzgerald, Richard, 61, 66
Fitzgerald, Thomas (seventh earl of Kildare), 48–9, 50
Fitzgerald, Thomas ('Silken Thomas'), 65, 66
Fitzgerald, Thomas (tenth earl of Kildare), 68
Fitzgerald, Thomas ('the Great Earl of Desmond'), 51
Fitzgerald, Thomas fitz Maurice, 91
Fitzgerald, Walter Reagh, 101
FitzHenry, Amabilis, 11
FitzHerbert, Elizabeth, 179
Fitzjames, Sir Piers, 101
FitzStephen, Robert, 6
FitzThomas, Maurice, 22–3
Fitzwilliam, Alison, 66
Fitzwilliam, Eleanor, 87
Fitzwilliam, Margaret, 66
Fitzwilliam, Michael, 67, 87
Fitzwilliam, Nicholas, 67
Fitzwilliam, Thomas, 66, 72, 77, 85, 87, 93
Fitzwilliam, Thomas (Viscount Fitzwilliam of Merrion), 152
Fitzwilliam, William, 44, 67, 93–4, 97
Fitzwilliams, Katherine, 75
FitzWilliams, Thomas, 80
Flatsbury, James, 93, 95, 138
Flatsbury, Margaret, 93, 138
Fleetwood, Charles, 138
Forde, Jane, 277
Forster, William, 74
Fort Philippine, 195
Fortescue, Sir Faithfull, 202
Fortuatha Laigen, 2
Fox, Robert, 168
Foxe, Thomas, 161–2
Frederick V (elector of the Palatinate), 121, 122, 124, 180
Frederik Hendrik of Nassau (prince of Orange), 177, 181, 186, 195, 196, 199, 200, 202, 219
Frederik IV (elector of the Palatinate), 113
Friedrich, Georg, 124
Fynne, John, 168

G

Gabhal Raghnaill, 68, 72, 73, 74

Galway, County, 151
Garristown, Co. Dublin, 245
Garvey, Christopher, 94
Garvey, John, 77, 95, 171
Gennep, 217, 218
George, duke of Clarence, lord of Richmond, 51
Gibson, Richard, 256, 258, 262, 267
Gibson, Seafoule, 246
Gilbert, Humphrey, 83, 183
Giraldus Cambrensis, 6, 7, 9
Glenamuck, 153, 281
Glencullen, 19
Glendalough, 10, 13
Glyn, John, 158
Gondomar, count of (Diego Sarmiento de Acuña), 118, 119
Goodman, Christopher, 163
Goodman, Elenor, 93
Goodman, James, 74, 76, 80, 85, 93, 163, 164, 171
Goodman, James the elder, 172
Goodman, James the younger, 170
Goodman, Roland, 80
Goodman, Rose, 81
Goodman, Rowland, 163
Goodman, William, 80
Goring, George, 196, 198, 202, 210, 211, 212, 213, 217, 230
Gortnaclea Castle, 105
Graney, Co. Kildare, 11
Great Assembly, 135–7
Gregory XIII, Pope, 89
Gregory XV, Pope, 120
Grenville, Sir Richard, 242, 251, 254, 256
Grey, Arthur, 89, 90
Grey, Leonard (Viscount Grane), 68, 69
Groll (Groenlo), siege of, 186–8
Gruffudd, 40–1
Gunpowder Plot (1605), 118
Gustavus Adolphus of Sweden, King, 125, 126, 127, 128
Guy, William, 253, 254

H

Hackett, George, 168
Hackettsland, 164
Haket, William, 25
Hallowes, John, 260, 262
Hamilton, James, 206, 207, 208
Hammond, Robert, 225, 260, 261, 280
Harcourt, Anne, **204**, 223, 278–80
Harcourt, Daniel, 171
Harcourt, Edward William, 192
Harcourt, Elizabeth, 179
Harcourt, Michael, 179
Harcourt, Philip, 205, 281
Harcourt, Robert de, 179, 180, 222–3
Harcourt, Simon (born 1661), 281
Harcourt, Simon (born 1684), 281
Harcourt, Simon (born 1714), 281
Harcourt, Sir Simon (born 1603), 219–20, 222–4, 226, 239, 250, 251, 260, 262, 269–72, 278, 279
    appointment to the privy council, 245, 275
    arrival in Dublin, 177–9, 224
    battle of Kallo, 205
    capture of vessels, 210
    at Carrickmines Castle, 255–8
    death of, 272, 282
    family background, 179–80
    in Ireland, 224–5
    letters to Anne, 205, 211, 219, 222, 224, 241–2, 243
    military service in the Low Countries, 182–5, 216–17
    Scottish campaign of 1640, 212–13
    siege of Maastricht, 192–3, 194
    siege of Schenkenschans, 198
    siege of 's-Hertogenbosch, 188, 191
    siege of Tienen, 196
    in the south of Ireland, 230–3
    voyage from Norfolk to Yorkshire, 207–8
Harcourt family, 179
Harold, Edmund, 57
Harold, Geoffrey, 50, 56
Harold, Margaret, 92
Harold, Nicholas, 56
Harold, Robert, 51
Harold, Thomas, 56
Harold, Walter, 29, 41
Harold, William, 51, 139
Harolds, 8
Harrington, Sir Henry, 84, 88, 101, 104, 139
Harrington, Mary, 88
Harrington, William, 139
Hart, Henry, 110
Harwood, Sir Edward, 189
Hay, James (first Lord Carlisle), 134
Hayes, John, 168
hearths, **19**
Heinrich, Gottfried (Graf zu Pappenheim), 126, 128
Henrietta Maria, Queen, 134–5, 206, 221
Henry II, King, 6, 9, 16
Henry IV, King, 40, 43, 44, 45, 50, 117
Henry V, King, 16, 46
Henry VI, King, 47
Henry VII, King, 56, 57, 58
Henry VIII, King, 58, 63–4, 65, 66, 68, 69, 162

Henshaw, Thomas, 93, 94
Henshaw, Ursula, 93, 94
Heyes, John, 171
Hibbotts, Thomas, 82
Historia Gruffud vab Kenan, 40
Hoare, James, 132
Hoare, Maria, 130, 132, 163
Hoare, Philip, 132
Hogg, Alice, 165
Holland, Thomas, 39
Holles, Arabella, 141, 142
Holles, Denzil, 141
Holles, John (first earl of Clare), 141
Holles, John (Lord Haughton), 188
Hollywood, Christopher, 238
Hollywood, Nicholas, 238
Holmes, Cecily, 166
Home, Sir James, 211
Hope, Sir Thomas, 215
Hopton, Ralph, 279
Hore, James, 163
Hovenden, Giles, 97
Howard, Thomas, 63, 207
Howel, Henry, 28
Howel, John, 28
Howel, Maurice, 27–8, 41
Howel, Peter, 27
Howels, 41

I

Inber Dea, 2
Inishannon, 230
Irby, Sir Anthony, 278
Ireland, map of, **97**

J

James I of England (VI of Scotland), King, 108, 115, 116–17, 119, 120, 133, 134, 180
Jamestown, 91, 138
John, King, 9, 11
John, Prince, 10
John of Gaunt, duke of Lancaster, 34, 40
Johnson, Christopher, 281
Jones, Michael, 274
Jones, Roger, 281
Joyce, John, 167, 168, 262, 263
Jülich, 185
Justin of Nassau, 185

K

Kallo, battle of, 202–5
Karmein, 15, 24
Kartmayn, 24
Kavanagh, Dermot Mac Maurice, 90
Kavanagh, Gerald, 34
Kavanagh, Morgh, 73
Keatingsland, alias *Kiltekerah*, 62, 154
Keenan, Patrick, 171
Kennedy, George, 141
Kennedy, Mary, 139, 141
Kennedy, Sir Richard, 140, 277
Kennedy, Sir Robert, 139, 140, 277
Keymis, Lawrence, 119
Kilbogget, 275
Kilbogoge, 112
Kilcullenbridge, 237
Kildare, County, 2, **71**, 234–8, 253–5
Kilgobbin, 20, 41, 91–5
    Walshes of, 91–5
Kilgobbin Castle, Co. Dublin, **92**, 138, 165, 175
Killincarrig, Co. Wicklow, 38, 99, 138, 168
    Walshes of, 99–100
Killincarrig Castle, Co. Wicklow, **99**
Killininny, 11
Killoughter, 38
Kilmacberne, Co. Wicklow, 10
Kilmallock, 83
Kilmartin, 38
Kilmashogue, 24, 56
kilns, corn-drying, 28, **29**
Kilpoole, 71, 77
Kilsallaghan Castle, 242–4, 245
Kiltiernan, 19, 24
Kindlestown, 38
King, George, 228
King, Matthew, 77
King's County, 75
Knights Hospitaller, 24
Knockangall, 90
Knocklyon, 11
Knollys, Sir Francis, 205
Knollys, Lettice, 205
Korkeran, 6

L

Lambart, Lord Charles, 234, 240, 243, 251
Lambay, 4
Langham, Edward, 84
Lany, Elizabeth, 159
Laud, William (archbishop of Canterbury), 150, 158, 178, 206
Lawless, Aveline, 79
Lawless, Johan (Joan), 79
Lawless, John, 79
Lawless, Richard, 79
Lawless, Thomas, 78
le Botiller, Geoffrey, 16
le Botiller, Theobald (I), 16
le Botiller, Theobald (V), 15
le Botiller, Thomas, 16, 21
le Bret, Milo, 19, 20

le Brun, Fromund, 20
le Grant, William, 23
le Gros, Raymond, 7, 8
le Poer, Eustace, 23
le Waleys, Elias, 41
le Waleys, Thomas, 42
Lehaunstown Castle, 170, 173
Leinster, 84–8, **236**
Leo XI, Pope, 120
Leopardstown, 51, 62, 86, 164
Les Avins, battle of, 199
Leslie, Alexander, 209, 210, 214, 233
Ley, John, 49
Liamain (Lyons, Co. Dublin), 1
Limbourg, 195
Lionel, earl of Ulster, 33
Lison, Elizabeth, 168
Lison, John, 168, 170, 172
Lissebon, Aunger de, 17–24, 26
Lissebon, John, 19, 20, 24
Lissebon, William, 20, 24
Little Bree (Little Bray), 169
Lockwood, Sir Thomas, 73
Loftus, Sir Adam, 111, 136, 138, 148–9, 152, 165, 239, 242, 273
London, Treaty of, 117
Long Parliament, 158
longhouse, 5
longphort, 2
Louis XIII, King, 117, 204, 219
Low Countries, 182–5
Lucas, Sir Thomas, 243, 250, 251
Lunsford, Thomas, 214–15
Luttrell, Richard, 77
Luttrell, Sir Thomas, 100
Lützen, battle of, 126–30
Lyons, Co. Dublin, 1, 236, 241, 253, 254

M

Maastricht, siege of, 192–4
Mac Adam, Henry, 46
Mc Da More, Phelim, 88
Mc Da More, Redmond, 88
Mac Firbhisigh, Dubhaltach, 2
Mac Gilla Mo-Cholmóc, 8, 9
Mac Gilla Mo-Cholmóc, Domnall (king of Uí Dúnchada), 8
Mac Gilla Mo-Cholmóc, Muirchertach ('lord of *Feara-Cualann*'), 8
Mac Hugh, Feagh, 74
Mac Maelmórda, Bran, 13
mac Máil na mBó, Diarmait (king of Leinster), 3
Mac Shane, Feagh, 73
Mac Shane, Hugh, 73, 78
McCarthy, Dominic, 230, 231
McDavid, Phelim Reagh, 110
McDonagh, Maria, 113
McDonnell, Randal, 206
McEdmond, Morgan, 168
McHugh, Nicholas, 86
McHugh, Shane, 86
McMorish, Hebbart, 86
McMoryce, Charles, 74
MacMurrough, Art, 37, 38, 39
MacMurrough, Art Mór, 37
MacMurrough, Diarmait (king of Leinster), 5–6, 7, 8, 82
MacMurrough, Murchertach, 33
MacMurrough-Kavanagh, Domhnall Spáinneach, 106, 162
MacMurrough-Kavanagh, Elinor, 162
McPhelim, Hugh, 172
McRedmond, Luke (or Feagh), 163
Máel Sechnaill (high-king), 3
Maghery, 59, 61
Maginnis, Sir Con, 245
Maguire, Hugh, 95, 98, 109
Maguire, Rory, 245
Mainwaring, Sir Henry, 207
Malene (Malone?), Philip, 171
Malone, Joan, 93
Malone, John, 93
Manneringe, Robert, 76–7
Mannheim, 182
Margaret of Austria, 200
Margaret of Parma, 182
Maritt, Thomas, 261, 262
Marrowe, John, 254
Marten, Christopher, 74, 77
Marward, Eleanor, 58–9
Marward, Walter, 59
Mary, Queen, 67, 75
Maurits, prince of Orange, 185, 186
Maximilian I, duke of Bavaria, 113
Mayneringe, Robert, 74
Mayo, County, 150
Meic Turcaills, 8
Mellifont, Treaty of, 98, 108
Meredith, Sir Robert, 273
Mey, John, 95
Mildmay, Sir Henry, 211
mills, horizontal watermills, 14
Molineux, Thomas, 167, 168
Molyneux, Daniel, 121, 122
Monaghan, County, 93
monastic settlements, 5
Monck, George, 202, 215, 216, 242, 256, 262
Monkstown parish, 24
Monolough (or *Monnelough*), 62
Monro, Robert, 209, 233
Mooney, James, 281

Moore, Lord Charles, 246, 249, 251, 252
Moore, Sir Garret, 108
Moore, Roger (alias Rory O'More), 237
Morgan, Sir Charles, 195
Morgan, Thomas, 183
Morrey, James, 192
Morrison, Sir Richard, 234
Mortimer, Roger, 39
Morton, Sir Thomas, 208
Mountjoy, Lord (Charles Blount), 98, 105, 108
Mowbray, Thomas, 40
Mullacash, 237
Munster, 83, 229–34
Murphy, Hugh, 163, 172, 264
Murphystown, 27, 28, 165

N
Naas, Co. Kildare, 236, 237
Nangle, Amy, 165
Nani, Agustino, 102
Nest (or Nesta), Princess, 6
Netherlands, the, 182–5
Nettirvill, Luke, 278, 279
Nettirvill, Nicholas, 250
Neville, Cicely, 48
Newcastle, Co. Dublin, 13, 215, 235
Newcastle Lyons, 41
Newcastle McKynegan (*Novum Castrum McKynegan*), 27, 31, 34, 45, 226
Newcomen, Sir Thomas, 234
Newland, 237
Newtownmount-Kennedy, 140
Nicholas, Sir Edward, 143
Nonsuch, Treaty of, 183
Norgate, Edward, 211
Norreys, Sir John, 102
North, the, 95–8
Northorp, Richard, 46
Nugent, Richard, 63

O
Oath of Supremacy, 116, 136
O'Brien, Brian, 27
O'Brien, Brian Bán, 21, 23
O'Brien, Toirdhealbach (king of Thomond), 57, 58
O'Byrne, Barnaby, 167
O'Byrne, Bran, 91
O'Byrne, Caher McPhelim, 166
O'Byrne, Cahir McArt, 166
O'Byrne, Domhnall, 45
O'Byrne, Donnchadh, 46
O'Byrne, Dowling McCahir, 167
O'Byrne, Edmond, 166
O'Byrne, Edmund, 139, 263
O'Byrne, Edmund McArt, 166
O'Byrne, Edmund Óg, 65
O'Byrne, Feagh, 72, 76, 88
O'Byrne, Feagh Mac Hugh, 84, 89, 90, 100–3, 166, 172
O'Byrne, Gerald, 38
O'Byrne, Honora, 78, 86
O'Byrne, Hugh, 76, 165
O'Byrne, Hugh Mac Shane, 73, 88
O'Byrne, Hugh McPhelim, 172, 237
O'Byrne, James, 139
O'Byrne, John, 139
O'Byrne, Sir John, 33
O'Byrne, John mac Taidhg, 31
O'Byrne, Luke, 163, 166, 169
O'Byrne, Mary, 90
O'Byrne, Murrough McEdmund, 138
O'Byrne, Patrick, 50
O'Byrne, Phelim, 103, 105
O'Byrne, Philip, 85
O'Byrne, Redmond, 103, 104
O'Byrne, Rose, 72
O'Byrne, Tadhg, 69
O'Byrne, Teige Óg, 167
O'Byrne, Turlough McFeagh McHugh, 138
O'Byrne, Walter, 262
O'Byrnes (Ua Broin), 13, 14, 72, 74, 111, 166
O'Carroll, Donnchadh Fionn (king of Ely), 21
O'Connor, An Calbhach (king of Offaly), 46
O'Connor, Ruaidrí, 10
O'Doherty, Sir Cahir, 109, 110
O'Donnell, Aodh, 58
O'Donnell, Hugh Albert, 190
O'Donnell, Red Hugh, 95, 97, 98, 101
O'Donnell, Rory, 108, 109
O'Kelly, Daniel, 90
Old Connaught, 24, 163
Oldcourt, Co. Wicklow, 154, 280
Oldcourt Castle, Co. Wicklow, **169**
Oldenzaal, siege of, 186, **187**
Olivares, count of (Gaspar de Guzmán), 120, 121, 198, 199
O'Mechair, Tadc, 45
O'More, Edmund, 186
O'More, Laoiseach, 23
O'More, Uaithne Mac Ruaidhrí, 105
O'Moriarty, Owen Mac Donnell, 90
O'Neill, Hugh, 95, **96**, 97, 101, 108, 109
O'Neill, Owen Roe, 199, 205, 219, 274
O'Neill, Sir Phelim, 247, 248
O'Nolan, Donal, 38
O'Rourke, Tiernán, 5
Orsoy, 195
O'Sullivan, Sir Owen, 88
O'Sullivan Beare, Philip, 103
O'Toole, Aodh, 31
O'Toole, Barnabas, 81, 100

O'Toole, Esmond Tibbot, 91
O'Toole, Felim, 38
O'Toole, Luke, 163, 165, 166, 167, 226, 239, 240, 241
O'Toole, Phelim, 78, 105, 106
O'Toole, Turlough, 63, 68, 69–71
O'Tooles (Ua Tuathail), 13, 14, 52, 111, 166
Owain ap Cadwgan of Powys, 6
Owain Glyndwr, Prince, 43
Owain Gwynedd, 41
Owen, William, 255, 258, 259
Oxmanstown, 8

P
Paget, Catherine, 278
Paget, Letitia (Lettice), 205
Paget, Thomas, 225, 232
Paget, William (fourth Baron Paget), 205
Paget, William (fifth Baron Paget), 213, 224
Pale, the, 55, 59–61
Pale Ditch, 59, 60, 61
Pallas, Alexander, 94
Paramour, Thomas, 254
Parker, Will, 254
Parliaments
    of 1613, 113–15
    of 1634, 145–9
    of 1640, 155–7
    'Short Parliament', 157
Parsons, Richard, 141
Parsons, Sir William, 141, 142, 152, 159, 160, 167, 224, 240, 257, 258, 273, 274
Paul V, Pope, 116, 120
Pawlett, Sir George, 109, 110
Pelham, Sir Edmund, 108
Pennington, Admiral John, 210
Pennington, John, 207
Peppard, Anthony, 87
Peppard, Mary, 87
Peppard, Walter, 73, 87
Percy, Algernon, 213
Perkins, Christopher, 116
Perrot, Sir John, 83
Phelim, Patrick, 163
Philip II, King, 75
Philip III, King, 109
Philip IV, King, 118, 120
Philips, William, 239
Phrompstown, 62, 66, 77, 86, 112, 153, 275
Piccolomini, Octavio, 128
Pickering, Robert, 231, 256
Piper, Owen, 86
Pithan, Frederik, 185
Pius II, Pope, 50
plantations, 111
Plumleigh, Sir Richard, 143
Pole (son of Thorkil), 8
Poore, Alice, 165
Poyning, Sir Edward, 56–7
Poyning's Law, 145
Preston, Albone Thomas, 99
Preston, Mary, 67
Preston, Nicholas, 217
Preston, Thomas, 116, 186, 199, 217, 273, 274
Price, Christopher, 262, 267
Price, Samuel, 267
Priorsland, 154
Protestant Union, 113
Pue, John, 141
Pugh, John, 166, 167
Puttock, Revd Rodger, 257
Pym, Sir John, 157, 158

Q
Queen's County, 75

R
Radcliffe, Sir George, 143, 149, 152
Radcliffe, Sir John, 131
Raleigh, Sir Walter, 89, 118–19, 179
Ranelagh, 111, 159
Ratcliffe, Sir Thomas, 75
Rathcoole, 238
Rathdown, 4, 24, 49, 50, 55, 76, 80, 82, 95, 100
Rathfarnham, 8
Rathmichael, 24
Rathmullan, Co. Donegal, 109
Rawdon, Sir George, 220
Reade, Sir John, 250, 252
rebellions
    First Desmond Rebellion, 83
    insurrection of 1534, 65–6
    Second Desmond Rebellion, 88–91
Reeves, Sir William, 172
Rempston, Thomas, 44
Rheinberg, 195
Riabhach, Brian, 103, 104
Rich, Frances, 213, 224
Rich, Henry, 133, 157, 207, 212
Rich, Robert, 157
Richard II, King, 34, 39, 40, 45
Richard of Baggotrath, 66
Richard of Bordeaux, 34
Richard Plantagenet, duke of York, 48
Rinuccini, Giovanni Battista, 273–4
Ripon, Treaty of, 158
Robert the Bruce (king of Scotland), 16–17
Roberts, Jane, 67
Roberts, Nicholas, 223
Roche, Sir Patrick, 233
Rocheford, William, 112

Rochford, Alexander, 163, 171
Rochford, Henry, 275
Rochford, James, 244
Rochford, Nicholas, 171
Rochfort, Elizabeth, 83
Rochfort, Henry, 112
Rocque, John, 63
Rodes, Elizabeth, 142, 143
Roe, Sir Thomas, 217
Roermond, 191–2, 198, 201
Roodstown, 253
Roper, Christopher, 226, 246
Roscommon, County, 150
Rownswell, Thomasina, 87, 88
Rupert, Prince, 195
Russell, Sir William, 101, 102

S

Saggart, 52, 238
St John, Elizabeth, 57
St John, Sir Oliver, 111
St Leger, Sir Anthony, 67, 68, 69
St Mary de Hogges nunnery, 82
St Mary's Abbey, 24
St Patrick's Cathedral, 85, 148
Saint-Omer, 203
Santry, 228–9
Sarsfield, Sir William, 93
Scaramelli, Giovanni Carlo, 118
Schenk, Martin, 197–9
Schenkenschans, 197–9
Schetz, Anthonie, 191
Schlick, Countess Barbara, 129
Scotland, 205–7
Scrope, Sir Stephen, 45
Scurlocke, Martin, 235
Scurlocke, Patrick, 235
Scurlocke, Thomas, 235
Seagrave, William, 86
Second Bishop's War, 157, 213, 216
Segrave, James, 82
Sentleger, Sir Warham, 89
Shakespeare, William, 105
Shanganagh, 49, 78–81, 139, 153, 154
  Walshes of, 78–81
Shankill, 24
Shelton, John, 94
Sherlock, Katherine, 171
's-Hertogenbosch (Bois-le-Duc), 188–91
Shirborne, Christopher, 51
Sidney, Sir Henry, 76, 77, 83
Sidney, Sir Philip, 151
Sidney, Robert (earl of Leicester), 224, 225
Sigginstown, Co. Kildare, 273
'Silken Thomas' (Thomas Fitzgerald), 65, 66
Silyard, Constance, 140
Simnel, Lambert, 56
Sitriuc, 8
Skeffington, Sir William, 64, 65, 66
Sligo, County, 150
Smithson, Joseph, 171
Smithson, Mary, 171–2
Spain, 102
Spinola, Ambrogio, 181, 185, 186, 200
Stachlorcan, 25
Stanley, Sir John, 43
Statute of Kilkenny, 33–4
Stillorgan, 25, 56, 68, 163, 164, 171
Stokes, Edward, 170
Stokes, George, 80
Strale, 191–2
Strongbow (Richard FitzGilbert de Clare), 6, 7–8
Stuart, Elizabeth (titular queen of Bohemia), 178–9, 180, 194, 217
Stutvill, Thomas, 247, 249
Sutton, Nicholas, 237
Swayne, John, 47
Swayne, Revd Simon, 170
Swords, 225–6
Sydney, Philip, 183
Sydney, Robert, 183, 185
Symondstown, 45
Synnott, Margaret, 138
Synnott, Sir William, 138

T

Taafe, Joan, 44
Talbot, Apoloner, 80
Talbot, Esmay, 86, 112
Talbot, Henry, 276
Talbot, Isobel, 86
Talbot, John, 46
Talbot, Katherin, 165
Talbot, Marion, 94
Talbot, Matthew, 164, 165
Talbot, Peter, 69, 76
Talbot, Richard, 46–7
Talbot, Robert, 63, 94
Tallow, 231–2
Tara, Hill of, 173
taxes, Ship Money, 157
Teil, 200
Temair (Tara), battle of, 3
Temple, Sir John, 255, 257, 260, 272, 273, 278
Temple, Sir Thomas, 232
Thirty Years' War, 180
Thomas of Lancaster, 16, 43, 46
Three Castles, Co. Wicklow, 74–5
Tichborne, Sir Henry, 246, 247, 251, 252
Tienen (Tirlemont), 195–7
Tilson, Henry, 154

Tinnapark demesne, 139
Toirdhealbach, son of Conn Ó Néill, 57
Touchet, James (earl of Castlehaven), 252
Tracy, Mary, 180
trade and productivity, 28–30
Travers, Sir John, 74, 76
Tredagh (Drogheda), 246
Tregury, Michael, 50, 52
Trewoff, Alexander, 52
Tserclaes, Johann (Count Tilly), 122, 124, 125, 126, 182
Tuathal Mac Augaire, 13
Tully Church, Co. Dublin, **267**
Tully parish, 24, **265**

U
Uí Briúin Chualann, 2, 8, 15
Uí Cheinnselaig, 1, 21
Uí Chellaig Chualann, 2
Uí Dúnchada, 1, 8
Uí Fáeláin, 1
Uí Máil, 2
Uí Muiredaig, 1, 2
Urban VIII, Pope, 134
Ussher, Christopher, 66
Ussher, Archbishop James, 131, 136, 150
Ussher, Walter, 141

V
van den Bergh, Hendrik, 185, 188, 190
van Gendt, Baron Otto, 190
van Nassau-Siegen, Willem, 202
Vane, Sir Henry, 156, 158, 196, 214
Venlo, 191–2
Vere, Anne, 195
Vere, Avery, 194
Vere, Edward, 191, 194
Vere, Frances, 179
Vere, Francis, 183–4, 185
Vere, Horace, 184
Vere, Horatio (first Baron Vere of Tilbury), 180, 181, 182, 184–5, 186, 195
Vere, John, 194
Vere, Peter, 194
Verney, Edmund, 226, 245
Vernon, Elizabeth, 105
Viking/Scandinavian settlements, 2–5
Villiers, George, 133, 206
von Anhalt, Christian, 122
von Hatzfeld, Melchior, 126
von Mansfeld, Count Ernst, 124
von Weimar, Bernard, 128
Voorn, 201
Vorn, 201

W
Wakefield, battle of, 50
Walker, Sir Thomas, 43
Wallenstein, Albrecht Wenzel Eusebius von, 124–5, 126, 128
Waller, Anne, 281
Waller, Sir Thomas, 279
Waller, Sir William, 279
Walsh, Adam, 44
Walsh, Ambros, 139
Walsh, Anastace, 100, 139
Walsh, Anne, 87, 94, 132
Walsh, Charles, 56, 79, 80, 140, 141
Walsh, Christopher, 50, 94
Walsh, David, 44
Walsh, Dorothy (née O'Byrne), 137–8
Walsh, Edmond (of Clonmannan, Co. Wicklow), 106, 162, 240, 241
Walsh, Edmund, 62, 63, 77, 78, 85, 86, 141
Walsh, Edmund (of *Ballyvan*, Co. Dublin), 77
Walsh, Edmund (of *Corkagh*), 80
Walsh, Edmund (of Shanganagh), 87, 140
Walsh, Edmund (son of Edward Walsh of *Clonmanin*), 240
Walsh, Edward, 87, 131, 140, 162, 166, 167, 240, 277
Walsh, Edward (of Three Castles), 75
Walsh, Edward (son of Edward the elder), 277
Walsh, Edward (the elder), 167, 168
Walsh, Eleanor, 132, 139, 168
Walsh, Elizabeth, 86, 112
Walsh, Esmond (Edmund of Shanganagh?), 52
Walsh, Esmund (brother of Henry Walsh), 63
Walsh, Esmund (of Shankill), 52, 56
Walsh, Francis, 140
Walsh, Geoffrey, 72
Walsh, Gerald, 80, 86, 141
Walsh, Gerrod, 80
Walsh, Gerrot, 87
Walsh, Giles, 141
Walsh, Henry, 63, 88, 240
Walsh, Henry fitz Adam, 275
Walsh, Henry (of *Arcloo*/Arklow), 75, 80
Walsh, Henry (of Carrickmines), 43–6, 56
Walsh, Henry (of *Clonmarninge*), 162
Walsh, Henry (of Dalkey), 106
Walsh, Henry (of Killincarrig, Co. Wicklow), 132, 138, 139, 140
Walsh, Henry (of *Suttoneston*), 99–100
Walsh, Henry (the second), 46–53
Walsh, Honora, 87, 141
Walsh, Howel, 112
Walsh, Howell, 82, 86, 112
Walsh, James, 62, 75, 81, 91, 113
Walsh, James (of Balally), 103, 137, 138, 276
Walsh, James (of Brenanstown), 72

Walsh, James (of Old Connaught), 163, 276
Walsh, James (of Shanganagh), 139, 140, 141
Walsh, Joan, 85, 87, 90
Walsh, John, 79, 81, 94, 95, 138, 276
Walsh, John (of Balally), 82–3, 137
Walsh, John (of Carrickmines), 263
Walsh, John (of Kilgobbin), 86, 93, 140
Walsh, John (of Killincarrig), 168
Walsh, John (of *Litle Bre*), 112
Walsh, John (of *Shagnogh*), 277
Walsh, John (of Shanganagh), 80, 85, 86, 139, 269
Walsh, John (of *Thorgeteston*), 44
Walsh, John (son of Henry Walsh), 52, 53, 56, 140
Walsh, John (son of James Walsh), 140
Walsh, John (son of Walter Walsh), 80
Walsh, John (Stillorgan), 56
Walsh, Katherin, 56, 93, 94, 132, 138, 139
Walsh, Luke, 140
Walsh, Margaret, 86, 88, 95, 112, 139, 140, 163
Walsh, Margaret (née Flatsbury), 93, 138
Walsh, Margery, 112
Walsh, Maria, 280
Walsh, Mary, 112, 132
Walsh, Maurice, 49, 52, 56, 75, 87, 91, 104, 106
Walsh, Michael, 132
Walsh, Nicholas, 56, 75, 93, 94, 106, 141
Walsh, Oliver, 80, 87, 90, 121, 129–30, 132, 140, 153
Walsh, Owen, 77
Walsh, Owen (Howell), 85
Walsh, Pearse, 162
Walsh, Peter, 50, 81, 92, 93, 95, 138, 140
Walsh, Pierce, 138, 141
Walsh, Piers, 92, 93, 140, 162
Walsh, Richard, 64, 72, 80, 104, 117, 139, 162, 166, 273, 278, 280
 application to the Court of Claims, 276
 of *Carrickmayne*, 77
 court of chancery, 112
 death of, 86
 description of *Kilbagog* as '*als Anadan*', 275
 holdings, 79, 85
 military career, 121–6, 128, 129, 130
 will of, 132, 169
Walsh, Richard (born 1583), 107
Walsh, Richard (of *Kilgobban*), 92
Walsh, Richard (of *Little Brea*), 140
Walsh, Richard (son of Gerald), 141
Walsh, Richard (son of Robert Walsh), 78
Walsh, Richard (son of Theobald), 153, 263
Walsh, Robert, 62, 65, 73, 75, 78, 85, 86, 141
Walsh, Robert (alias John), 112, 113
Walsh, Roger, 42
Walsh, Rose, 139, 263
Walsh, Shane, 52
Walsh, Symon, 81
Walsh, Theobald, 76, 106, 112, 130–3, 137, 140, 155, 168, 173, 175–6, 263–4, 269
 allegiance to the government, 57
 birth of, 107
 death of, 91
 estate, 275
 land owned by, 154
 life at Carrickmines, 151–3
 marriage of, 58
 military service, 121, 122, 129
 participation in raids, 161–3, 164
 raid on property, 273
Walsh, Theobald (of Killincarrig, Co. Wicklow), 80, 81, 86–7, 90, 100, 138–9
Walsh, Thomas, 42, 50, 52, 56, 82, 92, 94, 112, 113, 117, 137, 141
Walsh, Tibbot (Theobald), 52, 56, 57, 58, 62, 66, 73, 74–5, 86, 164
Walsh, Walter, 52, 71–2, 79, 80, 81, 86
Walsh, William, 44, 52, 56, 65, 71–2, 76, 77, 82, 85, 93, 104, 137
 assault on John Ley, 49
 as commissioner, 68–9
 death of, 84
 holdings, 66
 and the House of Kildare, 64
 land agreement with the dean of Holy Trinity, 73–4
 marriage of, 88
 pardon granted to, 106
 as witness to documents, 42
Walsh, William (of *Ballmadrought/Ballinadrought*), 112
Walsh cadet houses, 137–41
Walshes
 of Balally, 81–3
 of Carrickmines, 40–3
 of Clonmannan, 167
 of Kilgobbin, 91–5
 of Killincarrig, 99–100
 of Shanganagh, 78–81
 of Wicklow, 166–70
Walsingham, Frances, 151
Walsingham, Sir Francis, 151
Walter the Goldsmith, 19
Warbeck, Perkin, 56
Warburton, Elizabeth, 162
Warren, Henry, 163, 276
Washington, Henry, 262
Waterford, County, **231**
watermills, **13**, 154

Weames, Sir Patrick, 226, 246
Welden, Robert, 168
Welsh, James, 117
Wentworth, Thomas (earl of Strafford), 141–2, 150, 151, 153, 155, 156, 157, 158–9, 160, 206, 224
as lord deputy of Ireland, 142–5
Wentworth-Woodhouse, Sir William of, 141
Wexford, County, 111
Wharme, James, 164, 165
Wharme, William, 161
White, Thomas, 163
Whitechurch parish, 8
Wicklow, County, 111, 152, 160, 166–70, 226–7
map of, **70**, **71**
Walshes of, 166–70
Wicklow Castle, 34, 167
Wielant, Anna, 197
Willem of Nassau, 195
William de Karru, 19
William I, prince of Orange, 185
William of Nassau, prince of Orange, 200
William of Orange, 182, 183
William of Windsor, 37
Williams, Sir William, 101
Willis, Humphrey, 98
Willoughby, Ensign, 191
Willoughby, Sir Francis, 224
Wilmot, Charles, 147
Wilmot, Henry, 215
Wilson, Revd John, 171
Wilson, Susan, 171
Windebank, Sir Francis, 150
Windsor, Treaty of, 10
Wolferston, William, 133
Wolsey, Cardinal Thomas, 63
Wolverston, George, 163
Wolverston, James, 163
Wolverston, William, 163–4, 171, 172
Woodhouse, Michael, 225, 261
Woodstock Castle, 253
wool, 155
Wrenne, Christopher, 93
Wriothesley, Henry (earl of Southampton), 104, 105

Y
Yarner, Abraham, 277
Youghal, 232–3